LEADERSHIP & PROBLEM SOLVING

MILITARY SCIENCE AND LEADERSHIP   MSL 301

Edited by

Sheila Visconti

**McGraw-Hill Primis
Custom Publishing**

Boston   Burr Ridge, IL   Dubuque, IA   Madison, WI   New York   San Francisco   St. Louis
Bangkok   Bogotá   Caracas   Lisbon   London   Madrid
Mexico City   Milan   New Delhi   Seoul   Singapore   Sydney   Taipei   Toronto

McGraw-Hill Higher Education 🖉

*A Division of The **McGraw-Hill** Companies*

LEADERSHIP & PROBLEM SOLVING
Military Science and Leadership
MSL 301

McGraw-Hill's Primis Custom Publishing consists of products that are produced from camera-ready copy. Peer review, class testing, and accuracy are primarily the responsibility of the author(s).

3 4 5 6 7 8 9 0 QPD QPD 0 9 8 7 6 5 4 3

ISBN 0-07-284059-5

Sponsoring Editor: Judy A. Wetherington
Production Editor: Carrie Braun
Cover Design: Fairfax Hutter
Printer/Binder: Quebecor World

CONTENTS

INTRODUCTION

OVERVIEW OF THE ARMY ROTC ADVANCED COURSE

The Army ROTC Advanced Course is comprised of four courses, Military Science and Leadership (MSL) 301, MSL 302, MSL 401, and MSL 402 and the National Advanced Leadership Camp (NALC). The Advanced Course is designed to teach all knowledge, skills, and attitudes essential for commissioning as a new second lieutenant, and to establish a sound foundation for a career as a commissioned Army officer. The content and methods of the Advanced Course assume no prior cadet experience or other military training. This approach is taken because the Advanced Course comprises the minimum curriculum that an individual must complete in order to be commissioned.

Advanced Course lessons are carefully sequenced, linked, and progressive in their treatment of key officer knowledge and competencies. Students are encouraged to synthesize lessons to form broader perspectives, deeper insights, and more robust problem solving abilities, by the use of case studies and simulations that require the use of skills and knowledge learned in a wide variety of earlier lessons. The sequencing of lessons is also designed to meet the immediate needs of cadets by addressing topics needed for success in the performance of cadet responsibilities early in the MSL 301 term, and at the NALC, and topics designed to facilitate entry into active military service during the MSL 402 term.

OVERVIEW OF THE MSL 301 COURSE: LEADERSHIP AND PROBLEM SOLVING

The MSL 301 course is designed to enable a student with no prior military or cadet experience to quickly learn essential cadet knowledge and skills necessary for integration into the cadet battalion and successful performance of key cadet tasks. First you will be introduced to principles of physical fitness and healthy lifestyle so that you may effectively work to improve or maintain your physical fitness from the very beginning of the term. Next, you will be introduced to the Leader Development Program that will be used to evaluate your leadership performance and provide you developmental feedback for the rest of your cadet years. To help prepare you for their responsibilities in teaching and participating in Military Science and Leadership Labs, you will then be taught how to plan and conduct individual and small unit training, as well as basic tactical principles. Following these important introductory modules, the course turns to a four-week study of reasoning skills and the military-specific application of these skills in the form of the Army's troop leading procedure. The term concludes its final four weeks with a detailed examination of officership, which culminates in a five-hour officership case study. This treatment of officership is especially appropriate in this term because MSL 301 is the first term that *all* cadets must take, regardless of their route of entry into ROTC.

COURSE STRUCTURE: A MODULAR APPROACH

This course is structured in modules and lessons. There are five modules containing 36 one-hour (50 minute) lessons as follows:

MODULE	TRACK
Module I	Physical Well-being (Lessons 1–3)
Module II	Personal Development (Lessons 4, 5 and 13–16)
Module III	The Army Profession: Army Operations (Lessons 6–12 and 17–24)
Module IV	The Army Profession: Officership (Lessons 25–36)

In addition, Leadership Labs that provide practical experience are scheduled during each semester. Leadership Labs meet a minimum of 1 hour per week.

HOW TO USE THIS TEXT

This textbook is divided by sections/modules, and is organized according to the Cadet Command class schedule model. Scope statements for each module are found on the module title pages. Within each module is a series of lessons that support the module. Each lesson begins with a purpose statement and a list of topics covered by the lesson, followed by the learning objectives identified for that. Readings for each lesson follow.

WHAT IS EXPERIENTIAL LEARNING?

Experiential learning simply means learning from an experience.

When participants are provided the opportunity to "experience" their learning rather than being told what they are to learn, experiential learning is taking place. Experiential Learning is rewarding; yet demanding, for both learners and teachers because the learning takes place during class as much as it does outside the classroom, from unstructured as well as structured experiences. Experiential learning, is founded on the belief that interaction is central to the learning process: cadet/faculty interaction, cadet/cadet interaction, and cadet/instructional material.

Helpful synonyms are: direct experience, discovery learning, experience-based learning, action learning, active learning, and participatory learning.

THE CADET COMMAND APPROACH TO ACADEMIC INSTRUCTION

The Military Science and Leadership program is designed to focus on the student (cadet), rather then the instructor or the subject matter. Focusing on the cadet requires student-centered objectives and conscious attention to how cadets react to the instruction received. For effective instruction, students need feedback that reinforces learning while identifying and correcting errors. Students need the opportunity to try to work with what has been taught. Too often instruction is limited to the delivery of information, either through reading assignments, lectures, or slide presentations.

Typically, we think of successful experiential learning as consisting of five steps:

1. Readiness/openness to the experience
2. The experience itself
3. Reflection upon the experience
4. Analysis, theory or additional information to clarify the relationship between theory and actions, with an understanding of lessons learned regarding any needed changes
5. The opportunity to re-experience (practice in new situations/practical exercises)

STUDENT RESOURCES

a. *Cadet text.* The Cadet text contains the readings that support the MSL 301 course: Leadership and Problem Solving.
b. *Cadet CD-ROM.* A CD-ROM is included in each cadet textbook and contains additional reference materials, readings and multimedia that support the MSL program.
c. *Cadet Workbook.* Packaged with cadet text of readings, this workbook contains the worksheets that support the exercises woven throughout the course. In addition, the workbook contains checklists and lesson overview statements for use by the cadet when preparing for class.
d. *Blackboard* (Bb). The Blackboard course site, *http://rotc.blackboard.com,* contains Military Science and Leadership course materials.

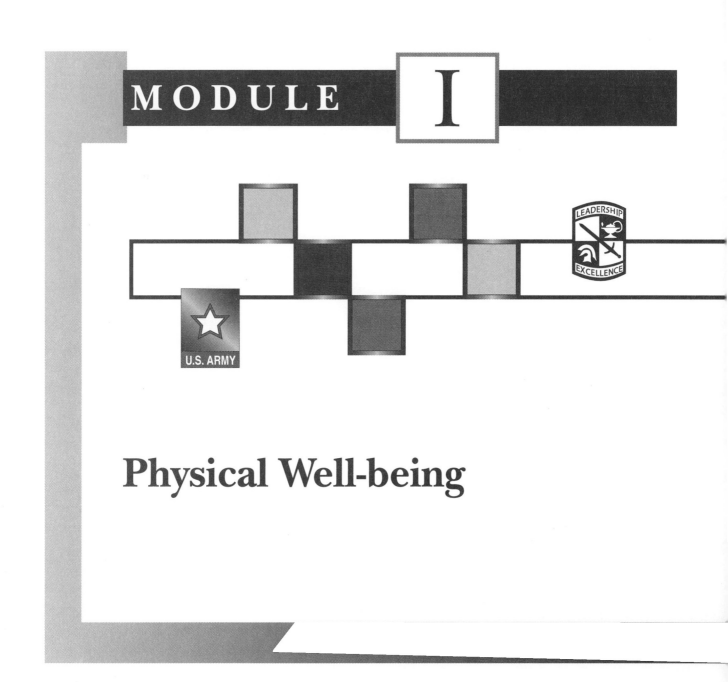

MODULE I

Physical Well-being

The Physical Well-being module is comprised of three lessons designed to introduce you to the standards of fitness that will be expected of you and to provide basic principles of fitness and diet that support a healthy lifestyle. Lesson one sets the tone for the importance of physical well-being as essential to the profession of the Army. The second lesson in the Physical Well-being module focuses on wellness while the third lesson emphasizes nutrition. Combined, these three lessons give you what you need to build and implement a total physical fitness program. The ultimate goal is you will willingly pursue a healthy lifestyle including a diet and fitness plan designed to achieve Army standards and individually established fitness goals.

Physical Fitness and Bearing

This lesson is intended to accomplish the following: 1) raise your awareness of the Army's physical fitness requirements; 2) relate personal assessment to physical wellness; and, 3) provide a set of tools for you to use to monitor and improve your own physical fitness.

The following topics are addressed in this lesson:

- Fitness components
- Principle of exercise
- Personal responsibility for fitness

The following Terminal Learning Objective (TLO) is supported in whole or in part by this lesson:

- Implement a Total Fitness Program

Following this lesson you will be able to:

- Describe the components of fitness as they relate to the Army's APFT
- Assess current health status
- Assess methods for improving physical health
- Explain the physical and emotional aspects of bearing as it relates to leadership.

Physical Fitness and Wellness

The lesson is intended to accomplish the following: 1) raise your awareness of importance of health and wellness; 2) assess personal health and wellness status and discuss methods for improvement; and, 3) assess current stress level and techniques to manage stress.

The following topics are addressed in this lesson:

- Principles and Practices of Wellness

The following TLO is supported in whole or in part by this lesson:

- Implement a Total Fitness Program

Following this lesson you will be able to:

- Identify the elements of a balanced, healthy lifestyle
- Use assessment tools to determine fitness status
- Set personal health goals
- Analyze personal stress levels in terms of principles of wellness

PUTTING HEALTH IN PERSPECTIVE

BY REBBECA J. DONATELLE

Although we use the term **health** almost unconsciously, few people understand the broad scope of the term or what it really means. For some, *health* simply means the antithesis of sickness. To others, *health* means being in good physical shape and being able to resist illness. Still others use terms like **wellness,** or *well-being,* to include a wide array of factors that seem to lead to positive health status. Why all of these variations? In part, the differences are due to an increasingly enlightened way of viewing health that has taken shape over time. In addition, as our collective understanding of illness has improved, so has our ability to understand the many nuances of health. Our progress to current understandings about health has evolved over centuries, and we have a long way to go in achieving a truly comprehensive view of this complex subject.

HEALTH: YESTERDAY AND TODAY

Prior to the 1800s, if you weren't sick, you were not only regarded as lucky, but also healthy. When deadly epidemics such as bubonic plague, pneumonic plague, influenza, tuberculosis, and cholera killed millions of people, survivors were believed to be of hearty, healthy stock, and congratulated themselves on their good fortune. Poor health was often associated with poor hygiene and unsanitary conditions, and certain stigmas were attached to households that harbored any of these illnesses. It wasn't until the late 1800s and early 1900s that researchers slowly began to discover that victims of these epidemics were not simply unhealthy or dirty people. Rather, they were victims of environmental factors (microorganisms found in contaminated water, air, and human waste) that made them sick and over which they often had little control. Public health officials moved swiftly to address these problems, and as a result, the term *health* became synonymous with *good hygiene.* Colleges offered courses in health and hygiene, or hygiene, that were the predecessors of the course you are in today.

Health Dynamic, ever-changing process of achieving individual potential in the physical, social, emotional, mental, spiritual, and environmental dimensions.

Wellness The achievement of the highest level of health possible in each of several dimensions.

Mortality Death rate.
Morbidity Illness rate.

Investigation into the environment as the primary cause of diseases continued well into the early 1900s, as outbreaks of diseases such as tuberculosis, pneumonia, and influenza surged in many regions of the world. If people made it through the first few years of life without succumbing to an infectious disease, they usually were able to survive to "old age." Keep in mind, however, that the average life expectancy in 1900 was only 47 years. Continued improvements in sanitation brought about dramatic changes in life expectancy, and the development of vaccines and antibiotics added even more years to the average lifespan.

By the 1940s, progressive thinkers in public health began to note that there was more to health than hygiene or disease. At an international conference in 1947 focusing on global health issues, the World Health Organization (WHO) took the landmark step of trying to clarify what *health* truly meant: "Health is the state of complete physical, mental, and social well-being, not just the absence of disease or infirmity."[1] For the first time, the concept of health came to mean more than the absence of disease.

Not until the 1960s and 1970s, however, did critics of a narrow definition of health successfully argue that health included much more than physical, social, or mental elements of life, and that other elements, such as environmental, spiritual, emotional, and intellectual aspects, helped define whether a person was truly capable of optimal functioning in typical daily settings. In addition, these critics argued that it wasn't just length of life or the number of disease-free years that really mattered, but rather living life to the fullest and reaching your optimum potential for happy, healthy, and productive life.

Today, because most childhood diseases are preventable or curable and because massive public health efforts are aimed at reducing the spread of infectious diseases, many people are living well into their 70s and 80s. According to **mortality** (death rate) statistics, people are now living longer than at any previous time in our history. **Morbidity** (illness) rates also indicate that people less frequently contract the common infectious diseases that devastated previous generations. However, longer life and less frequent disease are not proof that people are indeed *healthier.*

René Dubos, biologist and philosopher, aptly summarized the thinking of his contemporaries by defining *health* as "a quality of life, involving social, emotional, mental, spiritual, and biological fitness on the part of the individual, which results from adaptations to the environment."[2] The concept of adaptability, or the ability to successfully cope with life's ups and downs, became a key element of the overall health definition. Eventually the term *wellness* became popular and not only included the previously mentioned elements, but also implied that there were levels of health in each category. To achieve *high-level wellness,* a person would move progressively higher on a continuum of positive health indicators. Those who fail to achieve these levels may move to the illness side of the continuum. Today, the terms *health* and *wellness* are often used interchangeably to mean the dynamic, ever-changing process of trying to achieve one's individual potential in each of several interrelated dimensions.

- *Physical health.* This dimension includes characteristics such as body size and shape, sensory acuity and responsiveness, susceptibility to disease and disorders, body functioning, physical fitness, and recuperative abilities. Newer definitions of physical health also include our ability to perform normal **activities of daily living (ADLs),** or those tasks that are necessary to normal existence in today's society. Being able to get out of bed in the morning, being able to bend over to tie your shoes, or other usual daily tasks are examples of ADLs.
- *Intellectual health.* This dimension refers to the ability to think clearly, to reason objectively, to analyze critically, and to use "brain power" effectively to meet life's challenges. It means learning from successes and mistakes and making sound, responsible decisions that take into consideration all aspects of a situation.
- *Social health.* This dimension refers to the ability to have satisfying interpersonal relationships: interactions with others, adaptation to various social situations, and daily behaviors.
- *Emotional health.* This dimension refers to the feeling component—to express emotions when appropriate and to control emotions both when it is inappropriate to express them and to avoid expressing them in an inappropriate manner. Feelings of self-esteem, self-confidence, self-efficacy, trust, love, and many other emotional reactions and responses are all part of emotional health.
- *Environmental health.* This dimension refers to an appreciation of the external environment and the role individuals play in preserving, protecting, and improving environmental conditions.
- *Spiritual health.* This dimension may involve a belief in a supreme being or a specified way of living prescribed by a particular religion. Spiritual health also includes the feeling of unity with the environment—a feeling of oneness with others and with nature—and a guiding sense of meaning or value in life. It also may include the ability to understand and express one's purpose in life; to feel a part of a greater spectrum of existence; to experience love, joy, pain, sorrow, peace, contentment, and wonder over life's experiences; and to care about and respect all living things.

A well individual might display the following characteristics:

- A realistic sense of self, including personal capabilities and limitations
- An appreciation of all living things, no matter how ugly or beautiful, how unique or different, or how great or small
- A willingness to understand imperfection, to forgive others' mistakes, and to grow from personal mistakes or shortcomings
- The ability to laugh, to cry, and to genuinely "feel" emotions without getting lost in emotional upsets
- The ability to function at a reasonable level physiologically
- The ability to maintain and support healthy relationships with family, friends, intimate partners, and strangers
- An appreciation for one's role in preserving and protecting the environment
- A sense of satisfaction with life and an appreciation for the stages of the life experience
- A zest for living, coupled with a curiosity about what each new encounter, each new day will bring
- A respect for self, as well as a respect for others
- A realistic perspective about life's challenges and the skills to cope with life's stresses and challenges
- A balance in all things

Many people believe that wellness can best be achieved by the adoption of a *holistic* approach, in which a person emphasizes the integration of and balance among mind, body, and spirit. Persons on the illness and disability end of the continuum may have failed in one or more of these areas. This does not mean, however, that someone who is physically disabled can never achieve wellness. Rather, achieving wellness means attaining the optimum level of wellness for a given person's unique set of limitations and strengths. A physically disabled person may be functioning at his or her optimum level of performance; have satisfying interpersonal relationships; work to maintain emotional, spiritual, and intellectual health; and have a strong interest in environmental concerns. In contrast, those who spend hours lifting weights to perfect the size and shape of each muscle but pay little attention to nutrition may *look* healthy but may not maintain a healthy balance in all areas of health. Although we often consider physical attractiveness and other external trappings in measuring the overall health of a person, appearance and physical performance indicators are actually only two signs of physical health, indicating little about the other dimensions.

What Do You Think?

René Dubos, the renowned bacteriologist who developed many key philosophies about health, is credited with saying "Measure your Health by your sympathy with Morning and Spring." What do you think Dubos meant by this statement? Discuss how well your own health measures up when weighed against this criterion.

Activities of Daily Living (ADs)

Performance of tasks of everyday living, such as bathing, and walking up the stairs.

NEW DIRECTIONS FOR HEALTH

In response to the many indications that Americans were not as healthy as they should be, the Surgeon General of the United States proposed in 1990 a national plan for promoting health among individuals and groups.

HEALTHY PEOPLE 2000 *AND* 2010

Known as *Healthy People 2000,* the Surgeon General's plan outlined a series of long- and short-range goals and objectives.[3] Essentially, these goals included features such as improving the lifespan of all Americans by three years, reducing disparities in life expectancy, and improving access to health care for all Americans regardless of sex, race, socioeconomic status, and other variables. To realize these broad-based goals, *Healthy People 2000* provided hundreds of specific objectives for the nation to reach by the year 2000. For example, one goal was to reduce the average dietary-fat intake to

30 percent of calories consumed from the 40 percent average of the time. Other goals focused on specific priority areas relating to diet, smoking, exercise, immunizations, homicides, and other areas of concern. While *Health People 2000* was viewed as a landmark public health measure, the document also was criticized by many in the field for what were perceived as unreachable goals, a lack of national financial support, and no clear plan for achieving the goals. Since less than 5 percent of our national budget is allocated for prevention and we have historically spent most of our health care dollars on treatment, achieving these goals seems difficult.

Although many communities began working vigorously toward these goals soon after their initiation, as a nation, we still had a long way to go by as late as 1998. In an effort to continue working toward common goals, a new document, *Healthy People 2010,* took the initiative to the next level.[4] In the public sector, the Agency for Health Care, Research, and Quality (AHRQ) offered additional direction for national health care efforts through its *AHRQ Guidelines,* a set of objectives for health care providers to meet in specific area of practice.[5] For example, the guidelines related to tobacco specifically indicate what doctors should do when a patient who smokes visits them. Complete listings of the *Healthy People 2000* and *2010* documents, as well as area-specific guidelines, can be accessed through their respective websites. Visit this web-site for a direct link: *http://www. cdc.gov/nchs/ hphome.htm.*

BIBLIOGRAPHY

1. World Health Organization, "Constitution of the World Health Organization," *Chronicles of the World Health Organization* (Geneva, Switzerland, 1947).
2. R. Dubos, *So Human the Animal* (New York: Scribners, 1968), 15.
3. Department of Health and Human Services, *Healthy People 2000: National Health Promotion and Disease Prevention Objectives for the Year 2000* (Washington, DC: Government Printing Office, 1990).
4. Department of Health and Human Services, *Healthy People 2010 National Health Promotion and Disease Prevention Objectives for the Year 2010* (Washington, DC: Government Printing Office, 1998) (see DHHS website for specific information).
5. Agency for Health Care Policy and Research, Publications Clearinghouse, *Guidelines for Clinical Practice (by topic).* Phone: 800-358-9295. Also available through the Government Printing Office at 202-512-1800.

IMPROVING YOUR HEALTH

BY REBBECA J. DONATELLE

In the 1980s and 1990s, the United States made dramatic strides in identifying potential threats to health and in providing Americans with solid evidence, about health risks associated with various lifestyle behaviors.

BENEFITS OF OPTIMAL HEALTH

Table 2.1 on page 6 provides an overview of the leading causes of death in the United States, by age. Risks for each of these leading killers can be reduced significantly by the practice of specific lifestyle patterns—for example, consuming a diet low in saturated fat and cholesterol, exercising regularly, not smoking or consuming alcohol, and managing stress. Individual behavior is believed to be a major determinant of good health, but heredity, access to health care, and the environment are other factors that influence health status . When these factors are considered together and form the basis of a person's lifestyle choices, the net effect on health can be great.

For example, you may be predisposed to a less healthy lifestyle if you are unable to access the health care system because you have no health insurance, if your family doesn't believe in traditional medicine, or if family members or friends smoke, drink heavily, or take drugs. While you can't change your genetic history, and while improving your environment and the health care system can be difficult, you can influence your current and future health status by the behaviors you choose today.

HEALTH BEHAVIORS

Although mounting evidence indicates that there are significant benefits to being healthy, many people find it difficult to become and remain healthy. Most experts believe that several key behaviors will help people live longer, such as the following:

- Getting a good night's sleep (minimum of seven hours)
- Maintaining healthy eating habits

- Managing weight
- Participating in physical recreational activities
- Avoiding tobacco products
- Practicing safer sex
- Limiting intake of alcohol
- Scheduling regular self-exams and medical checkups

Although health professionals can statistically assess the health benefits of these behaviors, several other actions may not cause quantifiable "years added life" but may significantly result in "life added to years," such as the following:

- Controlling the real and imaginary stressors in life
- Forming and maintaining meaningful relationships with family and friends
- Making time for oneself
- Participating in at least one fun activity each day
- Respecting the environment and the people in it
- Considering alternatives when making decisions and assessing how actions affect others
- Valuing each day and making the best of opportunities
- Viewing mistakes as opportunities to learn and grow
- Being as kind to oneself as to others
- Understanding the health care system and using it wisely

Though it's easy to list things that one should do, change is not easy. All people, no matter where they are on the health/wellness continuum, have to start somewhere. All people have faced personal and external challenges to their attempts to change health behaviors—some have not done so well, some have been extremely successful, and some have made only small changes that may add up to significant improvements in how they feel and how they live. The key is to identify the behaviors most in need of change, determine goals and the actions necessary to accomplish them, set up a plan of action, and get started. But first, it is important to take a close look at factors that may contribute to current patterns of behavior.

TABLE 2.1 LEADING CAUSES OF DEATH IN THE UNITED STATES BY AGE (YEARS)

RANK	ALL AGES	1–4	5–14	15–24	25–44	45–65	65+
1	Diseases of heart	Unintentional injuries	Unintentional injuries	Unintentional injuries	Unintentional injuries	Malignant neoplasms	Diseases of heart
2	Malignant neoplasms	Congenital anomalies	Malignant neoplasms	Homicide and legal intervention	Malignant neoplasms	Diseases of heart	Malignant neoplasms
3	Cerebrovascular disease	Homicide and legal intervention	Homicide and legal intervention	Suicide	Diseases of heart	Unintentional injuries	Cerebrovascular diseases
4	Chronic obstructive disease	Malignant neoplasms	Congenital anomalies	Malignant neoplasms	Suicide	Cerebrovascular diseases	Chronic obstructive pulmonary diseases
5	Unintentional injuries	Diseases of heart	Diseases of heart	Diseases of heart	Human immunodeficiency virus infection	Diabetes mellitus	Pneumonia and influenza
6	Pneumonia and influenza	Pneumonia and influenza	Suicide	Congenital anomalies	Homicide and legal intervention	Chronic obstructive pulmonary diseases	Diabetes mellitus
7	Diabetes mellitus	Septicemia	Chronic obstructive pulmonary disease	Chronic obstructive pulmonary diseases	Chronic liver disease and cirrhosis	Chronic liver disease and cirrhosis	Unintentional injuries
8	Suicide	Conditions of perinatal period	Pneumonia and influenza	Pneumonia and influenza	Cerebrovascular diseases	Suicide	Nephritis, nephrotic syndrome, and nephrosis
9	Nephritis, nephrotic syndrome, and nephrosis	Cerebrovascular diseases	Benign neoplasms	Human immunodeficiency virus infection	Diabetes mellitus	Pneumonia and influenza	Alzheimer's disease
10	Chronic liver disease and cirrhosis	Benign neoplasms	Cerebrovascular diseases	Cerebrovascular diseases	Pneumonia and influenza	Human immunodeficiency virus infection	Septicemia

Source: Murphy, S. "Deaths: Final Data for 1998," National Vital Statistics Reports, vol. 48(11) from the Centers for Disease Control and Prevention (2000), National Center for Health Statistics, Hyattsville, MD. http://www.cdc.gov/nchs/data/nvs48_11_.pdf

DEFINING PSYCHOSOCIAL HEALTH

Psychosocial health encompasses the mental, emotional, social, and spiritual dimensions of health. It is the result of a complex interaction between a person's history and conscious and unconscious thoughts about and interpretations of the past. Psychosocially healthy people are emotionally, mentally, socially, intellectually, and spiritually *resilient* and are able to draw on deep reserves of wisdom in times of crisis. They have experienced pain and pleasure, and they have learned from these experiences and grown as individuals. They know when to call on friends for help, when to give help to others, and when it is okay to just be alone. They respond to challenges, disappointments, joys, frustrations, and pain in appropriate ways most of the time, despite occasional clips. Although definitions of psychosocial health vary, most authorities identify several basic elements shared by psychosocially healthy people.

- *The feel good about themselves.* Psychosocially healthy people are not typically overwhelmed by fear, love, anger, jealousy, guilt, or worry. They know who they are and have a realistic sense of their capabilities. They respect themselves even though they realize they aren't perfect.
- *They feel comfortable with other people.* Psychosocially healthy people have satisfying and lasting personal relationships and do not take advantage of others, nor do they allow others to take advantage of them. They can give love, consider others' interests, respect personal differences, and feel responsible for their fellow human beings.
- *They control tension and anxiety.* Psychosocially healthy people recognize the underlying causes and symptoms of stress and anxiety in their lives and consciously struggle to avoid illogical or irrational thoughts, unnecessary aggression, hostility, excessive excuse making, and blaming others for their problems.
- *They are able to meet the demands of life.* Psychosocially healthy people try to solve problems as they arise, to accept responsibility, and to plan ahead. They set realistic goals, think for themselves, and make independent decisions. Acknowledging that change is inevitable, they welcome new experiences.

They use their natural abilities to control their environment whenever possible and fit themselves into the environment when necessary.

- *They curb hate and guilt.* Psychosocially healthy people acknowledge and combat their tendencies to respond with hate, anger, thoughtlessness, selfishness, vengeful acts, or feelings of inadequacy. They do not try to knock others aside to get ahead but rather reach out to help others—even those they don't particularly care for. Rather than responding "in kind" to other people's negativity, they make honest attempts to listen, hear, and understand before jumping into the fray themselves.
- *They maintain a positive outlook.* Psychosocially healthy people try to approach each day with a presumption that things will go well. Since they believe that life is a gift, they are determined to enjoy it on a moment-to-moment basis rather than wander through it aimlessly. They block out most negative and cynical thoughts and give the good things in life star billing. They look to the future with enthusiasm rather than dread.
- *They enrich the lives of others.* Psychosocially healthy people recognize that there are others whose needs are greater than their own. They seek to ease these others' burdens by doing simple things such as giving a ride to an elderly neighbor who can't drive, bringing flowers to someone who's in pain, making dinner for someone who's too grief-stricken to cook, volunteering at a community agency, and making charitable donations.
- *They cherish the things that make them smile.* Psychosocially healthy people make a special place in their lives for memories of the past. Family pictures, high school mementos, souvenirs of past vacations, and other reminders of good experiences brighten their day. Fun is an integral part of their lives. So is making time for themselves.
- *They value diversity.* Psychosocially healthy people don't fear difference. They do not feel threatened by people who are of a different race, gender, religion, sexual orientation, ethnicity, or political party. They appreciate creativity in others as well as in themselves.

■ *They appreciate nature.* Psychosocially healthy people enjoy and respect natural beauty and wonders. They take the time to enjoy their surroundings and are conscious of their place in the universe.

Of course, few of us ever achieve perfection in these areas. Attaining psychosocial health and wellness involves many complex processes. The following sections of this chapter will help you understand not only what it means to be psychosocially well, but also why we often run into problems. In addition, learning how to assess your own health and to help yourself or seek help from others are important parts of psychosocial health (see Assess Yourself on page 13).

Psychosocial health The mental, emotional, social, and spiritual dimensions of health.
Mental health The "thinking" part of psychosocial health. Includes your values, attitudes, and beliefs.
Emotional health The "feeling" part of psychosocial health. Includes your emotional reactions to life.

What Do You Think?

What types of psychosocial qualities do you value the most in your friends? Do you think that you are strong in these areas yourself? Explain your answer.

MENTAL HEALTH: THE THINKING YOU

The term **mental health** is often used to describe the "thinking" part of psychosocial health. As a thinking being, you have the ability to reason, interpret, and remember events from a unique perspective; to sense, perceive, and evaluate what is happening; and to solve problems. In short, you are *intellectually* able to sort through the clutter of events, contradictory messages, and uncertainties of a situation and attach meaning (either positive or negative) to it (people often refer to this subset of mental health as *intellectual health.*) Your values, attitudes, and beliefs about your body, your family, your relationships, and life in general are usually—at least in part—a reflection of your mental health.

A mentally healthy person is likely to respond in a positive way even when things do not go as expected. For example, a mentally healthy student who receives a *D* on an exam may be very disappointed, but she will try to assess why she did poorly. Did she study enough? Did she attend class and ask questions about the things she didn't understand? Even though the test result may be very important to her, she will find a constructive way to deal with her frustration. She may talk to the instructor, plan to devote more time to studying before the next exam, or hire a tutor. In contrast, a mentally unhealthy person may take a distorted view and respond in an irrational manner. She may believe that her instructor is out to get her or that other students cheated on the exam. She may allow her low grade to provoke a major crisis in her life. She may spend the next 24 hours getting wasted, decide to quit school, try to get back at her instructor, or even blame her roommate for preventing her from studying.

When a person's mental health begins to deteriorate, he or she may experience sharp declines in rational thinking ability and increasingly distorted perceptions. The person may become cynical and distrustful, experience volatile mood swings, or choose to be isolated from others. The person's negative reactions to events may threaten the life and health of others. People showing such signs of extreme abnormal behavior or mental disorders are classified as having *mental illnesses,* discussed later in this chapter.

EMOTIONAL HEALTH: THE FEELING YOU

The term **emotional health** is often used interchangeably with *mental health.* Although emotional and mental health are closely intertwined, emotional health more accurately refers to the "feeling," or subjective, side of psychosocial health. **Emotions** are intensified feelings or complex patterns of feelings that we experience on a minute-by-minute, day-to-day basis. Loving, caring, hating, hurt, despair, release, joy, anxiety, fear, frustration, and intense anger are some of the many emotions we experience. Typically, emotions are described as the interplay of four components: *physiological arousal, feelings, cognitive (thought) processes,* and *behavioral reactions.* Each time you are put in a stressful situation, you react physiologically while your mind tries to sort things out. You consciously or unconsciously react based on how rationally you interpret the situation.

Psychologist Richard Lazarus has indicated that there are four basic types of emotions: (1) emotions resulting from harm, loss, or threats; (2) emotions resulting from benefits; (3) borderline emotions, such as hope and compassion; and (4) more complex emotions, such as grief, disappointment, bewilderment, and curiosity. Each of us may experience any of these

Assess Yourself

ASSESSING YOUR PSYCHOSOCIAL HEALTH

Being psychosocially healthy requires both introspection and the willingness to change or work on areas that need improvement. Often it is difficult to assess one's own behaviors and actions. Begin by completing the following assessment scale. When you've finished, ask someone who is very close to you to take the same test and respond with their perceptions of you. Carefully assess areas where your responses differ from those of your friend or family member. Which areas clearly need some work? Which areas are in good shape?

1 = never describes me	2 = describes me infrequently	3 = describes me fairly frequently	4 = describes me most of the time	5 = describes me all of the time

1. My actions and interactions indicate that I am confident in my abilities.	1 2 3 4 5
2. I am quick to blame others for things that go wrong in my life.	1 2 3 4 5
3. I am spontaneous and like to have fun with others.	1 2 3 4 5
4. I am able to give love and affection to others and show my feelings.	1 2 3 4 5
5. I am able to receive love and signs of affection from others without feeling uneasy.	1 2 3 4 5
6. I am generally positive and upbeat about things in my life.	1 2 3 4 5
7. I am cynical and tend to be critical of others.	1 2 3 4 5
8. I have a large group of people whom I consider to be good friends.	1 2 3 4 5
9. I make time for others in my life.	1 2 3 4 5
10. I take time each day for myself for quiet introspection, having fun, or just doing nothing.	1 2 3 4 5
11. I am compulsive and competitive in my actions.	1 2 3 4 5
12. I handle stress well and am seldom upset or stressed out by others.	1 2 3 4 5
13. I try to look for the good in everyone and every situation before finding fault.	1 2 3 4 5
14. I am comfortable meeting new people and interact well in social settings.	1 2 3 4 5
15. I would rather stay in and watch TV or read than go out with friends or interact with others.	1 2 3 4 5
16. I am flexible and can adapt to most situations, even if I don't like them.	1 2 3 4 5
17. Nature, the environment, and other living things are important aspects of my life.	1 2 3 4 5
18. I think before responding to my emotions.	1 2 3 4 5
19. I am selfish and tend to think of my own needs before those of others.	1 2 3 4 5
20. I am consciously trying to be a "better person."	1 2 3 4 5
21. I like to plan ahead and set realistic goals for myself and others.	1 2 3 4 5
22. I accept others for who they are.	1 2 3 4 5
23. I value diversity and respect others' rights, regardless of culture, race, sexual orientation, religion, or other differences.	1 2 3 4 5
24. I try to live each day as if it might by my last.	1 2 3 4 5
25. I have a great deal of energy and appreciate the little things in life.	1 2 3 4 5
26. I cope with stress in appropriate ways.	1 2 3 4 5
27. I get enough sleep each day and seldom feel tired.	1 2 3 4 5
28. I have healthy relationships with my family.	1 2 3 4 5
29. I am confident that I can do most things if I put my mind to them.	1 2 3 4 5
30. I respect others' opinions and believe that others should be free to express their opinions, even when they differ from my own.	1 2 3 4 5

Look at items 2, 7, 11, 15, and 19. Add up your score for these five items and divide by 5. Is your average for these items above or below 3? Did you score a 5 on any of these items? Do you need to work on any of these areas?

Now look at your scores for the remaining items (There should be 25 items.) Total these scores and divide by 25. Is your average above or below 3? On which items did you score a 5? Obviously you're doing well in these areas. Now remove these items from this grouping of 25 (scores of 5), and add up your scores for the remaining items. Then divide your total by the number of items included. Now what is your average?

Do the same for the scores completed by your friend or family member. How do your scores compare with those of the other person? Which ones, if any, are very different? How are they different? Which areas do you think you need to work on?

What actions can you take now to help improve your ratings in these areas?

emotions in any combination at any time. As rational beings, it is our responsibility to evaluate our individual emotional responses, the environment that is causing these responses, and the appropriateness of our actions.

Emotionally healthy people are usually able to respond in an appropriate manner to upsetting events. When they feel threatened, they are not likely to react in an extreme fashion, behave inconsistently, or adopt an offensive attack mode.

> **Emotions** Intensified feelings or complex patterns of feelings we constantly experience.

Even when their feelings are trampled upon or they suffer agonizing pain because of a lost love, they keep their emotions in check.

Emotionally unhealthy people are much more likely to let their feelings overpower them than are emotionally healthy people. Emotionally unhealthy people may be highly volatile and prone to unpredictable emotional outbursts and to inappropriate, sometimes frightening responses to events. An ex-boyfriend who becomes so angry that he begins to hit you and push you around in front of your friends because he is jealous of your new relationship is showing an extremely unhealthy and dangerous emotional reaction. Such violent responses have become a problem of epidemic proportions in the United States.

Emotional health also affects social health. Someone feeling hostile or withdrawn or displaying other mood fluctuations may be avoided by others. People in the midst of emotional turmoil may be grumpy, nasty, irritable, or overly quiet; they may cry easily or demonstrate other disturbing emotional responses. Since they are not much fun to be around, their friends may avoid them at the very time they are most in need of emotional support. Social isolation is just one of the many potential negative consequences of unstable emotional responses.

For students, a more immediate concern is the impact of emotional trauma or turmoil on academic performance. Have you ever tried to study for an exam after a fight with a close friend or family member? Emotional turmoil may seriously affect your ability to think, reason, or act in a rational way. Many otherwise rational, mentally healthy people do ridiculous things when they are going through a major emotional upset. Mental functioning and emotional responses are indeed intricately connected.

SOCIAL HEALTH: INTERACTIONS WITH OTHERS

Social health is the part of psychosocial health dealing with interactions with others and the ability to adapt to social situations. Socially healthy individuals have a wide range of social interactions with family, friends, acquaintances, and individuals with whom they may only occasionally come into contact. They are able to listen, to express themselves, to form healthy relationships, to act in socially acceptable and responsible ways, and to find the best fit for themselves in society.

Numerous studies have documented the importance of social life in achieving and maintaining health, and two aspects of social health have proven to be particularly important.

- *Presence of strong bonds.* **Social bonds,** or social linkages, reflect the general degree and nature of our interpersonal contacts and interactions. Social bonds generally have six major functions: (1) providing intimacy, (2) providing feelings of belonging to or integration with a group, (3) providing opportunities for giving or receiving nurturance, (4) providing reassurance of one's worth, (5) providing assistance and guidance, and (6) providing advice. In general, people who are more "connected" to others manage stress more effectively and are much more resilient when bombarded by life's crises.
- *Presence of key social supports.* **Social supports** refer to relationships that bring positive benefits to the individual. Social supports can be either expressive (emotional support, encouragement) or structural (housing, money). Families provide both structural and expressive support to children. Adults need to develop their own social supports.

> Psychosocially healthy people create a network of friends and family with whom they can give and receive support.

Social health also reflects the way we react to others. In its most extreme forms, a lack of social health may be represented by aggressive acts of prejudice and bias toward other individuals or groups. **Prejudice** is a negative evaluation of an entire group of people that is typically based on unfavorable (and often wrong) ideas about the group. In its most obvious manifestations, prejudice is reflected in acts of discrimination against others, in overt acts of hate and bias, and in purposeful intent to harm individuals or groups.

SPIRITUAL HEALTH

Although mental and emotional health are key factors in overall psychosocial functioning, it is possible to be mentally and emotionally healthy and still not achieve optimal levels of psychosocial well-being. What is missing? For many people, that difficult-to-describe element that gives zest to life is the spiritual dimension. For a complete discussion of spiritual health, see the section later in this material.

What Do You Think?

What are your strengths and weaknesses in the area of psychosocial health? What can you do to enhance your strengths? What does social and emotional health mean to you? What could you do to enhance your health in these areas?

FACTORS INFLUENCING PSYCHOSOCIAL HEALTH

Although it's relatively easy to say what psychosocial health is, it is much more difficult to assess why some people are psychosocially well virtually all the time, others are some of the time, and still others almost never are. What factors have influenced your own patterns of mental, emotional, social, and spiritual health? Are these factors changeable? Can you do anything to improve your health if you have problems? How can you enhance the positive qualities you already possess?

Social bonds Degree and nature of interpersonal contacts.

Social supports Structural and functional aspects of social interactions.

Prejudice A negative evaluation of an entire group of people that is typically based on unfavorable and often wrong ideas about the group.

Dysfunctional families Families in which there is violence; physical, emotional, or sexual abuse; parental discord; or other negative family interactions.

Most of our mental, emotional, and social reactions to life are a direct outcome of our experiences and social and cultural expectations. We often inter-pret situations based on learned reactions to certain environmental and social stimuli.

EXTERNAL FACTORS

Our psychosocial health is based on how we perceive life experiences. While some experiences are under our control, others are not. External influences are those factors in life that we do not control, such as who raised us and the physical environment in which we live.

The Family

Families have a significant influence on psychosocial development. Children raised in healthy, nurturing, happy families are more likely to become well-adjusted, productive adults. Children raised in families in which violence, negative behaviors, distrust, anger, dietary deprivation, drug abuse, parental discord, sexual, physical, or emotional abuse, or other characteristics of **dysfunctional families** are present may have a harder time adapting to life. In dysfunctional families, love, security, and unconditional trust are so lacking that the children in such families are often confused and psychologically bruised. Yet not all people raised in dysfunctional families become psychosocially unhealthy. Conversely, not all people from healthy family environments become well adjusted. Obviously, "more factors are involved in our" process of becoming than just our family.

The Wider Environment

While isolated negative events may do little damage to psychosocial health, persistent stressors, uncertainties, and threats may cause significant problems. Children raised in environments where crime is rampant and daily safety is in question, for example, run an increased risk of psychosocial problems. Drugs, crime, violent acts, school failure, unemployment, and a host of other bad things can happen to good people. But it is believed that certain protective factors, such as having a positive role model in the midst of chaos or high *self-esteem,* or level of self-evaluation and self-regard, may help children from even the worst environments remain healthy and well adjusted.

Another important influence on psychosocial health is access to health services and programs designed to maintain or enhance psychosocial health. Going to a support group or seeing a trained counselor or therapist is often a crucial first step in prevention and intervention efforts. Individuals from poor socioeconomic environments who cannot afford such services often find it difficult to secure help in improving their psychosocial health.

Social Supports and Social Bonds

Although often overlooked, a stable, loving support network of family and friends is key to psychosocial health. *Social supports* and the *social bonds* that come from close relationships help us get through even the most difficult times. Having those with whom we can talk, share thoughts, and practice good and bad behaviors without fear of losing their love is an essential part of growth.

INTERNAL FACTORS

Although life experiences influence people in fairly obvious ways, many internal factors also work more subtly to shape a person's development. Some of these factors are hereditary traits, hormonal functioning, physical health status (including neurological functioning), physical fitness level, and elements of certain mental and emotional health. If problems occur in relation to any of these factors, overall psychosocial health declines.

During our formative years, successes and failures in school, in athletics, in friendships, in intimate relationships, in our jobs, and in every other aspect of life subtly shape our perceptions and beliefs about our own personal worth and ability to act to help ourselves. These perceptions and beliefs in turn become internal influences on our psychosocial health. Psychologist Albert Bandura used the term **self-efficacy** to describe a person's belief about whether he or she can successfully engage in and execute a specific behavior. Prior success in academics, athletics, or achieving popularity will lead to expectations of success in these events in the future. Always being the last chosen to play basketball or long-term inability to make friends easily may make failure seem inevitable. In general, the more self-efficacious a person is and the more his or her past experiences have been positive, the more likely he or she will be to keep trying to execute a specific behavior successfully. A person having low self-efficacy may give up easily or never even try to change a behavior. People who have a high level of self-efficacy are also more likely to feel that they have **personal control** over situations, that their own internal resources allow them to control events.

Psychologist Martin Seligman has proposed that people who continually experience failure may develop a pattern of responding known as **learned helplessness** in which they give up and fail to take any action to help themselves. More recently, Seligman's theory has been expanded; just as we may learn to be helpless, so may we learn to be optimistic. His research on learned optimism provides growing evidence for the central place of mental health in overall positive development.

Personality

Your personality is the unique mix of characteristics that distinguish you from others. Hereditary, environmental, cultural, and experiential factors influence how each person develops. For each of us, the amount of influence exerted by any of these factors differs. Personality determines how we react to the challenges of life. It also determines how we interpret the feelings we experience and how we resolve the conflicts we feel on being denied the things we need or want.

Most of the recent schools of psychosocial theory promote the idea that we have the power not only to understand our behavior but also to actively change it and thus mold our own personalities. Yet although much has been written about the importance of a healthy personality, there is little true consensus on what that concept really means. People who have the following traits often appear to have key elements of what it takes to be psychosocially healthy:[5]

- *Extraversion.* This refers to the ability to adapt to a social situation and demonstrate assertiveness as well as power or interpersonal involvement.

- *Agreeableness.* This refers to the ability to conform, be likable, and demonstrate friendly compliance as well as love.

- *Openness to experience.* This refers to the ability to demonstrate curiosity and independence (also referred to as *inquiring intellect*).

- *Emotional stability.* Someone who demonstrates emotional stability is able to maintain social control.

- *Conscientiousness.* Someone who is conscientious demonstrates self-control and is dependable. This person has a need to achieve.[1]

Lifespan and Maturity

Although the exact determinants of personality are impossible to define, researchers do know that our personalities are not static. Rather, they change as we move through the stages of our lives. Our temperaments also change as we grow, as is illustrated by the extreme emotions experienced by many people in early adolescence. Most of us learn to control our emotions as we advance toward adulthood.

The college years mark a critical transition period for young adults as they move away from families and establish themselves as independent adults. For most, this step toward maturity entails changing the nature of the relationship to parents. The transition to independence will be easier for those who have successfully accomplished earlier developmental tasks such as learning how to solve problems, make and evaluate decisions, define and adhere to personal values, and establish both casual and intimate relationships. Management of personal finances, career strategies, interpersonal communication skills, and parenting skills (for those who choose to become parents) are among the developmental tasks college students must accomplish. Older students often have to balance the responsibilities of family, career, and school.

If you have not fulfilled earlier tasks, you will continue to grow but may find your life interrupted by recurrent "crises" left over from earlier stages. For example, if you did not learn to trust others in childhood, you may have difficulty establishing intimate relationships in late adolescence or early adulthood.

Self-efficacy Belief in one's own ability to perform a task successfully.

Personal control Belief that one's own internal resources can control a situation.

Learned helplessness Patterns of responding to situations by giving up because of repeated failure in the past.

Self-esteem Sense of self-respect or self-confidence.

What Do You Think?

Over which external factors does an individual have the most control? Which factors had the greatest impact on making you who you are today?

ENHANCING PSYCHOSOCIAL HEALTH

You may believe that your psychosocial health is fairly well developed by the time you reach college. However, you can always take steps to improve it. Your well-being is largely determined by your ability to respond to life's challenges and can be defined by your level of self-fulfillment or self-actualization. Attaining self-fulfillment is a lifelong, conscious process that involves building self-esteem, understanding and controlling emotions, and learning to solve problems and make decisions.

DEVELOPING AND MAINTAINING SELF-ESTEEM AND SELF-EFFICACY

Self-esteem

Self-esteem refers to one's sense of self-respect or self-worth. It can be defined as how one evaluates oneself and values one's own personal worth as an individual. People with high self-esteem tend to feel good about themselves and have a positive outlook on life. People with low self-esteem often do not like themselves, constantly demean themselves, and doubt their ability to succeed.

Our self-esteem is a result of the relationships we have with our parents and family during our formative years, our friends as we grow older, our significant others as we form intimate relationships, and with our teachers, coworkers, and others throughout our lives. If we felt loved and valued as children, our self-esteem may allow us to believe that we are inherently "lovable individuals" as we reach adulthood (see the Skills for Behavior Change box).

Finding a Support Group

The best way to maintain self-esteem is through a support group—peers who share your values and offer the nurturing that your family can no longer provide. The prime prerequisite for a support group is that it makes you feel good about yourself and forces you to take an honest look at your actions and choices. Although the idea of finding a support group seems to imply establishing a wholly new group, remember that old ties are often among the strongest. Keeping in contact with old friends and with important family members can provide a foundation of unconditional love that may help you through the many life transitions ahead.

Try to be a support for others, too. Join a discussion, political action, or recreational group. Write more postcards and "thinking of you" notes to people who matter. This will build both your own self-esteem and that of your friends.

Completing Required Tasks

A way to boost your self-efficacy is to learn how to complete required tasks successfully and develop a history of success. You are not likely to succeed in your studies if you leave term papers until the last minute, fail to keep up with the reading for your courses, and do not ask for clarification of points that are confusing to you. Most college campuses provide study groups and learning centers for various content areas. These groups offer tips for managing time, understanding assignments, dealing with professors, and preparing for test taking. Poor grades, or grades that do not meet expectations, are major contributors to diminished self-esteem and self-efficacy and to emotional distress among college students.

Forming Realistic Expectations

Having realistic expectations of yourself is another method of boosting self-esteem. College is a time to explore your potential. The stresses of college life may make your expectations for success difficult to meet. If you expect perfect grades, a steady stream of Saturday-night dates and a soap-opera-type romantic involvement, and the perfect job, you may be setting yourself up for failure. Assess your current resources and the direction in which you are heading. Set small, incremental goals that are possible to meet.

Taking and Making Time for You

Taking time to enjoy yourself is another way to boost your self-esteem and psychosocial health. Viewing each new activity as something to look forward to and an opportunity to have fun is an important part of keeping the excitement in your life. Wake up focusing on the fun things you have to look forward to each day, and try to make this anticipation a natural part of your day.

Maintaining Physical Health

Maintaining physical health also contributes to self-esteem and self-efficacy. Regular exercise fosters a sense of well-being. Nourishing meals can help you avoid the weight gain experienced by many college students. (See Chapter 10 for more information on the role of exercise on health.)

Examining Problems and Seeking Help

Knowing when to seek help from friends, support groups, family, or professionals is another important factor in boosting self-esteem. Sometimes life's problems are insurmountable; sometimes you can handle them alone. Recognizing your strengths and acting appropriately are keys to psychosocial health.

What Do You Think?

Based on how self-esteem and self-efficacy develop, which do you think it would be easier to improve on in adulthood? Do you think special 1-week lessons designed to improve self-esteem among school-age children would be effective? Why or why not? What might work to improve self-esteem among young people?

SLEEP: THE GREAT RESTORER

Sleep serves at least two biological purposes in the body: *conservation* of energy so that we are rested and ready to perform during high-performance daylight hours, and *restoration* so that neurotransmitters that have been depleted during waking hours can be replenished. This process clears the brain of daily minutiae as a means of preparing for a new day. Getting enough sleep to feel ready to meet daily challenges is a key factor in maintaining optimal physical and psychosocial health.

All of us can identify with that tired, listless feeling caused by sleep deprivation during periods of high stress. Either we can't find enough hours in the day for sleep, or once we get into bed, we can't fall asleep or stay asleep. **Insomnia**—difficulty in falling asleep quickly, frequent arousals during sleep, or early morning awakening—is a common complaint among 20 to 40 percent of Americans. Insomnia is more common among women than among men, and its prevalence is correlated with age and low socioeconomic status.

Some people have difficulty getting a good night's rest due to other sleep disorders. **Sleep apnea,** a condition in which a person may experience hundreds of episodes of breathing stoppage during a normal night's sleep, is increasingly common. Typically caused by upper respiratory tract problems in which weak muscle tone allows part of the airway to collapse, sleep apnea results in poor air exchange. This in turn causes a rise in blood pressure and low oxygen supply in the blood. Sleep apnea may do more than just disrupt sleeping cycles; in some cases, it can actually pose a serious health risk.

How much sleep each of us needs to feel refreshed depends on many factors. There is a genetically based need for sleep, different for each species. Sleep duration is also controlled by *circadian*

Skills for Behavior Change

BUILDING SELF-ESTEEM

Because self-esteem develops over many years, it cannot be improved effortlessly in one brief self-help workshop. However, there are several things you can do in your day-to-day life that may seem unimportant but, when practiced regularly and added to other actions, can have a significant impact on the way you feel about yourself.

Squelch That Inner Critic We are often our own worst enemies. We harp at ourselves continually about how we look and how we should have behaved in certain situations. Begin squelching that inner voice now:

- *Examine your faults with a "mirror" rather than a magnifying glass.* Instead of saying, "I'm stupid and I'll never get through this class," say, "I didn't do so well on this last test, but I'm going to do better. I'm doing great in another class."
- *Recharacterize your "mistakes" as opportunities to know yourself better or as growth experiences that will teach you to do things differently next time.* If you find that you made careless mistakes on a test because you rushed through it, resolve to take more time on your next test to double-check your work.
- *Say thank you rather than mumbling something in protest next time someone compliments you.* Don't mumble, "It's just my job" or "What choice did I have but to do it?" Always respond positively to compliment.

Focus on the Positive Don't allow yourself to wallow in self-pity. Although it's probably impossible to be upbeat at all times, you can do a great deal to shorten the interlude between positive thoughts:

- *Don't sulk.* When upset, allow yourself 15 minutes to worry and be upset and then force yourself to do or think of something else.
- *Don't compare yourself with others.* Concentrate on improving your past performance.
- *Give yourself time to feel good.* When you reach an objective, allow time for fun before starting another project.
- *Spend time with a friend who cares about you and isn't afraid to let you know it.* Friends are crucial to positive self-esteem, say experts, because they make up your "psychic family"—an important source of support and objectivity.
- *Count your blessings.* Make a list of all of the people, events, and things in your life for which you are grateful. List your own accomplishments. Whenever you feel cheated by life, look at this list.

rhythms, which are linked to the hormone *melatonin.* People may also control sleep patterns by staying up late, drinking coffee, getting lots of physical exercise, eating a heavy meal, or using alarm clocks. The most important period of sleep, known as the time of *rapid eye movement, or REM sleep,* is essential to feeling rested and refreshed by sleep. This is the period of deepest sleep, during which we dream. If we miss this period of sleep, then we are left feeling groggy and sleep deprived.

Though many people turn to over-the-counter sleeping pills, barbiturates, or tranquilizers to get some sleep, the following methods for conquering sleeplessness are less harmful:[7]

- *If your sleeplessness arises from worry or grief, try to correct what's bothering you.* If you can't correct it yourself, confide in a friend, join a support group, or find a qualified counselor to help you.
- *Don't drink alcohol or smoke before bedtime.* Alcohol can disrupt sleep patterns and make insomnia worse. Nicotine also makes you wakeful.
- *Avoid eating a heavy meal in the evening, particularly at bedtime.* Don't drink large amounts of liquids before retiring, either.
- *Eliminate or reduce consumption of caffeinated beverages except in the morning or early afternoon.*
- *Try a midafternoon nap, when circadian rhythms make you especially sleepy.* But avoid taking multiple catnaps—a practice that will keep you awake at night when you should be sleeping.
- *Spend an hour or more relaxing before retiring.* Read, listen to music, watch TV, or take a warm bath.

- *If you're unable to fall asleep, get up and do something rather than lie there.* Don't bring work to bed. If you wake up in the middle of the night and can't fall asleep again, try reading for a short time. Counting sheep or reconstructing a happy event or narrative in your mind may lull you to sleep.
- *Avoid reproaching yourself.* Don't make your sleeplessness a cause for additional worry. Insomnia is not a crime. Not everyone needs eight hours of sleep. You can feel well—and be quite healthy—on less. Don't worry that you have to make up lost sleep. One good night's sleep will reinvigorate you.
- *Don't watch the clock at night.* Turn it to the wall to avoid the temptation to worry about the night slipping away.
- *Go to bed and rise on a regular schedule.* Keep this schedule no matter how much you have or haven't slept in the recent past.
- *Get daily exercise, but not within three hours of bedtime.*
- *Experiment . . .* Figure out how much sleep you need to feel good, and then schedule it.

Insomnia Difficulty in falling asleep or staying asleep.

Sleep apnea Disorder in which a person has numerous episodes of breathing stoppage during a normal night's sleep.

Spirituality A form of well-being in which a person acknowledges the need for having, relating, being, and transcendence in the quest for meaning and purpose in life.

SPIRITUALITY: AN INNER QUEST FOR WELL-BEING

Most of us have heard from others or recognized in our own lives the importance of a spiritual dimension; this might range from a tree-hugging zest for nature to a great love for a God-like deity. Philosophers and humanists have discussed spirituality, religious crusaders have promoted spirituality throughout the world, and today, researchers extol the virtues of spirituality for everything from saving interpersonal relationships to reducing stress, maintain health, and living in harmony with nature and other living entities. Countless people report that they are on a quest to get in touch with their spiritual side.

But what, exactly, does **spirituality** mean? Although numerous definitions exist, most experts agree that *spiritual health* refers to a belief in some unifying force that gives purpose or meaning to life, or a sense of belonging to a scheme of being that is greater than the purely physical or personal dimensions of existence. For some, this unifying force is nature; for others, it is a feeling of connection to other people coupled with a recognition of the eternal nature of the human race; for others still, the unifying force is a god or some other spiritual symbol. Dr. N. Lee Smith, internist and associate professor of medicine at the University of Utah, defines spiritual health in the following ways:

- The quality of existence in which one is at peace with oneself and in good stead with the environment
- A sense of empowerment and personal control that includes feeling heard and valued, and feeling in control over one's responses (but not necessarily in control of one's environment)
- A sense of connectedness to one's deepest self, to other people, and to all regarded as good
- A sense of meaning and purpose, which provides a sense of mission by finding meaning and wisdom in the here and now
- Enjoying the process of growth and having a vision of one's potential
- Having hope, which translates into positive expectations[2]

Many of us live on a rather superficial material plane, focused on satisfying basic human needs.

People tend to be rather *egocentric,* or self-oriented, during the formative years of life, acquiring material possessions because it feels good and seems right. It provides immediate gratification and emotional pleasure that keep the focus on one's immediate environment. Worrying about the car you drive, the house you live in, the stereo you listen to, and the clothes you wear are examples of this use of possessions to give meaning to life. According to psychologist and philosopher Carl Jung, our materialistic Western civilization leads us to deny spiritual needs for much of our lives.

But there comes a point, usually around midlife, when we discover that material possessions do not automatically bring happiness or a sense of self-worth. A crisis may trigger this realization earlier. A failed relationship, a terrible accident, the death of a close friend or family member, or other loss often prompts a search for meaning, for the answer to the proverbial question "Is that all there is?" We begin to recognize that material things, prestige, money, power, and fame count for little in the larger scheme of existence and do not give meaning to life. At this point, many people reach what is often called a *midlife crisis,* an experience characterized by a sense of spiritual bankruptcy.[3] According to Jung,

> we need not be devastated by this sudden recognition, for with it comes the opportunity to reach deep within ourselves in order to resolve and integrate the polarities of our nature. Within our creative and collective unconscious we may discover a richness and a strength and a wisdom that we have not been able to utilize before.[4]

It takes time and life experience to begin appreciating the great gift of life and caring about more than immediate self-gratification. Some individuals develop their spiritual side in youth; others find it later in life. Still others never really gain this spiritual awareness.

As we develop into spiritually healthy beings, we begin to recognize our identity as unique individuals. We reach a better understanding of our strengths and shortcomings and our place in the universe. Many find that families, the environment, friends, strangers who are suffering, and religion assume greater significance. Many become more conscious of other living creatures and place a greater value on animals; some may give up eating meat for spiritual reasons. By developing an understanding of spiritual health and how it is interwoven intricately into our existence, we may embrace its power to improve health and our overall perspective on life. In turn, we may begin to notice more, feel more, and experience more of life. Perhaps most important, we may gain an appreciation for the here-and-now, rather than living for aspirations that we may never achieve.

Usually, people who have gained insight into spirituality describe it as involving a connectedness to self, to others, to nature, and to a larger meaning or purpose. They also indicate that it is associated with creativity, play, love, forgiveness, compassion, respect, trust, wisdom, and reverence; for some, it may also include faith in a higher being or deity. In its purest sense, spirituality addresses four main themes: **interconnectedness,** the practice of **mindfulness,** spirituality as a part of everyday life, and living in harmony with the community. The following examples illustrate each of these themes:

- *Interconnectedness.* This concept includes connectedness to self, connectedness to others, and connectedness to a larger meaning or purpose. Connecting with oneself involves exploring feelings, taking time to consider how you feel in a given situation, assessing your emotional reactions to people and experiences, and taking mental notes when things or people cause you to lose equilibrium. It also involves considering your values and achieving congruence between what you consider important (your goals) and what you can do to achieve your goals without compromising your values. You may choose to connect with people on a physical, emotional, social, occupational, intellectual, or spiritual way.
- *Practice of mindfulness.* This includes the ability to be fully present in the moment. Mindfulness has been described as a way of nurturing greater awareness, clarity, and acceptance of present-moment reality or a form of inner "flow"—a holistic sensation felt when a person is totally involved in the moment. According to mindfulness experts, you can achieve this inner flow through an almost infinite range of opportunities for enjoyment and pleasure, either through the use of physical and sensory skills ranging from athletics to music to yoga, or through the development of symbolic skills in areas

such as poetry, philosophy, or mathematics. The psychologist Abraham Maslow referred to these moments as *peak experiences,* during which a person feels integrated, synergistic, and at one with the world.
- *Spirituality as a part of daily life.* This refers to the ability to develop spiritual nature to its fullest potential. This spirituality is embodied in the ability to discover and articulate our own basic purpose in life; to learn how to experience love, joy, peace, and fulfillment; and to help ourselves and others achieve their full potential. This ongoing process of growth fosters three convictions: *faith, hope,* and *love.* **Faith** is the belief that helps us realize our purpose in life; **hope** is the belief that allows us to look confidently and courageously to the future; and **love** involves accepting, affirming, and respecting self and others regardless of who they are. Love also encompasses caring for and cherishing our environment. Rather than setting these three convictions as a goal to attain in the future, we should accept them as part of life's ongoing journey at all times.[5]
- *Living in harmony with community.* This aspect of spirituality involves living in congruence, peace, and harmony with the values of the greater community. Our values are an extension of our beliefs about the world and attitude toward life. They are formed over time through a series of life experiences, and they are reflected in our hopes, dreams, desires, goals, and ambitions.[6] Though most people have some idea of what is important to them, until a life-altering event shakes up their usual perspective on life, many spend life largely unaware of how their values impact themselves or those around them.

Interconnectedness A web of connections, including our relationship to ourselves, to others, and to a larger meaning or purpose in life.

Mindfulness Awareness and acceptance of the reality of the present moment.

Faith Belief that helps each person realize a unique purpose in life.

Hope Belief that establishes confidence and courage in facing the future.

Love Acceptance, affirmation, and respect for the self and others.

SPIRITUALITY: A KEY TO HEALTH AND WELLNESS

Although many experts affirm the importance of the spirituality in achieving health and wellness, the specific impact of this dimension remains illusive. Some experts describe the spiritual dimension as a factor of well-being, which is achieved when four basic kinds of needs are satisfied:[7]

1. The need for having
2. The need for relating
3. The need for being
4. The need for transcendence, or that sense of well-being that is experienced when a person finds purpose and meaning in life; nonphysical in nature, it can best be described as spiritual.

Over recent decades, studies have shown that most Americans want spirituality in their lives, but for many, it does not necessarily take the form of religion. Many find spiritual fulfillment in music, poetry, literature, art, nature, and intimate relationships.[8] Researcher Wade Clark Roof, of the University of California at Santa Barbara, found that in the 1960s and 1970s, baby boomers dropped out of organized religion in large numbers: 84 percent of Jews, 69 percent of mainline Protestants, 61 percent of conservative Protestants, and 67 percent of Catholics.[9] Many dropped out of formal religious practice not because they lost interest in spirituality, but because they felt that organized religion was not meeting their spiritual needs. In the 1990s, national polls show that 9 out of 10 Americans believe in God and consider religion and/or spirituality to be important in their lives.[10] In fact, since the 1990s, a movement back toward formal religious participation has grown in number. Many religious groups have spawned new philosophies *that are more inclusive and often influenced by new-age ideas.* An estimated 32 million baby boomers remain unaffiliated with older schools of religion and instead have turned to Eastern practices, new-age philosophies, twelve-step programs, Greek mythology, Jungian psychology, shamanic practices, massage, yoga, and a host of other traditions and practices (see New Horizons in Health box).[11]

For some, spirituality means a "quest for self and selflessness"—a form of therapy and respite from a sometimes challenging personal environment. This quest for a "life force," which helps people deeply experience the moments of their lives rather than just living through them, has received much scholarly and popular attention. Self-help books that focus on spirituality consistently top the bestseller lists.

Television programs promote the virtues of a spiritual or natural existence. Writers and psychologists such as William James, Gordon Allport, Erich Fromm, Viktor Frankl, Abraham Maslow, and Rollo May have made spirituality a major focus of their work. Carl Jung went so far as to say that spirituality was such an essential ingredient in psychological health that he could heal only those middle-aged people who embraced a spiritual or religious perspective in their lives.

Spiritual health courses have emerged as offshoots of public health coursework and medical school training in recent years. For example, the Harvard Medical School of Continuing Education offers a course called "Spirituality and Healing in Medicine," which brings together scholars and medical professionals from around the world to discuss the role of spirituality in the treatment of illness and chronic pain. Self-help workshops focusing on spiritual elements of health and the prevention of premature death and illness continue to surface in cities throughout the world. Although courses and self-help books may point you in the right direction, integrating spirituality into your life requires concerted effort, considerable thought, and careful planning.

New Horizons in Health

HEALING THROUGH FAITH AND SPIRITUALITY

Though dozens of studies have begun to examine the effects of religion and spirituality on mental health, the subject has lacked sufficient funding for more in-depth research. Recently, however, the National Institute of Health Care Research, a nonprofit organization, began awarding grants of up to $15,000 in support of academic projects exploring spirituality and psychiatry. Although this small amount of money is not enough to conduct the randomized, controlled trials necessary to make serious inquiry into this topic, universities such as Harvard have made some interesting preliminary statements about the role that spirituality may have in health and healing. However, much of the research being done in this area lacks adequate controls, includes too small a sample size, and/or has substantive methodological problems that make conclusive statements about results impossible. Nevertheless, several provide some interesting preliminary results that could provide considerable insights, were they to be investigated more thoroughly. Some of these examples are included below:

- *Stress.* The Alameda County Study, which trails nearly 7,000 Californians, showed that West Coast worshippers who participate in church-sponsored activities are markedly less stressed over finances, health, and other daily concerns than nonreligious types (*Journal of Gerontology: Psychological Sciences, 1998*).

- *Blood pressure.* Elderly people in a Duke University study who attended religious services, prayed, or read the Bible regularly had lower blood pressure than their nonpracticing peers.

- *Recovery.* In a Duke University study, devout patients recovering from surgery spent an average of 11 days in the hospital, compared with nonreligious patients who spent 25 days.

- *Mortality.* Research on 1,931 older adults indicates that those who attend religious services regularly have a lower mortality rate.

- *Immunity.* Research on 1,700 adults found that those who attend religious services were less likely to have elevated levels of interleukin-6, an immune substance prevalent in people with chronic diseases.

- *Lifestyle.* A recent review of several studies suggests that spirituality is linked with low suicide rates, less alcohol and drug abuse, less criminal behavior, fewer divorces, and higher marital satisfaction.

- *Depression.* Women with pious mothers are 60 percent less likely to be depressed over the course of 10 years than women whose mothers aren't so reverent, according to a Columbia University study. Daughters belonging to the same religious denomination as their mothers are even less likely (71 percent) to suffer the blues; sons were 84 percent less likely.

- A Duke University study of 577 men and women hospitalized for physical illness showed that the more patients used positive coping strategies (seeking spiritual support from friends and religious leaders, praying, meditating, etc.), the lower the level of their depressive symptoms and the higher their quality of life.

Source: From "Spirituality: It's What's Missing in Mental Health," by D. N. Elkins, September/October, 1999, *Psychology Today*, p. 48.

THE MIND-BODY CONNECTION

Can negative emotions make a person physically sick and positive emotions boost the immune system? Researchers have explored the possible interaction between emotions and health, especially in conditions of uncontrolled, persistent stress. According to the simplest theory of this interaction, the brain of an emotionally overwrought person sends signals to the adrenal glands, which respond by secreting cortisol and epinephrine (adrenaline), the hormones that activate the body's stress response. These chemicals are also known to suppress immune functioning, so it has been surmised that the persistently overwrought person undergoes subtle immune changes. What remains to be shown is how these changes affect overall health, if they do at all.

HAPPINESS: A KEY TO WELL-BEING

Although we can list the actions that we should perform to stay physically healthy, such as eating the right foods, getting enough rest, exercising, avoiding harmful substances, and so on, most of us wonder how to achieve that "feeling-good state" that researchers call **subjective well-being (SWB).** This refers to that all-too-uncommon uplifting feeling of inner peace, wonder, and unadulterated happiness we experience when walking on a remote trail after a rain and smelling fresh pine needles or the first flowers of spring. For most of us, those unexpected moments catapult us out of lethargy and give us bursts of energy. Although numerous studies of SWB have been done to determine what gives people satisfaction, makes us feel alive, and elevates our mood to a state called "happiness," researchers argue over what it really means to achieve a state of subjective well-being. Psychologists David Myers and Ed Deiner completed a major study of this thing called happiness and noted that people experience it in many different ways, based on age, culture, gender, and so on.[12] However, in spite of differences, SWB is defined by three central components.[13]

- *Satisfaction with present life.* People who are high in SWB tend to like their work and are satisfied with their current personal relationships. They are sociable, outgoing, and willing to open up to others. They also like themselves and enjoy good health and self-esteem.

- *Relative presence of positive emotions.* High SWBs more frequently feel pleasant emotions, mainly because they evaluate the world around them in a generally positive way. They have an optimistic outlook, and they expect success in what they undertake.

- *Relative absence of negative emotions.* Individuals with a strong sense of subjective well-being experience fewer and less severe episodes of negative emotions such as anxiety, depression, and anger. They like what they do, have a good control over life events, and are able to enjoy the "flow" of engaging work.

What Do You Think?

How you rate on each of the components of subjective well-being? How has your SWB level changed or stayed the same over the course of your life? What factors influence SWB? Who is most likely to experience it? Would some groups or individuals find it more difficult than others to achieve SWB? What could be done to help them achieve it?

Myths and Misperceptions About Happiness

Does a person have to be happy all of the time to have overall subjective well-being? Of course not. Everyone experiences disappointments, unhappiness, and time when life seems particularly harsh and unfair. However, people with SWB are typically resilient, able to look on the positive side and get themselves back on track fairly quickly, and less likely to fall into deep despair over disappointments and setbacks than are their fundamentally unhappy counterparts. Several other myths about happiness are worth noting:[14]

- *There is no "happiest age."* Age is not a predictor of SWB. Most age groups exhibit similar levels of life satisfaction, although the causes of happiness and the things that bring joy often change with age.

- *Happiness has no "gender gap."* Although women are more likely than men to suffer from anxiety and depression, and men are more at risk for alcoholism and personality disorders, equal numbers of men and women report being fairly satisfied with life.

- *There are minimal racial differences in happiness.* African Americans and European

Americans report nearly the same levels of happiness; in fact, African Americans are even slightly less vulnerable to depression. Despite racism and discrimination, members of disadvantaged minority groups generally seem to "think optimistically" by making realistic self-comparisons and attributing problems less to themselves than to unfair circumstances.

- *Money does not buy happiness.* Wealthier societies report greater well-being. However, once the basic necessities of food, shelter, and safety are provided, there is a very weak correlation between income and happiness. Having no money is a cause of misery, but wealth itself does not guarantee happiness.

Fortunately, humans are remarkably resourceful creatures. We can respond to great loss, such as the death of a loved one, a disabling injury or illness, or a traumatic event with an initial period of grief, mourning, and abject rage; yet with time and the support of loving family and friends, we can pick ourselves up, brush off the bad times, and manage to find satisfaction and peace. Typically, humans learn from suffering and emerge even stronger and more ready to deal with the next crisis. Most find some measure of happiness after the initial shock and pain of loss. Those who are otherwise healthy, in good physical condition, and part of a strong social support network can adapt and cope effectively.

Does Laughter Enhance Health?

How long has it been since you laughed so hard that you cried? Remember how relaxed you felt when you were done? Scientists are just beginning to understand the role of humor in our lives and on our health. Some emerging pieces of the laughter-mental health puzzle include the following points:

- Stressed-out people with a strong sense of humor become less depressed and anxious than those whose sense of humor is less well developed.
- Students who use humor as a coping mechanism report that it predisposes them to experiencing a positive mood.
- In a study of depressed and suicidal senior citizens, patients who recovered were the ones who demonstrated a sense of humor.

- Telling a joke, particularly one that involves a shared experience, increases our sense of belonging and social cohesion.

While laughter may not be a panacea for everything that prevents happiness, it helps us in many ways. People like to be around people who are fun-loving and laugh easily. Learning to laugh often puts more joy into everyday experiences and increases the likelihood that fun-loving people will keep company with us.

The notion that laughter can save your life gained wide acceptance with the 1979 publication of *Anatomy of an Illness,* by magazine editor Norman Cousins. In this book, Cousins recounted his recovery from a rheumatic disease of the spine—ankylosing spondylitis—with the aid of Marx Brothers movies and *Candid Camera* videos that made him laugh.[15] Similarly, in his 1988 bestseller, *Love, Medicine, and Miracles,* surgeon Bernie Siegel argued that a fighting spirit and the determination to survive are vital adjuncts to standard cancer therapy.[16] Other researchers, such as Lee Berk, M.D., and Stanley Tan, M.D., have noted that laughter sharpens our immune systems by activating T-cells and natural killer cells and increases production of immunity-boosting interferon.[17] It also reduces levels of the stress hormone cortisol.

In the 1970s and 1980s, a number of widely publicized studies of the health of widowed and divorced people showed that their rates of illness and death are higher than those of married people. Moreover, their lab tests revealed below-normal immune-system functioning. Several follow-up studies have shown unusually high rates of cancer among depressed people.[28] But are these studies conclusive evidence of the mind–body connection? Probably not, because they do not account for many other factors known to be relevant to health. For example, some researchers suggest that people who are divorced, widowed, or depressed are more likely to drink and smoke, to use drugs, to eat and sleep poorly, and to fail to exercise—all of which may affect the immune system. Another possibly relevant factor is that such people may be less tolerant of illness and more likely to report their problems.

Among the work most widely cited as proof that psychosocial treatment can help patients fight disease is an experiment involving women with advanced breast cancer. David Spiegel, professor of psychiatry at Stanford University, reported in 1989 that 50 women randomly assigned to a weekly support group lived an average of 18 months longer than 36 similarly afflicted women not in the support group. The implication of this finding is that the women in the support group cheered each other on while they endured agonizing therapy and that this allowed them to sleep and eat better, which promoted their survival. But a significant flaw in Spiegel's study was his failure to specifically measure immune functioning.[18]

In fact, the immune system changes measured in various other studies of the mind–body connection are relatively small (they are nowhere near as large as the disruptions that occur in people with AIDS, for example.) The health consequences of such minute changes are difficult to gauge because the body can tolerate a certain amount of reduced immune function without contracting illness. The exact amount it is able to tolerate and under what circumstances are still in question.[19]

Probably the boldest theory put forward in mind–body research is the notion that certain psychosocial behaviors actually make people vulnerable to cancer. In her book on the mind–cancer link, *The Type C Connection,* psychologist Lydia Temoshok reported that among the patients she studied who had malignant melanoma (a potentially deadly skin cancer), 75 percent shared common traits. They tended to be unfailingly pleasant, to repress their negative feelings and emotions, to put others' needs ahead of their own, and to make extraordinary attempts to accommodate others. She hypothesized that this "Type C" personality signals emotional repression, which may work to suppress the immune system.[20]

In summary, although a large body of evidence points to at least a minor association between the emotions and physical health, there is still no definitive proof of such a relationship. Another unresolved question is the actual mechanism. Does an emotional state trigger negative behaviors that in turn lead to decreased immune functioning? Or do emotions directly affect health by stimulating the production of hormones that tax the immune system? One more controversial issue in mind–body theory concerns personal responsibility. If, in fact, your emotions make you sick, is it then somehow your own fault that you got sick? Some professionals argue that mind–body theorists are too quick to blame patients for succumbing to the negative emotions that supposedly made them ill. They point out that illness itself causes negative feelings of guilt and anxiety, and it is often impossible to tell which preceded and precipitated which. Clearly, we still have a lot to learn in this area. In the meantime, however, maintaining an optimistic mind-set is probably a sound idea.

WHEN PSYCHOSOCIAL HEALTH DETERIORATES

In spite of attempts to be better people and get a grip on our occasionally erratic behavior, circumstances and events in our lives sometimes overwhelm us. In fact, they may overwhelm us to such a degree that we may need outside assistance to help us get through the difficult times and get back on track toward healthful living.

DEPRESSION: THE FULL-SCALE TUMBLE

In a recent meeting of the American Psychological Association, the organization's president remarked. "Depression has been called the common cold of psychological disturbances, which underscores its prevalence, but trivializes its impact."[21] According to experts, major depression is, in fact, one of the most common psychiatric disorders among people in the United States, affecting over 15 million Americans, many of whom are misdiagnosed, underdiagnosed, and not receiving treatment, despite its availability.[22]

Though it is normal to feel blue, sad, or depressed in response to many of life's common experiences, such as the death of a loved one, divorce, loss of a job, or an unhappy ending to a long-term relationship, people with **major depressive disorder** experience a form of **chronic mood disorder** that involves, on a day-to-day basis, extreme and persistent sadness, despair, and hopelessness. People with this disorder usually lose the ability to experience pleasure. They typically feel discouraged by life and circumstances, and experience sleep disturbances, loss of appetite, weight loss or gain, loss of energy, extreme exhaustion, and difficulty in thinking and concentrating. In addition, they may experience feelings of intense guilt and worthlessness and may become suicidal. In fact, approximately 15 percent of those suffering from severe depression will eventually attempt suicide or succeed in committing suicide. Usually, people with major depression show at least some impairment of social and occupational functioning, although their behavior is not necessarily bizarre.[23]

> **Major depressive disorder** Severe depression that entails chronic mood disorder, physical effects such as sleep disturbance and exhaustion, and mental effects such as the inability to concentrate.

> **Chronic mood disorder** Experience of persistent sadness, despair, and hopelessness.

Prevalence rates indicate the percentage of a population that experience a specific disorder. According to the National Institutes of Mental Health (NIMH), major depressive disorder strikes about 14–15 million Americans per year. Typically, women experience depression at nearly two times the rate of men, or between 8–11 percent of men and 19–23 percent of women. About 6 percent of women and 3 percent of men have experienced episodes severe enough to require hospitalization.[24] There is one notable exception to these findings, however. Among Jews, males are equally as likely as females to have major depressive episodes.[25] In recent years, there has also been a noteworthy increase in depression among adolescents, particularly among adolescent girls, and perhaps in Native American and homosexual young people as well.[26] Writers, composers, and entertainers also seem to have higher than expected rates of major depression, and people experiencing chronic, unrelenting pain have the highest rates of any group.[27]

Typically, major depressive episodes can occur at any age, but the first episode usually occurs before the age of 40. Some people experience one bout of depression and never have problems again; however, many others have recurrences throughout their lives. Stressful life events are often catalysts for these recurrences. Of particular note is the fact that depression appears to be increasing in prevalence among children and adolescents as well as among the elderly.

Risks for Depression

Most experts believe that major depressive disorders are caused by a combination of biology, learned behavioral responses, and cognitive factors. Biological theories suggest that chemical and genetic processes account for depression. Learning theories suggest that people develop faulty behaviors that make them predisposed to depression. Finally, cognitive theories suggest that irrational ideas and beliefs guide people to negative coping behaviors.[28] More progressive researchers suggest that combinations of the above variables interact to increase risk for depression. Some people, because of genetic history, their environment, situational triggers and stressors, poor behavioral skills, and brain–body chemistry, may be particularly vulnerable to depression.

Getting Evaluated for Depression

For the past decade, mental health specialists have come under fire for their sometimes cursory diagnosis of depression and tendency to prescribe powerful antidepressants far too quickly. If you suspect that you are suffering from depression, you should see a credentialed health professional for a complete clinical examination, which should include the following three parts:

- *A physical examination,* which will rule out thyroid disorders, viral infection, and anemia—all of which can result in depressive-like symptoms, and a *neurological check* of coordination, reflexes, and balance, to rule out brain disorders.
- *A psychiatric history,* which will attempt to trace the course of the apparent disorder, genetic or family factors, and past treatments
- *A mental status examination,* which will assess thoughts, speaking processes, and memory, as well as an in-depth interview with tests for other psychiatric symptoms[29]

In short, don't simply go to a therapist, say that you're depressed because you've broken up with a partner, and ask for a quick-fix antidepressant. You need to ask questions, demand a thorough assessment, and ask for assistance with follow-up therapy. Also, get recommendations for therapists through your doctor or someone that you trust.

Are You Depressed?

Regardless of the type of depression a person encounters, depressed individuals share many of the same symptoms. Sadness and despair are the main indicators, but the following are also among the more common symptoms:

- Loss of motivation or interest in pleasurable activities
- Preoccupation with failures and inadequacies; concern over what others are thinking
- Difficulty concentrating; indecisiveness; memory lapses
- Loss of sex drive or interest in close interactions with others
- Fatigue and loss of energy; slow reactions
- Sleeping too much or too little; insomnia
- Feeling agitated, worthless, or hopeless
- Withdrawal from friends and families

- Diminished or increased appetite
- Recurring thoughts that life isn't worth living, thoughts of death or suicide
- Significant weight loss or weight gain

A person who is depressed may display any or all of these symptoms, or, instead, mask the symptoms with a forced, upbeat sense of humor or high energy levels. Usually, the depressed person suffers from low self-esteem, loneliness, or detachment. Communication may cease or seem frantic at times. After a while, depression becomes a vicious cycle in which a person may feel helpless or trapped, sometimes coming to believe that the only way out is through death.

Facts and Fallacies About Depression

Depression among young Americans has come to be known as the "common cold" of mental illnesses. It is one of the fastest-growing problems in U.S. culture, yet it is among the most misunderstood of mental disorders. Myths and misperceptions about the disease abound. Here are some corrections to typical misunderstands about depression:[30]

1. *True depression is not a natural reaction to crisis and loss.* Depression is a pervasive and systemic biological problem that results in deep-seated pessimism and feelings of helplessness, despair, and lethargy, sometimes coupled with agitation. Victims may have problems at work or difficulties in relationships. Symptoms may come and go, and the severity will fluctuate, but they do not simply go away. Depressed people forget what being normal feels like. Crisis and loss can lead an already depressed person over the edge to suicide or other problems, but crisis and loss do not inevitably result in depression.

2. *People will not snap out of depression by using a little willpower.* Telling a depressed person to "snap out of it" is like telling a diabetic to produce more insulin. Medical intervention in the form of antidepressant drugs and therapy is often necessary for recovery. Remember that depression is the leading cause of suicide in the United States, and even with treatment, more than half of those who have it will eventually get it again. Understanding the seriousness of the disease and supporting victims in their attempts to recover are key elements of support.

3. *Frequent crying is not a hallmark of depression.* Some people who are depressed bear their burdens in silence, or may even be the life of the party. Some depressed individuals don't cry at all. Rather, biochemists theorize that crying may actually ward off depression by releasing chemicals that the body produces as a positive response to stress.

4. *Depression is* not *"all in the mind."* Depression isn't a disease of weak-willed, powerless people. In fact, research has shown that genetics plays a critical role in the development of severe depression. Data suggest that depressive illnesses originate with an inherited chemical imbalance in the brain. In addition, some physiological conditions, such as thyroid disorders, multiple sclerosis, chronic fatigue syndrome, and certain types of cancer, often have depressive side effects. Certain medications also are known to prompt depressive-like symptoms.

5. *It is* not *true that only in-depth psychotherapy can cure long-term clinical depression.* No single psychotherapy method works for all cases of depression.

Depression and Gender

For reasons that are not well understood, two thirds of all people suffering from depression are women. Researchers have proposed biological, psychological, and social explanations for this fact. The biological explanation rests on the observation that women appear to be a greater risk for depression when their hormone levels change significantly, as during the premenstrual period, the period following the birth of a child, and the onset of menopause. Men's hormone levels appear to remain more stable throughout life. Researchers therefore theorized that women were inherently more at risk for depression. Yet evidence to support this theory is either inconsistent or contrary.

Although adolescent and adult females have been found to experience depression at twice the rate of males, the college population seems to represent a notable exception, with equal rates experienced by males and females. Why? Several theories have been suggested to explain this anomaly:[31]

- The social institutions of the college campus provide a more egalitarian sex-role status for men and women.
- College women experience fewer negative events than do high school females. Males in

college report more negative events than they experienced in high school.
- College women report smaller and more supportive social networks.

Depression is often preceded by a stressful event. Some psychologists therefore theorized that women might be under more stress than are men and thus more prone to become depressed. However, women do not report more stressful events than do men.

Finally, researchers have observed gender differences in coping strategies, or the response to certain events or stimuli, and have proposed the explanation that women's strategies put them at more risk for depression than do men's strategies. Presented with "a list of things people do when depressed," college students were asked to indicate how likely they were to engage in the behavior outlined in each item on the list. Men were more likely to assert that "I avoid thinking of reasons why I am depressed," "I do something physical," or "I play sports." Women were more likely to assert that "I try to determine why I am depressed," "I talk to other people about my feelings," or "I cry to relieve the tension." In other words, the men tried to distract themselves from a depressed mood whereas the women tended to focus attention on it. If focusing on depressed feelings intensifies these feelings, women's response style may make them more likely than men to become clinically depressed. This hypothesis has not been directly tested, but some supporting evidence suggest its validity.[32]

Treating Depression

Different types of depression require different types of treatment. Selecting the best treatment for a specific patient involves determining his or her type and degree of depression and its possible cause. Both psychotherapeutic and pharmacological modes of treatment are recommended for clinical (severe and prolonged) depression. Drugs often relieve the symptoms of depression, such as loss of sleep or appetite, while psychotherapy can improve a depressed person's social and interpersonal functioning (see Table 2.2). Treatment may be weighted toward one or the other mode depending on the specific situation. In some cases, psychotherapy alone may be the most successful treatment. The two most common psychotherapeutic therapies for depression are cognitive therapy and interpersonal therapy.

Reality Check

DEPRESSION STRIKES INCREASING NUMBERS OF YOUNG PEOPLE

Based on recent statistics, depression and a host of other psychological problems are extremely common in the United States, affecting large numbers of people at any given time. While some statistics indicate a rising incidence of depression among all age groups, the most alarming aspect of these numbers is that they are probably gross "underestimations" of the true problem. Many people suffer silently; others are totally unaware that their cynical, unhappy attitudes are really part of a much greater problem. Consider the following:

- The known suicide rate among 15- to 19-year olds has more than doubled since 1950. In the United States, suicide rates are higher among whites than blacks, and higher among males than females. Rates for suicide among black women are very low.

- Suicide rates among elementary school children and high school students and on college campuses have increased dramatically in the past decade, forcing educational institutions to take significant steps to improve counseling services, teach teachers to recognize and refer high-risk students, and include communities and families in suicide prevention and intervention programs.

- Depression strikes over 17 million Americans each year, with less than half of those who suffer from it receiving the treatment they need.

- Many of the drug and alcohol problems facing Americans have their roots in a hopeless, depressed psychological state in which victims turn to drugs to ease their suffering. In addition, many drugs cause victims to be depressed.

- More than 80 percent of people with depression can be treated successfully with medication, therapy, or a combination of both; however, most people never seek treatment.

- Nearly 20 percent of Americans will seek psychological help from trained professionals during their lifetimes. Many of those who seek help will be suffering from depression-related problems.

- The risk of depression increases for those who have a parent or sibling who suffered from depression before age 30.

- Suicide is one of the leading causes of death in the United States, and more than 40,000 depressed people in the United States kill themselves every year.

- Antidepressant medications are among the most-prescribed drugs in the United States, with dramatic increases in the numbers of prescriptions filled and the length of time that patients are on these medications.

Sources: From *U.S. Health,* by the U.S. Department of Health and Human Services, 1999, Washington, DC: Author; and "How Healthy Are We?" by M. Clements, September 7, 1997, *Parade Magazine,* pp. 4–7.

Cognitive therapy aims to help a patient look at life rationally and to correct habitually pessimistic thought patterns. It focuses on the here and now rather than analyzing a patient's past. To pull a person out of depression, cognitive therapists usually need 6 to 18 months of weekly sessions comprising reasoning and behavioral exercises.

Interpersonal therapy has also proved successful in the treatment of depression and is sometimes combined with cognitive therapy. It also addresses the present but differs from cognitive therapy in that its primary goal is to correct chronic human relationship problems. Interpersonal therapists focus on patients' relationships with their families and other people.

Antidepressant drugs relieve symptoms in nearly 80 percent of people with chronic depression. Several types of the antidepressant drugs known as *tricyclics* are available and work by preventing the excessive absorption of mood-lifting neurotransmitters. Tricyclics can take from six weeks to three months to become effective. Newer antidepressant drugs, called *tetracyclics,* work in one or two weeks.

In recent years, words like *Zoloft* and *Prozac* have become such a common part of our vocabulary that it doesn't seem at all unusual to know someone who is taking an antidepressant. Such frequency of use could lead one to think that antidepressants can be taken like aspirin. However, countless emergency room visits occur when people misuse antidepres-

TABLE 2.2   DRUG TREATMENTS FOR DEPRESSION

ANTIDEPRESSANT CLASS	INDICATIONS/ CONTRAINDICATIONS	SIDE EFFECTS
Tricyclics (TCAs) Desipramine (Norpramin) Nortriptyline (Pamelor) Imipramine (Trofranil) Amitriptyline (Elavil) Protriptyline (Vivactil) Doxepin (Sinequan)	Due to their sedating effects, TCAs are useful for patients with insomnia. They may pose a risk for individuals with cardiovascular disease such as arrhythmias.	Most common: dry mouth, constipation. Others: weight gain, dizziness caused by a drop in blood pressure on sitting or standing up (orthostatic hypotension), changes in sexual desire, difficulty urinating, increased sweating, and sedation. TCAs can be lethal in overdose.
Selective Serotonin Reuptake Inhibitors (SSRIs) Fluoxetine (Prozac) Sertraline (Zoloft) Paroxetine (Paxil) Fluvoxamine (Luvox) Serzone	SSRIs are generally the first line choice because they have fewer side effects than other antidepressants, do not require blood monitoring, and are safe in overdose. Newer versions have fewer side effects.	Insomnia, agitation, sexual dysfunction, occasional nausea or heartburn, headache, occasional drowsiness, dizziness, tremor, diarrhea/constipation, and dry mouth (rare).
Monoamine Oxidase Inhibitors (MAOIs) Isocarboxazid (Marplan) Tranylcypromine (Parnate) Phenelzine (Nardil)	MAOIs can cause severe and sudden rise in blood pressure if ingested with certain drugs (e.g., over-the-counter cold preparations, diet pills, and amphetamines) or foods containing thramine (e.g., red wines, aged cheeses). They interact with epinephrine in some topical anesthetics and are not advised with other antidepressants.	Agitation, insomnia, sexual dysfunction, disturbed appetite, faintness (like orthostatic hypotension). Weight gain is most prominent with MAOIs.
Bupropion (Wellbutrin)	This drug doesn't interact significantly with other drugs. At high doses it can cause seizures in some people, most commonly those who have seizure disorders, anorexia, or bulimia. It has been used experimentally to counteract sexual side effects of SSRIs.	Agitation, insomnia, sedation, blurred vision, dizziness, headache/migraine, dry mouth, tremor, appetite loss, weight loss, excessive sweating, rapid heartbeat, constipation, rashes.
Trazodone (Desyrel)	Trazodone is often used with another antidepressant to alleviate insomnia induced by the initial drug.	Drowsiness, faintness, nausea, and vomiting.
Maprotiline (Ludiomil)	This drug is used to treat agitation and anxiety associated with depression, but is not advised for people with seizure disorders. It is somewhat risky for patients with cardiovascular disease.	Similar to those of TCAs.
Serotonin and Norephinephrine Reuptake Inhibitors (SNRIs) Venlafaxine (Effexor)	SNRIs work something like a combination of an SSRI and a TCA and are useful for patients who don't respond to other antidepressants.	Similar to those of SSRIs.
Nefazodone (Serzone)	This drug shouldn't be taken with the non-sedating antihistamines terfenadine (Seldane) and astemizone (Hismanal).	Headache, dry mouth, nausea, drowsiness, faintness, constipation.

Source: Table of antidepressant drugs in "Antidepressants" excerpted by permission from the December 1995 issues of Harvard Women's Health Watch, *Vol. 3, No. 4, p. 3. © 1995, President and Fellows of Harvard College. Nichols, Mark. "The Quest for a New Cure: New Drugs and Therapies Join the Battle against Depression."* Maclean's, *December 1, 1997, V. 110, No. 48, pp. 60–63.*

sants, decide to quit by going "cold turkey," or react to the type of antidepressant they are taking. The potency and dosage of each vary greatly. Antidepressants should be prescribed only after a thorough psychological and physiological examination. If your doctor suggests putting you on an antidepressant, ask these questions first:

- What biological indicators are you using to determine whether I really need this drug? *(Beware of the health professional who gives you a 5-minute exam, asks you if you are feeling down or blue, and prescribes an antidepressant to fix your problems.)*
- What is the action of this drug? What will it do, and when will I start to feel the benefits?
- What is your rationale for selecting this antidepressant treatment over other antidepressants that are available?
- What are the side effects of using this drug?
- How long can I be on this medication without significant risk to my health?
- What happens if I stop taking this medication?
- How will you follow up or monitor the levels of this drug in my body? How often will I need to be checked?

Electroconvulsive therapy (ECT) is another treatment for depression. A patient given ECT is sedated under light general anesthesia, and electric current is applied to the patient's temples for five seconds at a time for a period of about 15 or 20 minutes. Between 10 and 20 percent of people with depression who do not respond to drug therapy are responsive to ECT, but because a major risk associated with ECT is permanent memory loss, some therapists do not recommend its use under any circumstances.

Clinics have been established in large metropolitan areas to offer group support for depressed people. Some clinics treat all types of depressed people; others restrict themselves to specific groups, such as widows, adolescents, or families and friends of people with depression.

ANXIETY DISORDERS: FACING YOUR FEARS

On a recent trip to a professional conference, Marilyn Erickson (fictitious name) boarded a connecting flight at O'Hare International Airport. Her husband, John, a professor at a major university, did not get back on the plane. Her worry over her husband's whereabouts prompted Marilyn to get off the plane and search frantically throughout the airport for him. Finally, long after the plane had departed, she found him sitting on a bench outside the terminal, having become sick (vomiting), extremely dizzy, and distraught over the mere thought of boarding the plane. When Marilyn suggested taking another flight to continue their journey, he began to shake violently and, in his terror, refused to budge from his bench. Later, they boarded a bus to travel back to their home on the West Coast and missed their scheduled conference appearance.

Professor Erickson suffered an acute form of one of several **anxiety disorders,** known as a panic attack, a little-understood yet extremely common psychological problem faced by many Americans. Consider John Madden, former head coach of the Oakland Raiders and a true "man's man" who has outfitted his own bus and drives every weekend across the country to serve as commentator on NFL football games. What's the reason behind this exhausting driving schedule? Madden is terrified of getting on a plane.

Each of us has undoubtedly experienced such anxiety or known others with similar problems. In fact, anxiety disorders are the number one mental health problem in the United States, affecting over 19 million people of ages 18–54 each year, or about 13 percent of all adults.[33] Some sources estimate that these numbers may be even higher and may include about 1 of every 4 adults in America. The problem doesn't affect adults only. Anxiety is also a leading mental health problem among adolescents, affecting 13 million youngsters of ages 9–17. Costs associated with an overly anxious populace are growing rapidly; conservative estimates cite nearly $50 billion a year spent in doctors' bills and workplace losses in America. According to a study by the World Health Organization, the odds of developing an anxiety disorder have doubled in the past four decades.[34] These numbers don't begin to address the human costs incurred when a person is too fearful to leave the house or afraid to talk to anyone outside of the immediate family.

What makes members of our society anxious, ever vigilant, fearful? One only needs to listen to the news, read the newspaper, or observe the events in cities and towns across the country to understand. Constant, intense stressors, such as heavy traffic, noise, an ever-changing dose of pressure at work, job changes, changes in management, uncertainty, and a host of other factors make people uneasy, queasy, or downright sick. Headaches abound, nervous skin rashes are on the rise, and people daily ingest gallons of caffeine-laden beverages such as coffee and cola, exacerbating any potential tendency toward anxiety.

According to a new *USA Weekend* report, "edginess" is epidemic; the following real-world scenarios serve as evidence: a man is so anxious about driving over a bridge that he asks his wife to shut him in the trunk of the car before crossing, a woman is so fearful of heights that she won't befriend anyone who lives above the tenth floor, a man is so nervous about using public restrooms that he needs a therapist to accompany him to the toilet and talk him through it, and the list goes on. According to the same source, the numbers of "hits" on the website of the Anxiety Disorders Association of America skyrocketed from 500,000 in 1997 to over 21.6 million in 1999.[35]

Typically, anxiety disorders do not consist of one single ailment, but encompass several different types of problems. The common ones include generalized anxiety disorders, panic disorders, specific phobias, and social phobias.

Generalized Anxiety Disorders

A common form of anxiety disorders, **generalized anxiety disorders (GAD)** are severe enough to significantly interfere with the routine activities of daily life. They often do not have discrete, apparent causes. Generally, the person with the disorder is a consummate "worrier" and may develop a debilitating level of anxiety. Often multiple sources of worry exist, and it is hard to exactly pinpoint the root cause of the worry. To be labeled as having GAD, a person must meet the *DSM-IV (Diagnostic and Statistical Manual for Mental Disturbances)* criterion of having three or more of the following six symptoms for more days than not during a period of six months.[36]

1. Restlessness or feeling keyed up or on edge
2. Being easily fatigued
3. Difficulty concentrating or mind going blank
4. Irritability
5. Muscle tension
6. Sleep disturbances (difficulty falling or staying asleep or restless sleep)

Often GAD runs in families and is readily treatable with benzodiazepines such as Librium, Valium, and Xanax, which calm the person for short periods. More effective long-term treatments are achieved through individual therapy.

Panic Disorder

Panic attacks are typically described as sudden bursts of disabling terror. Unfortunately for many, a typical distinguishing feature of panic disorder is a feeling of panic that has no connection with events in the person's present experience. The feeling is often labeled as "free-floating anxiety."[37] According to the DSM-IV, a panic attack may be described as a discrete period of fear or discomfort, in which at least four of the following symptoms develop abruptly and reach a peak within 10 minutes:[38]

- Palpitations, pounding of the heart, or accelerated heart rate
- Sweating
- Trembling or shaking
- Sensations of shortness of breath or smothering
- Feeling of choking
- Chest pain of discomfort
- Nausea or abdominal distress
- Feeling dizzy, unsteady, lightheaded, or faint
- Derealization (feeling of unreality) or depersonalization (being detached from oneself)
- Fear of losing control or going crazy
- Fear of dying
- Paresthesias (numbness or tingling sensations)
- Chills or hot flashes

Specific Phobias

In contrast with panic disorders, **phobias,** or phobic disorders, involve a persistent and irrational fear of a specific object, activity, or situation, often out of proportion to the circumstances. About 13 percent of Americans suffer from phobias, such as fear of spiders or snakes, fear of public speaking, and so on. Social phobias are perhaps the most common phobic response.

Social Phobias

A **social phobia** is an anxiety disorder characterized by the persistent fear and avoidance of social situations. Essentially, the person dreads these situations for fear of being humiliated, embarrassed, or even looked at.[39] These disorders vary in scope. Some cause difficulty only in specific situations, such as getting up in front of the class to give a report. In more extreme cases, a person avoids all contact with others. These phobias can be very problematic for individuals who suffer from them.

Sources of Anxiety Disorders

Because these disorders vary in complexity and degree, scientists have yet to find clear reasons why one person develops them and another doesn't. The following factors are often cited as possible sources of the problems.

Biology

Some scientists trace the origin of anxiety to the brain and brain functioning. Using sophisticated positron emission tomography scans (PET scans), scientists can analyze areas of the brain that react during anxiety-producing events. Families appear to display similar brain and physiological reactivity, leading some to indicate that we may inherit our tendencies toward anxiety disorders.

Environment

Others indicate that anxiety is a learned response. Though genetic tendencies may exist, it is experiencing a repeated pattern of reaction to certain situations that programs the brain to respond in a certain way. For example, monkeys separated from their mothers at an early age are more fearful, and their stress hormones fire more readily, than those that stayed with their mothers. If your mother (or father) screamed and carried on whenever a large spider loped into view, or if other anxiety-raising events occured very frequently, you might be predisposed to react with anxiety to similiar events later in your life. Animals also experience such anxieties—perhaps from being around their edgy owners.

Social and Cultural Roles

Because men and women are taught to assume different roles in society (such as man as protector, woman as victim), women may find it more acceptable to scream, shake, pass out, and otherwise express extreme anxiety. Men, on the other hand, have learned to "stuff" such anxieties rather than act upon them; thus culture and social roles may also be a factor in risks for anxiety.

SEASONAL AFFECTIVE DISORDER

An estimated 6 percent of Americans suffer from **seasonal affective disorder (SAD),** a type of depression, and an additional 14 percent experience a milder form of the disorder known as the winter blues. SAD strikes during the winter months and is associated with reduced exposure to sunlight. People with SAD suffer from irritability, apathy, carbohydrate craving and weight gain, increases in sleep time, and general sadness. Researchers believe that SAD is caused by a malfunction in the hypothalamus, the gland responsible for regulating responses to external stimuli. Stress may also play a role in SAD.

> **Anxiety disorders** Disorders characterized by persistent feelings of threat and anxiousness in coping with everyday problems.
>
> **Generalized anxiety disorder (GAD)** A constant sense of worry that may cause restlessness, difficulty in concentrating, and tension.
>
> **Panic disorder** Severe anxiety disorder in which a particular situation, often for unknown reasons, causes terror.
>
> **Phobia** A deep and persistent fear of a specific object, activity, or situation that results in a compelling desire to avoid the source of the fear.
>
> **Social phobia** A phobia characterized by fear and avoidance of social situations.
>
> **Seasonal affective disorder (SAD)** A type of depression that occurs in the winter months, when sunlight levels are low.

Certain factors seem to put people at risk for SAD. Women are four times more likely to suffer from SAD than are men. Although SAD occurs in people of all ages, those between ages 20 and 40 appear to be most vulnerable. Certain families appear to be at risk. And people living in northern states in the United States are more at risk than are those living in southern states. During the winter, there are fewer hours of sunlight in northern regions than in southern areas. An estimated 10 percent of the population in northern states such as Maine, Minnesota, and Wisconsin, experience SAD, whereas fewer than 2 percent of those living in southern states such as Florida and New Mexico suffer from the disorder.

There are some simple but effective therapies for SAD. The most beneficial appears to be light therapy, in which a patient is exposed to lamps that stimulate sunlight. Eighty percent of patients experience

Women's Health/Men's Health

WOMEN'S AND MEN'S EMOTIONS: A CULTURAL DIFFERENCE?

If you felt depressed, would you tell your friends? Whether you know it or not, your answer to that question depends, in part, on your gender and culture. In the United States, males and females often learn different lessons about emotional control. Stereotyped gender roles have often dictated that men and boys receive reinforcement for emotional displays of dominance such as anger and aggression. In contrast, they may be chastised and ridiculed for emotional displays that show weakness, such as crying or sadness. Women on the other hand, have often been rewarded for appear to be vulnerable and weak and have been chastised when they show dominance and controlling emotions.

While it is clear that there are differences in how men and women are allowed to show their emotions in the United States, different cultures teach different *display rules*—the permissible ways of showing emotions. In fact, it is likely that different cultures vary much more in how they express emotions than do the sexes within a given culture. Among the peoples of Europe, the Americas, and the Middle East, the display rules typically depend on the emotion being expressed. In Israel and Italy, for example, men more often than women hide their feelings of sadness. The opposite holds true in Britain, Spain, Switzerland, and Germany, where women are more likely than men to hide their emotions. In many Asian cultures both sexes learn to restrain all their emotional expressions. Emotional expression is also situational and depends on issues of power and control. For example, an American man is just as likely as an American woman to control an outburst of anger if the target is a supervisor or other person in power.

What is the source of the emotional differences between males and females? It is difficult to distinguish biological from cultural influences. We know that men and women often give different emotional interpretations to the same situation, especially when the situation involves an encounter between a man and a woman. We know that women suffer more panic attacks, report crying more often than their male counterparts, and so on, but that men are more likely to show anger and display more physiological signs of emotional arousal than do women.

In spite of all of our insight into the differences between men and women, most authorities indicate that far too many stereotypes about differences may not be scientifically defensible. What is known is that the sexes often differ in their emotional experiences, both within and across cultures. We cannot say conclusively, however, that one sex has more emotional intensity than the other.

Source: Adapted from *Psychology* (3rd ed., p. 309), by P. Zimbardo, A. Weber, and R. Johnson, 2000, Boston: Allyn and Bacon.

---

relief from their symptoms within four days of treatment. Other forms of treatment for SAD are diet change (eating more foods high in complex carbohydrates), increased exercise, stress management techniques, sleep restriction (limiting the number of hours slept in a 24-hour period), psychotherapy, and antidepressants.

SCHIZOPHRENIA

Perhaps the most frightening of all mental disorders is **schizophrenia,** a disease that affects about 1 percent of the U.S. population. Schizophrenia is characterized by alterations of the senses (including auditory and visual hallucinations); the inability to sort out incoming stimuli and to make appropriate responses; an altered sense of self; and radical changes in emotions, movements, and behaviors. Victims of this disease often cannot function in society.

Schizophrenia

A mental illness with biological origins that is characterized by irrational behavior, severe alterations of the senses (hallucinations), and, often, an inability to function in society.

For decades, scientists believed that schizophrenia was an environmentally provoked form of madness. They blamed abnormal family interactions or early childhood traumas. Since the mid-1980s, however, when magnetic resonance imaging (MRI) and positron emission tomography (PET) began to allow scientists to study brain function more closely, scientists have recognized that schizophrenia is a biological disease of the brain. It has become evident that the brain damage involved occurs very early in life, possibly as early as the second trimester of fetal development. However, the disease most commonly has its onset in late adolescence.

Schizophrenia is treatable but not curable at present. Treatments usually include some combination of hospitalization, medication, and supportive psychotherapy. Supportive psychotherapy, as opposed to psychoanalysis, can help the patient acquire skills for living in society.

Even though environmental theories of the causes of schizophrenia have been discarded in favor of biological theories, a stigma remains attached to the disease. Families of people with schizophrenia often experience anger and guilt associated with misunderstandings about the causes of the disease. They often need help in the form of information, family counseling, and advice on how to meet the schizophrenic person's needs for shelter, medical care, vocational training, and social interaction.

GENDER ISSUES IN PSYCHOSOCIAL HEALTH

Studies have shown that gender bias often gets in the way of correct diagnosis of psychosocial disorders. In one study, for instance, 175 mental health professionals, of both genders, were asked to diagnose a patient based upon a summarized case history. Some of the professionals were told that the patient was male, others that the patient was female. The gender of the patient made a substantial difference in the diagnosis (though the gender of the clinician did not). When subjects thought the patient was female, they were more likely to diagnose hysterical personality, a "women's disorder." When they believed the patient to be male, the more likely diagnosis was antisocial personality, a "male disorder."

PMS: Physical or Mental Disorder?

A major controversy regarding gender bias has been the inclusion of a "provisional" diagnosis for premenstrual syndrome (PMS) in the American Psychiatric Association's *Diagnostic and Statistical Manual of Mental Disorders* (fourth edition; know as *DSM-IV*). The provisional inclusion, in an appendix to *DSM-IV*, signals that PMS merits further study and may be included as an approved diagnosis in future editions of the *DSM*. In other words, PMS could be considered a mental disorder in the future.

PMS is characterized by depression, irritability, and other symptoms of increased stress typically occurring just prior to menstruation and lasting for a day or two. A more severe case of PMS is known as *premenstrual dysphoric disorder*, or PMDD. Whereas PMS is somewhat disruptive and uncomfortable, it does not interfere with the way a woman functions from day to day; PMDD does. To be diagnosed with PMDD, a woman must have at least five symptoms of PMS for a week to 10 days, with at least one symptom being serious enough to interfere with her ability to function at work or at home. In these more severe cases, antidepressants may be prescribed. The point of contention lies in whether administering this treatment indicates that PMDD is viewed as a mental disorder rather than a physical disorder.[40] The controversy involves the legitimacy of attaching a label indicating dysfunction and disorder to symptoms experienced only once or twice a month. Further controversy stems from the possible use (or misuse) of the diagnostic label to justify systematic exclusion of women from certain desirable jobs.

SUICIDE: GIVING UP ON LIFE

There are over 35,000 reported suicides each year in the United States. Experts estimate that there may actually be closer to 100,000 cases; due to the difficulty in determining many causes of suspicious deaths, many suicides are not reflected in the statistics. More lives are lost to suicide than to any other single cause except cardiovascular disease and cancer. Suicide is often a consequence of poor coping skills, lack of social support, lack of self-esteem, and the inability to see one's way out of a bad or negative situation. Risks are much higher among those who suffer from depression.

College students are more likely than the general population to attempt suicide; suicide is the third leading cause of death in people between the ages of 15 and 24. In fact, this age group now accounts for nearly 20 percent of all suicides. The pressures, joys, disappointments, challenges, and changes of the college environment are believed to be in part responsible for these rates. However, young adults who choose not to go to college but who are searching for direction in career goals, relationship goals, and other life aspirations are also at risk for suicide.

Risk factors for suicide include a family history of suicide, previous suicide attempts, excessive drug and alcohol use, prolonged depression, financial difficulties, serious illness in the suicide contemplator or in his or her loved ones, and loss of a loved one through death or rejection. Societal pressures often serve as a catalyst for those at risk. Although women attempt suicide at four times the rate of men, more than three times as many men as women actually succeed in ending their lives. The elderly, divorced people, former psychiatric patients, and Native Americans have a higher risk of suicide than others. In fact, the elderly make up 23 percent of those who commit suicide. Alcoholics also have a high rate of suicide.

Depression is often a precursor of suicide. People who have been suffering from depression are more likely to attempt suicide while they are recovering, when their energy level is higher, than while they are

Health in a Diverse World

SUICIDE: A NEGLECTED PROBLEM AMONG DIVERSE POPULATIONS

One of the most underrated public health problems facing America today, suicide accounts for more than 35,000 preventable deaths each year, nearly 10,000 more than deaths from homicide. It touches all ages, all races, and all social groups, and is on the rise in many segments of the population.

- Recent reports from the Centers for Disease Control showed the rate of suicides among black teens of ages 15 to 19 more than doubled between 1980 and 1995.
- For every successful suicide, another 17 are attempted.
- Elderly men use the most violent means of suicide and are the most likely to be successful.
- After age 75, suicide rates are three times the national average, and after age 80, six times the national average.
- The average teen suicide is a white male who uses a firearm to kill himself. Males outnumber females five to one in completed suicides, while females are two times more likely to attempt suicide, often by using less lethal means, such as drugs or alcohol. Native Americans have a higher suicide rate than whites of all ages.
- Teen suicides often occur in clusters, particularly when friends or prominent national figures, such as rock stars, commit suicide.
- Rates of suicide are considerably higher in the western states, followed by the South, Midwest, and Northeast.
- People who have never been married are twice as likely to commit suicide as currently married people; the highest rates of all occur among the divorced or widowed.
- Suicide rates are lower in rural areas than in cities.
- Suicide rates are highest in German-speaking countries, Switzerland, Scandinavia, Eastern Europe, and Japan, and lowest in Greece, Italy, and Spain.

Sources: From "The Surgeon General Calls for Suicide Prevention," by S. Stapleton, 1998, *American Medical News,* 41, p. 9; and "Suicide Among Black Youth, 1980–1995," *Journal of the American Medical Association,* 279, p. 1431.

in the depths of depression. Although only 15 percent of depressed people are suicidal, most suicide-prone individuals are depressed.

Due to the growing incidence of suicide, many of use will be touched by a suicide at some time. In most cases, the suicide does not occur unpredictably. In fact, between 75 and 80 percent of people who commit suicide give a warning of their intentions.

WARNING SIGNS

Recognizing the signs of depression and possible suicide risks is an important aspect of prevention. Although predicting suicide is difficult, it is *not* impossible. Common signs include the following:

- Recent loss and a seeming inability to let go of grief
- Change in personality—sadness, withdrawal, irritability, anxiety, tiredness, indecisiveness, apathy
- Change in behavior—inability to concentrate, loss of interest in classes
- Diminished sexual interest—impotence, menstrual abnormalities
- Expressions of self-hatred
- Change in sleep patterns
- Change in eating habits
- A direct statement about committing suicide, such as "I might as well end it all"
- An indirect statement about committing suicide, such as "You won't have to worry about me anymore"
- Final preparations," such as writing a will, repairing poor relationships with family or friends, giving away prized possessions, or writing revealing letters
- A preoccupation with themes of death
- A sudden and unexplained demonstration of happiness following a period of depression
- Marked changes in personal appearance
- Excessive risk taking and an "I don't care what happens to me" attitude

TAKING ACTION TO PREVENT SUICIDE

Most people who attempt suicide really want to live, but see suicide as the only way out of an intolerable situation. Crisis counselors and suicide hotlines may be helpful temporarily, but the best way to prevent suicide is to get rid of conditions that may precipitate attempts, including alcoholism, drug abuse, loneliness, isolation, and access to guns.

If someone you know threatens suicide or displays any of the typical warning signs, take the following actions:

- *Monitor the warning signals.* Try to keep an eye on the person involved, or see that there is someone around the person as much as possible.
- *Take any threats seriously.* Don't just brush them off.
- *Let the person know how much you care about him or her.* State that you are there if he or she needs help.
- *Listen.* Try not to be shocked by or to discredit what the person says to you. Empathize, sympathize, and keep the person talking. Talk about stressors and listen to the responses.
- *Ask the person directly, "Are you thinking of hurting or killing yourself?"*
- *Do not belittle the person's feelings or say that he or she doesn't really mean it or couldn't succeed at suicide.* To some people, these comments offer the challenge of proving you wrong.
- *Help the person think about other alternatives.* Be ready to offer choices. Offer to go for help with the person. Call your local suicide hotline and use all available community and campus resources. Recommend a counselor or other person to talk to.
- *Remember that your relationships with others involve responsibilities.* If you need to stay with the person, take the person to a health care facility, or provide support, give of yourself and your time.
- *Tell your friend's spouse, partner, parents, brothers and sisters, or counselor.* Do not keep your suspicions to yourself. Don't let a suicidal friend talk you into keeping your discussions confidential. If your friend is successful in a suicide attempt, you will have to live with the consequences of your inaction.

What Do You Think?

If your roommate showed some of the warning signs of suicide, what action would you take? Whom would you contact first? Where on campus might your friend get help? What if someone in class whom you hardly know gave some of the warning signs? What would you then do?

BIBLIOGRAPHY

1. G. H. Wilson, P. Nathan, K. O'Leary and L. E. Clark, *Abnormal Psychology* (Boston: Allyn and Bacon, 1996), 137.

2. S. Hawks, M. Hull, R. Thalman, and P. Richins, "Review of Spiritual Health: Definition, Role, and Intervention Strategies in Health Promotion," *American Journal of Health Promotion* 9 (5) (1995): 371-378.

3. Ibid.

4. Ibid.

5. Ibid., 122.

6. Ibid., 124.

7. P. Sloan, B. Bagiella, and T. Powell, "Religion, Spirituality, and Medicine," *The Lancet* 353-9153 (1999): 664-672.

8. D. Elkins, *Beyond Religion—A Personal Program for Building a Spiritual Life Outside the Walls of Traditional Religion,* (Wheaton, IL: Quest Books, 1998).

9. Ibid.

10. Ibid.

11. D. Elkins, "Spirituality: It's What's Missing in Mental Health," *Psychology Today* (September/October, 1999), 48.

12. D. G. Myers and E. Diener, "Who Is Happy?" Psychological Science 6 (1995): 10-19.

13. Ibid.

14. Ibid.

15. D. Grady, "Think Right, Stay Well," *American Health xi* (1992): 50-54.

16. B. Siegel, *Love, Medicine, and Miracles* (New York: Harper Collins, 1988).

17. P. Doskoch, "Happily Ever Laughter," *Psychology Today* 29 (1996): 32-34.

18. Ibid., 50-54.

19. L. Cool, "Is Mental Illness Catching?" *American Health For Women* 16 (1997) 72-74.

20. L. Temoshock, *The Type C Connection* (New York: Random House, 1989).

21. L. A. Lefton, *Psychology* 7th ed. (Boston: Allyn and Bacon, 2000).

22. R. Hirshchfeld et al., "The National Depressive and Manic Depressive Association Consensus Statement on the Understatement of Depression. *Journal of the American Medical* 277 (4) (1997): 333-340.

23. Lefton, op. cit., 540.

24. National Institute for Mental Health (2000) (see http://www.nimh.nih.gov/); Lefton, op. cit., 541.

25. I. Levav, R. Kohn, J. Golding, and M. Weissman, "Vulnerability of Jews to Affective Disorders," *American Journal of Psychology* 154 (1997). 941-947.

26. S. Wood and E. Wood, *The World of Psychology* (Boston: Allyn and Bacon, 1999), 513.

27. S. Banks and R. Hems, "Explaining High Rates of Depression in Chronic Pain: A Diathesis–Stress Framework," *Psychological Bulletin* 119 (1996): 995-110.

28. Lefton, op. cit., 543.

29. Ibid., 542.

30. Adapted by permission of the author from Kathryn Rose Gertz, "Mood Probe: Pinpointing the Crucial Differences between, Emotional Lows and the Gridlock of Depression," *Self* (November 1990): 165-168, 204.

31. R. G. Gladstone and L. Koenig, "Sex Differences in Depression Across the High School to College Transition," *Journal of Youth and Adolescence* 23 (1994): 643-669.

32. S. Scott, "Biology and Mental Health: Why Do Women Suffer More Depression and Anxiety?" *Maclean's* (January 12, 1998): 62-64.

33. NIMH, op. cit.

34. "Anxiety Disorders," *USA Weekend* (October 12, 2000): 12.

35. Ibid., 13.

36. Zimbardo et al., op. cit., 505.

37. Ibid, 506.

38. Ibid., 506.

39. Ibid., 147.

40. R. Saltus, "The PMS Debate," *Boston Globe Magazine* (July 25, 1999): 8-9.

Physical Fitness and Nutrition

This final Physical Well-being lesson examines the influence of diet and lifestyle on total fitness. The lesson is intended to accomplish the following: 1) raise your awareness of the nutrition as it relates to health and physical fitness and wellness; 2) assess personal eating habits for their nutritional value; 3) assess personal attitudes towards nutrition and weight management; and, 4) discuss nutritional foods and the importance of fluid intake.

The following topics are addressed in this lesson:

- Nutrition
- Incorporating healthy eating into everyday life

The following TLO is supported in whole or in part by this lesson:

- Implement a Total Fitness Program

Following this lesson you will be able to:

- Describe elements of nutrition and a healthy diet
- Explain the food pyramid and how to make proper food choices
- Design a personal nutrition program

NUTRITION BASICS

BY PAUL INSEL AND WALTON ROTH

In your lifetime, you'll spend about 6 years eating—about 70,000 meals and 60 tons of food. What you choose to eat can have profound effects on your health and well-being. Of particular concern is the connection between lifetime nutritional habits and the risk of major chronic diseases, including heart disease, cancer, stroke, and diabetes. Choosing foods that provide adequate amounts of the nutrients you need while limiting the substances linked to disease should be an important part of your daily life. The food choices you make will significantly influence your health—both now and in the future.

Choosing a healthy diet that supports maximum wellness and protects against disease is a two-part process. First, you have to know which nutrients are necessary and in what amounts. Second, you have to translate those requirements into a diet consisting of foods you like to eat that are both available and affordable. Once you have an idea of what constitutes a healthy diet for you, you may want to make adjustments in your current diet to bring it into line with your goals.

This lesson provides the basic principles of **nutrition.** It introduces the six classes of essential nutrients, explaining their roles in the functioning of the body. It also provides different sets of guidelines that you can use to design a healthy diet plan. Finally, it offers practical tools and advice to help you apply the guidelines to your own life. Diet is an area of your life in which you have almost total control. Using your knowledge and understanding of nutrition to create a healthy diet plan is a significant step toward wellness.

NUTRITIONAL REQUIREMENTS: COMPONENTS OF A HEALTHY DIET

When you think about your diet, you probably do so in terms of the foods you like to eat—a turkey sandwich and a glass of milk or a steak and a baked potato. What's important for your health, though, are the nutrients contained in those foods. Your body requires proteins, fats, carbohydrates, vitamins, minerals, and water—about 45 **essential nutrients.** The word *essential* in this context means that you must get these substances from food because your body is unable to manufacture them at all, or at least not fast enough to meet your physiological needs. Plants obtain all the chemicals they need from air, water, soil, and sunlight. Animals, including humans, must east foods to obtain the nutrients necessary to keep their bodies growing and functioning properly. Your body obtains these nutrients through the process of **digestion,** in which the foods you eat are broken down into compounds your gastrointestinal tract can absorb and your body can use . A diet containing adequate amounts of all essential nutrients is vital because various nutrients provide energy, help build and maintain body tissues, and help regulate body functions.

The energy in foods is expressed as **kilocalories.** One kilocalorie represents the amount of heat it takes to raise the temperature of 1 liter of water 1°C. A person needs about 2000 kilocalories per day to meet his or her energy needs. In common usage, people usually refer to kilocalories as *calories,* which is a much smaller energy unit: 1 kilocalorie contains 1000 calories. We'll use the familiar word *calorie* in this chapter to stand for the larger energy unit.

Three classes of nutrients supply energy: protein, carbohydrates, and fats. Fats provide the most energy, at 9 calories per gram; protein and carbohydrates each provide 4 calories per gram. The high caloric content of fat is one reason experts continually advise against high fat consumption; most of us do not need the extra calories. Alcohol, though it is not an essential nutrient and has no nutritional value, also supplies energy—7 calories per gram.

But just meeting energy needs is not enough; our bodies require adequate amounts of all the essential nutrients to grow and function properly. Practically all foods contain mixtures of nutrients, although foods are commonly classified according to the predominant nutrient; for example, spaghetti is thought of as a "carbohydrate" food. Let's take a closer look at the function and sources of each class of nutrients.

PROTEINS—THE BASIS OF BODY STRUCTURE

Proteins form important parts of the body's main structural components: muscles and bones. Proteins also form important parts of blood, enzymes, some hormones, and cell membranes. As mentioned above, proteins can provide energy for the body (4 calories per gram).

Amino Acids

The building blocks of proteins are celled **amino acids.** Twenty common amino acids are found in food; nine of these are essential: histidine, isoleucine, leucine, lysine, methionine, phenlalanine, threonine, tryptophan, and valine. The other 11 amino acids can be produced by the body, given the presence of the needed components supplied by foods.

Complete and Incomplete Proteins

Individual protein sources are considered "complete" if they supply all the essential amino acids in adequate amounts and "incomplete" if they do not. Meat, fish, poultry, eggs, milk, cheese, and soy provide complete proteins. Incomplete proteins, which come from other plant sources such as **legumes** and nuts, are good sources of most essential amino acids but are usually low in one or two.

Terms

nutrition The science of food and how the body uses it in health and disease.

essential nutrients Substances the body must get from foods because it cannot manufacture them at all or fast enough to meet its needs. These nutrients include proteins, fats, carbohydrates, vitamins, minerals, and water.

digestion The process of breaking down foods in the gastrointestinal tract into compounds the body can absorb.

kilocalorie A measure of energy content in food; 1 kilocalorie represents the amount of heat needed to raise the temperature of 1 liter of water 1°C; commonly referred to as *calorie.*

protein An essential nutrient; a compound made of amino acids that contain carbon, hydrogen, oxygen, and nitrogen.

amino acids The building blocks of protein.

legumes Vegetables such as peas and beans that are high in fiber and are also important sources of protein.

Combining two vegetable proteins, such as wheat and peanuts in a peanut butter sandwich, allows each vegetable protein to make up for the amino acids missing in the other protein. The combination yields a complete protein. Your concern with amino acids and complete protein in your diet should focus on what you consume throughout the day, rather than at each meal. It was once believed that vegetarians had to "complement" their proteins at each meal in order to receive the benefit of a complete protein. It is now known, however, that proteins consumed throughout the course of the day can complement each other to form a pool of amino acids the body can draw from to produce the necessary proteins.

Recommended Protein Intake

The leading sources of protein in the American diet are (1) beef, steaks, and roasts; (2) hamburger and meatloaf; (3) white bread, rolls, and crackers; (4) milk; and (5) pork. About two-thirds of the protein in the American diet comes from animal sources; therefore, the American diet is rich in essential amino acids. Most Americans consume more protein than they need each day. Protein consumed beyond what the body needs is synthesized into fat for energy storage or burned for energy requirements. Consuming somewhat above our needs is not harmful but it can contribute fat to the diet because protein-rich foods are often fat-rich as well. The amount of protein you eat should represent 10–15% of your total daily calorie intake.

FATS—ESSENTIAL IN SMALL AMOUNTS

Fats, also known as *lipids,* are the most concentrated source of energy, at 9 calories per gram. The fats stored in your body represent usable energy; they help insulate your body, and they support and cushion your organs. Fats in the diet help your body absorb fat-soluble vitamins, as well as add important flavor and texture to foods. Fats are the major fuel for the body during rest and light activity. Two fats—linoleic acid and alpha-linolenic acid—are essential components of the diet. They are key regulators of such body functions as the maintenance of blood pressure and the progress of a healthy pregnancy.

Types and Sources of Fats

Most of the fats in food are in the form of triglycerides, which are composed of a glycerol molecule (an alcohol) plus three fatty acids. A fatty acid is made up of a chain of carbon atoms with oxygen attached at one end and hydrogen atoms attached along the length of the chain. Fatty acids differ in the length of their carbon atom chains and in their degree of saturation (the number of hydrogens attached to the chain). If every available bond for each carbon atom in a fatty acid chain is attached to a hydrogen atom, the fatty acid is said to be **saturated.** If not all the available bonds are taken up by hydrogens, the carbon atoms in the chain will form double bonds with each other. Such fatty acids are called unsaturated fats. If there is only one double bond, the fatty acid is called **monounsaturated.** If there are two or more double bonds, the fatty acid is called **polyunsaturated.** The essential fatty acids, linoleic and alpha-linolenic acids, are both polyunsaturated. The different types of fatty acids have different characteristics and different effects on your health.

Food fats are often composed of both saturated and unsaturated fatty acids; the dominant type of fatty acid determines the fat's characteristics. Food fats containing large amounts of saturated fatty acids are usually solid at room temperature; they are generally found naturally in animal products. The leading sources of saturated fat in the American diet are red meats (hamburger, steak, roasts), whole milk, cheese, hot dogs, and lunch meats. Food fats containing large amounts of monounsaturated and polyunsaturated fatty acids are usually from plant sources and are liquid at room temperature. Olive, canola, safflower, and peanut oils contain mostly monounsaturated fatty acids. Soybean, corn, and cottonseed oils contain mostly polyunsaturated fatty acids.

There are notable exceptions to these generalizations. When unsaturated vegetable oils undergo the process of **hydrogenation,** a mixture of saturated and unsaturated fatty acids is produced. Hydrogenation turns many of the double bonds in unsaturated fatty acids into single bonds, increasing the degree of saturation and producing a more solid fat from a liquid oil. Hydrogenation also changes some unsaturated fatty acids to **trans fatty acids,** unsaturated fatty acids with an atypical shape that affects their behavior in the body. Food manufacturers use hydrogenation to increase the stability of an oil so it can be reused for deep frying; to improve the texture of certain foods (to make pastries and pie crusts flakier, for example); and to extend the shelf life of foods made with oil. Hydrogenation is also used to transform a liquid oil into margarine or vegetable shortening.

Many baked and fried foods are prepared with hydrogenated vegetable oils, so they can be relatively high in saturated and trans fatty acids. Leading sources of trans fats in the American diet are deep-fried fast foods such as french fries and fried chicken (typically fried in vegetable shortening rather than oil); baked and snack foods such as pot pies, cakes, cookies, pastries, doughnuts, and chips; and stick margarine. In general, the more solid a hydrogenated oil is, the more saturated and trans fats it contains; for example, stick margarines typically contain more saturated and trans fats than do tub or squeeze margarines. Small amounts of trans fatty acids are found naturally in meat and milk.

Hydrogenated vegetable oils are not the only plant fats that contain saturated fats. Palm and coconut oils, although derived from plants, are also highly saturated. On the other hand, fish oils, derived from an animal source, are rich in polyunsaturated fats.

Fats and Health

Different types of fats have very different effects on health. Many studies have examined the effects of dietary fat intake on blood **cholesterol** levels and the risk of heart disease. Saturated and trans fatty acids raise blood levels of **low-density lipoprotein (LDL),** or "bad" cholesterol, thereby increasing a person's risk of heart disease. Unsaturated fatty acids, on the other hand, lower LDL. Monounsaturated fatty acids, such as those found in olive and canola oils, may also increase levels of **high-density lipoproteins (HDL),** or "good" cholesterol, providing even greater benefits for heart health. In large amounts, trans fatty acids may lower HDL. Thus, to reduce the risk of heart disease, it is important to substitute unsaturated fats for saturated and trans fats.

Most Americans consume more saturated fat than trans fat (11% versus 2–5% of total daily calories). However, health experts are particularly concerned about trans fats because of their double negative effect on heart health—they both raise LDL and lower HDL—and because there is less public awareness of trans fats. The saturated fat content of prepared foods has been listed on nutrition labels since 1994. The FDA has proposed that information on trans fat content also be listed on food labels, included with the amount of saturated fat. Consumers would thus be able to determine the total amount of unhealthy fats that a food contains. Until trans fat content appears on food labels, consumers can check for the presence of trans fats by examining the ingredient list of a food: If a food contains "partially hydrogenated oil" or "vegetable shortening," it contains trans fat.

For heart health, it's important to limit your consumption of both saturated and trans fats. The best way to reduce saturated fat in your diet is to lower your intake of meat and full-fat dairy products (whole milk, cream, butter, cheese, ice cream). To lower trans fats, decrease your intake of deep-fried foods and baked goods made with hydrogenated vegetable oils; use liquid oils rather than margarine or shortening for cooking; and favor tub or squeeze margarines or those labeled low-trans or trans-free over standard stick margarines. Remember, the softer or more liquid a fat is, the less saturated and trans fat it is likely to contain.

Although saturated and trans fats pose health hazards, other fats are beneficial. Monounsaturated fatty acids, as found in avocados, most nuts, and olive, canola, peanut, and safflower oils, improve cholesterol levels and may help protect against some cancers. **Omega-3 fatty acids,** a form of polyunsaturated fat found primarily in fish, may be even more healthful. Omega-3s are produced when the endmost double bond of a polyunsaturated fat occurs three carbons from the end of the fatty acid chain. Omega-3s have a number of heart-healthy effects: They reduce the tendency of blood to clot, inhibit inflammation and abnormal heart rhythms, and reduce blood pressure and risk of heart attack and stroke in some people. Because of these benefits, nutritionists recommend that Americans increase the proportion of omega-3s in their diet by eating fish two or more times a week. Salmon, tuna, trout, mackerel, herring, sardines, and anchovies are all good sources of omega-3s; lesser amounts are found in plant sources, including dark-green leafy vegetables; walnuts; flaxseeds; and canola, walnut, and flaxseed oils.

Terms

saturated fat A fat with no carbon-carbon double bonds, usually solid at room temperature.

monounsaturated fat A fat with one carbon-carbon double bond; liquid at room temperature.

polyunsaturated fat A fat containing two or more carbon-carbon double bonds, liquid at room temperature.

hydrogenation A process by which hydrogens are added to unsaturated fats, increasing the degree of saturation and turning liquid oils into solid fats. Hydrogenation produces a mixture of saturated fatty acids and standard and trans forms of unsaturated fatty acids.

trans fatty acid A type of unsaturated fatty acid produced during the process of

hydrogenation; trans fats have an atypical shape that affects their chemical activity.

cholesterol A waxy substance found in the blood and cells and needed for cell membranes, vitamin D, and hormone synthesis.

low-density lipoprotein (LDL) Blood fat that transports cholesterol to organs and tissues; excess amounts result in the accumulation of deposits on artery walls.

high-density lipoprotein (HDL) Blood fat that helps transport cholesterol out of the arteries, thereby protecting against heart disease.

omega-3 fatty acids Polyunsaturated fatty acids commonly found in fish oils that are beneficial to cardiovascular health, the endmost double bond occurs three carbons from the end of the fatty acid chain.

Another form of polyunsaturated fat, omega-6 fatty acid, is produced if the endmost double bond occurs at the sixth carbon atom. Most of the polyunsaturated fats currently consumed by Americans are omega-6s, primarily from corn oil and soybean oil. Foods rich in omega-6s are important because they contain the essential nutrient linoleic acid. However, some nutritionists recommend that people reduce the proportion of omega-6s they consume in favor of omega-3s. To make this adjustment, use canola oil rather than corn oil in cooking, and check for corn, soybean, or cottonseed oil in products such as mayonnaise, margarine, and salad dressing.

In addition to its effects on heart disease risk, dietary fat can affect health in other ways. Diets high in fatty red meat are associated with an increased risk of certain forms of cancer, especially colon cancer. A high-fat diet can also make weight management more difficult. Because fat is a concentrated source of calories (9 calories per gram versus 4 calories per gram for protein and carbohydrate), a high-fat diet is often

COMMUNICATE! Fast-food restaurants are convenient, fast, and inexpensive—but feature many high-fat, high-sodium options. The next time your friends or family want to go get a burger, try persuading them to make a different choice. Engage both their minds and their emotions by pointing out the facts about fat and salt and appealing to their desire to be fit and active. End with specific suggestions, such as going to a salad bar or an ethnic restaurant or cooking a meal together at home.

a high-calorie diet than can lead to weight gain. In addition, there is some evidence that calories from fat are more easily converted to body fat than calories from protein or carbohydrate.

Although more research is needed on the precise effects of different types and amounts of fat on overall health, a great deal of evidence points to the fact that most people benefit from lowering their overall fat intake to recommended levels and substituting unsaturated fats for saturated and trans fats.

Recommended Fat Intake

You need only about 1 tablespoon (15 grams) of vegetable oil per day incorporated into your diet to supply the essential fats. The average American diet supplies considerably more than this amount; in fact, fats make up about 33% of our total calorie intake. (This is the equivalent of about 75 grams, or 5 tablespoons, of fat per day for someone who consumes 2000 calories.) Although the percentage of calories from fat has declined in the American diet in recent years, the simultaneous increase in total calorie intake means that we're actually consuming more total grams of fat.

The 2000 Dietary Guidelines for Americans recommend that most people limit their total fat intake to 30% or less of total calories, with less than 10% coming from saturated fat. A 2001 report by the National Cholesterol Education Program (NCEP) suggests total fat intake of 25–35%, with less than 7% coming from saturated fat, up to 10% from polyunsaturated fat, and up to 20% from monounsaturated fat. The NCEP diet also recommends that trans fat intake be kept low and that total calorie intake allow for the maintenance of a healthy weight.

The number of calories and grams of fat that correspond to the 30% (total fat) and 10% (saturated fat) limits are shown in Table 3.1 for diets consisting of 1600, 2200, and 2800 calories per day. For example, if you consume about 2200 calories per day, you should limit your total fat intake to 73 grams per day, of which no more than 24 grams should be saturated fat; recommended intakes for protein and carbohydrate are also provided in Table 3.1. To determine how close you are to meeting these intake goals for fat, keep a running total over the course of the day. For prepared foods, food labels list the number of grams of fat, protein, and carbohydrates. Nutrition information is also available in many grocery stores,

published in inexpensive nutrition guides, and online. By checking these resources, you can keep track of the total grams of fat, protein, and carbohydrate you eat and assess how close your current diet is to the recommended intake goals.

In reducing fat intake to recommended levels, the emphasis should be on lowering saturated and trans fats. You can still eat high-fat foods, but it makes good sense to limit the size of your portions and to balance your intake with low-fat foods. For example, peanut butter is higher in fat, with 8 grams (72 calories) of fat in each 90-calorie tablespoon. Two tablespoons of peanut butter eaten on whole-wheat bread and served with a banana, carrot sticks, and a glass of nonfat milk makes a nutritious lunch—high in protein and carbohydrate, relatively low in fat (500 calories, 18 grams of total fat, 4 grams of saturated fat). Four tablespoons of peanut butter on high-fat crackers with potato chips, cookies, and whole milk is a less healthy combination (1000 calories, 62 grams of total fat, 15 grams of saturated fat). So although it's important to evaluate individual food items for their fat content, it is more important to look at them in the context of your overall diet.

CARBOHYDRATES—AN IDEAL SOURCE OF ENERGY

Carboyhydrates are needed in the diet primarily to supply energy for body cells. Some cells, such as those found in the brain and other parts of the nervous system and in blood, use only carbohydrates for fuel. During high-intensity exercise, muscles also use primarily carbohydrates for fuel. When we don't eat enough carbohydrates to satisfy the needs of the brain and red blood cells, our bodies synthesize carbohydrates from proteins. In situations of extreme deprivation, when the diet lacks a sufficient amount of both carbohydrates and proteins, the body turns to its own organs and tissues, breaking down proteins in muscles, the heart, kidneys, and other vital organs to supply carbohydrate needs. This rarely occurs, however, because consuming the equivalent of just three or four slices of bread supplies the body's daily minimum need for carbohydrates.

Simple and Complex Carbohydrates

Carbohydrates are classified into two groups: simple and complex. Simple carbohydrates contain only one

TABLE 3.1 RECOMMENDED DAILY INTAKE FOR FAT, PROTEIN, AND CARBOHYDRATE

	ENERGY/GRAM	PERCENT OF TOTAL CALORIES	Recommended Daily Nutrient Intake Goal or Limit — Calories and Grams for Three Levels of Energy Intake		
			1600 CALORIES	2200 CALORIES	2800 CALORIES
Fat	9 calories/gram	30% or less	480 calories = 53 grams	660 calories = 73 grams	840 calories = 93 grams
Saturated fat	*9 calories/gram*	*less than 10%*	*160 calories = 18 grams*	*220 calories = 24 grams*	*280 calories = 31 grams*
Protein	4 calories/gram	15%	240 calories = 60 grams	330 calories = 83 grams	420 calories = 105 grams
Carbohydrate	4 calories/gram	55%	880 calories = 220 grams	1210 calories = 303 grams	1540 calories = 385 grams
Added sugars	*4 calories/gram*		*6 teaspoons = 24 grams*	*12 teaspoons = 48 grams*	*18 teaspoons = 72 grams*

or two sugar units in each molecule; they include sucrose (table sugar), fructose (fruit sugar), maltose (malt sugar), and lactose (milk sugar). Simple carbohydrates provide much of the sweetness in foods and are found naturally in fruits and milk and are added to soft drinks, fruit drinks, candy, and sweet desserts. There is no evidence that any type of simple sugar is more nutritious than others.

Complex carbohydrates consist of chains of many sugar molecules; they include starches and most types of dietary fiber. Starches are found in a variety of plants, especially grains (wheat, rye, rich, oats, barley, millet), legumes (dry beans, peas, and lentils), and tubers (potatoes and yams). Most other vegetables contain a mixture of starches and simple carbohydrates. Dietary fiber, discussed in the next section, is found in grains, fruits, and vegetables.

During digestion in the mouth and small intestine, your body breaks down starches and double sugars into single sugar molecules, such as **glucose,** for absorption. Once glucose is in the bloodstream, the pancreas releases the hormone insulin, which allows cells to take up glucose and use it for energy. The liver and muscles also take up glucose to provide carbohydrate storage in the form of **glycogen.** Some people have problems controlling blood glucose levels, a disorder called diabetes mellitus.

Refined Carbohydrates Versus Whole Grains

Complex carbohydrates can be further divided between refined, or processed, carbohydrates and unrefined carbohydrates, or whole grains. Before they are processed, all grains are **whole grains,** consisting of an inner layer of germ, a middle layer called the endosperm, and an outer layer of bran. During processing, the germ and bran are often removed, leaving just the starchy endosperm. The refinement of whole grains transforms whole-wheat flour to white flour, brown rice to white rice, and so on.

Terms

carbohydrate An essential nutrient; sugars, starches, and dietary fiber are all carbohydrates.

glucose A simple sugar that is the body's basic fuel.

glycogen An animal starch stored in the liver and muscles.

whole grain The entire edible portion of a grain such as wheat, rice, or oats, including the germ, endosperm, and bran. During milling or processing, parts of the grain are removed, often leaving just the endosperm.

dietary fiber Carbohydrates and other substances in plants that are indigestible by humans.

Refined carbohydrates usually retain all the calories of their unrefined counterparts, but they tend to be much lower in fiber, vitamins, minerals, and other beneficial compounds. Unrefined carbohydrates tend to take longer to chew and digest than refined ones; they also enter the bloodstream more slowly. This slower digestive pace tends to make people feel full sooner and for a longer period, lessening the chance that they will overeat. Also, a slower rise in blood glucose levels following consumption of complex carbohydrates may help in the management of diabetes. Whole grains are also high in dietary fiber and so have all the benefits of fiber. Consumption of whole grains has been linked to reduced risk for heart disease, diabetes, high blood pressure, stroke, and certain forms of cancer. For all these reasons, whole grains are recommended over those that have been refined. This does not mean that you should never eat refined carbohydrates such as white bread or white rice, simply that whole-wheat bread, brown rice, and other whole grains are healthier choices. See the box "Choosing More Whole-Grain Foods" for tips on increasing your intake of whole grains.

Recommended Carbohydrate Intake

On average, Americans consume over 250 grams of carbohydrate per day, well above the minimum of 50–100 grams of essential carbohydrate required by the body. However, health experts recommend that most Americans increase their consumption of carbohydrates to 55–60% of total daily calories, or about 275–300 grams of carbohydrates for someone consuming 2000 calories per day. The focus should be on consuming a variety of foods rich in complex carbohydrates, especially whole grains.

Experts also recommend that Americans alter the proportion of simple and complex carbohydrates in the diet, lowering simple carbohydrate intake from about 25% to 10–15% of total daily calories. To accomplish this change, reduce your intake of foods like soft drinks, candy, sweet desserts, and sweetened fruit drinks, which are high in simple sugars but low in other nutrients. The bulk of the simple carbohydrates in your diet should come from fruits, which are

excellent sources of vitamins and minerals, and milk, which is high in protein and calcium.

Athletes in training can especially benefit from high-carbohydrate diets (60-70% of total daily calories), which enhance the amount of carbohydrates stores in their muscles (as glycogen) and therefore provide more carbohydrate fuel for use during endurance events or long workouts. In addition, carbohydrates consumed during prolonged athletic events can help fuel muscles and extend the availability of the glycogen stored in muscles. Caution is in order, however, because overconsumption of carbohydrates can lead to feelings of fatigue and underconsumption of other nutrients.

DIETARY FIBER—A CLOSER LOOK

Dietary fiber consists of carbohydrate plant substances that are difficult or impossible for humans to digest. Instead, fiber passes through the intestinal tract and provides bulk for feces in the large intestine, which in turn facilitates elimination. In the large intestine, some types of fiber are broken down by bacteria into acids and gases, which explains why consuming too much fiber can lead to intestinal gas. Because humans cannot digest dietary fiber, fiber is not a source of carbohydrate in the diet; however, the consumption of dietary fiber is necessary for good health.

Types of Dietary Fiber

Nutritionists classify fibers as soluble or insoluble. **Soluble fiber** slows the body's absorption of glucose and binds cholesterol-containing compounds in the intestine, lowering blood cholesterol levels and reducing the risk of cardiovascular disease. **Insoluble fiber** binds water, making the feces bulkier and softer so they pass more quickly and easily through the large intestine.

Both kinds of fiber contribute to disease risk reduction and management. A diet high in soluble fiber can help people manage diabetes and high blood cholesterol levels. A diet high in insoluble fiber can help prevent a variety of health problems, including constipation, hemorrhoids, and **diverticulitis.** Some studies have linked high-fiber diets with a reduced risk of colon and rectal cancer; more recent evidence suggests that other characteristics of diets rich in fruits, vegetables, and whole grains may be responsible for this reduction in risk.

Take Charge

CHOOSING MORE WHOLE-GRAIN FOODS

Whole grain foods are good weapons against heart disease, diabetes, high blood pressure, stroke, and certain cancers. They are also low in fat and so can be a good choice for managing weight. Federal dietary guidelines recommend 6–11 total servings of grain products every day, with at least several of these servings from whole grains. However, Americans currently average less than one serving of whole grains per day.

What Are Whole Grains?

The first step in increasing your intake of whole grains is to correctly identify them. The following are whole grains:

whole wheat	whole-grain corn
whole rye	popcorn
whole oats	brown rice
oatmeal	barley

More unusual choices include bulgur (cracked wheat), millet, kasha (roasted buckwheat kernels), quinoa, wheat and rye berries, amaranth, graham flour, whole-grain kamut, whole-grain spelt, and whole-grain triticale.

Wheat flour, unbleached flour, enriched flour, and degerminated corn meal are not whole grains. Wheat germ and wheat bran are also not whole grains, but they are the constituents of wheat typically left out when wheat is processed and so are healthier choices than regular wheat flour, which typically contains just the endosperm.

Reading Food Packages to Find Whole Grains

To find packaged foods rich in whole grains, read the list of ingredients and check for special health claims related to whole grains. The *first* item on the list of ingredients should be one of the whole grains listed above. In addition, the FDA allows manufactures to include special health claims for foods that contain 51% or more whole-grain ingredients. Such products may contain a statement such as the following on their packaging; "Rich in whole grain," "Made with 100% whole grain," or "Diets rich in whole-grain foods may help reduce the risk of heart disease and certain cancers." However, many whole-grain products will not carry such claims.

Don't be misled by a foods name of description. Products named or described as 9-gram, stoned wheat, wheat bran, cracked wheat, wheat berry, rye, oatmeal, or multigrain or as being *made with* whole wheat or whole grains often contain mostly refined grains. Color can also be misleading: Although many whole-grain breads and cereals are darker than their refined counterparts, manufactures may use ingredients such as molasses or caramel coloring to darken a product. *When in doubt, always check the list of ingredients, looking for "whole" as the first word on the list.*

Incorporating Whole Grains into Your Daily Diet

There are many opportunities to choose whole-grain foods. For maximum nutrition, look for whole-grain foods that are also low in fat.

- *Bread:* Look for sandwich breads, bagels, English muffins, buns, and pita breads with a whole-grain listed as the first ingredient.
- *Breakfast cereals:* Check the ingredient list for whole grains. Whole-grain choices include oatmeal, muesli, shredded wheat, and some types of raisin bran, bran flakes, wheat flakes, toasted oats, and granola.
- *Rice:* Choose brown rice or rice blends that include brown rice.
- *Pasta:* Look for whole-wheat, whole-grain kamut, or whole-grain spelt pasta.
- *Tortillas:* Choose whole-wheat or whole-corn tortillas.
- *Crackers and snacks:* Some varieties of crackers are made from whole grains, including some flatbreads or crispbreads, woven wheat crackers, and rye crackers. Other whole-grain snack possibilities include popcorn, popcorn cakes, brown rice cakes, whole-corn tortilla chips, and whole-wheat fig cookies. Be sure to check food labels for fat content, as many popular snacks are also high in fat.
- *Mixed-grain dishes.* Combine whole grains with other foods to create healthy mixed dishes. Possibilities include taboult, soups made with hulled barley or wheat berries; and pilafs, casseroles, and salads made with brown rice, whole-wheat couscous, kasha, millet, wheat bulgur, and quinoa.

If your grocery store doesn't carry all of these items, try your local health food store.

Sources of Dietary Fiber

All plant foods contain some dietary fiber. Fruits, legumes, oats (especially oat bran), barley, and psyllium (found in some cereals and laxatives) are particularly rich in soluble fiber. Wheat (especially wheat bran), cereals, grains, and vegetables are all good sources of insoluble fiber. However, the processing of packaged foods can remove fiber, so it's important to depend on fresh fruits and vegetables and foods made from whole grains as sources of dietary fiber.

Recommended Intake of Dietary Fiber

Although it is not yet clear precisely how much and what types of fiber are ideal, most experts believe the average American would benefit from an increase in daily fiber intake. Currently, most Americans consume about 16 grams of dietary fiber a day, whereas the recommended daily amount is 20-35 grams of fiber. However, too much fiber—more than 40-60 grams a day—can cause health problems, such as excessively large stools or the malabsorption of important minerals. Fiber should come from foods, not supplements, which should only be used under medical supervision. In fiber intake, as in all aspects of nutrition, balance and moderation are key principles.

To increase the amount of fiber in your diet, try the following:

- Choose whole-grain foods instead of those made from processed grains. Select high-fiber breakfast cereals (those with 5 or more grams of fiber per serving).
- Eat whole, unpeeled fruits rather than drinking fruit juice. Top cereals, yogurt, and desserts with berries, unpeeled apple slices, or other fruit.
- Include legumes in soups and salads. Combine raw vegetables with pasta, rice, or beans in salads.
- Substitute bean dip for cheese-based or sour cream—based dips or spreads. Use raw vegetables rather than chips for dipping.

Vitamins—Organic Micronutrients

Vitamins are organic (carbon-containing) substances required in very small amounts to regulate various processes within living cells (Table 3.2). Humans need 13 vitamins. Four are fat-soluble (A, D, E, and K), and nine are water-soluble (C, and the eight B-complex vitamins; thiamin, riboflavin, niacin, vitamin B-6, folate, vitamin B-12, biotin, and pantothenic acid). Solubility affects how a vitamin is absorbed, transported, and stored in the body. The water-soluble vitamins are absorbed directly into the bloodstream, where they travel freely; excess water-soluble vitamins are detected and removed by the kidneys and excreted in urine. Fat-soluble vitamins require a more complex absorptive process; they are usually carried in the blood by special proteins and are stored in the body in fat tissues rather then excreted.

Functions of Vitamins Many vitamins help chemical reactions take place. They provide no energy to the body directly but help unleash the energy stored in carbohydrates, proteins, and fats. Vitamins are critical in the production of red blood cells and the maintenance of the nervous, skeletal, and immune systems. Some vitamins act as **antioxidants,** which help preserve healthy cells in the body. Key vitamin antioxidants include vitamin E, vitamin C, and the vitamin A precursor beta-carotene.

Terms

> **soluble fiber** Fiber that dissolves in water or is broken down by bacteria in the large intestine.
>
> **insoluble fiber** Fiber that does not dissolve in water and is not broken down by bacteria in the large intestine.
>
> **diverticulitis** A digestive disorder in which abnormal pouches form in the walls of the intestine and become inflamed.
>
> **vitamins** Carbon-containing substances needed in small amounts to help promote and regulate chemical reactions and processes in the body.
>
> **antioxidant** A substance that can lessen the breakdown of food or body constituents by free radicals; actions include binding oxygen, donating electrons to free radicals, and repairing damage to molecules.

Sources of Vitamins

The human body does not manufacture most of the vitamins it requires and must obtain them from foods. Vitamins are abundant in fruits, vegetables, and grains. In addition, many processed foods, such as

TABLE 3.2 FACTS ABOUT VITAMINS

Vitamin	Important Dietary Sources	Major Functions	Signs of Prolonged Deficiency	Toxic Effects of Megadoses
Fat-Soluble				
Vitamin A	Liver, milk, butter, cheese, and fortified margarine; carrots, spinach, and other orange and deep-green vegetables and fruits	Maintenance of vision, skin, linings of the nose, mouth, digestive and urinary tracts, immune function	Night blindness; dry scaling skin; increased susceptibility to infection; loss of appetite; anemia; kidney stones	Headache, vomiting and diarrhea, vertigo, double vision, bone abnormalities, liver damage, miscarriage and birth defects
Vitamin D	Fortified milk and margarine, fish liver oils, butter, egg yolks (sunlight on skin also produces vitamin D)	Development and maintenance of bones and teeth, promotion of calcium absorption	Rickets (bone deformities) in children; bone softening, loss, and fractures in adults	Kidney damage, calcium deposits in soft tissues, depression, death
Vitamin E	Vegetable oils, whole grains, nuts and seeds, green leafy vegetables, asparagus, peaches	Protection and maintenance of cellular membranes	Red blood cell breakage and anemia, weakness, neurological problems, muscle cramps	Relatively nontoxic, but may cause excess bleeding or formation of blood clots
Vitamin K	Green leafy vegetables; smaller amounts widespread in other foods	Production of factors essential for blood clotting	Hemorrhaging	Anemia, jaundice
Water-Soluble				
Vitamin C	Peppers, broccoli, spinach, brussel sprouts, citrus fruits, strawberries, tomatoes, potatoes, cabbage, other fruits and vegetables	Maintenance and repair of connective tissue, bones, teeth, and cartilage; promotion of healing; aid in iron absorption	Scurvy, anemia, reduced resistance to infection, loosened teeth, joint pain, poor wound healing, hair loss, poor iron absorption	Urinary stones in some people, acid stomach from ingesting supplements in pill form, nausea, diarrhea, headache, fatigue
Thiamin	Whole-grain and enriched breads and cereals, organ meats, lean pork, nuts, legumes	Conversion of carbohydrates into usable forms of energy, maintenance of appetite and nervous system function	Beriberi (symptoms include muscle wasting, mental confusion, anorexia, enlarged heart, nerve changes)	None reported
Riboflavin	Dairy products, enriched breads and cereals, lean meats, poultry, fish, green vegetables	Energy metabolism; maintenance of skin, mucous membranes, and nervous system structures	Cracks at corners of mouth, sore throat, skin rash, hypersensitivity to light, purple tongue	None reported
Niacin	Eggs, poultry, fish, milk, whole grains, nuts, enriched breads and cereals, meats, legumes	Conversion of carbohydrates, fats, and protein into usable forms of energy	Pellagra (symptoms include diarrhea, dermatitis, inflammation of mucous membranes, dementia)	Flushing of the skin, nausea, vomiting, diarrhea, liver dysfunction, glucose intolerance
Vitamin B-6	Eggs, poultry, fish, whole grains, nuts, soybeans, liver, kidney, pork	Protein and neurotransmitter metabolism; red blood cell synthesis	Anemia, convulsions, cracks at corners of mouth, dermatitis, nausea, confusion	Neurological abnormalities and damage
Folate	Green leafy vegetables, yeast, oranges, whole grains, legumes, liver	Amino acid metabolism, synthesis of RNA and DNA, new cell synthesis	Anemia, weakness, fatigue, irritability, shortness of breath, swollen tongue	Masking of vitamin B-12 deficiency
Vitamin B-12	Eggs, milk, meats, other animal foods	Synthesis of blood cells; other metabolic reactions	Anemia, fatigue, nervous system damage, sore tongue	None reported
Biotin	Cereals, yeast, egg yolks, soy flour, liver; widespread in foods	Metabolism of fats, carbohydrates, and proteins	Rash, nausea, vomiting, weight loss, depression, fatigue, hair loss	None reported
Pantothemic acid	Animal foods, whole grains, broccoli, legumes; widespread in foods	Metabolism of fats, carbohydrates, and proteins	Fatigue, numbness and tingling of hands and feet, gastrointestinal disturbances	None reported

Sources: Food and Nutrition Board, National Academy of Sciences. 2000. *Dietary Reference Intakes for Vitamin C, Vitamin E, Selenium, and Carotenoids.* Washington, D.C.: National Academy Press. Food and Nutrition Board, National Academy of Sciences. 1998. *Dietary Reference Intakes for Thiamin, Riboflavin, Niacin, Vitamin B₆, Folate, Vitamin B₁₂, Pantothenic Acid, and Choline.* Washington, D.C.: National Academy Press. National Research Council. 1989. *Recommended Dietary Allowances,* 10th ed. Washington, D.C. National Academy Press, Shils, M. E., et al., eds. 1998. *Modern Nutrition in Health and Disease,* 9th ed. Baltimore: Williams & Wilkins.

flour and breakfast cereals, contain added vitamins. A few vitamins are made in certain parts of the body: The skin makes vitamin D when it is exposed to sunlight, and intestinal bacteria make vitamin K. Nonetheless, you sill need to obtain vitamin D and vitamin K from foods.

Vitamin Deficiencies and Excesses

If your diet lacks sufficient amounts of a particular vitamin, characteristic symptoms of deficiency develop (see Table 3.2). For example, vitamin A deficiency can cause blindness, and vitamin B-6 deficiency can cause seizures. The best-known deficiency disease is probably **scurvy,** caused by vitamin C deficiency. In the eighteenth century, it killed many sailors on long ocean voyages, until people realized that eating citrus fruits could prevent it. Even today people develop scurvy; its presence suggests a very poor intake of fruits and vegetables, which are rich sources of vitamin C.

Vitamin deficiency diseases are most often seen in developing countries; they are relatively rare in the United States because vitamins are readily available from our food supply. People suffering from alcoholism and malabsorption disorders probably run the greatest risk of vitamin deficiencies. However, intakes below recommended levels can have adverse effects on health even if they are not low enough to cause a deficiency disease. For example, low intake of folate and vitamins B-6 and B-12 has been linked to increased heart disease risk. Many Americans consume less-than-recommended amounts of several vitamins, including vitamins A, C, and B-6; vitamin E intake is also low among some groups, especially African Americans. Table 3.2 lists good food sources of vitamins.

Extra vitamins in the diet can be harmful, especially when taken as supplements. High doses of vitamin A are toxic and increase the risk of birth defects, for example. Vitamin B-6 can cause irreversible nerve damage when taken in large doses. Megadoses of fat-soluble vitamins are particularly dangerous because the excess will be stored in the body rather than excreted, increasing the risk of toxicity. Even when vitamins are not taken in excess, relying on supplements for an adequate intake of vitamins can be a problem. There are many substances in foods other than vitamins and minerals, and some of these compounds may have important health effects. Later in the chapter we will discuss specific recommendations for vitamin intake and when a vitamin supplement is advisable. For now, keep in mind that it's best to obtain most of your vitamins from foods rather than supplements.

Keeping the Nutrient Value in Food

Vitamins and minerals can be lost or destroyed during the storage and cooking of foods. To retain nutrients, consume or process vegetables as soon as possible after purchasing. Store fruits and vegetables in the refrigerator in covered containers or plastic bags to minimize moisture loss; freeze foods that won't be eaten within a few days. (Frozen and canned vegetables are usually as high in nutrients as fresh vegetables because nutrients are "locked in" when produce is frozen or canned.) To reduce nutrient losses during food preparation, minimize the amount of water used and the total cooking time. Develop a taste for a crunchier texture in cooked vegetables. Baking, steaming, broiling, and microwaving are all good methods of preparing vegetables.

Minerals—Inorganic Micronutrients

Minerals are inorganic (non–carbon-containing) elements you need in relatively small amounts to help regulate body functions, aid in the growth and maintenance of body tissues, and help release energy (Table 3.3). There are about 17 essential minerals. The major minerals, those that the body needs in amounts exceeding 100 milligrams, include calcium, phosphorus, magnesium, sodium, potassium, and chloride. The essential trace minerals, those that you need in minute amounts, include copper, fluoride, iodide, iron, selenium, and zinc.

Characteristic symptoms develop if an essential mineral is consumed in a quantity too small or too large for good health. The minerals most commonly lacking in the American diet are iron, calcium, zinc, and magnesium. Focus on good food choices for these (see Table 3.3). Lean meats are rich in iron and zinc, while low-fat or fat-free daily products are excellent choices for calcium. Plant foods such as whole grains and leafy vegetables are good sources of magnesium. Iron-deficiency **anemia** is a problem in many age groups, and researchers fear poor calcium intakes are sowing the seeds for future **osteoporosis,** especially in women.

TABLE 3.3   FACTS ABOUT SELECTED MINERALS

Mineral	Important Sources	Major Functions	Signs of Prolonged Deficiency	Toxic Effects of Megadoses
Calcium	Milk and milk products, tofu, fortified orange juice and bread, green leafy vegetables, bones in fish	Maintenance of bones and teeth, control of nerve impulse and muscle contraction	Stunted growth in children, bone mineral loss in adults, urinary stones	Constipation, calcium deposits in soft tissues, inhibition of mineral absorption
Fluoride	Fluoride-containing drinking water, tea, marine fish eaten with bones	Maintenance of tooth and bone structure	Higher frequency of tooth decay	Increased bone density, mottling of teeth, impaired kidney function
Iodine	Iodized salt, seafood	Essential part of thyroid hormones, regulation of body metabolism	Goiter (enlarged thyroid) cretinism (birth defect)	Depression of thyroid activity, hyperthyroidism in susceptible people
Iron	Meat, legumes, eggs, enriched flour, dark-green vegetables, dried fruit, liver	Component of hemoglobin, myoglobin, and enzymes	Iron-deficiency anemia, weakness, impaired immune function, gastrointestinal distress	Liver and kidney damage, joint pains, sterility, disruption of cardiac function, death
Magnesium	Widespread in foods and water (except soft water), especially found in grains, legumes, nuts, seeds, green vegetables	Transmission of nerve impulses, energy transfer, activation of many enzymes	Neurological disturbances, cardiovascular problems, kidney disorders, nausea, growth failure in children	Nausea, vomiting, diarrhea, central nervous system depression, coma, death in people with impaired kidney function
Phosphorus	Present in nearly all foods, especially milk, cereal legumes, meat, poultry, fish	Bone growth and maintenance, energy transfer in cells	Impaired growth, weakness, kidney disorders, cardiorespiratory and nervous system dysfunction	Drop in blood calcium levels, calcium deposits in soft tissues, bone loss
Potassium	Meats, milk, fruits, vegetables, grains, legumes	Nerve function and body water balance	Muscular weakness, nausea, drowsiness, paralysis, confusion, disruption of cardiac rhythm	Cardiac arrest
Selenium	Seafood, meat, eggs, whole grains	Protection of cells from oxidative damage, immune response	Muscle pain and weakness, heart disorders	Hair and nail loss, nausea and vomiting, weakness, irritability
Sodium	Salt, soy sauce, salted foods, tomato juice	Body water balance, acid-base balance, nerve function	Muscle weakness, loss of appetite, nausea, vomiting, deficiency is rarely seen	Edema, hypertension in sensitive people
Zinc	Whole grains, meat, eggs, liver, seafood (especially oysters)	Synthesis of proteins, RNA and DNA, wound healing, immune response, ability to taste	Growth failure, loss of appetite, impaired taste acuity, skin rash, impaired immune function, poor wound healing	Vomiting, impaired immune function, decline in blood HDL levels, impaired copper absorption

Sources: Food and Nutrition Board, National Academy of Sciences, 2001. *Dietary Reference Intakes for Vitamin A, Vitamin K, Arsenic, Boron, Chromium, Copper, Iodine, Iron, Manganese, Molybdenum, Nickel, Silicon, Vanadium, and Zinc.* Washington, D.C.: ©2000 by the National Academy of Sciences. Courtesy of the National Academy Press. Food and Nutrition Board, *Deitary Reference Intakes for Vitamin C, Vitamin E, Selenium, and the Carotenoids.* Washington, D.C.: National Academy Press. Food and Nutrition Board. National Academy of Sciences. 1997. *Dietary Reference Intakes for Calcium, Phosphorus, Magnesium, Vitamin D, and Fluoride.* Washington, D.C.: Shils, M. E., et al., eds. 1998. *Modern Nutrition in Health and Disease,* 9th ed. Baltimore; Williams & Wilkins.

Take Charge

EATING FOR HEALTHY BONES

Osteoporosis is a condition in which bones become dangerously thin and fragile over time. It currently afflicts over 28 million Americans, 80% of them women, and results in over 1.5 million bone fractures each year. Most bone mass is built by age 18, and after bone density peaks between the ages of 25 and 35, bone mass is slowly lost over time. To prevent osteoporosis, the best strategy is to build as much bone as possible during your young years and then do everything you can to maintain it as you age. Up to 50% of bone loss is determined by controllable lifestyle factors, especially diet and exercise habits. Key nutrients include the following:

Calcium Consuming an adequate amount of calcium is important throughout life to build and maintain bone mass. Americans average 600-800 mg of calcium per day, only about half of what is recommended. Milk, yogurt, and calcium-fortified orange juice, bread, and cereals are all good sources. Nutritionists suggest that you obtain calcium from foods first and then take supplements only if needed to make up the difference.

Vitamin D Vitamin D is necessary for bones to absorb calcium; a daily intake of 400-800 IU is recommended by the National Osteoporosis Foundation. Vitamin D can be obtained from foods and is manufactured by the skin when expose to sunlight. Candidates for vitamin D supplements include people who don't eat many foods rich in vitamin D, those who don't expose their face, arms, and hands to the sun (without sunscreen) for 5-15 minutes a few times each week, and people who live north of an imaginary line roughly between Boston and the Oregon–California border (the sun is weaker in northern latitudes).

Vitamin K Recent studies have linked high vitamin K intake to a lower risk of fractures. Vitamin K promotes the synthesis of proteins that help keep bones strong. Broccoli and leafy green vegetables are rich in vitamin K.

Other Nutrients Several other nutrients may play an important role in bone health.

- *Vitamin C* works with calcium and other minerals to build bone, it also helps produce the connective tissue collagen, which forms the scaffolding in bones.
- *Magnesium* aids in bone formation.
- *Potassium* helps bones retain calcium.
- *Manganese* may help lessen calcium losses.
- *Zinc* and *copper* help maintain collagen.
- *Boron* may increase calcium absorption.

Several dietary substances may have a *negative* effect on bone health. Alcohol reduces the body's ability to absorb calcium and may interfere with the bone-protecting effects of the hormone estrogen. A high intake of protein and sodium has been shown to increase calcium loss in the urine, especially when calcium intake is low, and thus may lead to loss of calcium from the skeleton. Caffeine may also cause small losses of urinary calcium, and experts often recommend that heavy caffeine consumers take special care to include calcium-rich foods in their diet. Adding milk to coffee or tea may offset the effect of caffeine on calcium loss. Chronic excess intake of retinol, one form of vitamin A, is associated with decreased bone density; if you consume a vitamin supplement or vitamin A–fortified foods, try to limit your daily intake of retinol to no more than 100% of the RDA. (You may need to check labels to determine what form of vitamin A is present; beta-carotene, which the body can convert to vitamin A, is not associated with problems.) Drinking lots of soda, which often replaces milk in the diet and which is high in phosphorus (a mineral that may interfere with calcium absorption), has been shown to increase the risk of bone fracture in teenage girls. For healthy bones, then, it is important to moderate in your consumption of alcohol, protein, sodium, caffeine, retinol, and sodas.

Finally, it is important to combine a healthy diet with regular exercise. Weight-bearing aerobic activities, if performed regularly, help build and maintain bone mass throughout life. Strength training improves bone density, muscle mass, strength, and balance, protecting against both bone loss and falls, a major cause of fractures.

Terms

scurvy A disease caused by a lack of vitamin C, characterized by bleeding gums, loosening teeth, and poor wound healing.

minerals Inorganic compounds needed in relatively small amounts for regulation, growth, and maintenance of body tissues and functions.

anemia A deficiency in the oxygen-carrying material in the red blood cells.

osteoporosis A condition in which the bones become extremely thin and brittle and break easily.

Water—Vital but Often Ignored

Water is the major component in both foods and the human body: You are composed of about 60% water. Your need for other nutrients, in terms of weight, is much less than your need for water. You can live up to 50 days without food, but only a few days without water.

Water is distributed all over the body, among lean and other tissues and in blood and other body fluids. Water is used in the digestion and absorption of food and is the medium in which most of the chemical reactions take place within the body. Some water-based fluids like blood transport substances around the body, while other fluids serve as lubricants or cushions. Water also helps regulate body temperature.

Communicate! Changing our eating and cooking habits is hard work, and getting others to change is even harder. If your parents, roommates, or friends could be preparing food in healthier ways, you may want to suggest some changes. For example, "I saw some pump sprays for cooking oil at the store. You spray oil on the frying pan instead of pouring the oil in. It cuts back on the amount of oil you have to use. Would you try it if I picked one up?" Or, "Some people I know have stopped cooking with salt, mostly because they're worried about high blood pressure, which extra salt can sometimes make worse. They have salt at the table; they just don't cook with it. Since we have high blood pressure in our family, I'm wondering if you'd consider using less salt when you cook." You might also offer to cut up some fresh fruit, prepare a green salad, or buy whole-grain bread.

Water is contained in almost all foods, particularly in liquids, fruits, and vegetables. The foods and fluids you consume provide 80-90% of your daily water intake; the remainder is generated through metabolism. You lose water each day in urine, feces, and sweat and through evaporation from your lungs. To maintain a balance between water consumed and water lost, you need to take in about 1 milliliter of water for each calorie you burn—about 2 liters, or 8 cups, of fluid per day—more if you live in a hot

BEHAVIOR CHANGE STRATEGY
Improving Your Diet by Choosing Healthy Beverages

After reading this lesson and completing the dietary assessment, you can probably identify several changes you could make to improve your diet. Here, we focus on choosing healthy beverages to increase intake of nutrients and decrease intake of empty calories from added sugars and fat. However, this model of dietary change can be applied to any modification you'd like to make to your diet.

Gather Data and Establish a Baseline

Begin by tracking your beverage consumption in your health journal. Write down the types and amounts of beverage you drink, including water. Also note where you were at the time and whether you obtained the beverage on-site or brought it with you.

At the same time, investigate your options. Find out what other beverages you can easily obtain over the course of your daily routine. For example, what drinks are available in the dining hall where you eat lunch or at the student union where you often grab snacks? How many drinking fountains do you walk by over the course of the day? This information will help you put together a successful plan for change.

climate or engage in vigorous exercise. Many Americans fall short of this recommended intake.

Thirst is one of the body's first signs of dehydration that we can actually recognize. However, by the time we are thirsty, our cells have been needing fluid for quite some time. A good motto to remember, especially when exercising is: Drink *before* you're thirsty. Severe dehydration causes weakness and can lead to death.

Other Substances in Food

Many substances in food are not essential nutrients but may influence health.

Antioxidants

When the body uses oxygen or breaks down certain fats or proteins as a normal part of metabolism, it gives rise to substances called **free radicals.** Environmental factors like cigarette smoke, exhaust fumes, radiation, excessive sunlight, certain drugs, and stress can increase free radical production. A free radical is a chemically unstable molecule that is missing an electron; it will react with any molecule it encounters from which it can take an electron. In their search for electrons, free radicals react with fats, proteins, and DNA, damaging cell membranes and mutating genes. Because of this, free radicals have been implicated in aging, cancer, cardiovascular disease, and other degenerative diseases like arthritis.

Antioxidants found in foods can help protect the body from damage by free radicals in several ways. Some dietary antioxidants prevent or reduce the formation of free radicals; other remove free radicals from the body by reacting with them directly by donating electrons. Antioxidants can also repair some types of free radical damage after it occurs. Some antioxidants, such as vitamin C, vitamin E, and selenium, are also essential nutrients; others, such as carotenoids, found in yellow, orange, and deep-green vegetables, are not. Obtaining a regular intake of these nutrients is vital for maintaining the health of the body. Many fruits and vegetables are rich in antioxidants.

Phytochemicals

Antioxidants are a particular type of **phytochemical,** a substance found in plant foods that may help prevent chronic disease. Researchers have just begun to identify and study all the different compounds found in foods, and many preliminary findings are promising. For example, certain substances found in soy foods may help lower cholesterol levels. Sulforaphame, a compound isolated from broccoli and other **cruciferous vegetables,** may render some carcinogenic compounds harmless. Allyl sulfides, a group of chemicals found in garlic and onions, appear to boost the activity of cancer-fighting immune cells. Further research on phytochemicals may extend the role of nutrition to the prevention and treatment of many chronic diseases.

If you want to increase your intake of phytochemicals, it is best to obtain them by eating a variety of fruits, vegetables, and grains rather than relying on supplements. Like many vitamins and minerals, isolated phytochemicals may be harmful if taken in high doses. In addition, it is likely that their health benefits are the result of chemical substances working in combination.

Analyze Your Data and Set Goals

Evaluate your beverage consumption by dividing your typical daily consumption between healthy and less healthy choices. Use the following guide as a basis, and add other beverages to the lists as needed.

Choose less often:

- Regular soda
- Sweetened bottled iced tea
- Fruit beverages made with little fruit juice (usually labeled fruit drinks, punches, beverages, blends, or ades)
- Whole milk

Choose more often:

- Water—plain, mineral, and sparkling
- Low-fat or nonfat milk
- Fruit juice (100% juice)
- Unsweetened herbal tea

How many beverages do you consume daily from each category? What would be a healthy and realistic goal for change? For example, if your beverage consumption is currently evenly divided between the "choose more often" and "choose less often" categories (four from each list), you might set a final goal for your behavior change program of increasing your healthy choices by two (six from the "more often" list and two from the "less often" list).

Develop a Plan for Change

Once you've set your goal, you need to develop strategies that will help you choose healthy beverages more often. Consider the following possibilities:

- Keep healthy beverages on hand; if you live in a student dorm, rent a small refrigerator or keep juice, nonfat milk, and other healthy choices in the dorm's kitchen refrigerator.
- Plan ahead, and put a bottle of water or 100% juice in your backpack every day.
- Check foods labels on beverages for serving sizes, calories, and nutrients; comparison shop to find the healthiest choices, and watch your serving sizes. Use this information to make your "choose more often" list longer and more specific.
- If you eat out frequently, examine all the beverages available at the placed you typically eat your meals. You'll probably find that healthy choices are available; if not, bring along your own drink or find somewhere else to eat.
- For a snack, try water and a piece of fruit rather than a heavily sweetened beverage.
- Create healthy beverages that appeal to you; for example, try adding slices of citrus fruit to water or mixing 100% fruit juice with sparkling water.

You may also need to make some changes in your routine to decrease the likelihood that you'll make unhealthy choices. For example, you might discover from your health journal that you always buy a soda after class when you pass a particular vending machine. If this is the case, try another route that allows you to avoid the machine. And try to guard against impulse buying by carrying water or a healthy snack with you every day.

To complete your plan: Develop and sign a contract, set up a system of rewards, involve other people in your program, and develop strategies for challenging situations. Once your plan is complete, take action. Keep track of your progress in your health journal by continuing to monitor and evaluate your beverage consumption.

MODULE II

Personal Development Overview

The Personal Development module is comprised of six lessons divided into two parts: Part I consists of lessons four and five; Part II consists of lessons 13 through 16.

PART I

Lessons four and five are designed to introduce the Leadership Development Program (LDP) that will be used to evaluate your leadership performance and provide you developmental feedback for the rest of your cadet years.

PART II

Lessons 13 through 16 provide you with a set of broadly applicable problem solving concepts, principles, and procedures. A generic model of problem solving is first presented. This problem solving model is later shown to provide the underlying structure for Army-specific problem solving methods. Consideration of the importance of creative and critical thinking, as well as methods information management are added to the problem solving model to better equip you to engage in a brief problem solving practical exercise at the end of the module.

MODULE II

Personal Development (Part I)

Goal Setting, Feedback, and Introduction to the Leadership Development Program

This class emphasizes the importance of goal setting in producing desirable individual and group outcomes. The importance of the leader's role in goal setting and in providing feedback as the basis for goals is also stressed. The lesson then shifts to Cadet Command's implementation of these principles in the form of the Leadership Development Program.

The following topics are addressed in this lesson:

- Importance of goal setting
- Leader's role in goal setting
- Importance of feedback in goal setting and achievement
- LDP system of feedback and goal setting

The following TLO is supported in whole or in part by this lesson:

- Seek self improvement

Following this lesson you will be able to:

- List the four characteristics of goal setting theory
- Analyze personal goals
- Describe Cadet Command's method of feedback using the Blue Card

SETTING GOALS

BY R.L. HUGES, R.C. GINNET, & C.J. CURPHY

Goals Should Be Specific and Observable

Goals Should Be Attainable but Challenging

Goals Require Commitment

Goals Require Feedback

The Roman philosopher Seneca wrote, "When a man does not know what harbor he is making for, no wind is the right wind." Setting goals and developing plans of action to attain them are important for individuals and for groups. For example, the purpose or goal is often the predominant norm in any group. Once group goals are agreed on, they serve to induce member compliance, act as a criterion for evaluating the leadership potential of group members, and become the criteria for evaluating group performance (Bass, 1990).

Perhaps the most important step in accomplishing a personal or group goal is stating it right in the first place. The reason many people become frustrated with the outcomes of their New Year's resolutions is not any character flaw on their part (e.g., "I don't have any willpower"), but that their resolutions are so vague or unrealistic they are unlikely to ever lead to demonstrable results. It is possible to keep New Year's resolutions, but one must set them intelligently. In a more general sense, some ways of writing goal statements increase the likelihood that someone will successfully achieve the desired goals. Goals should be specific and observable, attainable and challenging, based on top-to-bottom commitment, and designed to provide feedback to personnel about their progress toward them. The following is a more detailed discussion of each of these points.

GOALS SHOULD BE SPECIFIC AND OBSERVABLE

Research provides strong support for the idea that specific goals lead to higher levels of effort and performance than general goals. General goals do not work as well because they often do not provide enough information regarding which particular behaviors are to be changed or when a clear end-state has been attained. This may be easiest to see with a personal example.

Assume that a student is not satisfied with her academic performance and wants to do something about it. She might set a very general goal, such as "I will do my best next year" or "I will do better in school next year." At first, such a goal may seem fine; after all, as long as she is motivated to do well, what more would be needed? However, on further thought you can see that "do my best" or do "better" are so ambiguous as to be unhelpful in directing her behavior and ultimately assessing her success. General goals have relatively little impact on energizing and directing immediate behavior, and they make it difficult to assess, in the end, whether someone has attained them or not. A better goal statement for this student would be, for example, to attain a B average or to get no deficient grades this semester. Specific goals like these make it easier to chart one's progress. A more business-oriented example might deal with improving productivity at work. Specific goal statements in this case might include a 20 percent increase in the number of products being produced by the work unit over the next three months or a 40 percent decrease in the number of products being returned by quality control next year.

The idea of having specific goals is closely related to that of having observable goals. It should be clear to everyone when the goal has or has not been reached. It is easy to say your goal is to go on a diet, but a much better goal is "to lose 10 pounds by March." Similarly, it is easy to say the team should do better next season, but a better goal is to say the team will win more than half of next season's games. It is important to note that specific, observable goals are also time limited. Without time limits for accomplishing goals, there would be little urgency associated with them. Neither would there be a finite point at which it is clear a person or group has or has not accomplished the goals. For example, it is better to set a goal of improving the next quarter's sales figures than just improving sales.

GOALS SHOULD BE ATTAINABLE BUT CHALLENGING

Some people seem to treat goals as a sort of loyalty oath they must pass, as if it would be a break with one's ideals or be a reflection of insufficient motivation if any but the loftiest goals were set for oneself or one's organization. Yet to be useful, goals must be realistic. The struggling high school student who sets a goal of getting into Harvard may be unrealistic; but it may be realistic to set a goal of getting into the local state university. A civil rights activist may wish to eliminate prejudice completely, but a more attainable goal might be to eliminate racial discrimination in the local housing project over the next five years. A track team is not likely to win every race, but it may be realistic to aim to win the league championship.

The corollary to the preceding point is that goals should also be challenging. If goals merely needed to be attainable, then there would be nothing wrong with setting goals so easy that accomplishing them would be virtually guaranteed. As we have seen previously, setting easy goals does not result in high levels of performance; higher levels of performance come about when goals stretch and inspire people toward doing more than they thought they could. Goals need to be challenging but attainable to get the best out of oneself and others.

GOALS REQUIRE COMMITMENT

There is nothing magical about having goals; having goals per se does not guarantee success. Unless supported by real human commitment, goal statements are mere words. Organizational goals are most likely to be achieved if there is commitment to them at both the top and the bottom of the organization. Top leadership needs to make clear that it is willing to put its money where its mouth is. When top leadership sets goals, it should provide the resources workers need to achieve the goals and then should reward those who do. Subordinates often become committed to goals simply by seeing the sincere and enthusiastic commitment of top leadership to them. Another way to build subordinate acceptance and commitment to goals is to have subordinates participate in setting the goals in the first place. Research on the effects of goal setting demonstrates that worker acceptance and satisfaction tend to increase when workers are allowed to participate in setting goals (Erez, Earley, & Hulin, 1985; Locke, Latham, & Erez, 1987).

On the other hand, research is less conclusive about whether participation in goal setting actually increases performance or productivity. These mixed findings about participation and performance may be due to various qualities of the group and the leader. In terms of the group, groupthink may cause highly cohesive groups to commit to goals that are unrealistic and unachievable. Group members may not have realistically considered equipment or resource constraints, nor have the technical skills needed to successfully accomplish the goal. In addition, group members may not have any special enthusiasm for accomplishing a goal if the leader is perceived to have little expert power or is unsupportive, curt, or inept (House, 1984; Latham & Lee, 1986; Locke, Latham, & Erez, 1987). However, if leaders are perceived to be competent and supportive, then followers may have as much goal commitment as they would if they had participated in setting the goal. Thus, participation in goal setting often leads to higher levels of commitment and performance if the leader is perceived to be incompetent, but it will not necessarily lead to greater commitment and performance than is achieved when a competent leader assigns a goal. Again, these findings lend credence to the importance of technical competence in leadership effectiveness.

GOALS REQUIRE FEEDBACK

One of the most effective ways to improve any kind of performance is to provide feedback about how closely a person's behavior matches some criterion, and research shows that performance was much higher when goals were accompanied by feedback than when either goals or feedback were used alone. Goals that are specific, observable, and time limited are conducive to ongoing assessment and performance-based feedback, and leaders and followers should strive to provide and/or seek feedback on a fairly regular basis. Moreover, people should seek feedback from a variety of sources or provide feedback using a variety of criteria. Often, different sources and criteria can paint very different pictures about goal progress, and people can get a better idea of the true level of their progress by examining the information provided and integrating it across the different sources and criteria.

PUNISHMENT

BY R.L. HUGES, R.C. GINNET, & C.J. CURPHY

Myths Surrounding the Use of Punishment

Punishment, Satisfaction, and Performance

Administering Punishment

In an ideal world, perhaps everyone would be dependable, achievement oriented, and committed to the organization's goals. The fact is, however, that leaders sometimes will need to deal with followers who are openly hostile or insubordinate, create conflicts among co-workers, do not work up to standards, or openly violate important rules or policies. In such cases leaders may need to administer punishment to change the follower's behavior.

Of all of the different aspects of leadership, few are as controversial as punishment. Some of the primary reasons for this controversy stem from myths surrounding the use of punishment, as well as the lack of knowledge regarding the effects of punishment on followers' motivation, satisfaction, and performance. This section is designed to shed light on the punishment controversy by (*a*) addressing several myths about the use of punishment, (*b*) reviewing research findings concerning the relationships between punishment and various organizational variables, and (*c*) providing leadership practitioners with advice on how to properly administer punishment.

MYTHS SURROUNDING THE USE OF PUNISHMENT

Punishment is the administration of an aversive event or the withdrawal of a positive event or stimulus, which in turn *decreases* the likelihood a particular behavior will be repeated (Arvey & Ivancevich, 1980). Examples of punishment might include verbal reprimands, being moved to a less prestigious office, having pay docked, being fired, being made to run several laps around the athletic field, or losing eligibility for a sport entirely. We should note that according to this definition, only those aversive events administered on a contingent basis are considered to be forms of punishment; aversive events administered on a noncontingent basis may constitute harsh and abusive treatment but are not punishment. Additionally, punishment appears to be in the eye of the beholder; aversive events that

effectively change the direction, intensity, or persistence of one follower's behavior may have no effect on another's (Curphy, Gibson, Asiu, McCown, & Brown, 1992). It is even possible that some followers may find the administration of a noxious event or the removal of a positive event to be reinforcing. For example, it is not uncommon for some children to misbehave if that increases the attention they receive from parents, even if the latter's behavior outwardly may seem punishing to others. (To the children, some parental attention of any kind may be preferable to no attention.) Similarly, some followers may see the verbal reprimands and notoriety they receive by being insubordinate or violating company policies as forms of attention. Because these followers enjoy being the center of attention, they may find this notoriety rewarding. From an operant perspective, they may be even more likely to be insubordinate in the future.

We will examine four myths surrounding the use of punishment. Three of these myths were reviewed by Arvey and Ivancevich (1980) and included beliefs that the use of punishment resulted in undesirable emotional side effects on the part of the recipient, was unethical and inhumane, and rarely worked anyway (i.e., seldom eliminated the undesirable behavior).

B. F. Skinner's (1938) work in behavioral psychology lent support to the idea that punishment was ineffective and caused undesirable side effects. He based his conclusions on the unnatural behaviors manifested by rats and pigeons punished in various conditioning experiments. Despite the dangers of generalizing from the behavior of rats to humans, many people accepted Skinner's contention that punishment was a futile and typically counterproductive tool for controlling human behavior. This was so despite the fact that considerable research regarding the emotional effects of punishment on humans did not support Skinner's claim (Kazdin, 1975; Johnston, 1972; Solomon, 1964). Parke (1972), for example, suggested that undesirable emotional side effects of punishment might occur only when punishment was administered indiscriminately or was particularly harsh.

With respect to the myth that punishment is unethical or inhumane, Arvey and Ivancevich (1980) maintained there is an ethical distinction between "future-oriented" and "past-oriented" punishment. Future-oriented punishment, intended to help improve behavior, may be effective in diminishing or eliminating undesirable behavior. Past-oriented punishment, or what we commonly think of as retribution, on the other hand, is simply a payback for past misdeeds. This sort of punishment may be more questionable ethically, especially when it is intended *only* as payback and not, say, as deterrent to others. Moreover, when considering the ethics of administering punishment, one must also consider the ethics of *failing* to administer punishment. The costs of *failing* to punish a potentially harmful behavior, such as unsafe workplace practices, may far outweigh those associated with the punishment itself (Arvey & Ivancevich, 1980).

A third myth concerns the efficacy of punishment. Skinner (1938, 1985), and more recently Campbell (1977) and Luthans (1989), claimed that punishment did not result in a permanent behavior change but instead only temporarily suppressed behavior. Evidence to support this claim was found by Huberman (1964), who reported that incarcerated prisoners had a recidivism rate of 85 percent. However, this high recidivism rate may be due to the fact that criminals may have received punishment primarily for retribution rather than for corrective purposes. Judicious administration of sanctions, combined with advice about how to avoid punishment in the future, may successfully eliminate undesirable behaviors on a more permanent basis (Arvey & Ivancevich, 1980). Furthermore, it may be a moot point to argue (as Skinner did) that punishment only temporarily suppresses behavior; so long as sanctions for misdeeds remain in place, their impact on behavior should continue. In that regard, it's relevant to note that the "temporary" effects of punishment on behavior are no different from the "temporary" effects of reinforcement on behavior.

PUNISHMENT, SATISFACTION, AND PERFORMANCE

It appears that properly administered punishment does not cause undesirable emotional side effects, is not unethical, and may effectively suppress undesirable behavior. However, we also should ask what effect punishment has on followers' satisfaction and performance. Most people probably would predict that leaders who use punishment more frequently will probably have less-satisfied and lower-performing followers. Interestingly, this does not appear to be

the case—at least when punishment is used appropriately. Let us look a little more closely at this issue.

Several researchers have looked at whether leaders who administer punishment on a contingent basis also administered rewards on a contingent basis. Generally, researchers have found that there is a moderate positive relationship between leaders' contingent reward behaviors and contingent punishment behaviors (Arvey, Davis, & Nelson, 1984; Podsakoff & Todor, 1985; Strasser, Dailey, & Bateman, 1981). There also are consistently strong negative correlations found between leaders' contingent reward and non-contingent punishment behaviors. Thus, leaders meting out rewards on a contingent basis were also more likely to administer punishment only when followers behaved inappropriately or were not performing up to standards.

Keller and Szilagyi (1976, 1978) maintained that punishment can serve several constructive organizational purposes. They said it can help clarify roles and expectations, as well as reduce role ambiguity. Several other authors have found contingent punishment either was unrelated to followers' satisfaction with their supervisor ratings or had a low positive relationship with it (Arvey, Davis, & Nelson, 1984; Podsakoff, Todor, Grover, & Huber, 1984). In other words, leaders who follow certain rules in administering punishment need not have dissatisfied subordinates. As a matter of fact, judicious and appropriate use of punishment by leaders may result in somewhat *higher* satisfaction of followers overall. These findings make sense when the entire work unit is considered; failing to use punishment when it seems called for in most followers' eyes may lead to perceptions of inequity, which may in turn lead to lower group cohesiveness and satisfaction (Curphy et al., 1992; Dobbins & Russell, 1986).

With respect to followers' work behaviors, Arvey and Jones (1985) reported that punishment has generally been found to reduce absenteeism and tardiness rates. Nevertheless, the evidence about punishment's impact on performance appears mixed. Some authors report a strong positive relationship between punishment and performance (Beyer & Trice, 1984; Katz, Maccoby, Gurin, & Floor, 1951; Podsakoff & Todor, 1985; Schnake, 1986), whereas others found either no relationship between punishment and performance or a negative one (Curphy et al., 1992; Curtis, Smith, & Smoll, 1979).

Despite such mixed findings, there are several points about the relationship between punishment and performance findings still worth noting. First, the level of punishment as well as the manner in which it was administered across studies could have differed dramatically, and these factors could have affected the results. Second, of the studies reporting positive results, Schnake's (1986) experiment of the vicarious effects of punishment is by far the most provocative. Schnake hired college students for a temporary job, and after several hours at work, publicly reduced the pay or threatened to reduce the pay of a confederate in the work group. As predicted, the more severe the punishment witnessed (either the threat of reduced pay or the reduction of pay), the higher the subsequent performance of other work-group members.

Although these findings demonstrated that merely witnessing rather than receiving punishment could result in increased performance, these results should be interpreted with some caution. Because most of the individuals in the experiment did not know each other and had only been working together for several hours, there was probably not enough time for group cohesiveness or norms to develop. It is not at all clear whether members of cohesive groups or groups with strong norms would react in the same way if they had observed another group member being punished (Curphy et al., 1992).

Third, of the studies reporting less favorable punishment-performance results, the Curtis, Smith, and Smoll (1979) study made an important point about the opportunities to punish. Curtis, Smith, and Smoll examined the relationships between Little League coaches' behaviors and their teams' win–loss records. They found coaches who punished more often had less-successful teams. These coaches also, however, had less-talented players and therefore had many more opportunities to use punishment. Coaches of successful teams had little if any reason to use punishment. Fourth, many behaviors that do get punished may not have a direct link to job performance. For example, being insubordinate, violating company dress codes, and arriving late to meetings are all punishable behaviors that may not be directly linked to solving work-related problems or producing goods or services.

Finally, almost all these studies implicitly assumed punishment enhanced performance (by correcting problem behaviors), but Curphy and his associates (1992) were the only researchers who actually tested this assumption. They collected over 4,500 incidents of documented punishment and perform-ance data from 40 identical organizations over a three-month period. (The punishment and performance data were collected monthly.) They found that low performance led to higher levels of punishment. Moreover, they found that inexperienced leaders administered almost twice as much punishment as experienced leaders. The authors hypothesized that inexperienced leaders used punishment (i.e., relied on their coercive power) more frequently because by being the newest arrivals to the organization, they lacked knowledge of the organizational norms, rules, and policies (i.e., expert power); had not yet established relationships with followers (i.e., referent power); and were severely limited in the rewards they could provide to followers (i.e., reward power).

In summary, the research evidence shows that punishment can lead to positive organizational outcomes if administered properly. When administered on a contingent basis, it may help increase job satisfaction; may decrease role ambiguity and absenteeism rates; and depending on the behaviors being punished, may have a positive effect on performance. However, administering intense levels of punishment in a noncontingent or capricious manner can have a devastating effect on the work unit. Group cohesiveness may suffer, followers are likely to become more dissatisfied and less apt to come to work, and they may perform at a lower level in the long term. Thus, learning how to properly administer punishment may be the key to maximizing the benefits associated with its use.

ADMINISTERING PUNISHMENT

Usually, leaders administer punishment in order to rectify some type of behavioral or performance problem at work. However, not every behavior or performance problem is punished, and leaders probably weigh several different factors before deciding whether or not to administer punishment. Green and Mitchell (1979) maintained that leaders' decisions concerning punishment depended on whether leaders made internal or external attributions about a subordinate's substandard performance. Leaders making internal attributions were more likely to administer punishment; leaders making external attributions were more likely to blame the substandard performance on situational factors beyond the follower's control.

Attribution theory (Mitchell, Green, & Wood, 1981; Mitchell & Wood, 1980) maintains that leaders weigh three factors when making internal or external attributions about a follower's substandard performance. More specifically, leaders would be more likely to make an internal attribution about a follower's substandard performance (and administer punishment) if the follower had previously completed the task before, if other followers had successfully completed the task, and if the follower had successfully completed other tasks in the past. Moreover, Mitchell, Green, and Wood (1981) and Mitchell and Wood (1980) reported that leaders were biased toward making internal attributions about followers' poor performance (i.e., the fundamental attribution error) and thus more likely to use punishment to modify a follower's behavior.

Because leaders are biased toward making internal attributions about followers' substandard performance, leaders can administer punishment more effectively by being aware of this bias and getting as many facts as possible *before* deciding whether or not to administer punishment. Leaders also can improve the manner or skill with which they administer punishment by using tips provided by Arvey and Ivancevich (1980), who said punishment is administered most effectively when it focuses on the act, not the person. Followers probably cannot change their personalities, values, or preferences, but they can change their behaviors. By focusing on specific behaviors, leaders minimize the threat to followers' self-concepts. Also, punishment needs to be consistent across *both* behaviors and leaders; the same actions need to have the same consequences across work groups, or feelings of inequity and favoritism will pervade the organization. One way to increase the consistency in punishment is through the establishment of clearly specified organizational policies and procedures.

Administering punishment properly depends on effective two-way communication between the leader and follower. Leaders need to provide a clear rationale for punishment and indicate the consequences for unacceptable behavior in the future. Finally, leaders need to provide followers with guidance about how to improve. This guidance may entail role-modeling proper behaviors for followers, suggesting followers take additional training courses, or just giving followers accurate feedback about their behavior at work (Arvey & Ivancevich, 1980).

Overall, it may be the manner in which punishment is administered, rather than the level of punishment, that has the greatest effect on followers' satisfaction and performance. Leaders need to realize that they may be biased toward administering punishment to rectify followers' substandard performance, and the best way to get around this bias is to collect as much information as possible before deciding whether or not to punish. By collecting the facts, leaders will be better able to focus on the act, not the person; be able to administer a punishment consistent with company policy; provide the rationale for the punishment; and give guidance to followers on how to improve.

A final caution which leaders need to be aware of concerns the reinforcing or rewarding nature of punishment. As stated earlier in the discussion of the operant approach to motivation, behaviors that are rewarded are likely to be repeated. When leaders administer punishment and subsequently see improvement in a follower's behavior, the leader will be rewarded and be more apt to use punishment in the future. Over time, this may lead to an overreliance on punishment and an underemphasis of the other motivational strategies as the means for correcting performance problems. Again, by collecting as much information as possible and by carefully considering the applicability of goal setting, the operant approach, job characteristics theory, and so on, to the problem, leaders may be able to successfully avoid having only one tool in their motivational tool kit.

Leadership Development Program and Self-Assessment

The purpose of this lesson is to ensure you understand the Leadership Development Program (LDP). The sixteen leadership dimensions and the seven Army Values, used to assess your leadership potential within the context of the LDP, will be addressed. The Cadet Evaluation System (CES) will be explained to ensure you are familiar with the evaluation system to include self-assessments.

The following topics are addressed in this lesson:

- 23 assessment dimensions (leadership dimensions & Army Values)
- Operation of Cadet Evaluation System
- Use of Blue & Yellow cards
- Observing, classifying, & rating performance

The following TLOs are supported in whole or in part by this lesson:

- Seek self improvement
- Conduct a self-assessment

Following this lesson you will be able to:

- Describe the Army Leadership Framework—values, attributes, skills, and actions of the "BE, KNOW, and DO" of a leader
- Explain the use of the LDP "blue" and "yellow" cards in relation to cadet self assessment
- Classify performance indicators using the 23 leadership dimensions
- Perform a self-assessment, applying the performance indicators and using the LDP yellow self-assessment card

MODULE III

The Army Profession: Army Operations Overview

This module consists of fifteen lessons divided into two parts: Part I consisting of lessons 6-12; and Part II consisting of lessons 17-24).

PART I

Lesson six and seven are designed to teach you how to plan a block of instruction to be delivered to a small unit. These lessons are intended to prepare you for your responsibilities to prepare and deliver instruction in Military Science and Leadership Labs.

Lessons eight through twelve are designed to introduce you to tactical theory and its battlefield applications. These lessons constitute your classroom introduction to tactics. The principles taught in this module serve as the broad theoretical underpinning to the solution of tactical problems. Historical case studies are used to illustrate tactical principles of offensive and defensive operations and as a capstone exercise for the module. The tactical drills and practice of the MSL Labs complement the theoretical focus of this module.

PART II

Lessons 17 through 24, build on the preceding Personal Development module (Problem Solving lessons 13–16) by examining the Army's adaptation of general problem solving and decision making principles to military operational problems and decisions. The lessons of this module take you through the eight steps of the troop leading procedure including mission analysis, planning, and execution. Sample missions are used throughout this module to give you practical experience in conducting the eight troop leading steps.

MODULE III

The Army Profession: Army Operations (Part I)

Train a Team I

This is the first of two lessons on Training a Team, and it is the first lesson in the Army Operations track. As such, it lays the foundation for your success in a key aspect of leadership—training. The lesson is intended to do the following: 1) familiarize you with learning styles, multiple intelligences and information about how you can use soldiers' learning styles to provide more effective training; 2) provide you with information about the Army Training Management System and how leaderships' responsibilities for training and the principles of Army training form the framework for that system; and 3) teach you how to use the Army's crawl-walk-run training process to plan, implement, and assess a training session, including determining whether retraining is a requirement and how it should be conducted.

The following topics are addressed in this lesson:

- Plan training addressing soldiers' learning styles and multiple intelligences
- Establish pre-execution checklists
- Conduct resource coordination
- Train a task
- Assess training
- Conduct retraining

The following TLO is supported in whole or in part by this lesson:

- Apply the Army Training Management System

Following this lesson you will be able to:

- Describe the Army Training Management System
- Plan a training session
- Identify assessment strategies for training

DISCOVERING YOUR LEARNING STYLES

BY ROBERT S. FELDMAN

Consider what it would be like to be a member of the Trukese people, a small group of islanders in the South Pacific.

Trukese sailors often sail hundreds of miles on the open sea. They manage this feat with none of the navigational equipment used by Western sailors. No compass. No chronometer. No sextant. They don't even sail in a straight line. Instead, they zigzag back and forth, at the mercy of the winds and tides. Yet they make few mistakes. Almost always they are able to reach their destination with precision. How do they do it?

They can't really explain it. They say it has to do with following the rising and setting of the stars at night. During the day, they take in the appearance, sound, and feel of the waves against the side of the boat. But they don't really have any idea of where they are at any given moment, nor do they care. They just know that ultimately they'll reach their final destination.

It would be foolhardy to suggest that the Trukese don't have what it takes to be successful sailors. The fact that they don't use traditional Western navigational equipment when they're sailing does not mean that they are any less able than Western navigators. Certainly, if they took a test of Western navigational skills, they would do badly. But their ultimate success cannot be questioned.

What about academic success? Isn't it reasonable to assume that there are different ways to reach academic goals? Wouldn't it be surprising if everyone learned in exactly the same way, without any differences in what worked best for them?

It turns out that we don't all learn in the same way. Each of us has preferred ways of learning, approaches that work best for us. And our success is not just dependent on how *well* we learn, but on *how* we learn.

Learning styles reflect our preferred manner of acquiring, using, and thinking about knowledge. These styles are not abilities, but types of learning. They represent the ways we approach these tasks.

We don't have just one learning style, but a profile of styles. Even though our ability may be identical to someone else's, our learning styles might be quite different.

You probably already know quite a lot about your learning styles. Maybe you do particularly well in your biology classes while struggling with English. Or it may be the other way around. Because biology tends to be about natural processes, teachers present the subject as a series of related facts. English, however, requires you to think more abstractly, analyzing and synthesizing ideas presented in a variety of ways. Whichever subject you prefer, it is almost certain you prefer it because of your learning style.

Though we may have general preferences for fact-based learning or learning that requires more abstract thinking, we all use a variety of learning styles.

Some involve our preferences regarding the way information is presented to us, some relate to how we think and learn most readily, and some relate to how our personality traits affect our performance. Different approaches to learning overlap one another, and there are few distinct categories. We'll start by considering the preferences we have for how we initially perceive information.

ARE YOU A PRIMARILY VISUAL, AUDITORY, OR TACTILE LEARNER?

One of the most basic aspects of learning styles concerns the way in which we initially receive information from our sense organs—our **receptive learning style.** Some of us have primarily **visual learning styles,** recalling the spelling of a word, for example, or the structure of a chemical compound by reviewing a picture in our head. Or maybe you learn best when you have the opportunity to read about a concept rather than listening to a teacher explain it. Students with visual learning styles find it easier to see things in their "mind's eye"—to visualize a task or concept—than to be lectured about them.

Have you ever asked a friend to help you put something together by having her read the directions to you while you worked? If you did, you may have an **auditory learning style.** People with auditory learning styles prefer listening to explanations rather than reading about them. They love class lectures and discussions, because they can easily take in the information that is being talked about.

Students with a **tactile learning style** prefer to learn by doing—touching, manipulating objects, and doing things. For instance, some people enjoy the act of writing because of the feel of a pencil or a computer keyboard—the tactile equivalent of "thinking out loud" (which would be preferred by someone with an auditory learning style). Or they may find that it helps them to make a three-dimensional model to understand a new idea.

Having a particular receptive learning style simply means that it will be easier to learn material that is presented in that style. It does not mean you cannot learn any other way!

Receptive learning styles also have implications for effective studying. For instance, students with an auditory learning style may have greater success if they recite material out loud when studying. In contrast, a visual learner might do better producing time lines, charts, or other graphical study aids. Tactile learners may learn best by tracing or using other hands-on methods of studying.

HANDLING INFORMATION: DO YOU FOCUS ON PIECES OR THE WHOLE?

When you are putting a jigsaw puzzle together, do you focus more on the individual pieces and how each one fits together with the one next to it, or is your strategy to concentrate on the whole picture, keeping the finished product in mind?

The way you approach a jigsaw puzzle provides a clue to the process by which you fit together bits of information. Specifically, the strategy you use suggests which of the following two learning styles you are more comfortable with:

- People with **analytic learning styles** learn most easily if first exposed to the individual components and principles behind a phenomenon or situation. Once they have identified the underlying components involved, they find it easier to figure out and grasp the broad picture and determine whether particular cases exemplify the principle.
- Those with **relational learning styles** learn most readily if exposed to the full range of material that they are aiming to learn. Rather than focusing on the individual components of a problem, as those with analytic styles prefer to do, people with relational learning styles do best when they are first given the full picture. They can then take this broad view and break it down into its individual components.

For example, consider trying to understand the way that food is converted to energy in a cell. A more analytic learner would approach the task by learning each individual step in the process, first to last. In contrast, a more relational learner would consider the big picture, focusing on the general, overall process and its purpose.

Students who use an analytic style study most effectively by focusing on facts and specific principles, for they excel at organizing information. They often work best on their own, and science and math may come particularly easy to them. On the other hand, students with a relational style perceive concepts globally, thinking in terms of the "big picture." They may be drawn to subject areas that demand the ability to forge a broad overview of material, such as English and history. You probably already have a good idea of whether you have an analytic or relational learning style, but Try It 1 on page 82, "Assess Your Analytical and Relational Learning Styles," will help you understand your learning style further.

PERSONALITY STYLES

Our learning styles are also influenced by our personality. Are you a person who is likely to try out for school productions? Or is the idea of getting on a stage something that is totally lacking in appeal (if not completely terrifying)? Do you relate to the world around you primarily through careful planning or by spontaneously reacting?

According to the rationale of the *Myers-Briggs Type Indicator,* a questionnaire frequently used in business and other organizations, our personality type plays a key role in determining how we react to different kinds of situations. Specifically, the idea is that we work best in situations in which others—both students and instructors—share our preferences and in which our personality preferences are most suited to the particular task on which we are working.

According to studies done on personality, four major dimensions are critical. Although we'll describe the extremes of each dimension, keep in mind that most of us fall somewhere in between each of the endpoints of each dimension.

- **Introverts versus extroverts.** A key difference between introverts and extroverts is whether they enjoy working with others. Independence is a key characteristic of introverted learners. They enjoy working alone and they are less affected by how others think and behave. In contrast, extroverts are outgoing and more affected by the behavior and thinking of others. They enjoy working

Try It! 1

ASSESS YOUR ANALYTICAL AND RELATIONAL LEARNING STYLES

Consider the following pairs of statements. Place a check next to the statement in each pair that more closely describes your style.

_____ 1a. Before tackling a complex task that I'm unfamiliar with, I prefer to have detailed instructions on how to do it.

_____ 1b. I prefer to "dive into" a new task, trying things out to see what happens and finding my way as I go.

_____ 2a. I like watching movies a second time because then I know where they're going.

_____ 2b. I generally don't like watching movies a second time because I know their plots already.

_____ 3a. I prefer to solve math or science problems using formulas and directions.

_____ 3b. I prefer to figure out why formulas work.

_____ 4a. When I read mystery stories, I usually let the author tell the story and reveal the mystery.

_____ 4b. When I read mystery stories, I like to try figuring out the mystery before the author reveals it.

_____ 5a. I usually read the instruction booklet before trying out a new piece of software.

_____ 5b. I never read the instruction booklet before trying out a new piece of software.

_____ 6a. I prefer to have someone who knows about a subject explain it to me before I try my hand at it.

_____ 6b. I'm impatient when others try to explain things to me, preferring to get involved in them myself without much explanation.

_____ 7a. Whenever I see a really amazing special effect in a movie, I like to sit back and enjoy it.

_____ 7b. Whenever I see a really amazing special effect in a movie, I try to figure out how they did it.

If you tended to prefer the "A" statements in most pairs, you probably have a relational style. If you preferred the "B" statements, you probably have a more analytic style. Remember that no one is purely analytical or purely relational.

---

with others, and they are energized by having other people around.

■ **Intuitors versus sensors.** Intuitors enjoy solving problems and being creative. They get impatient with details, preferring to make leaps of judgment, and they enjoy the challenge of solving problems and taking a "big-picture" approach. People categorized as sensors, on the other hand, prefer a concrete, logical approach in which they can carefully analyze the facts of the situation. Although they are good with details, they sometimes miss the big picture.

■ **Thinkers versus feelers.** Thinkers prefer logic over emotion. They reach decisions and solve problems by systematically analyzing a situation. In contrast, feeling types rely more on their emotional responses. They are aware of others and their feelings, and they are influenced by their personal values and attachments to others.

■ **Perceivers and judgers.** Before drawing a conclusion, perceivers attempt to gather as much information as they can. Because they are open to multiple perspectives and appreciate all sides of an issue, they sometimes have difficulty completing a task. Judgers, in comparison, are quick and decisive. They like to set goals, accomplish them, and then move on to the next task.

Each personality type has specific likes and dislikes when it comes to learning preferences. For example, introverts enjoy working alone, while extroverts enjoy cooperative learning and projects involving many people. Intuitors most enjoy creative problem solving, while sensors flourish with assignments that are concrete and logical. Thinkers prefer to systematically use logic to analyze a problem, and feelers enjoy assignments that involve others and their emotional reactions. Finally, perceivers favor work on which there are multiple sides to an issue, while judgers' preferences are to be decisive, determining goals and sticking to them.

THE ORIGINS OF OUR LEARNING STYLES

For many of us, our learning style preferences result from the kind of processing our brain "specializes" in. **Left-brain processing** concentrates more on tasks requiring verbal competence, such as speaking, reading, thinking, and reasoning. Information is processed sequentially, one bit at a time. For instance, people who are naturally inclined to use left-brain processing might be more likely to prefer analytic learning styles, because they first like to look at individual bits of information and *then* put them together.

On the other hand, **right-brain processing** tends to concentrate more on the processing of information in nonverbal domains, such as the understanding of spatial relationships, recognition of patterns and drawings, music, and emotional expression. Furthermore, the right hemisphere tends to process information globally, considering it as a whole. Consequently, people who naturally tend toward right-brain processing might prefer relational learning styles.

FACTS TO REMEMBER ABOUT LEARNING, PERSONALITY, AND PROCESSING STYLES

- **You have a variety of styles.** For any given task or challenge, some types of styles may be more relevant than others. Furthermore, success is possible even when there is a mismatch between what you need to accomplish and your own pattern of preferred styles. It may take more work, but learning to deal with situations that require you to use less-preferred styles is important practice for life after college.
- **Your style reflects your preferences regarding which abilities you like to use—*not* the abilities themselves.** Styles are related to our preferences and the mental approaches we like to use. You may prefer to learn tactilely, but that in itself doesn't guarantee that the products that you create tactilely will be good—you still have to work!
- **Your style will change over the course of your life.** You can learn new styles and expand the range of learning experiences in which you feel perfectly comfortable. In fact, you can conceive of this material as one long lesson in learning styles because it provides you with strategies for learning more effectively in a variety of ways.

- **You should work on improving your less-preferred styles.** Although it may be tempting, don't always make choices that increase your exposure to preferred styles and decrease your practice with less-preferred styles. The more you use approaches for which you have less of a preference, the better you'll be at developing the skills associated with those styles.
- **Work cooperatively with others who have different styles.** If your instructor asks you to work cooperatively in groups, seek out classmates who have styles that are different from yours. Not only will your classmates' differing styles help you to achieve collective success, but you can learn from observing others' approaches to tackling the assignment.

USING YOUR INSTRUCTORS' TEACHING STYLES

In the same way that each of us has preferred learning styles, instructors have their own styles of teaching. They may not even be aware of them, but their learning styles have an important impact on the way they teach—and that, in turn, will help determine how well you do in their classes.

Instructors who make frequent requests to "list," "label," "diagram," "outline," or "define," may favor a more analytic learning style. In contrast, if their tendency is to ask you to "compare," "analyze," "discuss," "criticize," or "evaluate," they may be more in tune with relational learning.

Similarly, instructors who assign frequent projects that involve oral presentations and demonstrations might be indicating that their learning style is somewhat auditory. On the other hand, instructors whose assignments consist of frequent written work may have a more visual style. Work on "Instructor Styles" (Try It 2 on page 85) to get a sense of your instructor's learning style.

What if your learning styles are mismatched with those of your instructor? Several approaches might improve the situation:

TABLE 6.1 LEARNING, PERSONALITY, AND PROCESSING STYLES.

All of us have particular learning, personality, and processing styles that we tend to rely on. At the same time, we also have capabilities in less-preferred styles. So, for example, although you may be primarily a visual learner, you have the capacity to use auditory and tactile approaches. Note in particular that the four categories under "Personality Styles" are considered independent of each other. For example, you may be an extrovert and at the same time a sensor, a feeler, and a judger.

CATEGORY	DESCRIPTION
Receptive Learning Styles	
Visual	A style that involves visualizing information in the mind, favoring reading and watching over touching and listening
Auditory	A style in which the learner favors listening as the best approach
Tactile	A style that involves learning by touching, manipulating objects, and doing things
Information Processing Styles	
Analytic	A style in which the learner starts with small pieces of information and uses them to build the big picture
Relational	A style in which the learner starts with the big picture and breaks it down into its individual components
Personality Styles	
Introvert versus Extrovert	Independence is a key characteristic of introverted learners, who enjoy working alone and are less affected by how others think and behave. In contrast, extroverts are outgoing and more affected by the behavior and thinking of others. They enjoy working with others.
Intuitor versus Sensor	Intuitors enjoy solving problems and being creative, often taking a "big-picture" approach to solving problems. Sensors, on the other hand, prefer a concrete, logical approach in which they can carefully analyze the facts of the situation.
Thinker versus Feeler	Thinkers prefer logic over emotion, reaching decisions and solving problems by systematically analyzing a situation. In contrast, feelers rely more on their emotional responses and are influenced by their personal values and attachments to others.
Perceiver versus Judger	Before drawing a conclusion, perceivers attempt to gather as much information as they can and are open to multiple perspectives. Judgers, in comparison, are quick and decisive; they enjoy setting goals and accomplishing them.
Brain Processing Styles	
Left-Brain Processing	Information processing that focuses on tasks requiring verbal competence, such as speaking, reading, thinking, and reasoning; information is processed sequentially, one bit at a time.
Right-Brain Processing	Information processing focusing on information in nonverbal domains, such as the understanding of spatial relationships, recognition of patterns and drawings, music, and emotional expression. Information is processed globally.

Try It! 2

WORKING IN A GROUP: INSTRUCTOR STYLES

Working as a group with your classmates, try to determine your course instructor's learning style by answering the following questions:

1. What clues does the language your instructor uses give you about his or her learning style?

_____

_____

_____

_____

_____

2. What assignments has the instructor scheduled, and what do they tell you about the instructor's learning style?

_____

_____

_____

_____

_____

3. Are there constraints (such as class size, scheduling factors, school traditions) that also influence the instructor's teaching style, apart from his or her underlying learning style?

_____

_____

_____

_____

_____

■ **Consider the instructor's learning styles when studying.** If your natural tendency is to stick to the facts, and your instructor appears to prefer broad, conceptual views of the material, then be sure to consider the material from the instructor's broader view. In contrast, if your instructor's learning preferences lean toward factual views of material, pay special attention to the details that your instructor will likely be more interested in. For example, an instructor who focuses on the broad view is not likely to ask you to repeat a detailed series of dates of particular events during the French Revolution. Yet this may be exactly what another instructor, more focused on the details, is interested in.

In short, if your instructor doesn't seem to share your learning preferences, pay particular attention to approaches that *don't* come naturally to you. They are the ones that may prove the most successful in the course.

■ **Seek out alternative assignments.** A second approach to a mismatch between your learning styles and those of your instructor is to seek out alternative assignments. Occasionally instructors are willing to provide substitute assignments that tap into your preferences and strengths.

What if your instructor is unwilling to accommodate your learning preferences? Instructors have many students, and it would be nearly impossible to come up with independent assignments for each one. Furthermore, many instructors feel that it is part of their job to maximize student exposure to various learning approaches—which leads to the final point about mismatches between student and instructor styles: *Understand that there are benefits to discomfort.*

- **Accept discomfort as a necessary evil.** Real learning is often difficult and uncomfortable. To become an accomplished student,

you'll have to use a variety of strategies and approaches. Although you'll always have certain learning preferences, it is important to develop flexibility in the form of strategies that we'll be considering in future chapters.

Learning styles are just one example of how your personal characteristics affect your academic success. We now turn to a broader consideration of who you are as we examine how your understanding of yourself influences your success in college.

Train a Team II

This is the second of two lessons on Training a Team. Together, the pair lay the foundation for your success in a key aspect of leadership—training. Where the first lesson laid out the principles and practices of effective training, this lesson focuses on practice time with guidance and mentoring from the instructor, and feedback from other cadets.

The following topics are applied in this lesson:

- Reinforcement of leaders' responsibilities for Army training
- The framework of the Army Training Management System
- Feedback in preparing, conducting, and assessing training

The following TLO is supported in whole or in part by this lesson:

- Apply the Army Training Management System

Following this lesson you will be able to:

- Train others in a task, based on a training plan
- Select an assessment strategy
- Assess the training session's effectiveness
- Describe needed retraining
- Implement retraining

SOLDIER'S MANUAL OF COMMON TASKS-SKILL LEVEL 1

DOCUMENT AND SECTION

STP 21-1-SMCT SOLDIER'S MANUAL OF COMMON TASKS SKILL

LEVEL 1 (1994/10/01)

SUBJECT AREA: SEE

TASK: REPORT INFORMATION OF POTENTIAL INTELLIGENCE VALUE 301-348-1050

SUBJECT AREA: COMMUNICATE

TASK: PERFORM VOICE COMMUNICATIONS 113-571-1022

SUBJECT AREA: NAVIGATE

TASK: ORIENT A MAP TO THE GROUND BY MAP TERRAIN ASSOCIATION 071-329-1012

TASK: IDENTIFY TERRAIN FEATURES ON A MAP 071-329-1001

TASK: DETERMINE A LOCATION ON THE GROUND BY TERRAIN ASSOCIATION 071-329-1005

TASK: MEASURE DISTANCE ON A MAP 071-329-1008

TASK: DETERMINE THE GRID COORDINATES OF A POINT ON A MILITARY MAP 071-329-1002

TASK: DETERMINE DIRECTION WITHOUT A COMPASS 071-329-1018

TASK: DETERMINE A MAGNETIC AZIMUTH USING A LENSATIC COMPASS 071-329-1003

TASK: IDENTIFY TOPOGRAPHIC SYMBOLS ON A MILITARY MAP 071-329-1000

SUBJECT AREA: SHOOT, M16A1 or M16A2 Rifle

TASK: PERFORM A FUNCTION CHECK ON AN M16A1 OR M16A2 RIFLE 071-311-2026

TASK: ENGAGE TARGETS WITH AN M16A1 OR M16A2 RIFLE 071-311-2007

TASK: ZERO AN M16A1 RIFLE 071-311-2004

TASK: MAINTAIN AN M16A1 OR M16A2 RIFLE 071-311-2025

TASK: ZERO AN M16A2 RIFLE 071-311-2030

TASK: CORRECT MALFUNCTIONS OF AN M16A1 OR M16A2 RIFLE 071-311-2029

TASK: UNLOAD AN M16A1 OR M16A2 RIFLE 071-311-2028

TASK: LOAD AN M16A1 OR M16A2 RIFLE 071-311-2027

SUBJECT AREA: SHOOT, M60 Machine Gun

TASK: ENGAGE TARGETS WITH AN M60 MACHINE GUN 071-312-3031

TASK: CORRECT MALFUNCTIONS OF AN M60 MACHINE GUN 071-312-3029

TASK: UNLOAD AN M60 MACHINE GUN 071-312-3028

TASK: MAINTAIN AN M60 MACHINE GUN 071-312-3025

TASK: LAY AN M60 MACHINE GUN USING FIELD EXPEDIENTS 071-312-3003

TASK: PREPARE A RANGE CARD FOR AN M60 MACHINE GUN 071-312-3007

TASK: PERFORM A FUNCTION CHECK ON AN M60 MACHINE GUN 071-312-3026

TASK: LOAD AN M60 MACHINE GUN 071-312-3027

SUBJECT AREA: SHOOT, Hand Grenades

TASK: EMPLOY HAND GRENADES 071-325-4407

TASK: PERFORM SAFETY CHECKS ON HAND GRENADES 071-325-4401

SUBJECT AREA: SHOOT, Land Mines

TASK: RECOVER AN M18A1 CLAYMORE MINE 071-325-4426

TASK: EMPLOY AN M18A1 CLAYMORE MINE 071-325-4425

SUBJECT AREA: SURVIVE, Techniques

TASK: PERFORM INDIVIDUAL CAMOUFLAGE 051-191-1501

TASK: DRIVE VEHICLE WITH OR WITHOUT TRAILER/SEMITRAILER IN BLACKOUT CONDITIONS 551-721-1363

DOCUMENT AND SECTION

TASK: DRIVE VEHICLE IN A CONVOY 551-721-1359

TASK: PERFORM VEHICLE PREVENTIVE MAINTENANCE CHECKS AND SERVICES (PMCS) 551-721-1352

TASK: IDENTIFY UNEXPLODED ORDNANCE (UXO) HAZARDS 093-401-5000

TASK: CLEAR A FIELD OF FIRE 071-331-0852

TASK: PERFORM SURVEILLANCE WITHOUT THE AID OF ELECTRONIC DEVICES 071-331-0804

TASK: CHALLENGE PERSONS ENTERING YOUR AREA 071-331-0801

TASK: CONSTRUCT INDIVIDUAL FIGHTING POSITIONS 071-326-5703

TASK: SELECT TEMPORARY FIGHTING POSITIONS 071-326-0513

TASK: PRACTICE NOISE, LIGHT, AND LITTER DISCIPLINE 071-331-0815

TASK: REACT TO FLARES 071-326-0511

TASK: REACT TO INDIRECT FIRE WHILE DISMOUNTED 071-326-0510

TASK: MOVE OVER, THROUGH, OR AROUND OBSTACLES (EXCEPT MINEFIELDS) 071-326-0503

TASK: MOVE UNDER DIRECT FIRE 071-326-0502

TASK: IMPLEMENT DEFENSIVE PROCEDURES WHEN UNDER ENEMY ATTACK OR AMBUSH IN A TRUCK CONVOY 551-721-1408

TASK: LOCATE MINES BY PROBING 051-192-1135

SUBJECT AREA: SURVIVE, Protect Against NBC Attack

TASK: PROTECT YOURSELF FROM CHEMICAL AND BIOLOGICAL INJURY/ CONTAMINATION USING YOUR M40-SERIES PROTECTIVE MASK WITH HOOD 031-503-1025

TASK: REPLACE CANISTER ON YOUR M40-SERIES PROTECTIVE MASK 031-503-1024

TASK: PROTECT YOURSELF FROM NBC INJURY/CONTAMINATION WHEN CHANGING MISSION-ORIENTED PROTECTIVE POSTURE (MOPP) GEAR 031-503-1023

TASK: REACT TO CHEMICAL OR BIOLOGICAL HAZARD/ATTACK 031-503-1019

TASK: REACT TO A NUCLEAR HAZARD 031-503-1018

TASK: PROTECT YOURSELF FROM NBC INJURY/CONTAMINATION WITH MISSION-ORIENTED PROTECTIVE POSTURE (MOPP) GEAR 031-503-1015

TASK: IDENTIFY CHEMICAL AGENTS USING M8 DETECTOR PAPER 031-503-1014

TASK: PROTECT YOURSELF FROM CHEMICAL AND BIOLOGICAL INJURY/CONTAMINATION USING YOUR M24 OR M25-SERIES PROTECTIVE MASK WITH HOOD 031-503-1012

TASK: MAINTAIN YOUR M24 OR M25-SERIES PROTECTIVE MASK WITH HOOD 031-503-1011

TASK: PROTECT YOURSELF FROM CHEMICAL AND BIOLOGICAL INJURY/ CONTAMINATION WHILE ELIMINATING BODYWASTE WHEN WEARING MOPP4 031-503-1008

TASK: DETECT CHEMICAL AGENTS USING M9 DETECTOR PAPER 031-503-1020

TASK: DECONTAMINATE YOUR SKIN AND PERSONAL EQUIPMENT USING AN M258A1 DECONTAMINATION KIT 031-503-1007

TASK: PROTECT YOURSELF FROM NBC INJURY/CONTAMINATION WHEN DRINKING FROM YOUR CANTEEN WHILE WEARING YOUR PROTECTIVE MASK 031-503-1006

TASK: MAINTAIN YOUR M17-SERIES PROTECTIVE MASK WITH HOOD 031-503-1005

TASK: MAINTAIN YOUR M40-SERIES PROTECTIVE MASK WITH HOOD 031-503-1026

TASK: PROTECT YOURSELF FROM CHEMICAL AND BIOLOGICAL INJURY/ CONTAMINATION USING YOUR M17-SERIES PROTECTIVE MASK WITH HOOD 031-503-1004

TASK: PROTECT YOURSELF AND OTHERS FROM CHEMICAL AND BIOLOGICAL INJURY/CONTAMINATION BY USING (ENTERING OR EXITING) A COLLECTIVE PROTECTION SHELTER 031-506-1052

TASK: DECONTAMINATE YOUR INDIVIDUAL EQUIPMENT USING THE M295 INDIVIDUAL EQUIPMENT DECONTAMINATION KIT (IEDK) 031-503-1034

DOCUMENT AND SECTION

TASK: DECONTAMINATE YOUR SKIN USING THE M291 SKIN DECONTAMINATING KIT (SDK) 031-503-1033

TASK: PROTECT YOURSELF FROM CHEMICAL AND BIOLOGICAL INJURY/ CONTAMINATION USING YOUR M42 PROTECTIVE MASK WITH HOOD 031-503-1028

SUBJECT AREA: SURVIVE, Give First Aid

TASK: PERFORM MOUTH-TO-MOUTH RESUSCITATION 081-831-1042

TASK: TRANSPORT A CASUALTY USING A TWO-MAN CARRY OR AN IMPROVISED LITTER 081-831-1041

TASK: TRANSPORT A CASUALTY USING A ONE-MAN CARRY 081-831-1040

TASK: SPLINT A SUSPECTED FRACTURE 081-831-1034

TASK: APPLY A DRESSING TO AN OPEN HEAD WOUND 081-831-1033

TASK: ADMINISTER NERVE AGENT ANTIDOTE TO SELF (SELF-AID) 081-831-1030

TASK: APPLY A DRESSING TO AN OPEN CHEST WOUND 081-831-1026

TASK: APPLY A DRESSING TO AN OPEN ABDOMINAL WOUND 081-831-1025

TASK: PUT ON A TOURNIQUET 081-831-1017

TASK: PUT ON A FIELD OR PRESSURE DRESSING 081-831-1016

TASK: ADMINISTER FIRST AID TO A NERVE AGENT CASUALTY (BUDDY-AID) 081-831-1031

TASK: GIVE FIRST AID FOR FROSTBITE 081-831-1009

TASK: GIVE FIRST AID FOR HEAT INJURIES 081-831-1008

TASK: GIVE FIRST AID FOR BURNS 081-831-1007

TASK: PREVENT SHOCK 081-831-1005

TASK: CLEAR AN OBJECT FROM THE THROAT OF A CONSCIOUS CASUALTY 081-831-1003

TASK: EVALUATE A CASUALTY 081-831-1000

SUBJECT AREA: CUSTOMS AND LAWS OF WAR

TASK: CONDUCT COMBAT OPERATIONS ACCORDING TO THE LAW OF WAR 181-906-1505

SUBJECT AREA: HANDLE REMAINS

TASK: PERFORM MORTUARY AFFAIRS OPERATIONS 101-515-1900

Introduction
to Tactics

This is the first in a series of five lessons that provide the framework for tactical principles. This lesson introduces you to basic definitions and concepts of tactics.

The following topics are addressed in this lesson:

- Definition of tactics as both an art and a science
- Relationship and differentiation of the tactical, operational, and strategic levels of warfare
- Definition and description of the battlefield framework and organization
- Battlefield Operating Systems

The following TLO is supported in whole or in part by this lesson:

- Apply tactical principles and doctrine to the solution of tactical problems

Following this lesson you will be able to:

- Define the term tactics
- Describe the differences between the art and science of tactics
- Differentiate among the levels of war
- Describe the basic battlefield framework and organization
- Identify the characteristics of deep, close, and rear operations
- List the Battlefield Operating Systems

FRIGHT NIGHT:

TASK FORCE 2/34 ARMOR

BY COL GREGORY FONTENOT, US ARMY

Numerous articles have been written about the "100-hour" ground phase of Operation *Desert Storm;* the author commanded Task Force 2/34 Armor during operations *Desert Shield* and *Desert Storm.* He discusses his unit's involvement during the ground war, highlighting techniques that worked for the task force and also some techniques that did not do so well. In doing so he conveys the sense of confusion and friction in combat. He concludes with some suggestions for training for future battles.

Before daybreak on 26 February 1991, the 1st Infantry Division (ID) (Big Red One) moved north to join the 1st and 3d Armored divisions (ADs) in a three-division attack on the Republican Guard. During the previous two days, the Big Red One breached prepared positions of two Iraqi divisions. The 1st AD (UK) passed through the breach to attack the tactical reserves of the frontline Iraqi corps defending the western end of the Saddam Line. The remainder of VI Corps, led by the 2d Armored Cavalry of VII Corps, led by the 2d Armored Cavalry Regiment (ACR), streamed around the western flank of the Iraqi defenses and moved north.

The corps plan required the Big Red One to Move in a corridor, between the 1st AD (UK) and the 3d AD, which 2d ACR had cleared. The first order of business was to close on the 2d ACR, which was 40 kilometers (km) north of the division and moving. The 1st ID commander, Major General Thomas G. Rhame, ordered the 1st Squadron, 4th Cavalry (1/4 CAV) to lead, followed by 1st Brigade. Because the zone was narrow, Rhame directed the rest of the division to follow in column until clear of the British rear area north of Phase Line (PL) New Jersey.[1] (See fig. 1)

The 1st Brigade moved out at 0530 toward PL Harz, approximately 60 km north. At Harz, the brigade planned to assume hasty defensive positions prepared to attack the Republican Guard, probably on 27 February. Initially, space constrained the brigade's movement. Accordingly, 1/34 Armor (AR) (1st Battalion, 34th Armor) led the way, followed by Task Force (TF) 2/34 AR (2d Battalion, 34th Armor). Behind them trailed 1st Battalion, 5th (1/5) Field Artillery (FA) and TF 5/16 Infantry (5th Battalion, 16th Infantry). The brigade service support assets brought up the rear.[2]

This article traces the operations of TF 2/34 (Dreadnought) during the Big Red One's movement forward and attack on elements of the Iraqi *Tawakalna Mechanized Division* and *12th AD* on the night of 26–27 February 1991. Journalist have referred to the Big Red One's night attack as the "Battle of Objective Norfolk." The soldiers call it "Fright Night," which far better describes the events of that night which, among other things, resulted in the destruction of nearly 300 Iraqi armored vehicles. During an all-night battle of immense dimensions and enormous confusion, the division destroyed two Iraqi brigades, and penetrated the positions of both the Republican Guard and scratch forces for the Iraqi Jihad Corps.

The Dreadnoughts played a key role in the battle, destroying approximately 70 armored vehicles, two dozen trucks and an undetermined number of enemy infantry while capturing 728 enemy soldiers, including 308 during the night fighting. A balanced task force of nearly 1,000 soldiers, TF 2/34 had gone into action on 18 February 1991, firing their first shots against an enemy outpost. From then until cease-fire, the Dreadnoughts remained in constant contact with the enemy. On the morning of 26 February, still mourning the loss of two dead and four wounded comrades, they faced a new phase of war. No more fending off enemy reconnaissance or overwhelming demoralized dismounted infantry; now they were joining the main battle against Iraq's best troops.[3]

During the Gulf War, coalition forces waged the largest tank battles since World War II, testing doctrine, equipment and readiness. The Dreadnoughts' experiences during Fright Night provide the opportunity to consider the unique nature of armored warfare at night. Their tale is told in the belief that insights may be developed which will form part of the Army's evaluation of its performance during Operation *Desert Storm.* Learning from the experiences of TF 2/34, and those of the many other units that headed north in February 1991 may help the Army to meet the chief's goal of "No more Task Force *Smiths!*"

At 0330, 26 February, the Dreadnought orders groups convened to complete orders for the day. Both enemy and friendly situations remained vague. Brigade only knew that 1st AD (UK) was in contact to the east of the division zone and that 2d ACR had made contact with enemy reconnaissance late on 25 February. The update received by radio from the 1st Brigade commander, Colonel Lon E. Maggart, con-

FRIGHT NIGHT

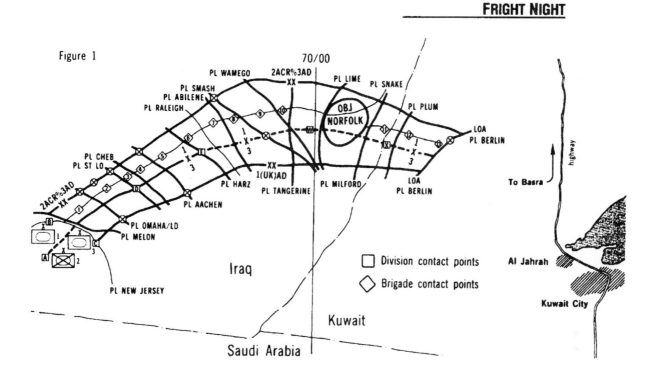

Figure 1

firmed that the brigade would occupy reserve positions, vicinity PL Larz, some 60 km north, which meant the 2d ACR was at least that far or moving. With this limited information, task force leadership completed movement planning and plans for occupation of positions on PL Harz. The Dreadnoughts would advance in a box formation with platoons in column, bringing along all of the fuelers in the battalion combat trains. Following this short meeting, the task force mounted up and moved out.

The brigade motored along at 20–30 km per hour in a nearly impenetrable murk produced by intermittent showers, blowing sand and smoke from the oil fires in Kuwait. Periodically, flashes of lightning streaked across a greenish, dull sky, followed by continuous peals of thunder. Punctuated a few times by the discovery of Iraqis trudging south, 26 February lasted forever and seemed foreboding. Only the task force scouts, maintaining contact with 1/34 AR, could provide evidence that other "friendlies" were in Iraq.

Closing on PL Harz at approximately 1200 hours, 1/34 AR (Centurions) destroyed two tanks and captured a handful of Iraqi prisoners. On arrival, both units occupied hasty positions, tied in with each other and began collecting large numbers of prisoners presumably disarmed and sent south by the 2d ACR. In addition to 200 Iraqis captured along the way to PL Harz, the Dreadnoughts processed 220 more, including four with wounds serious enough to require air evacuation. Refueled, fed and settling in, the Dreadnoughts and Centurions were ready for business soon after 1400.

Instead of orders or information, the "mother" of all sandstorms struck with amazing violence. The storm howled steadily for two hours before dissipating into occasional gusts of wind. During the storm, the remainder of the brigade continued to close on the two lead battalions. The forward area support team moved close enough to top off fuel trucks so that once again the lead battalions had fuel. TF 5/16 (Devil Rangers) and 4/5 FA, assigned to reinforce 1/5 FA, still had not closed at 1630 when Maggart issued new orders by radio.

The new mission required almost immediate movement toward a link-up point some 20 km away. At 1800, the Dreadnoughts and the Centurions were to join on the move and head for an as yet undetermined passage point through the 2d ACR. At midafternoon, as the remaining 1st ID units closed on FL Harz, the decision had been made to commit the division. The 1st ID would attack that night with 1st Brigade in the north or left and 2d AD (Forward) in the south or right. The division placed 2d Brigade in reserve. The 1/4 CAV had orders to screen the northern flank. On the way to the passage point, the division would wheel east onto a nearly due east direction of attack. The mission was to destroy elements of the 17th AD and the *Tawakalna Mechanized Division* of the Republican Guard. According to the order, 2d ACR was in contact with the 17th AD along PL Smash some 40 km northeast of PL Harz.

Attacking at night made perfect sense. Clearly, time was of the essence. All indications were that the Iraqis were on the run. Obviously, if the corns defeated the Republican Guard quickly, then those enemy units fleeing north on the Basra highway could be cut off. The technological advantages of the M1 should assure victory. Spirited discussions at the club in Fort Riley, Kansas, often centered around the conviction held by most of the Big Red One's leadership that the night belonged to the US Army. Now everyone who made that argument would get to demonstrate the courage of those convictions.

But debates at the club were not on Maggart's mind when he issued his order. Maggart assigned each of the forward units a zone of action and instructed them to destroy the enemy in zone. He also assigned objectives along PL Milford, the limit of advance, to orient maneuver. TF 5/16 would follow and support. Details on the passage would be forthcoming once brigade could talk to 2d ACR. First, however, the Dreadnoughts had to link up with the Centurions.

Both of the forward battalions were off and running in minutes. The first problem to solve was how to effect the linkup. Moving on the inside of a slow turn to the east, the Centurions covered ground more rapidly than TF 2/34. Lieutenant Colonel Pat Ritter, commander of 1/34 AR, adjusted speed and passed headings that would allow the Dreadnoughts to close the distance. In short, the rendezvous would occur by maneuvering the two battalion formations as though they were ships at sea. At sunset, Bravo Company, 1/34 AR pumped smoke that confirmed the last heading, allowing the Dreadnoughts to form on the Centurions' left flank, with neither battalion having to halt.

At nightfall, both task forces were abreast and scouts were out and moving at 30 km per hour toward a still undetermined passage point. Maggart continued to work with division while his S3 (operations officer), Major Kevin Huddy, struck out for 2d

ACR to arrange the passage. Meanwhile, the brigade S2 issued overlays of enemy positions on Objective Norfolk that were by then a month old. Whether the information was still valid was unknown, but old information seemed better than none. SFC Mike Schulte, the 'TF 2/34 liaison officer, departed the brigade Tactical Operations Center (TOC) with this gem in pursuit of the task force, unsure where or whether he would find them.

In the dark, maintaining formation with the Centurions proved challenging. They seemed to move in starts and stops. After a few minutes of frustration, a call reduced the confusion immediately. Bravo Team, TF 2/34 was guiding on a tank that was having maintenance problems and not on the actual flank of 1/34 AR. Upon learning this, the greatly chagrined team commander found the "real" Centurion left flank. Captain Juan Toro, Bravo Team commander, also put a radio on his counterpart's net. Eventually, the pace settled to an even 30 km per hour. Finally, having attained control, time was available to exercise command. Bouncing along in their respective turrets, company team commanders briefed their units, and the task force leadership reviewed the essentials of conducting a forward passage of lines.

Maggart, too, had these matters on his mind. Initially, he planned to pass the brigade through a 10-km gap in the 2d ACR forward line of troops. Within minutes that proved impossible, as did passage through a series of lanes the cavalry had prepared. At 2100, he ordered both units to move through a single passage point at the 70/00 grid lines. Here, 3d Squadron, 2d ACR would funnel through both of the lead maneuver units. Once forward of the 2d ACR, the Dreadnoughts would break out of movement formation and accept the battle at a grid line to be agreed upon mutually with the passed unit.

Maggart based his decision to use a single passage point partly on speculation, guidance from division and Huddy's trip to the 2d ACR. There was no time to send forward control parties or the jump command post, since the brigade barely had time to reach the 70/00 grid line intersection by 2200, the time specified for the passage. However, the 2d AUK was helpful and informative, passing clear data on the passage point and battle handoff in the Centurions' sector. Similar information was not forthcoming for the Dreadnoughts' zone, because it apparently was forward of a different squadron. For reasons that remain unknown, brigade was unable to obtain solid

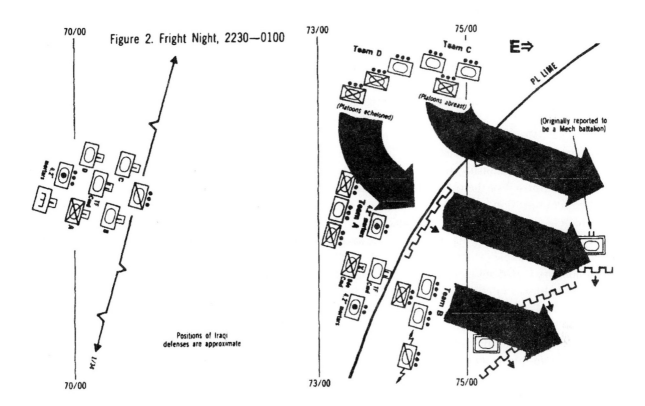

Figure 2. Fright Night, 2230—0100

Positions of Iraqi
defenses are approximate

handoff information or provide a frequency so that the task force could talk to the passed unit. Finally, since the cavalry had broken direct fire contact with the enemy, few details were available on current enemy dispositions.

As these deliberations occurred, the brigade passed corps artillery units firing in support of the 2d ACR. The Multiple Launch Rocket System produced the usual dazzling display, while the less glamorous howitzers banged and boomed away. The corps artillery and the great sprawl of the cavalry's support area were the only heartening sights during a bleak day that showed every sign of becoming bleaker. Threading a way through the cavalry's rear area stowed the brigade to a crawl, which allowed me supporting artillery and TF 5/16 to catch up.

At 2145, as the 2d ACR fired the first set of pyrotechnics to guide the brigade to the passage point, the brigade S2 issued an intelligence summary update. The information included center of mass grids to three battalions believed to be composed of T-55s and BMPs (Soviet armored personnel carriers) belonging to the *17th AD*. According to the S2, one mechanized battalion lay in the zone of TF 2/34. An armor battalion seemed to be situated just inside 1/34 AR's

zone. The Centurions also faced a mechanized battalion in the southern half of their zone. Both of the two northern battalions actually defended ground in the Dreadnought zone and were armed primarily with T-72s. Dug-in infantry reinforced all three positions to the tune of 300–400 infantrymen in each zone. In fact, all three battalions probably belonged to the southernmost brigade of the *Tawakalna Division*.

It was time to issue the operations order for the attack. The task force order stressed that the mission was to destroy enemy forces in zone. The concept of the operation was simple. The Dreadnoughts would attack with Bravo Team (tank) on line on the right. Charlie Team (tank), also on line, would attack on Bravo's left. On the far left, Delta Team (infantry) would echelon left with his tank platoon leading. Both tank teams' infantry would trail the tanks to keep enemy antitank teams off the friendlies and to provide dismounted infantry as required. The task force command group, including my tank, the air liaison officer (ALO) and the S3—both in M113s—would follow Charlie Team. Alpha Team (infantry) in reserve would follow Delta Team just to the right and rear of its echelon formation. (See fig. 2)

The battalion mortars would bound sections on either side of the command group, Alpha Company,

1st Engineers (-) would follow Bravo Team. Alpha Company, with one engineer platoon, two combat engineer vehicles and other equipment, would provide reinforcement to the forward units in the event a breach was required, clear bunkers and assist in the evacuation of prisoners.

Once through the 2d ACR, the scout platoon would move from forward of the task force to the task force's right flank. The scouts' job would be to maintain contact with 1/34 Armor and to screen the task force boundary. Additionally, the scouts were to keep both units apprised of the other's location. To that end, the scout platoon leader directed one of his sections to become the Centurions' left flank unit.

Execution of the scheme of maneuver was also intended to be simple. Once contact was made, the Dreadnoughts would advance by task force bounds. Weapons hold was in effect until released following battle handoff. The intent was to fight engagements from 2,000 to 1,500 meters to allow certainty both in target identification and target hits. This decision stemmed from information on T-72 fire control and night fighting capability. I simply did not believe Iraqis could see well enough to hit targets at 1,500 meters or greater, and I considered the M1A1 the most dangerous thing in the desert. Finally, engagements would be cleared by unit commanders and fired in platoon volleys any time multiple targets were acquired. In short, while this was a hasty attack, I directed deliberate execution.

Issued by 2200, the task force order evoked no surprise. Warning orders specifying this approach had gone out earlier and, in any case, the Order reflected well-rehearsed formations and movement techniques. Time now slowed to a standstill. The strobe effect of the rockets, muzzle flashes of the artillery to the rear and the 2d ACR ahead cast an eerie light, further adding to the surrealistic quality of the night. Just before 2230, the battlefield quieted down and the light show, except for a green star cluster to mark the passage point, ended.

At the passage point, the Centurions moved out, with the Dreadnoughts trailing at their left rear. As the passage occurred, Ritter provided details regarding recognition signals the 2d ACR was using. Additionally, Captain Marvin Meek, assistant S3, 1/34 AR, entered the Dreadnought command net to assure effective cross communications. Meek stayed on the net all night,

passing and receiving information as required. On the brigade operations and intelligence net, the two maneuver S2s and the brigade S2 shared battle tracking and assessment, further reducing the load on the commanders. As the Dreadnoughts began crossing the passage point, Major Larry Steiner, task force executive officer, dropped off the combat trains out of the 2d ACR's way and hopefully out of harms way. Steiner and the TOC, now joined by the liaison officer (LNO) and his precious overlay, planned to jump as required to maintain contact with the task force.

At almost the exact grid of the passage point, I encountered two Bradleys marked as advertised by the 3d Squadron, 2d ACR. In sight and just beyond the Bradleys, a T-72 lay smoldering with the tank commander still at his station. I pulled up to confirm the passage point in my tank, only to learn that the task force was north of the actual passage point. Nonetheless, the cavalrymen on the ground promised to report the passage of TF 2/34.[4] Incongruously, the young troopers began to cheer and yell as the tank motored off toward the burning hulk and its grisly crew.

By 2330, the Dreadnoughts had passed through the cavalry and reached the 73 Easting. At that point, the task force began to deploy out of the box formation used through the passage. Bravo Team and the scouts moved out without incident as did Alpha Team, the mortars and the engineers. Charlie and Delta, however, went astray. As the two teams broke out from columns of platoons, their tanks and Bradleys moved left away from Bravo Team in order to have room to deploy. What resulted as the effect spread was that Charlie and Delta wound up facing north. Eventually, the two teams broke off from Bravo Team altogether. (See fig. 2)

Confused, I stopped and called Bravo Team to complain that they were not keeping up with Charlie, the base team. Toro reported that he was oriented east and in contact with enemy infantry. By this time, Bravo was out of sight to the east and Charlie and Delta had disappeared to the north. Slowly it dawned on me that Toro was right. A call to Charlie resulted in the team commander, Captain Bob Bums, getting off his tank with a compass. In short order, he called to report he was indeed facing north. This information confirmed that the Dreadnoughts were in enemy contact, with two teams misoriented.

Moreover, the task force was floundering around forward of friendly troops who were probably a bit nervous.

The two team commanders believed they could straighten it out and be back on line in 30 minutes. Meanwhile, Toro launched a star cluster to mark his position, with immediate results of enemy fire and recognition from the two "lost" teams. I was out of sight of Bravo, Charlie and Delta Teams and could only wait and advise brigade. Maggart was not happy to hear this news, but he offered no criticism and agreed to warn the 2d ACR that TF 2/34 was pirouetting forward of their positions.

During the interminable wait for Charlie and Delta, Bravo fought dismounts and what they believed were BMPs, killing some infantry and at least one armored vehicle. Toro moved up and down the perimeter of his hasty defense to assure control of his company, which was spread over a kilometer of ground and fighting both north and east. Charlie and Delta turned around, but still could not see the rest of the task force. To orient them, I launched a star cluster, which drew Iraqi fire but also attracted the misoriented, chastened and still missing company teams. A second star cluster fired from my tank got them home and produced two kills for Toro's company. Bravo destroyed a tracked vehicle and truck, both of which were firing heavy machineguns on the blissfully ignorant and illuminated command group.

Still, the ordeal was not over. As Charlie and Delta passed the command group closing on Bravo's left rear, they encountered infantrymen in spider holes who wanted to fight. Burns, leading his company team back into the fight, discovered a rocket propelled grenade (RPG) team to his direct front. He announced he would run them down and not fire, since that would endanger Bravo. I told Burns, who was passing to my direct front, to engage them with machineguns. Bravo buttoned up, and Charlie Team went to work. Burns attempted to run over one Iraqi soldier while a Bradley to his rear scrubbed other infantrymen off his backside. Burns missed his man, who then rose and shouldered an RPG, but one of Charlie Team's Bradleys killed the would-be tank killer with a burst of 25mm fire.

Both tank platoons fired machineguns on Iraqi infantry running between bunkers, who apparently believed they could not be observed. In less than two

minutes the fire fight ended. Charlie Team's infantry platoon dismounted and swept through the area, killing those who wanted to fight and taking prisoner those who wanted to quit. At one point, one of Burns' infantry squad leaders climbed onto C-66 to report, "There's an awful lot of dead infantry out there."[5]

Under small arms fire from both the Iraqis and Charlie, Toro could not imagine how things could get worse until a flash of orange revealed the destruction of a 1/34 AR scout platoon Bradley. The scout platoon leader maneuvered his Bradley to shield the burning Bradley while Ritter moved up a tank company in support. Shortly after arriving on the scene, the platoon leader's vehicle drew heavy caliber machinegun fire that badly wounded him and killed his gunner. Nonetheless, the platoon leader remained at his post, organized the evacuation of his wounded and vectored in the supporting tanks.

The brigade attack seemed stalled, with the Dreadnoughts first lost and then dogged by dismounts. More seriously, the Centurions were coping with five wounded and one dead soldier. Maggart remained, as he did throughout the night, calm and patient while the two battalions got on with it. By 0100, both were moving again and in contact. The Centurions seemed to be in the thick of it, dispatching tracks and tanks with abandon. In the Dreadnought sector, the pace quickened about 0130 as they reached the 78 Easting. The overlay brought by Schulte revealed infantry here and armor to their north and east.

Delta Team promptly began killing what they believed to be BMPs while Charlie Team drew RPG fire. Charlie quickly reduced the enemy in the trenches, Charlie's formation had now been constricted so that their tanks were only a few feet apart. That close together, with the Bradleys backing them up, they hosed down the trenches and rolled right over the enemy infantry. A few sporadic rounds of small arms from the survivors were silenced by coax and 25mm. Seconds later, Charlie and Bravo turned on enemy armor to their front.

From 0130 until 0430, the night settled into a desperate rhythm of targets reported and divided among the teams, followed by volleys of tank rounds, Bushmasters or TOWs (tube-launched, optically tracked, wire-guided missile), as appropriate. In the first hour, the task force destroyed 35 armored vehicles, 10 trucks, an unknown number of dismounted infantrymen and captured nearly 100 Iraqi troops. The enemy seemed to be arrayed in belts of company-size positions, with dismounted company positions between the belts. In fact, the Dreadnoughts were attacking down the flank of a reinforced tank battalion that was oriented south. Delta Team was nearly astride those positions. Bravo Team, at the southern end of the task force, was killing vehicles and troops from the second of two tank battalions. Charlie Team, in the center, fought through two infantry positions, and the southernmost tank company in the battalion Delta Team attacked. (See fig. 3)

None of this was apparent to anyone in the task force until they actually began to pass the enemy positions. In itself, this was no small feat since the enemy vehicles continued to explode and burn with great violence. Learning from passing their burning hulks that virtually all of the targets destroyed were tanks, explained why the Bushmasters had been relatively ineffective. At one point, Delta Team had banged away for nearly 30 minutes at six or more targets believing they were BMPs. Delta Team ultimately destroyed all of them with a combination of 25mm and tank fire and discovered, as they passed, that all six targets were tanks. By now, 1f/34 AR reported enemy prisoners who claimed they were being supported by T-72s—a fact borne out by Delta Team's engagements.

A second key learning point for the task force occurred in the first hour after 0130. Several of the targets were cold. Believing they were destroyed by the US Air Force, I ordered them bypassed. One of the scouts, forward on the right flank, entered the net to report that he could see people trying to man those very vehicles from nearby bunkers. From that time on, the Dreadnoughts fired on cold and hot targets.

The system of engagement is perhaps best described in the words of one of those executing it. Sergeant First Class Kevin W. Lemon recalls the attack as a "series of repetitions." According to Lemon, "once a group of targets were spotted and confirmed, the battalion would stop on line (about 1,500 to 2,000 meters), and engage on the order of the Team Commanders. Once all of the targets were destroyed the battalion then again moved out on line (usually about another 2,000 meters) to the next firing line."[6]

This system worked but had serious flaws. Since Charlie served as the base team, Burns coordinated movement that took him off his net, often when his subordinates needed him. To prevent fratricide, team

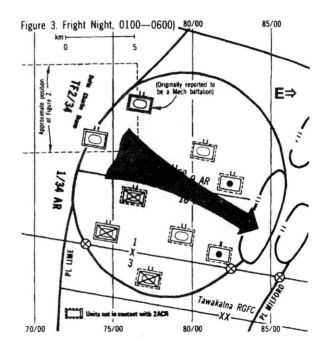

Figure 3. Fright Night, 0100—0600)

commanders had to clear all fires, which took time. Finally, distributing fires also consumed time. All of these things reduced the speed of attack to a crawl, during which each soldier believed that surely the Iraqis would kill him.

Betting on the enemy being slower was a safe bet, but the soldiers in tanks and Bradleys could not be sure and, as the night wore on, it became increasingly hard for them to believe it. Lemon believed, at the time, that this system endangered the task force unnecessarily. According to Lemon, "The adverse weather, difficult communications within the unit, control of fires, reduced capabilities of the Thermal Imaging System that kept overheating and shutting off, in addition to reduced visibility, battlefield fatigue and stress all contributed to our frustration."[7]

To add to that frustration, an unexplained phenomenon also occurred at intervals during the night. Several targets were struck, glowed and then cooled without ever exploding. Again, I concluded these were victims of the US Air Force. However, the next morning Lieutenant Colonel Daniel A. Magee, 1st Brigade executive officer, found dead crews in several tanks that had neither exploded nor burned, but which did show sabot holes. Some of these were probably killed by the Dreadnoughts, but not all of them since the Dreadnoughts, believing they were fighting T-55s and BMPs, fired relatively few of their "Silver Bullets." All but a handful of the 40 tanks destroyed that night turned out to be T-72s. The Dreadnoughts did change ammunition after confirming the presence of T-72s, but that occurred fairly late in the battle. The good news is that 120mm high explosive antitank rounds do just fine against T-72s. Who or what killed the tanks that did not explode cannot be determined with any certainty.

After 0330, the enemy thinned out. By this time, the Centurions had reached the limit of advance, having destroyed part of the centermost of the three battalions in the brigade sector and part of the southernmost of the three battalions. From 0330 until 0430, the Dreadnoughts labored on, picking off a couple of tanks fleeing the battlefield and slowing to destroy the odd abandoned vehicle. In the middle of all this, the task force reached the enemy brigade support area and began machinegunning trucks and grabbing fleeing mechanics and truck drivers. Machinegunning trucks proved foolish. Ammunition trucks went up like volcanos, raining burning and exploding ammunition down on the task force. The Dreadnoughts asked for and received permission to leave the rest for TF 5/16 to destroy at a more leisurely pace as they came through.

The other chief excitement of the night occurred when two Iraqi BMPs suddenly emerged from the darkness between Alpha and Delta teams. Both BMPs turned east behind Delta's trailing platoon. Alpha's lead platoon quickly dispatched the two BMPs. As soon as the two BMPs exploded, Captain Johnny Womack, Alpha Team commander, came upon the battalion net to swear he was not shooting at Delta. By 0430, the task force had destroyed another 17 armored vehicles. After 0430, the task force encountered relatively few enemy, reaching the limit of advance at 0600 destroying another two tanks and four enemy tracked vehicles.

What a night! The good news was the brigade was in reserve. At last, rest and the opportunity to refuel and rearm. At 0630, as TF 2/34 settled in at FL Milford, Lieutenant Colonel Sydney F. "Skip" Baker moved forward of his task force to come up to the brigade command post. Moving east through the area "cleared" by the Dreadnoughts, Baker encountered a southbound T-55. Quick action by Charlie Team, TF 5/16 saved their commander and provided a topic of conversation for the two task force commanders. However, backslapping and open hostilities had to wait. The brigade was off again by 0930 and in contact by noon. Nearly two more days of skirmishes and still another night of fighting remained before cease-fire would allow a decent night's sleep and contemplation of just what had happened at Objective Norfolk.

The fight at Norfolk, at least in the TF 2/34 zone, was probably not as fierce as the fight on the Medinah Ridge or at 73 Easting. The fight at Norfolk was also one-sided, as the paucity of Iraqi return fire demonstrated. The Dreadnoughts fired 115 tank-killing rounds but reported only a dozen or so rounds returned. Delta Team, 2/34, trailing the Dreadnoughts as part of TF 5/16, reported seeing a great many rounds fired at the task force. Several Dreadnought soldiers traveling in the trains also claimed to have seen substantial amounts of return fire. Still, the frontline units saw no more than 10 to 12 main gun rounds and a half-dozen RPGs. It is possible that the enemy was firing at 1/34 AR. The Iraqis did fire a lot of small arms, heavy machineguns and RPGs, but they only landed with small arms and so did no damage.

Despite ineffectual resistance, courage, skill and discipline were shown all around. To start with, the soldiers held to the fire discipline despite the fact they believed it endangered their lives as some of them later told Esquire reporter John Sack.[8] They did not fire unless cleared by a unit commander or were fired upon by an identifiable enemy. As a consequence, the Dreadnoughts did not shoot at each other or at 1/34 AR to the south or 1/4 CAV operating to their north.

Charlie Team was brilliant in close quarters against RPG teams. At one point, Burns crawled all over his infantry platoon leader for firing on C-66 with a Bushmaster. The platoon leader calmly replied he was killing enemy infantry, a fact to which I can attest. Toro's soldiers destroyed two enemy vehicles shooting at the illuminated and very nervous task force commander. Delta Team did most of the shooting and did it very effectively. Alpha Team stayed alert in reserve and destroyed two BMPs that might have wreaked havoc on the task force.

The scouts got a few kills, but they maintained contact with the Centurions and coolly reported enemy positions not visible to the task force and, thus, prevented surprise. The mortars never fired a round that night, but always had a section set to fire if required. The engineers had the least glorious task of keeping the enemy prisoners moving and remaining far enough forward to support. Shortly after 0600, 27 February, the ever-vigilant engineers grabbed four Iraqis spooked by HQ-66 driving over their bunker without killing any of them despite the Iraqis showing an initial inclination to fight.

There are several possible lessons that can be gleaned from TF 2/34's experience during Fright Night. First, developing mission essential task lists (METL) suited to European general defense plans have broad applicability. Nearly every METL task developed in the 1st ID proved valid, including esoteric tasks such as deploying and building combat power. Obviously, conducting tactical movements and training to pass or assist passage paid off both for the 2d ACR and the 1st Brigade. Moreover, the regiment accomplished superbly the classic cavalry mission of finding and fixing the enemy.

Drills and standard tactical techniques also worked well. In TF 2/34, logistics package drills saved time day and night. Rehearsal of day and night movement, occupation of hasty defensive positions and actions on contact, reinforced drills and enabled execution when tired, frightened and under fire. Firing in platoon volleys also proved effective. Task force gunnery, in the spring of 1990, assured that the attached infantry understood the technique as well. The benefit of volley fire on multiple targets is shock and suppression of the enemy. On more than one occasion during that long night in February 1991, two or more targets exploded simultaneously.

The theory that the Iraqis could not acquire targets at ranges over 1,500 meters at night seems to have been validated by the Dreadnoughts' experience. Only Bravo Team reported multiple near misses from enemy tank fire. It is possible, however, that enemy orientation and the fact that some of their tank crews remained in bunkers is the reason TF 2/34 took no main gun hits. On the down side, it often took too long for commanders to sort out contact and clear fires. This resulted, in part, because there is no way to determine direction accurately from a tank.

When in contact, the Dreadnoughts advanced using the technique of position improvement. Simply put, the entire task force made a short bound of 2,000 meters or less to firing positions. Modeled on the Israeli technique and not unlike the movement of the National Training Center (NTC) opposing forces firing lines, this method worked well in the open desert. In Europe or in broken terrain, this technique would probably not be effective.

Pyrotechnics, despite the fact that they attracted fire, proved essential at the passage point and in reorienting the two companies that had strayed. Chemical lights, too, proved their utility in providing visual evidence of flank units. Visual signals will remain useful for some time to come. Running lights, or at least lights on the backs of turrets, would also prove useful in maintaining control during night operations. Most Iraqi tanks and tracks were equipped with such a system. Simple to install and relatively cheap, they appear to be a useful modification for the Army to consider.

Cross talk at brigade and between the attacking battalions assured effective command and prevented fratricide. Meek not only kept TF 2/34 apprised of what his commander was thinking, but did the same for Ritter. The brigade operations and intelligence net provided a venue for analysis and assured rapid dissemination of combat information. For example, the first clue TF 2/34 had about the presence of T-72s in large numbers came from the Centurions' interrogation of a prisoner they took. Finally, Maggart's cool demeanor and patience on the radio helped restore order from confusion when both battalions were hung up shortly after the attack began. Throughout the night, he provided calm support and reached sound decisions which he communicated clearly.

There were other systems that did not work well or, in some cases, could not be used effectively. Chief among these was that despite the herculean efforts of the FA battalions to keep up, the brigade could find no useful way to use artillery during the night attack. The preparation fired by corps artillery prior to 2230 were the only rounds of artillery fired that night. By the time targets were acquired, the task force was committed to a direct fire battle.

Clearly, had resistance been stiffer, artillery would have been used, but the fire support team (FIST) platform is not adequate for acquiring targets at night on the move. At one point during the night, the Delta Team commander observed four tracked vehicles fleeing east at a range of just over 4,000 meters. Unfortunately, no one could get a decent azimuth on which to call a polar plot. Adjusting fire from an interpolated grid, based on a guess for direction, also made no sense. Those four targets got away. If every tank were equipped with an on-board direction finding device, waiting for the FIST to get its hammerhead up would never be a problem again.

Unreliable FM communications produced problems throughout the war. Burns frequently had to come up on battalion command because his XO's radio worked intermittently. At one point, when Burns was on the battalion net, First Lieutenant Bennie McRae acquired targets dangerously close to the company. McRae lost valuable time waiting to talk to Burns before concluding correctly that he should fire. McRae and his platoon destroyed two tanks at ranges under 1,000 meters—too close for comfort if the enemy had been oriented toward the company.

The failure of brigade to disseminate a corps intelligence overlay of the Norfolk area that it had received prior to the start of the ground war could have had serious consequences. When Schulte caught up with the task force and handed over the three-week-old overlay, it proved useful. However, time to study it before the attack would have revealed orientation and composition of key enemy positions, enabling the task force to conduct the attack with far more confidence and a great deal less confusion. The lesson here is to pass information if you have it and supersede it as necessary.

Finally, both the corps and division commanders believed the 1st ID would reap benefits from attacking at night. The Big Red One justified their confidence by destroying nearly 3 armored vehicles before dawn. But some units in the division suffered several fratricide incidents. It is impossible to account for the root cause of those incidents. Navigation, target identification, fire discipline and the confusion of battle all contributed. However, the most important factor was that neither the Big Red One nor 2d AD (Forward) had been able to conduct adequate night training prior to deployment.

Fort Riley is a great training reservation, but maneuver space and the capability to conduct battalion mounted night operations are simply not available. The Garlstedt units had even fewer opportunities to conduct battalion-level night training than did their Fort Riley counterparts. Only at the NTC can the Army train large formations at night. Because of safety constraints and controller limitations, night training is minimal even at Fort Irwin. The Army must find a way to conduct more tactical training at night.

No doubt other conclusions will be drawn by critical and thoughtful readers. Equally important, uncritical application of the ideas suggested here would be a mistake. To benefit from our technological advantages, we must develop systems that enable us to use them and train to implement those systems. If we do that, we will have gone a long way toward our part of meeting Army Chief of Staff Gordon R. Sullivan's goal of "No More Task Force *Smiths*!"

NOTES

1. Regarding the VII Corps tactical plan, see LTC Peter S. Kindsvatter, "VII Corps in the Gulf War: Ground Offensive," *Military Review* February 1992): 16-37. Kindsvatter's article provides a first-rate overview of the corps plan. Dependent on executive overviews of division after-action reports (AARs) for the tactical picture below XXXXXXXX For example, Kindsvatter notes XXXXXX the breach. TF 2/34 Armor received artillery tire on three separate occasions on 24 February. One soldier was wounded by Iraqi artillery, and evacuated on the afternoon of the 24th. Despite the problems of executive overviews of AARs, the author of his article, too, must rely on them. Information on 1st ID plans is taken from "Executive Summary 1st ID AAR." Except as otherwise cited, the remainder of the details provided came from AAR materials and/or journals of 1st Brigade, 1/34 Ar and TF 2/34 Ar.

2. For Maggart's perspective on the battle, see COL Lon E. Maggart, "A Leap of Faith," *Armor* (January–February 992): 24-32.

3. Statistics are taken mainly from TF 2/34 Ar jounals but, like all statistics in combat, are suspect

4. See 1LT John Hillen, "2d Armored Cavalry. The Campaign to Liberate Kuwait" *Armor* (July–August 1991): 8-12. See also Vince Crawley, Ghost Troop's Battle at the 73 Easting," *Armor* (May–June 1991): 7-12, 1st Brigade actually passed through 3/2 ACR.

5. Undated letter from CPT Robert A. Burns to the author.

6. Undated letter from SFC Kevin W. Lemon to the author.

7. Ibid.

8. See John Sack. "C Company," *Esquire* (Dec 1991): 107-121, 186-93.

Colonel Gregory Fontenot is assigned to Headquarters, US Army Training and Doctrine Command, Fort Monroe, Virginia. He received a B. A. from Kansas State University, an M.A. from the University of North Carolina at Chapel Hill, an M.M.A.S. from the US Army Command and

General Staff College (USACGSC) and is a graduate of the USACGSC, the School of Advanced Military Studies and the National Defense College of Canada. He has served in a variety of command and staff positions in the United States, West Germany and commanded 2d *Battalion, 34th Armor during operations* Desert Shield *and* Desert Storm.   *His article "The Promise of Cobra: The Reality Manchuria,"* *appeared in the September 1985 issue of* Military Review.

Army Principles of War

This is the second in a series of five lessons that provide the framework for tactical principles. The first lesson introduced you to basic definitions and concepts, whereas this lesson focuses on types of military operations (offense, defense, stability, and support).

The following topics are addressed in this lesson:

- Principles of war
- Types of tactical operations—offense, defense, stability, and support
- Security and reconnaissance in support of offensive and defensive operations
- Force protection

The following TLO is supported in whole or in part by this lesson:

- Apply tactical principles and doctrine to the solution of tactical problems

Following this lesson you will be able to:

- List the four basic types of military operations
- Define stability operations
- Summarize the army's role in stability operations
- List the nine principles of war and define each
- Define support operations
- Summarize the Army's role in support operations

FULL CIRCLE

WORLD WAR II TO THE PERSIAN GULF

by Colonel Harry Summers Jr., US Army, Retired

The author finds many striking similarities between the US prosecution of the Gulf War and that of World War II. He analyzes the performance of the nation, its leadership and its Armed Forces in the wars of the last half-century against the enduring measure of the Principles of War. He draws several positive comparisons of US actions in World War II and the Gulf War.

Paradoxical as it may sound, from a strategic military perspective, the Japanese attack on Pearl Harbor on 7 December 1941 and the world war that followed is closer to us in 1991 than it has been for many years. One cannot fully understand the significance of the recent Persian Gulf War, for example, without an appreciation of World War II, for in a very real sense the Gulf War was closer to World War II than it was to either the Korean or Vietnam wars.

Indeed, the very leitmotiv of the Gulf War was the phrase, "for the first time since World War II," a refrain repeated time and again to describe the dynamics of that conflict. The reason for that time warp is that for more than a generation, the World War II experience was sidetracked, first by the so-called atomic age and then by the advent of the Cold War.

And it has been obscured by the shadows of time as well. It is hard to believe today that when World War II began on 1 September 1939, the United States ranked 17th in the world in terms of military power. Not only were US military capabilities pitifully inadequate, America's military authority—the degree to which other nations in the world were deterred by the possibility of US military action—was in even worse shape.

In *Dragon By the Tail,* John Paton Davies Jr. tells how this military and political weakness prompted the Japanese attack on Pearl Harbor. An "old China hand" who served as political adviser to General Joseph W. 'Vinegar Joe' Stilwell in the China-Burma-India theater in World War II (and who was later vilified as one of those who "lost" China), Davies decries what he called America's prewar "diplomacy by incantation." In response to Japanese expansion into China

and Southeast Asia, America lacked what was needed most, "a tremendous military force in being, backed by an evident will to use it." In its absence, Davies noted, "The American government complained, moralized and bluffed. That could not and did not stop the Japanese." It was a policy that lead inexorably to Pearl Harbor.[1]

That pusillanimous policy was reinforced by American public opinion. Many believed we had been hoodwinked into involvement in World War I, and isolationistic sentiment in the United States was particularly powerful. Most Americans today believe that such antiwar activities as opposing US military aid for beleaguered allies abroad, anti-draft protests and student demonstrations to kick the ROTC (Reserve Officers' Training Corps) off college campuses were hallmarks of the Vietnam War. But such actions were common across America in the years immediately preceding Pearl Harbor.

These antiwar and isolationistic sentiments were so strong that when President Franklin D. Roosevelt asked for a declaration of war against Japan on 8 December 1941, he did not ask for a declaration of war against Germany for fear it would not pass the Congress. Adolf Hitler settled the issue on 11 December 1941 when Nazi Germany declared war against the United States. It was a strategic miscalculation that would not be equalled until almost a half-century later when Saddam Hussein also misread the United States and launched his blitzkrieg against Kuwait.

Tellingly, it was again the fecklessness of US foreign policy (this time toward the Middle East) and the lack of American military *authority* that precipitated that miscalculation. In East Asia in the 1930s, the failure of the United States to react to the Japanese conquest of Manchuria in 1931, to their invasion of China in July 1937, and to the December 1937 Imperial Japanese Navy's brazen daylight bombing and strafing of the USS *Panay,* a gunboat on Yangtze River patrol, convinced Japan that the United States lacked the backbone to resist its aggression.

The pattern was repeated in the Middle East. United States failure to react to the 1976 assassination of United States Ambassador Francis C. Meloy in Lebanon, to the killing of 241 American servicemen when the Marine barracks in Beirut was bombed in 1983, to the kidnapping and murder of CIA station chief William Buckley in 1985, and to the kidnapping and murder of Marine Colonel William Higgins in 1989, convinced Saddam Hussein of US gutlessness.

While US military capabilities had increased dramatically, its military authority was as weak in August 1990 as it had been in December 1941. "America was regarded as a paper tiger," an Asian diplomat in Beijing told *Washington Times* reporter Michael Breen. "It was beaten like a wet rat in Vietnam and because of that we tended to underestimated it. . . . [W]hile mindful of superior United States muscle [we] had until now figured that the United States would lack the will to fight."

"But the Gulf War changed all that," he said.[2] And the reason it changed was that for the first time since World War II the United States was able to decisively bring its combat power—the combination of physical strength and moral authority—to bear.

THE PRINCIPLES OF WAR

A useful framework to analyze why and how that came about is provided by the nine classic principles of war, principles used by the American military since World War I as tools for understanding the dynamics of war.

Objective. The first and most important of these principles is the *objective,* which poses the fundamental question: "What are you trying to accomplish with the use of military force?" In World War II, the answer was obvious—ensure the survival of the nation. But in the postwar world, the answer became more and more confused. The beginning of the atomic age and the advent of the Cold War shortly thereafter had seemingly changed everything.

With the explosion of the atomic bombs at Hiroshima and Nagasaki in 1945, all the feats of conventional arms up to that time were seemingly rendered meaningless. The very definition of military strategy—the use of battles to gain the political objectives of the war—was called into question. Nuclear destruction was so absolute, said the civilian academic nuclear theorists, that the primary atomic age utility of military forces was not in warfighting but in signaling national intentions.

This viewpoint was reinforced by the advent of the Cold War in 1946, and particularly by the later Soviet and Chinese acquisition of nuclear weaponry which, as will be discussed below, threw the United States on the strategic defensive. Instead of the clear-cut objectives of World War II—total victory, unconditional enemy surrender, occupation of the enemy homeland and the trial and execution of those responsible for the war—the objectives in both Korea and Vietnam were cloudy and unclear.

"My whole effort since Red China came in them has been to get some definition, military definition, of what I should do," complained General of the Army Douglas MacArthur, the former allied commander in Korea, during the 1951 Senate hearings following his relief from command.[3] And the most damning statistic of the Vietnam War was the finding of Brigadier General Douglas Kinnard (later the Army's Chief of Military History) that "almost 70 percent of the Army generals who managed the war were uncertain of its objectives."[4]

While this lack of objectives was disastrous in a military sense, it was even more damaging in a political sense. As the great theorist of war Carl von Clausewitz had preached a century-and-a-half earlier, it is the object of war that determines its value, and it is that value which determines the sacrifices to be made in pursuit of it, both in magnitude and duration. In World War II, the object was national survival, a value so high that the American people supported the mobilization of the entire nation for war and willingly paid the price of over one million battlefield casualties. In both Korea and Vietnam, the objectives were never made clear and, as a result, the price in both wars—157,530 casualties in Korea, 211,324 in Vietnam—was deemed exorbitant and public opinion turned against the war.

And this equation held at the international level as well. The value of the objective—defeat of the Axis powers—was so immense that it brought such mortal enemies as the Soviet Union and the Western democracies together in common cause and held them together until Germany and Japan were totally defeated.

Instead of the powerful coalitions of World War II, the confusing objectives of the Korean and Vietnam wars spawned what *The New Republic's* Charles Krauthammer called "pseudomultilaterlism."[5] In both cases, the host country and the United States carried the majority of the load and allies contributed only token forces to give the conflict an international appearance.

For example, at theft peak strength in July 1953, United Nations (UN) ground forces in Korea included 590,911 from South Korea, 302,483 US Army and Marine Corps personnel and 39,145 from other UN countries. In 1969, the peak year for United States and allied participation in the Vietnam War, South Vietnamese forces stood at 897,000, US forces at 543,400 and allied "Free World Military Forces" at 68,889.[6]

By comparison, in the Persian Gulf War some 40 allied nations furnished over 205,000 troops, almost 28 percent of the 737,000 men and women who fought the war.[7] The reason for the difference is that for the first time since World War II, there was a genuine coalition effort. What caused that alliance to coalesce was an objective so powerful that, as in World War II, it could bring former enemies together to work toward a common goal.

That objective was clearly articulated—the Iraqi invaders must withdraw from Kuwait, the legitimate government there must be restored, and regional peace and security must be secured. For the first time since World War II, the permanent members of the UN Security Council—the allied partnership that fought World War II—stood united to oppose aggression. In the past, the Soviet Union could have been expected to veto any action against its erstwhile ally, Iraq. But on 2 August 1990, it voted in favor of UN Security Council Resolution 660 to condemn Iraq's invasion of its neighbor.

Like the Japanese attack on Pearl Harbor almost a half-century earlier, that action marked a sea change (that is a change of enormous magnitude) in the international strategic environment. Taking advantage of that change, US diplomatic efforts rapidly forged a political and military alliance against Iraq in the UN Security Council, among Arab nations in the Middle East and among America's European allies.

The changes were equally dramatic at home. For the first time since World War II, the American people were mobilized for war. President George Bush not only waged a major campaign to drive home the objectives of the war but, in a politically courageous move, made the decision to call America's reserve military forces to active duty. As a result, the entire nation was involved in the war and, as in World War II, that made all the difference in the world. "The early decision to call up the reserves . . . turned out to be a major catalyst in consolidating American public opinion firmly behind our strategy in the gulf," noted General Crosbie E. Saint. "The moral ascendancy that US forces had when they knew their country was behind them cannot be discounted."[8]

And in the KTO (Kuwaiti Theater of Operations), the clarity, of the political goals made possible the formulation of a coherent military campaign to achieve those objectives. Instead of the battlefield stalemates and negotiated settlements of the Korean and Vietnam wars, the war in the Persian Gulf, as in World War II, was won by force of arms on the field of battle.

The Offensive. It was won by force of arms because for the first time since World War II, the US military was able to apply a key principle of war, the *offensive,* which holds that the best way to win a war is to carry the fight to the enemy, destroy his armed forces and thereby break his will to resist. That is the way America has fought most of its wars, especially World War II. Indeed, to most Americans, World War II is the very paradigm of war, the model against which all subsequent wars are compared.

But in November 1950, when the Chinese Communist Forces (CCF) massively intervened in the Korean War, the strategic offensive was abandoned. Fearful of provoking a nuclear war with the Soviet Union and becoming inexorably involved in a land war with China, the US national policy changed from "rollback and liberation" (the policy it had pursued until that time) to "containment." US military strategy, which by definition must be in consonance with US national policy, changed from the strategic offensive to the strategic defensive, a posture it would maintain throughout the Korean and Vietnam wars.

Reaffirmed by Dwight D. Eisenhower during the 1956 Hungarian uprising and endorsed by every president since, as a national policy, containment well served long-term US interests. It not only avoided a nuclear confrontation with China and the Soviet Union, but forced communism back upon itself as well.

As American diplomat George Kennan had predicted in his famous 1946 "Long Telegram" from Moscow, containing Communist expansion and allowing the contradictions inherent in Marxist-Leninist doctrine to destroy itself from within proved to be the best strategy to achieve victory in the Cold War.[9] But the consequences for military strategy were never well understood.

By forcing the military onto the strategic defensive, the policy of containment guaranteed that war could not be won on the battlefield. The best possible result was stalemate. And that's precisely what happened in both the Korean and Vietnam wars. The Korean battlefield was stalemated in 1951 in the wake of the CCF's abortive 27-division spring offensive. Two years of diplomatic negotiations ended with the Korean Armistice of 1953.

Likewise in Vietnam, the battlefield was again stalemated, this time in the wake of the North Vietnamese Army/Viet Cong's disastrous 1968 Tet Offensive. Five years of diplomatic negotiations ended with the Paris Peace Accords of 1973.

Because they did not fit the World War II paradigm, both of these wars were unpopular with the American people. The Korean War was seen as a tie at best, and the Vietnam War was seen as a national disgrace after the North Vietnamese violated the "peace" agreement with their tank-led, multidivision cross-border blitzkrieg that overran South Vietnam in the spring of 1975.

Almost unnoticed, especially by Saddam Hussein, was that with the end of the Cold War the US policy of containment had been obviated. With Soviet cooperation in the United Nations, the 40-year constraint imposed by fear that massive application of military force would provoke a nuclear confrontation no longer applied. Thus, for the first time since World War II, the United States was once more on the strategic offensive, and the full fury of America's military might was brought to bear to destroy the Iraqi military on the battlefield and thus break their will to resist.

Mass and Economy of Force. The reason the United States was able to bring the full fury of its military to bear was that, for the first time since World War II, it was able to apply the principles of *Mass and Economy of Force.* These two principles of war are reciprocal—*Mass* dictates that one should mass—that is bring the bulk of one's forces to bear—on the primary objective and use an *Economy of Force* against secondary objectives.

For a half-century, the United States massed its forces in Europe and used an economy of force elsewhere in the world. Even though American military involvement in World War II began with the Japanese attack on Pearl Harbor, America massed its forces in Europe to defeat Nazi Germany and used an economy of force against Japan.

The same thing happened in the Korean War. Believing that the North Korean invasion of South Korea in June 1950 had been orchestrated by Moscow as a diversion and that the Soviet main attack would come in Europe, the United States sent more forces to bolster NATO defenses in Europe than it did to fight the actual war in Korea. And although the United States did mass its troops in South Vietnam, it never devoted full-time attention to that conflict until it was too late. In 1967, for example, two years after our ground combat involvement in Vietnam began, the Army's Command and General Staff College taught no classes on Vietnam. Its attention, like that of the entire Defense Department, was still concentrated on countering the Soviet threat in Europe.

But in the Gulf, for the first time since World War II, the United States was able to mass both physically and mentally on the field of battle. No longer was there the need to devote the majority of its assets and attention to guard against the Soviet threat.

With the Soviet Union now on its side, the United States could commit not only its contingency XVIII Airborne Corps and 1st Marine Expeditionary Force, but also its heavy divisions at home previously earmarked for NATO reinforcement. Most important, it could withdraw its VII Corps from Europe (where it had been stationed for decades to guard against Soviet attack) and also move it to the Gulf, where its 1st and 3d Armored divisions and 2d Armored Cavalry Regiment could provide the muscle for the main attack.

Maneuver. America's ability to mass was contingent on its ability to *maneuver,* for at the strategic level this principle has to do with the movement and transport of military forces to the critical point on the battlefield. It is an especially important principle for the United States, for in strategic terms America is a world island which must first traverse the oceans to bring its forces to bear. Therefore, sealift and airlift are essential.

In World War II, the first task was to seize control of the oceans so that a sea bridge could be constructed to bring America's mobilization capability to bear. Then the transport had to be built to move America's military into action. It was not until the North African invasion in November 1942, almost a year after Pearl Harbor, that US military ground forces first went into battle against Nazi Germany. But despite the almost total decline in the US Merchant

Marine since World War II, the Gulf buildup was completed in six months. One reason was strategic airlift, a negligible (actor in World War II. In the Gulf War, the Military Airlift Command flew more than 15,800 missions, moving more than a half-million passengers and almost a half-million tons of supplies to the Gulf. These planes included not only the cargo aircraft of the active Air Force, Air National Guard and Air Force Reserve, but also some 55 civilian transports of the Civil Reserve Air Fleet (CRAF), which for the first time was mobilized for war.[10]

But, as in World War II, the majority of supplies moved by sea. "It was the quickest and largest military sealift buildup since World War II," said General H. Norman Schwarzkopf, "an 8,000 mile, 250-ship haze-grey bridge, one ship every 50 miles from the shores of the United States to the shores of Saudi Arabia. And they offloaded some nine million tons of equipment and petroleum products for our forces.[11]

Security and Surprise. According to the experts, *surprise* is supposed to be a rarity at the strategic level of warfare. But three of America's last four wars began with a surprise attack—the December 1941 Japanese sneak attack on Pearl Harbor, the June 1950 North Korean invasion of South Korea and the August 1990 Iraqi invasion of Kuwait.

While these surprises are well known, less noted is the attacker's surprise at the ferocity of the American response. "If we surprise the enemy with faulty measures," remarked Clausewitz, "we may not benefit at all, but instead suffer sharp reverses." That was certainly the end result of the Japanese attack on Pearl Harbor, the North Korean attack on South Korea and the Iraqi attack on Kuwait. The reason, as Clausewitz noted, "is that only the commander who imposes his will can take the enemy by surprise," and in every case it was the American will that prevailed.

"The worse the situation is, the better it may turn out," Clausewitz said.[12] The surprise attacks on Pearl Harbor, on South Korea and on Kuwait did not break the American will. They energized it. Saddam Hussein, like Hideki Tojo and Kim Il Sung before him, had been deceived as to the true nature of the American people. Ironically, the unintended instrument of that deception had been the American media.

Security is the reciprocal of the principle of surprise, and the conventional wisdom is that the media are the main threat to American military security. The

problem of achieving strategic surprise, says the Army's strategy manual, "is compounded in an open society such as the United States, where freedom of the press is ensured."[13] But the conventional wisdom is wrong.

Stories about US pacifism, American isolationism, draft resistance and antiwar protests on the eve of World War II, and particularly accounts of President Roosevelt's 1940 campaign promises not to get involved in the war, certainly helped to convince Japan and Germany that the United States lacked the backbone to fight. And similar stories about President Harry Truman's drastic cuts in the American defense budgets and partisan political wrangling over US Asian policy encouraged North Korea in its aggression.

Likewise, "At every juncture in the Persian Gulf war," noted *The New Republic's* Fred Barnes, "Saddam sold Bush short. Maybe he'd read some of the wimp stories in the American press."[14] There was more than a little truth in that remark.

On the battlefield itself, security measures in the Gulf War were tighter than they had been since World War II, and newsmen wistfully talked about "the good old days" during the Vietnam War when access to the front was relatively unrestricted. But even though there had been almost no violations of security by newsmen in World War II, Korea or Vietnam, access to the Gulf battlefield was severely restricted. These tight security measures aided deception of the enemy and facilitated operational and tactical surprise. But they came at a price.

In its discussion of the principle of security, the 1981 edition of the Army's strategy manual warned that "at the strategic level . . . implementation of . . . security measures must be balanced against the need to prevent them from severing the link between the American people and its Army."[15] That caveat fell out of subsequent editions, but its truth was revealed once more during the Gulf War. The Navy claimed that although it had flown 23 percent of the war's combat missions, that fact was almost unknown. The reason was that the Navy avoided the press.

Security restrictions notwithstanding, the Gulf War was the most thoroughly reported conflict since World War II. "A Gallup public opinion poll in early 1991 showed 85% of the public had a high level of confidence in the military," noted Rear Admiral Brent Baker, the Navy's Chief of Public Affairs. "Where did the public get its perception of the military's professionalism? They got it from news media reports."[16]

Simplicity. "If one has never personally experienced war," Clausewitz remarked, "everything looks simple; the knowledge required does not look remarkable, the strategic options are so obvious that by comparison the simplest problem of higher mathematics has an impressive scientific dignity." But, he went on to say, "Everything about war is very simple, but the simplest thing is difficult."[17]

The task imposed by the principle of *simplicity* is to take this difficulty and translate it into terms as simple as it appears on the surface. Thus it serves as a kind of litmus test against which the other principles can be measured. Given that test, the war in the Gulf, as with World War II, was simplicity itself compared to the Korean and Vietnam Wars.

For the first time since World War II, the political and military *objectives* of the war were clear and unambiguous, and progress toward their attainment could be followed on a map. Once again the war was waged on the strategic *offensive* with no sanctuaries and political restrictions to hamper the application of force. Because for the first time since World War II the entire world, especially including the Soviet Union, was united against a common enemy, the United States could *mass* its forces on the battlefield, leaving only an *economy of force* behind to guard its other interests in the world. Thus all of its *maneuver* airlift and sealift assets could be applied to the task at hand.

Tight *security* control of the news media, as in World War II, helped ensure operational and tactical *surprise* on the battlefield. Free of its Cold War convolutions, the military was able, for the first time since World War II, to decisively apply the principles of war. Nowhere was this more true than with the principle of *unity of command.*

Unity of Command. "Who will command the force?" That is the question posed by *unity of command,* the final principle of war. As in World War II, the number of nations involved and their political sensitivities made it obvious that the textbook solution—"ensure unity of effort under one responsible commander"—would not work. In World War II, this problem was solved with the creation of the "Combined Chiefs of Staff" in Washington, where US and British commanders shaped coalition strategy and provided strategic guidance for the conduct of the war.

That experience provided the model for the Gulf War. In an agreement reached by Secretary of State James A. Baker and King Fahd of Saudi Arabia in November 1990, a similar system was created in the Gulf Schwarzkopf, the commander of all US forces in the gulf, would work in tandem with Saudi Lieutenant General Khalid bin Sultan, who commanded all Saudi and Arab forces there. All allied forces in the Gulf would be under one of these two headquarters.

While Schwarzkopf and Khalid were given authority over operational matters, the decision of when to launch the air and ground campaigns, as in World War II, remained "at the highest political levels." The doubts that had been raised as to whether this system would work were dispelled on the first day of the air war when aircraft of seven different nations made a coordinated air strike on Iraq. While there was no one single commander, there was no doubt that unity of effort had been achieved.

And unity of effort had been achieved within the United States military chain of command as well. Command and control during the Vietnam war had been disastrous. Unlike General Eisenhower in World War II, General William C. Westmoreland was not the theater commander. That post was held by the Commander in Chief, Pacific Command in Honolulu, 6,000 miles from the battlefield.

The Goldwater-Nichols Department of Defense Reorganization Act of 1986 changed all that. Returning to the successful relationship of World War II, that law strengthened the role of the chairman of the Joint Chiefs of Staff and the role of the combatant CINCs (commanders in chiefs) in the field. The result was that when the war in the Gulf began, there was a clear-cut chain of command.

Authority flowed from the president, as Commander in Chief, through Defense Secretary Richard B. Cheney and General Colin L. Powell, the chairman of the Joint Chiefs of Staff, to Schwarzkopf, the CINC of the US Central Command.

Like Eisenhower in the European Theater of Operations in World War II, Schwarzkopf was in total command of all US forces in the Kuwaiti Theater of Operations. His ground component commander was the commander, Third Army. His air component commander was the commander, Ninth Air Force; his Marine component commander the commander, 1st Marine Expeditionary Force; and his Naval component commander the commander, Seventh Fleet.

In Washington, Powell was able to reprise the World War II roles of Army chief of staff General

George C. Marshall and Admiral Ernest J. King, the chief of naval operations. Working closely with his civilian superiors, Powell provided strategic direction to the field commander without attempting to micromanage the war.

And then there was the president himself. In the Gulf War, as in World War II, there was no reference to "national command authority," a Vietnam-era euphemism for whoever, if anybody, was making the key decisions for the war. In a remarkable transformation, Bush changed from the "wimp in the White House" to one of America's most effective wartime presidents. As was the case with Roosevelt in World War II, there was no doubt who was running the war. As the Constitution provided, it was President George Herbert Walker Bush, the Commander in Chief of the United States.

BUT WHAT GOOD CAME OF IT AT LAST?

The bottom line for all wars is little Peterkin's question to his grandfather in Robert Southey's famous poem about the Battle of Blenheim—"But what good came of it at last?"[18] The dreams for lasting peace following the end of World War IF were dashed by the onset of the Cold War that followed closely on its heels. But the war in the Gulf may provide yet another chance.

"[F]or the first time since World War II, the international community is united," said Bush in his State of the Union address in January 1991. "The leadership of the United Nations, once only a hoped-for ideal, is now confirming its founders' vision." In words that could have been spoken almost verbatim in 1945, Bush laid out the charge for the future. "And when we [succeed in the Gulf]," he said, "the world can . . . seize the opportunity to fulfill the long-held promise of a new world order where brutality will go unrewarded and aggression will be met with collective resistance."

"Yes, the United States bears a major share of leadership in this effort. Among the nations of the world, only the United States of America has both the moral standing and the means to back it up. We are the only nation on this Earth that could assemble the forces of peace."[19]

Whether this time we can indeed form a new world order remains to be seen. The only thing we know for sure about the future is that the past is still prologue.

NOTES

1. John Paton Davies Jr., *Dragon By the Tail* (NY: W. W. Norton and Company, 1972), 89, 219-20.

2. Michael Breen, "North Korea in Gulf 'Shock,'" *The Washington Times*, 12 March 1991, A1.

3. General Douglas MacArthur, *Military Situation in the Far East,* 82d Congress, 1st Session, Senate Joint Committee on Armed Services and Foreign Relations, vol. 1, (Washington, DC: US Government Printing Office [GPO]. 1951), 30-31.

4. Douglas Kinnard, *The War Managers* (Hanover, NH: University Press of New England, 1977), 25.

5. Charles Krauthammer, "The Lonely Superpower," *The New Republic* (19 July, 1991): 23.

6. For Korean War statistics see Harry G. Summers Jr., "United Nations Ground Force," *Korean War Almanac* (NY: Facts on File Publications, 1990), 269. For Vietnam War statistics see Summers, "Free World Military Forces" and "SVNAF" (South Vietnamese Armed Forces), *Vietnam War Almanac* (NY: Facts on File Publications, 1985), 173, 327-28. South Vietnamese forces ultimately peaked at 1.1 million in January 1973.

7. Joseph P. Englehardt, *Desert Storm and Desert Shield: A Chronology and Troop List For the 1990-1991 Persian Gulf Crisis,* (Carlisle Barracks, PA: Strategic Studies Instituted, US Army War College, 25 March 1991), 5, 8-10. See also "Allied Forces in the Gulf Theater," *Triumph in the Desert,* ed. Ray Cave and Pat Ryan, (NY: Random House, 1991), 64.

8. General Crosbie E. Saint, "Thoughts on the Victory in Desert Storm," Message 260800Z Mar 91, CINCUSAREUR, Heidelberg, Germany, 1.

9. George F. Kennan, *Memoirs: 1925-1950* (Boston, MA: Little, Brown and Company, 1967), 271-91, 354-67.

10. Airlift statistics provided by Major Jim Bates, US air Force, Public Affairs Office, Military Airlift Command, Scott Air Force Base, IL, 12 March 1991.

11. General H. Norman Schwarzkopf, "A Tribute to the Navy—Marine Corps Team," *U.S. Naval Institute Proceedings,* (August 1991): 44.

12. Carl von Clausewitz, *On War,* ed. and trans. Michael Howard and Peter Paret, (Princeton, NJ: Princeton University Press), 1976, 200-201.

13. US Department of the Army Field Manual (FM) 100-1, *The Army* (Washington, DC: US GPO, 1986), 17.

14. Fred Barnes, "The Unwimp," *The New Republic* (18 March 1991): 17-18.

15. FM 100-1, *The Army* (Washington, DC: US GPO, 1981), 16.

16. Rear Admiral Brent Baker, "Last One in the Pool . . .," *U.S. Naval Institute Proceedings* (August 1991): 71.

17. Clausewitz, 199.

18. Robert Southey, "The Battle of Blenheim," in John Bartlett, *Familiar Quotations* (Boston, MA: Little, Brown and Company, 1951), 322.

19. George Bush, "Text of the State of the Union Address," *Washington Post*, 30 January 1991, A14.

Colonel Harry G. Summers Jr,. US Army, Retired, is editor of Vietnam *magazine and a syndicated columnist for the Los Angeles Times. He received a B.S. from the University of Maryland and an M.M.A.S. from the US Army Command and General Staff College (USACGSC). A combat infantry veteran of the Korean and Vietnam wars, he taught strategy at USACGSC and later held the General Douglas MacArthur Chair of Military Research at the US Army War College. His article, "Leadership in Adversity: From Vietnam to Victory in the Gulf," appeared in the May 1991 issue of* Military Review.

Offensive Operations

This is the third in a series of five lessons that provide the framework for tactical principles. The first two lessons introduced you to basic definitions and concepts. At the conclusion of this lesson will be expected to understand the purposes of offensive operations, the forms of maneuver, and types of offensive operations. Analysis of a case study exposes you to an example of the US Army's offensive role in a recent actual combat operation.

The following topics are addressed in this lesson:

- Purposes of the offense
- Forms of offensive maneuver
- Types of offensive operations
- Offensive operations in Desert Storm

The following TLO is supported in whole or in part by this lesson:

- Apply tactical principles and doctrine to the solution of tactical problems.

Following this lesson you will be able to:

- List and define the characteristics of offensive operations
- Analyze an offensive situation
- Compare and contrast forms of maneuver
- Compare and contrast types of offensive operations

Defensive Operations

This is the fourth in a series of five lessons that provide the framework for tactical principles. This lesson focuses on defensive operations—their purposes, characteristics, and the various types of defensive operations. Like the previous lesson, this lesson also provides an example of the US Army's defensive role in an actual historical combat operation where the defense was instrumental in turning the tide of battle.

The following topics are addressed in this lesson:

- Purposes of the defense
- Types of defensive operations
- Defensive operations in the Pusan Perimeter

The following TLO is supported in whole or in part by this lesson:

- Apply tactical principles and doctrine to the solution of tactical problems

Following this lesson you will be able to:

- Identify the characteristics of defensive operations
- Analyze a defensive situation
- List and define types of defensive operations
- Define the terms decisive, shaping and sustaining as they relate to defensive operations

THE KOREAN WAR

INTRODUCTION

The Korean War was the first major armed clash between Free World and Communist forces, as the so-called Cold War turned hot. The half-century that now separates us from that conflict, however, has dimmed our collective memory. Many Korean War veterans have considered themselves forgotten, their place in history sandwiched between the sheer size of World War II and the fierce controversies of the Vietnam War. The recently built Korean War Veterans Memorial on the National Mall and the upcoming fiftieth anniversary commemorative events should now provide well-deserved recognition. I hope that this series of brochures on the campaigns of the Korean War will have a similar effect.

The Korean War still has much to teach us: about military preparedness, about global strategy, about combined operations in a military alliance facing blatant aggression, and about the courage and perseverance of the individual soldier. The modern world still lives with the consequences of a divided Korea and with a militarily strong, economically weak, and unpredictable North Korea. The Korean War was waged on land, on sea, and in the air over and near the Korean peninsula. It lasted three years, the first of which was a seesaw struggle for control of the peninsula, followed by two years of positional warfare as a backdrop to extended cease-fire negotiations. The following essay is one of five accessible and readable studies designed to enhance understanding of the U.S. Army's role and achievements in the Korean conflict.

During the next several years the Army will be involved in many fiftieth anniversary activities, from public ceremonies and staff rides to professional development discussions and formal classroom training. The commemoration will be supported by the publication of various materials to help educate Americans about the war. These works will provide great opportunities to learn about this important period in the Army's heritage of service to the nation.

This brochure was prepared in the U.S. Army Center of Military History by William J. Webb. I hope this absorbing account, with its list of further readings, will stimulate further study and reflection. A complete listing of the Center of Military History's available works on the Korean War is included in the Center's online catalog: *www.army.mil/cmh-pg/catalog/brochure.htm.*

JOHN S. BROWN
Brigadier General, USA
Chief of Military History

THE OUTBREAK
27 JUNE–15 SEPTEMBER 1950

Korea, a small country numbering 30 million people in 1950, lies at the point where three great Asian powers meet—Japan, China, and the former Soviet Union. Japan ruled Korea from 1910 to 1945. Following the defeat of Japan in World War II, the United States and the Soviet Union jointly occupied the country, the United States south of the 38th Parallel and the Soviet Union north. Preoccupied with Soviet intentions in western Europe, the United States attached little strategic importance to Korea in the late 1940s. America did assist the South Koreans in national elections and in formation of the Republic of Korea (ROK). The Soviet Union, on the other hand, took an active role in governing North Korea and in formation of the Democratic People's Republic of Korea (DPRK). The United States Army withdrew its combat forces from South Korea in 1949 but left a military advisory group to assist the ROK Army. In early 1950 the Soviets supplied weapons to and assigned several thousand Russian soldiers as trainers for the *North Korean People's Army (NKPA)*. Armed clashes between North and South Korea were common along the 38th Parallel, but in June 1950 American observers did not anticipate an invasion of the South. Determined to unite Korea by force, the North Koreans invaded South Korea on 25 June. An initially hesitant United States decided that it must take a stand against this armed aggression. American military intervention was ineffective at first, but by September 1950 the combined efforts of the U.S. and ROK Armies, complemented by air and naval superiority, held the North Koreans in check at the Pusan Perimeter.

Strategic Setting

Korea is a mountainous peninsula jutting from the central Asian mainland with a shape that resembles the state of Florida. Water outlines most of this small country, which has more than 5,400 miles of coast-line. The Yalu and Tumen Rivers define much of its northern boundary, while major bodies of water are located on its other sides: the Sea of Japan on the east, the Korea Strait on the south, and the Yellow Sea on the west. China lies above the Yalu and Tumen Rivers for 500 miles of Korea's northern boundary as does the former Soviet Union for some eleven miles along the lower Tumen River. Korea varies between 90 and 200 miles in width and 525 to 600 miles in length. High mountains drop down abruptly to deep water on the east where there are few harbors, but a heavily indented shoreline on the south and west provides many harbors. Summers are hot and humid, with a monsoon season that lasts from June to September, but in the winter cold winds roar down from the Asian interior. A rugged landscape, a lack of adequate roads and rail lines, and climatic extremes make large-scale modern military operations in Korea difficult. In 1950 the country's population totaled about 30 million: 21 million south of the 38th Parallel, with 70 percent of the people engaged in agriculture, and 9 million north.

Japan annexed Korea in 1910 and ruled the country until the end of World War II. Unlike the Soviet Union, in 1945 the United States attached little strategic importance to Korea. At the Potsdam Conference Soviet authorities told American representatives that the Soviets would attack Korea after declaring war on Japan, but the collapse of Japan in August 1945 made a major assault unnecessary. As a line to divide Korea into Soviet and American areas for accepting Japanese surrender, the U.S. War Department selected the 38th Parallel, roughly splitting the country in half. The Soviets agreed to operate in the north, and the American forces would operate in the south. Also in August 1945 the Joint Chiefs of Staff designated General of the Army Douglas MacArthur, as Supreme Commander for the Allied Powers, to receive the Japanese surrender. MacArthur selected Lt. Gen. John R. Hodge, XXIV Corps commander, to command the United States Army Forces in Korea (USAFIK), which administered South Korea on behalf of the United States. The foreign ministers of the United States, Great Britain, and the Soviet Union met in Moscow in December 1945 and developed a plan for a four-power trusteeship of Korea for up to five years. Many South Koreans wanted their independence

immediately and protested violently. The Soviets had their own special plans, which involved strong support for the Korean Communist Party that assumed political power in the North under Kim Il Sung.

In August 1947 the United States, Great Britain, and China agreed to reconsider establishment of a four-power trusteeship to facilitate Korean unification, but the Soviet Union refused to cooperate. The United States then proposed that the United Nations (UN) supervise elections in both zones of Korea and that it oversee the formation of a national government. Elections took place in South Korea in May 1948, but the North Koreans neither participated in nor recognized the results of the elections. The South Koreans chose representatives for the National Assembly of the new Republic of Korea, which then elected Syngman Rhee as its chairman. In July 1948 the assembly produced a constitution and elected Rhee as president of the republic. USAFIK's governmental authority then came to an end. In September 1948 the North Koreans formed their own government, the Democratic People's Republic of Korea under the leadership of Kim Il Sung, that claimed jurisdiction over all of Korea. The National Security Council recommended that all U.S. combat troops leave Korea by the end of June 1949, and President Harry S. Truman approved the recommendation.

Attempts to build a native defense force in South Korea began shortly after the end of World War II. In January 1946 the Joint Chiefs of Staff authorized General MacArthur to form a Korean police force and, despite problems with equipment and training, the Korean Constabulary grew to 20,000 men by the close of 1947. Washington asked MacArthur about the advisability of creating a South Korean army. MacArthur proposed instead in February 1948 an increase of the Constabulary to 50,000 men. President Rhee asked in November for an American military mission, and the Provisional Military Advisory Group established by MacArthur in August 1948 was redesignated in July 1949 the United States Military Advisory Group to the Republic of Korea (KMAG) and authorized 472 soldiers. In November 1948 South Korea passed the Armed Forces Organization Act, which created a department of national defense. By March 1949 the South had converted its Constabulary brigades into an Army of 65,000 men assigned to eight tactical divisions—the 1st, 2d, 3d,

5th, 6th, 7th, 8th, and Capital Divisions. In June 1950 the ROK armed forces consisted of the following: Army, 94,808; Coast Guard, 6,145; Air Force, 1,865; and National Police, 48,273.

In the early summer of 1950 four ROK divisions held positions along the 38th Parallel: the 1st, 6th, 7th, and 8th. The 17th Regiment of the Capital Division was on the western extreme in the Ongjin Peninsula. The other four divisions were scattered about the interior and southern parts of the country. The headquarters of the Capital Division was located at Seoul, the 2d near Taejon, the 3d at Taegu, and the 5th at Kwangju in southwest Korea. When U.S. Armed Forces in Korea withdrew from South Korea in 1949, it transferred equipment to the ROK Army sufficient for 50,000 men. The weapons of the ROK divisions stationed along the 38th Parallel included the American M1 rifle, .30-caliber carbine, 60-mm. and 81-mm. mortars, 2.36-inch rocket launchers, and the M3 105-mm. howitzer. The South Korean armed forces had no tanks, no medium artillery, and no fighter aircraft or bombers. In October 1949 the ROK minister of defense had requested M26 Pershing tanks from the United States, but the KMAG staff concluded that the rough Korean terrain and inadequate roads would not allow efficient tank operations. In June 1950 the ROK Army possessed some 2,100 serviceable U.S. Army motor vehicles—830 2½-ton trucks and 1,300 ¼-ton trucks (jeeps). The ROK Air Force consisted of twelve liaison-type aircraft and ten advance trainers (AT6). The ROK Navy had a sprinkling of small vessels that included patrol craft along with mine layers and sweepers.

The *North Korean People's Army* was officially activated in February 1948. The Soviets exercised close control over its organization and training, and Soviet advisers worked directly with units. At that time 150 Soviets were assigned to each division; the number dropped to 20 per division in 1949 and to a lesser number by 1950 as trusted North Korean officers were developed. By June 1950 the *NKPA* and the *Border Constabulary* numbered about 135,000. The primary tactical units consisted of eight full-strength infantry divisions of 11,000 men each, two more infantry divisions at half strength, a separate infantry regiment, a motorcycle-reconnaissance regiment, and an armored brigade. The *NKPA* benefited from some 20,000 North Koreans who were veterans of the Chinese civil war of the late 1940s, which gave its units a combat-hardened quality and efficiency.

The Soviet Union supplied much of the materiel for the *NKPA*. Of primary importance was the T34 medium tank, a mainstay of the Soviet armored force in World War II that weighed 32 tons and mounted an 85-mm. gun. The Soviets also supplied artillery support that resembled the weaponry of the older Soviet division of World War II: 76-mm. and 122-mm. howitzers, 45-mm. antitank guns, and 82-mm. and 120-mm. mortars. At the outset of the war North Korea had about 180 Soviet aircraft—60 YAK trainers, 40 YAK fighters, 70 attack bombers, and 10 reconnaissance planes. Like the ROK Navy, the North Korean naval forces had only a few small vessels—sixteen patrol craft and several coastal steamers.

U.S. strategic planning after World War II centered on the Soviet Union and its satellite nations. In 1950, as the single most powerful nation in the North Atlantic Treaty Organization, America gave first claim for its military resources to the defense of western Europe. Not only did the United States give priority to Europe over the Pacific and Far East, in April 1948 President Truman had approved a policy that no problems within Korea could become a *casus belli* for the United States. In January 1950, in a speech to the National Press Club in Washington, D.C., Secretary of State Dean G. Acheson announced an American defensive strategy in the Far East that excluded both Korea and Formosa.

The Joint Chiefs of Staff had designated General MacArthur as Commander in Chief, Far East Command (FEC), effective January 1947. The boundaries of FEC were not specific, but MacArthur commanded forces in Japan, Korea, the Philippines, and other island groups. He was responsible for the American occupation of and for general emergencies in those areas. Along with United States Army Forces, Far East, MacArthur also controlled Far East Air Forces and Naval Forces, Far East.

In June 1950 the active United States Army had an authorized strength of 630,201 with an actual strength of about 591,000 and ten combat divisions. Some 360,000 troops were at home, while the remaining 231,000 were in overseas commands with 80,000 in Germany and 108,500 in the Far East. The force designated to handle the Army's emergency assignments was the General Reserve, which consisted mainly of five combat divisions stationed in the United States: 2d Armored Division, 2d and 3d Infantry Divisions, and the 11th and 82d Airborne Divisions. The Far East Command had four tactical divisions and a regimental combat team (RCT)—the 1st Cavalry Division, the 7th, 24th, and 25th Infantry Divisions, and the 29th RCT—that operated under the command of the Eighth U.S. Army in Japan. Each division was short of its authorized war strength of 18,900 by nearly 7,000 men and had major shortages in artillery batteries and equipment. The FEC had received no new vehicles, tanks, or other equipment since World War II. Army personnel stationed in Japan had performed primarily occupation duties, and no serious effort had been made to attain combat efficiency at battalion level or higher. Convinced that a purely occupational mission was no longer needed, MacArthur issued a policy directive in April 1949 that called for an intensified training program for ground, naval, and air units in FEC. By May 1950 Eighth Army's divisions had reportedly reached combat readiness levels that ranged from 65 to 84 percent.

As early as 1947 the North Korean Communists employed propaganda and even armed violence to instigate the overthrow of the South Korean government. On 3 May 1949, the North Koreans launched their first open attack across the 38th Parallel in the vicinity of Kaesong, but ROK units repulsed them. Hundreds of small-scale assaults occurred across the parallel during the first half of 1950; however, some encounters inflicted heavy casualties on both sides. A series of guerrilla uprisings on the island of Cheju-do spread to the mainland by late 1948, but by June 1950 the ROK Army had virtually eliminated them, claiming to have killed about 5,000 insurgents. By late 1949 talk of a North Korean invasion was almost routine in intelligence circles, but it went unnoticed against the background of threatening Communist activities in other parts of the world- Southeast Asia, western Europe, and the Middle East. In the early summer of 1950 senior American observers discounted the likelihood of a North Korean invasion. Both Maj. Gen. Charles A. Willoughby, the FEC G-2 (intelligence officer), and the American embassy in Seoul opined that an attack was unlikely and that the North Koreans would continue to employ guerrillas and psychological warfare. The officers of the KMAG felt that an attack by North Korea was not imminent and, if it happened, they thought that the South Koreans could repel it. Since the United States had no plan to counter an invasion, any debate about an American intelligence failure regarding the North Korean attack was academic.

Operations

During 15-24 June 1950, the North Korean High Command assembled some 90,000 men—7 infantry divisions, 1 armored brigade, 1 separate infantry regiment, 1 motorcycle regiment, and 1 *Border Constabulary* brigade—supported by 150 Soviet T34 tanks near the 38th Parallel. At 0400 on 25 June the North Koreans launched a coordinated attack on South Korea that ran from coast to coast. The assault began on the Ongjin Peninsula on the western extreme of the parallel, but the North Koreans concentrated half of their forces on the Uijongbu Corridor, an ancient invasion route that led directly south to Seoul. The ROK 1st, 2d, 7th, and Capital Divisions defended the area north of Seoul, but the suddenness of the North Korean attack and the shock of enemy armor rapidly pushed the ROK Army back toward Seoul. In the early hours of 28 June the South Korean vice minister of defense ordered a premature blowing of the Han River bridges, located on the southern edges of Seoul, to slow the North Korean advance. This was catastrophic for the ROK Army. Much of the Army was still north of the river and had to abandon transport, supplies, and heavy weapons and cross the Han River in disorganized groups. The ROK Army numbering 95,000 on 25 June could account for only 22,000 men at the end of June.

The UN Security Council met on 25 June and passed a resolution that called on North Korea to cease hostilities and withdraw to the 38th Parallel. President Truman authorized ships and airplanes to protect the evacuation of American dependents in Korea and also use of American air and naval forces to support the Republic of Korea below the 38th Parallel. On 27 June the UN Security Council passed another resolution that recommended UN members assist South Korea in repelling the invasion. The Joint Chiefs of Staff issued a directive that authorized MacArthur to assume operational control of all American military activities in Korea. MacArthur then sent the General Headquarters Advance Command and Liaison Group in Korea (ADCOM), headed by Brig. Gen. John H. Church, from Japan to South Korea to administer KMAG and assist the ROK Army. On 29 June MacArthur personally inspected the situation at the Han River and urged the immediate commitment of American ground forces. President Truman then authorized the employment of Army combat troops to ensure a port and air base at Pusan, South Korea, and more importantly, approved sending two Army divisions from Japan to Korea and the establishment of a naval blockade of North Korea.

Following the breakdown of the ROK Army at Seoul, elements of the North Korean *3d* and *4th Divisions* captured the South Korean capital on 28 June. The North Koreans then repaired a railroad bridge over the Han River, and by 4 July these two divisions, with T34 tank support, were poised to resume their drive south. In Tokyo on 30 June General MacArthur instructed Lt. Gen. Walton H. Walker, Eighth U.S. Army commander, to order the 24th Infantry Division, stationed on Kyushu, to Korea at once. Maj. Gen. William F. Dean, commander of the 24th, was to send immediately to Korea by air a delaying force of about 500 men, and the rest of the division would soon follow by water. General Dean would assume command of USAFIK, reinstated as a provisional headquarters, upon his arrival. Lt. Col. Charles B. Smith, commander of the 1st Battalion, 21st Infantry, of the 24th Division, led the delaying force, called Task Force Smith. On 5 July he established a defensive position three miles north of Osan, assisted by elements of the 52d Field Artillery Battalion. Task Force Smith took on two regiments of the North Korean *4th Division* and thirty-three T34 tanks. Badly outnumbered and without armor, effective antitank weapons, or air support, the U.S. force was overrun. The next day, Colonel Smith could assemble only 250 men, half his original force.

On 4 July General Dean assumed command of USAFIK and established his headquarters at Taejon. The 34th Infantry, another organic regiment of Dean's 24th Division, and the rest of the 21st Infantry arrived in Korea during the first week of July. During that week General MacArthur ordered General Walker to deploy from Japan and assume operational control of the campaign in Korea. Walker set up his headquarters for the Eighth U.S. Army in Korea at Taegu and on 13 July assumed command of USAFIK. Shortly thereafter, he also took command of ROK ground forces. Walker's objectives were to delay the enemy advance, secure the current defensive line, and build up units and materiel for future offensive operations. On 7 July the UN Security Council passed a resolution that recommended a unified command in Korea. President Truman then appointed MacArthur commanding general of the military forces under the unified command that became the United Nations Command. MacArthur's strategy in the early stages of the Korean War was first to stop the North Koreans and then use naval and air superiority to support an amphibious operation in their rear. Once he realized that the *North Korean People's Army* was a formidable force, MacArthur estimated to the Joint Chiefs of Staff that to halt and hurl back the North Koreans would require four to four-and-a-half full-strength infantry divisions, an airborne regimental combat team, and an armored group of three medium tank battalions and reinforcing artillery.

After the defeat of Task Force Smith, General Dean employed the 34th and 21st Infantries in additional delaying actions against the advance of the North Korean *3d* and *4th Divisions* along the corridor that ran south of Osan toward Taejon. Fighting occurred at P'yongt'aek, Ch'onan, Chonui, and Choch'iwon. Dean sought to delay the enemy's approach to the Kum River to support the ROK forces' left flank that was retreating through the central mountains of South Korea. By early July the ROK Army, which became badly disorganized after the fall of Seoul, had re-formed to some extent. From west to east, the ROK Army line was held by the 17th Regiment; the 2d, Capital, 6th, and 8th Divisions; and the 23d Regiment of the 3d Division. The major part of the *NKPA* conducted a main attack on a wide front against ROK-defended territory, which was everything east of the main Seoul-Taegu railroad and highway. Five divisions moved south over the two mountain corridors, while a sixth, the *2d Division,* followed the road from Ch'ongju through Poun to Hwanggan where it entered the Seoul-Taegu highway. The North Korean *1st, 13th,* and *15th Divisions* moved over one mountain corridor and across the Mun'gyong plateau, while the *8th* and *12th Divisions* came down the eastern corridor. On the east coast along the Sea of Japan, the North Korean *5th Division* and the *766th Independent Infantry Regiment* marched south and met virtually no opposition. The trackless mountains of the Taebaek Range effectively separated the east coast of Korea below the 38th Parallel from the rest of the country.

In mid-July 1950 General Dean's 24th Division continued as the primary U.S. Army fighting force in Korea. Taejon, located 100 miles south of Seoul, served as an important road and communications center. The Kum River makes a semicircle to the north around Taejon that constitutes a protective moat. Dean placed his 24th Division in a horseshoe-shaped arc in front of Taejon—the 34th Infantry on the left, the 19th Infantry on the right, and the 21st Infantry in reserve. By positioning elements of the 34th at Kongju, located about twenty miles northwest of Taejon, Dean hoped to prevent the North Koreans from an early crossing of the Kum River and an immediate drive on Taejon. Since the division had only about 4,000 men at Taejon, the 24th could not effectively delay two enemy divisions. During 14-16 July the North Korean *4th* and *3d Divisions,* operating west to east, penetrated the 34th and 19th Infantries' forward defensive positions on the south side of the Kum River and inflicted substantial casualties. Dean then pulled his regiments into a tighter defensive perimeter around Taejon, and the North Koreans launched their attack on Taejon on 19 July. The men of the 24th at Taejon enjoyed one positive development. They had just received a weapon that was effective against the T34 tank, the new 3.5-inch rocket launcher. The five-foot hand-carried launcher fired a two-foot-long eight-and-a-half-pound rocket with a shaped charge designed to burn through any tank then known. U.S. Army soldiers destroyed ten enemy tanks in Taejon on 20 July, eight of them with the 3.5-inch rocket launcher.

The superior numbers and relentless assault of the North Koreans forced the men of the 24th Division to abandon Taejon on 20 July and withdraw to the south. General Dean experienced one of the most dramatic adventures of the withdrawal. Moving down the road to Kumsan, Dean and a small party encountered an enemy roadblock. Forced back, Dean's party, with some wounded, set out on foot after dark. While trying to fetch water for the injured, Dean fell down a steep slope, was knocked unconscious, and suffered a gashed head and a broken shoulder. Separated from his men, Dean wandered alone in the mountains for thirty-six days trying to reach the American lines and was betrayed by two South Koreans to the North Koreans. He would spend the next three years as a prisoner of war. Dean was awarded the first Medal of Honor for service in the Korean War for his leadership and personal bravery with the 24th Division at Taejon. The division suffered a 30 percent casualty rate there and lost all of its organic equipment. The unit had endured many deficiencies since its arrival in Korea. Among them were new subordinate unit commanders who were unfamiliar with their men, poor communications equipment, a shortage of ammunition, outdated

maps, and large numbers of young soldiers in the ranks who were inadequately trained for combat. As for the North Koreans, in five days they had executed two highly successful envelopments of American positions, one at the Kum River and other at Taejon. Each time, they combined strong frontal attacks with movements around the left flank to establish roadblocks and obstruct the escape routes.

The 24th Division would soon share the defense of South Korea with the rebuilt ROK Army and two newly arrived U.S. Army divisions, the 25th Infantry Division and the 1st Cavalry Division. On 24 July the ROK Army reorganized itself into two corps and five divisions. The ROK I Corps controlled the 8th and Capital Divisions, while the ROK II Corps controlled the 1st and 6th Divisions. A reconstituted ROK 3d Division was placed under direct ROK Army control. The ROK II Corps headquarters was at Hamch'ang with its 1st and 6th Divisions on line from west to east, and the I Corps headquarters was at Sangju with the 8th and Capital Divisions on line from west to east. The 3d Division operated on the east coast of South Korea. Large numbers of recruits and replacements had entered the ROK Army, which had regained its prewar strength of about 95,000. The U.S. 25th Division, with its three regiments—24th, 27th, and 35th—commanded by Maj. Gen. William B. Kean, arrived during 10-15 July 1950 at Pusan. General Walker ordered the 25th to bolster ROK defenses of the central mountain corridors. The 1st Cavalry Division, with its three regiments—5th, 7th, and 8th—sailed from Japan and landed at P'ohang-dong north of Pusan during 15-22 July. The unit assumed responsibility for blocking the enemy along the main Taejon-Taegu corridor. In late July both the 25th Division and the 1st Cavalry Division withdrew steadily in the face of aggressive North Korean attacks. On 29 July General Walker, with the support of General MacArthur, issued what the press called a "stand or die" order to the Eighth Army. Walker emphasized that the retreating must stop. The Eighth Army had been trading space for time and was running out of space.

One of the major problems of the retreat was the volume of refugees moving through Eighth Army lines. Their numbers were greater during July and August 1950 than at any other time in the war. During the middle two weeks of July about 380,000 refugees crossed into ROK-held territory. The North Koreans often exploited the situation by launching attacks that began with herding groups of refugees across minefields and then following up with tanks and infantry. The enemy also infiltrated U.S. Army lines by wearing the traditional white civilian clothing and joining groups of refugees, thus enabling him to commit a variety of surprise attacks on American soldiers. The commanders of the 25th Infantry and 1st Cavalry Divisions attempted unsuccessfully to control the volume of refugees and enemy infiltration by searching displaced civilians and limiting the times and routes available for their movements. In late July General Walker, with the cooperation of ROK authorities, set explicit rules for the organized removal of refugees to the rear by the ROK National Police. By the end of July the ROK government had established fifty-eight refugee camps, most of them in the Taegu-Pusan area, to care for the homeless. But even with these efforts, refugees continued to hamper the movement of U.S. and ROK troops throughout the battlefield.

As the Eighth Army neared a natural defensive position along the Naktong River, the North Koreans accelerated their efforts to cut off elements of that army. After the fall of Seoul in late June the North Korean 6th Division had crossed the Han River and rapidly moved south over the western coastal roadnet. Eighth Army intelligence lost track of the 6th. The only UN forces situated at the time southwest of the Taejon-Taegu-Pusan highway were a few hundred ROK 7th Division survivors along with some scattered ROK marines and local police. On 21 July General Walker learned that a North Korean unit, presumed to be the 4th Division, was operating in the southwest area. Walker ordered the 24th Division, despite its deficiencies in manpower and equipment after the loss of Taejon, to serve as a blocking force in the area from Chinju in deep south central Korea northward to Kumch'on. Two battalions of the 29th Infantry, then stationed on Okinawa, and the ROK 17th Regiment would reinforce the 24th Division. On 23 July the North Korean *4th Division* moved south from Taejon with the intent of supporting the *6th Division* in an envelopment of the United Nations' left flank and driving to Pusan. The *4th* pushed as far as the Anui-Koch'ang area, about fifty miles southwest of Taegu, by the end of July. During 25-28 July the two battalions of the 29th were driven back by elements of the *6th* at Hadong, located about twenty-five miles west of Chinju. On 31 July the Eighth Army finally became aware of the *6th Division's* presence after the *6th*

took Chinju and forced one battalion of the 29th and the 19th Infantry of the 24th Division to withdraw to the east. Eighth Army rushed the 27th Infantry of the 25th Division, which had been in reserve, to reinforce American units in the Chinju-Masan corridor. The 24th and 25th Divisions, aided by the ROK 17th Regiment, finally managed to slow the progress of the North Korean *4th* and *6th Divisions* at what would become the southernmost sector of the Pusan Perimeter. By 3 August U.S. and ROK units had averted the immediate threat of a North Korean drive all the way to Pusan.

On 1 August the Eighth Army issued an operational directive to all UN ground forces in Korea for their planned withdrawal east of the Naktong River. UN units would then establish main defensive positions behind what was to be called the Pusan Perimeter. The intent was to draw the line on retreating and hold off the *NKPA* while the U.S. Army could build up its forces and wage a counteroffensive. The Pusan Perimeter assumed by U.S. and ROK forces on 4 August involved a rectangular area about 100 miles from north to south and 50 miles from east to west. The Naktong River formed the western boundary except for the southernmost 15 miles where the Naktong turned eastward after its confluence with the Nam River. The ocean formed the eastern and southern boundaries, while the northern boundary was an irregular line that ran through the mountains from above Waegwan to Yongdok. From the southwest to the northeast the UN line was held by the U.S. 25th and 24th Infantry and 1st Cavalry Divisions, and then by the ROK 1st, 6th, 8th, Capital, and 3d Divisions. From south to northeast the North Korean units positioned opposite the UN units were the *83d Motorized Regiment of the 105th Armored Division* and then the *6th, 4th, 3d, 2d, 15th, 1st, 13th, 8th, 12th, and 5th Divisions* and the *766th Independent Infantry Regiment.* The 5th Regimental Combat Team from Hawaii and the phased arrival of the 2d Infantry Division from the United States augmented U.S. Army forces. A third major reinforcement arrived in Korea on 2 August, the 1st Provisional Marine Brigade, about 4,700 men. UN combat forces at this point actually outnumbered the North Koreans, 92,000 to 70,000.

The North Koreans had four possible avenues of advance leading to Pusan that could result in the defeat of U.S. and ROK forces, and in August they tried them all simultaneously. These approaches went through Masan south of the confluence of the Nam and Naktong Rivers, through the Naktong Bulge to the rail and road lines at Miryang, through Kyongju and down the east coast corridor, and through Taegu. During the first week of August General Walker decided to launch the first American counterattack of the war in the Chinju-Masan corridor. One of his purposes was to break up a suspected massing of enemy troops near the Taegu area by forcing the diversion of some North Korean units southward. On 6 August the Eighth Army issued the operational directive for the attack by Task Force Kean, named for the 25th Division commander. Task Force Kean consisted of the 25th Division, less the 27th Infantry and a field artillery battalion, with the 5th RCT and the 1st Provisional Marine Brigade attached. The Army plan of attack required the force to move west from positions then held near Masan, seize the Chinju Pass, and secure the line as far as the Nam River. Task Force Kean launched its strike on 7 August but ran head-on into one being delivered simultaneously by the North Korean *6th Division.* After a week of heavy fighting, neither Kean's troops nor their opponents had made any appreciable progress. Even so, the Eighth Army had launched its first offensive in Korea and successfully halted an assault by an enemy division.

Seven air miles north of the point where the Naktong River turns east and the Nam River enters it, the Naktong curves westward opposite Yongsan in a wide semicircular loop. This loop became known to the American troops as the Naktong Bulge during the bitter fighting there in August and September. On 6 August the North Korean *4th Division* crossed the Naktong at Ohang with the intent of driving to Yongsan located about ten miles to the east. The 24th Division defended that sector and the 24th commander, Maj. Gen. John H. Church, who had succeeded General Dean as division commander, placed the defense of the Naktong Bulge under Task Force Hill. Task Force Hill consisted of the 9th Infantry of the 2d Infantry Division along with the 34th and 19th Infantries and a battalion of the 21st Infantry of the 24th Division. Despite the efforts of Task Force Hill, by 11 August the *4th Division* had penetrated to the vicinity of Yongsan.

General Walker then added to the fray the 23d Infantry of the 2d Division, the 27th Infantry of the 25th Division, and the 1st Provisional Marine Brigade. General Church led the coordinated attack of Army

and Marine Corps troops against the North Koreans that began on 17 August. By the eighteenth the American forces had decisively defeated the *4th Division,* which had lost half its original strength of about 7,000 men.

Located about twenty miles south of P'ohang-dong on the east coast, Kyongju was an important rail and highway center situated within the Taegu-P'ohang-dong-Pusan triangle inside the Pusan Perimeter. The capture of P'ohang-dong and the nearby Yonil Airfield, used by the Far East Air Force, would open a natural and essentially undefended corridor for the *NKPA* to move directly south through Kyongju to Pusan. General Walker had only lightly fortified the east coast corridor because the enemy threat was more immediate on the western perimeter, and he doubted that the North Koreans could mount a major successful drive through the trackless mountains. In early August the enemy almost proved Walker wrong when three North Korean divisions—the *5th, 8th,* and *12th*—and the *766th Independent Infantry Regiment* mounted strong attacks against the ROK defenders. By 12 August the North Koreans had pressed to P'ohang-dong and also threatened Yonil Airfield. The North Korean *5th Division* cut off the ROK 3d Division above P'ohang-dong, and the 3d Division had to be evacuated by sea to positions farther south. General Walker reinforced the ROK units in the area with elements of the U.S. 2d Infantry Division. By 17 August ROK units and the 2d Division had managed to check the enemy drive at P'ohang-dong. A primary factor in stopping the North Koreans was logistics, as the enemy had outrun his supply line during the difficult trek southward through the mountains.

The natural corridor of the Naktong Valley from Sangju to Taegu presented another principal axis of attack for the *NKPA.* The sizable enemy forces assembled in an arc around Taegu in early August from south to north consisted of the *10th, 3d, 15th, 13th,* and *1st Divisions* and elements of the *105th Armored Division.* Opposite the North Korean divisions were the U.S. 1st Cavalry Division and the 1st and 6th Divisions of the ROK II Corps. The North Koreans crossed the Naktong River in several places within the arc around Taegu during the second week of August. When several enemy artillery shells landed in Taegu on 18 August, President Rhee ordered movement of the Korean provincial government, then in Taegu, to Pusan. The North Korean *1st* and

13th Divisions posed the primary threat as they pressed toward Taegu by overland routes from the north and northwest. General Walker moved up the 23d and 27th Infantries, both fresh from defensive action in the Naktong Bulge, to reinforce the ROK 1st Division, which confronted the North Korean *1st* and *3d Divisions* in its sector. Although the North Korean *1st Division* pushed to within nine miles of Taegu, the combined efforts of the ROK 1st Division and the U.S. 23d and 27th Infantries frustrated enemy efforts to penetrate to Taegu.

Even though the *North Korean People's Army* had seriously threatened the United States and ROK Armies within the Pusan Perimeter during August 1950, the defenders both successfully resisted the enemy attacks and continued the buildup of forces for a counteroffensive. The Far East Air Force had established air supremacy over the North Koreans early in the war and continued to influence the outcome of battles by multiple sorties in close support of ground troops, 4,635 in July and 7,397 in August. By late August there were more than 500 American medium tanks within the Pusan Perimeter. The tanks in tank battalions were equally divided between M26 Pershings and M4A3 Shermans, except for one battalion that had the newer M46 Pattons. On 1 September the United Nations Command had a strength of 180,000 in Korea: 92,000 were South Koreans and the balance were Americans and the 1,600-man British 27th Infantry Brigade. In August the North Koreans continued the plan and tactics begun at the Han River in early July with a frontal holding attack, envelopment of the flank, and infiltration to the rear. When the Eighth Army stabilized the line at the Pusan Perimeter, these tactics no longer worked and success could come only by frontal attack, penetration, and immediate exploitation. Generals MacArthur and Walker countered with classical principles of defense—interior lines of communications, superior artillery firepower, and a strong air force. By 1 September the North Koreans had assembled a 98,000-man army for a massive offensive against the Pusan Perimeter. However, they experienced substantial problems: a third of their ranks manned by forcibly conscripted and untrained South Koreans, a major shortage of small arms, and only enough rations for one or sometimes two meals a day.

In early September as during August, General Walker faced dangerous situations in essentially the same places along the Pusan Perimeter: in the east at P'ohang-dong to include a potential severing of the corridor between Taegu and P'ohang-dong, north of Taegu where the enemy made disturbing gains, at the Naktong Bulge, and in the Masan area in the extreme south. Also as he had during the fighting in August, Walker continued his masterful tactics of shifting his forces from one threatened enemy penetration to another. In early September the ROK 3d, Capital, 8th, and 6th Divisions held the line farthest to the east against the North Korean *5th, 8th, 12th,* and *15th Divisions.* Maj. Gen. John B. Coulter, newly appointed deputy commander, Eighth Army, assumed command of American units in the eastern sector and employed the 21st Infantry of the U.S. 24th Division and other supporting units to bolster the ROK divisions. On 7 September General Church replaced Coulter as American commander in the eastern sector after General Walker ordered the entire 24th to reinforce the ROK divisions. A combination of ground fighting, predominantly by the South Koreans, along with American close air support and naval gunfire from offshore inflicted serious losses on the enemy divisions. The North Korean *1st, 3d,* and *13th Divisions* pressed the attack north of Taegu against the U.S. 1st Cavalry Division, which prompted Walker on 5 September to move the main Eighth Army headquarters from Taegu to Pusan. The 1st Cavalry Division essentially checked the thrusts of the North Koreans north of Taegu, but fighting continued there into mid-September.

At the end of August the *North Korean People's Army* also planned a crushing blow against the U.S. 2d and 25th Divisions in the southern part of the Pusan Perimeter. The enemy's *6th Division* would attack through Haman, Masan, and capture Kumhae, fifteen miles west of Pusan. The *7th Division* was to strike north of the Masan highway, wheel left to the Naktong River, and wait for the *6th Division* on its right and the *9th* on its left and then resume the attack toward Pusan. The 25th Division held the southernmost sector that ran from the confluence of the Naktong and Nam Rivers to the southern coast, while the 2d Division was positioned in the area across the Naktong River north of the 25th. The North Korean *9th Division* faced the 2d Division at the Naktong Bulge and had the mission of capturing the towns of Miryang and Samnangjin, thereby cutting off the Eighth Army route of withdrawal between Taegu and Pusan. During the first week of September the *9th Division* penetrated the Naktong

Bulge as far east as Yongsan, but a counterattack by the 2d Division together with the U.S. 1st Provisional Marine Brigade pushed back the *9th* almost to the Naktong River. The 2d Division's 23d Infantry beat back the North Korean *2d Division* six miles north of Yongsan at Changnyong. At the same time the *6th* and *7th Divisions* mounted strong attacks against the 25th Division. Despite enemy penetrations into the sectors of the 25th's regiments—the 35th Infantry's sector west of Ch'irwon and the 24th Infantry's sector near Haman that was effectively stopped by the 27th Infantry—the 25th Division repelled the NKPA's offensive in the south. The Naktong River line held, and the Pusan Perimeter was secure.

Analysis

Within the space of a few months in 1950, the United States had taken the big leap from attaching no strategic importance to Korea to active involvement there in a major armed conflict. Its active Army of 591,000 had been focused on Soviet intentions in western Europe and occupation duty in Europe and the Far East. The four divisions under MacArthur's Far East Command in Japan were performing primarily occupation duties, and their actual readiness level for conventional combat was even lower than their marginal statistical ratings indicated. Each of MacArthur's divisions was about 7,000 men short of its authorized strength of 18,900, and none of them had received any new equipment since World War II. MacArthur had not fully supported development of the ROK Army, and in 1948 he had suggested merely expanding the ROK Constabulary. When the ROK minister of defense in 1949 requested M26 Pershing tanks from America, the KMAG argued that the Korean terrain and roads would not allow tank operations, a clearly inaccurate prediction of the Soviet T34 tank's performance in South Korea during the war's early stages. When USAFIK withdrew from South Korea in 1949, it did transfer to the ROK Army individual weapons and equipment sufficient for 50,000 men, but these small arms were incapable of repelling enemy armored attacks.

America failed to anticipate the North Korean invasion, and KMAG erred in concluding that the ROK Army could withstand an invasion if it happened.

Nevertheless, when the attack came the United States decided to intervene on behalf of South Korea. President Truman authorized air and naval support early in the conflict and the progressive introduction of ground troops. The defeat of Task Force Smith underscored the importance of adequate prewar training along with armored and air support in combat operations. Further, MacArthur underestimated the skill and determination of the North Koreans but recognized his error when he concluded that more than four U.S. divisions were needed to defeat the enemy. The combined efforts of the U.S. and ROK Armies led by General Walker, complemented by air and naval superiority, slowed the southward drive of the North Koreans and ended in a difficult but successful defense of the Pusan Perimeter. The fighting was intense as reflected in American casualties to mid-September 1950—4,599 battle deaths, 12,058 wounded, 401 reported captured, and 2,107 reported missing in action. The bitter weeks of retreat and death would soon change, however, with MacArthur's "hammer against the anvil": the breakout from the Pusan Perimeter coupled with the landing at Inch'on by the 1st Marine Division and the Army's 7th Infantry Division during the third week of September.

FURTHER READINGS

Appleman, Roy E. *South to the Naktong, North to the Yalu.* United States Army in the Korean War. Washington, D.C.: U.S. Army Center of Military History, 1961.

Blair, Clay. *The Forgotten War: America in Korea.* New York: Time Books, 1988.

Collins, J. Lawton. *War in Peacetime: The History and Lessons of Korea.* Boston: Houghton Mifflin, 1969.

Dean, Major General William F. *General Dean's Story.* New York: Viking Press, 1954.

Edwards, Paul M. *The Pusan Perimeter, Korea, 1950: An Annotated Bibliography.* Westport, Conn.: Greenwood Press, 1994.

Ridgway, Matthew B. *The Korean War.* Garden City, N.Y.: Doubleday, 1967.

Schnabel, James F. *Policy and Direction: The First Year.* United States Army in the Korean War. Washington, D.C.: U.S. Army Center of Military History, 1972.

Tactical Analysis Case Study

This is the last in a series of five lessons that provide the framework for tactical principles. This lesson is intended to build the four previous lessons in tactics and to get you to analyze an operation using the principles of war. The analysis of a case study will enable you to pull together, review, reinforce, and apply definitions, concepts, and characteristics of tactical operations to one famous engagement during the Gettysburg Campaign—the Battle for Little Round Top.

The following TLO is supported in whole or in part by this lesson:

■ Apply tactical principles and doctrine to the solution of tactical problems

Following this lesson you will be able to:

■ Determine the level of war impacted by an operation
■ Analyze an operation using the principles of war
■ Determine which characteristics of the offense or defense are present during an operation
■ Distinguish between the forms of maneuver on the offense and types of operations on the defense

MANTLED IN FIRE AND SMOKE

BY DAVID F. CROSS

The Battle of Gettysburg, and perhaps the fate of the Union, was decided in one hour of desperate fighting on the rocky ledges of Little Round Top. In June 1863, Confederate military fortunes in the East were at their zenith. The Union Army of the Potomac had just been defeated at the Battle of Chancellorsville; flushed with victory, the Army of Northern Virginia began an invasion of the North. It seemed that one more decisive victory, this time on the soil of a Northern state, might crush the already sagging will of the North and force Abraham Lincoln's government to the bargaining table, where a negotiated peace could win the war for the Confederacy.

On July 1, in swift, dramatic consequence, General Robert E. Lee's army met the Army of the Potomac, commanded now by Maj. Gen. George Gordon Meade, at the Battle of Gettysburg. On the first day of the encounter, Lee's legions drove the Federal troops back through the town to a defensive position on Cemetery Ridge. Lee's army seemed invincible. At the end of the day, it looked like another great Confederate victory was in the making. More than just another battle might be won this time, however—possibly the entire war.

It did not turn out that way, of course. Better generalship by Meade, superior tactical decisions by his field officers and, most important, stubborn fighting by Federal troops, defeated the Confederates and drove them back to Virginia. With the retreating Rebel army, the specter of peace faded forever.

But it was close. Ever since, the "what ifs" of Gettysburg have haunted historians of the most momentous battle of the Civil War. One of the greatest imponderables surrounds the fateful struggle for Little Round Top. The Union defensive position on the second day of the battle resembled an inverted "J," extending from Culp's Hill on the north, around Cemetery Hill and irregularly south along Cemetery Ridge to Little Round Top. Geographically and strategically, the 650-foot-high Little Round Top anchored the left end of the Union Line. In Confederate hands, Lee's troops would have a springboard to attack the Union rear and force evacuation of Cemetery Ridge.

On the morning of July 2, the second day of the battle, Little Round Top was occupied by a division of the XII Corps commanded by Brig. Gen. John W. Geary. Meade ordered Geary's unit to rejoin the rest of the XII Corps at Culp's Hill and troops of Maj. Gen. Daniel E. Sickles' III Corps to take over Geary's position. But in the confusion, III Corps troops failed to arrive and Geary pulled his men out too soon, leaving Little Round Top undefended. Lee, with a sense for Federal weakness, chose to attack the southern end of the Union line. If the Confederate troops could crush this portion of the Union defenses and occupy Little Round Top, the whole Union line would become indefensible.

There were many crucial moments in the three-day battle at Gettysburg, but none more so than the defense of Little Round Top by the 20th Maine Regiment. Had the Maine Yankees been driven off Little Round Top, the Battle of Gettysburg might have had a different outcome. At least, Meade thought so, saying later, "But for the timely advance of the Fifth Corps and the prompt sending of a portion to Round Top, where they met the enemy almost on the crest and had a desperate fight to secure the position—I say but for these circumstances the enemy would have secured Round Top planted his artillery there, commanding the whole battlefield, and what the result would have been I leave to you to judge."

Fortunately for the Federal forces, it took Lee most of the day to assemble his troops and get them to the attack staging areas. His plan was to attack the Union left with 20,000 men while the rest of his army pressured the Union right. Major General John B. Hood's division, composed of Brig. Gen. E.M. Law's Alabama Brigade on the right and Brig. Gen. J.B. Robertson's Texas/Arkansas Brigade on the left, advanced first at about 4:30 p.m. They headed toward the southern end of the Union line defended by Maj. Gen. George Sykes' V Corps. As Law's brigade advanced, it wheeled obliquely to the left, hitting the western slope of Little Round Top and pouring into the gorge of Plum Run; it threatened to envelop the entire Union left flank. Lieutenant General James Longstreet later described this advance of Hood's division as the "best 3 hours of fighting ever done by any troops on any battlefield."

Meanwhile, Meade was feeding troops into his line as fast as they arrived on the battlefield. He was concerned about the Union left flank and sent his chief of engineers, Brig. Gen. Gouverneur K. Warren, to Little Round Top to assess the situation. Warren arrived at 3:30 p.m. and—to his utter surprise—found the hill undefended. Recognizing a disaster in the making, he frantically sent riders to

Meade and Sickles commanding the adjacent III Corps, requesting immediate assistance. Sickles, whose troops were already hotly engaged, replied that he had none to spare. Fortuitously, Colonel Strong Vincent, who commanded the 3rd Brigade of the 1st Division, V Corps, intercepted one of the messages for help. He immediately recognized the strategic importance of the hill and led the 1,350 men of his brigade at the "double quick" to Little Round Top. Vincent positioned the four regiments of his brigade—the 20th Maine, 83rd Pennsylvania, 44th New York and 16th Michigan—along the southern and western slope facing the oncoming Rebels. His last words to the 389 men of the 20th Maine were: "This is the left end of the Union line. You understand? You are to hold this ground at all costs!"

Advancing against them were the 15th Alabama Regiment and seven companies of the 47th Alabama Regiment, under the command of Colonel William C. Oates. He had been ordered to "pass up between the Round Tops, find the Union left, turn it and capture Little Round [Top]." His men were drawn to their right by fire from a detachment of Major Homer R. Staughton's 2nd U.S. (Berdan's) Sharpshooters at the base of Round Top. Pushing them back, the Alabama regiments drove to the top of Round Top.

Pausing to rest, Oates aligned his men and sent them crashing down the northern slope of Round Top into the saddle between the hills. Suddenly, what he described as a "heavy force" of the enemy poured "a most destructive fire" into his troops from the slope of Little Round Top—it was Chamberlain's 20th Maine Regiment.

Oates had the advantage in numbers, 644 riflemen to 358 from Maine. He described the 15th Alabama as the "strongest and finest regiment in Hood's division." His men were battle hardened and supremely confident, boasting they'd "never been whipped." When they attacked, they struck hard, "with an impetuosity which betrayed the anticipation of an easy triumph." They must have been tired, however, having marched 28 miles in the previous 24 hours to get to the battlefield. Oates himself was not a professional soldier, having only become colonel of the 15th Alabama in May 1863, but he was known as a fearless and aggressive leader.

The men of the 20th Maine, in contrast to the Alabamians, were not veteran troops, having had little battlefield experience. These men were also tired; they had marched 107 miles in the past five days,

including 26 miles the previous day, to get to the battlefield. Their colonel had been a professor of religion and romance languages at Bowdoin College. However, Joshua Lawrence Chamberlain sought to offset Oates' advantage with strength of position, better handling of his men, and iron determination. Chamberlain reported that every man who could carry a rifle, including "every pioneer and musician," was placed in the line. Two soldiers from the 2nd Maine Regiment being guarded by the 20th Maine Regiment while awaiting court-martial were also given rifles and willingly joined the battle line.

Chamberlain sent Company B, commanded by Captain Walter G. Morrill, out to the left as skirmishers to protect his flank. Cut off by the advancing Rebels, Morrill's men hid behind a stone wall. There they were joined by 14 of Berdan's Sharpshooters, who had previously been driven from in front of Round Top. This occurrence was subsequently to have important consequences.

The Alabama troops struck at 6 p.m., and the fighting immediately became intense. Oates later described the struggle: "I ordered my regiment to drive the Federals from the ledge of rocks, gain the enemy's rear, and drive him from the hill. My men obeyed and advanced about half way to the enemy's position, but the fire was so destructive that my line wavered like a man trying to walk against a strong wind, and then slowly, doggedly, gave back a little."

Oates ordered another advance: "We drove the Federals from their strong defensive position; five times they rallied and charged us, twice coming so near that some of my men had to use their bayonet." Another charge by the Alabama troops and the "20th Maine was driven back from the ledge but not farther than to the next ledge on the mountainside."

Fighting was now at close quarters, so close that—for once—the fabled bayonet actually became a weapon instead of a mere threat. One 20th Maine private, emboldened or maddened by the fight, tried to grab the colors from the 15th Alabama's color-bearer, John G. Archibald. As the Yankee made a sudden lunge for the flag, Sergeant Pat O'Connor coolly stepped forward and jabbed a bayonet into the Federal's head.

The noise of battle, as might be imagined, was deafening. Captain James H. Ellison, commanding Company C, cupped his hand to his ear as Oates shouted an order. Then, in the process of executing the ordered maneuver, Ellison suddenly fell with a bullet through the head. He turned over onto his back, raised his arms, gave a shudder and died. The rest of the company, horrified by the sight, lost momentum and gathered around their fallen leader until Oates got them started forward again.

Another company commander, Captain Henry C. Brainard of Company G, fell among the rocky ledges of Little Round Top. His last words were, "O God, that I could see my mother!"

Even more grievous to Oates, on a personal level, was the loss of his younger brother John, who now succeeded to Brainard's command. The younger Oates had been sick that day and had only reached the battlefield after his brother found him a horse to ride. Colonel Oates then came upon him Lying sick in a field and suggested that he could, with honor, remain behind the lines. "Brother, I will not do it," said John Oates. "If I were to remain here people would say that I did it through cowardice; no, sir, I am an officer and will never disgrace the uniform I wear; I shall go through, unless, I am killed, which I think is quite likely." John Oates fell dead, struck by several bullets, moments later.

"Theodore Gerrish of the 20th Maine described the battle from his side: "Ten minutes have passed since we formed the line...but we have no indications of the enemy: 'But look! Look! Look!' exclaim half a hundred men in our regiment at the same time; and no wonder, for right in our front...we see the lines of the enemy. The conflict opens...the carnage began. Our regiment was mantled in fire and smoke.

"I wish that I could picture with my pen the awful details of that hour—how rapidly the cartridges were torn from the boxes and stuffed in the smoking muzzles of the guns; how the steel rammers clashed and clanged in the heated barrels; how the men's hands and faces grew grim and black with burning powder; how our little line, baptized with fire, reeled to and fro as it advanced or was pressed back; how our officers bravely encouraged the men to hold and recklessly exposed themselves to the enemy's fire—a terrible medley of cries, shouts, cheers, groans, prayers, curses, bursting shells, whizzing rifle bullets and clanging steel. "

The enemy was pouring a terrible fire upon us, his superior forces giving him a great advantage.... The air seemed to be alive with lead. The lines at times were so near each other that the hostile gun barrels almost touched.... At one time there was a brief lull in the carnage, and our shattered line was

closed up, but soon the contest raged again with renewed fierceness....Many of our companies have suffered fearfully....But there is no relief and the carnage goes on."

Oates now decided to concentrate the 15th Alabama on his right in an effort to outflank the left end of the Union line. Warned that "something very strange was going on" behind the attacking Confederates, Chamberlain climbed atop a large boulder and saw Oates' flanking column moving to attack the left flank. The 20th Maine was in a very tight spot. Chamberlain had to maneuver to protect his left flank while actively engaged with the 47th Alabama along his entire front. He reported, "Without betraying our peril to any but one or two officers, I had the right wing move by the left flank, taking intervals of a pace or two...extending so as to cover the whole front then engaged; and at the same time moved the left wing to the left rear, making a large angle at the color which was now brought up to the front where our left had first rested."

The 20th Maine's line now resembled a "V" composed of a single rank of men. "We were not a moment too soon," reported Chamberlain, for the 15th Alabama rushed forward against what they expected to be an unprotected left flank, reaching within 10 paces before being stopped by a sudden deadly volley by the new left wing of the 20th Maine. "From that moment began a struggle fierce and bloody beyond any that I have witnessed and which lasted in all its fury a full hour," reported Chamberlain. Each side fought like madmen. The 20th Maine regimental history simply states, "No one could ever describe this part of the fight coherently." Chamberlain remembered that "the edge of the conflict swayed to and fro, with wild whirlpools and eddies. At times I saw around me more of the enemy than of my own men."

The Confederates somehow broke through the Union line in several places; there was hand-to-hand fighting. Somehow the 20th Maine line held, but the left wing had been forced back so far that the line now resembled a hairpin and incoming fire on the left was landing in the rear of the right wing. It was now after 7 p.m. and the 20th Maine was in bad shape.

The regiment had fired 15,000 rounds, and the 60 rounds allotted per man were almost exhausted. Three hundred and fifty-eight riflemen had gone into the battle and only 228 remained effective. The enemy appeared to be massing for another charge, one that would certainly overwhelm the left wing of the 20th Maine. Private Gerrish remembered: "Our line is pressed back so far that our dead are within the lines of enemy. Our ammunition is nearly all gone, and we are using the cartridges from the boxes of our wounded comrades. A critical moment has arrived, and we can remain as we are no longer; we must advance or retreat."

For Chamberlain there was only one thing left—a counterattack. He gave the order, "Fix bayonets!" Gerrish describes it this way: "Every man understood in a moment that the movement was our only salvation, but there is a limit to human endurance . . . and the little line seemed to quail under the fearful fire that was being poured upon it. In that moment of supreme need...Lieutenant Holman S. Melcher with a cheeer and a flash of his sword, full ten paces to the front he sprang—ten paces—more than half the distance between hostile lines. 'Come on! Come on! Come on, boys!' he shouts. The color sergeant and the brave color guard follow, and with one wild yell of anguish wrung from it's tortured heart, the regiment charged."

In a brilliantly executed maneuver, Chamberlain's men charged forward and across the hill from the left wing of their line while those on the right swung with them in an extended "right wheel forward" movement. Chamberlain described the charge as having the effect of "a reaper cutting down the disconcerted foe." Stunned, the Confederate troops in the front ranks dropped their rifles and surrendered. The rest broke and retreated toward a stone wall in their rear.

"Suddenly," said Chamberlain, "to our mutual surprise, two scores of rifle barrels gleam over the rocks, and a murderous volley was poured in upon them at close quarters." Captain Morrill's lost Company B and Staughton's wandering sharpshooters rose up out of their hiding place, and with a shout they too charged into the Confederate flank, making such a commotion that the Rebels thought they were a whole regiment. Oates described the situation: "My position rapidly became untenable. The Federal infantry were reported to be coming down on my right and certainly were closing in on my rear." He ordered his staff officers to "return to your companies; we will sell out as dearly as possible."

What was left of the 15th and 47th Alabama Regiments fled to Round Top. Oates collapsed while climbing the hill and might have been captured had not two of his men carried him to safety. He described the retreat simply and honestly, saying, "We ran like a herd of cattle."

Chamberlain reported capturing 400 prisoners. In addition, 150 dead or wounded Rebels were found in his front. These numbers seem exaggerated; at least Oates thought so. He admitted that in a roll call after the battle only 223 enlisted men and half the officers (19) of his regiment responded. The 20th Maine had only 200 of 386 officers and men still effective. The Confederate assault on the south slope of Little Round Top had been repulsed.

However, the battle was not going as well on the right, where Law's men were pushing up the west slope of Little Round Top. The 44th New York and 83rd Pennsylvania in the center stood firm against repeated attacks, but on the right, part of the 16th Michigan fell back. When Vincent saw signs of faltering by the 16th Michigan, he rushed forward and, while encouraging his men, fell, mortally wounded. He died five days later.

It appeared that the Confederate drive might succeed despite the heroic defense by the 20th Maine. Warren, on the crest of Little Round Top, received a call for immediate help. He searched for reinforcements and found Colonel Patrick H. O'Rorke and the 140th New York Regiment in the rear. These 526 men, dressed in jaunty new Zouave uniforms, scrambled up the hill. Without taking time to align ranks, O'Rorke yelled, "Down this way, boys!" and led them down the western slope. His men drove back the Confederate troops, but O'Rorke fell with the first volley, fatally hit in the neck by a Minie bullet.

By the time the Confederates could regroup, more Union reinforcements had poured into position. This discouraged further attempts by the Southerners to take Little Round Top. The golden opportunity to turn the Union left was gone. Little Round Top had been saved for the Union, and in saving Little Round Top, its courageous defenders had saved the left end of the Union line, the Battle of Gettysburg, and perhaps the entire Union.

Oates said later, "General Lee was never so close to victory as that day on Little Round Top. "And he summed it up: "There was no better regiment in the Confederate Army than the 15th Alabama, and if it failed to carry any point against which it was thrown, no other single regiment need try it. It fought hard and persistently. The other regiments of the brigade did their duty at Gettysburg, but the 15th struck the hardest knot. There never were harder fighters than the 20th Maine and their gallant Colonel. His skill and persistence and the great bravery of his men saved Little Round Top, and the Army of the Potomac, from defeat. Great events sometimes turn on comparatively small affairs."

Perhaps because of his showing at Gettysburg, Oates was never officially confirmed a colonel by the Confederate Congress. Instead, his command was taken over by another officer in the regiment, Major Alexander A. Lowther, who managed to formally receive his colonelcy ahead of Oates. Reduced to major, Oates was transferred to the 48th Georgia Regiment, and while leading it he was shot in the right arm in June 1864 during the Wilderness Campaign. The limb was amputated and Oates subsequently left the service. After the war he served seven terms as an Alabama congressman and one term as governor. He later served, improbably, as a brigadier general during the Spanish-American War.

As for Chamberlain, the college professor-turned-warrior survived two wounds at Little Round Top and a more serious wound 11 months later at Petersburg, where commanding general Ulysses S. Grant, thinking Chamberlain was about to die, promoted him to brigadier general on the field. Chamberlain survived that wound, as well, and had the signal honor of receiving the formal surrender of Robert E. Lee's army at Appomattox Court House in April 1865.

Like Oates, his young opponent that memorable day, Chamberlain entered politics after the war, serving four terms as governor of Maine before returning to Bowdoin College as its president. In a sense, Chamberlain had made it full circle. A grateful Congress bestowed him with the Medal of Honor in 1893, exactly 30 years after his quick thinking and gallant action saved Little Round Top—and the Union.

Like Joshua Chamberlain, author David Cross is an "Up East" Yankee, residing in Rutland, Vt. Further reading: Harry W. Pfanz's Gettysburg: The Second Day, or William Oates' firsthand account, The War Between the Union and the Confederacy.

THE ATTACK AND DEFENSE OF LITTLE ROUND TOP

GETTYSBURG, JULY 2, 1863

Report of Col. Joshua L. Chamberlain, Twentieth Maine Infantry.

"FIELD NEAR EMMITTSBURG, July 6, 1863.

"In compliance with the request of the colonel commanding the brigade, I have the honor to submit a somewhat detailed report of the operations of the Twentieth Regiment Maine Volunteers in the battle of Gettysburg, on the 2d and 3d instant.

"Having acted as the advance guard, made necessary by the proximity of the enemy's cavalry, on the march of the day before, my command on reaching Hanover, Pa., just before sunset on that day, were much work, and lost no time in getting ready for an expected bivouac. Rations were scarcely issued, and the men about preparing supper, when rumors that the enemy had been encountered that day near Gettysburg absorbed every other interest, and very soon orders came to march forthwith to Gettysburg.

"My men moved out with a promptitude and spirit extraordinary, the cheers and welcome they received on the road adding to their enthusiasm. After an hour or two of sleep by the roadside just before daybreak we reached the heights southeasterly of Gettysburg at about 7 A.M., July 2.

"Massed at first with the rest of the division on the right of the road, we were moved several times farther toward the left. Although expecting every moment to be put into action, and held strictly in line of battle, yet the men were able to take some rest and make the most of their rations.

"Somewhere near 4 P.M. a sharp cannonade, at some distance to our left and front, was the signal for a sudden and rapid movement of our whole division in the direction of this firing, which grew warmer as we approached. Passing an open field in the hollow ground in which some of our batteries were going into position, our brigade reached the skirt of a piece of woods, in the farther edge of which there was a heavy musketry fire, and when about to go forward into line we received from Colonel Vincent, commanding the brigade, orders to move to the left at the double-quick, when we took a farm road crossing Plum Run in order to gain a rugged mountain spur called Granite Spur, or Little Round Top.

"The enemy's artillery got range of our column as we were climbing the spur, and the crashing of the shells among the rocks and the tree tops made us move lively along the crest. One or two shells burst in our ranks. Passing to the southern slope of Little Round Top, Colonel Vincent indicated to me the ground my regiment was to occupy, informing me that this was the extreme left of our general line, and that a desperate attack was expected in order to turn that position, concluding by telling me I was to 'hold that ground at all hazards.' This was the last word I heard from him.

"In older to commence by making my right firm, I formed my regiment on the right into line, giving such direction to the line as should best secure the advantage of the rough, rocky, and stragglingly wooded ground.

"The line faced generally toward a more conspicuous eminence southwest of ours, which is known as Sugar Loaf, or Round Top. Between this and my position intervened a smooth and thinly wooded hollow. My line formed, I immediately detached Company B, Captain Morrill commanding, to extend from my left flank across this hollow as a line of skirmishers, with directions to act as occasion might dictate, to prevent a surprise on my exposed flank and rear.

"The artillery fire on our position had meanwhile been constant and heavy, but my formation was scarcely complete when the artillery was replaced by a vigorous infantry assault upon the center of our brigade to my right, but it very soon involved the right of my regiment and gradually extended along my entire front. The action was quite sharp and at close quarters.

"In the midst of this an officer from my center informed me that some important movement of the enemy was going on in his front, beyond that of the line with which we were engaged. Mounting a large rock, I was able to see a considerable body of the enemy moving by the flank in rear of their line engaged, and passing from the direction of the foot of Great Round Top through the valley toward the front of my left. The close engagement not allowing any change of front, I immediately stretched my regiment to the left, by taking intervals by the left flank, and at the same time 'refusing' my left wing, so that it was nearly at right angles with my right, thus occupying about twice the extent of our ordinary front, some of the companies being brought into single rank when the nature of the ground gave sufficient strength or shelter. My officers and men understood my wishes so well that this movement was executed under fire, the right wing keeping tip fire, without giving the enemy any occasion to seize or even to suspect their advantage. But we were not a moment too soon; the enemy's flanking column having gained, their desired direction, burst upon my left, where they evidently had expected an unguarded flank, with great demonstration.

"We opened a brisk fire at close range, which was so sudden and effective that they soon fell back among the rocks and low trees in the valley, only to burst forth again with a shout, and rapidly advanced, firing as they came. They pushed up to within a dozen yards of us before the terrible effectiveness of our fire compelled them to break and take shelter.

"They renewed the assault on our whole front, and for an hour the fighting was severe. Squads of the enemy broke through our line in several places, and the fight was literally hand-to-hand. The edge of the fight rolled backward and forward like a wave. The dead and wounded were now in front and then in our rear. Forced from our position, we desperately recovered it, and pushed the enemy down to the foot of the slope. The intervals of the struggle were seized to remove our wounded (and those of the enemy also), to gather ammunition from the cartridge-boxes of disabled friend or foe on the field, and even to secure better muskets than the Enfields, which we found did not stand service well. Rude shelters were thrown up of the loose rocks that covered the ground.

"Captain Woodward, commanding the Eighty-third Pennsylvania Volunteers, on my right, gallantly maintaining his fight, judiciously and with hearty co-operation made his movements conform to my necessities, so that my right was at no time exposed to a flank attack.

"The enemy seemed to have gathered all their energies for their final assault. We had gotten our thin line into as good a shape as possible, when a strong force emerged from the scrub wood in the valley, as well as I could judge, in two lines in echelon by the right, and, opening a heavy fire, the first line came on as if they meant to sweep everything before them. We opened on them as well as we could with our scanty ammunition snatched from the field.

"It did not seem possible to withstand another shock like this now coming on. Our loss had been severe. One-half of my left wing had fallen and a third of my regiment lay just behind us dead or badly wounded. At this moment my anxiety was increased by a great roar of musketry in my rear, on the farther or northerly slope of Little Round Top, apparently on

the flank of the regular brigade, which was in support of Hazlett's battery on the crest behind us. The bullets from this attack struck into my left rear, and I feared that the enemy might have nearly surrounded the Little Round Top, and only a desperate chance was left for us. My ammunition was soon exhausted. My men were firing their last shot and getting ready to 'club' their muskets.

"It was imperative to strike before we were struck by this overwhelming force in a hand-to-hand fight, which we could not probably have withstood or survived. At that crisis I ordered the bayonet. The word was enough. It ran like fire along the line from man to man, and rose into a shout, with which they sprang forward upon the enemy, now not thirty yards away. The effect was surprising; many of the enemy's first line threw down their arms and surrendered. An officer fired his pistol at my head with one hand while he handed me his sword with the other. Holding fast by our right, and swinging forward our left, we made an extended 'right wheel,' before the enemy's second line broke, and fell back, fighting from tree to tree, many being captured, until we had swept the valley and cleared the front of nearly our entire brigade.

"Meantime, Captain Morrill with his skirmishers (sent out from my left flank), with some dozen or fifteen of the U.S. Sharpshooters who had put themselves under his direction, fell upon the enemy as they were breaking, and by his demonstrations, as well as his well-directed fire, added much to the effect of the charge.

"Having thus cleared the valley and driven the enemy up the western slope of the Great Round Top, not wishing to press so far out as to hazard the ground I was to hold by leaving it exposed to a sudden rush of the enemy, I succeeded (although with some effort to stop my men, who declared they were on the road to Richmond') in getting the regiment into good order and resuming our original position.

"Four hundred prisoners, including two field and several line officers, were sent to the rear. These were mainly from the Fifteenth and Forty-seventh Alabama regiments, with some of the Fourth and Fifth Texas. One hundred and fifty of the enemy were found killed and wounded in our front.

"At dusk Colonel Rice informed me of the fall of Colonel Vincent, which had devolved the command of the brigade on him, and that Colonel Fisher had come up with a brigade to our support. These troops were massed in our rear. It was the understanding, as

Colonel Rice informed me, that Colonel Fisher's brigade was to advance and seize the western slope of Great Round Top, where the enemy had shortly before been driven. But after considerable delay this intention for some reason was not carried into execution.

"We were apprehensive that if the enemy were allowed to strengthen himself in that position he would have a great advantage in renewing the attack on us at daylight or before. Colonel Rice then directed me to make the movement to seize that crest.

"It was now 9 P.M. Without waiting to get ammunition, but trusting in part to the very circumstance of not exposing our movement or our small front by firing, and with bayonets fixed, the little handful of 200 men pressed up the mountain side in every extended order, as the steep and jagged surface of the ground compelled. We heard squads of the enemy falling back before us, and, when near the crest, we met a scattering and uncertain fire, which caused us the great loss of the gallant Lieutenant Linscott, who fell, mortally wounded. In the silent advance in the darkness we laid hold of 25 prisoners, among them a staff officer of General (E. M.) Law, commanding the brigade immediately opposed to us during the fight. Reaching the crest, and reconnoitering the ground, I placed the men in a strong position among the rocks, and informed Colonel Rice, requesting also ammunition and some support to our right, which was very near the enemy, their movements and words even being now distinctly heard by us.

"Some confusion soon after resulted from the attempt of some regiment of Colonel Fisher's brigade to come to our support. They had found a wood road up the mountain, which brought them on my right flank, and also in proximity to the enemy, massed a little before. Hearing their approach, and thinking a movement from that quarter could only be from the enemy, I made disposition to receive them as such. In the confusion which attended the attempt to form them in support of my right, the enemy opened a brisk fire, which disconcerted my efforts to form them and disheartened the supports themselves, so that I saw no more of them that night.

"Feeling somewhat insecure in this isolated position, I sent in for the Eighty-third Pennsylvania, which came speedily, followed by the Forty-fourth New York, and, having seen these well posted, I sent a strong picket to the front, with instructions to report to me every half hour during the night and allowed the rest of my men to sleep on their arms.

"At some time about midnight two regiments of Colonel Fisher's brigade came up the mountain beyond my left, and took position near the summit; but as the enemy did not threaten from that direction I made no effort to connect with them.

"We went into the fight with 386, all told—358 guns. Every pioneer and musician who could carry a musket went into the ranks. Even the sick and footsore, who could not keep up in the march, came up as soon as they could find their regiments and took their places in line of battle, while it was battle, indeed. Some prisoners I had under guard under sentence of court-martial, I was obliged to put into the fight, and they bore their part well, for which I shall recommend a commutation of their sentence.

"The loss, so far as I can ascertain it, is 136—30 of whom were killed, and among the wounded are many mortally.

"Captain Billings, Lieutenant Kendall, and Lieutenant Linscott are officers whose loss we deeply mourn—efficient soldiers and pure and high-minded men.

"In such an engagement there were many incidents of heroism and noble character which should have place even in an official report; but, under present circumstances, I am unable to do justice to them. I will say of that regiment that the resolution, courage, and heroic fortitude which enabled us to withstand so formidable an attack have happily led to so conspicuous a result, that they may safely trust to history to record their merits.

"About noon on the 3d of July we were withdrawn, and formed on the right of the brigade, in the front edge of a piece of woods near the left center of our main line of battle, where we were held in readiness to support our troops, then receiving the severe attack of the afternoon of that day.

"On the 4th we made a reconnaissance to the front, to ascertain the movements of the enemy, but finding that they had retired, at least beyond Willoughby's Run, we returned to Little Round Top, where we buried our dead in the place where we had laid them during the fight, marking each grave by a head-board made of ammunition boxes, with each soldier's name cut upon it. We also buried 50 of the enemy's dead in front of our position of July 2. We then looked after our wounded, whom I had taken the responsibility of putting into the houses of citizens in the vicinity of Little Round Top, and on the morning of the 5th took up our march on the Emmittsburg road."

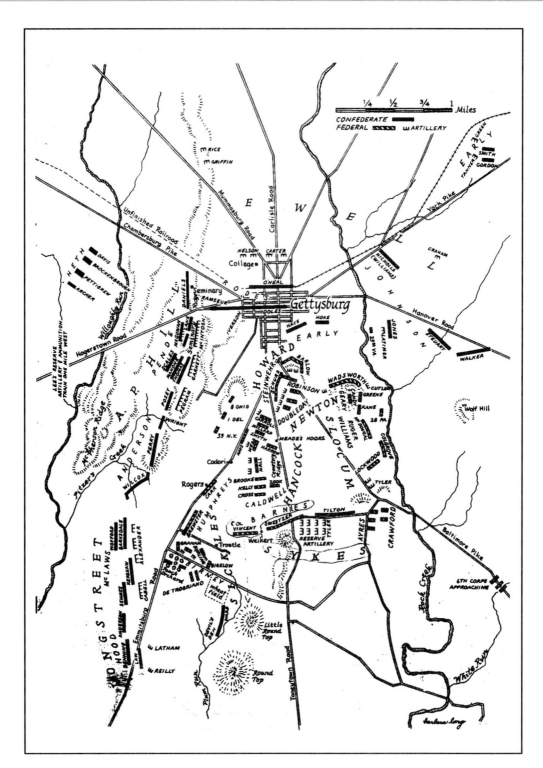

Chamberlain at Gettysburg July 2, 1863

MODULE II

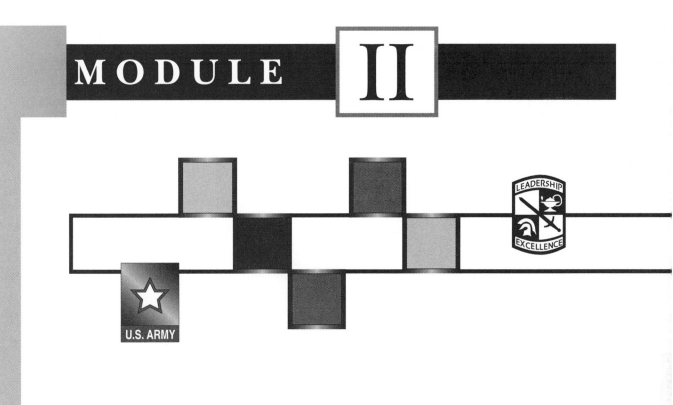

Personal Development (Part II)

Part II of the Personal Development module consists of lessons 13 through 16, which focus developing reasoning skills. This series of four lessons provides a foundation for developing leadership skills by providing you with a set of broadly applicable problem solving concepts, principles, and procedures. All four lessons address the seven-step Army problem-solving process described in FM 22-100. The first lesson provides an overview and begins a step-by-step examination of the process. The step-by-step examination continues through the third lesson and allows you to practice the skills of each step. The fourth lesson provides higher-level practice by requiring you to work in teams, and apply the entire process to a moderately complex problem situation. This problem-solving module provides a sound foundation for the problem-solving aspects of the lessons in the Army Operations module that immediately follows.

Problem Solving— Identifying the Problem

This lesson provides an overview and begins a step-by-step examination of the Army problem solving process. The intent of this lesson is not to make you an expert problem solver, but rather to expose you to a formalized and general process that you can adapt and apply to both military and daily life situations.

The following topics are addressed in this lesson:

- General model of problem solving
- Problem solving heuristics
- Problem statements
- The Army problem solving model

The following TLO is supported in whole or in part by this lesson:

- Solve problems

Following this lesson you will be able to:

- Describe the seven-step Army problem-solving process
- Identify specified, implied, and critical tasks for a given problem or mission
- Develop a problem statement from a situational description

THE ARMY PROBLEM SOLVING PROCESS

INTRODUCTION

Good decision making is an essential leadership skill regardless of whether the decision maker is a corporate executive faced with a problem in the production of a product or a military commander faced with a tactical problem on the battlefield. Each analyzes the problem and makes a decision that affects the welfare of the organization. Each knows that such problem analysis and decision making are among the most important things he or she does. Consequently, each leader consciously or unconsciously uses a system that assists in the problem solving process.

Because few commanders or executives recognize the phases involved in problem analysis and decision making, their methods are rarely foolproof. Often, in times of stress, they abandon their processes altogether in favor of snap decisions based on intuition and "gut feel," thus falling into one of the many traps that block good decisions. In such instances, they argue that a systematic approach is too slow to meet the needs of the situation. They forget that a systematic approach is always more efficient than a disorderly approach that may require repeated attempts to solve the problem in order to get it right. Good leaders and managers, regardless of profession, recognize this. They are aware that the key to good decision making is a systematic and logical approach to problems.

THE PROBLEM SOLVING PROCESS

The problem solving process has been written about extensively and a number of problem solving models have been proposed by various authors. Although the models vary in the number of steps that they use to describe the problem solving sequence, they all promote a similar underlying process. This process requires that the problem first be clearly identified. After the problem is understood, relevant information is gathered, potential solutions to the problem are developed, the solutions are examined to determine the best, and then the selected solution is implemented and monitored. This generic problem solving sequence serves as the basis for the Army Problem Solving Process that is the subject of this paper, and also for the more specialized Troop-Leading Procedure, Military Decision-Making Process, Staff Estimate, and Staff Study methods that are used throughout the Army.

The Army Problem Solving Process, as described in Army Field Manual 22-100, Army Leadership: Be, Know, Do, follows this general sequence, dividing it into seven steps.

Although the steps of the Army Problem Solving Process appear to be sequential, it is important to understand that information or insights gained at almost any step may require that the problem solver go back to a previous step to, for example, revise the problem statement, gather additional information, or develop additional solutions.

Step One—Identify the Problem

A problem may be thought of as an unsettled question, a source of confusion, a troublesome situation, or the difference between what you want to happen and what actually is happening.

Problems may be well structured, ill structured, or possess some intermediate level of structure. A well structured problem is one in which all of the information needed to solve the problem is available, the problem is clear and well defined, a solution method is available, and there is a correct and verifiable answer. The engineering problem of how to design a bridge is an example of a well-structured problem. Ill structured problems, on the other hand, may be difficult or impossible to define and have answers that cannot be verified. The question of how to achieve peace in the Middle East is an example of an ill structured problem. Most of the problems that we face in our personal and professional lives offer an intermediate level of structure. Some information may be known, the problem may be at least partially defined, and a solution can be achieved by routine problem solving methods in combination with critical and creative thinking.

The Army Problem Solving Process

Identify the problem
Identify facts and assumptions
Generate alternatives
Analyze the alternatives
Compare the alternatives
Make and execute your decision
Assess the results

Identifying the problem involves recognizing what the root problem really is and defining the problem in as precise terms as is possible. It is important that the symptoms of the problem not be mistaken for the problem itself. The problem statement should help you focus on the cause of the problem rather than its effect. There are several things you can do to help identify the problem:

1. Compare the problem situation to the desired outcome, goal, or end state.
2. Define the problem boundaries by asking:
   - Who is affected?
   - What is affected?
   - When did it occur?
   - Where is the problem?
   - Why did it occur?
3. Consider how to eliminate obstacles.
4. Phrase the problem statement as a "How to…" or "How can…" question. For example, "How can I minimize the amount of debt that I accrue as a result of attending college?"
5. Ask someone else to define the problem to benefit from his or her experience and perspective.
6. Use visualization aids such as sketches, diagrams, mental maps, or models.
7. Use brainstorming techniques.
8. Take your time and do it right the first time.

Step Two – Identify Facts and Assumptions

Gather information to determine what is already known about a problem, identify gaps in your knowledge of the problem, provide direction for required research into the problem, and serve as standards for evaluating the feasibility and suitability of the alternative problem solutions developed in step three.

The information you gather can be classified into five categories:

1. **Fact:** Information that you know about the situation. An event, past or present, that has been personally observed or has been observed and reported to you is a fact. Documents such as Army manuals, regulations, and policies, as well as references and texts may also provide relevant facts. When using such sources, you must determine whether the publication is providing information that is always true, sometime true, or simply conjecture or opinion.
2. **Assumption:** A statement that you believe to be true but do not have facts to verify its truth.

When solving problems, assumptions should be kept to a minimum. You should make only those assumptions that are essential to generating solutions to the problem. Scrutinize each assumption and ask yourself, "Do I have to make this assumption in order to solve the problem?" Do not adopt overly optimistic assumptions that lead you to "assume away" the problem.

3. **Criteria:** The information that defines the limits within which the solution to a problem must fall. Criteria are used to determine which solution is best. There are two types of criteria:

   - **Screening Criteria:** Essential features that any acceptable solution to the problem must possess. If a potential course of action fails to meet even a single screening criterion, that course of action is rejected. For example, a course of action that would not result in the problem being solved by a critical deadline would not be adopted.
   - **Evaluation Criteria:** Features that we desire the problem solution to provide, but which are not truly essential. For example, if the problem that we face is which lawn tractor to purchase, the lawn aerator attachment that comes with Brand X may be desirable, but not essential. Evaluation criteria and screening criteria often deal with the same aspect of the problem and differ only in degree. For example, if we only have $1,800 for the purchase of our lawn tractor, we would apply the $1,800 limit as a screening criterion and eliminate from our consideration any lawn tractors that cost more than $1,800. When examining the remaining lawn tractors, we would consider the cost of the lawn tractor as an evaluation criterion and look more favorably on those lawn tractors that cost less.
   - **Benchmark:** A value that represents the preferred state of an evaluation criterion. Benchmarks help us determine if an alternative is good enough or desirable. Benchmarks can be established through reasoning, historical data, current allocation, and averaging. Averaging is the least preferred method. Using the lawn tractor purchase example, we might find that the optimum size engine produces 12 horsepower, although lawn tractors with as little as 8 horsepower will serve adequately. We

might then use the 12 horsepower figure as a benchmark for evaluating the engine size of the various lawn tractors we are considering.

4. **Opinion:** A personal judgment that you have made or that some other individual has made.

5. **Definition:** Used to clarify technical terms, to provide precise nomenclature on particular equipment, or to describe specific operations or procedures that may not be familiar to you or others involved in the problem solving situation.

Of these categories of information, facts and criteria are the most important. Facts establish the truths upon which solutions can confidently be based, and criteria establish the limits within which problem solutions must fall and allow us to select from among alternative solutions. Opinions are of the least value in problem solving

Step Three—Generate Alternatives

Alternatives are ways to solve the problem. The best possible solution to a problem can be determined only after considering alternative solutions. The goal in this step is to produce as many alternative solutions to the problem as possible within existing time constraints. Alternative solutions should be different from each other in some significant way. Identifying acceptable alternative solutions is accomplished by analyzing the effect of the possible alternative solutions on the problem environment. An analysis of the total problem environment facilitates this step.

Developing possible solutions requires creativity and imagination. A recognition and avoidance of the barriers to creative thinking, adoption of a questioning attitude, and use of brainstorming techniques will facilitate this process. Barriers affecting the creative thinking process include:

1. **Habit:** A reluctance to change from the old or the accepted way of doing things.

2. **Fear:** The apprehension of adopting new ways or discarding old ways.

3. **Inertia:** A lack of desire to expend the energy necessary to effect change.

4. **Prejudice:** The enmity toward or the affection for something.

Step Four—Analyze the Alternatives

Examine each alternative solution to identify its intended and unintended consequences, resource or other constraints, and advantages and disadvantages. It is especially important that each alternative solution be analyzed in terms of the screening and evaluation criteria identified in step two. It is also critical that all alternatives be considered and objectively analyzed. Do not prejudge the situation by favoring any one alternative over the others.

Step Five—Compare the Alternatives

All alternative solutions are evaluated and compared simultaneously, not sequentially, by first applying screening criteria to eliminate any alternatives that fail to meet essential minimum standards.

The next step is to apply evaluation criteria to the remaining alternatives to determine the degree of benefit that each provides. A convenient way to compare alternatives is to use a raw data matrix. A raw data matrix lists the courses of action down the left column of a grid and the names of the evaluation criteria across the top row of the grid. Each cell of the grid contains a value or quality of the evaluation criterion for a course of action. For example (see following table):

When comparing alternatives, you should consider how much difference on a given evaluation criterion is significant. For example, when considering the purchase of a lawn tractor that costs nearly $1,800, a difference in price of only $15 between Brand X and Brand Y is probably not a significant difference, and the two brands should be considered as

LAWN TRACTOR PURCHASE					
Name	Cost	Cutting Width	Speed	Aerator Attachment?	Horsepower
Brand X	$1,795	48 in.	7 mph	Yes	11 hp
Brand Y	$1,780	48 in.	4 mph	No	12 hp
Brand Z	$1,625	42 in.	5 mph	No	10 hp

		Cutting		Aerator	
LAWN TRACTOR PURCHASE					
Name	**Cost**	**Width**	**Speed**	**Attachment?**	**Horsepower**
Criterion Weight	4	2	1	1	2
Brand X	$1,795	48 in.	7 mph	Yes	11 hp
Brand Y	$1,780	48 in.	4 mph	No	12 hp
Brand Z	$1,625	42 in.	5 mph	No	10 hp

equal on the cost criterion. You should decide how much difference you will consider to be significant for each of your evaluation criteria before you compare the alternatives. In fact, you should decide this when you develop the evaluation criteria in step two. By making this decision before you begin to compare the alternatives, you can help avoid inadvertently establishing criterion standards that lead to a biased decision. Benchmarks can also help you decide if an alternative offers a significant benefit on each evaluation criterion.

Step Six—Make and Execute Your Decision

The best solution to a problem is that solution which meets the screening criteria and ranks highest against the evaluation criteria. It can be difficult to compare several alternative courses of action on many screening criteria. This difficulty is compounded when the screening criteria are not all of equal importance. It may be useful to numerically weigh the screening criteria to reflect their importance. Criteria that are of equal and basic importance are given a weight of 1 and criteria that are more important are given higher numeric weights to reflect their degree of importance. For example, if cost was very important, and cutting width and horsepower were moderately important, the raw data matrix for the lawn tractor purchase might look like this (See table above):

Even after the evaluation criteria information is displayed in a raw data matrix and weighted according to importance, it may still be difficult to clearly determine which alternative solution is the best. It

may be necessary to convert the raw data matrix into a decision matrix to facilitate the comparison and selection. The use of decision matrices is addressed in a future lesson.

Once you have decided which course of action to implement, it will be necessary to translate your decision into a plan of action and implement this plan. If you are not the deciding authority, you may have to prepare a decision paper or decision briefing for the individual who must make the final decision. In this decision paper or briefing, you will lay out the steps you followed in deciding on your recommended course of action. You should define the problem; provide essential facts, assumptions, criteria, opinions, and definitions; describe the alternatives you developed; describe the results of your analysis of each alternative; and provide the results of your comparison of alternative courses of action.

Step Seven—Assess the Results

The Army Problem Solving Process does not end with the implementation of the selected course of action. You must monitor the progress of the implementation plan and be prepared to make adjustments as needed to keep the plan moving forward. Monitoring the execution of the plan is made easier if, before execution begins, you identify the critical events of the plan and essential standards of performance for the elements of the plan. This step of the Army Problem Solving Process also provides an opportunity for observation and learning that can better prepare you for future problem solving efforts.

Problem Solving–
Developing Solutions

This lesson continues the step-by-step examination and practice of the seven steps of the Army problem-solving process. The lesson is divided into two main parts. In the first part, you will apply analytic skills to identify needed information, categorize information, and evaluate the validity and utility of information. In the second part, you will apply creative thinking skills to generate potential solutions to a problem situation. In doing this, you will gain practical experience in brainstorming. Impediments to creative thinking are also illustrated as part of pre-class activity assignments.

The following topics are addressed in this lesson:

- Application of the general model of problem solving
- Creative thinking
- Brainstorming methods to identify courses of action
- Use of screening and evaluation criteria

The following TLOs are supported in whole or in part by this lesson:

- Apply critical thinking skills
- Solve problems

Following this lesson you will be able to:

- Classify information as fact, assumption, criterion, opinion, or definition
- Assess the importance and accuracy of information using critical thinking skills
- Apply brainstorming techniques to generate potential problem solutions
- List common impediments to creative thinking

SOLVING PROBLEMS

BY J. S. NAIRNE

In this section we'll consider some of the thought processes people use when they consciously seek to solve problems. Obviously, problem solving is an extremely adaptive skill. When you're faced with a problem, such as how to get your car started in the morning, there is a goal, a running motor, and a certain amount of uncertainty about how to reach that goal. To study the solution process, psychologists typically use problems like the following:

> It's early morning, still dark, and you're trying to get dressed. Your 2-month-old baby, snuggled in her crib at the foot of the bed, sleeps peacefully after a night of sustained wailing. You can't turn on the light—she'll wake up for sure—but the black socks and the blue socks are mixed up in the drawer. Let's see, you recall, I have 5 pairs of black socks and 4 pairs of blue socks. How many socks do I need to take out of the drawer in order to guarantee myself a pair of matching colors?

Notice there is a goal (selecting a pair of matching socks), and it's not immediately obvious how to get from the problem to the solution. Psychologists call this a **well-defined problem** (even though you

may have no idea how to solve it) because there is a well-stated goal, a clear starting point, and a relatively easy way to tell when a solution has been reached. Other kinds of problems do not have well-stated goals, clear starting points, or effective mechanisms for evaluating progress—these are called **ill-defined problems.** Ever wonder about the secret of happiness? Maybe you can agree on the startingpoint (I'm not happy enough), but the goal (happiness) is pretty tough to define, and it's not at all clear how to reach that goal or measure progress.

Most of the research done on the thought processes involved in problem solving has been conducted using well-defined problems, such as our sock problem or those involving math or logic. We'll mainly consider these types of problems in this section, but ill-defined problems can be tackled with some of the same strategies. It's believed that ill-defined problems may sometimes require unique cognitive processes (Jausovec, 1997), but generally the same psychological processes are assumed to operate in the vast majority of problem-solving settings.

THE IDEAL PROBLEM SOLVER

Let's start by considering a set of guidelines that highlight the psychological processes relevant to problem solving. These particular guidelines were developed

CONCEPT SUMMARY   The IDEAL Problem Solver

STATE OF PROBLEM SOLVING	DESCRIPTION	EXAMPLE
Identify	Recognize that a problem exists.	In the basement, Greg notices a small amount of water underneath the washing machine.
Define	Represent the problem information in the most efficient way.	Greg notices that there is water dripping down from a pipe above him, just under where the bathroom is.
Explore	Consider possible solutions.	Greg considers trying to fix it himself, asking his handy friend to help, or calling a plumber.
Act	Employ the chosen strategy.	Greg decides to give his friend a call, and watches as he diagnoses and fixes the problem.
Look	Evaluate the effectiveness of the chosen strategy.	Greg notices that the pool of water is gone, and that the pipe has stopped leaking.

by psychologists John Bransford and Barry Stein and are recommended in their book *The Ideal Problem Solver* (1993). Bransford and Stein use the letters of the acronym IDEAL to stand for the five major steps that underlie effective problem solving. These steps are briefly described here and are summarized in the concept summary table.

1. *Identify* the problem. Obviously, before you can solve a problem, you need to recognize that there is, in fact, a problem that needs solving. Strange knocking sounds, little spots of oil, and uneven acceleration are signs of car problems, but if they need to be recognized as symptoms before the necessary diagnosis and repairs can begin.

2. *Define,* or represent, the problem information in the most efficient way. Not only is it important to define the goal—What exactly are you trying to solve?—it's also important to correctly interpret the problem components you have to work with. As we discussed previously, the ticket scalping problem that opened the chapter is difficult because most people fail to see that Wayne actually made two *separate* ticket transactions. They tend to think about just *one* pair of tickets, so the cost of the second transaction is applied incorrectly to the first.

3. *Explore* a variety of problem strategies. Once you have identified the problem, defined the goal, and developed some understanding of the information you have to work with, it's time to try to move forward toward a possible solution. To do this, you must decide on a strategy. Most solution strategies amount to "rules of thumb." They don't guarantee a solution, but they can speed up the problem-solving process or at least move you closer to your goal.

4. *Act* on the problem strategy that you chose in step 3. Work through the solution strategy, and as part of the process try to anticipate any dead ends or obstacles that might prevent you from reaching the goal.

5. *Look* back and evaluate the effectiveness of your selected strategy. Have you in fact solved the problem? It's important to identify and correct any errors that have occurred before moving on and trying something new.

If you follow these five problem-solving guidelines, you have approximated the IDEAL problem solver (Bransford & Stein, 1993). Now let's consider some of the processes involved in greater detail.

IDENTIFYING AND DEFINING: PROBLEM REPRESENTATION

To identify and define a problem correctly it's essential to represent the problem information in the correct way. By *problem representation,* psychologists mean that you need to understand exactly what information is given and how that information can potentially be used. Solving a problem is like building a house. If you can't find the right tools or if you don't know how to use the tools. once you've found them, you're unlikely to ever complete the house.

Take the sock problem, for example. The correct answer is three. There are only two colors, so with three samples, you will get two that match. If you're like most people, you let the math get in your way. Did you start worrying about the four to five ratio of blue to black? Did you briefly consider calculating some sort of probability? To solve this problem, you must pay attention to the right problem components—you need to see the problem in the right way. Most people simply fail to detect which information is relevant and which is not. They get hung up with ratios and probabilities and the like. Let's consIder another example.

> Dr. Adams is interrupted from his daily rounds by the arrival of a new patient, a child, who has been injured in a fall. "My god!" Adams cries, "It's my son!" Moments later, Dr. Henderson arrives with the same sense of panic and grief. "My son, my dear son," Henderson moans in despair. Is it a tragic mix-up?

You probably solved this one almost immediately, but it demonstrates the point. The two doctors are the mother and the father, which makes it easy to see why both are panicked about their injured son. But the word *doctor,* with its powerful gender connotations, can create an obstacle to correct problem representation. If you initially identify and define the doctors as men, the solution becomes more involved. Seeing the problem in the right way is even more difficult because the doctors have different last names.

Functional Fixedness

The two-doctor problem illustrates a common obstacle to correct problem representation. People allow their preconceptions, even their prejudices, to lock them into an incorrect view of the problem information (Bassok et al., 1995; Dixon & Moore, 1997). Consider another example called the Maier two-string problem (after Maier, 1931). Imagine you are standing in a room with two lightweight strings hanging from the ceiling. The strings are hung such a distance apart that, when holding one of the strings, you cannot reach the other. Using only a pair of pliers, which happens to be sitting on a table in the room, can you tie the strings together?

This is a reasonably difficult problem because most people have a certain set, or fixed, way of viewing the function of pliers. The solution is to tie the pliers to one of the strings and swing it, like a pendulum, while you hold onto the other string. The correct solution, however, requires you to *restructure* the way that you normally think about pliers. Pliers are good for grabbing and holding, but in this case they can serve as pendulum weights, too.

Psychologists use the term **functional fixedness** to refer to this tendency to see objects, and their functions, in certain fixed and typical ways. Doctors are men, pliers are for grabbing, and so on. Functional fixedness is an obstacle to problem solving because it prevents you from recognizing the problem-solving tools that are present in the situation. Now try solving the problem this problem. You enter a room in which a candle, a box of tacks, some matches, and a hammer lie on a table. You are told to mount the candle on the wall so that it will still burn properly, using only the objects on the table. Work on the problem for a while; we'll return to its solution shortly.

First, let's stop for a moment and think about the adaptive significance of a concept like functional fixedness. How can such a tendency possibly be adaptive? Wouldn't it be better to consider all possible object uses? Actually, the answer is "no." Most of the time, if you view objects in fixed ways or use fixed strategies that have worked well in the past, you're likely to be successful. After all, pliers usually do solve problems having to do with holding and grabbing, don't they? The problems we've been considering are actually quite artificial—they're set up by psychologists to lead the mind astray in order to provide insight into normal problem-solving methods. Generally, the fact that people tend to rely on well-established habits of perception and thought (sometimes called **mental sets**) is probably an effective overall problem-solving strategy.

Were you able to solve the candle-mounting problem? The correct solution is to dump the tacks out of the box, mount the box on the wall with one of the tacks, and then put the candle in the box (Duncker, 1945). The problem is difficult because most people see the box only as a device for holding the tacks, not as a potential problem-solving tool. They become *fixed* in their views about the *functions* of objects, and thereby fail to identify and define all of the available problem tools correctly.

EXPLORING AND ACTING: PROBLEM STRATEGIES

It's important to represent a problem correctly, but problem representation alone cannot guarantee a solution. You also need an arsenal of problem *strategies*—techniques that allow you to move systematically toward a problem solution. Two classes of problem strategies can be used to solve problems: *algorithms* and *heuristics.*

Algorithms and Heuristics

For some well-defined problems you can use **algorithms,** which are step-by-step roles or procedures that guarantee a solution. You can use algorithms to solve simple math problems, for example, because there are fixed rules for addition, subtraction, and so on. As long as you use the rules properly, you will always arrive at the correct solution. Solving anagrams, such as MBLOPRE, is another case in point. There are seven letters in the word, which means there are 5040 possible combinations of the letters. If you systematically work out each of the possible sequences, one will eventually provide a solution to the PROBLEM. But it could take a long time.

Computers are often programmed to use algorithms because computers are capable of examining lots of information very quickly. But algorithms are not always practical strategies for problem solution, even for computers. Consider chess, for example. In principle, it would be possible to use algorithms to play chess—the computer would simply need to consider all of the possible consequences of a particular move. But practically, computers cannot examine all possible outcomes in a chess game; they can examine only some of them. Consider that there are some 10^{40} possible game sequences, so even if a computer could calculate a game in under one-millionth of one-thousandth of a second, it would still require 10^{21}

Inside the Problem

TRANSFERRING STRATEGIES ACROSS PROBLEMS

Solving problems through analogy is one of the most valuable heuristics you can use. But it requires that you see the connection between the problems that you've solved before and the current task at hand. Unfortunately, making the connection turns out to be quite difficult, even if the previous and current problems share many problem features. Consider the following problem, taken from Gick and McGarry (1992):

> One Saturday night, at a local country dance, 40 people, 20 men and 20 women, showed up to dance. The dance was a "contra dance," in which men and women face each other in lines. From 8 to 10 P.M., there were 20 heterosexual couples (consisting of one man and one woman each; i.e., two men or women cannot dance together) dancing on the floor. At 10 P.M., however, two women left, leaving 38 people to dance. Could the dance caller make arrangements so that the remaining people could all dance together at the same time in 19 heterosexual couples ?

This problem is quite easy for most people to solve. They recognize that 20 men and 18 women cannot be divided into 19 mixed-sex couples, so the answer is "no" (this is sometimes called a "parity" problem).

> You are given a checkerboard and 32 dominoes. Each domino covers exactly two adjacent squares on the board. Thus, the 32 dominoes can cover all 64 squares of the checkerboard. Now suppose two squares are cut off at diagonally opposite corners of the board. If possible, show how you would place 31 dominoes on the board so that all of the 62 remaining squares are covered. If you think it is impossible, give a proof of why (Gick and McGarry, 1992, p. 625).

This problem turns out to be much more difficult to solve, even though it's actually very similar to the dance problem (it's also a "parity" problem). Just substitute the word "man" for black and the word "woman" for red, and think of the domino as the pairing of a mixed-sex couple. The first problem should serve as an effective analogy for solving the second. But most people fail to see the connection. In the study by Gick and McGarry (1992), people were first shown how to solve the dance-partner problem and were then asked to solve the checkerboard problem. Very few solved the second problem correctly even though they understood the solution to the first.

What kinds of factors promote successful transfer from one problem-solving situation to another? For one thing, people who have a great deal of experience in a particular area seem better able to draw connections across situations relevant to their expertise than do nonexperts. Experts are able to see what amounts to the deep structure of a problem (its true meaning representation), and they can therefore map one kind of problem to another by noting how the problems are similar (Novick, 1988). Cognitive scientists familiar with parity problems, for example, will have little trouble recognizing the common link between the dance and checkerboard problems.

It also helps if problem-solving hints are provided. In our checkerboard problem, if subjects are told to try using the dance-partner solution as a way of solving the checkerboard problem, performance improves significantly. Finally, it may even help transfer somewhat if your initial attempts at solving the first problem fail. If you get stuck while you're solving one kind of problem and then find yourself stuck in a similar way during a later problem, you tend to use your earlier failure as a way of reminding yourself how you solved the first (Gick & McGarry, 1992).

centuries to examine all the game possibilities (Best, 1989). It could do so; it would just take a very long time. Another problem with algorithms is that they work for only certain kinds of well-defined problems—there is no algorithm, for example, for deciding how to be happy, or for deciding on an appropriate career.

In cases in which it's not feasible to use an algorithm, or in cases in which one is not readily available, it's possible to use **heuristics,** which are essentially problem-solving "rules of thumb." To solve an anagram, especially one with seven letters, it's

hardly expedient to use an algorithmic approach, examining all 5040 possible letter sequences. Instead, you turn to heuristics. You know that English words don't usually begin with MB, or end with BL, so you can avoid checking out those possibilities. You can use your knowledge about English words to make guesses about the most likely solution possibilities. Heuristics are extremely adaptive problem-solving tools because they often open the door to a quick and accurate solution. In natural environments, quick solutions can mean the difference between life and death. An organism cannot spend its time wrapped in thought, systematically working through a long list of solution possibilities. Instead, it's adaptive for the organism to guess, as long as the guess is based on some kind of logic.

Means–Ends Analysis

One common heuristic that people use to solve problems is **means–ends analysis,** which attacks problems by devising *means,* or actions, that are designed to reduce the gap between the current starting point and the desired goal, or *ends* (Newell & Simon, 1972). Usually, this strategy requires breaking down the problem into a series of simpler subgoals, in which the appropriate means to an end are more immediately visible. Let's assume that Peter, a normally nonachieving undergraduate, wants to start a relationship with Jill, the brightest student in his psychology class. Obviously, asking Jill out immediately is unlikely to succeed, so Peter breaks the problem down into more manageable components.

First, he reasons, he'll impress her in class by making an insightful comment during the lecture. He now has a new goal, acting intelligent in class, for which there is relatively straightforward means—he needs to study hard so he can master the material. Assuming he is successful (everyone now thinks he is an amazingly insightful young man), he devises a new subgoal: making some kind of sustained contact with Jill. Forming a small study group would be a good means to that end, he surmises, so he approaches the recently impressed Jill with the idea. Notice the key ingredients of the problem-solving strategy: Establish where you are, figure out where you want to be, and then devise a means for effectively getting you from here to there. Often, as in Peter's case, means—ends analysis is made more effective by working systematically through subgoals.

Working Backward

Another effective heuristic is **working backward**—starting at the goal state and trying to move back toward the starting point. Suppose someone asked you to generate a set of anagrams. How would you proceed? Would you try to generate sets of randomly arranged letters and then see whether a particular sequence forms a word? Of course not. You would start with the solution, the word, and work backward by mixing up the known sequence.

Let's consider another example. You're working on a biology project tracking the growth of bacteria in a petri dish. You know that this particular strain of bacteria doubles every 2 hours. After starting the experiment, you discover that the petri dish is exactly full after 12 hours. After how many hours was the petri dish exactly half full? To solve this one, it's better to work backward. If the dish is full after 12 hours, and it takes 2 hours for the bacteria to double, what did the dish look like after 10 hours? This turns out to be the answer, which is arrived at rather simply if the problem is attacked in reverse.

Check your knowledge about problem solving by answering the following questions.
1. Decide whether each of the following problems is *well defined* or *ill defined.* Justify your answer.
    a. Finding your way to a new restaurant in town: _____
    b. Receiving an "A" in your psychology course: _____
    c. Making your lab partner in chemistry fall madly in love with you: _____
    d. Baking a cherry cheesecake that won't taste like plumber's caulk: _____
2. Try to identify the problem-solving strategy at work in each of the following examples. Choose from the following terms: algorithm, means–ends analysis, working backward, searching for analogies.
    a. On the final exam Myka looks for connections between the physics problem on the test and the ones he worked on while studying. _____
    b. Rachel needs a three-letter word that begins with R to complete the crossword puzzle. She mindlessly considers all possible two-letter combinations, placing them after R until she arrives at an acceptable word. _____
    c. Hector really needs an A in his philosophy class, but he has no idea what it takes. He decides to concentrate on writing a really top-notch first paper. _____
    d. Courtney needs to generate a set of anagrams for a school project. To generate each anagram, she starts with a word and then scrambles the letters. _____

Searching for Analogies

Finally, another useful heuristic for problem solving is **searching for analogies.** If you can see a resemblance between the current problem and some task that you to solved in the past, you can quickly obtain an acceptable solution. Imagine that a man buys a horse for $60 and sells it for $70. Later, he buys the same horse back for $80 and sells it again for $90. How much money did the man make in the horse-trading business?

LOOKING AND LEARNING

The ideal problem solver identifies and defines the problem, seeks the best problem representation, and explores and acts on problem strategies. But the whole process is incomplete unless you also *look and learn* from your experience (Bransford & Stein, 1993). Think about a student who tries to use the principles of psychology to improve a test score. The goal is clear—an improved test score—and the student could develop a variety of possible study strategies to enhance performance. However, the ideal problem solver doesn't stop at the final score; the ideal problem solver "debugs" performance in an effort to maximize the information gained.

By analyzing your performance in detail, noting where you made mistakes as well as correct answers, you can determine whether your strategy helped solve one kind of problem, but not another. Through an after-the-fact analysis, you can gain insight into *why* a particular heuristic failed or succeeded. Look and learn from your experience so that the next time, you can do better still.

MAKING DECISIONS

BY J. S. NAIRNE

We turn our attention now to the topic of **decision making,** which deals with the thought processes involved in evaluating and choosing from among a set of alternatives. Obviously, decision making and problem solving are closely related. When you make a decision, you're confronted with a set of alternatives and you must make a choice. The choice is almost always accompanied by *risk,* so it's in your interest to evaluate and select among the alternatives with care. Think about the military strategist on the brink of conflict who must determine whether to attack with vigor or pull back in retreat. Or consider the physician who must choose between a risky treatment that may kill or save a patient with some unsettling probabilities.

Like problem solving, decision making is influenced by how you represent the alternatives in your mind, and by your choice of decision-making strategies. Let's examine how each of these processes affects the choices we make.

THE FRAMING OF DECISION ALTERNATIVES

It turns out that the way the alternatives are structured, called **framing,** has a dramatic influence on the decision-making process. In a study by McNeil and colleagues (1982), practicing hospital physicians were asked to choose between two forms of treatment for a patient with lung cancer: either a surgical operation on the lungs, or a six-week treatment with radiation. Half of the physicians received the following information prior to making the choice:

Of 100 people having surgery, 10 will die during treatment; 32 will have died by one year, and 66 will have died by five years. Of 100 people having radiation therapy; none will die during treatment, 23 will have died by one year, and 78 will have died by five years.

Put yourself in the doctor's shoes—which would you choose? The other half of the physicians were given the following:

Of 100 people having surgery, 90 will be alive immediately after the treatment, 68 will be alive after one year, and 34 will be alive after five years. Of 100 people having radiation therapy, all will be alive immediately after treatment, 77 will be alive after one year, and 22 will be alive after five years.

Do you want to change your mind? Actually, exactly the same information is given in each of the choice scenarios. The only difference is that in the first description the treatment outcomes are described, or framed, in terms of who will die, whereas the second description emphasizes who is likely to survive. The treatment consequences are exactly the same in each case. Believe it or not, practicing physicians are more than twice as likely to choose radiation when the choices are death based than when the choices are framed around who will live. Why? The reason probably has to do with the fact that death is abhorrent to physicians. The surgery alternative in the first example clearly states that people will die during the treatment, so it is to be avoided. Interestingly, doctors are even more susceptible to these framing effects than patients who are given the same choices!

This example reinforces the point that human decision making is not always a rational process (at least from an objective perspective). People are prone to inconsistency in their judgments, in part, because our minds weigh information differently in different situations (Kahneman et al., 1982). Let's consider another example. Suppose you were given the choice of winning $40 with a probability of 0.40 or winning $30 with a probability of 0.50. Which would you choose? From a statistical perspective, there is a rational choice based on the *expected value* or each alternative. An expected value is simply the value that you would expect to gain, on average, by choosing one particular alternative many times. Winning $40 with a probability of 0.40 leads to an expected average gain of $16 ($40 × 0.40); winning $30 with a probability of 0.50 leads to an expected value of $15 ($30 × .50). The rational choice, then, is to pick the first alternative, which is what most people do.

But suppose you were given a choice of winning $40 with a probability of 0.80 or winning $30 with a probability of 1.00. Again, the rational choice is to pick the first alternative (expected values of $32 versus $30), but people tend to act differently in this context. They go for a sure thing. How people weigh decision-making alternatives depends on the particular situation. In general, when people are confronted with situations in which they think they can gain something (such as winning money), they tend to avoid taking risks—they choose certainty. But if the outcomes potentially lead to a loss of some kind (such as someone dying), people are much more likely we take a risk that will limit or avoid the loss.

Another factor to be considered is the decision maker's interpretation of the problem. In the medical example, the doctors seemed to be acting irrationally, switching choices depending on how the same information was framed. But the treatment problem might have been interpreted quite differently by the doctors in the two situations. For example, when the alternatives were death based, perhaps the doctors readily connected the deaths to the treatment (surgery will kill 10 people and radiation none). In contrast, when the alternatives were framed around who was living, they might have focused on long-term survival and not thought too much about the hazards of treatment (34 people who receive surgery will be alive after five years, but only 22 radiation patients will survive this long). Thus, you cannot assume that the problem information was identical in the two framings—you need to take into account how the problem was actually represented in the mind of the decision maker (Berkeley & Humphreys, 1982; Einhorn & Hogarth, 1981; Jou et al., 1996).

DECISION-MAKING HEURISTICS

When people are forced to choose from among a set of alternatives, most rely on heuristics, or rules of thumb, just as they do when solving problems. These strategies simplify the decision-making process and often lead to correct judgments, but they can sometimes lead you to the wrong decision.

Representativeness

Suppose you're asked to judge the likelihood of some event falling into class A or B. In such a case people often rely on a rule of thumb called the **representativeness heuristic.** They arrive at their decision by comparing the similarity of the object or event in question to the average, or prototypical, member of each class. It's easiest to demonstrate with an example. Let's assume that your friends, the Renfields, have six children. If B denotes boy and G denotes girl, which of the following two birth order sequences do you think is more likely?

1. B B B G G G
2. B G G B G B

If you said the second alternative, you're like most people. Actually, according to the rules of probability, the two outcomes are equally likely. Whether your next child will be a boy or a girl doesn't depend on the sex of your previous children—each event is independent of the other. Still, people favor the second alternative because the first sequence clashes with their worldview of randomness. The first sequence just doesn't look like the outcome of a random process—it's not *representative* of randomness.

What if you flipped a coin six times and you got six heads? You'd probably think it was a crooked coin. Again, a sequence of six heads isn't similar to, or representative of, what you think of as a random sequence. You have taken the outcome and compared it to some standard and made your decision accordingly. People use the representativeness heuristic all the time to make decisions in real-world settings. For example, clerks in stores use the type of products that a shopper buys as a way of judging age. If someone loads his or her shopping cart with products normally thought to be representative of an older consumer, the clerk's estimate of the shopper's age increases (McCall, 1994).

Using a heuristic such as representativeness is adaptive and beneficial most of the time, but it can lead to irrational decisions. Imagine that you're leafing through a stack of questionnaires that have been filled out by some adult men. One of the respondents lists his height as 6 feet 5 inches, but his answers are so sloppily written that you can't make out his circled profession—it's either bank president or basketball player (NBA). You need to make a choice: Which is he? Most people choose NBA player because the applicant is tall and apparently not interested in careful writing (Beyth-Marom & Lichtenstein, 1984). But this is actually an illogical choice, because the odds of someone in the sample being a professional basketball player is extremely low—bank presidents outnumber NBA players by a wide margin (probably at least 50 to 1). In choosing basketball player, people have ignored the *base rate,* or the proportion of times that an object or event is likely to occur in the population being sampled.

The representativeness heuristic also dupes people into committing what is called the *conjunction error.* Consider the following: Linda is 31 years old, single, outspoken, and very bright. She majored in philosophy. As a student she was deeply concerned with issues of discrimination and social justice and participated in antinuclear demonstrations. Which of the following alternatives is more likely?

1. Linda is a bank teller.
2. Linda is a bank teller and active in the feminist movement.

CONCEPT SUMMARY   Decision-Making Heuristics

HEURISTIC	DESCRIPTION	EXAMPLE
Representativeness	We arrive at a decision by comparing the similarity of the object or event to the average member of each class.	Juan meets his new college roommate, Bryce, who is 6′10″ and very athletic-looking. Juan assumes that Bryce is a basketball player, probably on scholarship.
Availability	We estimate the odds of some event occurring based on the ease with which examples come to mind.	Stella reads so much in the newspaper about car accidents that she believes her chances of dying in a car accident are greater than her chances of dying from a stroke.
Anchoring and adjustment	Judgments are influenced by initial estimates.	Stacey holds a garage sale and sells two big items early for a total of $150. Throughout the day, she overestimates how much she is making, and is disappointed to learn her actual profit.

In a study conducted by Tversky and Kahneman (1983), 85% of the participants judged alternative 2 to be the more likely. Why? Because Linda's description is more representative of someone active in the feminist movement than it is of a bank teller. But think about it—how can the odds of two things happening together be higher than the likelihood of anyone of those events happening alone? Notice that the second alternative is actually a subset of the first alternative and therefore cannot be more likely. Those who choose alternative 2 have acted illogically, at least from the standpoint of the rational decision maker.

Availability

At other times, when asked to estimate the odds of some event occurring, we rely on our memories to help us make our decisions. You are using an **availability heuristic** when you base your estimates on the ease with which examples of the event come to mind. Imagine you're asked to estimate the likelihood that you will forget to turn off your alarm clock on Friday night. If you can easily remember lots of instances in which your Saturday morning sleep was interrupted by a blasting alarm, your estimate of for-

getting is likely to be high. You have relied on your previous experiences—particularly those experiences that easily come to mind—as a basis for judging probability.

Once again, the availability heuristic is likely to be an adaptive strategy much of the time. But, as with the representativeness heuristic, researchers can arrange situations which make this decision-making practice ineffective. Which do you think is more likely, an English word that begins with the letter K or an English word with K in the third position? By now you're probably skeptical about your first choice, but most people think that English words that begin with K are more likely (Tversky & Kahneman, 1973). In fact, English words that have K in the third position are much more common (the ratio is about 3 to 1). Which do you think is more likely, someone dying from any kind of accident or someone dying from a stroke? Accidents, right? It's not even close. Over twice as many people are likely to die from stroke than from any kind of accident (Slovic et al., 1982). People make the error because examples of the incorrect alternative are more likely to come to mind. It's easier to think of an English word with K in the first position, and accidental deaths get much more publicity than deaths due to stroke.

Anchoring and Adjustment

Judgments are also influenced by starting points—that is, by any initial estimates that you might be given. For example, Tversky and Kahneman (1974) asked people to estimate the number of African countries belonging to the United Nations. Prior to answering, subjects were given a number (between 0 and 100) and were asked to pick the number of countries by moving up or down from this starting point. So, you might be given the number 10 and asked to estimate the number of countries using 10 as a base. For groups that received 10 and 65 as the initial starting points, the estimated number of African countries was 25 and 45, respectively. The judgments were apparently adjusted based on initial estimates, or *anchors,* in a direction that stayed close to the starting point. The smaller the base, the fewer the countries that were estimated.

In another experiment described by Tversky and Kahneman (1974), one group of people was asked to estimate the product of the following numbers:

$$1 \cdot 2 \cdot 3 \cdot 4 \cdot 5 \cdot 6 \cdot 7 \cdot 8$$

whereas a second group was asked to estimate the product of the same numbers presented in reverse order:

$$8 \cdot 7 \cdot 6 \cdot 5 \cdot 4 \cdot 3 \cdot 2 \cdot 1$$

The correct answer in both cases is 40,320. But the first group gave an average estimate of 512, whereas the second group's estimate averaged 2250—quite a difference, given that it's the same problem in both cases. In this example, the early numbers in the sequence serve as the anchors leading to either low or more moderate estimates.

THE VALUE OF HEURISTICS

What are we to make of such an imperfect decision maker? As psychologist Reid Hastie (1991) noted, the heuristic tool user described by Kahneman and Tversky is "an image of a decision maker of 'small brain' attempting to make do with a limited set of useful, imperfect, and not-too-demanding cognitive subroutines".

However, imperfect as heuristics may be there are several points worth making in their favor. First, the use of heuristics may lead to systematic errors under some circumstances, but, as Tversky and Kahneman (1974) have argued, they are usually surprisingly effective. Second, heuristics are economical. Optimal, or rational, decision making can be a complex, time-consuming activity. Strategies that lead to quick decisions with little cost are adaptive even if they sometimes lead to error. Third, to act optimally, in the sense of rational probability theory, you must possess all the information needed to calculate a choice; unfortunately, you often don't have all this information. In these cases, heuristics become useful tools for pointing you in the right direction.

Moreover, as we discussed in the section on framing effects, the fact that people make errors in artificial laboratory situations is somewhat misleading. We can define what the rational decision might be, based on objective information, but people do not always interpret the decision alternatives in the way the researcher intends. We all bring background knowledge to a situation which affects how we think and behave. In the "Linda is a bank teller" example, for instance, people know that there are more bank tellers in the world than feminist bank tellers. People understand a great deal about the frequencies of events in the world—the mistake is made because they're thinking about a single case, Linda, rather than about probabilities in general (Fielder, 1988; Gigerenzer, 1996).

It's important to recognize that just because you make decision errors doesn't mean you're using maladaptive processes. It's easy to arrange situations in which you might see or hear things that aren't really there, but there is still wide agreement that your visual system is highly adaptive. Just because your visual system can be tricked by an illusion doesn't mean it's a bad system. Similarly, when you make decisions you're relying on adaptive systems that serve you very well in the majority of situations (Gigerenzer, 1997).

BRAINSTORMING

BY G. EGAN

INTRODUCTION

Step three of the Army problem solving process, Generate Alternatives, requires the use of divergent and creative thinking to generate the maximum number of innovative potential solutions to the problem. The focus of this step is on the production of both quantity and innovativeness of ideas. When time permits, step three should be conducted using a group of creative individuals familiar with the problem situation. In the generation of ideas, many heads are usually better than one.

Brainstorming is a time-proven group method of generating ideas for the solution of problems. The goal of brainstorming is to produce the maximum number of ideas possible that are related to the solution of the problem. During the brainstorming session, the only concern of the group is the quantity of ideas. Concern with the quality or feasibility of the ideas is completely set aside until after the brainstorming session is completed. Members of the group engaged in brainstorming must feel uninhibited as they develop ideas and offer them to the group. Even though many ideas may seem silly or impossible, there is often a subordinate idea, principle, or concept that is useful to catalyze the generation of additional ideas or to employ in the solution to the problem.

RULES OF BRAINSTORMING

- Personnel roles in a brainstorming session:
  - Facilitator—Understands and enforces the rules of brainstorming. Asks open-ended questions to prompt the creative thinking and elicit the ideas of the group members. Seeks clarification of ideas as necessary but avoids adding personal bias or interpretations to the ideas of the group members.
  - Recorder—Makes a comprehensive and accurate written record of all of the ideas offered by the group members. Ideas are usually recorded in the form of bullet comments in a way that is visible to all members of the group (e.g. on a chalk board, white board, chart paper, etc.).

- Members—Consider the brainstorming question, develop as many ideas as possible to address the question, and offer the ideas to the group. Maximum member participation is essential.
- Start with a clear written definition of the problem, but be careful to avoid a statement of the problem that puts unnecessary restrictions on the solution. For example, if XYZ Organization is having financial difficulties, it should consider solutions that increase income and solutions that reduce debt. If the problem statement is written as, "To develop ways of increasing XYZ Organization sales," the brainstorming group might not even consider ways of reducing debt.
- The goal of brainstorming is to produce the largest quantity of ideas possible.
- All ideas, even wild ideas, are accepted and recorded. No criticisms, judgments, or qualitative assessments, however subtle, are allowed during the brainstorming session. Such judgments tend to stifle ideas and work against the goal of maximum quantity of ideas. Ideas will be reviewed for usefulness and feasibility after the brainstorming session is over. It is much easier to eliminate ideas later than it is to add ideas.
- Leaders should encourage the free flow of ideas and let it be known that even the wild ideas are welcome. Members must know that leaders will not think less of them if the members offer unusual ideas.
- Leaders and other influential members of the group should not express a preference or opinion. Members of the brainstorming group may self-censor by not offering ideas that they know are contrary to the opinions of influential others.
- Members are encouraged to piggyback on the ideas of others. That is, to use the concepts and perspectives evident in the ideas of other members as the basis for additional ideas. Members should also consider how other ideas can be combined to form yet additional ideas.
- Being careful to avoid the appearance of judgment or criticism, ask members to clarify or

explain their ideas. This may lead to additional ideas.

- The group should persist. Often, after an initial flurry of ideas, new ideas will slow to a trickle and it will be tempting to conclude that all ideas have been identified. However, if the group persists in its effort to generate ideas it will frequently find that it gains a "second wind" and the ideas begin to flow more rapidly again.

- When the allocated time is consumed or the group agrees that they have sufficiently exhausted their ideas, the brainstorming session can end. After the brainstorming session has finished, the group then turns to the task of examining the ideas generated to evaluate their utility and feasibility for answering the question that the group faces. The group considers ideas singly and in combination.

Problem Solving—
Evaluating Solutions

This is the third in a series of four lessons on problem solving. This lesson focuses on the identification and application of screening and evaluation criteria to compare and to select the best problem solution from among alternatives. The intent of this lesson is to enhance your ability to solve problems by introducing the concepts of screening and evaluation criteria and practicing the systematic application of criteria to select the best solution to a problem from among alternatives.

The following topics are addressed in this lesson:

- Screening and evaluation criteria
- Simply decision matrices
- Application of solution alternatives

The following TLOs are supported in whole or in part by this lesson:

- Apply critical thinking skills
- Solve problems

Following this lesson you will be able to:

- Analyze a problem
- Identify screening and evaluation criteria appropriate to problem solving
- Apply simple decision matrices to select the best course of action

COMPARING ALTERNATIVES

BY J. S. NAIRNE

INTRODUCTION

The product of the brainstorming activities of step three, Generate Alternatives, of the Army problem solving process is a large number of ideas that may be useful in solving the problem. You combine these ideas to form alternative courses of action that you might use to solve the problem. Ideally, at the end of step three, you will have several distinct courses of action from which to choose to solve the problem. The next task is to compare alternatives and select the best from among the several courses of action that you have developed. Steps four, five, and part of step six of the Army problem solving process deal with this selection process.

The remainder of this reading examines the comparison and selection process of steps four, five, and six by continuing the problem of deciding which lawn tractor to purchase. You previously encountered this example problem in the pre-class reading for Lesson 13.

COURSE OF ACTION COMPARISON
AND SELECTION

Step Four—Analyze the Alternatives

Examine each alternative solution to identify its intended and unintended consequences, resource or other constraints, and advantages and disadvantages. It is especially important that each alternative solution be analyzed in terms of the screening and evaluation criteria identified in step two. It is also critical that all alternatives be considered and objectively analyzed. Do not prejudge the situation by favoring any one alternative over the others.

It is important to keep the purpose of criteria in mind and to differentiate between screening and evaluation criteria as you analyze the alternative courses of action:

Criteria: The information that defines the limits within which the solution to a problem must fall. Criteria are used to determine which solution is best. There are two types of criteria:

- Screening Criteria: Essential features that any acceptable solution to the problem must possess. If a potential course of action fails to meet even a single screening criterion, that course of action is rejected. For example, a

course of action that would not result in the problem being solved by a critical deadline would not be adopted.

- **Evaluation Criteria:** Features that we desire the problem solution to provide, but which are not truly essential. For example, if the problem that we face is which lawn tractor to purchase, the lawn aerator attachment that comes with Brand X may be desirable, but not essential. Evaluation criteria and screening criteria often deal with the same aspect of the problem and differ only in degree. For example, if we only have $1,800 for the purchase of our lawn tractor, we would apply the $1,800 limit as a screening criterion and eliminate from our consideration any lawn tractors that cost more than $1,800. When examining the remaining lawn tractors, we would consider the cost of the lawn tractor as an evaluation criterion and look more favorably on those lawn tractors that cost less.

- **Benchmark:** A value that represents the preferred state of an evaluation criterion. Benchmarks help us determine if an alternative is good enough or desirable. Benchmarks can be established through reasoning, historical data, current allocation, and averaging. Averaging is the least preferred method. Using the lawn tractor purchase example, we might find that the optimum size engine produces 12 horsepower, although lawn tractors with as little as 8 horsepower will serve adequately. We might then use the 12 horsepower figure as a benchmark for evaluating the engine size of the various lawn tractors we are considering.

Step Five—Compare the Alternatives

All alternative solutions are evaluated and compared simultaneously, not sequentially, by first applying screening criteria to eliminate any alternatives that fail to meet essential minimum standards.

The next step is to apply evaluation criteria to the remaining alternatives to determine the degree of benefit that each provides. A convenient way to compare alternatives is to use a raw data matrix. A raw data matrix lists the courses of action down the left column of a grid and the names of the evaluation criteria across the top row of the grid. Each cell of the grid contains a value or quality of the evaluation criterion for a course of action. For example:

LAWN TRACTOR PURCHASE					
Name	Cost	Cutting Width	Speed	Aerator Attachment?	Horsepower
Brand X	$1,795	48 in.	7 mph	Yes	11 hp
Brand Y	$1,780	48 in.	4 mph	No	12 hp
Brand Z	$1,625	42 in.	5 mph	No	10 hp

When comparing alternatives, you should consider how much difference on a given evaluation criterion is significant. For example, when considering the purchase of a lawn tractor that costs nearly $1,800, a difference in price of only $15 between Brand X and Brand Y is probably not a significant difference, and the two brands should be considered as equal on the cost criterion. You should decide how much difference you will consider to be significant for each of your evaluation criteria before you compare the alternatives. In fact, you should decide this when you develop the evaluation criteria in step two. By making this decision before you begin to compare the alternatives, you can help avoid inadvertently establishing criterion standards that lead to a biased decision. Benchmarks can also help you decide if an alternative offers a significant benefit on each evaluation criterion.

Step Six—Make and Execute Your Decision

The best solution to a problem is that solution which meets the screening criteria and ranks highest against the evaluation criteria. It can be difficult to compare several alternative courses of action on many screening criteria. This difficulty is compounded when the screening criteria are not all of equal importance. It may be useful to numerically weight the screening criteria to reflect their importance. Criteria that are of equal and basic importance are given a weight of 1 and criteria that are more important are given higher numeric weights to reflect their degree of importance. For example, if cost was very important, and cutting width and horsepower were moderately important, the raw data matrix for the lawn tractor purchase might look like this:

LAWN TRACTOR PURCHASE					
Name	Cost	Cutting Width	Speed	Aerator Attachment?	Horsepower
Criterion Weight	4	2	1	1	2
Brand X	$1,795	48 in.	7 mph	Yes	11 hp
Brand Y	$1,780	48 in.	4 mph	No	12 hp
Brand Z	$1,625	42 in.	5 mph	No	10 hp

Even after the evaluation criteria information is displayed in a raw data matrix and weighted according to importance, it may still be difficult to clearly determine which alternative solution is the best. It may be necessary to convert the raw data matrix into a decision matrix to facilitate the comparison and selection.

The simplest type of decision matrix uses + and - symbols (or any other similar symbols such as green and red dots, up and down arrows, etc.) to indicate advantages and disadvantages. For example, our weighted raw data matrix above might be converted to the following +/- decision matrix:

LAWN TRACTOR PURCHASE					
Name	Cost	Cutting Width	Speed	Aerator Attachment?	Horsepower
Criterion Weight	4	2	1	1	2
Brand X	–		+	+	
Brand Y	–		–		+
Brand Z	+	–			

Alternatively, the criterion weights can be applied to the symbols to produce a more meaningful visual impression:

LAWN TRACTOR PURCHASE					
Name	Cost	Cutting Width	Speed	Aerator Attachment?	Horsepower
Criterion Weight	4	2	1	1	2
Brand X	– – – –		+	+	
Brand Y	– – – –		–		+ +
Brand Z	+ + + +	– –			

It should be obvious from an examination of these matrices that while a +/– decision matrix does simplify the comparison of courses of action, much of the quality and quantity of the information contained in the raw data matrix is lost. The +/– decision matrix is a crude tool at best because it eliminates so much information from the comparison.

The relative values decision matrix eliminates many of the problems of the +/– decision matrix. In a relative values decision matrix, the values in the raw data matrix are converted to numbers that indicate the relative value (i.e. the rank order) of the courses of action on each of the evaluation criteria. For each evaluation criterion, you simply assign a 1 to the course of action that is best, a 2 the course of action that is second best, and so on. Remember that for some evaluation criteria it is better to have a high value (e.g. a higher horsepower engine) and for other evaluation criteria it is better to have a lower value (e.g. a lower cost). It is important that you assign numbers based on which is best, next best, and so on, so that, for example, the course of action with the highest horsepower receives a 1 and the course of action with the lowest price receives a 1. If two or more courses of action are tied on an evaluation criterion, the values that the courses of action would have spanned, had they had different but adjacent values, are averaged and each of the tied courses of action receives the same average value. When we convert our raw data matrix to a relative values matrix it becomes:

LAWN TRACTOR PURCHASE					
Name	Cost	Cutting Width	Speed	Aerator Attachment?	Horsepower
Criterion Weight	4	2	1	1	2
Brand X	3	1.5	1	1	2
Brand Y	2	1.5	3	2.5	1
Brand Z	1	3	2	2.5	3

Note the treatment of tied values in this matrix. Both Brand X and Brand Y have the same cutting width. Since Brand Z has the narrowest (least desirable) cutting width, it receives the relative value of 3. If Brands X and Y had had different but adjacent cutting widths, they would have relative values of 1 and 2. Since Brands X and Y are tied, we average the relative values 1 and 2 and assign the average value (1.5) to Brand X and Brand Y. The same process was followed for the aerator attachment evaluation criterion.

We can weight the relative values by multiplying them by the criterion weights. To determine which course of action is best, we then add the weighted relative values across the matrix to determine the total for each course of action. Since lower numbers indicate better outcomes in our relative values matrix, the course of action with the lowest total is the preferred course of action:

LAWN TRACTOR PURCHASE						
Name	Cost	Cutting Width	Speed	Aerator Attachment?	Horsepower	Total
Criterion Weight	4	2	1	1	2	
Brand X	12	3	1	1	4	21
(Brand Y)	8	3	3	2.5	2	18.5
Brand Z	4	6	2	2.5	6	20.5

In this case, Brand Y is the preferred choice because it has the lowest score of 18.5 as compared to 20.5 for Brand Z and 21 for Brand X. However, as discussed above, if you decide that the $15 dollar difference in price between Brand X and Brand Y is not significant, you could choose to consider Brand X and Brand Y to be tied on cost. This would mean that they would receive the same relative values. Since the cost evaluation criterion is weighted so heavily, this decision would lead to choosing Brand X instead of Brand Y, as the decision matrix on the following page shows:

LAWN TRACTOR PURCHASE					
Name	Cost	Cutting Width	Speed	Aerator Attachment?	Horsepower	Total
Criterion Weight	4	2	1	1	2	
Brand X	10	3	1	1	4	19
Brand Y	10	3	3	2.5	2	20.5
Brand Z	4	6	2	2.5	6	20.5

As you can see, small differences and simple decisions can have a significant effect on the outcome of the decision matrix. It is important that you carefully make all relevant decisions before you construct the decision matrix. You should determine all of the evaluation criteria that are important to the decision, carefully decide how each evaluation criterion should be weighted, and decide for each evaluation criterion how much of a difference in value is required in order for courses of action to be given different relative values (e.g. Will you give the lawn tractors different relative values if their prices differ by $1, $10, $25, or some other value? Is a 47-inch cutting width given the same relative value as a 48-inch cutting width?). Thinking through and making these decisions in advance can help avoid bias or the appearance of bias that might come from altering decision criteria after the decision matrix has been developed.

Problem Solving— Practical Exercise

This is the last in the series of four lessons on problem solving. This lesson provides you with the opportunity to apply what has been learned in previous lessons and to practice several aspects of problem solving. This lesson fosters practice in the application of the Army problem-solving process to a moderately complex real-world situation.

The following topics are addressed in this lesson:

- Application of the Army problem solving model
- Use of time and information management techniques
- Development and use of screening and evaluation criteria
- Application of creative and critical thinking

The following TLOs are supported in whole or in part by this lesson:

- Apply critical thinking skills
- Solve problems

Following this lesson you will be able to:

- Apply the seven-step Army problem solving process
- Communicate the seven step problem-solving process to peers

MODULE III

U.S. ARMY

LEADERSHIP EXCELLENCE

The Army Profession: Army Operations (Part II)

Part II of The Army Profession: Army Operations module consists of lessons 17 through 24. These lessons build on the preceding Personal Development module (Problem Solving lessons 13 through 16) by examining the Army's adaptation of general problem solving and decision making principles to military operational problems and decisions. The lessons in Part II of this module take you through the eight steps of the troop leading procedure including mission analysis, planning, and execution. Sample missions are used throughout this module to give you practical experience in conducting the eight troop leading steps.

Troop Leading Procedures

This is a transition lesson between the Personal Development module on Problem Solving and the Army Operations module. This lesson is the first in a group of eight lessons dealing with military planning and the application of problem-solving principles to military operations. The purpose of this lesson is to show the relationship between troop leading procedures and the problem solving process. You will have worked in teams, have a basic familiarity with practices of problem-solving, and should be in a position to begin to integrate basic problem-solving skills with the specific steps and actions of the troop-leading procedures and military operations orders.

The following topics are addressed in this lesson:

- The eight troop leading procedures steps
- Relationship between troop leading procedures and the problem solving process
- Types and functions of military orders (warning order, operations order, & fragmentary order)
- The five paragraph OPORD structure and general content of each paragraph
- Military aspects of terrain

The following TLO is supported in whole or in part by this lesson:

- Conduct troop leading procedures

Following this lesson you will be able to:

- Describe the eight steps of the Army troop-leading procedure
- List the elements of METT-T
- Analyze the five military aspects of terrain according to OCOKA

Receive Mission: METT-T

This is the second in a series of eight lessons on Troop Leading procedures within the Army Operations Module. This is the first in a two-part set on Mission analysis, METT-T. The purpose of this lesson is to have you analyze a Higher Headquarters (HQ) Operations Order and then extract specified tasks as well as constraints and limitations.

The following topics are addressed in this lesson:

- Identify specified, implied, and essential tasks from a higher headquarters OPORD
- Identify related constraints and limitations

The following TLO is supported in whole or in part by this lesson:

- Follow military planning considerations

Following this lesson you will be able to:

- Analyze a Higher HQ Operations order: Step one of the Troop Leading Procedures (Receive the Mission)
- Extract and classify tasks and limitations

Mission Analysis

This is the third in a series of eight lessons on Troop Leading Procedures within the Army Operations module. This lesson continues the mission analysis phase of the military problem solving process introduced in the previous lesson. It focuses on terrain analysis and map reading.

The following topics are addressed in this lesson:

- METT-T analysis
- Military aspects of terrain (OKOCA)
- Time management for mission planning
- Restated Mission Statement

The following TLO is supported in whole or in part by this lesson:

- Follow military planning considerations

Following this lesson you will be able to:

- Analyze an order: Step one of the TLP (Receive the Mission)
- Use OKOCA to analyze Military Aspects of Terrain
- Write a Platoon Mission Statement

Issue Warning Order

This is the fourth in a series of eight lessons on Troop Leading procedures within the Army Operations module. This lesson focuses on step two of the Troop Leading Procedures, issuance of a warning order. During this lesson, you will use the five-paragraph OPORD format to develop warning orders. You will practice creating warning orders for scenarios that also reinforce understanding of OCOKA.

The following topic is addressed in this lesson:

- Preparation of a warning order

The following TLO is supported in whole or in part by this lesson:

- Conduct Troop Leading Procedures

Following this lesson you will be able to:

- Relate Step 1 of the TLP to Step 2
- Use mission analysis to develop the basis for a warning order
- Issue a warning order

Make a Tentative Plan

This is the fifth in a series of eight lessons on Troop Leading procedures within the Army Operations module. This lesson focuses on step three of the Troop Leading Procedures, make a tentative plan. This lesson builds on your familiarization with OCOKA and the practice of issuing warning orders.

The following topics are addressed in this lesson:

- Develop Courses of Action
- Analyze and Compare Courses of Action
- Select a course of action and develop a tentative plan

The following TLO is supported in whole or in part by this lesson:

- Conduct troop leading procedures

Following this lesson you will be able to:

- List the four steps of The Estimate of the Situation
- Explain how mission analysis contributes to development of the tentative plan
- Develop a tentative plan for a platoon defensive operation

Movement, Recon, and Complete Plan

This is the sixth in a series of eight lessons on Troop Leading procedures within the Army Operations module. It builds on the foundations set out in the previous lesson involving the formulation of a tentative plan. This lesson is designed to familiarize you with steps four through six of the troop leading procedures. It addresses the purpose, supervision, and execution of movement in the absence of the primary unit (squad/platoon) leader; the purpose and execution of a map or ground reconnaissance; and completion of the OPORD in light of mission updates and the results of the reconnaissance.

The following topics are addressed in this lesson:

- Purpose, supervision, and execution of preparatory unit movement
- Purpose, methods, and execution of map and ground reconnaissance
- Considerations in the completion of the OPORD

The following TLO is supported in whole or in part by this lesson:

- Conduct troop leading procedures

Following this lesson you will be able to:

- Describe when and under what circumstances to initiate movement and recon
- Identify the steps to develop a plan
- Develop a complete plan

Issue Operations Order

This is the seventh in a series of eight lessons on Troop Leading procedures within the Army Operations module. The purpose of this lesson is to have you apply what you learned from previous lessons about gathering information, analyzing the situation, including constraints and limitations. Guided by the instructor, you will complete a final operations order and deliver the order to subordinates.

The following topics are addressed in this lesson:

- Prepare an operations order
- Prepare OPORD briefing aids (sketches, overlays, terrain models, etc.)
- Issue an operations order
- Receive and correct an OPORD brief-back from a subordinate

The following TLO is supported in whole or in part by this lesson:

- Conduct troop leading procedures

Following this lesson you will be able to:

- Identify when and under what circumstances to issue an operations order
- List the characteristics of an operations order
- Issue an operations order

Supervise, Inspect, and Rehearse

This is the last in a series of eight lessons on Troop Leading procedures within the Army Operations module. The purpose of this lesson is to have you take what you learned from previous Troop Leading Procedures and apply it in issuing orders and preparing the platoon to carry out those orders. You will also integrate what you have learned in Leadership Labs and practice sessions so that you can carry out inspections and required rehearsals.

The following topics are addressed in this lesson:

- Purpose, planning, and execution of pre-operational rehearsals
- Purpose, focus, and execution of pre-operational inspections

The following TLO is supported in whole or in part by this lesson:

- Conduct Troop Leading Procedures

Following this lesson you will be able to:

- List characteristics of supervision
- Identify those items in the approved plan that need to be inspected
- Identify those items in the approved plan that need to be rehearsed
- Summarize the steps involved in Troop Leading Procedures

MODULE IV

The Army Profession: Officership

This module consists of twelve lessons that focus on The Army Profession, and Officership. The first seven lessons, 25 through 31, provide an extensive examination of the unique purpose, roles, and obligations of commissioned officers. This series of lessons covers history, source documents, organizational structure, and the Army's source of authority—the Congress. The aim is to convey a clear and complete understanding of what it means to be a commissioned officer. Special emphasis is given to the officer's role in shaping and guiding the growth and evolution of the Army through decisions, policies, and personal example.

Lessons 32 through 36 consist of a series of case studies, designed to enable you to examine the Officer Corps and the Evolution of the United States Army from Vietnam and the years following to its emerging strength during the Gulf War. The case studies focus on how organizations change and the important role leaders play in effecting change for the better in the Army.

By tracing the successes and failures of the force as it evolved from the Vietnam War to the present, the previous Army Profession and Officership lessons topics are placed in a real-world context that directly affect your future.

Each of the lessons that make up this case study cover a specific phase of the Army's evolution: The Vietnam War, The Army of the 70's, The Transformation, Desert Shield/Desert Storm, and Into the Twenty First Century. Identifying and tracing the critical elements of the transformation phase serves as the mechanism by which the various phases are tied together. Nine of these critical elements are then used as threads of continuity by which you trace the evolution of the Army and the responsibilities, influences, successes, and failures of the officer corps. These nine threads of continuity include: quality of people, war fighting doctrine, force structure, continuous modernization, leader development, empowerment of the NCO Corps, integration of reserve forces, and institutional values.

Foundations of Officership

This is the first of a series of seven lessons on the Army Profession and Officership. This series of lessons covers history, source documents, organizational structure, and the Army's source of authority—the Congress. Specifically, this lesson addresses the obligations and the legal basis of the commissioned officer corps through an examination of the United States Constitution, the Officers Commission, and the Oath of Office.

The following topics are addressed in this lesson:

- Army officer traditions
- The Constitution, commission, and oath of office as they relate to officers
- Legal responsibilities of officers
- The Army Profession and Officership through history

The following TLO is supported in whole or in part by this lesson:

- Relate the characteristics of a profession to military service as an officer

Following this lesson you will be able to:

- Identify the source of the authority to commission officers
- Identify the source of Commissioned Officers' authority
- Identify the source of the Commissioned Officers Oath
- Summarize the officers commission
- Summarize the Oath of Office

ARMY OFFICER'S GUIDE

PREFACE

Address by General of the Army Douglas MacArthur

General Westmoreland, General Groves, distinguished guests, and gentleman of the Corps.*

As I was leaving the hotel this morning, a doorman asked me, "Where are you bound for, General?" and when I replied, "West Point," he remarked, "Beautiful place, have you ever been there before?"

No human being could fail to be deeply moved by such a tribute as this [Thayer Award]. Coming from a profession I have served so long, and a people I have loved so well, it fills me with an emotion I cannot express. But this award is not intended primarily to honor a personality, but to symbolize a great moral code—the code of conduct and chivalry of those who guard this beloved land of culture and ancient descent. That is the meaning of this medallion. For all eyes and for all time, it is an expression of the ethics of the American soldier. That I should be integrated in this way with so noble an ideal arouses a sense of pride and yet of humility which will be with me always.

Duty—Honor—Country. Those three hallowed words reverently dictate what you ought to be, what you can be, what you will be. They are your rallying points: to build courage when courage seems to fail; to regain faith when there seems to be little cause for faith; to create hope when hope becomes forlorn. Unhappily, I possess neither that eloquence of diction, that poetry of imagination, nor the brilliance of metaphor to tell you all that they mean. The unbelievers will say they are but words, but a slogan, but a flamboyant phrase. Every pedant, every demagogue, every cynic, every hypocrite, every troublemaker, and, I am sorry to say, some others of an entirely different character, will try to downgrade them even to the extent of mockery and ridicule. But here are some of the things they do. They build your basic character, they mold you for your future roles as the custodians of the nation's defense, they make you strong enough to know when you are weak, and brave enough to face yourself when you are afraid.

*To the Members of the Association of Graduates, U.S.M.A., The Corps of Cadets and Distinguished Guests upon his acceptance of THE SYLVANUS THAYER AWARD, United States Military Academy, West Point, New York, 12 May 1962. Published by permission of General MacArthur.

OATH OF OFFICE - MILITARY PERSONNEL

For use of this form, see AR 135-100, the proponent agency is ODCSPER

DATA REQUIRED BY THE PRIVACY ACT OF 1974

AUTHORITY: 5 USC 3331, 552, 552a; 10 USC 10204.

PRINCIPAL PURPOSE: To create a record of the date of acceptance of appointment.

ROUTINE USES: Information is used to establish and record the date of acceptance. The SSN is used to identify the member. The date of acceptance of appointment is used in preparing statements of service and computing basic pay date.

DISCLOSURE: Completion of form is mandatory. Failure to do so will cause the appointment to be invalid.

INSTRUCTIONS

INDICATE THE APPOINTMENT FOR WHICH OATH IS BEING EXECUTED BY PLACING AN "X" IN APPROPRIATE BOX. REGULAR ARMY COMMISSIONED OFFICERS WILL ALSO SPECIFY THE BRANCH OF APPOINTMENT WHEN APPOINTED IN A SPECIAL BRANCH.

This form will be executed upon acceptance of appointment as an officer in the Army of the United States. Immediately upon receipt of notice of appointment, the appointee will, in case of acceptance of the appointment, return to the agency from which received, the oath of office *(on this form)* properly filled in, subscribed and attested. In case of non-acceptance, the notice of appointment will be returned to the agency from which received, *(by letter)* indicating the fact of non-acceptance.

COMMISSIONED OFFICERS	WARRANT OFFICERS
☐ REGULAR ARMY _____ *(Branch, when so appointed)*	☐ REGULAR ARMY
☐ ARMY OF THE UNITED STATES, WITHOUT COMPONENT	☐ ARMY OF THE UNITED STATES, WITHOUT COMPONENT
☐ RESERVE COMMISSIONED OFFICER	☐ RESERVE WARRANT OFFICER

I, _____ *(First Name, Middle Name, Last Name)*   _____ *(Social Security Number)*

having been appointed an officer in the Army of the United States, as indicated above in the grade of _____ do solemnly swear *(or affirm)* that I will support and defend the Constitution of the United States against all enemies, foreign and domestic, that I will bear true faith and allegiance to the same; that I take this obligation freely, without any mental reservation or purpose of evasion; and that I will well and faithfully discharge the duties of the office upon which I am about to enter; SO HELP ME GOD.

_____ *(Signature - full name as shown above)*

SWORN TO AND SUBSCRIBED BEFORE ME AT _____

THIS _____ DAY OF _____ , _____ .
(Day)   *(Month)*   *(Year)*

_____ *(Grade, component, or office of official administering oath)*   _____ *(Signature)*

FOR THE EXECUTION OF THE OATH OF OFFICE

1. Whenever any person is elected or appointed to an office of honor or trust under the Government of the United States, he/she is required before entering upon the duties of his/her office, to take and subscribe the oath prescribed by 5 USC 3331.

2. 10 USC 626 and 14309 eliminate the necessity of executing oath on promotion of officers.

3. The oath of office may be taken before any commissioned officer of any component of any Armed Force, whether or not on active duty *(10 USC 1031)*, or before any commissioned warrant officer when acting as an adjutant, assistant adjutant, acting adjutant, or personnel adjutant in any of the Armed Forces *(See UCM,*

Article 136; 10 USC 936). A commissioned warrant officer administering the oath of office will show his/her title in the block to the left of his/her signature.

4. Oath of office may also be taken before any civil officer who is authorized by the laws of the United States or by the local municipal law to administer oaths, and if so administered by a civil official, the oath must bear the official seal of the person administering the oath, or if a seal is not used by the official, the official's capacity to administer oaths must be certified to under seal by a clerk or court or other proper local official.

DA FORM 71, JUL 1999   EDITION OF DEC 1988 IS OBSOLETE   USAPA V1.00

To all who shall see these presents, greeting:

Know Ye, that reposing special trust and confidence in the patriotism, valor,
fidelity and abilities of _____ . *I do*
appoint   **SAMPLE**   *in the*

United States Army

to _____ *as such from the* _____ *day of* _____ , *two*
thousand _____ . *This officer will therefore carefully*
and diligently discharge the duties of the office to which appointed by doing and
performing all manner of things thereunto belonging.
And I do strictly charge and require those officers and other personnel of lesser
rank to render such obedience as is due an officer of this grade and position. And,
this officer is to observe and follow such orders and directions, from time to time, as
may be given by the President of the United States of America or other superior
officers, acting in accordance with the laws of the United States of America.
This commission is to continue in force during the pleasure of the President of the
United States of America under the provisions of those public laws relating to
officers of the **Armed Forces of the United States of America**
and the component thereof in which this appointment is made.

Done at the city of Washington, this _____ *day of* _____
in the year of our Lord two thousand _____ *and of the*
Independence of the United States of America the _____
By the President:

HOW MILITARIES TRANSFORM— VARIOUS SCHOOLS OF THOUGHT VS. INTRODUCTION

BY DON M. SNIDER AND GAYLE L. WATKINS

INTRODUCTION

The Army that won the battles of the Gulf War in 1991 was one of the most professional ever fielded by America. As Gen. Norman Schwarzkopf commented, "We could have traded equipment with the Iraqis and still won."[3] The extraordinary success met by the Army in the Gulf was based on the quality and training of its people.

A decade later, as the Army continues to transform from a Cold War force to one appropriate for the 21st century, it must grapple with many issues. In this book, we propose that the most critical challenge the Army now faces in its planned transition is to reinforce the professional nature of the institution and to provide the opportunity for its soldiers to be members of a profession—the Army profession. The Army is neither a public-sector bureaucracy manned by civil servants nor is it a business with employees. It has been and must continue to be a profession, one in which military professionals serve with deep pride and immense personal satisfaction.

HOW MILITARIES TRANSFORM— VARIOUS SCHOOLS OF THOUGHT

History shows that many armies do not adapt well in peacetime to changing environments; some do not adapt at all and no longer exist as armies. And even for those that are able to innovate and adapt in order to remain effective militarily and relevant to the societies they defend, the process is often long and difficult. Such processes take at least a decade or longer and often are not resolved when the next war starts, thus requiring the even more difficult process of wartime innovation and adaptation.

Since modern armies reflect the national culture from which they are drawn and its state of technology, and since they each have unique relationships with the civilian society and the nation defended, it is not surprising that there is little consensus in the scholarly literature on just how military transformations occur in peacetime—the specific causal relationships. In fact, there are three rather distinct schools of thought that address the phenomena of military transformations, each with its own historical literatures and each recently renewed and invigorated since the end of the Cold War.

The most recent and popular school of thought on military transformations—populated by historians, defense and policy analysts, technologists, and futurists—tends to view military institutions in relation to the changing conduct of warfare and how militaries fight—particularly the influence of technology.[4] This school claims that the military services of the United States are now undergoing a true "revolution in military affairs" (RMA).[5] Such claims started during the last decade of the Cold War based on the conventional arms race then occurring between the Soviets and NATO (largely American), and gained momentum as a result of the remarkably successful one-hundred-hour Gulf War, in which the high-tech American-led forces overwhelmed the Iraqi army.[6]

Then in 1996, all three U.S. services adopted a vision of future warfare—*Joint Vision 2010*[7]—that required a peacetime transformation in all of their conventional capabilities. Both the joint vision and the subsequent service visions focused on gaining for their forces significant increases in military effectiveness, increases to be brought about by creating a "system of systems" integrating ubiquitous sensors and strike systems in real-time decision cycles more compact than those of any enemy. Situational awareness within the battle space, sometimes described as "dominant battlefield knowledge," became the term to describe the uniquely American high-technology advantage in future conventional warfare.

But whether such a transformation is actually occurring today, or even should, is contested both within the three services themselves, by the larger community of defense policy-makers in recent administrations, and within the powerful defense industries.[8] Thus the service perspectives on transformation have often been, not surprisingly, more related to the endless political game of near zero-sum resource allocations within the Department of Defense than to future war-fighting realities.[9] Currently, within this school there simply is no consensus on an RMA other than the general agreement that, if affordable, one is desirable. Moreover, what role current conventional force structures—the so-called "legacy" forces left over from the Cold War—will play in such transformations, and at what opportunity costs, remain undecided. The war in Afghanistan, following the "first modern war"— Kosovo—by less than two and a half years, is drawing to a close as this chapter is written.[10] It will doubtless heighten within this school the relevance of asymmetric responses to an RMA-led transformation of U.S. defense capabilities. All of which can only leave the future of Army transformation even more uncertain, but no less urgent.

The second school of thought—populated by political scientists and organizational theorists—views armies as large, standing institutions whose behaviors in peacetime can be best understood in strategic context by the application of evolving organizational theories originally found in business, economics, and public administration literatures.[11] According to this school, major influences on an army's decisions issue from its own intrinsic character and its relationships with the external environment, particularly its structural relationship with the other governmental institutions (executive and legislature) with authority over it.

Of particular interest regarding this school is its emphasis on the culture of the military institution, the relationships between culture and strategic doctrines, and the influence such organizational culture has in interpreting the external environments in which the army is operating, both domestic and international. In this school one of the roles of strategic leaders is to influence organizational cultures in such a manner as to make profound change more acceptable and likely, such as abetting "learning" within the organization.[12] A recent Army Chief of Staff, Gen. Gordon Sullivan, adopted such an approach to Army modernization during his tenure.[13] In our view, this school places more emphasis on the human resources of the Army than does the technology-oriented RMA school.

The third school has focused on civil-military relations, those observable relationships in the post-Westphalian western world between military institutions and the states they serve. The scholars within this school—historians, political scientists, sociologists, and anthropologists—have long focused on the central issue of a state's ability to control a military institution sufficiently strong to defend that state.[14] The challenge has been to maintain equilibrium between the two imperatives introduced by Samuel Huntington forty-five years ago, that is, to balance the *military* imperative of a strong, effectively coercive military institution of immense power, with the *social* imperative for that same institution to remain legitimate before the society served and subordinate to its elected and appointed civilian officials.[15] How different and how separate the military should be

from civil society, and to what degree it has the need for a different culture and ethos, have long been issues of concern to this school.

More recently, as western societies have entered the post-industrial era and states have abandoned mass conscripted armies in the tremulous hope that major land warfare is obsolete, this school has widened its interests. Now, this school's salient themes are "post-modern militaries," the influence on them of "other-than-war" missions,[16] and the potential of new cultural gaps growing between such militaries and the societies they serve.[17] It is fair to say that scholars of the civil-military school have focused on human resources more than the other two, both in terms of individual soldiers and leaders and collectively as social organizations. Today, however, their focus has largely narrowed to a sociologically identifiable set of Army soldiers—women, gays, single-parents—and the equity and ethics involved in their military service, or the lack thereof.[18]

KEY TO MILITARY TRANSFORMATIONS— "PEOPLE"

As can be inferred from our review of the second and third schools—organizational and civil-military—they share certain characteristics. One such is the proposition advanced by General Shinseki in the introductory quotation: *people count*. In his view they count more than technology and readiness when it comes to transforming the U.S. Army. Unfortunately, the currently popular RMA school is almost devoid of considerations of human resources, beyond the notion that they constitute "cultural impediments" to change.[19]

But it is not clear in General Shinseki's vision and its implementing White Paper who those "people" are.[20] Are they the Army's soldiers and their leaders who count in military transformations, i.e., just the uniformed people? Or do civilian contractors and Department of the Army civilians count also as "people"? And what of retired soldiers, now increasingly contracted back into the Army? Further, General Shinseki has not told us *how* these people count. What identities, roles, attitudes, and behaviors will they need to effect such a transition? Do they now have them? How are the before-and-after roles different, especially for the Army officer corps? And, most importantly, what relationship must these "people" have with the Army, and the Army with them, to be effective at transformations?

We suggest in the present book—in fact, it is the major theme—that General Shinseki is entirely correct in his judgment that "people count" most in the transformation of the U.S. Army. But we go even further by suggesting that in recent decades none of the three schools of thought about military transformations has emphasized sufficiently, *nor in policy relevant ways*, in what sense "people count." And until that is done, the necessary roles that "people" must play in order for any transformation effort to be successful within the U.S. Army, and the policies necessary to enable them to fulfill those roles, cannot be determined, thus rendering futile such transformation efforts.

We believe the reason the various schools of thought have neglected the roles and policies of people is that *they have failed to view these "people" as "professionals" and the U.S. Army as a "profession," or calling.* They have not introduced the analytical frameworks and necessary understandings of how modern professions prepare and compete for the opportunity to apply their expertise that would facilitate, indeed enable, such a people-oriented perspective.

Accordingly, we present in this book the results of a collective research effort, undertaken by over a score of military and civilian scholars, to renew study of the U.S. Army as a profession, its "people" as members of a profession, and its transformation as one that, if it is to occur, will have to occur within a highly competitive system of military professions of which the Army profession is only one. As will become clear, our thesis is that competitive professions are quite different from other producing organizations in America, and the three military professions even more so. Thus they must be studied, understood, and led in light of this difference. Simply stated, the transformation of a military profession is not the same as that of a business or other type of organization, and cannot be approached in the same way.

THE U.S ARMY AS A PROFESSION

America has three military professions: army, maritime, and aerospace. These professions are generally (but not wholly) contained within the Departments of the Army, Navy, and Air Force and surrounded by the immense bureaucracies of the Department of Defense, the Congress, and the Executive. Therefore, the military services are simultaneously professions and government bureaucracies. For example, a newly promoted major of infantry stationed in Korea has developed professionally to the same level of expertise as a newly promoted major of infantry stationed in Germany. By promoting them to the rank of major, the Army as a profession has certified their competence at the field grade level to the client, American society. But the Army as a bureaucracy uses its personnel management system when making the two majors' future assignments, considering them merely as "faces" to be matched with a particular manpower "space." This dual nature—profession and bureaucracy—creates a challenging but healthy tension within all such military institutions.

Before considering how the Army can better deal with this tension, let us review briefly the nature of military professions. First, expertise and the knowledge underlying it are the coins of the professional realm. More so than other occupations and organizations, professions focus on generating expert knowledge and the ability of its members to apply that expertise to new situations.[21] Medical professionals perfect medical techniques to apply to patients, lawyers apply legal expertise in trying cases, and the military develops new technologies, capabilities, and strategies to "provide for the common defense," most often in places and under circumstances that cannot be foreseen. Such professional expertise is ultimately validated by the client (or professions would not exist!), and forms the basis for the trust between the profession and the society served. Given such trust, professions are granted limited autonomy to establish and enforce their own professional ethics, the maintenance of which further enhances such trust. Furthermore, success in professional practice stems from effective and ethical application of the expertise—the patient is cured, the case is won, conflict is deterred, or if fought, settled on terms favorable to the United States. Thus measures of efficiency, while important, rank behind effectiveness as measures of success for professions.

Although they may appear static, modern professions also have a hidden, dynamic, and occasionally indecorous side. They are continuously engaged in fierce competitions for control over the jurisdictions in which they apply their expertise.[22] A well-publicized current example of these competitions is occurring in the medical arena where physicians and HMOs battle over the right to make patient-care decisions. Other professions face similar challenges as they seek to gain legitimacy in new fields while retaining legitimacy in their traditional areas.

Competitive Jurisdictions of The Army Profession

FIGURE 1-1. *Competitive Jurisdictions of the Army Profession.*

Since the end of the Cold War, the Army has been embroiled in such competitions in a variety of settings. These include counter-drug operations on our southern border, operations other than war in the Balkans, and now homeland security and counter-terrorism. The Army's competitors within these jurisdictions range from other professions (the other military services and foreign armies) to other governmental agencies, private contractors, and non-governmental organizations, both American and international. Simultaneously the Army has continued to compete in its traditional jurisdiction, conventional war-fighting, where its ability to do so has been compromised by a legacy force that is now too strategically immobile to be fully relevant to the new global situations.

Figure 1-1 presents a schematic of the four external jurisdictions in which the Army profession competes. Also displayed are the internal jurisdictions in which the Army as a profession develops and maintains its expert knowledge and teaches it to the members of the profession and their units. Since the end of the Cold War even these internal jurisdictions have become more competitive as the Army increasingly "contracts out" such professional services as doctrinal studies, the training of foreign armies, staff functions within the Army General Staff, and the leadership of ROTC detachments.

THE U.S. ARMY AS A BUREAUCRACY

In contrast to the more traditional professions, which have not normally been lodged within a controlling organization, the Army is also a huge hierarchical bureaucracy, only one of many within the U.S. government. Unlike professions, bureaucracies focus on application of knowledge embedded in organizational routine and process rather than in their employees. The extreme of this is represented by government bureaucracies—think of a state department of motor vehicles in one of the 50 states. Bureaucracies implant such knowledge in their structures through standing operating procedures, operating routines, personnel policy handbooks, regulations, pay structures and bonuses, equipment, and machinery more so than in the development of their employees and their functional competence.[23] Efficiency and survival are normally the dominant organizational goals within bureaucracies.

Herein lies the natural tension within the Army's dual character. On the one hand, the Army is a profession focused on effectively developing military expertise and its members' ability to collectively apply their expertise to new situations. On the other hand, it is a hierarchical bureaucracy focused on efficiency, "doing more with less." This dual nature is unavoidable and healthy for the nation, although it may be cause for considerable tension both for the individual professional and for the institution as a whole.

Maintaining an appropriate balance between the Army's two natures is elusive; at any point in time, one is likely to predominate over the other. The result is an Army whose leaders, self-concepts, decisions, and organizational climate for soldiers reflect either a high degree of military professionalism and effectiveness or a high degree of bureaucracy and efficiency. In the former, the self-concept of the Army's members is likely to be one of "professional," while in the latter their self-concept is one of "employee." The Army of Desert Storm was a case of the former. Historically, militaries that do not resolve this tension in favor of their professional nature can experience the "death" of their professional character. As their bureaucratic nature comes to dominate, they cease to be a profession and become little more than an obedient military bureaucracy.[24]

WHAT IS DOMINANT TODAY WITHIN THE ARMY—PROFESSION OR BUREAUCRACY?

For a number of reasons, most having to do with the past decade of downsizing and budget cuts, the Army of the late 1990s has behaved more like a bureaucracy than a highly effective military profession. We have argued this point elsewhere, with our rationale resting on indicators of reduced Army effectiveness in applying its expertise to tasks at hand (e.g., the 1999 deployment of Task Force Hawk to Albania where the force was never subjected to the hazards of combat; reports from the Army's combat training centers of declining proficiency among tested battalions and task forces; declining readiness ratings among Army divisions; and a study by the RAND Arroyo Center documenting declining tactical proficiency among combat arms captains).[25] Our rationale also rested on indicators of low morale caused by an excessively bureaucratic personnel management system (e.g., the exodus of captains from the Army; the Army's own reports of declining soldier morale; and increased declinations by lieutenant colonels and colonels selected for command).

Also weighing heavily in our conclusion was an independent study of American military culture by retired senior officers and defense policy-makers who documented within the active Army a serious gap in trust between junior and senior Army officers. The gap is worsened by the rise of a "zero-defects"

mentality too often displayed by commanding officers at all levels, just the opposite of what is needed in military organizations if the developmental processes of professions are to flourish.[26]

Now, however, such conclusions about the state of the Army profession need not rest primarily on external analyses. Early in 2000, in response to several of the issue studies just cited, the Army Chief of Staff directed an internal panel of general officers to study officer perceptions and understandings of the Army's training and leader development systems to determine the scope of current problems and to recommend corrective actions. Not surprisingly, after extensive field work the panel thoroughly documented by the fall of 2000 many of the same deficiencies earlier indicated by the external studies, as well as several not previously aired, particularly in Army training systems.[27]

With respect to the Army's culture, the panel concluded that the gap between the institution's professed ideals and its actual practices in the areas of training and leader development had spread outside the Army officer corps' "band of tolerance," within which there is no loss of trust between officers and the institution. Seven specific conclusions supported this overall finding:

1. "Within the Army Officer Corps, the service ethic and concepts of officership are neither well-understood nor clearly defined;
2. An excessive operational pace is a major source of the degradation. [It is] detrimental to readiness, leader development, and officer job satisfaction; leads to micromanagement; and is a major reason for attrition among all cohorts;
3. Retention is a significant issue across [all commissioned grades below flag rank], a result of a perceived lack of commitment from the Army, limitations on spouse employment and a perceived imbalance between Army expectations and the family, the lack of work predictability, and only limited control over assignments;
4. Micromanagement has become part of the Army culture [, producing] a growing perception that lack of trust stems from the leader's desire to be invulnerable to criticism and blocks the opportunity for subordinates to learn through leadership experiences;
5. The officer efficiency report (OER) is a source of mistrust and anxiety [and] is not yet meeting officer expectations as a leader development tool . . . aspects of the OER are seldom used, and senior raters seldom counsel subordinates;

6. Assignment requirements, instead of individual leader development needs, drive officer personnel management; and

7. Officers believe mentoring is important for both personal and professional development, yet a majority of officers report not having mentors."[28]

While the panel did not study the Army as a profession nor use the language of professions in their report, there can be no doubt that they are describing quite accurately an Army that is behaving far more bureaucratically than professionally. There are, of course, many causes of the bureaucratic state of the Army. The panel noted "excessive operational tempo"; the Center for Strategic International Studies study earlier noted several other causes, both internal and external to the Army. The primary research presented in Chapter 5 invokes the words of Army officers themselves to describe this phenomenon. One of our most striking findings is that the Army has bureaucratized its professional knowledge into checklists and forms to such a degree that it has reduced the expertise of its officers by reducing their opportunities to exercise it, frustrated them in their attempts to apply their knowledge and experience, and decreased the effectiveness of professional decisions. All of these sources clearly indicate that *the Army profession is seriously compromised by excessive bureaucratization of major leadership and management systems and is so perceived by the individual members of the Army officer corps.*

PROFESSION OR BUREAUCRACY—WHAT DIFFERENCE DOES IT MAKE?

One might argue that for purposes of efficiency or even to make the planned transformation "easier," the Army should simply continue to deprofessionalize, becoming an obedient but nonprofessional military bureaucracy. One need look no further than Europe to see Western democratic societies readily accepting this outcome. But America has a different role to play in the world. If deprofessionalization happened here, American society would lose two key benefits of military professionalism: (1) the development and adaptation of expert knowledge and the expertise of military professionals; and (2) social control of individuals within an institution capable of terrible destruction.

One reason for the nearly unanimous public support for the current war on terrorism in Afghanistan and elsewhere is that the leaders commissioned to be responsible for the most powerful army in the world are considered to be experts at their art and unquestionably under the control of elected and appointed civilian officials. Professions excel where bureaucracies do not in the creation, adaptation, and application of abstract expert knowledge to new situations. Therefore, if the Army is to remain on the cutting edge of military strategy, applied technology, and operations, its professional nature must be renewed, adapted, and preserved. Other nations may be willing to renounce the leadership role in military theory and practice, but America cannot.

With regard to social control, by nurturing the profession's ethic within its members, a profession offers a better means of shaping human behavior in situations of chaotic violence, stress, and ambiguity than bureaucratic management can ever hope to achieve. In other words, within the culture of a profession is embedded an ethos that strongly informs the actions of the individual professionals, even in the direst of circumstances. A good example appears in a letter then Maj. Gen. George Patton wrote from North Africa in 1942 to classmates in the states after his division had fared poorly against the Germans:"We did not turn and run, because we were more afraid of our consciences than we were of the enemy."[29] Such social control within the Army profession—by development of professional ethics—has been under stress during the past decade owing to political guidance to deployed forces to avoid any casualties, particularly in unpopular peacekeeping operations.[30] Such risk-averse behavior is natural and fitting for a bureaucracy. In contrast, restoring the discretion of the Army officer corps to do its duty in combat as best fits the needs of mission accomplishment, always the first priority, is vital to renewing the ethos of the Army profession.

Since the continual development of military expertise and effective control of an Army operationally engaged on behalf of American society are both essential to the nation's future security, a nonprofessional Army is certainly not in America's best interest. Equally important, neither is it in the Army's best interest. To remain relevant to the nation it serves and to effect the transformation it plans, the Army must renew its essence as a profession.

	Expert Knowledge of the Army Profession			
Level of Analysis	Military-Technical	Moral-Ethical	Political-Social	Human Development
Societal National and global context in which Army exists	National and international uses of military forces	National and international values and beliefs	National and international political and societal systems	
Civil-Military Tensions				
Institutional Internal context and systems	Internal Army systems supporting military-technical capabilities	Internal Army systems that establish, communicate, and maintain the profession's norms and values	Internal Army systems focused on political and societal actions	Internal Army systems focused on developing, educating, training, and managing the Army's human resources
Army-Soldier Tensions				
Individual People who constitute the Army	Individual knowledge and skills needed to be successful in the Army	Individual moral-ethical values	Political and social knowledge and skills held by or necessary for Army members	Individual commitment, motivation, and expectations of the Army

FIGURE 1-2. *Framework for Analysis of the Army Profession.*

FROM BUREAUCRACY TO PROFESSION— THE MISSING COMPONENT OF ARMY TRANSFORMATION

The research project serving as the basis of this book was designed to study the Army as a profession, to assess the state of the profession, and to make recommendations for the redefinition and renewal of the Army's professional character as an essential part of its planned transformation. Surprisingly, of all the studies done both by the Army and for the Army in recent years, this is the first time since 1970 that the Army has been studied *as a profession*. However, it was no surprise to discover that many of the ideas offered the last time the Army undertook to renew its professionalism—after Vietnam and the end of the draft in the early 1970s—were quite responsive to what is needed today.[31]

To coordinate the efforts of such a diverse group of researchers in the conduct of a substantive review of the state of the Army profession, we applied a common framework for the individual research as reflected in the chapters of this book (see Figure 1-2).

This framework, which incorporates both the traditional view of military professions as well as the newer view of professions as competitive vocations, allows visualization of several factors vital to the Army officer corps' successful introspection and dialogue regarding the planned transformation.

First, it becomes clear that each broad area of expert knowledge of the profession—the military-technical, the moral-ethical, the political-social, and human development—should be analyzed and understood from three different perspectives: the client's (society); the professional institution's (the Army); and that of the individual professional (officer, noncommissioned officer, Army civilian). Second, owing to the significant differences between these perspectives, the two horizontal boundaries dividing them are loci of recurrent tensions (civil-military relations and the gap in trust between the Army and its junior professionals) about which our researchers could develop policy-relevant conclusions and recommendations.

To this framework we added the new understanding of the Army profession as operating within a competitive systems of professions.[32] As discussed earlier, modern professions are competitors—for members, resources, and, most important, jurisdiction— within a "system of professions." This system includes other professions, occupations seeking professional status, and other producing organizations, each of which vies for jurisdiction and a legitimated claim to apply their expertise to specific situations. It is in the context of such jurisdictional competitions that strategic leaders of the profession must develop the detailed requirements for professional systems— education, ethics, oversight, and credentialing, to name but a few.

FINIS: IN ARMY TRANSFORMATION, PEOPLE COUNT BUT PROFESSIONALS COUNT EVEN MORE

There are many fine professionals in the Army, those who go to work each day seeking no more personally than the opportunity to serve their country by improving their expertise and applying it to the tasks at hand. To us, these professionals include anyone who has made and is living a resolute commitment to a lifetime of ethical service in the Army profession— officer, noncommissioned officer, or Department of Army civilian. Many others aspire to such status, and will doubtless someday attain it.

But among these professionals one group must be singled out for special responsibility in the planned transformation. From the members of the Army officer corps, as the commissioned agents of the American people responsible for the continued stewardship of the profession and for the development of the sons and daughters of America who serve in it, more is expected, legally and morally. It is in behalf of these officers' professional education and preparation for the role of Army steward, and equally in behalf of reinforcing professionalization for the superb noncommissioned officers with whom they serve, that this book has been prepared.

We have no doubt that, under their leadership in the years ahead, the Army profession will be redefined and renewed as the fundamental precondition for a successful Army transformation.

NOTES

1. The views and opinions expressed in this chapter are those of the authors and are not necessarily those of the Department of the Army or any other U.S. government entity.

2. Speech by Gen. Eric Shinseki, Army Chief of Staff, AUSA Symposium, 8 November 2001, accessed on 10 November at *http://www.army. mil/leaders/csa/speeches/20011108CSARE-MARKSAUSA.doc.*

3. Stephen Biddle, "Victory Misunderstood: What the Gulf War Tells Us about the Future of Conflict," *International Security* 21 (Fall 1996): 139-79.

4. For examples see Adm. William Owens, *Lifting the Fog of War* (Baltimore, MD: Johns Hopkins University Press, 2001); Michael O'Hanlon, *Technological Change and the Future of Warfare* (Washington, DC: The Brookings Institution, 2000); Stuart J.D. Swartzstein, *The Information Revolution and National Security* (Washington, DC: Center for Strategic and International Studies, 1996); and Williamson Murray and Allen R. Millett, eds., *Military Innovation in the Interwar Period* (Cambridge: Cambridge University Press, 1996).

5. See Richard O. Hundley, *Past Revolutions, Future Transformations* (Washington, DC: RAND, National Defense Research Institute, 1999).

6. For the Army's version of the war, see Robert H. Scales, Jr., *Certain Victory* (Washington, DC: Office of the Chief of staff, U.S. Army, 1993).

7. See Gen. John Shalikashvili, *Joint Vision 2010* (Washington, DC: Office of the Chairman, JCS, 1996). There is now an updated version, *Joint Vision 2020*, but the emphasis remains the same.

8. For the best summary of this debate, see O'Hanlon, Chapter 2.

9. See George C. Wilson, *This War Really Matters* (Washington, DC: CQ Press, 2000); and William Greider, *Fortress America* (New York: PublicAffairs Press, 1998).

10. For the first "modern" war, see Chapter 1 of Wesley K. Clark, *Waging Modern War* (New York: Public Affairs Press, 2001).

11. See Deborah D. Avant, *Political Institutions and Military Change* (Ithaca, NY: Cornell University Press, 1994); Elizabeth Kier, *Imagining War: French and British Military Doctrines between the Wars* (Princeton, NJ: University Press, 1999); Stephen Peter Rosen, *Innovation and the Modern Military: Winning the Next War* (Ithaca, NY: Cornell University Press, 1991); Theo Ferrell, "Figuring Out Fighting Organizations," *Journal of Strategic Studies* 19, No. 1 (March 1996): 122-135; and Michael James Meese, "Defense Decision Making Under Budget Stringency: Explaining Downsizing in the United States Army," (Ph.D. diss., Princeton University, May 2000).

12. See Peter Senge, *The Fifth Discipline* (New York, NY: Doubleday, 1990); and Emily O. Goldman, "The U.S. Military in Uncertain Times: Organizations, Ambiguity, and Strategic Adjustment," *Journal of Strategic Studies* 20, No. 2 (June 1997): 41-74.

13. See Gordon R. Sullivan and Michael V. Harper, *Hope is Not a Method* (New York: Random House, Times Business, 1996).

14. Peter D. Feaver, "The Civil-Military Problematique: Huntington, Janowitz, and the Problem of Civilian Control," *Armed Forces and Society* 23, No.2 (Winter 1996): 149-78.

15. The classics of the civil-military school include: Alfred Vagts, *A History of Militarism* (rev. ed.; New York: Free Press, 1959); Samuel P. Huntington, *The Soldier and The State* (Cambridge, MA: Harvard University Press, 1959); Morris Janowitz, *The Professional Soldier: A Social and Political Portrait* (Glencoe, NY: The Free Press, 1960); Bengt Abrahamsson, *Military Professionalism and Political Power* (Beverly Hills, CA: Sage Publishing, 1972). For more recent literature see also Samuel Sarkesian and Robert E. Connor, Jr., *The U.S. Military Profession into the Twenty-First Century* (London: Frank Cass Publishers, 2000); Michael C.

Desch, *Civilian Control of the Military* (Baltimore, MD: Johns Hopkins University Press, 1999); and Don M. Snider and Miranda Carleton-Carew, eds. *U.S. Civil-Military Relations: In Crisis or Transition* (Washington DC: Center for Strategic and International Studies, 1995).

16. See James Burk, ed., *The Adaptive Military: Armed Forces in a Turbulent World* (London: Transaction Publishers, 1998); Charles C. Moskos, "Toward a Post-Modern Military: The United States as Paradigm," in *The PostModern Military*, ed. Charles C. Moskos, John Allen Williams, and David R. Segal (Oxford, Eng.: Oxford Univ. Press, 2000): 14-31; and Don M. Snider, "America's Post-Modern Military," *World Policy Journal* 18, No. 1 (Spring 2000): 47-56.

17. For the widening gap in political identity, see Oli R. Holsti, "A Widening Gap Between the US Military and Civilian Society? Some Evidence, 1976-1996," *International Security* 23 (Winter 1998/99): 8; and commentary and reply by Joseph J. Collins and Oli Holsti, *International Security* 24 (Fall 1999): 199-207. For other gaps, see Peter D. Feaver and Richard D. Kohn, eds., *Soldiers and Civilians* (Cambridge, MA: MIT Press, 2001).

18. For example, Mary Katzenstein and Judith Reppy, *Beyond Zero Tolerance: Discrimination in Military Culture* (New York: Rowman and Littlefield Publishers, 1999). For an alternative view see Don M. Snider, "The Uninformed Debate on Military Culture," *Orbis* (Winter 1999): 11-26.

19. See discussion between the Defense press corps and newly appointed Director of Force Transformation, Rear Adm. (Ret.) Arthur K. Cebrowski, 27 November 2001 accessed at *http://www.defenselink.mil/news/Nov2001/t11272001_t1127ceb.html*.

20. See "U.S. Army White Paper: Concepts for the Objective Force," 8 November 2001 accessed at *http://www.army.mil/features/WhitePaper/default.html*.

21. See A. P. Carr-Saunders and P. A. Wilson, *The Professions* (Oxford, Eng.: Oxford University Press, 1933) for initial case studies on professions. H.L. Wilensky's "The Professionalization of Everyone?" *American Journal of Sociology* 70 (1964), 137-58, presents the professionalization sequence for American professions. For more recent literature, see Eliot Freidson, *Professional Powers: A Study of the Institutionalization of Formal Knowledge* (Chicago, IL: University of Chicago Press, 1986).

22. This discussion is drawn primarily from Andrew Abbott's, *The System of Professions: An Essay on the Division of Expert Labor* (Chicago, IL: University of Chicago Press, 1988). Additional sources include Elliott Krause, *Death of the Guilds: Professions, States, and the Advance of Capitalism, 1930 to Present* (New Haven, CT: Yale University Press, 1996); Eliot Freidson, *Professionalism Reborn: Theory, Prophecy and Policy* (Chicago, IL: University of Chicago Press, 1994).

23. For bureaucratic behavior within military institutions, see David C. Kozak and James M. Keagle, eds., *Bureaucratic Politics and National Security: Theory and Practice* (Boulder, CO: Lynne Reiner Publishers, 1988).

24. One need only look to the armies of the post-Cold War Western Europe nations for examples of this phenomenon.

25. See Don M. Snider and Gayle L. Watkins, "The Future of Army Professionalism: A Need for Renewal and Redefinition," *Parameters* 30 (Autumn 2000): 5-20.

26. See Edwin Dorn and Howard D. Graves, *American Military Culture in the 21st Century* (Washington, DC: Center for Strategic and International Studies, 2000).

27. See the Executive Summary to *The ATLDP Study Report to the Army*, accessed at *http:// www.army. mil/features/ATLD/ATLD.htm*.

28. ATLDP, Executive Summary, OS-10 and OS-11.

29. The quotation is from an unpublished manuscript, "The Inadvertent Demise of the Traditional Academy, 1945-1995," dated November 1995, by Professor Roger H. Nye, Department of History, USMA.

30. See Don M. Snider, John Nagl, and Tony Pfaff, "*Army Professionalism, the Military Ethic and Officership in the 21st Century*" (Carlisle Barracks, PA: Army War College, Strategic Studies Institute, 2000).

31. See *Study on Military Professionalism* (Carlisle Barracks, PA: U.S. Army War College, 1970). For the official history of this period, see Robert K. Griffith, *Today's Army Wants to Join You: The US Army's Transition from the Draft to an All-Volunteer Force* (Washington, DC: Center of Military History, 1995); and Anne W. Chapman, *The Army's Training Revolution, 1973-1990* (Ft. Monroe, VA: TRADOC, 1990). For a very readable current history of the same events, see James Kitfield, *Prodigal Soldiers* (New York: Simon and Schuster, 1995).

32. As noted earlier, this understanding is drawn primarily from Andrew Abbott, *The System of Professions*.

Officer Duties

This is the second of a series of seven lessons on the Army Profession and Officership. Whereas the first lesson focused on the Army's source of authority and laid historical foundations for the authority and role of the officer, this lesson expands on moral duties and responsibilities of officership.

The following topics are addressed in this lesson:

- The social contract and expectation of selfless service
- The nobility of profession
- Duty, Honor, Country
- The concept of officership as a unique calling in society

The following TLO is supported in whole or in part by this lesson:

- Relate the characteristics of a profession to military service as an officer

Following this lesson you will be able to:

- List the basic duties of an officer
- Describe and give examples of Duty, Honor, Country
- Explain how the concept of Duty, Honor, Country is significant

THE COMMANDER'S CONCEPT OF DUTY

BY ROGER NYE

> *Duty, Honor, Country. These three hallowed words reverently dictate what you ought to be, what you can be, what you will be.*

> —General of the Army Douglas MacArthur
> Thayer Award Address, May, 1962.

Shortly before the 1942 American invasion of North Africa, the Task Force commander, George S. Patton, wrote in his diary, "I hope that, whatever comes up, I shall be able to do my full duty. If I can do that, I have nothing more to ask. Fate will deliver what success I shall attain . . ." Three centuries earlier, the Frenchman Pierre Corneille advised in *El Cid,* "Do your duty, and leave the rest to heaven." Since the Age of Pericles, philosophers, playwrights, and generals have never doubted that duty was the central virtue of the professional military man. But this was not so in 1984, when two Washington study groups wrote 500-word statements of philosophy for Army systems that governed officer personnel management and professional development—never using the word Duty. Moreover, they did not mention Honor or Country. Instead, they wrote of commitment, selfless service, loyalty, and candor.

Was this a mere substitution of modern words for antique ones? Or was there a new message, a departure from a long tradition?

Subordinating "duty" to newer Army values seems to have evolved from the American experience in Vietnam. In 1980, the Chief of Staff of the Army, General Edward C. Meyer, spoke and wrote of Army values, emphasizing not duty but, rather, loyalty to institution, loyalty to unit, personal responsibility, and selfless service. A year later, General Donn A. Starry also omitted duty from his assessment of important military values; he expanded the Chief's list to include competence, commitment, candor, and courage. ("In Pursuit of an Ethic," *Army,* Sep., 1981, 11) The goal of this new language was to correct an evil that had come upon the Army—too many officers misbehaving and thinking it necessary to lie, cheat, and steal in order to get ahead.

The new language might well achieve this goal, for it underscored those values that would assure obedience to authority, be it to regulations, superior commanders or institutions. The new words said little about mutual trust and obligations, about the professional growth of officers and NCO's, or about the importance of the strong individual in creativity, leadership, and command. The new language was the answer to a special problem in the Officer Corps. It was apparently necessary, because the old traditional concepts were too difficult to be taught and grasped by young people from contemporary American society.

The substantive difference between old and new was in the concept of self, the worth of the person, and the place of the individual in a shared human enterprise. While the new word "commitment," for example, implied giving over one's will to the cause (be it institution, ideal, or group), the old word "duty" implied that the individual should determine the nature and extent of his obligation, and then give the obedience and allegiance that reason dictated.

While the new "candor" called for truthfulness and frankness, it did so as an institutional requirement, for automatic conformance by the individual involved. The old word "honor" called for truthfulness and honesty to sustain, not only the institution, but the honor or reputation of the individual, whose most valuable asset was his good name for integrity and trustworthiness.

In the new language, loyalty to institution and unit became a requirement of conduct boldly demanded by superiors. In the old language, loyalty was subordinated to other values, a commodity to be earned by authority, and then offered as a duty by the individual because the object of his loyalty merited it.

Finally, the introduction of the new concept of "selfless service" seemed to advocate that the strong, self-centered personalities like Patton and MacArthur be avoided, as subversive to loyalty and good morals. In contrast, the old language did not necessarily probe into the motivations of the individual, but assumed that selfishness was ever-present and ineradicable, and that the self, while inviolable, was always in need of discipline, restraint, and temperance. The old philosophy wisely coped with "weakness of character," rather than foolishly trying to order evil into oblivion. In so doing, it nurtured the strong-willed and often self-centered personalities that breathed creativity, leadership, and discipline into Army life. The strength and meaning of these "old school" military values were delineated by Edgar F. Puryear in

Nineteen Stars, a comparison of the ideals and careers of Marshall, MacArthur, Patton, and Eisenhower.

The future commander, looking for a settled philosophy about military conduct, might well ask whether he would prefer the old or new language in counseling subordinates. If he accuses a wayward lieutenant of not giving "selfless service" in the performance of his tasks, the junior officer may well assume that he has been insulted, ask for proof, and effectively terminate the conversation. If, on the other hand, the commander suggests that he and the lieutenant talk about the latter's conception of what his duty is and how it might be performed, no insult about motives need be inferred and some progress might be made. In the traditional language of duty, personalities could be left out, and an impartial discussion of a third entity entertained.

In the early chapters of these commentaries on military command, the lieutenant who thought his commanders too self-centered might have had a different view if he had been trained to think in terms of duty rather than of selfless service. If asked, "Does your commander carry out his duty in a worthy manner?," the lieutenant would have had to assess the nature of the senior's duty and whether he handled it well. The old language provided for distance between ranks, more suitable for cool assessment and dispassionate appraisal.

For the commander who would organize his thoughts and actions around the concept of duty, military memoirs and biographies offer a wide array of mentors. *The Eisenhower Diaries,* for example, reveal a five-star general's arguing within himself as to whether he should be a candidate for the Presidency. In August, 1951, as Supreme Allied Commander in Europe, Ike wrote that Republican leaders had come to persuade him to run for the job.

> They recognize that I have an important duty in this post. They believe that I have (rather, will have) a more important duty, to accept the Republican nomination.... I've told them, as I tell all, that I'll certainly always try to do my duty to the country, when I know what that duty is. As of now I have a duty; I cannot yet even describe the circumstances that would be conclusive in convincing me that my duty had changed to that of assuming a role in a political field. (198-199)

Two months later he wrote:

> I entered upon this post only from a sense of duty—I certainly had to sacrifice much in the way of personal convenience, advantage, and congenial constructive work when I left New York [as president of Columbia University]. I will never leave this post for any other governmental task except in response to a clear call to duty. I will not be a participant in any movement that attempts to secure for me a nomination because I believe that the presidency is something that should never be sought, just as I believe, of course, that it could never be refused.... I would consider the nomination of which they speak, if accomplished without any direct or indirect assistance or connivance on my part, to place upon me a transcendent duty.... As of now I see nothing to do but keep my mouth shut. (204)

In the early part of 1952, Ike agreed that a nomination by the Republican Party constituted a valid call to a more important duty. His diary entries reflected three characteristics of the person who has guided his life toward a star of duty. First was his ingrained desire to do the right thing—to obey the law, to meet obligations, to await a mandate from others. Second was his determination to uphold principles that he had adopted for himself—to serve his country, and keep out of politics when in uniform. Third was his awareness that one has many duties, which may often be in conflict. One must make choices about which duty is transcendent at any give time.

THE NATURE OF SOLDIERLY DUTY

While few men have the burden of deciding if it is their duty to become President of the United States, all Army officers face challenges to their sense of duty every day. At the working levels of the Army, the questions are quite mundane: Is it my duty to see that this Hispanic soldier learns to read English? Is it my duty to volunteer for a combat assignment? Is it my duty to stay in the company overnight, to see that we are ready for tomorrow's inspection? Is it my duty to stand in for a fellow officer when he is unaccountably absent?

Each of these questions arises from the demands of duty which, for military people, has at least eight faces, or varieties that must be honored. Chart 5 is a quick summary of the scope of the soldier's duty.

The first four varieties of duty stem from the officer's commissioning warrant, the oath of office, and acceptance into a profession with a special responsibility. The remainder are the responsibilities of any human being, although they take on greater meaning because of the public nature of the officer's work; it is the duty of military leaders to set an example. They do not have the freedom of civilians to ignore these charges. Only the eighth duty is self-selected, since it is for those officers whose God and religion are a fundamental allegiance in their lives; they adhere to Ecclesiastes XII, 13: "Fear God and keep His Commandments, for this is the whole duty of man."

The Chart's listing of the varieties of a soldier's duty includes both professional and personal obligations. This is considerably at variance with those who would speak only of professional matters, leaving the officer's private life to "his own time." Human beings are not divided into such neat categories; they each have one mind and one character, weigh their decisions and actions as a total person. To some degree, officers are "on duty" twenty-four hours a day, and are never entirely professional or entirely personal. Rather, military people must consider all facets of their duty concurrently, as though holding a cut diamond to the light and looking at each of its facets as an expression of the whole.

CHART 5

The Varieties of the Soldier's Duty

1. The duty to obey orders and carry out assigned missions.
2. The duty to care for subordinates and build strong units.
3. The duty to defend the nation, its people, and its values.
4. The duty to uphold the profession and its ethical code.
5. The duty of self-development to one's highest potential.
6. The duty of fidelity to family, friends, and colleagues.
7. The duty to uphold the moral principles of civilized man.
8. The duty to one's God and religion.

It is normal for these varieties of duty to be in conflict with each other. For those concerned with doing their duty, life is a succession of choices that relegate the myriad of obligations and duties to their proper time, place, and importance. Often, choices result in compromise. The combat commander, for example, may estimate that his mission will produce excessive casualties if conducted according to the operations order; he may seek to resolve this conflict between duty to mission and duty to the troops by requesting an alternative timing or route of advance, which can complete the same mission with fewer casualties.

In 1951, General Douglas MacArthur, who spoke more about duty than any other soldier, felt that he had to choose between obeying the orders of President Truman and defending the nation's interest by waging war more aggressively against the Chinese. He found no compromise, persisted in his dogma, and was relieved of his command. In succeeding years, he argued that the soldier's first duty is to the Constitution rather than to the men temporarily in power. The same "higher duty" argument was used by officers dissenting from service in Vietnam. This pressing problem of disobedience in the sixties is analyzed in Michael Walzer's *Obligations: Essays on Disobedience, War, and Citizenship.*

When claims of duty are used to govern decisions and actions, the soldier becomes aware of the limits and terminal points of one's duty. Like MacArthur, some take their dissent to the point of giving up their commissions and leaving active service. More customary is the decision to limit one's dissent at the point where argument over policy has ceased, a decision is made, and unity is needed to carry out the policy.

Another important limitation of the duty to obey is the code clearly stating that an officer should not obey an unlawful order. Whether one can prove that the order is or could be illegal may be very difficult. Unless the issue involves murder or some other equally heinous crime, the refusal to obey is usually worked out between contending parties before a court must decide whether or not an order is legal. The important effect of the code is to deter commanders from issuing illegal orders, rather than to safeguard those who disobey.

The most significant limitations of the soldier's duty are those that must be self-imposed by the soldier himself. Duty to the family cannot be met fully if one's duty to subordinates and units is to be fulfilled effectively. Each professional finds his own individual compromises between these claims. Soldiers often feel that they must limit the duty owed to friends and colleagues, particularly when such friends misuse a friendship to ask for favors bordering on unethical, illegal, or immoral activities. In these cases, one "discharges" the duty with which one has previously "charged" oneself.

How do commanders judge between the demands of conflicting duties? Some do it well; others, poorly. Many barely recognize that the problem exists, and are continually surprised to find their decisions ill-advised and not carried out. These commanders are usually out of touch with their people, although they may talk with them every day. They appear to be without strong moral convictions, are easily swayed by the last person they talked to, and are pliable in the hands of their seniors. They react to fear for their popularity and to opportunities for immediate gain. They are at the beginning stages of moral growth, as suggested in Lawrence Kohlberg's *Essays on Moral Development: Moral Stages and the Idea of Justice.*

The majority of American military commanders fit into Kohlberg's intermediate moral stages much better; they adhere to the set of moral principles brought to the Army from their early years of family and religious training. They make their judgments heavily in favor of the values of the institutions that they serve—the Army, the nation, and the units to which they are assigned. Obedience, patriotism, loyalty to the mission and the unit: these are the duties weighing the most in the judgments. For some, however, the results are often crude and misguided—decisions that reflect the jargon of the trade, such as "I go by the book," and "We accept only zero defects." This narrow orientation produces old responses to new challenges, a failure to serve the real needs of the Army, and a cookie-cutter standard reaction to problems rather than the creative solutions that are needed.

In contrast, the best commanders tend to put strong emphasis on their duty "to uphold the moral principles of civilized man," using it to make judgments about the many varieties of duty they face. They are aware of the moral principles that have been passed down through the ages. They believe in the efficacy of these principles in sustaining worthy

CHART 6

Moral Principles of Primary Concern to Military Commanders

Beneficence towards others, as reflected in:

- not inflicting evil or harm on others, killing, stealing, bearing false witness
- preventing evil or harm from coming to others
- removing evil from institutions and society

Fidelity towards others, as reflected in:

- truth-telling
- promise-keeping.
- reparation for previous wrongful acts
- gratitude for previous beneficial arts, such as giving and preserving life.

Justice towards others, as in assuring a proper distribution of rights, benefits, and injuries

communities and institutions, and act in accordance with them. Through this knowing, believing, and doing, they are identified with Kohlberg's higher levels of moral development. Chart 6 presents a listing of these moral principles, derived from Dr. Arthur Dyke's *On Human Care,* a textbook that has been used in courses in military ethics at the U.S. Army War college.

It is evident from this Chart that moral principles have to do with one's actions towards other human beings, whether beneficence, fidelity, or justice. These "rules" govern the actions of men and women in dealing with each other as human beings—as part of a society of mankind. Commanders who adhere to these principles see themselves as leaders of a community over which they have the authority to act. Here there is little room for the ego-gratification or self-aggrandizement that afflicts commanders who see themselves standing in splendid isolation above the masses.

PERFORMING DUTY FOR REASONS OF JUSTICE

Cadets who came into the Army in the fifties often listened to the following story told by a chaplain. There was once a traveler on the road to Jericho who had been beaten, robbed, and left to die. Two noble citizens passed him by as if they did not see him. Then a Samaritan, a stranger in the land, came by. He stopped, dressed the traveler's wounds, and took him to an inn to recover. The chaplain finished his story of The Good Samaritan with an observation. Had there been a soldier stationed on the road to Jericho, whose duty was to protect travelers from evil, the victim would have never been assaulted, the passerby would not have been mocked for their hypocrisy, and the Samaritan would not have been tested for his compassion, nor delayed on his journey. The cadets left the sermon convinced that the life of the soldier was worthy, made so by his duty to safeguard the citizenry of a nation.

But the chaplain did not go quite far enough. How do we know that the soldier posted on the road to protect travelers would actually carry out his duty? Might not the soldier ignore the robbers if they were better armed than he? Was there any guarantee that he would not join them in their plundering? Or suppose that a group of citizens came to the soldier one day, saying, "The government is corrupt and exploits the people. You have more important things to do than to protect this road. It is your higher duty to join us and employ your weapons to pull down this evil government." What, if anything, will cause the soldier to resist such temptations?

Obedience and discipline, if properly understood and enforced, can keep the soldier aware of his duty in ordinary times. But the commitment to duty that is necessary under exceptional circumstances must be reinforced by values that tie the soldier to the service of other human beings. Chief among these soldierly values is a sense of justice.

In 1939, General Sir Archibald Wavell foretold an audience, at Cambridge University:

> In a future war . . . discipline should be a different matter from the old traditional military discipline. It has changed greatly since I joined, and is changing still. But, whatever the system, it is the general's business to see *justice* done. The soldier does not mind a severe code, provided it is administered fairly and reasonably.
> —Wavell, *Soldiers and Soldiering, 28.*

Like Wavell, most soldiers equate justice with fairness, the fairness of one's dealing with other human beings. This is *distributive justice,* wherein equal individuals merit equal shares of social goods and evils. The commander, however, is also concerned with two other kinds of justice. One is *contributive justice,* wherein each person must contribute equally to the sustaining of institutions that benefit him, such as his government or his infantry company. The other is the justice of *human rights,* wherein every human being is entitled to certain inalienable rights, such as freedom from murder, bondage, theft, and libel. The legal justice that must be provided by the military commander is largely in the justice of human rights. The inquiring commander finds further analysis of these three concepts of justice in Mortimer J. Adler's *Six Great Ideas* and John Rawls' *A Theory of Justice.*

Aristotle argued that man is governed by love in his dealings with his family and very close friends. But beyond this tight inner circle, in the absence of love, man must be governed by justice, as promulgated by a tribal, institutional, or state government. Through justice, each receives according to what is due him; the determination of "just dues" within the organization may be based on law, merit, or fairness.

Not everyone agrees with Aristotle that rewards should be based on merit, and that those who are unequal should receive unequal shares of the rewards or punishments. By the test of fairness, however, each man is entitled to equal treatment with others, and if some are given disproportionate shares of material wealth, power, or freedom, this inequality must be justified on the grounds that it benefits everyone in the organization. Hence, a commander acquires more power or physical comforts than that of his subordinates only if the least advantaged man in the organization benefits from this unequal distribution.

Justice is said to be the first virtue of social institutions, just as truth is of systems of thought. Wise commanders of military "social institutions" know that justice demands fairness as well a lawfulness, and that they must insist that every soldier willingly contributes his fair share of the work to the cooperative enterprise of the unit. But they also know that every obligation of the soldier has an earned right attached to it. These are obverse sides of the same coin, and for every sacrifice of freedom of movement and speech that a soldier makes, he can rightfully expect commanders to use restraint in curbing the soldier's fundamental liberty.

Understanding the citizen-soldier's right to basic freedoms has been most difficult for American commanders of the past two generations. All citizens are guaranteed freedom of thought and conscience; freedom of speech, assembly, and personal movement; freedom to participate equally in political affairs; and a variety of basic civil liberties. But if men are to act as one in a fighting organization, obedient to civilian and military command and able to live together in close quarters without harming each other, they are required to forego some of their inherent freedoms.

The wise commander, however, knows that subordinates need sufficient freedom to develop their capacities and to avoid losing their identities as men and women. He also knows that the protection of this freedom is the fundamental reason for America's wars with Naziism, Japanese militarism, and communism in Korea and Vietnam. Such commanders recognize that to curb the soldier's liberty beyond what is demanded by real military necessity is to perpetrate injustice and unfairness among the troops. Commanders who substitute personal whim and craving for power for military necessity in determining the liberties of their subordinates suffer the consequences—a decline in unit morale and effectiveness.

The respect for an individual's dignity that causes the commander to give a subordinate extensive freedom also causes him to resist the temptation to manipulate the soldier into shameful or wrongful deeds. To lead, we are told, is to cause others to do willingly what one wants them to do. Commanders who are unused to power find security in manipulating men through fear, intimidation, or false promises, thereby manipulating them into "willing" performances. Such commanders may misunderstand the writings of psychologists (such as B. F. Skinner in *About Behaviorism*) that describe how researchers can manipulate their human objects into certain behavioral patterns. Commanders who seek "the good" of their troops, however, are more prone to look upon manipulation of subordinates as the philosophers do; that is, as unethical and an assault upon the integrity and worth of other human beings. The trick is, of course, to distinguish between proper demands on subordinates and the unethical manipulation of them. A concern for justice and fairness makes this discernment easier.

In 1804 Napoleon wrote, "There is no strength without justice." Today, the strength of the American Army is sapped by the injustice that arises from neglect or miscalculation—errors in pay, promotion, rotation of assignments. Correcting injustice here is a matter of sensing the problem and pursuing it with skill through the labrynthine system. Much of the injustice is also due to bad policy decisions, ordering conflicting requirements without providing the time and resources for accomplishment, until men are senselessly overworked, deprived of deserved liberty, or wrongly rated on their performances. These injustices call for a quick policy change; only commanders who are aware of the real price paid for injustice can avoid or correct such wrongdoing.

When neither miscalculations nor erroneous policy are to blame, we look for the villain who forces injustice on subordinates for a variety of ego-gratifying reasons—the desire to see lackeys jump, the urge to keep other races or ethnic groups in servility, the hankering to savor anachronistic rules long after they have become unjust, only because they are symbolic of a more comfortable past. Nevertheless, the villains argue that they are only acting in the organization's best interest, in which they crave a more generous share of power and privilege. It is most difficult to avoid or correct injustice coming from this source. But the process of eradicating these miscreants goes on. In the words of the Naval Board investigating the mutiny on H.M.S. Bounty: "If justice be not in the mind of the Captain, it be not aboard."

THE DUTY OF SELF-DEVELOPMENT

On 7 July, 1970, Captain John Alexander Hottell was strapped in a helicopter that was caught up in a tropical storm and slammed into a hillside in a remote mountain area of Vietnam. Shortly before, while commanding a company of the 1st Cavalry Division, he had written a sealed letter to his wife, Linda, which began:

> I am writing my own obituary . . .
> [because] I am quite simply the last authority on my own death.
>
> I loved the Army: it reared me, it nurtured me, and it gave me the most satisfying years of my life. Thanks to it I have lived an entire lifetime in 26 years. It is only fitting that I should die in its service. We all have but one death to spend, and insofar as it can have any meaning it finds it in the service of comrades in arms.
>
> And yet, I deny that I died FOR anything—not my Country, not my Army, not my fellow man, none of those things. I LIVED for these things, and the manner in which I chose to do it involved the very real chance that I would die in the execution of my duties. I knew this and accepted it, but

my love for West Point and the Army was great enough—and the promise that I would someday be able to serve all the ideals that meant anything to me through it was great enough—for me to accept this possibility as a part of a price which must be paid for all things of great value. If there is nothing worth dying for—in this sense—there is nothing worth living for.

The Army let me live in Japan, Germany, and England, with experiences in all of these places that others only dream about . . . I have climbed Mount Fuji, visited the ruins of Athens, Ephesus, and Rome . . . and earned a master's degree in a foreign university. I have known what it is like to be married to a fine and wonderful woman and to love her beyond bearing with the sure knowledge that she loves me: I have commanded a company and been a father, priest, income-tax advisor, confessor, and judge for 200 men at a time; I have played college football and rugby, won the British national Diving Championship two years in a row, boxed for Oxford against Cambridge only to be knocked out in the first round. . . . I have been an exchange student at the German Military Academy, and gone to the German Jumpmaster school. I have made thirty parachute jumps from everything from a balloon in England to a jet at Fort Bragg. I have written an article for *Army* magazine, and I have studied philosophy.

I have experienced all these things because I was in the Army and because I was an Army brat. The Army is my life, it is such a part of what I was that what happened is the logical outcome of the life I lived. I never knew what it was to fail, I never knew what it is to be too old or too tired to do anything. I lived a full life in the Army, and it has exacted the price. It is only just.

Just, yes, in the personal philosophy of Alex Hottell. When the obituary eventually appeared in the press, it was admired for its expression of gratitude for being permitted such opportunities to learn, and for the sense of justice in the tradeoff of a life well lived for a cause well merited. Some felt that it expressed well the sixties' absorption with self. They could not, however, attribute selfishness to his willingness to give up life in fulfillment of that self. This was not "selfless service," but "self-in-service."

Hottell had been an excellent commander at the company level. He had earned two Silver Stars, and some said that he had been "rescued from himself" by sudden orders to division headquarters. If there was an explanation for his nascent capacity to command, it lay in his incessant desire to learn—to read, to experience new phenomena, to question, to experiment. The duty of "self-development to one's highest potential," although stated crudely in Chart 5, symbolized Hottell's personal philosophy of daily living. His enforcement of it, however, was more in keeping with Theodore Ropp's reason for reading military history—"because it is fun."

Learning about the role of a military commander must start early enough for a person to acquire a vision of himself in command roles at several levels higher than then held. Hottell saw a model in Major General George W. Casey, who died in the crash with him: He is imaginative, aggressive, charming, and has a more complete grasp of the complex missions that confront the American division commander than I would have thought possible. It will be almost a religious experience for me to serve with the Cav when this man commands it." Such visions of what a commander should be came not only from Hottell's reading of military biography, but also from his study of philosophy and literature; he had read not only Plato's description of the "man of virtue," but also the modern expressions of same theme, such as John F. Kennedy's *Profiles in Courage*.

The duty of self-development for commanders seems to call for three study objectives. First is the acquisition of knowledge and skills associated with the several roles of the commander—leader, manager, tactician, warrior, strategist, and moral standard bearer. Second is the acquisition of knowledge, insights, and values associated with the virtuous human being, perhaps best stated in Plato's ideal of the man of wisdom, courage, temperance, and justice. Third is the acquisition of insights gained from thought about oneself the personal style that is suited best to a commander's role in the twentieth century Army environment.

For pursuing the first of these objectives, the early chapters of these commentaries cite books useful in developing one's vision as a tactician, warrior, professional, leader, and manager. In addition to these, future commanders will want to read the recent mind-expanding popular works that widen the vision of the management expert, such as John Naisbit's *Megatrends: Ten New Directions Transforming Our*

Lives, Scott and Hart's *Organizational America;* and Peters and Austin's *A Passion for Excellence.* In the field of leadership, some of the best works deal with political leaders, such as James McGregor Burns' *Leadership,* Field Marshal Bernard Montgomery's *The Path to Leadership,* and Dankwart A. Rustow's *Philosophers and Kings: Studies in Leadership.*

In order to develop a more complete understanding of Plato's "virtuous leader," commanders must turn to some of the classic and popular works of philosophy, religion, literature, and history. Mortimer J. Adler has made some of the best ideas on justice and duty readable in *Six Great Ideas* and *Aristotle For Everybody: Difficult Thought Made Easy.* For a remarkably penetrating analysis of the relationship between justice and man's ability to cope with modern society, there is Alasdair MacIntyre's *After Virtue: A Study of Moral Theory.* Recent popular works exploring the problem of self and its place in the philosophy of public leaders include Erich Fromm's *Man For Himself* and C. S. Lewis' *The Abolition of Man.* The problems of holding power, with its dangers of corruption by hubris and arrogance, are explored by Thucydides, Macchiavelli, Hobbes, Lord Acton, and the fathers of the American Revolution; David Kipnis attempts to pull these ideas into some understandable pattern in *The Powerholders.*

The most dramatic portrayals of military commanders who have lost track of their sense of justice and the reality of their duty are Cecil Woodham-Smith's *The Reason Why* and C.S. Forester's *The General.* In contrast, Forester's story of *Rifleman Dodd* portrays the trials of a private soldier trapped behind the lines in the Napoleonic Wars, and driven to heroic feats by his sense of duty.

The third objective for commander self-development is the most difficult. It requires the creative generation of insights about one's strengths and limitations, and the finding of a person style of command that best matches one's personality with the demands of the job in the reality of modern times. Not all are to be Pattons, some might be Marshalls, none should be Custers. All should assume that command may be thrust on them in time of need; many should stp aside, so that commanders of greater potential can get experience.

Assessing self, present and potential, requires the intake of ideas generated by first-hand experience, and by the vicarious experience of reading. But the gestation and analysis of this intake often requires writing. "I do not know what I think until I try to write it down," is the byword of men and women intent on probing into their beliefs and competencies. Nearly all the inquiring soldiers discussed in these commentaries in military command have been writers as well as readers; Clark and Hottell started personal journals before entering cadet training. Writing articles for professional periodicals seems to be standard fare for future commanders. Senior commanders finish their careers by publishing books. All reflect a lifetime of note-taking, research, experimental speeches, records of conversations, summaries of reading, diaries of current thoughts, file-drawers of trial paragraphs and short talks, and "commonplace books" of poems, quotations, and speeches. These are the tools of inquiring minds, who look upon books as fuel for the mind, as gasoline is to the internal combustion engine. Reading is a means, not an end; expressing one's thoughts is the end. Xenophon's *Anabasis,* Caesar's *Commentaries,* and Napoleon's *Maxims* are summary statements of thinker-doers who were writers. Modern military men and women who are writers customarily have a reference shelf of best books alongside their dictionaries; there is distillation of these military writers' reference collections at the end of this chapter.

Alexander Pope wrote that the proper study of mankind is man. It then follows that the proper study of military command is military commanders. The biographies and memoirs provide such a study. There is, however, a special way of thinking about other men's battle experiences if one asks, "How am I suited for this and what is my best style?" Questions form in the reader's mind, and he asks them of the biographies and memoirs, which then become a goldmine of research, as well as a task undertaken "because it is fun." Each researcher has his own questions, based on his own particular inventory of hopes, fears, biases, and ambitions. In the final analysis, it remains true that there is no stereotypical commander around whom all must model their lives. Command is so unique a blend of personality and task that no two commanders should mirror each other. To the extent that they share common qualities, it is their common search for courage, truth, duty, and justice.

GENERAL MACARTHUR'S DUTY, HONOR, COUNTRY SPEECH

This speech was delivered to the member of the Association of Graduates of the United States Military Academy (USMA), the Corps of Cadets, and distinguished guests upon his acceptance of the Sylvanus Thayer Award in 1962.

DUTY, HONOR, COUNTRY

General Westmoreland, General Groves, distinguished guests, and gentlemen of the Corps (Corps of Cadets at the United States Military Academy at West Point New York). As I was leaving the hotel this morning, a doorman asked me, "Where are you bound for, General?" and when I replied, "West Point," he remarked, "Beautiful place, have you ever been there before?"

No human being could fail to be deeply moved by such a tribute as this [Thayer Award]. Coming from a profession I have served so long and a people I have loved so well, it fills me with an emotion I cannot express. But this award is not intended primarily to honor a personality, but to symbolize a great moral code-a-code of conduct and chivalry of those who guard this beloved land of culture and ancient descent. That is the animation of this medallion. For all hours and for all time, it is an expression of the ethics of the American soldier. That I should be integrated in this way with so noble an ideal arouses a sense of pride, and yet of humility, which will be with me always.

Duty, honor, country: Those three hallowed words reverently dictate what you ought to be, what you can be, what you will be. They are your rallying point to build courage when courage seems to fail, to regain faith when there seems to be little cause for faith, to create hope when hope becomes forlorn.

Unhappily, I possess neither that eloquence of diction, that poetry of imagination, nor that brilliance of metaphor to tell you all that they mean.

The unbelievers will say they are but words, but a slogan, but a flamboyant phrase. Every pedant, every demagogue, every cynic, every hypocrite, every troublemaker, and, I am sorry to say, some others of an entirely different character, will try to downgrade them even to the extent of mockery and ridicule.

But these are some of the things they do. They build your basic character. They mold you for your future roles as the custodians of the Nation's defense. They make you strong enough to know when you are weak, and brave enough to face yourself when you are afraid.

WHAT THE WORDS TEACH

They teach you to be proud and unbending in honest failure, but humble and gentle in success; not to substitute words for actions, not to seek the path of comfort, but to face the stress and spur of difficulty and challenge; to learn to stand up in the storm, but to have compassion on those who fall; to master yourself before you seek to master others; to have a heart that is clean, a goal that is high; to learn to laugh, yet never forget how to weep; to reach into the future, yet never neglect the past; to be serious, yet never to take yourself too seriously; to be modest so that you will remember the simplicity of true greatness, the open mind of true wisdom, the meekness of true strength.

They give you a temperate will, a quality of the imagination, a vigor of the emotions, a freshness of the deep springs of life, a temperamental predominance of courage over timidity, of an appetite for adventure over love of ease.

They create in your heart the sense of wonder, the unfailing hope of what next, and joy and inspiration of life. They teach you in this way to be an officer and a gentleman.

And what sort of soldiers are those you are to lead? Are they reliable? Are they brave? Are they capable of victory?

Their story is known to all of you. It is the story of the American man-at-arms. My estimate of him was formed on the battlefield many, many years ago, and has never changed. I regarded him then, as I regard him now, as one of the world's noblest figures; not only as one of the finest military characters, but also as one of the most stainless.

His name and fame are the birthright of every American citizen. In his youth and strength, his love and loyalty, he gave all that mortality can give. He needs no eulogy from me; or from any other man. He has written his own history and written it in red on his enemy's breast.

But when I think of his patience in adversity of his courage under fire and of his modesty in victory, I am filled with an emotion of admiration I cannot put into words. He belongs to history as furnishing one of the greatest examples of successful patriotism. He belongs to posterity as the instructor of future generations in the principles of liberty and freedom. He belongs to the present, to us, by his virtues and by his achievements.

WITNESS TO THE FORTITUDE

In 20 campaigns, on a hundred battlefields, around a thousand camp fires, I have witnessed that enduring fortitude, that patriotic self-abnegation, and that invincible determination which have carved his statue in the hearts of his people.

From one end of the world to the other, he has drained deep the chalice of courage. As I listened to those songs [of the glee club], in memory's eye I could see those staggering columns of the first World War, bending under soggy packs on many a weary march, from dripping dusk to drizzling dawn, slogging ankle deep through the mire of shell-pocked roads to form grimly for the attack, blue-lipped, covered with sludge and mud, chilled by the wind and rain, driving home to their objective, and for many to the judgment seat of God.

I do not know the dignity of their birth, but I do know the glory of their death. They died, unquestioning, uncomplaining, with faith in their hearts, and on their lips the hope that we would go on to victory.

Always for them: Duty, honor, country. Always their blood, and sweat, and tears, as we sought the way and the light and the truth. And 20 years after, on the other side of the globe, again the filth of murky foxholes, the stench of ghostly trenches, the slime of dripping dugouts, those boiling suns of relentless heat, those torrential rains of devastating storms, the loneliness and utter desolation of jungle trails, the bitterness of long separation from those they loved and cherished, the deadly pestilence of tropical disease, the horror of stricken areas of war.

SWIFT AND SURE ATTACK

Their resolute and determined defense, their swift and sure attack, their indomitable purpose, their complete and decisive victory - always through the bloody haze of their last reverberating shot, the vision of gaunt, ghastly men, reverently following your password of duty, honor, country.

The code which those words perpetuate embraces the highest moral law and will stand the test of any ethics or philosophies ever promulgated for the things that are right and its restraints are from the things that are wrong. The soldier, above all

other men, is required to practice the greatest act of religious training–sacrifice. In battle, and in the face of danger and death, he discloses those divine attributes which his Maker gave when He created man in His own image. No physical courage and no greater strength can take the place of the divine help which alone can sustain him. However hard the incidents of war may be, the soldier who is called upon to offer and to give his life for his country is the noblest development of mankind.

You now face a new world, a world of change. The thrust into outer space of the satellite, spheres, and missiles marks a beginning of another epoch in the long story of mankind. In the five or more billions of years the scientists tell us it has taken to form the earth, in the three or more billion years of development of the human race, there has never been a more abrupt or staggering evolution.

We deal now, not with things of this world alone, but with the illimitable distances and as yet unfathomed mysteries of the universe. We are reaching out for a new and boundless frontier. We speak in strange terms of harnessing the cosmic energy, of making winds and tides work for us, of creating unheard of synthetic materials to supplement or even replace our old standard basics; to purify sea water for our drink; of mining ocean floors for new fields of wealth and food; of disease preventatives to expand life into the hundred of years; of controlling the weather for a more equitable distribution of heat and cold, of rain and shine; of spaceships to the moon; of the primary target in war, no longer limited to the armed forces of an enemy, but instead to include his civil populations; of ultimate conflict between a united human race and the sinister forces of some other planetary galaxy; of such dreams and fantasies as to make life the most exciting of all times.

And through all this welter of change and development your mission remains fixed, determined, inviolable. It is to win our wars. Everything else in your professional career is but corollary to this vital dedication. All other public purposes, all other public projects, all other public needs, great or small, will find others for their accomplishment; but you are the ones who are trained to fight.

THE PROFESSION OF ARMS

Yours is the profession of arms, the will to win, the sure knowledge that in war there is no substitute for victory, that if you lose, the Nation will be destroyed, that the very obsession of your public service must be duty, honor, country.

Others will debate the controversial issues, national and international, which divide men's minds. But serene, calm, aloof, you stand as the Nation's war guardian, as its lifeguard from the raging tides of international conflict, as its gladiator in the arena of battle. For a century and a half you have defended, guarded, and protected its hallowed traditions of liberty and freedom, of right and justice.

Let civilian voices argue the merits or demerits of our processes of government: Whether our strength is being sapped by deficit financing indulged in too long, by Federal paternalism grown too mighty, by power groups grown too arrogant, by politics grown too corrupt, by crime grown too rampant, by morals grown too low, by taxes grown too high, by extremists grown too violent; whether our personal liberties are as thorough and complete as they should be.

These great national problems are not for your professional participation or military solution. Your guidepost stands out like a ten-fold beacon in the night: Duty, Honor, Country.

You are the leaven which binds together the entire fabric of our national system of defense. From your ranks come the great captains who hold the Nation's destiny in their hands the moment the war tocsin sounds.

The long, gray line has never failed us. Were you to do so, a million ghosts in olive drab, in brown khaki, in blue and gray, would rise from their white crosses, thundering those magic words: Duty, Honor, Country.

PRAYS FOR PEACE

This does not mean that you are warmongers. On the contrary, the soldier above all other people prays for peace, for he must suffer and bear the deepest wounds and scars of war. But always in our ears ring the ominous words of Plato, that wisest of all philosophers: "Only the dead have seen the end of war."

The shadows are lengthening for me. The twilight is here. My days of old have vanished–tone and tint. They have gone glimmering through the dreams of things that were. Their memory is one of wondrous beauty, watered by tears and coaxed and caressed by the smiles of yesterday. I listen vainly, but with thirsty ear, for the witching melody of faint bugles blowing reveille, of far drums beating the long roll.

In my dreams I hear again the crash of guns, the rattle of musketry, the strange, mournful mutter of the battlefield. But in the evening of my memory always I come back to West Point. Always there echoes and re-echoes: Duty, Honor, Country.

Today marks my final roll call with you. But I want you to know that when I cross the river, my last conscious thoughts will be of the corps, and the corps, and the corps.

I bid you farewell.

Role of the Army

This is the third of a series of seven lessons on the Army Profession and Officership. This lesson explains and places the organizational structure of the Army in relation to the larger context of the Armed Forces and national security and defense.

The following topics are addressed in this lesson:

- The mission and role of the Army and sister services
- National Security Act of 1947
- Constitutional and legal basis for the Army
- The value of selfless service as part of the Army tradition

The following TLO is supported in whole or in part by this lesson:

- Relate the characteristics of a profession to military service as an officer

Following this lesson you will be able to:

- Explain in general terms, the National Command structure
- Explain the role of the Army, and the Army's mission
- Compare and contrast the role of the Army in relation to its sister organizations

MISSIONS, PURPOSE, AND ORGANIZATION

BY KEITH E. BONA

> Army forces are the decisive component of land warfare in joint and multinational operations. The Army organizes, trains, and equips its forces to fight and win the nation's wars and achieve directed national objectives. Fighting and winning the nation's wars is the foundation of Army service—the Army's nonnegotiable contract with the American people and its enduring obligation to the nation.
> —Field Manual 3-0, *Operations* (14 June 2001)

The U.S. Army consists of 23 combat division equivalents: 10 active-duty divisions, 8 National Guard divisions, and 15 National Guard enhanced combat brigades, which equate to 5 more combat divisions. These units are formed under one of the Army's four corps headquarters. There are in addition, hundreds of combat, combat support, and combat service support units that are available for assignment to corps and higher-level support commands. As of 2002, the Army has 482,000 soldiers on active duty, 206,000 in the reserves, and 352,000 in the National Guard for a total strength of 1,040,000 soldiers. In addition, there are 222,000 direct-hire Department of the Army civilian employees.

This impressive force represents the landpower of the United States. It is the Army that must be ready to fight today, with the weapons and equipment on hand, anywhere in the world, as directed by the nation's civilian leaders. It's purpose is to provide for the security of the nation, and of our people, and to accomplish assigned tasks related to the attainment of America's national and international interests. If war—or combat operations short of war—cannot be deterred, the mission of the Army and the other armed forces of the United States is to fight the enemy and win the conflict as quickly as possible.

In carrying out its combat missions, the Army forces always operates under the command of a U.S. joint commander. They operate in close cooperation with other U.S. military forces in *joint* operations; with the forces of other nations in *multinational* operations; and with a variety of governmental agencies and non-governmental organizations in *interagency* operations. Never have the demands on an Army officer's skills been greater than they are today.

OBJECTIVES OF THE ARMY

The objectives, or purpose, of the Army should be understood clearly by all members of the Army, and by each of our nation's citizens. It is firmly established in Title 10, USC, as follows:

It is the intent of Congress to provide an Army that is capable, in conjunction with the other armed forces, of—

(1) preserving the peace and security and providing for the defense of the United States, the Territories, Commonwealths, and possessions and any areas occupied by the United States;

(2) supporting the national policies;

(3) implementing the national objectives; and

(4) overcoming any nations responsible for aggressive acts that imperil the peace and security of the United States.

In general, the Army, within the Department of the Army, includes land combat and service forces and such aviation and water transport as may be organic therein. It shall be organized, trained, and equipped primarily for prompt and sustained combat incident to operations on land. It is responsible for the preparation of land forces necessary for the effective prosecution of war except as otherwise assigned and, in accordance with integrated joint mobilization plans, for the expansion of the peacetime components of the Army to meet the needs of war.

MISSION-ESSENTIAL TASKS

Army Field Manual (FM) 1, *The Army* (14 June 2001), identifies six core competencies the Army must be prepared to accomplish in order to fulfill its Title 10 responsibilities. These are: "Shape the security environment; prompt response; mobilize the army; forcible entry operations; sustained land dominance; and support civil authorities." These are identified more clearly in the Army's mission-essential task list (Army METL) found in FM 3-0, *Operations,* and are summarized here. The Army's performance of these tasks generates the credible landpower necessary to preclude and deter enemy action, win decisively if deterrence fails, and establish a rapid return to sustained post-conflict stability. Tasks in the Army METL are:

Shape the Security Environment. The U.S. will remain politically and militarily engaged in the world and will maintain military superiority over potential adversaries. International military engagement in peacetime shapes the international environment in a manner that promotes and protects U.S. national security interests and is a form of deterrence. Forward basing; forward presence; force projection; peacetime military engagement activities, such as hosting foreign military personnel at our military schools and military assistance missions abroad, are examples of military engagement that shape the international security environment in a manner conducive to U.S. interests.

Respond Promptly to Crisis. Commanders organize actions in time and space to present the enemy with simultaneous, multidimensional threats— on land, and from the air, the sea, and space. Responsive Army forces are ready to conduct operational and tactical maneuver on land, early in the operation, to seize and retain the initiative, to dictate the terms of land combat, and to quickly build and maintain the momentum to win decisively. Army forces respond to crises in all environments, and Army commanders tailor and train forces to react quickly in any crisis, regardless of its nature or the circumstances.

Mobilize the Army. The Army maintains the ability to mobilize reserve component forces to meet contingent needs or the requirements of war and national emergencies. The Army also has the facilities, equipment, systems, procedures, and manpower necessary to expand its combat power rapidly and effectively, to meet either planned or unexpected contingencies, and to confront unforeseen threats to national security.

Conduct Forcible Entry Operations. Army forces are prepared to fight their way into and seize land areas previously denied them by the enemy force. Army forces can strike contested areas from the air, land, and sea. They can establish secure lodgments. The airborne and air assault capabilities of the Army allow it to seize airfields and other important facilities. In conjunction with the Navy and the other services, Army forces can conduct amphibious operations.

Dominate Land Operations. For a military operation to be successful, its outcome must be decisive. Army forces today are the best in the world and have the ability to dominate operations on most of the world's land areas and achieve decisive results. Land forces dominate when they seize the enemy's territory and resources, destroy his armed forces, and eliminate his means of controlling his population. Domination is achieved when enemy leaders conclude that close combat with U.S. forces will have only one of two possible outcomes—surrender or destruction.

Provide Support to Civil Authorities. Army forces adapt and tailor their warfighting capabilities to complement and support civil authorities and agencies at home and abroad with resources beyond local capabilities. The presence of trained and ready Army forces also contributes to security and defense of the U.S. homeland. The Army can rapidly respond to natural or manmade disasters, and to security threats at home and abroad, because it maintains a substantial presence in the United States, and has forces based or deployed forward in every theater.

Events in the wake of the September 2001 terrorist attacks in New York City and Washington, D.C., only underscore the multiplicity of roles and missions for which the Army must be prepared. To attain and retain the flexibility required to perform its roles and accomplish its mission, the Army must be in a continual state of change, adapting its thinking, organization, doctrine, and equipment. This is called Army Transformation.

The weapon systems and other equipment issued to Army units are excellent, but they are evolving. Not surprisingly, the Army's future warfighting doctrine is based on the advantages that accrue from information systems. Equipment and ordinance—from communications systems to weapons—are also changing accordingly. As newer weapons, equipment, and doctrine become available, the Army will change as necessary to make the best use of what is furnished, always with the view of performing the tasks assigned to it.

It takes trained and determined personnel to do the vital jobs of the Army, a fact that must be remembered by civil, industrial, and educational leaders, by those who mold public opinions, and by our citizens generally. Army power means power applied by soldiers in person, at close range, as the nation's mission demands.

The heart of the Army is the officer and the soldier. The soldier's training, pride in service, confidence in the excellence of equipment, and conviction as to the worthiness of the national cause are all matters that must concern our government, our leaders, and our citizens.

HEADQUARTERS, DEPARTMENT OF THE ARMY

The Headquarters, Department of the Army, in the Pentagon, Washington. D.C., is the place of final decision as to Army affairs, and it is the nerve center for control of execution of the military missions pertaining to the Army. It is an organizational component of the Department of Defense. The command and control elements of the Department of Defense and the Departments of Army. Navy, and Air Force are located together so they can work as a team and take part in jointly planned and executed combined operations (AR 10-5).

As a result of legislation passed in 1986, the Goldwater-Nichols Department of Defense Reorganization Act, a major restructuring of the Department of the Army staff and the staff of the Secretary of the Army was implemented in 1987. As a result, more immediate control of Army activities was given to the Secretary of the Army as part of a larger effort to enhance the role of the Joint Chiefs of Staff and the Secretary of Defense. The organizations for the Secretary of the Army and the Army staff are shown in the accompanying charts.

As of spring 2002, the Army is considering a further reorganization of the headquarters.

Secretary of the Army. The Secretary of the Army, a civilian, is the head of the Army and has primary responsibility for all affairs of the Army establishment. The position illustrates the application of civilian control under our Constitution. The Secretary is assisted by other civilian officials as follows:

Under Secretary of the Army. This official acts as deputy to the Secretary and is the Secretary's principal assistant. The Under Secretary also is the Army's acquisition executive and, in that capacity, reports directly to the Under Secretary of Defense for Acquisition. Two Deputy Under Secretaries are provided, one designated specifically to handle operations research matters.

Assistant Secretaries of the Army. There are five Assistant Secretaries of the Army responsible for the following areas: Acquisitions, Logistics, and Technology; Civil Works; Financial Management and Comptroller; Installations and Environment; and Manpower and Reserve Affairs.

Other Assistants to the Secretary. The following are also responsible directly to the Secretary: Director of Information Systems for C⁴ (command,

control, communications, and computers); the Inspector General; Auditor General; Chief of Legislative Liaison; Chief of Public Affairs; Director of Office of Small and Disadvantaged Business Utilization, and General Counsel.

In this staff restructuring, responsibility was transferred from the Chief of Staff to the Secretary of the Army in the areas of acquisition, auditing, comptroller activities, information management, Inspector General functions, and research and development.

Army Staff. The Secretary of the Army is assisted by the Army staff, which is the professional military staff at the Headquarters, Department of the Army. It consists of the Chief of Staff, the Army General Staff, the Special Staff, and the Personal Staff.

Chief of Staff. The Chief of Staff is the highest military assistant or adviser to the Secretary of the Army. He or she occupies the pinnacle position within the Army. He or she is a member of the Joint Chiefs of Staff. As Army Chief of Staff, his or her responsibility is to the Secretary of the Army and includes the worldwide Army mission as well as its administration, training, and supply.

Office of the Chief of Staff. The Office of the Chief of Staff includes the Vice Chief of Staff, Director of the Army Staff, and other staff members as may be required.

Army General Staff. The Chief of Staff is assisted by other staff officers, each heading a general staff agency charged with a particular function. These functions pertain to the people, planning, logistics, and intelligence aspects of the Army. The general staff officers are the Deputy Chief of Staff for Operations and Plans (DCSOPS), the Deputy Chief of Staff for Personnel (DCSPER), the Deputy Chief of Staff for Logistics (DCSLOG), the Deputy Chief of Staff for Intelligence (DCSI), the Deputy Chief of Staff for programs, and the Assistant Chief of Staff for Installation Management.

Special Staff. The Chief of Staff also is assisted by staff officers heading special staff agencies, each of which is charged with exercising responsibility for specialized activities. The special staff consists of the following officers: Chief of Engineers; Surgeon General; Chief, National Guard Bureau; and Chief, Army Reserve.

Personal Staff. The personal staff assists the Chief of Staff in specifically designated areas. It consists of the aides to the chief, other individual staff officers whose advice and assistance he or she desires to

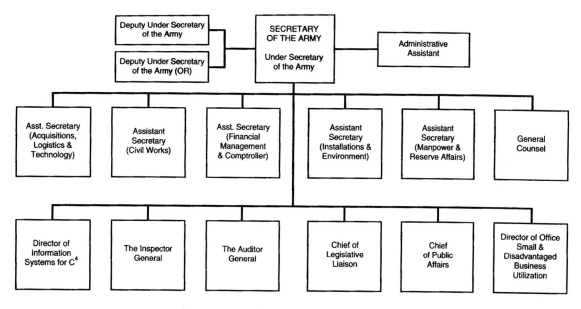

Department of the Army—Secretariat

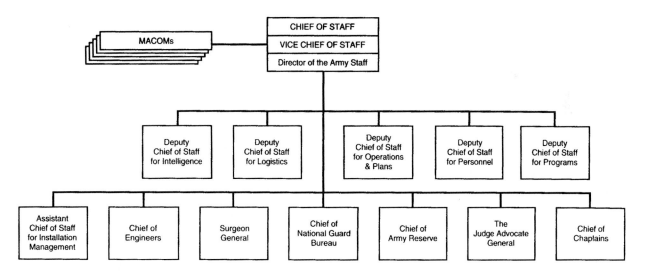

Department of the Army—Army Staff

receive directly, and those staff agencies whose functions and activities he or she desires to coordinate and administer directly.

The Personal Staff officers include the Chief of Chaplains, and the Judge Advocate General. The heads of the following staff agencies command personnel, facilities, and organizations in addition to their staff duties: the Chief of Engineers, the Surgeon General, and the Judge Advocate General.

MAJOR ARMY FIELD COMMANDS

Many of the missions of the Army are carried out through nine major Army field commands, whose missions are described below.

U.S. Army Forces Command (FORSCOM). With headquarters at Fort McPherson, Georgia, FORSCOM is the largest major command (MACOM) in the Department of the Army. FORSCOM supervises the training of almost 800,000 active Army, Army National Guard, and U.S. Army Reserve soldiers to prepare them for combat. FORSCOM provides Army support to Joint Forces Command (JFC) in its role as the joint force integrator and supplies Army forces during a crisis to other CINCs for operations elsewhere. Forces Command has four major missions:

• Supply combat-ready units to warfighting commanders-in-chief to meet their strategic, operational, and tactical needs.

• Execute contingency missions as directed by the President and Secretary of Defense through the commander-in-chief of USACOM.

• Defend the United States land mass, which includes protecting key national assets, assisting in civil defense, and helping to protect the nation from terrorism. It also works with Canadian forces to prepare for a combined defense.

• Respond to federal, state, and local officials during emergencies, natural disasters, and the war against drugs.

In recent years, FORSCOM soldiers have been dispatched to virtually every contingency operation in which Army forces participated. In the United States, FORSCOM provides aid to flood and hurricane victims, fights forest fires, and controls riots. FORSCOM is a leader in maintaining this country's quality forces through reengineering to become the most efficient organization possible by maximizing limited resources. It sets the example for other Army commands.

In today's force-projection era, FORSCOM has several major subordinate headquarters that help lead the nation's strategic, combat-ready forces: USARC, CONUSAs, and the Third U.S. Army.

United States Army Reserve Command (USARC). The United States Army Reserve Command, headquartered in Atlanta, Georgia, is responsible for all conventional Army Reserve units in the continental United States and Puerto Rico. Its commander is also Chief of the Army Reserve and is responsible for the training, equipment, and funding of Army Reserve units.

Continental United States Armies (CONUSAs). The Continental United States Armies are regional commands responsible for the operations, mobilization, and deployment of reserve units from home stations to the areas of operations. There are two continental armies: First U.S. Army, with headquarters at Fort Gillem, Georgia; and Fifth U.S. Army, headquartered at Fort Sam Houston, Texas. The CONUSAs advise state national guard adjutants general on training so that they will be prepared if called into federal service by the President.

Third U.S. Army. The Third U.S. Army, located at Fort McPherson, Georgia, serves as the Army component headquarters of the U.S. Central Command. The mission of Third Army is to plan, exercise, and deploy Army forces in response to contingencies threatening vital U.S. interests in Southwest Asia. The commanding general of Third U.S. Army also serves as the deputy commanding general of FORSCOM.

Training Centers. Forces Command units engage in home station training and joint training throughout the year. FORSCOM has two major training centers.

The *National Training Center (NTC)* at Fort Irwin, California, provides realistic training in a desert environment for armored and mechanized task forces. In addition to the space needed to maneuver heavy forces, the NTC offers a highly proficient opposing force on an instrumented battlefield, Active and reserve component maneuver battalions training at the NTC receive immediate feedback on their performance. Such training was very valuable to the units sent to the Middle East to take part in the Gulf War.

The *Joint Readiness Training Center (JRTC)* at Fort Polk, Louisiana, provides realistic training for light forces in rugged terrain where armored vehicle access is limited. The JRTC uses techniques similar to those used at the NTC and trains brigade-sized units. Training includes integrated operations with the Air Force for deployment, close air support, and aerial resupply.

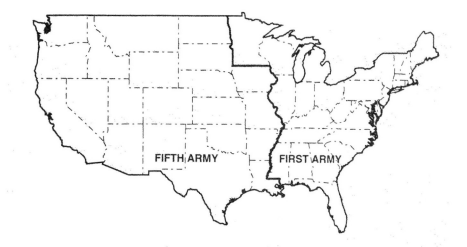

Two Continental United States Army Areas

U.S. Army Training and Doctrine Command (TRADOC). With headquarters at historic Fort Monroe, Virginia, the mission of TRADOC is to acquire and provide institutional training for the soldiers of the Army, to set the Army's training standards and requirements, and to prepare the Army for the future. TRADOC manages all institutional training for officers from basic officer courses through the Command and General Staff College, and for enlisted soldiers from basic training through the Sergeants Major Academy.

TRADOC functions through major subordinate organizations, including the Combined Arms Center (CAC) at Fort Leavenworth, Kansas; the Combined Arms Support Command (CASCOM) at Fort Lee, Virginia; the TRADOC Analysis Command (TRAC at Fort Leavenworth, Kansas; and the ROTC Cadet Command at Fort Monroe, Virginia. CAC and CASCOM direct and coordinate training (including training development and Army-wide training support), leader development, doctrine, force design, material requirements, and mission support functions. TRAC is the principal Army organization that provides in-depth analyses of Army training, doctrine, and combat developments.

Doctrine. TRADOC prepares the doctrine that determines how the Army will fight; how combat units will be supported; and how Army and joint service tactics, techniques, and procedures are standardized.

Training. Through training, soldiers and leaders are prepared to fight and win. TRADOC manages all institutional training and professional development for enlisted soldiers and officers. TRADOC commands the Army's service schools and manages officer procurement through the ROTC Cadet Command and the Officer Candidate School (OCS) program. Additionally, TRADOC supports total Army training by developing, producing, and distributing training support materials to commanders in the field.

Leader Development. TRADOC coordinates, integrates, and executes leader development matters through the Leader Development Support System.

Organizations. The TRADOC combat developments process sets requirements for how the Army organizes and equips units for battle.

Soldiers. TRADOC installations support mobilization of individual soldiers and support units during conflict, with training, processing, and logistical activities that support deployment of units and soldiers.

Architect of the Future. The uncertain and rapidly changing realities of a world in a new millennium demand that the Army embrace—indeed, lead—change, to maintain its ability to accomplish the nation's goals, policies, and objectives. To lead the Army into the future, TRADOC supervises major warfighting experiments and contributes in other ways to Army transformation.

Although high technology is key to future Army programs, combat will remain a dirty, bloody, and exhausting experience. That is why the TRADOC-avowed basis of all future Army success remains *soldiers*—competent, confident, tough, disciplined *American soldiers.* As the leaders of the 21st-century force, junior officers of today face the exciting possibilities provided by tomorrow's technologies, and the daunting and demanding requirements of leading and training the soldiers who will use them.

U.S. Army Materiel Command (AMC). The principal missions of the U.S. Army Material Command, with headquarters in Alexandria, Virginia, are to equip and sustain a trained, ready Army; to provide equipment and services to other nations through the security assistance program; to develop and acquire nonmajor systems and equipment; to provide development and acquisition support to program managers; to define, develop, and acquire superior technologies; to maintain the mobilization capabilities necessary to support the Army in emergencies; and to continue to improve productivity and quality of life.

AMC accomplishes its mission through a number of subordinate organizations, which are the Industrial Operations Command at Rock Island, Illinois; the Aviation and Missile Command at St. Louis, Missouri; the CommunicationsElectronics Command at Fort Monmouth, New Jersey; the Chemical and Biological Defense Command at Aberdeen Proving Ground, Maryland; the Army Research Laboratory at Adelphi, Maryland; the Missile Command at Redstone Arsenal, Alabama; the Tankautomotive and Armaments Command at Warren. Michigan; the Test and Evaluation Command at Aberdeen Proving Ground. Maryland; the Security Assistance Command at Alexandria, Virginia; the Simulation, Training, and Instrumentation Command at Orlando, Florida; AMCEurope at Seckenheim, Germany; and AMC-Far East at Seoul, South Korea.

U.S. Army Intelligence and Security Command (INSCOM). The U.S. Army Intelligence and Security Command, with headquarters at Fort Belvoir, Virginia, near Washington, D.C., has worldwide responsibilities for intelligence collection, electronic warfare, counterintelligence, and operations security.

U.S. Army Information Systems Command (USAISC). The U.S. Army Information Systems Command, with headquarters at Fort Huachuca, Arizona, provides information systems and services to the Army and to other Department of Defense and government organizations as directed.

U.S. Army Criminal Investigation Command (USACIC). The U.S. Army Criminal Investigation Command has its headquarters in Falls Church, Virginia, near Washington, D.C. The USACIC commands and controls worldwide Army investigations of serious crimes, provides a full range of investigative support to all Army elements, conducts sensitive and special-interest investigations, and provides personal security for selected Army and DOD officials.

U.S. Army Military District of Washington (MDW). The Military District of Washington commands Army units, activities, and installations in the national capital area and is responsible for designated Army functions in the metropolitan area of Washington, D.C. Its headquarters is located at Fort Leslie J. McNair in Washington, D.C.

U.S. Army Medical Command (MEDCOM). The U.S. Army Medical Command, with headquarters at Fort Sam Houston, Texas, is the Army's single manager for healthcare delivery and supportive services within CONUS and in Alaska and Hawaii, including command of the Army hospital system. It supervises all medical training for the Army.

U.S. Army Corps of Engineers (USACE). The U.S. Army Corps of Engineers, with headquarters in Washington, D.C., manages Army real property: manages and executes engineering, construction, and real estate programs for the Army and the Air Force, including research and development in support of these programs; and manages and executes the civil works program for the Army.

ARMY COMPONENTS OF UNIFIED COMMANDS

The bulk of the Army's soldiers are assigned to commands that are Army components of unified joint service commands. The Army furnishes units to these unified commands, which operate under the direction of the Secretary of Defense through the Joint Chiefs of Staff. The Secretary of the Army is responsible for administrative and logistical support of these component commands. There are now Army components of eight major unified commands.

In addition to the listed Army components of the major unified commands, there are Army components of a number of subordinate unified commands. These include Eighth U.S. Army, Korea (EUSAK), the Army component of U.S. Forces, Korea, which in turn is the U.S. component of the ROK/U.S. Combined Forces Command, U.S. Army, Japan (USARJ), the Army component of U.S. Forces, Japan, and U.S. Army, Alaska (USARAL), are subordinate elements of the U.S. Army, Pacific (USARPAC).

U.S. Army Forces Command (FORSCOM). FORSCOM, described earlier, serves as the Army component of the unified U.S. Joint Forces Command. FORSCOM is headquartered at Fort McPherson, Georgia.

Third U.S. Army. Also known as the U.S. Army Central Command (USARCENT), Third U.S. Army is the Army component of the unified U.S. Central Command. It is a part of FORSCOM and has its headquarters at Fort McPherson, Georgia.

U.S. Army, Europe (USAREUR). USAREUR, with headquarters in Heidelberg, Germany, is the Army component of the unified U.S. European Command.

U.S. Army, Pacific (USARPAC). USARPAC is headquartered at Fort Shatter, Hawaii. It is the Army component of the unified U.S. Pacific Command.

U.S. Army, South (USARSO). USARSO, with headquarters at Fort Clayton, Panama, is the Army component of the U.S. Southern Command.

U.S. Army Special Operations Command (USASOC). USASOC, with headquarters at Fort Bragg, North Carolina, is the Army component of the unified **U.S. Special Operations Command.** USASOC provides Army Special Forces, Rangers, Special Operations Aviation, Civil Affairs, and Psychological Operations forces to the U.S. Special Operations Command for deployment to other combatant unified commands and Joint Special Operations Task Forces around the world.

Military Traffic Management Command (MTMC). MTMC, with headquarters at Falls Church, Virginia, is the Army component of the unified U.S. Transportation Command. It functions as the single manager for the Department of Defense of all military traffic management, land transportation, and common-user ocean terminal service within CONUS, and for worldwide movement and storage of household goods for the Department of Defense.

U.S. Army Space and Missile Defense Command (SMDC). This command is the Army component of the unified U.S. Space Command. It is located at Colorado Springs, Colorado.

ORGANIZATION BY COMPONENT

The Army of the United States consists of the Regular Army, the Army National Guard, and the Army Reserve. The terms of service differ as to each of the three components, but the purposes for which each is formed and maintained are identical: the security of the United States, its Constitution, and its government and people.

The Regular Army. Members of the Regular Army, both officer and enlisted, are on active, full-time military duty, as volunteers. It is the permanent. professional force. The station and duty of members are as directed by military authority. In war or peace, in good times or bad, the Regular Army must he ready to undertake whatever mission is directed by proper governmental authority. Members of the Regular Army are the "United States Army."

The Reserve Components. The reserve components are the Army National Guard of the United States and the Army Reserve. Members of these components may be on inactive military status, at their homes or locations of their own choice, while receiving military instruction at times of minimum interference with their civilian vocations and professions. They may be called into active federal military service in time of war or other national emergency. when so determined by the President in accordance with law. That is to say. a member of the reserve forces may be inactive and perform part-time military service, or may be active and be as fully engaged in military affairs as a member of the regular service, with the same hazards and the same rewards.

The Active Army. That part of the Army of the United States that is on full-time service is called the active Army. It includes under all conditions the U.S. Army (the Regular Army) as our full-time professional force, plus those individuals or complete units drawn from the Army National Guard or Army' Reserve to serve on a full-time basis to meet conditions of war or overall strength requirements determined by the President and the Congress. Specified units of the reserve components are designated to round out or augment active Army units in an emergency.

The Army National Guard (ARNG). The Army National Guard traces its lineage back to 1636 when three militia units, the North, South, and East Regiments, were formed in the colony of Massachusetts. Since that time. National Guard units have been mobilized for national defense nearly two dozen times, including major participation in every war except Vietnam. For that conflict, a decision was made not to mobilize the ARNG, although a number of smaller units were called into federal service.

Since 1945, the ARNG has had a dual status. During peacetime, it is a state force under the control of the respective state governors, and is designed to preserve peace, order, and public safety in the state during emergencies. In wartime or a declared national emergency, the ARNG can be mobilized (called into federal service) by the President. In this latter role, the ARNG constitutes a major portion of the total force available to the Army of the United States.

The ARNG has a total strength of about 370,000 soldiers. The principal maneuver units include the following:

Unit	Headquarters
28th Infantry Division	Harrisburg, Pennsylvania
29th Infantry Division (Light)	Fort Belvoir, Virginia
34th Infantry Division	St. Paul, Minnesota
35th Infantry Division (Mechanized)	Fort Leavenworth, Kansas
38th Infantry Division	Indianapolis, Indiana
40th Infantry Division (Mechanized)	Los Alamitos, California
42nd Infantry Division	Troy, New York
49th Armored Division	Austin, Texas
27th Infantry Brigade (Light) (Separate)	Syracuse, New York
29th Infantry Brigade	Honolulu, Hawaii
30th Infantry Brigade (Mechanized) (Separate)	Clinton, North Carolina
39th Infantry Brigade (Light) (Separate)	Little Rock, Arkansas
41st Infantry Brigade (Light) (Separate)	Portland, Oregon
45th Infantry Brigade (Light) (Separate)	Edmond, Oklahoma
48th Infantry Brigade (Mechanized) (Separate)	Macon, Georgia
53rd Infantry Brigade (Light) (Separate)	Tampa, Florida
76th Infantry Brigade (Separate)	Indianapolis, Indiana
81st Infantry Brigade (Mechanized) (Separate)	Seattle, Washington
218th Infantry Brigade (Mechanized) (Separate)	Newberry, South Carolina
256th Infantry Brigade (Mechanized) (Separate)	Lafayette, Louisiana
31st Armored Brigade (Separate)	Northport, Alabama
155th Armored Brigade (Separate)	Tupelo, Mississippi
116th Cavalry Brigade (Separate)	Boise, Idaho

Unit	Headquarters
278th Armored Cavalry Regiment	Knoxville, Tennessee
66th Aviation Brigade	Fort Lewis, Washington
63rd Aviation Group (Lift)	Frankfort, Kentucky
185th Aviation Group (Lift)	Jackson, Mississippi
211th Aviation Group (Attack)	West Jordan, Utah
385th Aviation Group (Attack)	Phoenix, Arizona
449th Aviation Group (Lift)	Kinston, North Carolina

The ARNG is becoming increasingly involved with the wide variety of military missions to which Army units are being deployed. In 2000–01, ARNG units responded to 124 natural disasters, 35 civil emergencies, 39 missions in support of civil law enforcement agencies, and 208 other missions. Almost 19,000 ARNG soldiers were deployed outside the continental United States in training missions and military operations other than war. ARNG soldiers will be more, not less, closely involved with future Army operations.

U.S. Army Reserve (USAR). In contrast to the ARNG, reserve units are federal troops. The U.S. Army Reserve traces its beginnings to the Medical Reserve Corps, established in 1908, to provide a pool of trained physicians to meet Army wartime needs. The National Defense Act of 1916 authorized an Officers Reserve Corps and an Enlisted Reserve Corps and created the Reserve Officers' Training Corps (ROTC). More than 160,000 reservists served on active duty during World War I.

After that war a reserve force of 33 divisions was planned, but lack of funds and support prevented the planning from becoming reality. Training funds were scarce, and there were only limited funds available for paid drill periods. The result was that only small cadre groups were assigned to only some of the divisions. However, many officers coming out of the ROTC program were commissioned into the reserves during the period. As World War II got under way, many of these officers were called into active service, so that by the summer of 1941, about 90 percent of the active-duty company-grade officers were reservists who had been called to active duty. Almost the entire reserve mobilization for World War II was in the form of individual replacements rather than reserve units. The reserve units that were mobilized were staffed largely with personnel who had not been members of the units before the war.

About 240,000 soldiers of the Organized Reserve Corps were called to active duty during the Korean conflict, and more than 400 Army Reserve units served in Korea.

Problems encountered with the Korean War mobilization led to a major restructuring of the reserve forces. The U.S. Army Reserve was established in 1952, replacing the previous Officers Reserve Corps and Enlisted Reserve Corps. During the late 1950s and the 1960s, the Army Reserve became increasingly oriented toward combat support and combat service support missions.

The USAR today consists of about 460,000 soldiers, including the Individual Ready Reserve. The major USAR support and training units include the following.

Unit	Headquarters
9th Regional Support Command	Fort Schafter, Hawaii
63rd Regional Support Command	Los Alamitos, California
65th Regional Support Command	San Juan, Puerto Rico
70th Regional Support Command	Fort Lawton, Washington
77th Regional Support Command	Flushing, New York
81st Regional Support Command	Birmingham, Alabama
88th Regional Support Command	Fort Snelling, Minnesota
89th Regional Support Command	Wichita, Kansas
90th Regional Support Command	North Little Rock, Arkansas
94th Regional Support Command	Fort Devens, Massachusetts
96th Regional Support Command	Salt Lake City, Utah
99th Regional Support Command	Oakdale, Pennsylvania
3rd Medical Command	Decatur, Georgia
75th Division (Training Support)	Houston, Texas
78th Division (Training Support)	Edison, New Jersey
80th Division (Institutional Training)	Richmond, Virginia
84th Division (Institutional Training)	Milwaukee, Wisconsin

Unit	Headquarters
85th Division (Training Support)	Arlington Heights, Illinois
87th Division (Training Support)	Birmingham, Alabama
91st Division (Training Support)	Fort Baker, California
95th Division (Institutional Training)	Oklahoma City, Oklahoma
98th Division (Institutional Training)	Rochester, New York
100th Division (Institutional Training)	Louisville, Kentucky
104th Division (Institutional Training)	Vancouver Barracks, Washington
108th Division (Institutional Training)	Charlotte, North Carolina

The USAR has provided a great deal of support to the burgeoning number of deployments in which the Army has recently participated. Since 1995, over 11,000 USAR soldiers have been mobilized and deployed to Bosnia alone.

The Total Force. At about the time the draft ended in 1973, the Army adopted a total force concept that pared the strength of the active-duty forces to the minimum estimated to be required to maintain the peace and relied on well-trained, well-equipped reserve forces that could be mobilized on short notice to augment the active-duty forces. Under this total force policy, the ARNG now provides nearly all of the reserve component combat power available in emergencies to the Army of the United States. The USAR provides some 70 percent of the combat support and combat service support strength that would be required to support operations of a mobilized Army of the United States, as well as a pool of individual replacements who are already trained and who could be called into service as fillers in active Army units to help bring them up to full strength.

To ensure that the reserve forces are trained and ready for mobilization if necessary, much emphasis is being placed on training. In fact, 15 brigades of the ARNG are maintained in an enhanced state of readiness, with close association with active component trainers. These designated units receive supervision, training assistance, and guidance from the active Army. ARNG and USAR personnel are participating in the various Army exercises, including overseas training duty.

In sum, the active Army, the Army National Guard, and the U.S. Army Reserve each play a vital role in planning for the defense of U.S. interests around the world. The complementary missions of these three components of the total force provide assurance that the Army of the United States can successfully conduct such operations as may be assigned by our national authorities.

ORGANIZATION BY BRANCH

Officers of the Army are appointed into a basic or special branch, wear the branch insignia as a part of their uniforms, and are known, for example, as infantry officers, engineer officers, quartermaster officers, and so on. Officers may be temporarily detailed to another branch, such as to the Inspector General or to General Staff, but unless there is a transfer of branch, each officer remains assigned to the branch in which appointed throughout his or her career.

ORGANIZATION BY UNITS

The Army is organized into a number of units, from the smallest platoon to the largest theater army. The system and the terminology of these units are fairly uniform throughout the different arms and services, and once identified, the various terms fit readily into the total pattern.

Tables of organization and equipment (TOE), issued by the Department of the Army, establish for each category of Army unit its title, the number and grades of its officers and enlisted personnel, its organic equipment, and its interior organization. Using the TOE as the base document, units organized under modified tables of organization and equipment (MTOE) are tailored to the unit's requirements as determined by MACOM. Tables of distribution and allowances (TDA) prescribe the organization and equipment for special-purpose temporary units. A newly assigned officer should study his or her units TOE or TDA as soon as possible.

Below Company Level. In ascending order, crews of certain weapons systems, infantry fire teams, squads, and sections are the smallest units of the Army and are led by noncommissioned officers (NCOs). The smallest unit led by an officer is the platoon, which is led by a lieutenant and includes two or more squads.

Company. Companies, which usually consist of a headquarters and two or more platoons and/or sections, are usually commanded by captains (although some, such as corps headquarters companies and special forces companies, are commanded by majors). In the artillery, this sized unit is called a battery; in the armored cavalry, it is called a troop.

Battalion. Traditionally, the battalion has included its commander, his or her staff and headquarters elements, and two, three, or four companies, batteries (field artillery, air defense artillery), or troops

(cavalry). The cavalry unit corresponding to the battalion is called a squadron. In the Army of Excellence (AOE) divisions, there is a fixed number of combat battalions (infantry, airborne infantry, mechanized, tank, aviation), the number and type of battalions depending on the type of division and its mission. Also in the division are battalion-sized units of artillery, engineers, signal, and cavalry, with those in the support command providing maintenance, supply, and medical support.

Regiments. In the tactical sense, there are several armored cavalry regiments, which are combined arms teams of about brigade size, usually commanded by colonels. The 75th Ranger Regiment is also a tactical unit and is commanded by a colonel. Several infantry brigades, such as those in the 82nd Airborne Division and the 101st Airborne Division (Air Assault), that comprise the senior three battalions (i.e., 1st, 2nd, and 3rd) of the same regiment (under the Army's Regimental System) call themselves by their traditional regimental appellations, purely for the purposes of historical identification and the corollary esprit de corps.

All officers are assigned a regimental affiliation that has little or nothing to do with assignments. Regimental affiliation has become purely sentimental at most, although many officers respect and draw inspiration from the heritage of whichever battalion (of whichever regiment) they happen to be serving in at the moment. Combat support and combat service support officers generally all belong to the regiment that corresponds to their branch. Combat arms officers are generally assigned to whichever regiment they choose, so long as they have served with a battalion of that regiment previously.

Each regiment is allowed an honorary colonel and honorary sergeant major of the regiment. Held by retired soldiers who have previously served with battalions of the regiment, often in some distinguished capacity, these honorary positions are intended to be a living link to each regiment's past. When employed properly, regimental customs and traditions, along with the honorary colonel and sergeant major, can be of great value to unit morale and cohesion.

Soldiers affiliated with a regiment wear regimental distinctive insignia (see appendix C, Uniforms and Appearance).

Divisional Brigades. In the AOE divisions, there are four maneuver brigade headquarters (including the aviation brigade), each capable of controlling from two to five combat battalions. The necessary combat support and administrative elements are furnished to the brigade by the division.

Brigades and Groups. Field artillery, engineers, air defense artillery, special forces, and many combat support and combat service support units such as transportation and military police are organized into brigades and groups, most of which are "pure" (that is, single-arm) units designed to support particular corps. These brigades and groups are generally commanded by colonels.

Separate Maneuver Brigades and Groups. Usually commanded by brigadier generals, separate brigades are combined arms formations, with integral field artillery, engineer, support, and combat service support units. At the time of writing, the only separate infantry brigade left in the active component is the 172nd infantry Brigade in Alaska. There are no longer separate armored or mechanized infantry brigades in the active component, although two air cavalry combat brigades remain.

As shown previously in this chapter, the ARNG maintains separate light infantry, mechanized infantry, and infantry brigades and groups, as well as separate armored brigades. Many of these are "enhanced" brigades, with special readiness and deployment capabilities.

Division. Except for the armored cavalry regiment and separate maneuver brigades, the division is the smallest unit of the combined arms and services. In the active component, there are currently five types of combat divisions: armored, mechanized, light infantry, airborne, and air assault. Divisions are commanded by major generals. Strengths of the divisions range from about 11,000 for the light infantry division to about 16,500 for the larger armored and mechanized divisions. There are still infantry divisions in the ARNG as of this writing.

Each type of division has command and control, combat, combat support, and combat service support elements. The command and control element includes division headquarters and four brigade headquarters. The combat element includes varying proportions of combat battalions of the different types (armor, infantry, mechanized, air assault, airborne infantry, and aviation) to make up the division (armored, six tank and four mechanized battalions; mechanized, five mechanized and five tank battalions; light infantry, nine light infantry battalions; airborne, nine airborne infantry battalions; air assault, nine air assault infantry battalions). The mix of units can be further tailored to accomplish a specific task. The armored and mechanized divisions combine fast maneuver with tremendous firepower. The light infantry division is designed for rapid deployment to any contingency. It can be employed against enemy forces in all terrain and is especially useful in restrictive terrain where it can take maximum advantage of the terrain against enemy heavy forces. The airborne division is for vertical envelopment by airborne assault, using parachutes and Air Force troop carrier and assault landing aircraft. The air assault division with its helicopters demonstrated in Vietnam its ability to deliver firepower and maneuver units quickly anywhere. Combat support and combat service support elements are included in each division.

Army Corps. An army corps consists of its headquarters, two or more divisions, and such other organizations as its mission may require. The additional units may consist, for example, of artillery, aviation, engineer units, medical units, and a corps support command (COSCOM).

Field Army. If a numbered field army is required, it will consist of a TDA headquarters, two or more army corps, and other organizations of all kinds needed for sustained field operations.

Theater Army. This is the army component of a U.S. unified command in a theater of operations. An echelon above the corps organization, it provides combat support and combat service support to U.S. Army combat and combat support forces in the theater. It must be tailored for each theater.

ASSOCIATION OF THE UNITED STATES ARMY (AUSA)

Members of the Association of the United States Army (AUSA) believe that a strong Army, well led, of high morale, and provided with an adequate supply of weapons and equipment as good as or better than can be thrown against it, is essential to protect the United States during times of danger. The association's membership encompasses officers and soldiers of the regular and reserve components of the Army; leaders of government; leaders in industry, science, and education; and interested civilians. The essential characteristic of members is belief in the U.S. Army, its mission, and its capability of providing the necessary security for our nation and our people. Their convictions are sound. The organization corresponds to the Navy League and the United States Air Force Association.

A monthly magazine, *Army*, is essential reading for the active Army officer of regular or reserve component. Army officers and others interested in the Army should be members of the association. Headquarters of the association is at 2425 Wilson Boulevard, Arlington, VA 22201.

ORGANIZATION AND MISSIONS

In the euphoria following the end of World War II the United States rushed to dismantle the mightiest military force the world had ever seen in the belief that large military forces would no longer be required. Yet barely four years later, the remnants of that force, relatively unprepared and ill equipped, were thrust onto the Korean Peninsula to assist in repelling the attack by North Korea. During the ensuring four decades, the Army, along with its sister services, stood firm around the globe as the bulwark against the spread of communism. Throughout that period, the size of the force remained relatively high. With the end of the Cold War, however, the need for large, standing military forces was once again in question, and the Army entered a period of significant force reductions. The wisdom of these strength reductions may not become obvious until the next time military intervention is required to preserve or restore the peace. What is obvious to any student of history, however, is that there most certainly will be a future need for the Army to perform its role in the defense of our nation and our nation's interests.

The Army must be ready to fight today, with the weapons and equipment on hand today, anywhere in the world as directed by our nation's civil leaders. The mission continues to be to provide for the security of the nation, and of our people, and to accomplish assigned tasks in upholding the commitments made by our government in consonance with the United States' status as sole superpower. Prevention of war is the primary goal. But if war—or combat short of war—cannot be prevented, the mission of the Army and its sister services is to win the conflict as quickly as possible. *The Army must be ready to fight at once with the personnel and equipment we have ready for immediate deployment.*

At the same time, it is an era of new developments in weapons. C^{4}I systems, and doctrine, with the need for personnel specifically trained in their effective employment. Just as the Army must be ready and able to fight effectively and promptly, wherever ordered, with personnel and weapons available, it must also prepare itself to fight the battles of the future, with the weapons it will then have on hand. Soldiers expect that weapons and equipment provided for their use will be the very best our national capabilities can develop and produce.

OBJECTIVES OF THE ARMY

The objectives, or purpose, of the Army should be understood clearly by all members of the Army, and by each of our nation's citizens. It is firmly established in Title 10, USC, as follows:

> It is the intent of Congress to provide an Army that is capable, in conjunction with the other armed forces, of—
>
> (1) preserving the peace and security and providing for the defense of the United States, the Territories, Commonwealths, and possessions and any areas occupied by the United States;
>
> (2) supporting the national policies;
>
> (3) implementing the national objectives; and
>
> (4) overcoming any nations responsible for aggressive acts that imperil the peace and security of the United States.
>
> In general, the Army within the Department of the Army, includes land combat and service forces and such aviation and water transport as may be organic therein. It shall be organized, trained, and equipped primarily for prompt and sustained combat incident to operations on land. It is responsible for the preparation of land forces necessary for the effective prosecution of war except as otherwise assigned and, in accordance with integrated joint mobilization plans, for the expansion of the peacetime components of the Army to meet the needs of war.

Although the objectives of the Army remain the same over time, the Army itself undergoes continuing change to meet the challenges inherent in these objectives. The pace of change in our nation and world is accelerating; the information age is upon us, and the Army must keep pace. The United States is the world's only remaining superpower, and experts generally agree that this situation will continue until about 2015, when the appearance of a major competitor is likely. Until then, soldiers and units must be prepared to conduct an increasingly complex and diverse variety of missions across a broad spectrum from fighting and winning midintensity wars against regional powers to humanitarian relief missions—and everything in between, such as peacekeeping and peace enforcement, counterdrug missions, nation assistance, and military support to civil authorities.

To attain and retain this flexibility requires that the Army be in a continual sate of change, adapting its thinking and organization to new doctrine and equipment as they are developed. Failure to make these adjustments would result in a loss of the capability and flexibility so necessary to meet the exacting tasks assigned.

The strength of the active Army is established by our nation's leaders to meet the estimated need for Army forces in support of national goals. Recent policy has been to reduce the size of the active Army to about 480,000 soldiers organized into divisions, separate brigades, and support units as necessary to provide adequate defense for our nation and to reassure and support our allies. The enormous changes in eastern Europe since late 1989 and the easing of four decades of Cold War with the Soviet Union have led to reduced funding for the Department of Defense. The end result is a smaller Army with fewer forces deployed overseas, but the remaining active forces must be capable of rapid deployment to trouble spots as needed.

Active component forces are joined by forces from the reserve components (the Army National Guard and Army Reserve) in the conduct of more and more missions. The accelerating operational tempo implicit to the Army's expanding roles require this; gone are the days when soldiers of active component units saw reservists only on occasional weekends, as opposing forces (OPFOR) for exercises, or during annual training (AT). Today, teams and larger units of reserve component soldiers are likely to operate with active component units on most operational deployments, as well as major training events. Therefore, gone, too, are the days when differing standards and procedures were acceptable. The Total Army on which our nation depends—the Army Reserve, National Guard, and Regular Army—must, more than ever, be interoperable in every way.

The weapons systems and other equipment issued to Army units are excellent, but they are evolving. Not surprisingly, the Army's future warfighting doctrine is based on the tremendous advantages that accrue with information, and the equipment and ordnance—from communications systems to weapons—are changing accordingly. As newer weapons, equipment, and doctrine become available, the Army will change as necessary to make the best use of what is furnished, always with the view of performing in a superb manner the tasks assigned to it by the civil leaders of our government.

It takes trained and determined personnel to do these vital jobs. This is a fact to be remembered by civil leaders, industrial and educational leaders, members of vocations who mold public opinions, and our citizens generally. Understanding of the requirements to provide for our nation's security, or to keep its solemn commitments, is enhanced when a person thinks of the soldier behind the rifle who aims it and fires it, or the crew of a tank or helicopter who operate and guide, aim, and fire. The emphasis must remain upon equipping and training the soldier, not merely manning the equipment. Army power means power applied by soldiers in person, at close range, as the nation's mission demands. The heart of the Army is the officer and the soldier. The soldier's training, pride in service, confidence in the excellence of equipment, and conviction as to the worthiness of the national cause are all matters that must concern our government, our leaders, and our citizens.

HEADQUARTERS, DEPARTMENT OF THE ARMY

The Headquarters, Department of the Army, in the Pentagon, Washington, D.C., is the place of final decision as to Army affairs, and it is the nerve center for control of execution of the military missions pertaining to the Army. It is an organizational component of the Department of Defense. Located together are the command and control elements of the Department of Defense and the Departments of Army, Navy, and Air Force, so they can work together in easy teamwork and take part in jointly planned and executed combined operations (AR 10-5).

As a result of legislation passed in 1986, the Goldwater-Nichols Department of Defense Reorganization Act, a major restructuring of the Department of the Army staff and the staff of the Secretary of the Army was implemented in 1987. The resultant organ-ization at the highest levels of the Army brought more immediate control of Army activities by the Secretary of the Army; it is part of a larger effort to enhance the role of the Joint Chiefs of Staff and the Secretary of Defense. The organizations for the Secretary of the Army and the Army staff are shown in the accompanying charts.

Secretary of the Army. The Secretary of the Army, a civilian, is the head of the Army and has primary responsibility for all affairs of the Army establishment. The position illustrates the application of civilian control under our Constitution. The Secretary is assisted by other civilian officials as follows:

Under Secretary of the Army. This official acts as deputy to the Secretary and is the Secretary's principal assistant. The Under Secretary also is the Army's acquisition executive and, in that capacity, reports directly to the Under Secretary of Defense for Acquisition. Two Deputy Under Secretaries are provided, one designated specifically to handle operations research matters.

Assistant Secretaries of the Army (ASA). There are five Assistant Secretaries of the Army for the following: Civil Works; Manpower and Reserve Affairs; Research, Development, and Acquisition, Installations, Logistics, and Environment; and Financial Management.

Other Assistants to the Secretary. The following are also responsible directly to the Secretary: Administrative Assistant, General Counsel, Army Reserve Forces Policy Committee, Office of Small and Disadvantaged Business Utilization, Chief of Public Affairs, Chief of Legislative Liaison, the Inspector General, the Auditor General, and the Director of Information Systems, C^4 (command, control, communications, and computers).

In this staff restructuring, responsibility was transferred from the Chief of Staff to the Secretary of the Army in the areas of acquisition, auditing, comptroller activities, information management, Inspector General functions, and research and development.

Army Staff. The Secretary of the Army is assisted by the Army Staff, which is the professional military staff at the Headquarters, Department of the Army. It consists of the Chief of Staff, the Army General Staff, the Special Staff, and the Personal Staff.

Chief of Staff. The Chief of Staff is the highest military assistant or adviser to the Secretary of the Army. He or she occupies the pinnacle position within the Army, and is a member of the Joint Chiefs of Staff. As Army Chief of Staff, his or her responsibility is to the Secretary of the Army and includes the worldwide Army mission as well as its administration, training, and supply.

Office of the Chief of Staff. The Office of the Chief of Staff includes the Vice Chief of Staff, Director of the Army Staff, and other staff members as may be required.

Army General Staff. The Chief of Staff is assisted by other staff officers, each heading a general staff agency charged with a particular function. These functions pertain to the people, planning, logistics, and intelligence aspects of the Army. The general staff officers are the Deputy Chief of Staff for Operations and Plans (DCSOPS), the Deputy Chief of Staff for Personnel (DCSPER), the Deputy Chief of Staff for Logistics (DCSLOG), and the Deputy Chief of Staff for Intelligence (DCSI).

Special Staff. The Chief of Staff also is assisted by staff officers heading special staff agencies, each of which is charged with exercising responsibility for specialized activities. The Special Staff consists of the following officers: Chief of Engineers; Surgeon General; Chief, National Guard Bureau; and Chief, Army Reserve.

Personal Staff. The Personal Staff assists the Chief of Staff in specifically designated areas. It consists of the aides to the chief, other individual staff officers whose advice and assistance he or she desires to receive directly, and those staff agencies whose functions and activities he or she desires to coordinate and administer directly.

The Personal Staff officers include the Chief of Chaplains and the Judge Advocate General. The heads of the following staff agencies command personnel, facilities, and organizations in addition to their staff duties. These are separate and distinct functions: the Chief of Engineers, the Surgeon General, and the Judge Advocate General.

MAJOR ARMY FIELD COMMANDS

Many of the missions of the Army are carried out through nine major Army field commands, whose missions are described below.

U.S. Army Forces Command (FORSCOM). With headquarters at Fort McPherson, Georgia, FORSCOM is the largest major command (MACOM) in the Department of the Army. FORSCOM supervises the training of almost 800,000 active Army, Army National Guard, and U.S. Army Reserve soldiers to prepare them for combat. FORSCOM provides Army support to USACOM in its role as the joint force integrator and supplies Army forces during a crisis to other commanders for eopations elsewhere. Forces Command has four major missions:

- Supply combat-ready units to warfighting commanders-in-chief to meet their strategic, operational, and tactical needs.
- Carry out contingency missions as directed by the President and Secretary of Defense through the commander-in-chief of USACOM.
- Defend the United States land mass. That includes protecting key national assets, assisting in civil defense, and helping protect the nation from terrorism. It also works with Canadian forces to prepare for a combined defense.
- FORSCOM is required to respond to federal, state, and local officials during emergencies, natural disasters, and the war against drugs.

In recent years, FORSCOM soldiers have been dispatched in the United States to provide aid to flood and hurricane victims, fight forest fires, and control riots. Forces Command units have also deployed to Somalia for Operation Restore Hope, to Haiti for Operation Uphold Democracy, and to Guantanamo Bay, Cuba, and several Central American nations to provide humanitarian relief. Forces Command was given the mission to train for those roles more effectively when it was designated a Reinvention Center in January 1995.

In this role, FORSCOM is a leader in maintaining this country's quality forces through reengineering to become the most efficient organization possible by maximizing limited resources. It sets the example for other Army commands.

In today's force-projection era, FORSCOM has several major subordinate headquarters that help lead our strategic, combat-ready forces: USARC, CONUSAs, and the Third U.S. Army.

United States Army Reserve Command (USARC). The United States Army Reserve Command, headquartered in Atlanta, Georgia, is responsible for all conventional Army Reserve units in the continental United States and Puerto Rico. Its commander is also Chief of the Army Reserve and is responsible for the training, equipment, and funding of Army Reserve units.

Continental United States Armies (CONUSAs). The Continental United States Armies are regional commands responsible for the operations, mobilization, and deployment of reserve units from home stations to the areas of operations. There are two continental armies: First U.S. Army, with headquarters at Fort Gillem, Georgia; and Fifth U.S. Army at Fort Sam Houston, Texas. The CONUSAs advise state national guard adjutants general on training so that they will be prepared if federalized by the President.

Third U.S. Army. The third U.S. Army, located at Fort McPherson, Georgia, serves as the Army component headquarters of the U.S. Central Command. The mission of Third Army is to plan, exercise, and deploy Army forces in response to contingencies threatening vital U.S. interests in Southwest Asia. The commanding general of Third U.S. Army also serves as the deputy commanding general of FORSCOM.

Training Centers. Forces Command units engage in home station training and joint training throughout the year. FORSCOM has two major training centers.

The *National Training Center (NTC)* at Fort Irwin, California, provides realistic training in a desert environment for armored and mechanized task forces. In addition to the space needed to maneuver heavy forces, the NTC offers a highly proficient opposing force on an instrumental battlefield. Active and reserve component maneuver battalions training at the NTC receive immediate feedback on their performance. The training was very valuable to the units sent to the Middle East to take part in the Gulf War.

The *Joint Readiness Training Center (JRTC)* at Fort Polk, Louisiana, provides realistic training for light forces in rugged terrain where armored vehicle access is limited. The JRTC uses techniques similar to those used at the NTC and trains brigade-sized units. Training includes integrated operations with the Air Force for deployment, close air support, and serial resupply.

U.S. Army Training and Doctrine Command (TRADOC). With headquarters at historic Fort Monroe, Virginia, the mission of TRADOC is to prepare the Army for war, determine how the Army will be organized and equipped, and be the architect for the future Army. In fulfilling these responsibilities, TRADOC managers all institutional training for officers from basic officer courses through the Command and General Staff College, and for enlisted soldiers from basic training through the Sergeants Major Academy.

TRADOC functions through major subordinate organizations, including the Combined Arms Center (CAC) at Fort Leavenworth, Kansas; the Combined Arms Support Command (CASCOM) at Fort Lee, Virginia; the TRADOC Analysis Command (TRAC) at Fort Leavenworth, Kansas; and the ROTC Cadet Command at Fort Monroe, Virginia. CAD and CASCOM direct and coordinate training (including training development and Army-wide training support), leader development, doctrine, force design, material requirements, and mission support functions. TRAC is the principal Army organization that provides in-depth analyses of Army training, doctrine, and combat developments.

Doctrine. TRADOC prepares the doctrine that determines how the Army will fight; how combat units will be supported; and how Army and joint service tactics, techniques, and procedures are standardized.

Training. Through training, soldiers and leaders are prepared to fight and win. TRADOC manages all institutional training and professional development for enlisted soldiers and officers. TRADOC commands the Army's service schools and managers officer procurement through the ROTC Cadet Command and the Officer Candidate School (OCS) program. Additionally, TRADOC supports total Army training by developing, producing, and distributing training support materials to commanders in the field.

Leader Development. TRADOC coordinates, integrates, and executes leader development matters through the Leader Development Support System.

Organizations. The TRADOC combat developments process sets requirements for how the Army organizes and equips units for battle.

Soldiers. TRADOC installations support mobilization of individual soldiers and support units during conflict, with training, processing, and logistical activities that support deployment of units and soldiers.

Architect of the Future. The uncertain and rapidly changing realities of a world on the verge of the millennium demand that the Army embrace—indeed, lead—change, to maintain its ability to accomplish the nation's goals, policies, and objectives. To lead the Army into the future. TRADOC supervises two major programs.

Force XXI is the *process* of experimentation and analysis by which the Army is building the digitized force for the period 2005 to 2015; this *product* is called Army XXI. The 4th Infantry Division (Mechanized) at Fort Hood has been chosen as the main organizational vehicle for this process and has already conducted brigade- and division-level experiments with the digitized systems that will facilitate new tactics and operational doctrine. Essentially, by taking advantage of high-technology information systems, Army XXI units will operate with far greater mobility, lethality, and operational velocity across the entire spectrum of military operations. Information systems will engender a "common situational awareness"—about the enemy as well as friendly activities and units—that will significantly streamline decision making at all levels. If you can imagine cutting the time it takes to recon an objective by 90 percent (or even more), cut planning time by 75 percent (thanks to the extensive, constantly updated information piped into your vehicle's computer), and resupply time by 80 percent (because the logisticians are monitoring your rations, ammunition, and fuel status in real time), then you can grasp the possibilities or Army XXI.

The Army After Next (AAN) is a process by which TRADOC and associated agencies are examining the most promising possibilities allowed by developments in technology, the art of war, human behavior, and geopolitical trends for the Army of 2015 to 2025. Dramatic changes in all four are expected, and the Army will probably create some smaller, hybrid tactical organizations to take advantage of the far greater knowledge that will be available and the operational velocities that will be possible. As most experts forecast the reappearance of a major political-military competitor during this era, the AAN process is essential to building an Army that will be able to prevail against all challengers.

Even though high technology is key to both future Army programs, combat will remain a dirty, bloody, and exhausting experience. That is why the TRADOC-avowed basis of all future Army success remains *soldiers*—competent, confident, tough, disciplined *American soldiers.* As the leaders of the 21st-century force, junior officers of today face the exciting possibilities provided by tomorrow's technologies, and the daunting and demanding requirements of leading and training the soldiers who will use them.

U.S. Army Material Command (AMC). The principal missions of the U.S. Army Material

Command, with headquarters in Alexandria, Virginia, are to equip and sustain a trained, ready Army; to provide equipment and services to other nations through the security assistance program; to develop and acquire nonmajor systems and equipment; to provide development and acquisition support to program managers; to define, develop, and acquire superior technologies; to maintain the mobilization capabilities necessary to support the Army in emergencies; and to continue to improve productivity and quality of life.

AMC accomplishes its mission through a number of subordinate organizations. The major subordinate elements of AMC are the Industrial Operations Command at Rock Island, Illinois; the Aviation and Missile Command at St. Louis, Missouri; the Communications-Electronics Command at Fort Monmouth, New Jersey; the Chemical and Biological Defense Command at Aberdeen Proving Ground, Maryland; the Army Research Laboratory at Adelphi, Maryland; the Missile Command at Redstone Arsenal, Alabama; the Tank-automotive and Armaments Command at Warren, Michigan; the Test and Evaluation Command at Aberdeen Proving Ground, Maryland; the Security Assistance Command at Alexandria, Virginia; the Simulation, Training, and Instrumentation Command at Orlando, Florida; AMC-Europe at Seckenheim, Germany; and AMC-Far East at Seoul, South Korea.

U.S. Army Intelligence and Security Command (INSCOM). The U.S. Army Intelligence and Security Command, with headquarters at Fort Belvoir, Virginia, near Washington, D.C., has worldwide responsibilities for intelligence collection, electronic warfare, counterintelligence, and operations security.

U.S. Army Information Systems Command (USAISC). The U.S. Army Information Systems Command, with headquarters at Fort Huachuca, Arizona, provides information systems and services to the Army and to other Department of Defense and government organizations as directed.

U.S. Army Criminal Investigation Command (USACIC). The U.S. Army Criminal Investigation Command has its headquarters in Falls Church, Virginia, near Washington, D.C. The USACIC commands and controls worldwide Army investigations of serious crimes, provides a full range of investigative support to all Army elements, conducts sensitive and special-interests investigations, and provides personal security for selected Army and DOD officials.

U.S. Army Military District of Washington (MDW). The Military District of Washington commands Army units, activities, and installations in the national capital area and is responsible for designated Army functions in the metropolitan area of Washington, D.C. Its headquarters is located at Fort Leslie J. McNair in Washington, D.C.

U.S. Army Medical Command (MEDCOM). The U.S. Army Medical Command, with headquarters at Fort Sam Houston, Texas, is the Army's single manager for healthcare delivery and supportive services within CONUS and in Alaska and Hawaii, including command of the Army hospital system. It supervises all medical training for the Army.

U.S. Army Corps of Engineers (USACE). The U.S. Army Corps of Engineers, with headquarters in Washington, D.C., manages Army real property; manages and executes engineering, construction, and real estate programs for the Army and the Air Force, including research and development in support of these programs; and manages and executes the civil works program for the Army.

ARMY COMPONENTS OF UNIFIED COMMANDS

The bulk of the Army's soldiers are assigned to commands that are Army components of unified joint service commands. The Army furnishes units to these unified commands, which operate under the direction of the Secretary of Defense through the Joint Chiefs of Staff. The Secretary of the Army is responsible for administrative and logistical support of these component commands. There are now Army components of eight major unified commands.

In addition to the listed Army components of the major unified commands, there are Army components of a number of subordinate unified commands. These include Eighth U.S. Army, Korea (EUSAK), the Army component of U.S. Forces, Korea, which in turn is the U.S. component of the ROK/U.S. Combined Forces Command, U.S. Army, Japan (USARJ), the Army component of U.S. Forces, Japan, and U.S. Army, Alaska (USARAL), are subordinate elements of the U.S. Army, Pacific (USARPAC).

U.S. Army Forces Command (FORSCOM). FORSCOM, described earlier, serves as the Army component of the unified U.S. Atlantic Command. FORSCOM is headquartered at Fort McPherson, Georgia.

Third U.S. Army. Also known as the U.S. Army Central Command (USARCENT), Third U.S. Army is the Army component of the unified U.S. Central Command. It is a part of FORSCOM and has its headquarters at Fort McPherson, Georgia.

U.S. Army, Europe (USAREUR). USAREUR, with headquarters in Heidelberg, Germany, is the Army component of the unified U.S. European Command.

U.S. Army, Pacific (USARPAC). USARPAC is headquartered at Fort Shafter, Hawaii. It is the Army component of the unified U.S. Pacific Command.

U.S. Army, South (USARSO). USARSO, with headquarters at Fort Clayton, Panama, is the Army component of the U.S. Southern Command.

U.S. Army Special Operations Command (USASOC). USASOC, with headquarters at Fort Bragg, North Carolina, is the Army component of the unified U.S. Special Operations Command. USASOC provides Army Special Forces, Rangers, Special Operations Aviation, Civil Affairs, and Psychological Operations forces to the U.S. Special Operations Command for deployment to other combatant unified commands and Joint Special Operations Task Forces around the world.

Military Traffic Management Command (MTMC). MTMC, with headquarters at Falls Church, Virginia, is the Army component of the unified U.S. Transportation Command. It functions as the single manager for the Department of Defense of all military traffic management, land transportation, and common-user ocean terminal service within CONUS, and for worldwide movement and storage of household goods for the Department of Defense.

U.S. Army Space and Missile Defense Command (SMDC). This command is the Army component of the unified U.S. Space Command. It is located at Colorado Springs, Colorado.

ORGANIZATION BY COMPONENT

The Army of the United States consists of the Regular Army, the Army National Guard, and the Army Reserve. The terms of service differ as to each of the three components, but the purposes for which each is formed and maintained are identical: the security of the United States, its Constitution, and its government and people.

The Regular Army. Members of the Regular Army, both officer and enlisted, are on active, full-time mili-

tary duty, as volunteers. It is the permanent, professional force. The station and duty of members are as directed by military authority. In war or peace, in good times or bad, the Regular Army must be ready to undertake whatever mission is directed by proper governmental authority. Members of the Regular Army are the "United States Army."

The Reserve Components. The reserve components are the Army National Guard of the United States and the Army Reserve. Members of these components may be on inactive military status, at their homes or locations of their own choice, while receiving military instruction at times of minimum interference with their civilian vocations and professions. They may be called into active federal military service in time of war or other national emergency, when so determined by the President in accordance with law. That is to say, a member of the reserve forces may be inactive and perform part-time military service, or may be active and be as fully engaged in military affairs as a member of the regular service, with the same hazards and the same rewards.

The Active Army. That part of the Army of the United States that is on full-time service is called the active Army. It includes under all conditions the U.S. Army (the Regular Army) as our full-time professional force, plus those individuals or complete units drawn from the Army National Guard or Army Reserve to serve on a full-time basis to meet conditions of war or overall strength requirements determined by the President and the Congress. Specified units of the reserve components are designated to round out or augment active Army units in an emergency.

The Army National Guard (ARNG). The Army National Guard traces its lineage back to 1636 when three militia units, the North, South, and East Regiments, were formed in the colony of Massachusetts. Since that time, National Guard units have been mobilized for national defense nearly two dozen times, including major participation in every war except Vietnam. For that conflict, a decision was made not to mobilize the ARNG, although a number of smaller units were called into federal service.

Since 1945, the ARNG has had a dual status. During peacetime, it is a state force under the control of the respective state governors, and is designed to preserve peace, order, and public safety in the state during emergencies. In wartime or a declared national emergency, the ARNG can be mobilized (called into federal service) by the President. In this latter role, the

ARNG constitutes a major portion of the total force available to the Army of the United States.

The ARNG has a total strength of about 370,000 soldiers. The principal maneuver units include the following:

Unit	Headquarters
28th Infantry Division	Harrisburg, Pennsylvania
29th Infantry Division (Light)	Fort Belvoir, Virginia
34th Infantry Division	Rosemount, Minnesota
35th Infantry Division (Mechanized)	Fort Leavenworth, Kansas
38th Infantry Division	Indianapolis, Indiana
40th Infantry Division (Mechanized)	Los Alamitos, California
42nd Infantry Division	Troy, New York
49th Armored Division	Austin, Texas
27th Infantry Brigade (Light) (Separate)	Syracuse, New York
29th Infantry Brigade	Honolulu, Hawaii
30th Infantry Brigade (Mechanized) (Separate)	Clinton, North Carolina
39th Infantry Brigade (Light) (Separate)	Little Rock, Arkansas
41st Infantry Brigade (Light) (Separate)	Tigard, Oregon
45th Infantry Brigade (Light) (Separate)	Edmond, Oklahoma
48th Infantry Brigade (Mechanized) (Separate)	Macon, Georgia
53rd Infantry Brigade (Light) (Separate)	Tampa, Florida
76th Infantry Brigade (Separate)	Indianapolis, Indiana
81st Infantry Brigade (Mechanized) (Separate)	Seattle, Washington
92nd Infantry Brigade (Separate)	Juana Diaz, Puerto Rico
218th Infantry Brigade (Mechanized) (Separate)	Newberry, South Carolina
256th Infantry Brigade (Mechanized) (Separate)	Lafayette, Louisiana
207th Infantry Group (Scout)	Fort Richardson, Alaska
31st Armored Brigade (Separate)	Northport, Alabama
155th Armored Brigade (Separate)	Tupelo, Mississippi
116th Cavalry Brigade (Separate)	Boise, Idaho
278th Armored Cavalry Regiment	Knoxville, Tennessee
66th Aviation Brigade	Fort Lewis, Washington
63rd Aviation Group (Lift)	Frankfort, Kentucky
185th Aviation Group (Lift)	Jackson, Mississippi
211th Aviation Group (Attack)	West Jordan, Utah
385th Aviation Group (Attack)	Phoenix, Arizona
449th Aviation Group (Lift)	Kinston, North Carolina

The ARNG is becoming increasingly involved with the wide variety of military missions to which Army units are being deployed. In 1997–98, ARNG units responded to 146 natural disasters, 35 civil emergencies, 39 missions in support of civil law enforcement agencies, and 88 other missions. Almost 28,000 ARNG soldiers were deployed outside the continental United States in training missions and military operations other than war. ARNG soldiers will be more, not less, closely involved with future Army operations.

U.S. Army Reserve (USAR). In contrast to the ARNG, reserve units are federal troops. The U.S. Army Reserve traces its beginnings to the Medical Reserve Corps, established in 1908, to provide a pool of trained physicians to meet Army wartime needs. The National Defense Act of 1916 authorized an Officers Reserve Corps and an Enlisted Reserve Corps and created the Reserve Officers' Training Corps (ROTC). More than 160,000 reservists served on active duty during World War I.

After that war a reserve force of 33 divisions was planned, but lack of funds and support prevented the planning from becoming reality. Training funds were scarce, and there were only limited funds available for paid drill periods. The result was that only small cadre groups were assigned to only some of the divisions. However, many officers coming out of the ROTC programs were commissioned into the reserves during the period. As World War II got under way, many of these officers were called into active service, so that by the summer of 1941, about 90 percent of the active-duty company-grade officers were reservists who had been called to active duty. Almost the entire reserve mobilization for World War II was in the form of individual replacements rather than reserve units. The reserve units that were mobilized were staffed largely with personnel who had not been members of the units before the war.

About 240,000 soldiers of the Organized Reserve Corps were called to active duty during the Korean conflict, and more than 400 Army Reserve units served in Korea.

Problems encountered with the Korean War mobilization led to a major restructuring of the reserve forces. The U.S. Army Reserve was established in 1952, replacing the previous Officers Reserve Corps and Enlisted Reserve Corps. During the late 1950s and 1960s, the Army Reserve became increasingly oriented toward combat support and combat service support missions.

The USAR today consists of about 460,000 soldiers, including the Individual Ready Reserve. The major USAR support and training units include the following:

Unit	Headquarters
9th Army Reserve Command	Fort DeRussy, Hawaii
65th Army Reserve Command	Fort Buchanan, Puerto Rico
63rd Regional Support Command	Los Alamitos, California
70th Regional Support Command	Seattle, Washington
77th Regional Support Command	Fort Totten, New York
81st Regional Support Command	Birmingham, Alabama
81st Regional Support	Fort Jackson, South Carolina
88th Regional Support Command	Fort Snelling, Minnesota
88th Regional Support Group	Indianapolis, Indiana
89th Regional Support Command	Wichita, Kansas
90th Regional Support Command	North Little Rock, Arkansas
90th Regional Support Group	San Antonio, Texas
94th Regional Support Command	Fort Devens, Massachusetts
96th Regional Support Command	Salt Lake City, Utah
99th Regional Support Command	Oakdale, Pennsylvania
3rd Medical Command	Decatur, Georgia
75th Division (Exercise)	Houston, Texas
78th Division (Exercise)	Edison, New Jersey
80th Division (Institutional Training)	Richmond, Virginia
84th Division (Institutional Training)	Milwaukee, Wisconsin
85th Division (Exercise)	Arlington Heights, Illinois
87th Division (Exercise)	Birmingham, Alabama
91st Division (Exercise)	Fort Baker, California
95th Division (Institutional Training)	Oklahoma City, Oklahoma
98th Division (Institutional Training)	Rochester, New York
100th Division (Institutional Training)	Louisville, Kentucky
104th Division (Institutional Training)	Vancouver, Washington
108th Division (Institutional Training)	Charlotte, North Carolina

The USAR has provided a great deal of support to the burgeoning number of deployments in which the Army has recently participated. Since 1995, over 11,000 USAR soldiers have been mobilized and deployed in Bosnia alone.

The Total Force. At about the time the draft ended in 1973, the Army adopted a total force concept that pared the strength of the active-duty forces to the minimum estimated to be required to maintain the peace and relied on well-trained, well-equipped reserve forces that could be mobilized on short notice to augment the active-duty forces. Under this total force policy, the ARNG now provides nearly all of the reserve component combat power available in emergencies to the Army of the United States. The USAR provides some 70 percent of the combat support and combat service support strength that would be required to support operations of a mobilized Army of the United States, as well as a pool of individual replacements who are already trained and who could be called into service as fillers in active Army units to help bring them up to full strength.

To ensure that the reserve forces are trained and ready for mobilization if necessary, much emphasis is being placed on training. In fact, 15 brigades of the ARNG are maintained in an enhanced state of readiness, with close association with active component trainers. These designated units receive supervision, training assistance, and guidance from the active Army. ARNG and USAR personnel are participating in the various Army exercises, including overseas training duty.

In sum, the active Army, the Army National Guard, and the U.S. Army Reserve each play a vital role in planning for the defense of U.S. interests around the world. The complementary missions of these three components of the total force provide assurance that the Army of the United States can successfully conduct such operations as may be assigned by our national authorities.

ORGANIZATION BY BRANCH

Officers of the Army are appointed into a basic or special branch, wear the branch insignia as a part of their uniforms, and are known, for example, as infantry officers, engineer officers, quartermaster officers, and so on. Officers may be temporarily detailed to another branch, such as to the Inspector General or to General Staff, but unless there is a transfer of branch, each officer remains assigned to the branch in which appointed throughout his or her career.

ORGANIZATION BY UNITS

There follows a short discussion of Army units, from the smallest to the largest. The system and the terminology are fairly uniform throughout the different arms and services, and once identified, the various terms fit readily into the total pattern.

Tables of organization and equipment (TOE), issued by the Department of the Army, establish for each category of Army unit its title, the number and grades of its officers and enlisted personnel, its organic equipment, and its interior organization. Using the TOE as the base document, units organized under modified tables of organization and equipment (MTOE) are tailored to the unit's requirements as determined by MACOM. Tables of distribution and allowances (TDA) prescribe the organization and equipment for special-purpose temporary units. A newly assigned officer should study his or her unit's TOE or TDA as soon as possible.

THE AMERICAN ARMY

FROM CHAPTER 2 OF FM 100-1, THE ARMY

THE CONSTITUTIONAL AND LEGAL BASIS

The strength of the American political system stems from the explicit recognition that all legitimate authority is derived from the people. We acknowledge that each person has inalienable rights and is equal under the law. Appreciation for the worth of the individual affects all public institutions in America, including the armed forces. In every important aspect, the United States Army reflects the democratic nature of our social and political structure both directly, in the Army's purpose and legal basis, and indirectly, in the professional ethos that commits its members to serving the public good.

> "We the People of the United States, in Order to form a more perfect Union, establish Justice, insure domestic Tranquility, provide for the common defense, promote the general Welfare, and secure the Blessings of Liberty to ourselves and our Posterity, do ordain and establish this Constitution for the United States of America."
>
> The Constitution of the United States

The legal basis for a military establishment is clearly set forth in the Constitution. In Articles I and II, the framers codified the principle of civilian control over the armed forces of the United States. They specified that Congress alone would have the power to raise and support armies, to declare war, and to make rules concerning captures on land and water. They further provided that the President, as the Nation's Chief Executive, would be the Commander-in-Chief of the armed forces of the United States. This responsibility, coupled with treaty-making authority, the power to appoint federal officers, and the requirement to "take care that the laws be faithfully executed," provides the principal constitutional bases for Presidential direction of national security affairs. Thus, the responsibility for providing the nation's defense through the armed forces of the United States is constitutionally shared by civilian officials in the legislative and executive branches of the Federal Government.

> "As long as I hold a commission in the Army I have no views of my own to carry out. Whatever may be the orders of my superiors and the law, I will execute. No man can be efficient as a commander who sets his own notions above the law. . . and those he has sworn to obey."
>
> General Ulysses S. Grant
> 1862

While the Constitution recognizes the need for armed forces to protect the Nation, it does not establish a system or define how the Nation is to be protected. As a result, the national defense structure has taken many forms throughout our history. The National Security Act of 1947 (as amended), which is now codified in Titles 10 and 32, United States Code, established the current structure for national defense.

Enacted by Congress in recognition of the need for unity and coordination among the armed services, the National Security Act of 1947 established the National Security Council, the Central Intelligence Agency, the Department of Defense (DOD), and the organization of the Joint Chiefs of Staff (JCS). It also established the position of Secretary of Defense, the principal assistant to the President in all matters relating to DOD, and provided for Departments of the Army, the Navy (which includes the Marine Corps), and the Air Force, under the direction, authority, and control of the Secretary of Defense.

In enacting this law and later amending legislation, Congress intended to:

- Provide a legal framework for the establishment of integrated policies and procedures for the departments, agencies, and functions of the government relating to the national security.
- Provide for the establishment of unified and specified combatant commands and a clear and direct line of command to them from the President and the Secretary of Defense (the National Command Authorities).
- Provide for the unified strategic direction of the combatant forces, for their operation under unified command, and for their integration into an efficient joint team of land, sea, and air forces.

■ Establish the function of the Chairman, Joint Chiefs of Staff, as the principal military advisor to the National Command Authorities.

Title 10, United States Code, as amended, is also the source from which the broad functions of DOD are derived. As presently set forth in DOD Directive 5100.1, Functions of the Department of Defense and its Major Components, dated 25 September 1987, DOD maintains and employs armed forces to:

■ Support and defend the Constitution of the United States against all enemies, foreign and domestic.
■ Ensure, by timely and effective military action, the security of the United States, its territories, and areas vital to its interest.
■ Uphold and advance the national policies and interests of the United States.
■ Safeguard the internal security of the United States.

NATIONAL PURPOSE AND NATIONAL POWER

The Constitution and the Declaration of Independence set forth our national purposes. They include national independence, preservation and expansion of individual human freedoms, individual dignity, equality under the law, and human rights to life, liberty, and the pursuit of happiness.

> "We are determined that before the sun sets on this terrible struggle our flag will be recognized throughout the world as a symbol of freedom on the one hand—of overwhelming power on the other."
> General George C. Marshall
> 1942

From these broad, enduring purposes we derive national interests and objectives, the specific expressions of national purpose that provide the rationale for national security policies. The following basic national security objectives have remained essentially unchanged since the late 1940s:

■ To preserve the independence, institutions, and territorial integrity of the United States,
■ To preserve U.S. and allied vital interests abroad; and

■ To help shape a world in which freedom and democracy can flourish in an international community, in which states coexist without the use of force and in which citizens are free to choose their own governments.

National power, the aggregate capacity of a state to safeguard and advance its national interests and influence the behavior of other states, has diplomatic, economic, and military elements. Specific tasks supporting any national security strategy are accomplished through application of selected combinations of these elements of national power. The principal function of the military element of national power is to deter war and other threats to national interests.

NATIONAL MILITARY OBJECTIVES

Our basic national security objective is to preserve the United States as a free nation with our fundamental institutions and values intact. Translating this general goal into specific national military objectives requires an understanding of the total capabilities of the Nation in relation to potential threats. The Army, in concert with the other services and our allies and friends, must be prepared to support these and other national security objectives:

■ Deter any aggression against the United States, its citizens, interests, or allies, and defeat such aggression if deterrence fails.
■ Establish and maintain a balance between nuclear and conventional capabilities, while fostering responsible arms reductions and arms control measures. The United States will not use biological or chemical weapons.
■ Stem the flow of illegal drugs into the United States.
■ Protect free access and movement to markets worldwide.
■ Maintain stable regional military balances and aid allies and friends in combating threats from aggression, insurgencies, international terrorism, and traffic in illegal drugs.

The world must know that the United States has the forces and the will to counter any form of aggression when its vital interests are at stake. This knowledge comprises the essence of deterrence; it applies across the range continuum of military operations.

NATIONAL SECURITY AND MILITARY STRATEGY FORMULATION

The President is responsible for the development of national security strategy. The National Security Council assists the President in determining U.S. national security interests and in assessing the associated objectives, concepts, resources, commitments, and risks relative to our military, economic, and diplomatic power. The National Security Council integrates the contributions of all agencies of the government to form a coherent national security strategy.

The Chairman, Joint Chiefs of Staff, in consultation with the other members of the Joint Chiefs of Staff and the Commanders-in-Chief (CINCs), prepares the National Military Strategy and provides national security advice to the President, the Secretary of Defense, and the National Security Council. This advice contains recommendations on the National Military Strategy, the force structure required to implement it, and the risks associated with resource shortages. The Chairman directs the combatant commanders to develop theater strategies as well as theater war and contingency plans based on approved guidance.

To support the combatant commands and to fulfill its Title 10 role and DOD Directive 5100.1 functions, the Army organizes, trains, and equips Army forces for the conduct of prompt and sustained combat operations on land and, in conjunction with the other military services, for joint amphibious, airborne and space operations. It also provides forces for the occupation of territories abroad and, as a collateral function, trains forces for interdiction of enemy sea and air power and communications through operations on or from land. Through realistic joint and combined planning and training exercises, the Army refines its doctrine and hones its skills to ensure that its forces are ready to meet any contingency.

Military forces may be employed to promote and protect national interests across the full range of relationships among nations. These range from peacetime activities, such as disaster relief or nation assistance, to fundamental clashes over ideologies and national objectives. The majority of these conflicts are resolved peacefully through arbitration, negotiation, or compromise based on the judicious application of the elements of national power. In those situations that affect vital U.S. interests, the National Command Authorities may give first consideration to the employment of military power. Thus, the United States must prepare for the use of military power across the entire range of military operations, from humanitarian assistance to peace operations, through confrontations short of war, to a range of wartime conventional or even nuclear operations.

LAND, MARITIME, AND AEROSPACE FORCES

To achieve national security objectives, our military forces must be able to deter or defeat enemy forces. Land, maritime, and aerospace forces provide this capability jointly through visible readiness or through unified or joint action. Each service contributes according to its characteristics and the principal medium in which it operates.

The wartime objectives of Army forces are land force dominance, that is, to defeat the enemy's land forces, to seize, occupy and defend land area, and to assist in destroying the enemy's will to resist. Our enemies must know that when the shooting stops, they will still face an American soldier with a weapon in hand.

The wartime objectives of maritime forces are to gain and maintain control of vital sea areas and to protect sea lines of communication from surface, subsurface, and air threats. The ground element of the maritime force, the Marine Corps, seizes or defends advanced naval bases and conducts land operations essential to naval operations. The Army relies upon maritime forces for strategic sealift.

The wartime objectives of aerospace forces are to gain and maintain control of the aerospace and to project aerial combat power promptly wherever needed. These actions include deterring, neutralizing, or destroying the enemy's forces, his command and control mechanisms, and his capacity to wage war. The Army also counts on aerospace forces to provide interdiction, airlift, and close air support to the ground commander.

Military operations that do not warrant a declaration of war, but which could include combat operations, may be required in support of national security. Such operations will almost always be joint, and will most likely take place in conjunction with allies. These operations could occur as part of a U.S.-led coalition or in response to a United Nations' initiative.

COMMAND AND CONTROL OF THE ARMED FORCES

The Chain of Command. As discussed earlier, the Constitution clearly places the military under civilian control. Responsibility for exercising that control is shared by the President, as Commander-in-Chief, and the Congress.

The chain of command is further defined by the Goldwater-Nichols Defense Reorganization Act of 1986, which declares that the operational chain of command passes from the President to the Secretary of Defense to the combatant CINCs of the unified and specified commands. The departmental chain of command runs from the President through the Secretary of Defense to the service secretary to the chief of service. The Chairman, Joint Chiefs of Staff advises and assists the Secretary of Defense and is charged with various supporting functions.

A formal chain of command exists within each specified or unified command according to the needs of the command and the desires of the CINC. The degree of control over assigned forces is specified by the Secretary of Defense and ranges from combatant command (COCOM) to tactical control (TACON) as defined in Joint Publication 0-2, Unified Action Armed Forces.

Unified and Specified Operations. In unified commands, elements of two or more services are placed under a single commander who exercises combatant command or operational control over the forces (land, maritime, and aerospace) assigned to him. Service forces may be organized under subordinate joint commands. Specified commands have a broad continuing mission and are normally composed of forces from primarily one service. Within these unified and specified organizations, each military department (Army, Navy, and Air Force) retains responsibility for administration and logistical support of its assigned forces under the directive authority of the CINC.

Combined operations are conducted by forces of two or more nations acting together to attain the same objective. U.S. forces participating in combined operations are subject to command arrangements and authorities established by international agreement between and consultations among the participating nations. There are two general types of combined operations, those with forces of an alliance among whom formal agreements and procedures for coordination have been developed; and those with forces of nations friendly to the immediate undertaking who form a "coalition" without prior formal agreements or procedures for coordination. These latter combined operations are the most challenging and, at a minimum, require the support of an extensive liaison structure.

The Army will rarely operate or fight alone. The high probability that the Army will operate in concert or alliance with the forces of foreign nations, or even in support of United Nations operations whenever it is committed, is fully reflected in joint doctrine. In such combined operations, the U.S. Army must be sensitive to the likelihood of significant differences in equipment, capabilities, training, combat doctrine, and culture. When operating in support of the United Nations, Rules of Engagement (discussed in Chapter 4) have special importance. Combined operations require the exercise of greater tact, flexibility, and closer coordination and liaison than any other type of operations.

"As with a properly organized citizen army reserve no officers or men need be maintained in the Regular Army to perform duties which can be performed effectively and in time by reserve officers and reservists, the dimensions and cost of the peace establishment, under such a system, are necessarily reduced to a determinable minimum."

General George C. Marshall
1944

THE RESERVE COMPONENTS

Section 8, Article I, of the Constitution specifically charges the Congress "To provide for organizing, arming, and disciplining, the Militia ... and the Authority of training the Militia according to the discipline prescribed by Congress." The same article gives Congress the power "To raise and Support Armies." The role of reserve components is codified in Title 10, United States Code, Section 3062, which provides for an Army consisting of "the Regular Army, the Army National Guard of the United States, the Army National Guard while in the service of the United States. . . the Army Reserve and. . . all persons appointed or enlisted in, or conscripted into the Army without component."

The reduction in Army strength and the accompanying shift from a forward deployed to a force projection Army demands increasingly active cooperation and affiliation between Active and Reserve Components. While the Reserve Components increase the mobilization potential of the Army, they also provide substantial forces to respond to Army missions and contingencies short of wartime mobilization. Reserve Component readiness programs directly support the versatility required of an army that must be able to perform a wide variety of missions or be able to expand on short notice.

Historically, the Army cycles through periods of relative resource adequacy and constraint. In periods of scarcity, the tendency is to shift to the Reserve Component those tasks and force structures not needed immediately. For the Army to be truly versatile, there must be a high degree of compatibility between Active and Reserve Component training and equipment to build a seamless organization. This requires the Army to assess continually the balance of capabilities between the Active and Reserve Components.

DEPARTMENT OF THE ARMY CIVILIANS

Civilian employees are an indispensable part of the Army. Only through the integrated efforts of dedicated civilians and soldiers can the Army accomplish its assigned functions and make the most effective use of its resources. The several thousand Army civilian employees and contractor personnel who served with the armed forces in DESERT SHIELD and DESERT STORM demonstrated that civilians and the soldiers they support share the same sense of commitment and selfless service to the Army and to the Nation.

NATIONAL SECURITY STRUCTURE

Intention of the National Security Act of 1947

Title 50 U.S.C., Chapter 15, Sec. 401. - Congressional Declaration of Purpose

In enacting this legislation, it is the intent of Congress to provide a comprehensive program for the future security of the United States; to provide for the establishment of integrated policies and procedures for the departments, agencies, and functions of the Government relating to the national security; to provide a Department of Defense, including the three military Departments of the Army, the Navy (including naval aviation and the United States Marine Corps), and the Air Force under the direction, authority, and control of the Secretary of Defense; to provide that each military department shall be separately organized under its own Secretary and shall function under the direction, authority, and control of the Secretary of Defense; to provide for their unified direction under civilian control of the Secretary of Defense but not to merge these departments or services; to provide for the establishment of unified or specified combatant commands, and a clear and direct line of command to such commands; to eliminate unnecessary duplication in the Department of Defense, and particularly in the field of research and engineering by vesting its overall direction and control in the Secretary of Defense; to provide more effective, efficient, and economical administration in the Department of Defense; to provide for the unified strategic direction of the combatant forces, for their operation under unified command, and for their integration into an efficient team of land, naval, and air forces but not to establish a single Chief of Staff over the armed forces nor an overall armed forces general staff.

OVERVIEW OF NATIONAL SECURITY STRUCTURE

Numerous governmental organizations are involved in the formulation and implementation of U.S. national military strategy. To set the stage for an explanation of the role of the Joint Chiefs of Staff in national security, we begin with information on those organizations and agencies responsible for the planning and execution of military operations, including their history, organizational structure, and command relationships.

NATIONAL COMMAND AUTHORITIES (NCA)

Constitutionally, the ultimate authority and responsibility for the national defense rests with the President. Since the passage of the National Security Act of 1947, the President has used the Secretary of Defense as his principal assistant in all matters relating to the National Military Establishment (NME)—later the Department of Defense. The Secretary has statutory authority, direction, and control over the Military Departments and is responsible for the effective, efficient, and economical operation of the department.

The National Command Authorities (NCA) are the President and Secretary of Defense together with their duly deputized alternates or successors. The term NCA is used to signify constitutional authority to direct the Armed Forces in their execution of military action. Both inter-theater movement of troops and execution of military action must be directed by the NCA. By law, no one else in the chain of command has the authority to take such action.

NATIONAL SECURITY COUNCIL (NSC)

The National Security Act of 1947 established the National Security Council to consider national security issues that require Presidential decision. It has four statutory members: the President, the Vice President, the Secretary of State, and the Secretary of Defense. The Chairman of the Joint Chiefs of Staff (CJCS) and the Director of Central Intelligence serve as statutory advisers to the NSC.

DEPARTMENT OF DEFENSE (DOD)

World War II and its aftermath furnished the impetus for unification of the Military Departments under a single cabinet-level secretary. Anticipating the needs of a peacetime military organization, an in-depth review by congressional, executive, and military groups began even before the end of the war. The studies were influenced by Service interests that reflected the opinions of experienced wartime military and civilian leaders with vastly different views of the postwar future. Issues that dominated the search for a consensus included retention of air power in the Navy, maintenance of a separate Marine Corps, and the form and responsibilities of the new Department of the Air Force.

The National Security Act of 1947 was monumental legislation. After almost 50 years that included overseas wartime experience beginning with the Spanish-American War, a modern military organization came into existence. Unification of the Services under a single department was law and the powers of the Secretary of National Defense were identified but subject to broad interpretation. The roles and missions of the military Services were defined by Executive Order but would not be statutorily defined until 1958. The act created the NME under the leadership of a civilian secretary and created secretaries for the new Departments of the Army, Navy, and Air Force.

In 1949, the National Security Act was amended to change the name of the NME to the Department of Defense and to recognize it as an executive department. Further, it changed the role of the Services to Military Departments within DOD. The DOD Reorganization Act of 1958 strengthened the Secretary of Defense's direction, authority, and control over the department and clarified the operational chain of command from the President and Secretary of Defense to the combatant commanders.

The role of the Secretary of Defense has changed since the position was established in 1947. Originally, the Secretary had only general authority over the NME, an authority shared with the civilian secretaries of the Military Departments. In 1949, h is position was strengthened with his appointment as head of an executive department, reduction of the role of Military Department heads, and his assumption of budgeting responsibilities. Today, he is the principal assistant to the President for all matt ers relating to the Department of Defense. He has nearly plenary authority, direction, and control of the entire department. Moreover, the Goldwater-Nichols DOD Reorganization Act of 1986 makes clear his position in the operational chain of command.

MILITARY DEPARTMENTS

The Military Departments (Department of the Army, Department of the Navy, Department of the Air Force) are organized separately under civilian secretaries who are responsible for and have authority to conduct the affairs committed to their departments. The service secretaries are not in the operational chain of command.

The Military Departments have been significantly altered by legislation and Executive Order since the National Security Act of 1947. The Key West Agreement of March 1948 clarified the roles of the Military Departments and amplified their responsibil-

ities. In 1953, the President and the Secretary of Defense agreed to designate a Military Department to function as "executive agent" for the unified commands. The Reorganization Act of 1958 removed the Military Departments from the operational chain of command and clarified their support and administrative responsibilities for the unified commands.

COMBATANT COMMANDS

The term combatant command means a unified or specified command. Unified and specified combatant commands were first described by statute in the National Security Act of 1947.

Unified Combatant Command. A command which has a broad, continuing mission under a single commander composed of forces from two or more Services, and which is established and so designated by the President through the Secretary of Defense with the advice and assistance of the Chairman of the Joint Chiefs of Staff.

Specified Combatant Command. A command which has a broad, continuing (usually functional) mission normally composed of forces from a single military department, and is established and so designated by the President through the Secretary of Defense with the advice and assistance of the Chairman of the Joint Chiefs of Staff. Currently, there are no specified commands.

CHAIN OF COMMAND

By the Goldwater-Nichols DOD Reorganization Act of 1986, Congress clarified the command line to the combatant commanders and preserve civilian control of the military. The Act states that the operational chain of command runs from the President to the Secretary of Defense to the combatant commanders. The Act permits the President to direct that communications pass through CJCS. This authority places CJCS in the communications chain. Further, the Act gives the Secretary of Defense wide latitude to assign the Chairman oversight responsibilities over the activities of the combatant commanders.

AUTHORITY

The effective use of the nation's Armed Forces requires a unity of effort in the operation of diverse military resources. This goal is achieved through:

- strategic direction of the Armed Forces,
- operations under unified command,

- integration into an efficient team of land, naval, and air forces,
- prevention of unnecessary duplication of efforts or resources,
- coordination of operations, and
- effective combined operations.

Commensurate with the responsibility placed on combatant commanders to achieve unity of effort, they have been given increased authority by law (Title 10, U.S. Code) and DOD Directive.

The DOD Reorganization Act of 1986 makes the combatant commanders accountable to the NCA for performing their assigned missions. With this accountability comes the assignment of all authority, direction, and control that Congress considers necessary to execute the responsibilities of the combatant commanders. The Act defines the command authority of the combatant commanders to give authoritative direction to subordinate commands, including all aspects of military operations, joint training, and logistics:

- prescribe the chain of command within the command;
- organize commands and forces to carry out assigned missions;
- employ forces necessary to carry out assigned missions;
- coordinate and approve administration, support, and discipline; and
- exercise authority to select subordinate commanders and combatant command staff.

NOTE: List not complete; see UNAAF (Joint Pub 0-2) page III-3.

This authority is termed "combatant command" and resides only in the combatant commander.

COMBATANT COMMAND (COCOM)

Combatant command (COCOM) is the command authority over assigned forces vested in the MACOM Commanders by Title 10, U.S. Code, Section 164, and is not transferable.

COCOM is exercised only by the commanders of unified and specified combatant commands. It is the authority of a combatant commander to perform those functions of command over assigned forces involving organizing and employing commands and forces, assigning tasks, designating objectives, and giving authoritative direction over all aspects of military operations, joint training, and logistics necessary to accomplish the missions assigned to the command. COCOM furnishes full authority to organize and employ commands and forces as the Theater Commander considers necessary to accomplish assigned missions.

COCOM is not shared with other echelons of command. It should be exercised through the commanders of subordinate organizations, normally the Service component commanders, subordinate unified commanders, commanders of joint task forces, and other subordinate commanders.

Directive authority for logistics supports the combatant commander's responsibility to execute effectively operational plans, maintain effectiveness and economy of operation, and prevent duplication of facilities and resources. Military Departments a re still responsible for logistics and administrative support of forces assigned or attached to the combatant commands.

In peacetime, the scope of the logistic and administrative authority exercised by the MACOM commander is consistent with legislation, Department of Defense policy or regulations, budgetary considerations, local conditions and other specific conditions prescribed by the Secretary of Defense or the CJCS. The combatant commander refers disputes to the military department, if he fails to receive timely resolution there, the MACOM Commander may forward the matter through CJCS to the Secretary of Defense for resolution.

During crisis or war, the MACOM Commanders' authority and responsibility are expanded to include use of facilities and supplies of all forces under their command. Joint logistics doctrine developed by CJCS establishes wartime logistics policy.

The MACOM Commanders have approval authority over Service logistics programs that affect operational capability or sustainability within their theaters (e.g., base adjustments, force beddowns). Disputes in this area may be settled by the Secretary of Defense through CJCS.

OPERATIONAL CONTROL (OPCON)

Operational control is another level of authority used frequently in the execution of joint military operations. OPCON authority may be delegated to echelons below the combatant commander. Normally, this is authority exercised through component commanders and the commanders of established subordinate commands. Limitations on OPCON, as well as additional authority not normally included in OPCON, can be specified by a delegating commander.

OPCON is the authority delegated to a commander to perform those functions of command over subordinate forces involving the composition of subordinate forces, the assignment of tasks, the designation of objectives, and the authoritative direction necessary to accomplish the mission. It includes directive authority for joint training. Commanders of subordinate commands and joint task forces will normally be given OPCON of assigned or attached forces by a superior commander. OPCON normally provides full authority to organize forces as the operational commander deems necessary to accomplish assigned missions and to retain or delegate OPCON or tactical control as necessary. OPCON may be limited by function, time, or location. It does not, of itself, include such matters as administration, discipline, internal organization, and unit training.

TACTICAL CONTROL (TACON)

The term tactical control is used in execution of operations and is defined as: "the detailed and usually, local direction and control of movements or maneuvers necessary to accomplish missions or tasks assigned."

ROLE OF CJCS

The role of CJCS in the chain of command of the combatant commands is threefold: communications, oversight, and spokesman.

- Communications between the NCA and the combatant commanders may pass through CJCS. The Goldwater-Nichols DOD Reorganization Act of 1986 permits the President to place the Chairman in the communications chain and the President has in fact directed that such communications pass through the Chairman.
- Oversight of the activities of combatant commands may be delegated by the Secretary of Defense to CJCS.

- CJCS is the spokesman for the combatant commanders on the operational requirements of their commands.

FORCES

The Goldwater-Nichols Act requires that forces under the jurisdiction of the Military Departments be assigned to the combatant commands, with the exception of forces assigned to perform the mission of the military department, (e.g., recruit, supply, equip, maintain). In addition, forces within a Commanders geographic area of responsibility fall under the command of the combatant commander except as otherwise directed by the Secretary of Defense.

ORGANIZATIONAL RELATIONSHIPS

The unified command structure is flexible, and changes as required to accomodate evolving U.S. national security needs. A classified document called the Unified Command Plan (UCP) establishes the combatant commands, identifies geographic areas of responsibility, assigns primary tasks, defines authority of the commanders, establishes command relationships, and gives guidance on the exercise of combatant command. It is approved by the President, published by the CJCS, and addressed to the commanders of combatant commands.

Five combatant commanders have geographic area responsibilities. These Theater Commanders are assigned an area of operations by the Unified Command Plan and are responsible for all operations within their designated areas: U.S. Joint Forces Command, U.S. Central Command, U.S. European Command, U.S. Pacific Command, and U.S. Southern Command.

The MACOM Commanders of the remaining combatant commands have worldwide functional responsibilities not bounded by any single area of operations and they are U.S. Space Command, U.S. Special Operations Command, U.S. Strategic Command and U.S. Transportation Command.

BACKBONE VS. BOX: The Choice between Principled and Prescriptive Leadership[1]

BY ANNA SIMONS

Officers belong to what is often described as the world's oldest profession. Do soldiers really predate priests or chiefs? We'll never know for sure. But officership has to count as one of humanity's most enduring social inventions.

Without question, significant shifts have occurred in terms of whether officers command from the front or the rear, compel or impel, transform or transact, and manage or lead. However, this chapter will contend that the services which officers and only officers can provide haven't really changed. Nor can they. In addition to fulfilling organizational and functional requirements, officership meets bio-political as well as sociological demands—demands which will remain the same no matter how dramatically future battlescapes alter.

Though the Army must always worry about what looms ahead, I want to suggest that it is equally essential to consider what still lurks within, namely, the all-too-human desire to be directed, if not led. This chapter will suggest a way in which it may actually be possible to address both concerns via the same approach—principled leadership—thereby taking advantage of what we do know in order to address what we can't know.

My general thesis is this: not only does operating from a set of core convictions or principles grant leaders at all levels maximum flexibility while minimizing a range of different frictions, but having principled leaders satisfies soldiers' demands. Absent the flexibility and adaptability afforded by principled leadership, the Army's future success would depend on its present ability to foresee accurately tomorrow's operational concepts and scenarios. That is a tall order. No one could have forecast U.S. involvement in Somalia twelve or, arguably, even two months before the fact. Were we the least bit prepared for an exodus of over 630,000 refugees from Kosovo or for their later return? Who would have suspected in August 2001 that we'd be fighting a war in Afghanistan in the fall? As these or any number of other recent military interventions would suggest, the only thing we can say with assurance today is that we will be surprised again tomorrow. In terms of how to react, meanwhile, we can no more count on

controlling the what, where, and when of future confrontations than we can command the weather; we don't always understand others' motivations or their methods. What we should be able to rely on, though, is the extent to which we know ourselves. And where our own strengths lie *as* Americans *is* in principles, and not just in tactics, techniques, and procedures, vital as these are. This is yet another reason to (re)turn to principles, though the gist of my argument is more elemental still: in conditions of flux humans need to be able to count on something fixed, while what is fixed has to be flexible too, paradoxical as that may sound.

In what follows I contend that humans need a hierarchy of values even when, and perhaps especially when, circumstances call for maximum behavioral flexibility. From an anthropological perspective, I demonstrate the extent to which officers often resemble Big Men more than they do Chiefs (terms I'll return to below), which means that they impel rather than compel and employ carrots as well as sticks. I make the point that an officer's most effective tool is to engage in principled behavior. I then go on to examine some of the principles of officership which have withstood the test of time, as well as those which seem to be challenged by postmodern change. I use Special Forces teams and two superlative military advisors—T.E. Lawrence and Edward Lansdale—to illustrate that principled officership remains integral even in decentralized situations. These are exactly the kinds of situations which soldiers confront. The world, after all, lacks geopolitical balance, units increasingly experience turbulence, and combat always causes turmoil. In the face of this, principles, like a backbone, offer consistency, resilience, and strength.

THE HIERARCHICAL IMPERATIVE

As humans, we are, to borrow from Lionel Tiger and Robin Fox, "imperial animals."[2] We invariably form hierarchies. Even in what anthropologists call "stateless" societies, which by definition lack formal government—where there are no permanent government structures, police forces, or officials of any kind—leaders arise. In foraging societies, for instance, one man may be a better hunter. Someone else might be a better healer. In societies where elders, as a group, deserve respect some individuals will always be listened to more closely; inevitably there are a few who command more attention than their peers. Why? Because they strive for this? Or because others won't, don't want to, or can't measure up?

Interestingly, in much of the leadership literature little is said about the competition involved in rising to the top. Anthropologists' accounts, in contrast, describe strategic struggles among New Guinea Highlanders, Swat Pathans, Kwakiutl, with the list stretching on and on. In both sets of literature the focus tends to be on what makes leaders effective and what effects they then have on their followers. Occasionally there are discussions about followers' desires: what they want of, from, and in their leaders. But not even in leadership manuals is it explained why followers might want to be followers and not leaders themselves.[3]

The literature never explicitly labels leaders winners and followers losers, but reading between the lines this is what it strongly suggests. If leaders have such qualities as ambition, character, drive, and ideas, then followers must lack them. Or they lack something else, perhaps self-esteem, self-confidence, skills, or smarts. Yet, what if many simply prefer to not compete? What if, instead, they'd rather belong? Or what if they like being directed by someone else, and would rather work for someone they admire, and alongside others, rather than for (or by) themselves? To anyone with drive or ambition this must sound unreal, impossible, or false.[4]

Indeed, to most Americans "moving up" must seem to be a universal goal. However, hierarchicized divisions of labor that have existed for generations generally persist not only because those at the top manage to successfully constrain those below, but because there are costs associated with exerting control. Or, to turn this around, so long as the price paid by subordinates is not too high (or can be rationalized away), the contest to become superior (or even autonomous) may not be considered worthwhile. Concomitant with different values (and rewards) attached to different kinds of work are different expected behaviors. Generally speaking, individuals lower down the ladder are granted (or grant themselves) more latitude to express themselves freely, display emotions, and act out in public.[5] The obverse is true for those in control; they must act controlled. Ergo the stiff upper lip (at least in public).[6] In other words, regardless of—and maybe even in psychic proportion to—the benefits leaders accrue, leadership is presumed to exact what many regard as too burdensome or too difficult a toll (though not a toll those who become leaders must mind).

Despite our "take-charge" attitudes, American ambivalence toward leadership—and even toward leaders themselves—runs deep. At the moment, for instance, we are consumed with weighing, justifying, and bemoaning what might be lost as we choose greater responsibilities for higher pay but longer hours. Attaining power costs time; exerting power consumes energy. We constantly weigh the trade-offs. No less than the former Secretary of Labor himself, Robert Reich, has recently questioned the sacrifices he made during his own rise to the top. Yet, no matter how predisposed we might be to think in terms of quid pro quos, it is unclear whether rewards and sacrifices are ever directly proportional.

For instance, in the all-volunteer force the quid pro quo we might expect for leaders vis-à-vis followers, in terms of risks and rewards, is turned on its head. The playing field is even when it comes to who makes the ultimate sacrifice: everyone commits to it. Yet, having said this, do senior officers work harder than juniors? Or put in longer hours? Lieutenants and captains would probably scream No. But the seniors earn more money and receive innumerable additional benefits. How do they justify this? How would we?

The clear answer is that those higher up the chain of command are responsible for more lives, more equipment, and more weighty decisions.[7] The more heretical answer would be that the Army can't operate without chains of command and has to have something to make its leadership division of labor as perceptible as is the division of labor between, say, armor, artillery, and infantry. The irony is that the further away from low-level, hands-on troop command that one moves, the harder it may be to clearly define precise leadership responsibilities. All the more reason, then, to make the hierarchy look as strong and well-delineated as possible, though in significant ways the more removed from soldiers officers are, the more control over them they can have.

OFFICERS: BIG MEN OR CHIEFS?

Anthropologists often draw a distinction between two types of leaders: Big Men and Chiefs. Big Men have prestige. Chiefs hold power. Prestige is evanescent; it can't be consolidated over time or inherited without continual expenditure of effort. In the hunt for more prestige, Big Men strive to maintain and attract more and more followers from whom they solicit the makings of grand feasts where everything collected will then be consumed or given away. The point is to *seem* big, a point they must make over and over again in the face of never-ending, often-escalating competition. Reputation, in such a contest, is paramount. Thus, Big Men devote inordinate amounts of time to impression and image management, planning, plotting, and worrying. And for what ends? At best all they can do is dominate the social scene. They can't dominate anything else.[8]

Chiefs, in contrast, not only dominate, they domineer.[9] Unlike Big Men, Chiefs have coercive authority. Either they have armed forces at their disposal, who assist them in making others do what they want, and/or they possess divine powers. As a consequence, Chiefs have the capacity to inspire fear as well as command respect. They *are* in control. Or, to redraw the contrast, Chiefs can make people do things; at best, Big Men can only get them to want to help.

So which, would we say, describes officers? In today's Army, would we characterize officers as Big Men or as Chiefs? The academic answer is, of course, that they represent a bit of both, though the ratio of Big Manship to Chiefliness seems to increase as individuals rise through the ranks. All officers are Chieflike by virtue of being vested with command authority; those who command soldiers can not only give direct lawful orders but can also mete out nonjudicial punishment. And like leaders who wield coercive authority elsewhere, officers of all types and in all positions seek to maintain distance between themselves and their subordinates.[10] There are legions of ways in which they do this—physically, materially, ideologically, and/or symbolically.[11] The officer-enlisted divide itself exemplifies this, though as officers advance they make use of all sorts of distancing techniques to preserve separations even among themselves. This is written all over uniforms. But it is also made evident in, for instance, the size of higher-ups' staffs and how difficult gaining access to those higher-ups may be—or is made to be.

Of course, there are practical reasons for limited access, large staffs, and other perquisites of power which wind up reinforcing distance. But we also shouldn't forget that distinction is integral to hierarchy—something which is much easier to maintain (and cultivate) in garrison, during peacetime, and in higher

headquarters, than in the field, during war, and in operational units. Without question, the hierarchical hope is that patterns of deference, obedience, respect, and order established during peacetime and training will carry over into war. Or, alternatively, the goal is that no one should think that such patterns don't carry over. But consider: when a unit is on its own, confronting discomfort, danger, or disaster, its officers actually live no differently than their soldiers and wield no more power than a Big Man could.[12] Though officers may be in a position to tell subordinates what they want them to do, they can't force them to do those things, let alone make them do them well.[13] Nor can they prevent their soldiers from acting like the fictional Sergeant Svejk, an exemplary goldbricker.[14]

Everyone has heard stories about soldiers who have found ingenious ways to thumb their noses at commanders by following the letter rather than the spirit of the law (even in combat). Thus, regardless of the fact that the stick looms larger than the carrot in the sense that those who choose not to follow orders *will* be punished (Big Men, remember, can't punish), officers who hope to succeed in battle, to accomplish their missions, and/or to rise in the chain of command are far better off using incentives than threats. Field Manual 22-100, the Army's leadership bible, itself concentrates on carrots: how to treat and counsel subordinates in order to get the most out of them. Presumably this wouldn't be doctrinal advice if followers' enthusiasm and support wasn't understood to be essential to mission accomplishment and leaders' success.

Interestingly, when we examine how Chiefs (and kings, emperors, rulers, and dictators) tend to treat their armed forces—as opposed to their subjects—we see something very similar. In societies where a national leader depends directly on wielders of force for his authority he will dangle all sorts of incentives in front of them in order to keep them eager to work on his behalf, with him, and for him. Tellingly, in this country the higher up the chain one looks the less officers have to depend on subordinates to help secure their reputation or assure their longevity as leaders. Instead, where subordinates' impressions matter most is at the tip of the spear, in units. There, most officers realize, at least in theory (and certainly this is what they are taught), that how well they do depends on what they can get, *not force*, their soldiers to do, while to accomplish this—as all the manuals make clear—they must lead.

In classic Big Man societies, where the societal ideal is to be generous, Big Men lead by being big, with the selfish aim of proving themselves *bigger than*. In the Army, according to the most recent edition of FM 22-100, "lead" means "be, know, do."[15] Does this mean, as with Big Men, "be, know, do" *better than*?

TIME-TESTED PRINCIPLES

According to Raimondo Montecuccoli, a preeminent seventeenth-century commander and strategist, "The ideal commander was warlike, in good health, and of martial stature. He should possess moral strength, prudence, and above all have 'force,' a quality embracing courage, fortitude, energy, and determination, similar to the *virtu* demanded by Machiavelli and the *constantia* praised by Lipsius."[16] Some three centuries later, U.S. Army Chief of Staff Edward Meyer emphasized the importance of character: "Character is ingrained principle expressed consciously and unconsciously to subordinates, superiors, and peers alike—honesty, loyalty, self-confidence, humility, and self-sacrifice. Its expression to all audiences must ring with authenticity."[17] Tim O'Brien, a writer and veteran of Vietnam, describes a platoon leader he admired this way: "He was insanely calm. He never showed fear. He was a professional soldier, an ideal leader of men in the field."[18]

If we consider the continuities, two things stand out. First, the inner character and inner convictions leaders are said to have must be made manifest somehow. And second, the ideals they embody have to resonate. Is it mere coincidence that the traits Edgar Puryear finds in most top military leaders—integrity, humility, selflessness, concern for others, reverence, and showmanship—can all be outwardly displayed?[19] Hardly. Leaders have to give evidence, somehow, that they are worth following, as well as being personally worthy of the sacrifices they might (and likely will) demand. Those who would be leaders will therefore find it advisable to come across as confident, credible, courageous, decisive, just, honest, loyal, and selfless. Moreover, they should set the example and manifest self-control.

Leadership manuals and guides draw from at least two broad sources.[20] One is clearly the past: what character traits, attitudes, and behaviors have characterized exemplary military leaders through the ages? The second is human nature—or, to be more precise, the unchanging nature of social relations. At any rate, the profitable use of examples from the past implies that the nature of social relations is unchanging. For instance, even as FM 22-100 warns aspiring leaders about "the stress of change" ahead, it refers them to Field Manual 100-5, *Operations*, because:

> FM 100-5 provides a doctrinal framework for coping with these challenges while executing operations. It gives Army leaders clues as to what they will face and what will be required of them, but *as COL Chamberlain found on Little Round Top*, no manual can cover all the possibilities. The essence of leadership remains the same: Army leaders create a vision of what's necessary, communicate it in a way that makes their intent clear, and vigorously execute it to achieve success."[21]

I quote the passage above at such length because its claim—that the essence of leadership hasn't changed since the unexpected will always occur—tells only half of what we already know. It's really the essence of human relations that hasn't changed, but recurs in familiar ways. Otherwise, it would make little sense for the manual to use Colonel Chamberlain at Gettysburg to illustrate exemplary leadership. Gettysburg was fought 138 years ago. Presumably everything about war has changed since then. Except, of course, the human element.

Not surprisingly, John Mattox is able to trace "principles of moral military leadership" back to Augustine's day,[22] while, as Lloyd Matthews might add, it is not so much the "broad ethical ideals" themselves which have proliferated over the centuries but rather the literature about them.[23]

Yet, no matter how carefully the historical record has been plumbed to yield lists which double as guides, the catch for every officer is that he or she has to re-create this ideal past all over again in the present. And though the Army may offer all sorts of methods for assisting officers to do this, it can't control for all of the dynamics they will encounter. There is interpersonal chemistry to take into account. Also, individual officers may be no more adept at fieldcraft (or soldiering) than are their soldiers. Nevertheless, what soldiers still want officers to be *is* "better than."[24] And they want this without officers implying that they think they are "better than." Thus, the only realm in which officers can't be bested turns out to be the overarching realm of principled, moral, and ethical behavior.

Since there is no better-than-principled behavior, *being* principled amounts to a virtue in and of itself. Moreover, the fact that it is never easy to remain principled, especially in war, abroad, under stress, during crises, *and* when presented with contrary temptation, helps render the foregoing proposition that much more significant and lends incalculable worth to officers who are principled.

Soldiers need principled leaders for both noble and prosaic reasons. A leader who acts in a principled way represents order and inspires cohesiveness as well as confidence, which are the antitheses of what war promises. If we rethink the attributes desired in leaders—fortitude, strength, composure—they represent fixity in conditions of extreme flux. One can think of a range of related traits—dependability, trustworthiness, reliability, consistency, good judgment—to describe someone who is principled.

There is probably more tacit agreement in the combat literature about the significance of being principled than there is regarding which principles officers should adhere to. Some principles, such as those brought forward by Don Snider, John Nagl, and Tony Pfaff, are suggested as those from which officers "should draw both their vision and their motivation."[25] Other lists of principles describe how officers should act and what they should do to be considered leaders. All, again, have been carefully distilled from what has worked through time and across space. Significantly, though, not a single one of these tells officers what to do in specific situations;[26] they can't. Given the messiness of real world encounters, officers have to be able to apply situational ethics to whatever might confront them. But if we think about it, this means that the thing officers most need—which is to know *what* to do—no one else can provide, except possibly those subordinates who are there with them (on the spot, in the field, in combat, in the unit). Yet *to lead* means never having to be told by subordinates what is the "right" or "moral" thing to do.

This, I would argue, is the source of an officer's power. Whether he or she can *consistently* make the "right" decisions determines whether or not others will consistently follow. Soldiers expect officers to be the authority on what is the right thing to do—tactically, doctrinally, legally, morally. Whenever officers can prove soldiers correct about this, they lead.

One could almost argue that this renders officership a profession within a profession: officers' work is

leadership. Their survival in the system depends on their moral expertise, their maintaining control over the jurisdiction of deciding what is or is not the appropriate thing to do, and their being able to prove the legitimacy of their decision-making to subordinates (and civilian authorities) through journals, special schools, courses, and academies. However, there is at least one problem with such a comparison. Historically, professions never have formal, permanently fixed, and clearly ranked hierarchies. At most they display informal and fiercely contested pecking orders in which seniority matters, but in which senior partners do not *command* junior partners. Just consider: generals and their aides will never share the same status while still in uniform. This alone renders the kind of hierarchy the Army has—and requires—unique. At least thus far.

POSTMODERN CHALLENGES

However, hierarchy as an organizing principle, at the small unit level especially, may be in jeopardy. In 1974, Morris Janowitz was already noting that "the basis of authority has shifted from that of an authoritarian domination to manipulation, persuasion, and group consensus."[27] He attributes this shift to "changing societal values" and the "impact of technology." Writing more than a decade later, Daryl Henderson likewise comments on "a significant historical shift downwards in the locus of control."[28]

Even more recently, in describing postmodern leadership challenges, French sociologist Bernard Boëne and British sociologist Christopher Dandeker acknowledge remarkable congruence between their conclusions and those reached by two Israelis, Boas Shamir and Eyal Ben-Ari.[29] The latter's prediction is that:

> The military organization of the future is likely to be much more "organic" in nature. Organic organizations are characterized by a more flexible division of labor, decentralization of decision-making, low reliance on formal authority and hierarchy and on rules and regulations to coordinate work, and greater reliance on nonrestricted, two-way, informal communication and coordination systems.[30]

Along the same lines, but in an even more pointed way, David Ronfeldt and John Arquilla, among other war futurists, advocate a new and hybrid form of networked organization "in which 'all-channel' networks are fitted to flattened hierarchies."[31]

Those who take such a tack, predicting or promoting the (d)evolution of hierarchy (or its transformation into something else, or less), do so out of the belief that something fundamental has changed in the world at large. They cite young peoples' expectations and attitudes, the technological and organizational capabilities of our opponents (and ourselves), and/or the increasingly diffuse nature of conflict, which may involve state, parastate, and substate actors anywhere in the world. They argue that so long as potential missions run the gamut from coalitional war-making to coalitional peacekeeping, there is a "greater need for versatility, flexibility, and adaptability" in size, design, responsiveness, recruits, in—essentially—everything.[32]

To recast what they are saying in only slightly different terms: basically, as the world's youth become better-informed, more nonconformist, and more self-absorbed,[33] as our enemies become more politically, economically, and socially but not conventionally militarily disruptive—the more complex and multinational our missions will become, and the harder it will be to exert control. Experientially, militaries have long had to cope with challenges posed by entropy, the intrinsic tendency toward disorder. As Martin van Creveld points out, there have generally been two alternative responses when the ground shifts tectonically: tighten "command *and* control," or decentralize and delegate in turn.[34] The problem with the latter approach, though, is that to decentralize, and still win, vertical integration must somehow be maintained. At the very least, everyone has to be singing from the same sheet of music—something far easier to achieve when everyone already shares internalized "values and norms," and when there is already "unity of thought."

As an organizational principle, unity of thought has few parallels. It facilitates unity of effort among separated forces in fluid environments, and is liberating in at least two senses. Any part of the organization should know how to replicate (or repair) the whole. This has to offer psychic comfort. At the same time, with less structure to worry about, it should be easier for units to reconfigure in response to novel situations. The staff of Moltke the Elder, for instance, shared "ethical and even religious ideals which served as the basis for calm confidence."[35] John Gates credits the success of American Army vol-

unteers in the Philippine insurrection of 1899-1901 to their being a "self-assured group with a self-conscious progressive orientation and a commitment to such traditional values as Duty-Honor-Country."[36]

Since the days of Napoleon, armies have worked hard to instill common values and norms when these were not already present. However, as Shamir and Ben-Ari caution, "achieving coordination through culture" may be increasingly difficult today.[37] They make this comment in light of "the frequently changing composition of the organizational and interorganizational frameworks that bring together members of different organizational and sometimes national cultures."[38] However, their observation may be equally apt when applied to advice offered today's leaders: namely, to be sensitive to, and even appreciative of, subcultural, gender, and other differences, as well as differing opinions.

This cannot but complicate a leader's role, which among other things is to build consensus *for* (or consensus from) without soldiers discovering, in a Heisenbergian twist, that the act of trying to reach a consensus among themselves prevents its achievement. At the same time, the need to soften (never mind flatten) hierarchy to foster strength through diversity reveals the Army's default in what may well be its chief responsibility to those it commissions, which is to place them in charge of soldiers who, as individuals, should all regard themselves as members of the Army—their *national* Army—first, and members of other groups or subcultures a clear and distant second.[39]

At a minimum, soldiers should come to units already regarding themselves *as* soldiers.[40] Otherwise, unity of effort—which requires that individuals think in terms of the good-of-the-group and not themselves—won't always (and may seldom) be achieved. Under conditions of confused (or even multiple) allegiances, organized decentralization will never work. In his book, *Command in War,* van Creveld analyzes four armies which purposely disaggregated their units and succeeded.[41] Worth noting, however, is that authority was purposely diffused between units, not diluted within them.

ORGANIZED DECENTRALIZATION: A CONTRADICTION IN TERMS?

If organized decentralization (or some approximation thereof) is to be introduced, there are in the meantime at least two sets of examples worth paying attention to: that of the Special Forces, and two different "armies of one" symbolized by T.E. Lawrence and Edward Lansdale.

Curiously, despite all the discussion in the military leadership literature about teams and teamwork, and what may or may not be applicable from the realms of business and management, little is said about the fact that teams already exist in the Army, and have for decades. More to the point still, many do exactly what it is said conventional units will do in the future. For example, Special Forces operational detachments—the term "operational detachment" itself speaks volumes—are not only designed to "deal in the gray" but to be left on their own for long periods of time, as is presumably the case in Afghanistan today. Until the end of the Cold War, Special Forces (SF) could be considered distinctive thanks to its unconventional warfare, counterinsurgency, and foreign internal defense missions. These required that SF soldiers be adept at winning hearts and minds and building rapport. SF may no longer be quite so alone when it comes to plying these particular skills, since peacekeeping operations and humanitarian interventions make similar demands. But the label "unconventional" unquestionably holds when applied to the teams' organization and the officer-enlisted relationship.

The individual who is officially in charge of an "A" Detachment—the captain—is often only nominally in charge of the warrant officer and ten noncommissioned officers (NCOs) on his team. Usually, the team sergeant has the more commanding presence. In part, this is a function of the team's division of labor: the team sergeant (an E8) is responsible for the world inside the team room while the officer interfaces with the world beyond. But also, the captain is not just chronologically younger than many of the men who serve under him (sometimes by as much as a decade), he is more inexperienced than most. Thus, they are unlikely to automatically look up to him, nor can he often present himself as an authority on anything having to do with their job(s), though he can know more about their next mission, about the country where they might deploy, the people there, etc.

Special Forces NCOs joke that the definition of a good captain is someone who knows when to defer to them. And, indeed, smart captains seem to understand exactly how to do this to earn respect: they don't initiate competition they can't win and, ideally, they don't engage in competition at all. In other words, they don't act like experts, while when they defer to others *as* experts it is in only certain domains.

This is not quite what the Army's leadership manuals advise, or what these officers would have done previously when commanding soldiers younger and more inexperienced than themselves. So how do they know, when new to SF, to do this? How do they know *how* to do this? The short answer is, they don't. Their success is simply an outgrowth of principled behavior.

Perhaps the best way to illustrate what I mean by behaving in a principled way is to compare two of the unconventional world's most prominent and successful figures, T.E. Lawrence and Edward Lansdale, though in the course of achieving their successes (Lawrence in Arabia, Lansdale in the Philippines) neither led a team of compatriots.[42] Instead, both men were military advisors: they could not command, nor could they control. All they could reasonably do was exemplify, suggest, project, and, to an uncanny degree, fit FM 22-100's prescriptions for how to lead.

Each did so, though, using radically different techniques. Lawrence was adept at everything Bedouin; Lansdale never tried to live or speak like a Filipino. Lawrence was an expert about the Bedouins long before he began advising them; Lansdale was interested in reading people, not about them.[43] Each operated at what amounted to opposite ends of the advisory spectrum. Nevertheless, both knew their own strengths and weaknesses (again, as FM 22-100 advises), and both fully appreciated what they could and could not be expert in *from their advisees' point of view*.

Nothing spells this out better than Lawrence's "Twenty-seven Articles," his own lessons learned as distilled into principles for others to use. For instance, here is Article 18:

> Disguise is not advisable. Except in special areas let it be clearly known that you are a British officer and a Christian. At the same time if you can wear Arab kit when with the tribes you will acquire their trust and intimacy to a degree impossible in uniform. It is however dangerous and difficult. They make no special allowances for you when you dress like them. Breaches of etiquette not charged against a foreigner are not condoned to you in Arab clothes.[44]

In other words, Lawrence was not just savvy enough to know how to dress like a Bedouin (Articles 17, 19, and 20 offer more specific advice about what was best to wear), but he also understood what Bedouins would and wouldn't let him get away with as either a Briton (which he was) or a Bedu (which he knew he could never be).

In contrast, Lansdale never developed anything like Lawrence's expertise regarding what Filipinos would have allowed him to do or not do as an intimate. But, then, he never had to. He found that he didn't need to operate from a set of principles related to them (let alone a set of principles built around *how* to relate to them). He excelled instead by operating from his own core convictions about what it meant to be an American, and only had to understand what Filipinos expected *this* to mean. In other words—while Lawrence proved consistent regarding Bedouins' expectations of him as someone who knew what it meant to be Bedouin, and thus knew in which areas it was acceptable to best them (e.g., endurance, marksmanship, etc.), and when to not even try (e.g., in discussions about religion and women)—Lansdale's expertise was in democracy and in being American.[45]

Not surprisingly, Lansdale's approach turns out to be in keeping with how most Americans behave abroad. We invariably project American values and ideals. The fact that these include (if they don't revolve around) being and acting the same, no matter where or among whom we find ourselves, may itself be our defining principle, while the fact that we judge one another accordingly only reaffirms our commitment to that principle.[46]

FROM AMERICAN PRINCIPLES TO PRINCIPLED AMERICANS?

Although every society can be said to have a set of principles by which its members are expected to live, we regard ours as universal human truths. We not only place emphasis on our absolute equality as individuals, both before the law and before one another, but our expectation is to always be treated fairly, as anyone should be, regardless of position, status, or rank.

At first glance this might seem to make hierarchy unAmerican. However, as Gerald Linderman points out in a book chapter titled "Discipline: Not the American Way" (in his seminal work on combat experience during World War II), Americans will accede to

hierarchy so long as it's equitable. What American combat soldiers in World War II desired, for instance, "was not a standing equivalent to that of officers but acknowledgment of an equivalent worth."[47] As he explains elsewhere, what American soldiers have historically wanted (and needed) from officers is to know where officers stand, what they stand for, what they won't stand for, and that they will always be fair.[48] This was true during the Civil War, when officers were often elected, and still held a century later, with appointees in place.[49]

Why would soldiers be so consistent and adamant about this? No doubt because, as Lloyd Matthews has written,

> Such revered documents as the Declaration of Independence, the Preamble to the Constitution, and the Bill of Rights have given rise to an American political tradition in which liberty and equality remain vibrant touchstone ideals among U.S. citizens. Though these values obviously cannot receive full or even substantial expression in military service, they do instill boundary expectations in the minds of service members that military leaders ignore at their peril.[50]

Not all of this, of course, is particularly or peculiarly American. For instance, Linderman quotes a British soldier who says, "Trust depends on a man's knowing that his commander thinks of him as a person and therefore treats him fairly, and looks after him."[51] But we, being a longer-lived, more deeply-rooted meritocracy, may push this even further. Meritocracies work only when status is achieved, not ascribed. And the Army is a classic meritocracy. Therefore, the presumption among soldiers is that those above them must have, somehow, demonstrably proven that they deserve to be where they are. And like Big Men, officers must keep proving and demonstrating this worth. Yet, to whom? What superiors need from officers seems vastly different from what subordinates do, in part perhaps because what merits worth for superiors is not necessarily what merits worth for subordinates. Often, though, this leads to wildly different judgments by subordinates and superiors about the same officer. Must this be? Should this be?

If principled behavior binds us together as Americans, and particular principles (such as equity) define us as a nation, then surely being able to be counted on *to be* principled is the one standard by which the Army could—and should—measure fitness, up and down the chain of command. Arguably, this is how we all judge one another anyway—rank, status, position be damned.

If the Army doesn't do this more consistently—or explicitly—it runs two risks: first, that informal pecking orders will undermine its formal order; and second, that the trappings of hierarchy are shown to be just that—devices. Neither is something the Army can long afford, since without differentiating people—and making subordinates *want* those differences to matter—control won't stick.[52]

BACKBONE VS. BOX

Again, it seems important to bear in mind that the Army does not need to maintain control merely for its own sake, but for the sake of those it seeks to control. Not everyone wants to lead. Either people recognize their own limitations, or realize they can't (or don't want to) set limits for others. Limits is a shorthand way to think about officers' domain: they remind soldiers of and about limits, set limits, interpret limits, and help subordinates stay within or push beyond accepted limits.

Limits have always been critical, but today—given real-time scrutiny by the news media, international agencies, and concerned citizens—they may be more important than ever before, especially since the Army has never been confronted by so many culturally alien, morally messy, and potentially victoryless missions. All the more reason to grant more, not less, control to those on site, those who know what's happening on the ground and can better read the local situation. To be able to grant leaders at the tip of the spear more control, though, demands and requires trust. Trust, meanwhile, comes from knowing subordinates can be counted on. This is less tautological than it is self-reinforcing: if everyone operates from the same set of principles—and proves principled—there would be no need for doubt or second-guessing.

Also, principles, once internalized, are always there; doctrinal manuals and models may well not be. Not only does operating from a strong principled core/corps offer maximum flexibility, but it avoids artificially constraining (as may a model) or delimiting (as can doctrine). Perhaps the best way to conceptualize this is graphically. Think of principles as a Backbone. With deeply embedded core convictions, officers should be able to operate anywhere; they don't have to think about what *not* to do; they know

from within. But lacking such core convictions they would have to be told. Because command has to make sure that everyone understands where the limits are to what's acceptable, constraints would be set externally and generated from without, not within. Ergo the Box.

Without question this is what some people would prefer—the comfort of being in a Box. Boxes offer protection, among other things. Small wonder it's then difficult to pry people out of them. Or that the Army finds itself *needing* to tell leaders to "think outside the box."

Of course, if there were no Box, there'd be no reason to tell leaders to think outside it. If, instead, the Army trusted—and entrusted—officers to be principled it could think, talk, and operate in terms of Backbone instead.

Which would build and bolster confidence? Which represents the more positive approach? Surely having Backbone is the means test the Army needs to apply in peopling its hierarchy: only those with inner conviction have the strength, resiliency, wisdom, and courage to set limits for those who prefer that limits be set. By switching metaphors—from Box to Backbone—the Army would simply be acknowledging this and using to maximum advantage our human penchant to self-select the extent to which we'd rather lead or follow.

To summarize. What followers want is to be able to count on their leaders, while what the Army should ask of its leaders is that they be able to be counted on. At the very least, they must be able to be counted on to know what *not* to do—tactically, ethically, strategically, politically.[53]

If equity, consistency, and acting in a principled way are inherent to being American, then it only makes sense to apply this standard—of officers being able to be counted on *for* principled behavior—up and down the line.

So long as superiors no less than subordinates can count on officers for principled behavior, they can relax top-down control (though not monitoring). By granting units more autonomy, they then grant themselves more flexibility.

In a messy world, few things are more important than flexibility at the strategic level, where national interests are at stake, or at the operational level, where the outcomes of campaigns are at stake, or at the tactical level, where lives are at stake. But at the tactical level, down where the bullet meets the bone, soldiers have another need even more important than *flexibility*: they need something fixed, something they can trust and rely on no matter what. That something is their officer-leaders, officer-leaders who invariably are fair, morally courageous, and principled.

NOTES

1. Thanks to Reginald Davis for an important off-hand remark; to Joe Andrade, Nick Mullen, and Ben Higginbotham for insightful comments on my initial draft; to Leland Young for prompting me to rethink and rephrase any number of critical points; and to Gayle Watkins for generously offering better ways to think about more things than I've managed to discuss. I'm (alas) responsible for all advice not taken, and any errors.

2. Lionel Tiger and Robin Fox, *The Imperial Animal,* 2nd edition (New Brunswick, NJ: Transaction Publishers, 1998).

3. Followers of specific leaders, yes—there are ample testimonials to what first attracted people to famous and yet-to-be famous men (and women) and then what kept them enthralled. Charisma is prominently mentioned. But not even Max Weber, who introduced the concept, believes charisma can be defined.

4. Also, consider: as Americans we are socialized not only to compete—for grades in school, for attention from our parents, teachers, and one another— but we are taught from an early age that the harder we choose to work the more this will propel us ahead. Not everyone learns this lesson soon enough. Not everyone accepts it. Meanwhile, keeping up with the Joneses when the Joneses are a moving target creates a vastly different set of societal ideals and standards than keeping up with the Joneses would if the Joneses just stood still.

5. See Paul Riesman, *First Find Your Child a Good Mother: The Construction of Self in Two African Communities* (New Brunswick, NJ: Rutgers University Press, 1992).

6. See V.G. Kiernan, *The Lords of Human Kind: Black Man, Yellow Man, and White Man in an Age of Empire* (New York: Columbia University Press, 1969; reprint 1986).

7. As one infantry captain and former general's aide has pointed out: the higher up the chain one moves, the better prepared and not just compensated officers are, though (as he also notes) no one puts in longer hours than do generals.

8. Sociobiologists, evolutionary psychologists, and some biological anthropologists would argue that the more successful a Big Man is/remains, the more wives he would likely have, the more offspring, and the higher his inclusive fitness or reproductive success. However, inclusive fitness (as they point out) is not a conscious strategy. Instead it is the genes' way of disseminating themselves. Unfortunately, this explains everything but nothing at the same time. As much pleasure as a Big Man in the New Guinea Highlands may take in procreating (and recreating), it is surely not because he wants to make his genes happy. At most he wants as many children as possible to spread his name.

9. Most of those we think of, and still refer to, as chiefs in this country—e.g., Chief Joseph, Sitting Bull, Crazy Horse, Osceola, etc.—were Big Men. They had no coercive authority. They could never compel followers to stay with them. Nor could they order or command men in battle. This granted an immense advantage to the U.S. Army.

10. Some classic techniques of doing this: people might be forbidden to set eyes on a ruler, except from a distance. Or he might never be seen to eat, let alone engage in any bodily function, by anyone outside his retinue.

11. For examples, see Abner Cohen, *Two Dimensional Man: An Essay on the Anthropology of Power and Symbolism in Complex Society* (Berkeley: University of California Press, 1974). Also, David Kertzer, *Ritual, Politics, and Power* (New Haven, CT: Yale University Press, 1988).

12. To take an extreme example: an officer might threaten to shoot a soldier for disobeying a direct order in combat, but once dead the soldier will never be able to comply with that order. If the officer needs the soldier, can he afford to threaten to shoot him? When officers need coercion most, they can afford only to use it carefully, strategically, and sparingly.

The comparison between officers and Big Men actually holds in at least one other regard. In Big Man societies there may be status differentials, but these don't translate materially. Big Men eat the same, dress the same, and live the same as their dependents. More to the point still, there is a one-for-all, all-for-one ethos in Big Man societies (which is the ethos skillful Big Men work hard to reaffirm). Can't the same be said of officers at platoon and company levels, especially when they are in the field?

13. Soldiers themselves represent their only immediate means of force.

14. For more on this, see F.G. Bailey, *The Kingdom of Individuals: An Essay on Self-Respect and Social Obligation* (Ithaca, NY: Cornell University Press, 1993).

15. Though "exemplify, suggest, project" might be no less accurate, and seems to be what the manual itself suggests.

16. Gunther Rothenberg, "Maurice of Nassau, Gustavus Adolphus, Raimondo Montecuccoli, and the 'Military Revolution' of the Seventeenth Century," in *Makers of Modern Strategy: from Machiavelli to the Nuclear Age*, ed. Peter Paret (Princeton, NJ: Princeton University Press, 1986), 61-62.

17. Edgar Meyer, "Leadership: A Return to Basics," *Military Review:* 4 [journal online]; available from *http://www-cgsc.army.mil/milrev/english/janfeb97/meyer.html;* Internet; accessed 18 January 2001.

18. Richard Holmes, *Acts of War: The Behavior of Men in Battle* (New York: The Free Press, 1985), 347.

19. Edgar Puryear, *19 Stars: A Study in Military Character and Leadership* (Novato, CA: Presidio, 1994/1971), 396.

20. For examples of the literature I refer to, beyond sources already cited, see: Dandridge Malone, *Small Unit Leadership: A Commonsense Approach* (Novato, CA: Presidio Press, 1983); Lloyd J. Matthews and Dale Brown, eds., *The Challenge of Military Leadership* (Washington, DC: Pergamon-Brassey's, 1989); Robert Taylor and William Rosenbach, eds., *Military Leadership: In Pursuit of Excellence,* 2nd edition (Boulder, CO: Westview Press, 1992), in addition to FM 22-100.

21. Headquarters, Department of the Army, Field Manual 22-100, *Army Leadership: Be, Know, Do* (Washington, DC: Department of the Army, 1999), 3-51; emphasis mine.

22. John Mattox, "Fifth-century Advice for 21st Century Leaders," *Military Review* [journal online]; available from *http://www.cgsc.army.mil/milrev/English/MayJune98/mat.html;* Internet; accessed 18 January 2001.

23. Lloyd J. Matthews, "The Evolution of American Military Ideals," *Military Review* 78 (January-February 1998): 51-61.

24. As Bernard Boëne points out: "Of the rank and file combatant, a minimum amount of courage or valiancy is expected—the capacity to control fear in the face of danger, discomfort, pain or misfortune, and to transgress the social taboos of civilian life when ordered to do so—together with physical agility and stamina, loyalty, and good will. Mastery of fairly simple tactical and technical skills is required.

Of the leader, something more is expected: competence, composure, and self-control, inspiration by example, comprehension, and manipulation of human relations in the exercise of authority, formal (discipline) and informal (personality)." See "How 'Unique' Should the Military Be? A Review of Representative Literature and Outline of a Synthetic Formulation," *European Journal of Sociology* 31 (1990): 30; emphasis mine.

25. Don M. Snider, John A. Nagl, and Tony Pfaff, *Army Professionalism, the Military Ethic, and Officership in the 21ˢᵗ Century* (Carlisle Barracks, PA: U.S. Army War College, Strategic Studies Institute, December 1999), 36.

26. For instance, under the subheading "Integrity" FM 22-100 counsels, "People of integrity consistently act according to principles. . . . People of integrity do the right thing not because it's convenient or because they have no choice. They choose the right thing because their character permits no less. Conducting yourself with integrity has three parts:

• Separating what's right from what's wrong.

• Always acting according to what you know to be right, even at personal cost.

• Saying openly that you're acting on your understanding of right versus wrong."

However, nowhere is what *is* right described, delineated, or defined. See FM 22-100, 2-31.

27. Daryl Henderson, *Cohesion: The Human Element in Battle* (Washington, DC: National Defense University, 1985), 44.

28. John Johns, *Cohesion in the U.S. Military* (Washington, DC: National Defense University Press, 1984), 22.

29. Bernard Boëne and Christopher Dandeker, "Post-Cold War Challenges and Leadership Strategies in West European Military Institutions," in *Leadership for Change*, ed. Gwyn Harries-Jenkins (London/ Hull: European Research Office of the U.S. Army/ University of Hull, 1999), 11-29; Boas Shamir and Eyal Ben-Ari, "Leadership in an Open Army? Civilian Connections, Interorganizational Frameworks, and Changes in Military Leadership," in *Out of the Box Leadership: Transforming the Twenty-First-Century Army and Other Top-Performing Organizations,* eds. James G. Hunt, George E. Dodge, and Leonard Wong (Stamford, CT: JAI Press, 1999), 27.

30. Shamir and Ben-Ari, 27.

31. John Arquilla and David Ronfeldt, "Looking Ahead: Preparing for Information-age Conflict," in *In Athena's Camp: Preparing for Information Age Conflict,* eds. John Arquilla and David Ronfeldt (Santa Monica, CA: Rand, 1997), 440.

32. Shamir and Ben-Ari, 27.

33. See Boëne and Dandeker. Also, see Shamir and Ben-Ari. This is yet another reason to reinforce principles. Everyone, ideally, should be taught principled behavior—and particularly since it can't be taken for granted that this has been taught in schools or in homes. Also, principled, good-of-the-group, selfless behavior, as Snider, Nagl, and Pfaff point out, differs significantly from what is or would be acceptable principled behavior among civilians. This, too, has to be emphasized.

34. Martin van Creveld, *Command in War* (Cambridge, MA: Harvard University Press, 1985).

35. Van Creveld, 149.

36. John M. Gates, *The U.S. Army and Irregular Warfare* (1998), chapter 5, 5 [book on-line]; available from *http://www.wooster.edu/jgates/book-contents.html;* Internet; accessed 20 November 2000.

37. Shamir and Ben-Ari, 27.

38. Ibid, 28.

39. The Yugoslav army is an unfortunate example of a nationalist institution which wasn't quite nationalist enough. Although numbers of Yugoslav soldiers and officers regarded themselves as Yugoslavs first, and Croat, Bosniac, or Serb second, and many deserted and refused to fight for what rapidly became the Serb army, not enough either quit or refused to quit. Slobodan Milosevic was thus able to use paramilitaries to make up for his military shortfall, alongside Serb forces who remained in uniform.

40. As numerous people continually note, this is something the Marine Corps does extraordinarily well. The Army, interestingly enough, seems able to do this only in *selective* units, but even in these (e.g., the 82nd Airborne, Rangers, Special Forces) there is a self-selection process which is likely to attract only individuals who already think in these terms.

41. The four armies which purposely disaggregated with successful results were the French, Israeli, German, and Roman.

42. On Lawrence see John Mack, *A Prince of Our Disorder: The Life of T.E. Lawrence* (Cambridge, MA: Harvard University Press, 1976; reprint 1998). Also, T.E. Lawrence, *Seven Pillars of Wisdom* (New York: Dell Publishing, 1926; reprint 1963). On Lansdale see Cecil Currey, *Edward Lansdale: The Unquiet American* (Washington, DC: Brassey's, 1998). Also, Edward Lansdale, *In the Midst of Wars: An American's Mission to Southeast Asia* (New York: Fordham University Press, 1991).

43. The contrast could be summarized this way: Lawrence did because he could, while Lansdale didn't because he couldn't. Lansdale couldn't learn other languages. He was also a miserable shot. But he clearly excelled at communicating with people of all walks of life—in large part by always treating everyone as though they were of worth.

44. Mack, *A Prince of Our Disorder*, 465.

45. This is not to suggest that promoting democracy as vigorously as Lansdale did is what the U.S. should always do. Far from it. But this is what his mission called for; this is also what local leaders sought. Also, though Lansdale was not a Lawrence in his approach to local culture, he showed a keen interest in whatever Filipinos

were interested in. His natural curiosity, empathy, and the extent to which he treated everyone with respect won him more friends than any amount of prior scholarship could have. In an ideal world, of course, advisors should have both.

46. This also explains, in part, Lansdale's failure in Vietnam. Though some critics claim Lansdale mistakenly tried to apply the same cookie-cutter programs in Vietnam which had worked so well in the Philippines, the real problem was that he wouldn't compromise his beliefs about how to achieve democracy and security, and Diem wasn't sufficiently receptive. There is actually every indication that had he been able to convince Diem to do what had been done in the Philippines—namely, secure free and fair elections, professionalize the military, initiate land reform, and root out corruption—things might have turned out very differently.

47. Gerald Linderman, *The War Within War: America's Combat Experience in World War II* (New York: The Free Press, 1987), 199.

48. Gerald Linderman, *Embattled Courage: The Experience of Combat in the American Civil War* (New York: The Free Press, 1987).

49. Johns, 33, reiterates the importance of this: "A sense of fairness (not equality) is critical. All members must perceive . . . that they are being treated fairly in terms of rights and obligations."

50. Matthews, 59.

51. Linderman, *The World Within War*, 227.

52. Of course, the more obvious—and significant—the division of labor is, the less noticeable hierarchy needs to be. Although this would seem to fly in the face of business models for teamwork, in which individuals are allowed (and even encouraged) to define their own roles, this describes SF teams. The weapons sergeants are weapons specialists, the communications sergeants are communications specialists. Everyone but the team captain plays a clear and significant role, which is not to say that captains can't or don't. But the fact that some NCOs consider officers superfluous, extraneous, and unnecessary on teams reveals how much is expected of them. To lead, officers had better add something. To convert potential critics into followers they must find a way to contribute to the good of the group, and they must do so even while proving themselves first among equals. Outside of combat, the fastest way to do this is by *being principled* and recognizing that it is a leader's duty to ensure principled behavior by, for, and from everyone.

Organization of the Army

This is the fourth of a series of seven lessons on the Army Profession and Officership. This lesson looks specifically at the composition of the Army and its component parts. The purpose of this lesson is to provide insight on the organization of the Army, while continuing to reinforce the Constitutional and legal basis for the Army, as well as affirming the value of selfless service as part of the Army tradition.

The following topics are addressed in this lesson:

- Organization of the Army from squad through division
- Role and function of the active Army, the Army Reserves and National Guard

The following TLO is supported in whole or in part by this lesson:

- Understand the Army's organization and how the Army runs

Following this lesson you will be able to:

- List the three components of the United States Army
- Describe the composition of the Active Army
- Describe the composition of the Army Reserve
- List the components of the Army National Guard
- Describe the organization of the Army by unit through the division level
- Place the Army in relation to her sister organizations in the military service

The Profession of Arms I

This is the fifth of a series of seven lessons on the Army Profession and Officership. This lesson provides the conceptual framework of a profession. The lesson also reviews Huntington's model and clearly explains how Army officership is a profession with regulated duties and expectations.

The following topics are addressed in this lesson:

- The concept of officership as a unique calling in society
- Huntington's model of a profession
- Characteristics of the Profession of Arms

The following TLO is supported in whole or in part by this lesson:

- Relate the characteristics of a profession to military service as an officer

Following this lesson you will be able to:

- Describe Huntington's model of what constitutes a profession
- Differentiate what constitutes the difference between a profession and a job
- Distinguish professions from jobs
- Be able to explain why the military is a profession

OFFICERSHIP

BY HARRY THIE

OFFICERS AS PROFESSIONALS

What is an officer? The officer corps of the United States military is "professional" when using that term as an adjective to mean competent or nonamateurish. For this research, we are more interested in the use of the term as a noun to convey a calling of an occupational group that requires specialized knowledge and long and intensive preparation.[1] Officers seek careers in the profession of "officership." We use the term "officership" to describe a construct that deals with the standard, defining criteria of a profession as applied to military officers.

IS "OFFICERSHIP" A PROFESSION?

The professionalization of the officer corps, which began in the 19th century in Europe, increased dramatically in the United States after World War II. This development paralleled that of other professions (e.g., law and medicine), which have evolved from the 19th century to the present, with rapid development during the 1960s and 1970s. A variety of social, political, and economic changes have combined to alter the environment that facilitated the emergence and dominance of certain professions, military officers included.[2] As the military faces further uncertainty and change, it is useful to discuss the present status of the officer profession to help evaluate how change may affect the profession in the future.

What do we mean by *profession* and how do *officers* fit the defining characteristics of a profession? The term *professional* refers to occupational groups that have the capacity to control the production and distribution of certain kinds of goods and services. This control includes the ability to negotiate freedom from external intervention and to influence the conditions and content of the work. In the case of the officer profession, this general definition implies that officers, as an occupational group, have the capacity to control the production and distribution of U.S. national security. Of course, the capacity of the profession is limited; it is not a monopoly, but the officer profession can significantly shape the development and implementation of national security activities.

The general definition implies several criteria for determining whether officership is a profession. Does it require or possess

- knowledge and skill expertise gained by formal education and long-term experience in the workplace, validated by formal examinations and credentials?
- career commitment and a closed community with strong feelings of loyalty?
- accession, assignment, and promotion based on competence?
- a formal code of law and ethics developed, maintained, and applied by the profession?[3]

Knowledge and Skill

First, a prerequisite of even the most general definition of a profession includes specific occupational groups applying abstract knowledge to particular problems. In the development of other professions such as law and medicine, the increasing body of knowledge and the uneven quality of informal apprenticeship programs provided the impetus for establishing formal education programs. Similarly, in the military, as size, technology, and requisite skills changed, a need arose for establishing the military academies to train officers initially in military science, a body of knowledge and skill that is gained through formal education and experience. The military curriculum across services emphasizes both theory and practice. Some of the core components of the officer curriculum include military history, military science, operational art, military engineering, weapons design, personnel management, and leadership training, which facilitate teamwork, decision-making, and control of ambiguous environments during military maneuvers that promote national security.[4]

Although formal educational experiences are crucial in developing officers, additional professional development comes through experience—long-term experience. As former Army Chief of Staff General John Wickham stated,

> Out of a twenty-year career, most officers spend three years in military schools, but the bulk of their careers is spent with troops or in staff positions. The cumulative experience gained in repetitive assignments in branch, joint, and functional positions—at progressively higher levels of responsibility—continues the professionalization of the officer corps.[5]

Commitment

Second, career commitment, loyalty, and identification with a specific occupational group are also professional criteria. Ideally, commitment to an occupational community stems from a sense of a "calling" and responsibility to serve the common good. Officers' responsibility to serve the common good explicitly reflects their commissioning oath to serve nation and constitution. Interviews with officers have revealed comparisons between officership and the ministry, both of which involve long-term commitment to a set of values that transcend individual self-interest.[6] Furthermore, there is evidence that those who anticipate a career as an officer espouse pro-military values and that these values are held before exposure to the socializing effects of actual military service or training.[7]

The values that are the bedrock of the officer profession are loyalty, duty, selfless service, integrity, and subordination of the military to the authority of the civilian government.[8] Loyalty involves faithfulness and fidelity to the unit; the institution; and those above, below, and alongside in the hierarchy. Duty encompasses the moral and legal obligations that soldiers have to defend the United States. Doing what is best for nation, branch of service, and unit—in opposition to one's own interests—encapsulates the value of selfless service. It is the higher good that comes before selfish ambitions and individual desires. An additional value constituting the bedrock of the officer profession is integrity. Officers are to be honest with their superiors, officers of similar rank, and their subordinates. Finally, in a democracy, the military is subject to the authority of the civilian government, and this value is embedded in officers as they are socialized into the profession.

Commitment to a career as an officer entails entree into a closed community with strong feelings of loyalty. Sociologist Erving Goffman referred to this community as a "total institution," characterized by (1) all activities being carried out under a single authority, (2) the influence of the immediate company of others who hold the ideals of the institution, (3) a disciplined life fixed by a set of formal rules and procedures, and (4) all activities aimed toward fulfilling the official aims of the institution.[9] A former general officer describes this more bluntly: "There is only one military in our nation. You are either in or out. There are no lateral transfers to another military. In other words, the 'company' is also the entire profession!"[10]

Describing the development of a community within the military academy, the Superintendent of West Point stated in a recent speech,

> West Point succeeds in teaching . . . important values because its cadets are immersed

for four years in a value-rich, professional military culture. They live twenty-four hours-a-day within a military organization, subject to an honor Code and military regulations, as well as the Uniform Code of Military Justice. Throughout the four years, they are educated by predominantly-military faculty role models who exemplify the essential values of the profession.[11]

In a more general way, the following comments by an officer emphasizes the unique experiences that foster commitment to the military community,

> The Army is a total institution that replaces individual values with the institution's values. It does this by providing its members with experiences that are significantly different from those encountered in their past civilian lives. These experiences are attributed to powerful [psychological] processes, which create intense comradeship and egalitarianism.[12]

Commitment to the values of the officer corps profession and the periodic intense socialization events lead to a unity of experience and orientation, out of which develops a community loyal to a common purpose and action (i.e., professional culture).[13]

Competence

A third element of officership is competence. Not only must a professional apply abstract knowledge to specific problems, he or she must apply it proficiently. Samuel Huntington (1957) described the skills required by officers as being neither craft nor art, but "an extraordinarily complex intellectual skill requiring comprehensive study and training." Despite the varied array of departments and experts (engineers, doctors, pilots, intelligence, communications), a "distinct sphere of military competence" is common to officers. The duties of the officer include the organization, equipping, and training of the force; planning its activities; and the direction of its operation in and out of combat.[14] This unique competence is typically described as effective military experience.

Competence is emphasized throughout the career of a military officer. Centralized promotion boards that in principle make promotion decisions based on experience and competence in different roles promote those who have the greatest leadership potential to meet the challenges of increased responsibilities. In the current workings of the system, the best-qualified advance in the profession; those who are fully qualified may be allowed to continue in the profession, but most are separated "out." This separation of the fully qualified is atypical; in a profession, all who are qualified normally continue. Although debate continues about whether certain characteristics (e.g., gender, ethnicity, and race) remain significant determinants of officer career paths, ability and achievement have become critical as the officer profession has developed since the 19th century.[15]

Formal Code

A fourth element of the officer profession is that there is a formal code of law and ethics, which is developed, maintained, and applied by the profession. Each branch of the military has guidelines for behavior and conduct that are strictly enforced. Failure to comply leads to sanctions such as punishment or discharge. Formulation of the ethical standards, investigation of violations, and application of sanctions are also conducted by military officers. Self-regulation of ethical principles of conduct relating to the professional group's conduct of practice, behavior toward clients, interaction with colleagues, and relationships with allied professions is a professional criterion that applies to military officers as it does to other professions.[16]

In summary, given the criteria typically used for determining whether an occupational group is a profession, characteristics of military officers' roles, values, culture, and activities suggest that "officership" is a profession. Despite the debate in the sociology of the military literature about whether the military in general constitutes a profession, the consensus holds that the term profession is applicable to military officers.[17]

CHANGE AND THE DEFINING CHARACTERISTICS OF OFFICERSHIP

The nature and meaning of officership have as much importance as concepts for career flow structures and personnel functions in the design of an officer career management system, because the career management system must support the future construct of officership. Change affects requirements for officers, the objectives and structures of the career management system, and the defining characteristics by which one understands officership. One can assess the amount and direction of future change in officer-

ship by reviewing the defining characteristics and how they have changed and may change.

At present, the military is facing many changes that are interrelated in complex ways. The purpose here is simply to highlight some likely changes as they relate to the defining characteristics of officership that will have implications for future officer management. As previously stated, the national military strategy has changed from emphasis on the containment of the former Soviet Union and communism. The perceived threat will most likely no longer be primarily a single entity as it was in the past. Other changes in technology, the economy, demography and culture, and the demands of officers will affect the defining characteristics of the officer profession, particularly the knowledge, skills, and nature of the closed community. Amidst this complex web of change, it is unlikely that emphasis on a core of military values will change as much as some of the other defining characteristics of officership.

The movement away from large-scale wars to other types of conflict management is likely to change the requisite knowledge and skills of officer as they relate to military science and management. As van Creveld points out, the ability to fight and win a war—classic military effectiveness—has given way to much broader notions about military effectiveness including a redefinition of war as deterrence or as the "creation and maintenance of armed forces."[18] As this happened, the military profession started to alter in ways that have yet to completely play out.

> During the fifties *defense* and *security* gradually supplanted *war*, thus gaining a double advantage. First unlike war, defense and security were continuous and could be presented as of overriding importance even in peacetime. Second they included not only strategy (how to deploy one's forces), operations (how to maneuver them in the theater of war), and tactics (how to make them fight when in contact with the enemy) but almost every conceivable aspect of human existence.[19]

This broader notion of national security means that knowledge about it is not just in the purview of the military officer. Many academic institutions in the United States offer courses (apart from ROTC) that deal with national security. The national security community has come to include a vast array of politicians, academics, businessmen, and serving military officers.

Also, conflict is no longer left to the full-time uniformed military in the United States. It is no longer a case of being "in or out" of a total institution but a case of fuzzy boundaries about in and out. Beginning in 1970, the Total Force Policy stipulated that all sources of manpower—full time, reserve, civilian—should be considered in building forces. "Amateurs" and those without any prior military experience can count in a theater of operations. Indeed, a civilian, Robert Oakley, was described by the former Chairman of the Joint Chiefs of Staff as the CINC in Somalia; a DoD civilian was the first casualty in that operation. For the future, there is not "in and out" but maybe only some groups who are more "in" than others.

An additional strand in this change is technology, more specifically the merging of civilian and military technologies in the service of national security in the broadest sense. At the same time that the defense laboratories are attempting to adapt military technologies for civilian use in order to stay relevant to society, the military is moving toward greater use of commercially available technologies for military use. Communications is another example. Not only can the battlefield be monitored in real time from the White House or the Pentagon, but it can also be watched from the living rooms of the nation via CNN and other news sources. Everyone is more connected to military forces.

Economic constraints on the military (e.g., budget) are another change confronting the military. With a downward shift in resources allocated to the military and the changing nature of its mission, there will no doubt be changes in military priorities. How much will the military be able to spend on advanced technologies? Will cost constraints result in common, generalist platforms or specialized platforms? How many officers will the military be able to attract and retain? The answers to these questions will have significant implications for defining the nature of officers' knowledge, skills, and specialties and the managing of the military and officers' careers.

The relationship between the military and society is also likely to change, with significant effects on the closed nature of the military community. Over time, the military has become less isolated from society , making it more difficult to maintain a closed community. This relative autonomy of the military vis-à-vis society is likely to decrease even more if current trends continue. For example, military bases are less like islands in the sea of society and are becoming more integrated with local government and economic infrastructures for housing, schooling, medical care, banking, retail, restaurants, and many other goods and services. Some have argued that this integration of the military into local communities is helpful for generating the public's confidence, decreasing costs, increasing satisfaction, and decreasing dependence of officers and their families on the military alone.[20] Furthermore, as American society continues to become more diverse—demographically and culturally—the pressures on the military to accommodate these changes will increase. The recent debate over gays in the military is but one example. Public debate about what our nation's national security policy should be in the post–Cold War era is yet another example.

Finally the demands of officers themselves have shifted and altered the defining characteristics of the officer profession, and they will continue to do so. For example, the requirements for joint duty assignments may result in a culture of jointness that supplants the separate cultures of the Army, Navy, Air Force, and Marines.[21] In addition, if civilian spouses of military personnel increasingly seek employment on their own and if the number of dual military and single parent households within the military continues to rise, issues of rotations and deployment will be problematic. Also, if the vast majority of the U.S. military force becomes stationed on this continent as anticipated, those officers who are interested in mobility and adventure are likely to be disappointed. Furthermore, the nature of overseas missions may change from officers being the managers of warriors to soldier diplomats and soldier statesmen, especially if there is more involvement in peacekeeping missions.[22] All of these changing demands from within the military are likely to change both the knowledge and skills as well as the closed nature of the military community.

In short, changes in threat, military strategy, technology, societal demographics and culture, the economy, and the demands of officers themselves are likely to change the defining characteristics of officership. *Most likely to change are the needed knowledge, skills, and experience and the nature of the closed community.* But in the face of these changes, a defining characteristic of officership that is likely to be maintained is the core values of the military. The military is likely to continue promoting specific values: loyalty, duty, selfless service, integrity, and respect for the Constitution and what it means in civil-military relations. Management theory claims that values constitute the foundation of organizational cultures; the military has a long tradition of cultural acculturation of its members; officers will probably continue down this path. However, given the present national security issues, what this culture is oriented toward will change. No longer can the educational institutions and the officer profession assume a singular orientation characteristic of the Cold War era. Rather, the increasing complexity of national security priorities will have an effect on how the bedrock values of the military are carried out in flexible and adaptable ways.

FOOTNOTES

[1]This useful distinction between uses of the term "professional" is made by Terry Willett, "The Canadian Military: A Design for Tomorrow," *Canadian Defense Quarterly*, Spring 1993, p. 45.

[2]Robert A. Rothman, *Working: Sociological Perspectives*, Englewood Cliffs, NJ: Prentice-Hall, 1987; and Andrew Abbott, *The System of the Professions*, Chicago, IL: The University of Chicago Press, 1989.

[3]J. A. A. Van Doorn, "The Military Profession in Transition," in N.A.B. Wilson (ed.), *Manpower Research in a Defense Context*, New York: American Elsevier Publishing Company, Inc., 1969, pp. 451–459.

[4]Samuel P. Huntington, *The Soldier and the State: The Theory and Politics of Civil-Military Relations*, Cambridge, MA: Harvard University Press, 1957; Morris Janowitz, *The Professional Soldier*, New York: The Free Press, 1971.

[5]General John A. Wickham, Jr. (retired), "Address at the Army Command Academy, Nanjing, China: The American Army and Professionalism," *Collected Works of the Thirtieth Chief of Staff, United States Army*, Department of the Army, 1987, p. 200.

[6]Janowitz, *The Professional Soldier*, op. cit.; on the sociological concept of calling see Max Weber, *The Protestant Ethic and the Spirit of Capitalism*, New York: Charles Scribner's Sons, 1958, pp. 54, 62, 79–92.

[7]Jerald G. Bachman, Lee Sigelman, and Greg Diamond, "Self-Selection, Socialization, and Distinctive Military Values: Attitudes of High School Seniors," *Armed Forces & Society*, Vol. 13, No. 2, Winter 1987, pp. 169–187; David R. Segal, John D. Blair, Joseph J. Lengermann, and Richard C. Thompson, "Institutional and Occupational Values in the U.S. Military," in Franklin D.

Margiotta, James Brown, and Michael J. Collins (eds.), *Changing U.S. Military Manpower Realities*, Boulder, CO: Westview Press, 1983, pp. 107–127.

[8]Robert L. Maginnis, "A Chasm of Values," *Military Review*, February 1993, pp. 2–11; General John A. Wickham, Jr. (retired), "The Professional Army Ethic," *Collected Works of the Thirtieth Chief of Staff, United States Army*, Department of the Army, 1987, pp. 182–183; General Howard Graves, Superintendent of West Point, "Developing Leaders for the 21st Century," 1993; on the importance of the officer's sense of purpose, see Morris Janowitz, "From Institutional to Occupational: The Need for Conceptual Clarity," *Armed Forces & Society*, 1977, Vol. 4, No. 1, pp. 51–54.

[9]Goffman, *Asylums*, op. cit., and "The Characteristics of Total Institutions," in Amitai Etzioni (ed.), *Complex Organizations*, New York: Holt, Rinehart & Winston, 1969.

[10]Ulmer, *Inside View*, op.cit., p. 7.

[11]Graves, op. cit., p. 5.

[12]Maginnlis, *A Chasm of Values*, op. cit., pp. 2–3.

[13]Sanford M. Dornbusch, "The Military Academy as an Assimilating Institution," *Social Forces*, 1955, Vol. 33, pp. 316–321.

[14]Huntington, *The Soldier and the State*, op. cit., pp. 11, 13.

[15]Janowitz, *The Professional Soldier*, op. cit.; David R. Segal, *Recruiting for Uncle Sam*, Lawrence, KA: University Press of Kansas, 1989; Bruce A. Brant, "Vanguard of Social Change?" *Military Review*, February 1993, pp. 12–19.

[16]Rothman, *Working*, op. cit., pp. 71–76.

[17]Janowitz, *From Institutional to Occupational*, op. cit.; Cathy J. Downes, "To Be or Not to Be a Profession: The Military Case," *Defense Analysis*, 1985, 1, pp. 147–171.

[18]Van Creveld, *Command in War*, op. cit., p. 102.

[19]Ibid., p. 71.

[20]David R. Segal, *Organizational Designs for the Future Army*, U.S. Army Research Institute for the Behavioral and Social Sciences, Special Report 20, 1993.

[21]For a description of the different cultures of the military services, see Carl H. Builder, *The Masks of War: American Military Styles in Strategy and Analysis*, Baltimore, MD: The Johns Hopkins University Press, 1989.

[22]Segal, *Organizational Designs*, op cit., p. 39.

OFFICERSHIP AS A PROFESSION

BY SAMUEL P. HUNTINGTON

PROFESSIONALISM AND THE MILITARY

The modern officer corps is a professional body and the modern military officer a professional man. This is, perhaps, the most fundamental thesis of this book. A profession is a peculiar type of functional group with highly specialized characteristics. Sculptors, stenographers, entrepreneurs, and advertising copywriters all have distinct functions but no one of these functions is professional in nature. Professionalism, however, is characteristic of the modern officer in the same sense in which it is characteristic of the physician or lawyer. Professionalism distinguishes the military officer of today from the warriors of previous ages. The existence of the officer corps as a professional body gives a unique cast to the modern problem of civil-military relations.

The nature and history of other professions as professions have been thoroughly discussed. Yet the professional character of the modern officer corps has been neglected. In our society, the businessman may command more income; the politician may command more power; but tile professional man commands more respect. Yet the public, as well as the scholar, hardly conceives of the officer in the same way that it does the lawyer or doctor, and it certainly does not accord to the officer the deference which it gives to the civilian professionals. Even the military themselves are influenced by their image in the public mind and at times have refused to accept the implications of their own professional status. When the term "professional" has been used in connection with the military, it normally has been in the sense of "professional" as contrasted with "amateur" rather than in the sense of "profession" as contrasted with "trade" or "craft." The phrases "professional army" and "professional soldier" have obscured the difference between the career enlisted man who is professional in the sense of one who works for monetary gain and the career officer who is professional in the very different sense of one who pursues a "higher calling" in the service of society.

THE CONCEPT OF PROFESSION

The first step in analyzing the professional character of the modern officer corps is to define professionalism. The distinguishing characteristics of a profession as a special type of vocation are its expertise, responsibility, and corporateness.[1]

EXPERTISE. The professional man is an expert with specialized knowledge and skill in a significant field of human endeavor. His expertise is acquired only by prolonged education and experience. It is the basis of objective standards of professional competence for separating the profession from laymen and measuring the relative competence of members of the profession. Such standards are universal. They inhere in the knowledge and skill and are capable of general application irrespective of time and place. The ordinary skill or craft exists only in the present and is mastered by learning an existing technique without reference to what has gone before. Professional knowledge, however, is intellectual in nature and capable of preservation in writing. Professional knowledge has a history, and some knowledge of that history is essential to professional competence. Institutions of research and education are required for the extension and transmission of professional knowledge and skill. Contact is maintained between the academic and practical sides of a profession through journals, conferences, and the circulation of personnel between practice and teaching.

Professional expertise also has a dimension in breadth which is lacking in the normal trade. It is a segment of the total cultural tradition of society. The professional man can successfully apply his skill only when he is aware of this broader tradition of which he is a part. Learned professions are "learned" simply because they are an integral part of the total body of learning of society. Consequently professional education consists of two phases: the first imparting a broad, liberal, cultural background, and the second imparting the specialized skills and knowledge of the profession. The liberal education of the professional man is normally handled by the general educational institutions of society devoted to this purpose. The second or technical phase of professional education, on the other hand, is given in special institutions operated by or affiliated with the profession itself.

RESPONSIBILITY. The professional man is a practicing expert, working in a social context, and performing a service, such as the promotion of health, education, or justice, which is essential to the functioning of society. The client of every profession is society, individually or collectively. A research chemist, for instance, is not a professional man because the service he renders, while beneficial to society, is not essential to its immediate existence and functioning: only DuPont and the Bureau of Standards have a direct and immediate interest in what he has to offer. The essential and general character of his service and his monopoly of his skill impose upon the professional man the responsibility to perform the service when required by society. This social responsibility distinguishes the professional man from other experts with only intellectual skills. The research chemist, for instance, is still a research chemist if he uses his skills in a manner harmful to society. But the professional man can no longer practice if he refuses to accept his social responsibility: a physician ceases to be a physician if he uses his skills for antisocial purposes. The responsibility to serve and devotion to his skill furnish the professional motive. Financial remuneration cannot be the primary aim of the professional man *qua* professional man. Consequently, professional compensation normally is only partly determined by bargaining on the open market and is regulated by professional custom and law.

The performance of an essential service not regulated by the normal expectation of financial rewards requires some statement governing the relations of the profession to the rest of society. Conflicts between the professional man and his clients, or among members of the profession, normally furnish the immediate impetus to the formulation of such a statement. The profession thus becomes a moral unit positing certain values and ideals which guide its members in their dealings with laymen. This guide may be a set of unwritten norms transmitted through the professional educational system or it may be codified into written canons of professional ethics.

CORPORATENESS. The members of a profession share a sense of organic unity and consciousness of themselves as a group apart from laymen. This collective sense has its origins in the lengthy discipline and training necessary for professional competence, the common bond of work, and the sharing of a unique social responsibility. The sense of unity manifests itself in a professional organization which formalizes and applies the standards of professional competence and establishes and enforces the standards of professional responsibility. Membership in the professional organization, along with the possession of special expertise and the acceptance of special responsibility, thus becomes a criterion of professional status, publicly distinguishing the professional man from the layman. The interest of the profession requires it to bar its members from capitalizing upon professional competence in areas where that competence has no relevance and likewise to protect itself against outsiders who would claim professional competence because of achievements or attributes in other fields. Professional organizations are generally either associations or bureaucracies. In the associational professions such as medicine and law, the practitioner typically functions independently and has a direct personal relationship with his client. The bureaucratic professions, such as the diplomatic service, possess a high degree of specialization of labor and responsibilities within the profession, and the profession as a whole renders a collective service to society as a whole. These two categories are not mutually exclusive: bureaucratic elements exist in most associational professions, and associations frequently supplement the formal structure of bureaucratic professions. The associational professions usually possess written codes of ethics since each practitioner is individually confronted with the problem of proper conduct toward clients and colleagues. The bureaucratic professions, on the other hand, tend to develop a more general sense of collective professional responsibility and the proper role of the profession in society.

THE MILITARY PROFESSION

Social scientists have devoted considerable study to professional groups to discern certain common attributes that are characteristic of all "professionals" (e.g., lawyers, doctors, priests, engineers, etc.). The result of this study has been the development of "models" of professions—conceptual frameworks that better enable us to understand what makes a profession. There are many models. One model developed by a Harvard political scientist, Dr. Samuel Huntington, is described in his work, The Soldier and the State. This is a classic in the study of military professionalism.

This reading introduces you to the purpose of a profession in our society and the relationship that exists between a professional and the society that he or she serves. You are also introduced to the idea of a "professional organization" and the essential functions a professional organization performs for a profession.

According to Samuel Huntington, a group of individuals engaged in a common line of work can be called a profession only if the group exhibits three essential characteristics. He calls these characteristics "expertise," "responsibility," and "corporateness." We will consider each of these in turn.

Professional Expertise—A profession centers around a particular service which is performed by that profession for society, but not every "service" requires a profession to provide it. Rather, a profession performs an essential service: something that the society would have difficulty doing without. The ability to perform that service properly is what we call the "expertise" of the profession. This professional expertise involves a specialized knowledge, skill or ability which is acquired through extensive education and experience. By itself, this statement might apply to most fields of employment. However, a member of a profession has knowledge that is more than simply a practical skill; his knowledge is intellectual and scholarly in nature. He acquires the special knowledge through a continuing educational process - usually involving a college education and additional graduate training. For the purpose of this instruction, we can summarize the resulting professional expertise in terms of three components:

Technical Component—This part of professional expertise is a knowledge of the "tools of the trade." In scientific professions such as medicine, these are the technological aspects of practice (ability to perform laboratory tests, x-rays, etc.). In the less technical profession of law, these could include a knowledge of court procedures, rules of evidence, and elements of proof.

Theoretical or Intellectual Component—This involves an understanding of the "how" and "why" of the technical component, for example, the philosophy behind the law or the theories explaining the functioning of the human body. Professional knowledge is constantly evolving as a result of research and application. It is the theoretical/intellectual component of expertise that enables the professional to comprehend and apply new techniques. This component separates the professional from the "technician" (the technician does not need to know why his skills get the job done).

Broad-Liberal Component—This is probably the most complex component of expertise, but it is possibly the most important. The broad-liberal component of expertise involves the ability of the professional to understand the role of his profession—and his unique expertise in his society. This includes the knowledge of behavior, human relationships, standards of conduct, and human organizational structures which allow the professional to know when and how to offer his services to achieve the most desirable and effective results. We say that the broad-liberal component of expertise enables the professional to apply his skills in a "human context."

Professional Responsibility—The professional person, by definition, offers a service (or "expertise") that is vital to society. This service is performed for a person or group of persons known as "clients." Professional expertise requires intensive education in the particular service or skill that most members of society do not have. Indeed, professional expertise is so complex that laymen are not really capable of understanding what the professional does or how he does it. Therefore, he has a "monopoly" over his particular skill. Furthermore, we are not capable of adequately judging whether he is acting competently or ethically. Only another professional can make such a judgment. For this reason, society requires a special relationship between the professional and the client that is quite different from a normal business relationship. It is called a "professional - client relationship." It works like this:

- On the one hand, the client must accept the professional's definition of the problem and the solution that requires professional expertise. The client does not have the training to know exactly what the problem is or what to do about it. The professional's "monopoly on expertise" is accepted.

- On the other hand, just as the professional expects the client to place affairs completely in his hands, the client expects the professional to observe certain ethics or standards of professional behavior. Society expects the professional to fulfill three key obligations to the client:

(1) The professional *does not exceed* the bounds of *professional competence*. This means two things: first, the professional does not perform services that are beyond his specific expertise. For example, it would be unethical for a dentist to prescribe something for a stomach pain even though, as a doctor, he has access to certain drugs that might be effective. Second, a professional does not exert his own personal, non-professional beliefs or judgments upon the relationship. (As these would also lie outside his sphere of competence.) A doctor, for example does not refuse treatment to a patient who is suffering from Acquired Immune Deficiency Syndrome (AIDS) because he disapproves of the individual's life style. Similarly, a clergyman is not professionally competent to give sound tax advice.

(2) The professional must ensure that his *actions* are guided by motives which are wholly *within* his *client's* best *interests*. For example, a lawyer accepts a case because he intends to work conscientiously for his client and not because he stands to make a financial gain by selling transcripts of his private interviews with his client. Similarly, a medical doctor is expected to perform surgery, not because he will get rich from it, but because it really is needed.

(3) Finally, the professional incurs a responsibility for absolute *integrity* with the client. A lawyer can use legal tricks and courtroom theatrics, he can banter technicalities, and he can fight his case as far as his conscience and the prevailing practices within his profession will allow. But he will not lie to his client or cheat or steal from him. The requirement for integrity is essential in the professional-client relationship.

The three obligations which the professional owes to the client are collectively called professional responsibility. It should be apparent the professional has all the leverage in the relationship. If he is not competent or if he is a crook, who will be the wiser? So, we might ask, "What is it that insures the professional maintains his part of the professional-client relationship?" There are two major motivating factors:

- **"Calling"**—Most people enter a profession because of a sincere desire to serve their fellow man. This is often referred to as a "calling." Many professionals have endured great personal hardship and sacrifice in meeting this "calling."

- **"Autonomy"**—Most professionals recognize that their credibility as a group depends upon the willingness of individual members to uphold their end of the professional-client relationship. If the profession as a whole acts responsibly, society will hold it in esteem, allow it to practice without undue interference and give unqualified acceptance to the actions of its members. If its members cease to abide by ethical standards, however, society will begin to regulate the profession. The profession as a whole will lose its "autonomy." Professionals with a strong sense of calling want to provide their unique service in the way they know to be best, with as little interference as possible. In other words, they want to act "autonomously."

- **Professional Corporateness**—
"Corporateness" means that a group of people experience a sense of belonging—a common bond. Among professionals, corporateness tends to result from the following factors:

(1) *A common bond of work*. Professional people are likely to associate with one another, both professionally and socially.

Doctors may, for example, work together within a hospital while lawyers frequently encounter one another in a court house. Professional groups are also likely to share the same symbols of their profession, the same interests and similar life styles.

(2) *A desire for "autonomy."* Professionals share a common desire to be able to serve mankind in the way they think best without undue interference by non-professionals.

(3) *Professional knowledge.* Professionals desire to maintain contacts with one another to share experiences and learning.

The desire for corporateness tends to manifest itself in "professional organizations." For the medical profession in the United States, the professional organization is the American Medical Association (AMA), and for the legal profession it is the American Bar Association (ABA) with affiliated state bar organizations. Such organizations perform four essential services/functions for the profession and for the society served by that profession. Professional organizations:

—Police the profession
—Control recruitment
—Promote professional knowledge
—Represent the profession

ON ENTERING THE MILITARY PROFESSION

BY MARTIN BLUMENSON

> *When Bucknell University's cadets gradu-*
> *ated and were commissioned this year,*
> *ARMY'S Contributing Editor Martin*
> *Blumenson spoke to them on the origin*
> *and significance of the military profes-*
> *sion. Excerpts of his speech follow:*

Today is a day of celebration and congratulations. Young men and women of the university have completed their preliminary work. They have proved their merit. They have been admitted to and are entering into the military profession.

The origins of the modern military profession are to be found, like the other early professions, in the guilds and brotherhoods of medieval times. I speak of medicine, the law, theology and the military. As professions they all display the same characteristics.

Each exists to render beneficial service to the society, the community. Each requires special education, medical or law school, theological seminary and, for the military, an academy, officers candidate school or ROTC. The special education imparts not only practical knowledge but also theoretical understanding of the profession's activities, methods and endeavors. Each profession engages in full-time employment for pay. It is not only the pay that distinguishes professionals from amateurs; each profession provides its members with standard responses to given situations.

Each profession regulates its own procedures, code of behavior, style of dress. Each selects certain members for promotion and honor. Finally, each member of these professions requires a license to practice—the commission in your case. This is what we celebrate today, the commissioning of our ROTC graduates.

It used to be that military service was prerogative of class. Only members of the upper class, the nobility, the aristocracy, could be warriors. To be armed, to carry weapons was a special privilege limited to the elite. That idea, or traces of it, persisted until at least the 19 century.

Gradually, as the medieval structure gave way to the emergence of states, a higher level of education became necessary for the military. As technology developed and as new weapons came into being, one needed to know some mathematics in order to fire artillery with some degree of accuracy. Aristocrats who lived in isolated castles were less likely to be learned than certain non-nobles or member of the bourgeoisie, that is, wealthy commoners who lived in towns. Educated commoners were better equipped to handle technical matters of increasing complexity. And over the years, they were allowed to enter the military profession. Today, our democratic society imposes no test of class on those who can be commissioned. Anyone adequately qualified in the modern sense can be an officer. But the tradition of the aristocrat continues.

How are you who are new officers likely to function in your profession? Historically, the task of the military is to defend its society against threats, both internal and external. The military thus has a twin mission. Against internal threats, in domestic disturbances, the military aids in the police power. Troops also aid the civil power and protect lives and property in time of natural disaster or special crisis.

Allied to the police power in another distinct mission. Because the military is an organized force trained and ready to act immediately in any capacity, the federal and state governments may call upon it for a particular task such as responding to natural disasters. In earlier times, stringing telegraph wires in Alaska, flying the mail in the 1920s or building dams were jobs the military was asked to perform. These were special jobs—at a particular time and place— that only the military could undertake and carry through.

Of course, the main purpose of the military is to wage warfare against external enemies. This is what the military is trained to do. This is the area where the honors, the decorations, the recognitions of greatness and fame are won. War is, of course, a political act determined and shaped by the political authorities. This remains a constant, but the nature of warfare has changed over the years.

The history of modern warfare may be said to begin with the Thirty Years' War in the 17th century. This war was so brutal—there were so many deaths—that it threatened to destroy the aristocracy in Europe. The war was simply killing off members of the nobility. To save them from extinction, the Peace of Westphalia, which ended the war in 1648, set up new rules to regulate warfare. The main features of what has come to be termed the Westphalian system are these:

First, each state then in existence was sovereign. It was independent and free to govern itself within its borders.

Second, the state had a monopoly to wage war. Only the state could make war, and it did so by means of a regular, uniformed army. Since the state was responsible for all legitimate violence, all other groups resorting to war or violence were, per se, criminal.

Third, regular forces fought against enemy regular forces. Everyone else was a noncombatant.

Fourth, at the time of the Peace of Westphalia, because making war was expensive, regular forces or armies tended to be small and wars to be short. The objectives of a war were small—a piece of the enemy's territory or a seaport or a mine. We call this "limited" in the number of people involved and limited in objectives.

This is the essence of the Westphalian system, and it makes a great deal of sense. But since its inception, the principles have been eroding. For example, sovereignty has declined. The freedom of a state to govern itself within its borders is no longer regarded as quite so sacred as before. Whatever Nazi Germany did within its borders before World War II, even its campaign of genocide, was perfectly all right according to Westphalian doctrine. Thus, no outside state interfered. After World War II, human rights acquired great importance. Concern for human rights now transcends national borders. We are interested in human rights everywhere, and thus sovereignty no longer has the exclusivity it once had. In addition, the United Nations has assumed some of the powers of the state. Regular military forces are now operating under U.N. command throughout the world.

Another change in the Westphalian system has been the nature of the state and the war it wages. The American and French Revolutions, particularly the latter, changed states into nations. The inhabitants, instead of being subjects of the state, became citizens of the nation. The nation belonged to them, not to the royalty. All the owners of a nation wanted to participate in war, and warfare became democratized. Regular armies swelled to unheard-of size in wartime.

In France, *la patrie,* the country or the nation, became an emotional entity, and patriotism emerged, a special kind of love and respect and regard for one's country. Military campaigns were supported by public opinion and turned into emotional drives motivated by hatred for the enemy.

Passions rather than statecraft drove hostilities. Not only regular soldiers but also civilians became potential casualties. Weapons were no longer selective; they could no longer distinguish between combatants and noncombatants. War became total, total in the means employed to win, that is, total exertion to destroy the enemy. What was wanted was a total victory over the adversary.

During our Civil War, the North destroyed the South, politically as well as economically. In World Wars I and II, the Allies destroyed the German government both times. This kind of warfare, total war, lasted from about 1800 to 1945, the end of World War II. By then, technology had made that kind of war obsolete. The weapons of war, not only the atomic bombs, were simply too lethal, too destructive, for this kind of war to continue. For war is, as I have said, a political act, fought for political aims, and total destruction, potentially of our planet, is hardly a political objective except for the insane.

Still another Westphalian tenet has eroded. During the French expansion late in the 18th and early in the 19th century, French armies occupied much of Western Europe, including Spain. Spanish patriots objected to the occupying forces and instituted guerrilla warfare against them, small wars by irregular forces. When these irregular soldiers were captured, they were executed, shot or hanged because they were not the regular forces recognized by the Westphalian system. According to the doctrine, they were criminals.

During the Franco-Prussian War of 1870–71, Prussian regular troops occupied much of France. French patriots, irregular forces, attacked the occupiers. Once again, those who were captured were executed, for they were not regulars, and they had no rights as belligerents; they were criminals.

By the time of World War II, guerrilla warfare was legitimate. Under important Geneva Conventions, so long as partisan forces were organized into units with recognized leaders, so long as the members wore a distinctive identifying badge, armband, hat, shirt or bandanna, they were regarded, at least theoretically, as having the same rights as regular soldiers.

Today, states or nations no longer have the sole right to wage war. So long as organized troops, usually representing ethnic groups, fight for political aims and not purely for violence or for criminal ends, they have gained the right to be recognized as legitimate warriors.

The newest form of warfare is the use of terror to gain a political objective. Like the modern weapons of regular forces, terror is nonselective. It harms noncombatant civilians as well as legitimate targets.

For quite some time now, military forces have engaged in peacekeeping. Instead of using their weapons in a quest for force and violence, the military has been called upon to maintain peace. It is a new and nontraditional mission, and the military so engaged has been splendid in its performance.

During your active duty, however, you may participate in waging war. You have to be prepared to. In that pursuit, you can do no better than to emulate the great officers who have gone before you. What the future holds, no one knows. I believe that we have entered a new historical age and are not yet aware of its parameters, its regulations, its meaning.

Despite the fundamental alterations evident in our particular society, we still rely or the military to protect us, to defend us against the threat of violence and intimidation.

So we count on you. Serving in the military has always been and continues to be challenging work.

Martin Blumenson, *contributing editor of ARMY and the editor of the two-volume* Patton Papers, *is a graduate of Bucknell University, and the author of* Patton: The Man Behind the Legend, *1885–1945 and* The Battle of the Generals: The Untold Story of the Falaise Pocket–The Campaign That Should have Won World War II.

You who are entering the profession will have problems and difficulties. You will also enjoy finding solutions to crises of one sort or another. You will have great satisfaction in discharging enormous responsibilities, including responsibility for the lives of those who are placed in your charge. I urge you to read about your profession, to learn its history and traditions. And I wish you the best.

In conclusion, I should like to read an excerpt from a talk given by George S. Patton Jr., one of our greatest and most professional soldiers, to his officers in 1919. This is what he said.

"We as soldiers . . . are not only members of the oldest of honorable professions, but we are also the modern representatives of the den-d-gods and heroes of antiquity. Back of us stretches a line of men whose acts of valor, of self-sacrifice, and of service have been the theme of song and story since long before recorded history began . . . In the days of chivalry, knights-officers were noted as well for courtesy and gentleness of behavior, as for death defying courage. From their acts of courtesy and benevolence were derived the words, now pronounced as one, Gentle Man. Let us be gentle, that is, courteous and considerate of the rights of others. Let us be men, that is, fearless and untiring in doing our duty. Our calling is most ancient and like all other old things it has amassed through the ages certain customs and traditions which decorate and ennoble it, which render beautiful the otherwise prosaic occupation of being professional men at arms."

EXPERTISE, JURISDICTION, AND LEGITIMACY OF THE MILITARY PROFESSION

This reading critically reviews the concept of the "professional soldier" as it applies to the American military from the end of the nineteenth century to the present. There are many reasons why such a review is needed. First, the end of the Cold War closed a long period in which preparation to fight and win world wars was the primary mission of the military, thus defining the occupation of the professional soldier. It is natural to wonder whether (or how) the professional soldier's occupation has changed as a result of this historical event. Second, the two classic and still influential studies of the professional military—Samuel Huntington's *The Soldier and the State* and Morris Janowitz's *The Professional Soldier*—were written over forty years ago, in the shadow of the world wars and during the Cold War.[1] Neither is historically up to date, although that (in principle) is relatively easy to fix. The fundamental question about them is whether recent experience reveals flaws in the logic of their arguments or suggests that their influence on our thinking about the professional military should be qualified or limited. Third, since Huntington and Janowitz wrote, much new scholarly work has been done on the professions in general. This work has implications for contemporary studies of the military profession that have not yet been fully explored.

We should not pretend that a critical review of this issue is value-free or disinterested. To call an occupation a "profession" is usually to make a positive normative judgment about the work being done, and, since we think that professional work is a social good, whatever we call professional work also reveals something about what we believe is required for the well-being of society.[2] When we inquire about the state of the military profession, we do not want a simple description of what the military *does*; we want a description compared to particular standards that prescribe how military activities *ought* to be done if they are good. That comparison is essential. It lets us know whether the military is measuring up to (or falling short of) our normative expectations. As should be obvious, the quality of the comparison (and of the normative judgment reached) depends on the validity and currency of the prescriptive statements used to characterize professional work. Yet how do we know whether these statements are valid and current?

Our answer to that question depends largely on the theoretical position we take about what a profession is and how professions develop. We might hold that the concept of a profession is widely accepted, clear, and unchanging. If so, then the prescriptive statements are universal claims that define the essence of professional activity. Once they are stated, they are recognized as sufficiently authoritative to rely on and use without further question. The task of evaluating professional activity is limited to getting the description right and fairly comparing what is done with what ought to be done. If we suppose, however, that the profession is a contested concept whose definition is historically opaque and changing, then the authority and universality of prescriptive standards are questionable and require defense. This enormously complicates the task of evaluating professional activity because, in addition to description, we have to identify the normative standards appropriate to a particular period. Nevertheless, the most recent studies of professional development argue that this more complicated task is the one we face.[3] As the historian Samuel Haber tells us, statements defining professional activity are "social artifacts fashioned by public events and usage."[4] Their validity and currency are not given once for all time, but are socially constructed and reconstructed by the choices and chances affecting particular generations. In this case, substantive prescriptions about what the professions ought to be evolve historically, influencing and influenced by what the professions are.

Adopting the second position to guide this chapter, I argue that the military profession's role has expanded over the course of the last century, widening from the management of violence early in the century to encompass the management of defense following the Second World War and the management of peace after the Cold War. This role expansion has resulted largely from the changing nature of war, war being the object of professional expertise, and brought the military into closer contact and competition with other professions when it performs its tasks. No less important, when we examine historical fluctuations in the prescriptive factors that define what a profession ought to be and do, we find that changing public views of what constitutes legitimate expert knowledge pose a challenge to the military's claim to professional status. In short, compared to their counterparts early in twentieth century, military professionals today must work harder to define and defend the domain within which they work and to overcome public skepticism about the value of their expertise.

My argument is developed in four parts. The first examines the idea of the professional in general. Here I propose a definition of the professions that depends on three prescriptive factors. These factors can be used to guide and characterize historical changes in professional activity. The second part considers how debates about military professionalism are connected to these prevailing ideas about the professions. Here I consider in particular (though not exclusively) the classic models of the military professional proposed by Huntington and Janowitz. I argue that neither model provides a wholly reliable guide for thinking about the military profession today. The third part tells how the military profession has changed over time. The description is not a simple narrative, but is organized around the three prescriptive factors identified in the first part that characterize professional activity. This analytic narrative tests the usefulness of these prescriptive factors for interpreting long-term trends in professional development. The fourth and last part draws out the practical implications of this study for creating and maintaining an effective military profession at the present time.

THE IDEA OF A PROFESSION

Social scientists and historians agree that a profession is a distinct kind of work, but disagree about what actually distinguishes it from other kinds of work. Eliot Freidson suggests that we should not become preoccupied with this disagreement, as if it were a matter that might someday be resolved. A resolution would be possible only if the idea of a profession were a "generic" concept, the one true meaning of which we might someday finally discover. In fact, Freidson argues, a profession is a "historic concept."[5] What it means changes with the particular period of history we examine. The standing of medicine, law, and the clergy as professions meant one thing in medieval Europe, another thing in eighteenth-century British society, and something else again in present-day American society. The different meanings are telling. Beyond what they say about the progress

of the division of labor, they connote something about the evaluative and often conflictual processes that make professions occupations of higher rather than lower social status. In short, disagreement about what a profession is stems partly from the historical development of occupational structures and partly from social conflicts about the allocation of occupational prestige.

Embracing this historical view of the idea of the professions does not excuse us from offering a definition of the profession. Some working definition is needed, if only to clarify what a historical approach to the study of professions should consider. In this chapter, I rely on the following definition: *A profession is a relatively "high status" occupation whose members apply abstract knowledge to solve problems in a particular field of endeavor.* The definition identifies three elements as critical to the idea of a profession: high status, which I will link to a notion of legitimacy; applied abstract knowledge, the source of expertise; and a field of endeavor or jurisdiction for problem-solving. These three elements are commonly, though not always or exclusively, referred to by sociologists writing on this subject.[6] It will be worthwhile briefly to consider what these elements mean and how they are interrelated.

The British sociologist, T. H. Marshall, identified the importance of high status to the professions in an early essay on the subject, first published in 1939.[7] The professions, he wrote, were "occupations suitable for a gentleman," which in Britain meant a person of high status. We should not suppose that he meant doing professional labor necessarily gave one high status. In eighteenth-century British society it was rather the other way around. An occupation qualified as a profession if it entailed work that a gentleman would do, that is, if it were compatible with "the good life." The source of prestige, on this account, was the high status of the person who performed the activity. As commerce was then a disreputable activity, work could not be professional if it entailed striving for money (although professionals had to make a lot of money to meet "the needs of a gentlemanly life"). By the twentieth century, a profession's high status derived more from the work done than from the social standing of the worker. What counted were the effects of professional labor on the lives of the clients. "The idea of service," Marshall wrote, "became more important than the idea of freedom."[8] To ensure the quality of service, thus protecting their prosperity and respect, professionals organized into associations.

Professional associations guaranteed the technical competence of their members by controlling their training and testing their ability; they imposed a code of ethics that put the needs of clients in first place and limited intra-professional competition by barring customary commercial practices (haggling over fees, advertising, etc.); and they protected the domain of professional practice from encroachment by non-members, not to preserve the revenue for association members, but in order (they said) to protect clients from unqualified encroachers.

According to Marshall, then, the contemporary professions enjoyed high status because they were "functional" occupations organized to meet important social needs. His was an idea widely shared in the mid-twentieth century.[9] By the 1970s, as sociologists became more skeptical of functional explanations, they began to locate the source of professional status in monopolies maintained by the operation of power, income, and education.[10] The main idea was that control over these resources could be used to secure and defend an advantaged place in the social structure. Without denying the relevance of these resources, Andrew Abbott has shown that, by themselves, they provide no satisfactory account of professional status.[11] Writing in 1981, he was prepared to revive a functionalist account, agreeing with Edward Shils that professionals possess esoteric knowledge that allows them to confront disorders—disease, crime, sin, war, etc.—and often to impose order on them or bring them to heel.[12]

By the late 1980s, however, Abbott had reformulated this idea to de-emphasize the functionalist assumption that professions met needs found naturally in society. He came to emphasize rather a constructionist account, arguing that an occupation's identification as a profession and its standing within society were outcomes of social competition within a system of professions for control over abstract knowledge applied within particular jurisdictions.[13] In keeping with this account, he defined professions quite loosely as "exclusive occupational groups applying somewhat abstract knowledge to particular cases."[14] In contrast with my own definition, his focuses on just two elements, professional expertise and jurisdiction, ignoring social status (though he seems to acknowledge the importance of legitimacy, he never incorporates it in his definitional construct).[15] I think that is a mistake because it wrongly assumes that an occupation's struggle for professional standing rests entirely on possessing and applying abstract knowledge.

It is certainly true that professionals apply abstract knowledge to solve social problems. All professionals have been instructed in and mastered a body of knowledge; their entry into professional practice is predicated on receiving some form of higher education. But the *form* abstract knowledge takes varies by profession and within professions over time. This variation in the form of knowledge is important because it affects the social standing of a profession among other professions and nonprofessional occupations. The historian Bruce Kimball has shown for example that in mid-eighteenth century America, the highest-ranked profession was the clergy, but by the early nineteenth century the highest-ranked profession was the law, and by the early twentieth century it was medicine. While each of these professions masters an abstract body of knowledge, the *form* of the knowledge of the highest-ranked professions has moved from the logic of theology to the logic of jurisprudence to the logic of natural science.[16] This historical succession indicates that the prestige of professions does not depend only on the mastery of knowledge. Professional prestige also depends on the legitimacy society accords to the form that knowledge takes.

It may be tempting to argue, as sociologists used to do, that the historical succession from theology through jurisprudence to science represents the growth and triumph of reason over superstition or at least over claims that cannot be tested empirically or verified. Talcott Parsons argued this way; although the professions originally descended from a "religious matrix," he contended they were now committed to the primacy of "cognitive rationality."[17] If we succumbed to Parsons's reasoning, we would say that professional expertise (i.e., the mastery of abstract knowledge) was proven by the ability actually to solve problems faced by individuals and society. With apologies to Christian Science, we would then say that medicine is ranked higher than the clergy among professions in the twentieth century because the application of medical science to the problems of disease and public health is demonstrably more effective than the application, say, of prayer. Indeed, that was Parsons's view. By the twentieth century, he said, occupational groups anchored in religious commitments were not professions; they only approximated professions.[18]

Nevertheless, this is a temptation we should avoid. It is true that professional standing requires control over a domain of social life—a jurisdiction—

within which members of the profession try to solve particular problems by applying the special knowledge at their command. Because control over a jurisdiction is usually contested, as Abbott contends, professions are involved in competition to secure their place in society. They wage this competition by various means, from redefining the nature of the professional task to be performed to fostering legislation that bars competitors from practicing in the field. Still, the most important factor for gaining and maintaining control over a jurisdiction is demonstration that the professional activity succeeds, that it solves the problems it confronts.

Try as they might, however, professions do not perfectly control either the definition of problems to be solved or what counts as a solution. They cannot answer the question on their own. Consider the ascent of modern medicine among the professions. The rising social status of medicine rested in large part on its successful application of germ theory to the diagnosis and treatment of diseases. But the development of germ theory to approach the problem of disease reflected—it did not precede—the growing belief in society that science (not theology or jurisprudence) was *the* legitimate form of abstract knowledge, superior in practice to any other. In the future, should belief in the practical efficacy of scientific knowledge decline, as it has done over the last half-century, then professions whose abstract knowledge is scientific in form would lose status and legitimacy, even if they were demonstrably solving more problems than before.

In sum, my definition identifies three prescriptive factors that, when found together, mark an occupation as a profession. One is mastery of abstract knowledge, which occurs through a system of higher education. Another is control—almost always contested—over a jurisdiction within which expert knowledge is applied. Finally is the match between the form of professional knowledge and the prevailing cultural belief or bias about the legitimacy of that form compared to others, which is the source of professional status. We can refer to these three simply as expertise, jurisdiction, and legitimacy.

A final comment on my definition is warranted. Applying knowledge to solve social problems was thought by earlier students of the professions to entail a public service both to the client and to society. The idea of public service was an important element in their definition of the professions, because its demands supposedly overrode the dictates of the

marketplace and self-interest. Relations with clients were based on the principle of trust (not caveat emptor), and professionals were expected to perform their duties even if that required an element of self-sacrifice.[19] Recent studies of the professions, however, have defined the professions more sparely as occupations based on expert knowledge, with the connection of service to the public welfare dropped by the wayside. As Steven Brint argues, the idea that professionals were "social trustees," applying knowledge to serve the public good gave way in the 1960s to the idea that professionals were knowledge "experts" hired to serve organizational authorities or market forces without much regard for the public good.[20] This change in ideas, he says, reflects a change in reality. It is at least an important shift in our understanding of the professions and one to which we will return.

THE PROFESSION OF MILITARY SERVICE

Social science studies of the military as a profession began in the mid-twentieth century most notably with the work of Huntington and Janowitz. It is not difficult to say why military professionalism became an object of study at this time. The Cold War required that the United States maintain a large professional military during "peacetime." The country had never done this before. For a liberal political culture, traditionally ambivalent about war and standing armies, maintaining a large force in being posed questions about the quality of civil-military relations. Many thought that a high level of military professionalism was needed to ensure a technically competent military establishment and to ensure that the military establishment would act only to serve appropriate civilian authority. This thought was based on the idea that professionals were, to use Brint's term again, "social trustees" who were organized to serve the public good and not their own self-interest. But was this a reasonable idea? Was military service a profession, and if so what made military professionals effective?

The question of whether military service is a profession received different answers depending on who was asked for an answer and when. Scholars studying the professions in the first half of the twentieth century did not usually include military service in their field of inquiry. In their seminal survey of the professions, published in 1933, A. M. Carr-Saunders and P. A. Wilson explicitly refused to count the Army as a profession. They were concerned with the professions only in relation to the ordinary business of life. "The Army is omitted," they wrote, "because the service which soldiers are trained to render is one which it is hoped they will never be called on to perform."[21] Unless the military's expertise is applied, it does not count. This is a novel and, some might say, utopian ground for exclusion that tells us more about social thought between the world wars than it does about the professions. Other scholars pointed out that military service was not professional because the military was controlled by the state; military officers lacked professional autonomy, which the scholars thought was a critical trait of the professions.[22] But the ideal of autonomy as a characteristic of the professions has lost influence as professional work is increasingly embedded within corporate hierarchies. More typically, sociologists just ignored the military when they studied professions, failing to say why. It is likely that, for sociologists in this period, the prototype of a legitimate profession was science-based medicine; the military seemed unlikely to fit the mold. If the military was a profession, it was so only in the eighteenth-century sense that T. H. Marshall discussed. That is, it was a profession only because being a military officer was an occupation fit for the life of a gentleman. In the twentieth century, this idea of the profession was no longer relevant.

The public held a more inclusive view of the professions, one that had room for the military. They did not count it among the higher-ranked professions. In 1955, Janowitz notes, the public placed the prestige of the military officer "below that of the physician, scientist, college professor, and minister"—and also below the public school teacher.[23] Still, they thought the military was a profession. Indeed, public consensus on this point, though unnoticed by social scientists studying the professions, was not recent but had already formed by World War I.[24] Early in the twentieth century, it was plain that a cadre of professional military officers was necessary to train military forces in peacetime and to direct them during war.

What Huntington and Janowitz did was connect this public view of the professional military with then current social science theories about what a profession was. For them, it was largely rhetorical to ask whether military service was a profession. Neither had any doubt that it was. Huntington made a more explicit defense of the proposition than Janowitz, but both were engaged in a task of conceptual clarification, to place the military within the

bounds of the professions. At the very beginning of *The Soldier and the State*, Huntington states: "The modern officer corps is a professional body and the modern military officer a professional man."[25] He then argued that expertise, responsibility (or service to society), and corporateness (or group unity) are the marks of a profession and that the military possesses all three of these, just as do the prototypical professions, medicine and law. In *The Professional Soldier*, Janowitz simply took for granted that the military was a profession. He too identified the officer corps as a professional group like medicine or law, marked by expert skill acquired over time, the rendering of a specialized service, and a sense of group identity, which entails a system of internal administration and a professional ethic.[26] In short, they agreed that the military was a profession and about what made it so.

Where they disagreed was in their answer to the second question, what made the military profession effective? Huntington believed that military professionals were effective under conditions of objective control; by objective control he meant that civilians would dictate the military security policy but leave the military free to determine what military operations would secure the policy objectives. There was, in essence, a swap of military loyalty to civilian authority in return for professional autonomy to control one's work. The alternative, he thought, was subjective control in which civilians would meddle in military affairs, trying to make the military more like society; the military would by necessity become politicized, with the result being a decline in military effectiveness. Janowitz, in contrast, believed that no clear line could be drawn between the military and civilian realms. He thought that effective civil-military relations in a liberal democracy required that the military identify with and be representative of the society it served. Isolation of the military from the larger society would reduce professional effectiveness. He also thought that the development of weapons of mass destruction fundamentally changed the nature of war in ways that required professional soldiers explicitly to consider the political consequences of military operations. Effective military professionals redefined their understanding of successful problem-solving. They downplayed their role as "heroic warriors" in pursuit of absolute military victory to emphasize their role as pragmatic managers of the minimum use of force needed to achieve political settlements and maintain viable international relations. To achieve this latter ideal, Janowitz advocated the development of what he called a constabulary force.

Important as both these models are, neither stands without criticism today. Huntington argues that the military professional is to master the functional requirements of war, to organize and train the military to meet them, and to lead the military to fight when ordered by political authorities to do so. But the presumption that there is a clearly delineated military sphere defined by war-fighting that is independent of the social and political sphere is dubious at best, especially in an era when we possess weapons of mass destruction. There is no real distinction between the ends and means of war. What ends are possible to think about depend to a large extent on the means with which they are to be pursued. As a practical matter, this means that the distinction between the political sphere, where ends are decided on, and the military sphere, where means are deployed in pursuit of ends, is highly misleading. If so, then Huntington's theory of objective civilian control does not really tell us how military professionalism can be strengthened.

Also, Huntington's confidence in the value of military professionalism is uncritical. He ignores the possibility that professionals (like all social groups) may act in ways contrary to the interests of the larger group. But sociologists have identified a number of ways in which professionals may act in their own interest against the public good: cultivating an incapacity to grasp the insights from any perspective but one's own; treating the means of professional practice as if they were ends in themselves, forgetting the original purpose they were intended to fulfill; acting to protect the station and privileges of one's group— service or branch—above any other, simply because it is one's own; shirking those tasks one is assigned to undermine the assignment; or acting opportunistically to do what is required to advance one's career.[27] Taking these into account, we have to conclude that the degree of military professionalism varies for reasons other than the institution of objective or subjective control.

Janowitz's model is more helpful because it anticipates change in the character of the military profession, something Huntington fails to do. The change is driven by the need to adapt professional practice to the changing nature of war: that affects what counts as a solution to problems of military security. But he was perhaps naïve in expecting that the profession could alter its self-conception away from the heroic warrior to the pragmatic constabulary model without intensifying competition (from within the military and without) for control over its professional jurisdiction. And while he recognized that tensions existed among officers of differing specialties—e.g., work oriented primarily to management, technology, or combat—he did not thoroughly explore the difficulties encountered between bureaucratic and professional cultures.

Even more objectionable, Janowitz failed to resolve the problems his theory poses for military professionalism. If the changing nature of war blurred the boundaries between the military and political spheres, as Janowitz said, then how was military professionalism to be reformed to ensure that its expertise was applied in the service of the state? The question is a serious one. In a constabulary force, military officers were inevitably "politicized" as they prepared for their new roles to deliver strategic deterrence and fight limited wars. But a politicized military at least implicitly challenges civilian supremacy.[28] How was the challenge to be met? In *The Professional Soldier*, Janowitz's discussion of mechanisms of civilian control to ensure professional responsibility is extremely limited, being confined to control mechanisms that are easily worked around. The problem Janowitz faced was an old one in the theory of the professions, namely, how to ensure that professionals are acting in the best interests of society when those they serve lack the expertise to define the service they need, or even to know whether their needs have been adequately addressed. His answer was to strengthen the commitment of professional soldiers to the system of civilian control through programs of political education that would help them connect their professional training to national and transnational purposes.[29] But the thrust of this argument is circular: responsible military professionalism is made to depend on the strength of military professionalism.

When Huntington and Janowitz devised their pioneering models, they were both confident that strong military professionalism was essential to ensure the military security of American democracy. Their confidence rested in part on the logic of the functionalist theory of the professions that prevailed at mid-century and on which they both relied. According to that theory, professionals were thought to be social trustees, acting in a fiduciary capacity to ensure the public good. They possessed systematic knowledge acquired through a long period of training, and, as required by their occupational ethic, they applied it competently, objectively, and impartially to meet the needs of the client and improve public welfare.

A decade after Huntington's and Janowitz's classic works appeared, sociologists abandoned this simple functional theory. In its place, they conceived a more conflict-oriented, class-based model that saw professions as group "projects" to obtain social mobility. According to this conflict approach, the professions did not necessarily serve social needs found in the natural order of things. They rather imposed their own definitions of needs on society and created self-serving means for meeting them.[30] It is mere speculation to wonder how Huntington or Janowitz might have concluded differently about the military profession had they written from the perspective of these later models. But the effects of these more cynical models of the professions were incorporated (though not explicitly) in the work of Charles Moskos and his associates.[31] Beginning in the late 1970s, Moskos argued that the military profession was moving away from its traditional institutional principles of social organization to embrace occupational or market-based principles of organization. It has proven difficult to trace development of the military profession along this single theoretical dimension. Over the years, those working on this model have multiplied the number of dimensions taken into account. Yet, despite refinements, in the end, there is consensus that a significant change has taken place. The military profession in its current state is, we must conclude, more like Brint's "expert" profession simply doing its job for an organized authority than like a "social trustee" profession rendering self-sacrificial service to the country.

TRENDS IN MILITARY PROFESSIONALISM

My approach to the study of change in the military profession is guided by our definition of the factors that mark an occupation as a profession: expertise, jurisdiction, and legitimacy. My hypothesis is that when we examine military professionalism from the late nineteenth century to the present, we see first a convergence of these three factors to strengthen military professionalism, and then an unraveling of these factors, especially in the last half-century, that subjects the military profession to strain. The reasons for this pattern of change are interrelated. As we shall see, they are not factors always within the power of the military profession to control.

To develop these ideas, I concentrate on three pivotal periods in the history of the Army professionalism: the period between Reconstruction and World War I, when on most accounts the Army officer corps turned itself into a modern profession; the period just following World War II, when the Army faced a professional crisis centered largely on the problems of defining and defending its jurisdiction at a time when military roles and missions were hotly contested; and finally the period since the end of the Cold War, when the Army profession has been challenged by lost resources, increased deployments, and increased competition for control of its jurisdiction. The task is to identify the main themes that connect these three periods along the analytic dimensions of expertise, jurisdiction, and legitimacy.

Expertise

The period following Reconstruction was one in which the Army began seriously to cultivate the study of war as an applied science which officers must master if they were to be professional specialists in the management of violence. The emphasis on the *science* (not the art) of war, while not entirely new, was new in its scope. It underwrote the development of a new professional education system and the founding of professional associations and journals.[32] This movement within the Army had its parallels in the Navy and in the larger society. This was a period in which the "culture of professionalism"—a term used by Burton Bledstein—was widespread.[33] Many middle-class occupational groups were organizing themselves to stake a claim to professional status. The success of their claims often hinged on their being able to demonstrate expertise over an abstract body of knowledge that took the form of science. Here the themes of expertise and legitimacy are intertwined. By the late nineteenth century, science was believed to be *the* source of reliable knowledge about the world; claims to expertise were more readily recognized if they were obviously grounded in science. Even the ancient professions of theology and law were affected by this development—they began to recast the form of their specialized knowledge in a scientific mold.[34]

The scientific turn in the Army professional's claim to expertise was accepted without significant challenge until the end of World War II. Before then there was a close connection between the use of military force and the possibility of military success or victory. If superior resources did not prevail, it was thought to be a failure to apply the science of war, not a challenge to the idea that greater military strength yields greater military security. But the development of weapons of mass destruction in the wake of the world wars made plain (sooner for some than for others) that sheer military might was no longer a guarantee of security if the use of that might was so destructive that its use was self-defeating. This shift in outlook spurred development of a new and broader science of national security and strategic studies, and the experts in this new science were not confined to those in the uniformed services.[35] Nevertheless, the Army professional did not abandon the claim to expertise in military science, but if anything pursued the claim with increasing vigor, extending its system of professional military education and augmenting it by dispatching officers to pursue graduate degrees in fields ancillary to or supportive of the military sciences. At the end of the twentieth century, the Army's claim to expert knowledge in the management of violence, certified by science, was a foundation for its professional identity.[36] That is not to say, however, that the empirical challenge to that expertise posed by weapons of mass destruction had been successfully resolved.

Jurisdiction

A professional jurisdiction is defined by the boundaries of the domain within which expert knowledge is applied. It is sometimes an actual place, like a hospital, court room, or battlefield, and sometimes a slice or aspect of life. So, while an Army commander focuses on directing the course of battle, the chaplain is focused on the soldiers' souls and the medic on the soldiers' wounds. In broad strokes, the Army's jurisdiction narrowed over the late nineteenth century, as it shed domestic functions and focused on protecting the country's borders and fighting land wars abroad. Competitors who would ply their knowledge in this jurisdiction at the expense of the professional Army, notably volunteers and state militias, were effectively curbed early in the twentieth century. State militias were upgraded, but subordinated to professional Army control by the Militia Act of 1903 and the National Defense Act of 1916. By World War I, well-meaning amateurs like Theodore Roosevelt were no longer allowed direct entry into the officer corps. The Army was following an old practice of the professions, protecting its jurisdiction by resort to the law. The Navy was a rival for resources, but not a competitor to fight land battles.

This neat arrangement was disturbed by the advancing technology of war over the course of the twentieth century. The disturbance was severe at the end of World War II as evinced by the conflict over the creation of a "unified" Department of Defense and of an Air Force separated from the Army.[37] There was severe competition among the various services over what their roles and missions—their jurisdiction—should be. This contest arose because the technological development of war over the course of the twentieth century had the effect of homogenizing the theater of war, undermining the clear connection of the three major services with a particular environment of warfare—land, sea, and air—and so creating an impetus for "joint" military operations. One could say that there is just one military profession, but the services resist this more abstract identity, in part because (as Kenneth Allard has shown) their dominant operating environments continue to support different kinds of expertise and modes of intra-professional cooperation, even to this day.[38] The interservice competition over jurisdiction has blown hot and cold ever since, and it has certainly not gone away.

However, the more important competition over the Army's professional jurisdiction has come from external sources. In effect, I argue that the jurisdictional claims of the military in general, including the Army, have expanded since the end of the world wars. We can reduce that to slogan form by saying the Army has moved from the management of war early in the century to the management of defense (a wider concern) during the Cold War to the management of peace (an even wider concern) since the end of the Cold War. With each broadening of the Army's jurisdictional claims, competition over the Army's jurisdiction has increased. As already suggested, the growth of national security studies after the world wars was propelled by the threat of weapons of mass destruction; war narrowly conceived could no longer be seen as a tool in the kit of foreign policy. The outbreak of general war had to be averted, and civilian scientists in relevant disciplines began to develop expertise outside the military profession to determine how this might be done. Within the Department of Defense, new techniques of rational planning were introduced to determine the most efficient use of scarce resources. This eroded claims of the Army and other service professionals that such judgments should not be based on the more general, quantitative language of cost-benefit analysis but rather on particular service expertise. Since the end of the Cold War, encroachment of civilian experts on the Army's jurisdiction increased in large part because military operations were no longer confined to actual war but had spread to include peacekeeping missions, broadly defined. Unlike actions in a theater of war, peacekeeping operations are not an endeavor of "sole practice" by the Army professional; they occur within what Abbott called a "multi-professional workplace."[39] Successful peacekeeping requires cooperative action between the Army and a wide array of other civilian service providers who answer to no single authority.[40]

This new competition over the Army's jurisdiction could be limited if the boundaries of its jurisdiction were narrowed, as they were at the turn to the twentieth century. But this approach, preferred by some, is unlikely given the changing nature of war, the object of the Army's professional expertise. As Janowitz argued long ago, it is the changing nature of war that is driving the expansion of the Army's definition of its professional jurisdiction, thus inviting the conflicts just observed.

Legitimacy

We have noted that the Army's claim to be a modern profession a century ago was bolstered by its ability to develop its expertise in the form of military science. This new science encompassed the study of battle, logistics, weapons development, and even the mobilization, assignment, and leadership of military personnel. Science at the time, enjoying a high point of its prestige, was considered the most reliable form of practical knowledge. It was not only the Army that advanced its claim to professional status by showing that its expertise was scientific. A new source of strain for the Army professional—as for many professionals—has been society's increasing skepticism of the legitimacy of expert knowledge based on science and the ideal of objectivity.

In 1962, Thomas Kuhn, a historian of science, famously cast doubt on the claims of science to provide objective and reliable knowledge with his analysis titled *The Structure of Scientific Revolutions*.[41] His argument, however, was only one of a number of studies to show that scientific knowledge often rested on hidden nonrational social factors. In any case the stock of scientific knowledge was always tentative and subject to revision. Sometimes the revisions required were disturbing, because the science once relied on was shown now to threaten human

well-being. Rachel Carson documented the harmful unintended consequences of applying modern science to industry in her study, *Silent Spring*, which created a foundation for the ecology movement.[42] In the case of military science, even reliable knowledge was a threat to human welfare, symbolized powerfully by the threat of thermonuclear weapons and literally brought home to many whose milk contained strontium 90, a radioactive particle released in fallout from above-ground nuclear testing.

There are two important results of this increased skepticism about the legitimacy of science for the professions in general and for Army professionalism in particular. First, increased skepticism about science has encouraged nonexperts to question the exercise of professional authority more boldly than they had done in the past. Before World War II, students of the professions could write confidently, for example, of doctors giving orders that only foolhardy clients would ignore. By the end of the twentieth century, resort to alternative medicine was more common, and medical doctors found it more difficult to silence competing claims from the practioners, for example, of chiropractics, homeopathy, and acupuncture. More generally, professional pleas for deference had a hollow ring, resting, as they were accused of doing, on an ideological footing to secure the privileges associated with their practice. This is true for the military as well. A good illustration of the point can be found in debates over whether and how military technology and performance standards should be revised to accommodate greater integration of women.[43] Those skeptical of the wisdom of such integration regard the redesign, say, of airplane cockpits or basic training regimes as evidence that professionalism is on the decline, as expertise and technical competence are diluted for reasons of "political correctness." In contrast, those skeptical of professional expertise argue that the established standards are not universal, objective truths, but rest on social constructions of gender that can be modified without compromising military effectiveness.[44] Without a general belief in what constitutes a legitimate form of reliable knowledge, such debates are impossible to resolve except by the exercise of politics.

Second, when we lack common belief about what constitutes legitimate, truthful, and objective knowledge, it is difficult to sustain a professional ethic of service. Unquestioned trust between the professional and the client, which is needed to sustain the ethic, no longer exists. When professionals claim to be offering impartial, disinterested, even self-sacrificial service, their claims are not accepted at face value, but are examined cynically by clients and other interested observers who look for the self-interested "angle" in such claims, and find claims of self-interest more believable than claims of altruistic service. Uncertainty about "objective truth" also makes it more difficult for professionals to engage in self-sacrificing service with confidence that their self-sacrifice is justified, that the service is rendered in pursuit of what is unambiguously good. In the Army, such doubts show up at the end of the Cold War, with rising doubts about the value of losing life when engaged in peacekeeping operations. It is not enough to assert that self-sacrificing service is central to professional practice.[45] The norm of self-sacrifice must be grounded in a general belief that the application of expert knowledge within a particular jurisdiction is legitimate.

IMPLICATIONS FOR MILITARY PROFESSIONALISM

Professional practice is strong when the conditions of all three prescriptive factors are met, that is, when the application of expertise within a particular jurisdiction is uncontested and thought in general to be legitimate. Otherwise the quality of professional practice is cast into doubt. Applying this standard of evaluation to our historical analysis, it is clear that the military profession was strongest at the end of the nineteenth century through the end of World War II, but has weakened since then as a result of heightened jurisdictional competition and declining public confidence in science as a form of legitimate expertise.

Increased jurisdictional competition stems largely from the changing nature of war. The enormous destructive power of weapons of mass destruction has made clear the self-defeating character of unrestrained armed conflict; military security was no longer (if it ever really was) a simple function of military strength. The practical effect of this development, in the aftermath of World War II, did not diminish, but expanded the military's role. Still centrally concerned with the management of violence between armies at war, the military profession came also to manage defense, the aim of which was to avoid the outbreak of general war through a strategy of deterrence; and after the Cold War, the military began to manage the peace—not alone, but with oth-

ers—with the aim of limiting armed conflict to the maximum extent and using the least force possible to promote a political settlement of differences, maintain respect for human rights, and provide humanitarian relief. The difficulty here is that the military does not possess the same level of abstract knowledge about how to conduct peacekeeping missions (or how to deter global war) that it has for waging war. Even if it did, the military does not and cannot pretend to possess a monopoly of expert knowledge relevant for mission success in its expanded jurisdictions. To a greater extent than when fighting war, the management of defense and peace requires the military profession to cooperate and compete with other professions as it goes about its work.

To strengthen military professionalism under these circumstances, one might consider the obvious possibility of contracting the military's jurisdiction. The Army could attempt to restrict its professional role by confining itself to problems of war, traditionally understood as conventional warfare between uniformed armies of nation-states and fought for the control of land—and forsake all other concerns. When threats stem less from the prospects of interstate war than from irregular religious and ethnic conflicts and attacks by terrorists, this possibility seems unrealistic. The need to prepare for general war cannot be ignored, but the Army could not justify a return to its world war jurisdiction while retaining its contemporary relevance.[46] Alternatively, one might deny the problem and emphasize the military's evident success in defending its expanded jurisdiction. The absence of a general war over the last half-century, the military could assert, demonstrates its professional competence in managing defense. Yet it is difficult to say with certainty whether or to what degree the absence of general war in this period resulted from the application of military expertise to the problem of deterrence. In fact, many wonder whether deterrence based on a nuclear standoff is a viable strategy. Consideration of an antimissile defense system suggests there are doubts about that even within the defense community.

A third approach considers how the Army professional can operate most effectively in its multi-professional workplace. Within the broad jurisdiction of the management of peace, mission success, say in Bosnia or Kosovo, cannot be achieved by relying on the expertise of the Army professional alone. Success requires the combined expertise of all the relevant professionals involved. The analogy is imperfect, but one can think for example about the combined expertise required in a hospital operating room before any complex surgery can succeed. It cannot be assumed, however, that professionals engaged in a peacekeeping arena will wish to cooperate for a common goal. Even if they did, at the moment there is no well-established institutional authority with the expertise to identify, much less integrate, the various professional activities that are needed to maintain peace and substitute nonviolent for violent means of conflict resolution. Nevertheless, it is important that the various professional organizations on the mission employ their particular expertise in a way that contributes to the overall objective of building peace in the region.

It is becoming clear with experience that the military's role in building peace is highly circumscribed. David Last, a major in the Canadian military, observes that while "military forces are effective at guaranteeing military security against organized military opposition . . . they are impotent in the face of bricks through windows or threatening telephone calls in the night."[47] He also notes that other agencies are needed to police, govern, provide relief, and move toward reconciliation if the conflict is to be resolved. He does not deny that military expertise is required in peacekeeping operations, especially to stop and prevent organized physical violence. But suppressing violence is only one step in the process, providing temporary relief.[48] Jurisdictional competition is limited and professionalism enhanced if the military's role within peacekeeping and humanitarian interventions is limited to fit its peculiar expertise. The same is true for other agencies involved. Achieving this outcome requires deliberate coordination across professional boundaries in which respect for the capacity of the others is acknowledged. There is no benefit in this setting if the military professional maintains a false sense of its own autonomy or attempts to do everything it possibly can. [49]

The public's declining confidence in science as a reliable form of practical knowledge is another troubling trend for military professionalism. This decline is a problem for all science-based professions, not just the military, because it makes it more difficult for all to establish the legitimacy of their authority. While science-based expertise continues to be used, and will be used far into the future, its use is no longer inevitably considered to be self-justifying. To shore up their authority, professions spend time building "sustainable partnerships" with those outside the profession whose expertise is other than their own and yet affects what they do.[50] That requires entering into a dialogue across professions and with the public (including the news media). The purpose is to increase the public's understanding of the reasons for a particular course of professional action and the profession's understanding of the reasons why that course of action might be resisted. There is no reason to expect that dialogue alone will lead to consensus. But without such a dialogue, it is hard to gain the public's trust on which professional legitimacy depends or to create the professional self-confidence required to embrace an ethic of self-sacrificing service.

This course, however advisable, also has a utopian ring to it. It seems to presume the persistence of the professions as "social trustees," committed to serving the public good. It seems to ignore the rise of "expert" professionals who serve only the interests of organizational authorities and market forces. But, as Brint has shown, the presumption of social trusteeship and the ignoring of self-advancing experts are not warranted; social supports needed for social trustee professionalism to thrive have eroded. This erosion has helped to elevate the authority of the market over moral elements in the life of the professions.[51] Brint's argument suggests that the new competitor to science as the form of objective and reliable practical knowledge is the market itself: what is true, objective, and useful knowledge is what sells in the marketplace; anything else is fancy. However crude that sounds when stated baldly, it is not far away from ordinary experience. We are used to people asking about the "bottom line" of our arguments and having them conclude that they "buy it" or not.[52] Making the market the new form by which the legitimacy of professional knowledge is judged does not unseat the science-based professions. But it poses a challenge to the customary pecking order of the professions, with those that can wrap their expertise in marketable form rising to the top (as economists and clinical psychologists have risen in the profession of social science). It also means that pressures will build within professions to formulate their expertise in the vocabulary of the marketplace. Such a change is what Moskos and others observed in the military profession beginning in the 1970s. The seeds of change were planted perhaps with Robert McNamara's introduction of cost-benefit analysis to evaluate the military budget and procurement programs in the early 1960s.

The triumph of the market cannot be ignored because it arises from and is part of society itself.

Nevertheless, the triumph is not complete and so the choice is not between legitimating expertise based *either* on the market *or* on science (or other more traditional social forms). The problem is to recognize when market legitimation is an appropriate basis of action and when it is not. In principle, this problem is not difficult to solve. Markets provide effective and legitimate diagnoses and prescriptions about the worth and allocation of social goods when there is real uncertainty about what goods to pursue at what cost. Historically, the rise of market-based legitimation in modern liberal democracies is connected with the growing heterogeneity of their populations and the diversity of their cultures. With the prevailing commitment to the principle of toleration as a foundation for society, there is reluctance to impose definitions of what is good or which goods are to be preferred over others. Instead, these definitions and valuations are established by free exchange whether in the marketplace of commerce or in the marketplace of ideas. Whenever the military profession confronts such uncertainty—as it may do for instance in decisions about the design of future weapons systems or in calculations about how much money soldiers should be paid—there is no reason why the profession should not employ the language of the market. Doing so is not completely foreign to military experience. The battlefield, after all, is full of uncertainty, and battles are decided by the exchange of fire. A great deal of military science is devoted to the end of gaining and sustaining the advantage in this deadly competition.

Many times of course it is not clear whether expertise rooted in the logic of the market or expertise rooted in some other moral or scientific logic should prevail. That is true for instance with respect to privatizing activities that once were handled within the military. Market efficiencies may justify privatizing some health-care or finance functions or closing some bases. But other matters are more difficult to judge. For instance, Deborah Avant, in her chapter on privatizing military training in the present book (Chapter 9), questions whether market efficiencies justify privatizing initial training of cadets who will become Army officers. The efficiencies are tempting to a downsized force that must stretch resources. Still, when the military relies on private contractors for instructors, it may subtly teach new entrants into the profession that, despite the rhetoric of self-sacrificing leadership, market logic trumps other considerations. As a result, young officers may leave the profession, abandoning command for the pursuit of economic opportunity.[53]

But when there is relative certainty about the goods to be sought or about comparative worth, then the language of the marketplace may be superfluous and the legitimacy of expert knowledge may rest on other grounds. The higher the degree of certainty, the more likely the public will regard such justifications as legitimate. Examples here include scientific questions about how to build thermonuclear weapons or to treat the psychological consequences for individuals subjected to prolonged stress in combat. Once the decision is made to do either, then scientific expertise is required. Professional diagnoses and prescriptions based on this knowledge should be defended against the logic of economic efficiency and "market tests." The same is true with respect to certain moral issues that the military professional must face. Relying on forms of discourse borrowed from the marketplace, one cannot explain or justify self-sacrifice for the public good that military (and other professional) service often requires. This was a lesson that Robert McNamara had yet to learn as he tried to monitor the "progress" and "efficiency" of the war in Vietnam by relying in part on body counts and ratios of enemy to American losses.[54]

In short, when possible, the military should wrap its expertise in the language of the market to enhance its professional legitimacy. But when that is counterproductive or not possible, the military should patiently explain both to itself and to the public why that language is sometimes inappropriate and why we might sometimes wish to act on alternative forms of knowledge to pursue a social good. Such explanations are especially important when military missions of war or peace put lives at risk, whether our lives or the lives of others.

NOTES

1. Samuel P. Huntington, *The Soldier and the State* (Cambridge, MA: Harvard University Press, 1957); Morris Janowitz, *The Professional Soldier* (Glencoe, IL: Free Press, 1960).

2. I say usually because we sometimes use the adjective "professional" in a derisive way, as we do when we speak about "professional politicians" or "professional wrestlers." In these cases, we expect the word professional to denote a fulltime occupation that is somehow dishonorable—the politician because politicians are often required to compromise on principles in order

to rule and the wrestlers because we know that the outcome of the sporting events in which they compete is scripted. The use of the term professional in these cases is ironical; we use it to cast doubt on their integrity and on their contribution to the well-being of society.

3. See, for example, Edward M. Coffman, "The Long Shadow of *The Soldier and the State*," *Journal of Military History* 55 (January 1991): 69-82; and Matthew Moten, *The Delafield Commission and the American Military Profession* (College Station: Texas A&M University Press, 2000), 6-15.

4. Samuel Haber, *The Quest for Authority and Honor in the American Professions, 1750-1900* (Chicago, IL: University of Chicago Press, 1991), x.

5. Eliot Freidson, *Professionalism Reborn: Theory, Prophecy, and Policy* (Chicago, IL: University of Chicago Press, 1994), 16. Freidson is not the only one to argue so. A brief but important summary of the historical development and changing meaning of the professions is found in Talcott Parsons, "Professions," *International Encyclopedia of the Social Sciences*, 12: 536-47. More comprehensive treatments can be found in Haber, *Quest for Authority*; and Bruce A. Kimball, *The "True Professional Ideal" in America* (Lanham, MD: Rowman & Littlefield, 1995).

6. For a review of definitions of the professions, see Geoffrey Millerson, *The Qualifying Associations: A Study in Professionalisation* (London: Routledge & Kegan Paul, 1964); and Freidson, *Professionalism Reborn*.

7. T. H. Marshall, "The Recent History of Professionalism in Relation to Social Structure and Social Policy," in *Class, Citizenship, & Social Development* (Chicago, IL: University of Chicago Press, 1977).

8. Ibid., 160.

9. So, for instance, Talcott Parsons argued that the professions were an "institutional framework in which many of our most important social functions are carried on." Talcott Parsons, "The Professions and Social Structure," in *Essays in Sociological Theory*, Rev. Ed. (New York: Free Press, 1954), 48.

10. See Eliot Freidson, *Professional Dominance* (New York: Atherton Press, 1970); Jeffrey Berlant, *Profession and Monopoly* (Berkeley and Los Angeles: University of California Press, 1975); and Magalí Sarfatti Larson, *The Rise of Professionalism* (Berkeley and Los Angeles: University of California Press, 1977).

11. Andrew Abbott, "Status and Status Strain in the Professions," *American Journal of Sociology* 86 (January 1981), 828-29.

12. Ibid., 829. See also Edward Shils, "Charisma, Order, and Status," in *Center and Periphery* (Chicago, IL: University of Chicago Press, 1975), 267-71.

13. Andrew Abbott, *The System of Professions: An Essay on the Division of Expert Labor* (Chicago, IL: University of Chicago Press, 1988).

14. Ibid., 8.

15. See, ibid., 184-195. Abbott's discussion of legitimacy underscores his belief that legitimacy is peripheral—not central—to what constitutes the profession. He acknowledges that professional legitimacy rests on a fit between professional work and values in the larger culture. He notes that "changes in values can recast the meaning of a profession's legitimation arguments without any change occurring in the arguments themselves," as meaning changes when put in a different context (p. 187, original italics). And he shows how changing values have affected the professions. Nevertheless, he contends that value shifts over the last two centuries have had "surprisingly small effects on the actual history of [professional] jurisdiction" (p. 195)—a contention that ignores effects they may have had on the form of professional expertise.

16. Kimball, *The "True Professional Ideal" in America*.

17. Parsons, "Professions," 537-38.

18. Ibid., 539.

19. These ideas are expressed, for instance, in the writings of Marshall, Parsons, and Wilensky.

20. Steven Brint, *In an Age of Experts: The Changing Role of Professionals in Politics and Public Life* (Princeton, NJ: Princeton University Press, 1994).

21. A. M. Carr-Saunders and P. A. Wilson, *The Professions*, Repr. Ed. (London: Frank Cass, 1964).

22. See Arthur Larson, "Military Professionalism and Civil Control," *Journal of Political and Military Sociology* 2 (Spring 1972): 57-72; and Bernard J. Piecznski, "Problems in U.S. Military Professionalism, 1945-1950" (Ph.D. diss., State University of New York at Buffalo, 1985), 34.

23. Janowitz, *Professional Soldier*, 4. More current occupational prestige scores, part of the General Social Survey, do not include military officers as an occupational category.

24. Allan R. Millett, *Military Professionalism and Officership in America* (Columbus, OH: Mershon Center, 1977).

25. Huntington, *Soldier and the State*, 7.

26. Janowitz, *Professional Soldier*, 5-7.

27. These professional pathologies that might affect military effectiveness are taken mainly from Larson, "Military Professionalism," 65-66. The idea that the military professional is an agent who might shirk his responsibilities comes from Peter Feaver, "Crisis as Shirking: An Agency Theory Explanation of the Souring of American Civil-Military Relations," *Armed Forces & Society* 24 (Spring 1998): 407-34.

28. Peter D. Feaver, "The Civil-Military Problematique: Huntington, Janowitz, and the Question of Civilian Control," *Armed Forces & Society* 23 (Winter 1996): 149-178.

29. Morris Janowitz, "Civic Consciousness and Military Performance," in *The Political Education of Soldiers*, eds. Morris Janowitz and Stephen D. Wesbrook (Beverly Hills, CA: Sage, 1983), 74-76.

30. Abbott, *The System of Professions*, 3-6.

31. See Charles C. Moskos and Frank R. Wood, eds., *The Military: More Than Just a Job?* (Washington, DC: Pergamon-Brassey's, 1988); and Charles C. Moskos, John Allen Williams, and David R. Segal, eds., *The Postmodern Military: Armed Forces After the Cold War* (New York: Oxford University Press, 2000).

32. In 1877, Maj. Gen. John M. Schofield told an audience of Army officers: "It is the Science of War in the broadest sense, not simply the *Art* of War, that we are to study." Quoted in Carol Reardon, *Soldiers and Scholars: The U.S. Army and the Uses of Military History* (Lawrence: University Press of Kansas, 1990), 9. For overviews of military professionalization in this period, see in addition to Reardon, for example, Huntington, *Soldier and the State*, 222-88; Millett, *Military Professionalism*; Russell F. Weigley, *History of the United States Army* (New York: Macmillan, 1967), 313-54; and John M. Gates, "The 'New' Military Professionalism," *Armed Forces & Society* 11 (Spring 1985): 427-36. Historians have recently explored the seeds of American military professionalism in the first half of the nineteenth century. See, e.g., William B. Skelton, *An American Profession of Arms* (Lawrence: University Press of Kansas, 1992); Moten, passim; and, more briefly, Allan R. Millett and Peter Maslowski, *For the Common Defense* (New York: Free Press, 1984), 126-130.

33. Burton J. Bledstein, *The Culture of Professionalism* (New York: Norton, 1976).

34. Kimball, *The "True Professional Ideal" in America.*

35. For a broader discussion of these trends, see the chapters by Christopher Dandeker and James N. Rosenau in *The Adaptive Military*, ed. James Burk (New Brunswick, NJ: Transaction, 1998).

36. I am indebted to James S. Powell, a history graduate student at my university, for his content analysis of articles appearing in *Army* in 1980, 1990, and 2000. His analysis confirms the centrality of applied scientific expertise for professional identity within the Army.

37. "Piecznski, "Problems in U.S. Military Professionalism"; Townsend Hoopes and Douglas Brinkley, *Driven Patriot: The Life and Times of James Forrestal* (New York: Knopf, 1992).

38. Kenneth C. Allard, *Command, Control, and the Common Defense* (New Haven, CT: Yale University Press, 1990).

39. Abbott, *System of Professions*, 69-79, 151, 153.

40. See Ian Wing, *Refocusing Concepts of Security: The Convergence of Military and Non-military Tasks* (Duntroon ACT: Land Warfare Studies Centre, 2000).

41. Thomas S. Kuhn, *The Structure of Scientific Revolutions* (Chicago, IL: University of Chicago Press, 1962).

42. Rachel Carson, *Silent Spring* (Boston, MA: Houghton Mifflin, 1962).

43. James Burk, "Three Views on Women in the Military," *Society* (forthcoming).

44. See, e.g., Rachel N. Weber, "Manufacturing Gender in Military Cockpit Design," in *The Social Shaping of Technology*, second ed., eds., Donald MacKenzie and Judy Wajcman (Philadelphia, PA: Open University Press, 1999), 372-81.

45. For an interesting discussion of the current doubts about self-sacrificing service within the Army, see Don M. Snider, John A. Nagl, and Tony Pfaff, *Army Professionalism, the Military Ethic, and Officership in the 21st Century* (Carlisle Barracks, PA: U.S. Army War College, Strategic Studies Institute, 1999).

46. This means that the slogan—the Army's purpose is to fight and win the nation's wars—provides little guidance to any serious discussion of military professionalism.

47. David Last, "Twisting Arms or Shaking Hands? How to Put Peacekeepers Out of Business" (paper presented at conference, Taking Stock of Civil Military

Relations, sponsored by the Centre for European Security Studies [The Netherlands], the Centre for Security and Defence Studies [Canada], and the Geneva Centre for the Democratic Control of Armed Forces [Switzerland], held at The Hague, 9-11 May 2001), 4.

48. For a fuller discussion of these issues, see Thomas G. Weiss, *Military-Civilian Interactions: Intervening in Humanitarian Crises* (Lanham, MD: Rowman & Littlefield, 1999).

49. An official with the International Committee of the Red Cross (ICRC) observes that "it is somehow paradoxical that in several tragic situations over the past decade, when the need for military force to restore peace was critical . . . the military (implementing mandates assigned by their political masters) were more involved in activities of an essentially humanitarian nature. The most prominent example is the U.N. Protection Force in Bosnia (UNPROFOR)." Meinrad Studer, "The ICRC and Civil-Military Relations in Armed Conflict" (paper presented at conference, Taking Stock of Civil Military Relations), 5. See note 47 for complete citation.

50. The phrase is used in *The United Nations and Civil Society: The Role of NGOs,* Proceedings of the 30th United National Issues Conference (Muscatine, IA: The Stanley Foundation, 1999), 2, as quoted and discussed in Wing, *Refocusing Concepts of Security*, 99.

51. Brint, *In an Age of Experts*, 203-05.

52. On the importance of simple metaphors for the construction of practical knowledge, see George Lakoff and Mark Johnson, *Metaphors We Live By* (Chicago, IL: University of Chicago Press, 1980).

53. Thomas E. Ricks, "Younger Officers Quit Army at Fast Clip," *Washington Post*, 17 April 2000, A1 (available from Lexis-Nexis, academic edition; accessed 27 June 2001). For data on the rates of loss of officers from lieutenant through colonel, see the briefing by Lt. Gen. Timothy J. Maude, Deputy Chief of Staff for Personnel, U.S. Army, presented at the Commanders' Conference, 19 October 2000. Available from: *http://www.d-n-i.net/DCSPER_10_00/index.htm*; Internet; accessed 27 June 2001.

54. Robert S. McNamara, *In Retrospect: The Tragedy and Lessons of Vietnam* (New York: Times Books, 1995), 48. In his own words: "I always pressed our commanders very hard for estimates of progress—or lack of it. The monitoring of progress—which I still consider a bedrock principle of good management [a market-based principle]—was very poorly handled in Vietnam. . . . Uncertain how to evaluate the results in a war without battle lines, the military tried to gauge its progress with quantitative measurements such as enemy casualties (which became infamous as body counts)."

The Profession of Arms II

This is the sixth of a series of seven lessons on the Army Profession and Officership. The intent of this lesson is to acquaint you with the Customs and Traditions that makeup the culture of the Army. This lesson exposes you to the culture of the Army and those customs and traditions that give the Army its rich heritage.

The following topics are addressed in this lesson:

- Importance of Army customs and traditions as aspects of the Army's heritage and organizational culture
- Review and discussion of selected Army customs and traditions

The following TLO is supported in whole or in part by this lesson:

- Relate the characteristics of a profession to military service as an officer

Following this lesson you will be able to:

- Describe the Army Customs of Comradeship, Rank Has Its Privileges, and Welcomes and Farewells
- Describe those actions that the Army considers taboo
- Describe the Army Traditions of Public Service, Achieving the Mission, Leadership, Loyalty, the Officer's Word, Discipline, Readiness, Taking Care of Soldiers, Being a Lady or Gentlemen, Avoiding the Political, and Candor

HERITAGE, CUSTOMS, AND COURTESIES OF THE ARMY

BY KEITH BONN

SOLDIERING

It's 0400, and you are shivering in the freezing cold of another night on an observation post overlooking a desolate no-man's land, a very tentative zone of separation between two bitter rival factions. Melted snow is dripping down your neck; you haven't raised your parka hood because it degrades your hearing too much. You wish these guys would just sign the peace accords and stop trying to kill each other (for the first time in 700 years). You wish you had a candy bar. You wish you could get five hours of uninterrupted sleep. Maybe your soldiers won't notice if you don't come around again until dawn. You climb out of your muddy hole and start your rounds of the bunker line. . . .

■ ■ ■

It's a magnificent day, the first in weeks. The sun is shining, there's a light breeze blowing, and a band is briskly trilling and thumping out Sousa marches. Beaming parents, giggling kids, and excited "significant others" fill the grandstands. The units are formed, the VIPs have taken their seats, and the reviewing party is about to take its place. . . .

■ ■ ■

It's late on a Saturday night, and you are going over the hand receipts for the millionth time, matching them to the printouts, checking off lines as your NCO in charge calls them off to you. It's been about three months since you had a date, and at this rate, it's no wonder. After getting back from the last National Training Center rotation, you went straight into a mission cycle during which you were on two-hour call for a month; now that *that's* over, you're in a support cycle, getting ready for the first command inspection your unit has had in over a year. You took over as supply officer last month; the records are a wreck. When does the mess hall open for Sunday brunch, anyway? "You got that one, sir?" asks your NCO, a little loudly. . . .

The sun is just coming up over East Garrison as you and your soldiers limp into the company area. The honorary sergeant major of the regiment, a leathery old man with your division's patch on his right shoulder—from the Korean War, when he earned the

Distinguished Service Cross for saving the colonel's life with a Red Chinese bayonet stuck in his side—is smiling the eternal smile of a satisfied NCO. He walked over 120 miles through knee-deep snow in North Korea with that hole in his side, all the way back to the Imjin River line. Now he's going to hand you a regimental coin for humping a measly 25 miles, with no one shooting at you. Your legs and feet don't feel so bad all of a sudden. . . .

■ ■ ■

Your RTO has just told you the CO is coming down to your sector to inspect it. You've been trying to get these refugees—errr, dislocated civilians— through your positions with minimum hassle, and now the colonel's coming down to check you out. "When did he say he'd be here?" you ask PFC Haines, and he says, "Said about one five, sir. Says to have someone out on the road to guide him in." Great. Who can you spare? All the NCOs and officers are still trying to get their guys' stuff together, making last-minute checks. Wait. That kid in the supply section, the new one. Seems really conscientious, even if his English isn't so good yet. Send him, he doesn't have much to do right now. "Sergeant Rheinschmidt, send that new guy up to the road and tell him to bring back the Old Man." Twenty minutes later, your RTO yells to you, "Hey sir, the colonel wants to know where the ground guide is, and he sounds pissed." You look uncomprehendingly toward the road and see that the new kid from Supply is prodding an elderly gentleman toward you with the muzzle of his rifle; he's clearly a straggler from the last gaggle of refugees, and he's terrified. "Here you are, Captain! I bring the old man." Your RTO says, "Sir, the colonel wants to talk to you, right now."

■ ■ ■

You've just come back from the field and are getting reacquainted with your family on your first weekend back after 10 days in the woods. The new lieutenant will probably work out OK, you think, but that buck sergeant in 3d Platoon was still awfully weak during the live fire. Hope he stays off the booze, too, this being his first weekend back, and him being at the point of no return in his alcohol rehab. Well, no use thinking about it now. Kids are asleep; wife's on the phone with her folks; her dad's not so good again. After almost two weeks without PT, a run would feel pretty good about now. You're passing the parade ground when the strains of Taps waft across the immense green field. Hadn't realized it was that late. Where does that grenade come from, the one it always feels like you've half swallowed when you hear those notes?

■ ■ ■

It happened again last night, but it's the first time in a long while. It's the same dream, though, and you're sweating hard. He was looking at you again with that silent scream, and then he was gone. He wasn't the only one who bought it that afternoon, and at least he went fast. But he took the one meant for you, and he knew he was doing it, too. You had to write the letter, but you didn't say you'd had to bust him for three days AWOL right before you got on the airplane. It's going to be another long night.

■ ■ ■

That face. You've stared at it for years, but it never seems to get boring. It's older now, there are lines that weren't there on your wedding day, about 8,000 days, 10 duty stations, three kids, a million or so field problems and deployments, and a couple of "operations other than war" ago, but you never get tired of it. And the youngest one seems to be getting it, too, as those teeth come in. Sometimes, you wonder if it's all been worth it.

If these anecdotes sound familiar, you've been in the Army for a while. If they don't, wait a few years—most of them will, although with luck, the worst ones still won't. If they sound meaningless to you, if they don't evoke the slightest twinge of recognition or interest, then the Army is probably not for you. If, however, you are somehow moved, amused, amazed, or at least a little intrigued, then read on, because these are real soldiers' anecdotes. It is especially about the officer's brand of soldiering, which carries its own particular nuances, customs, and duties, but any American soldier will recognize the content.

Throughout this work, the world *soldier* refers to anyone serving in the U.S. Army. Further differentiation is made among officers, noncommissioned officers (NCOs), warrant officers, and junior enlisted soldiers, where necessary.

THE OATHS WE TAKE

Most human cultures take oaths seriously, and the Army culture is one in which they are taken quite seriously indeed. There are two reasons for this. First, lives frequently depend on leaders' given words;

even in peacetime, even in garrison, the actions of leaders leave impressions or convey lessons that may have their ultimate impact—for better or worse—on some future battlefield. Leaders' given words must be unimpeachable, and oaths must be the most sacred promises of all. And so they are. When they enlist or reenlist, here is the oath that American soldiers take:

> I do solemnly swear (or affirm) that I will support and defend the Constitution of the United States against all enemies, foreign and domestic; that I will bear true faith and allegiance to the same; and that I will obey the orders of the President of the United States and the orders of the officers appointed over me, according to regulations and the Uniform Code of Military Justice. So help me God.

And here is the Army officer's oath:

> I (your name), having been appointed a (rank) in the United States Army, do solemnly swear (or affirm) that I will support and defend the Constitution of the United States against all enemies, foreign and domestic; that I will bear true faith and allegiance to the same; that I take this obligation freely, without any mental reservation or purpose of evasion, and that I will well and faithfully discharge the duties of the office upon which I am about to enter. So help me God.

The difference is obvious, but its meaning may not be clear. First, though, let us recognize what all American soldiers have in common. All must support and defend the Constitution against its enemies and remain loyal to it and its corollary way of government and life. This requires courage, commitment, discipline, selflessness, and regard for fellow citizens on the part of all soldiers—as it has since the founding of the Republic. These values motivated American soldiers to the extraordinary acts that are now our heritage. These values, corollary to our oaths, combine with those fulfilling acts to constitute the reasons behind the vast majority of our customs and courtesies—but not quite all.

The key difference in the oaths—the omission of the promise to *obey*—is what defines the differences between Army officers and enlisted soldiers. Officers are *legally* bound by the same UCMJ requirement to obey as are all other soldiers, but by their oath, they are not *morally* bound. Although it at first sounds like Orwellian "doublethink," it most assuredly is not. Officers are trusted by the American people (including enlisted soldiers), through their congressional representatives who approve commissions, with the enormous moral responsibility of knowing when to *not* obey. No system, however well thought out, however seemingly perfect, can conjure rules that are appropriate for every situation, every day. Army regulations, orders, doctrine, and so forth, are almost always right, but it is impossible to build any code of law whose logic or good sense will not at some point require a variance. That's where the officer comes in.

Officers are expected to exercise sound judgment, which sometimes—*rarely,* but sometimes—requires them to bend or break rules; to not obey those instructions, regulations, or orders that are not in the best interest of the Army at that moment. This is the single most formidable responsibility an officer can bear. This moral dispensation must never be used for personal gain or other corrupt ends. Further, although officers may be morally empowered to not obey, they are still *legally* and *morally* responsible for their actions, and it is up to the commanding officer to decide whether to exercise his or her judgment to prosecute an officer for exercising judgment in one of these exceptional situations.

If it sounds dicey, it is. The decision to not obey must never be taken lightly, and in the case of almost every order, directive, SOP, regulation, and the like, swift, cheerful obedience is the appropriate response. But knowing when to do otherwise—and doing it—is the essence of what sets officers apart from enlisted soldiers in the U.S. Army. From this single corollary of the oath, all other responsibilities flow. Officers are assigned to their duty positions because these positions require this kind of responsibility and judgment. The American people are not willing to entrust the lives of their sons and daughters—or vast quantities of their other treasure—to martinets who inflexibly follow rules for their own sake.

These differences in moral authority and their concomitantly higher responsibilities are also the main reasons why officers are paid more than NCOs. If you think it's because of officers' innately higher intelligence or better education or some other superiority, think again. There are many enlisted soldiers with IQs that leave those of many officers in the dust, and many of them are better

educated, too. Certainly, most officers *are* better educated than most enlisted soldiers, but that's because the Army believes that certain levels of education are essential for developing the character and perspective required for the proper exercise of the judgment and moral courage the Army expects of its officers in peace and war.

Because of this extremely special moral expectation and authority, officers' personal and professional conduct must remain above reproach. It is what dictates how we develop, evaluate, and promote officers. Although it is true for our whole Army, this difference makes it especially important that our officer corps remain a strict meritocracy, a system in which only the most competent, most prudent, most mature, most committed, most courageous officers are selected for advancement or promotion. To choose otherwise— for example, by caste or birthright, or political orthodoxy, or some other factors used in many other armies that are irrelevant to how officers exercise their commissions—is to court disaster. Such a process not only is a disservice to the American people, but it breaks faith with our subordinates, especially our enlisted soldiers, who—by *their* sacred oaths—are legally *and* morally bound to obey and therefore must trust their officers to "do the right thing."

In the army of the old Austro-Hungarian Empire, the emperor or empress had a medal that was awarded to officers who, by *disobeying orders,* turned the tide and won important battles. In the U.S. Army, of course, there is no such medal; this sort of judgment, wrapped within a full, disciplined understanding of the legal and moral impact of decisions, is *expected.* It is the essence of the U.S. Army officer corps.

THE ARMY IN WHICH WE SERVE

The Army in which a soldier serves is much more than his or her current unit; it is more than the sum total of all soldiers on active duty and in the reserve components today; it is more, even, than all of them plus the Department of Defense and other civilians and family members who work for and with the Army right now. Tomorrow, new soldiers will enlist; some will depart; others will retire or go on their final leave; new officers will be commissioned; and civilians will embark on and depart for new jobs for the Army. In most civilian corporations, this would not matter, for the bottom line is almost always money;

that's the way it is in a capitalistic society, and few Americans would want it any other way.

But in the Army, the bottom line is something different, so the nature of the organization is different, too. The Army's bottom line is the defense of the Constitution, which is gained by true service to the Republic. It must be defended, come what may, and soldiers are sworn to defend it to the death. Few Americans—and no well-adjusted ones—can be paid enough to put their lives, their families' welfare, and their futures on the line in the way soldiers are routinely called on to do. Soldiers implicitly put their lives on the line every day by their very presence in the Army, and that makes the Army a very *human* institution. It is this inherently human nature that makes the Army unique.

The Army is thus the sum of all past and present soldiers, civilians, and loved ones who have served it. Americans may be attracted to join the Army by a multitude of reasons—adventure, challenge, pay and benefits, or opportunities for service—but they do not die for them. British soldiers may die for monarch and regiment, Russian soldiers for their holy motherland, and soldiers of other nations for a dozen different causes, but American soldiers are ultimately willing to put their lives on the line mainly *for one another.* They need not only the camaraderie of those present but also the inspiration of those who have gone before to be willing to make the ultimate sacrifice. Thus, the Army is a living, breathing entity, changing in form, scope of tasks, and operational doctrine, and changeless in mission and fundamental morality.

ARMY HERITAGE

Heritage is based on history, the truth about the past. It is more than a dry collection of dates, places, pictures, and names in books; it is more than the artifacts under glass, lights, lock and key in museums or unit historical holdings. These are only the bones that build the framework, or the touchstones that help each of us form a better comprehension of our heritage as American soldiers. Army heritage is the legacy of those who have preceded us; it is the deeds they did, the standards they set, and the expectations they left for all of us. Any comprehensive, objective look at the Army's past, however, must ultimately conclude that the 225-year heritage of the U.S. Army is one of unparalleled courage, selflessness, sacrifice, commitment, and loyalty—the very same values we

must adhere to and cherish today. It is with this in mind that we should look to our veterans, living and dead, for inspiration and guidance with which to meet the uncertainties of the onrushing millennium.

In the Army, heritage is not just history, or even the inspiration and insights one can derive from its study. It is part of how we do business, day to day. It not only should be reflected in our every action but is, in fact, reflected in our customs and courtesies. No mere quaint holdovers of an irrelevant past, these are the living connections to our forebears. To a large extent, they are what makes us different from our comrades in the other uniformed services, as well as police, firefighters, and others who put their lives on the line in service to the community or nation. Our heritage and corollary customs and courtesies help our uniqueness as soldiers and help us remember who we are, what we do, and why.

ARMY CUSTOMS AND THEIR IMPORTANCE

A custom is an established usage. Customs include positive actions—things to do—and taboos—things to avoid doing. Like life itself, the customs that mankind observes are subject to a constant but slow process of change. Many practices that were habitual a generation or two ago have passed through a period of declining observance, and then into limbo. New customs arise to supplant the old. Others live on and on without apparent change. Humans are eager to rely upon established practice, upon precedent or custom, to an astounding degree. The realization that the action they are taking coincides with that which has been followed by others in similar circumstances bolsters their confidence, thus encouraging them to adhere to their course. Customs change with need; during a war period this process is greatly accelerated. But, whether old or new, the influence of custom is profound. It is man's attempt to apply to the solution of his immediate problems the lessons of the past. It is itself a custom. Army customs conform to the code of the Army officer, as they also conform to the established rules of military courtesy.

As long as harmonious human relations continue to be important, which will be a very long time indeed, the observance of useful, gracious, thoughtful customs will be important in the lives of the Army's officers and their families. The established customs have come into general use by evolution and represent the preferences of officers and their spouses. Customs enrich our life of national service. The new-comers are made welcome, given prompt opportunity to become known and to know others, to feel welcome and to "belong." Those who are departing receive a pleasant farewell. There are ceremonial ways that add to the color of military life. There are things to do and things to avoid doing. The sum of these customs adds appreciably to the interests, the pleasures, and the unique quality of Army life.

Life in the Army is colorful, interesting, and rich with friends and experiences. The customs and the courtesies help to establish these patterns. The glory of the Army is its fine people and the rewarding associations that may flow in abundance from its work and its life. It is a good life, a wholesome, interesting, rewarding life, if you learn its ways and grasp the opportunities extended. It can never be more to you than you, yourself, make it.

Many customs originating in antiquity are observed in our Army. They are forms of military pageantry, most of which are followed in one way or another in many armies. Although most professional military people are convinced that their life has greater interest and stimulation than other vocations, it is a fact that it has its drab aspects. These old customs add color, pageantry, and ceremony to daily life and deserve careful perpetuation. For the most part they consist of acts honoring the nation's flag or the military dead, or of paying respects to comrades in arms. Each heightens the concept of purposeful men and women serving their country in an honorable profession. For instance:

- The *salute* has an interesting history and is one of the most ancient and universal military customs. It is discussed later in this lesson.
- The *evening gun* is fired at the time of the retreat ceremony. It signifies the end of the normal military day, at which time the flag is lowered. It is an extremely old custom of armies, and one that is particularly appropriate to signal the arrival of retreat throughout a military reservation. This precedent extends over centuries.
- The *retreat ceremony* honors the nation's flag at the end of day. It was in use during the American Revolution, at which time it was sounded with drums. The retreat

parade, in which a ceremonial parade is combined with the retreat ceremony, including the sounding of the evening gun, is one of the most inspiring Army ceremonies. It is appropriate for all members of a garrison outdoors at the time to pause for a moment in salute to the nation's flag and the national anthem.

- The *"Sound Off"* and the *Three Cheers* occur during ceremonial parades when the adjutant commands, "Sound Off." The band, in place, plays the Sound Off of three chords. It then moves forward and, changing direction while playing a stirring march, troops the line or marches past the troops in formation, then returns to its post. Upon halting it sounds the Three Cheers. Some scholars believe that this custom originated at the time of the Crusades. The legend appears to have substance. At that time, when detachments were sent away on those faraway campaigns, it was the custom to assemble the garrison in formation with the departing troops in the place of honor on the right. The band of the period marched past troops being honored, much as is now done during Sound Off. Three cheers for their departing comrades were then given by the troops remaining behind. The simple notes of the Three Cheers could very well have this symbolic meaning. In any event, it is a pretty legend with logic as to its authenticity.
- The *three volleys over graves* is a special graveside ceremony honoring a military deceased and is an ancient custom in itself. After the committal service is read by the chaplain, a firing party fires three volleys with rifles. This ceremony is followed by a bugler sounding Taps from a position at the head of the casket over the grave. This completes the military funeral. Historians believe that military people in the 17th century used this custom. In concept it traces to the Romans, who honored their dead by casting earth three times upon the grave, calling the name of the dead, and saying "farewell" three times. It is also likened to the intent of saying an honorable farewell by the Three Cheers as used during the Crusades, discussed above.

- The *raising of the right hand in taking oath* comes from the earliest days when taking an oath as to the truth of statements or testimony was a solemn and serious matter accompanied by ceremony. In essence, it has always meant that the taker of the oath called upon God to bear witness that the truth would be told. Ancient men bared their heads and raised their arms in appeal to their deity as a symbol of truth and honesty.
- The *wearing of decorations* by individuals who have performed acts of military valor is very old in armies of history.
- The *wearing of unit badges or emblems* originated into our service during the Civil War.
- The *silver dollar salute* is the tradition that a newly commissioned second lieutenant presents a silver dollar to the first enlisted soldier who salutes him or her. The coin symbolically acknowledges the receipt of respect due the new rank and position.

MILITARY COURTESY

Courtesy is essential in human relationships. It stimulates the harmonious association of individuals, smoothes the conduct of affairs, and adds a welcome note to all manner of human contacts, civilian as well as military. It pertains to wholesome relationships between juniors and seniors, between young and old—with all persons. An essential element of courtesy is a full and proper appreciation of the rights of others. Military courtesy includes special acts and ceremonial procedures, which are prescribed in official regulations.

This subject is far more inclusive than the newcomer or the poorly informed person might consider to be the case. It includes the respect paid to the national flag and the national anthem; the courtesies appropriate for a soldier to extend to an officer or for a junior officer to extend to a senior officer, as well as the answering courtesies paid as a matter of course by the senior; the honors extended to high military or civilian dignitaries; and finally, the honors and respectful procedures extended to the military dead. There are many things to learn about military courtesy; by learning them, you will replace the embarrassments of ignorance with the confidence of knowledge.

The courtesies enjoyed within the service include as a matter of course all those common acts of civility, good breeding, and thoughtfulness observed by ladies and gentlemen of the American scene. You will see that there is nothing wrong with being military or with military courtesy; you will understand that the prescribed courtesies are a part of the ceremonial procedures that contribute color and dignity to our lives; they are a part of the discipline needed for the attack to succeed and the defense to hold; and they are a part of the comradeship that binds together servicemembers of all grades and ages who share the common responsibility of the nation's security.

An officer is expected to be a lady or a gentleman, and ladies and gentlemen have been defined as persons who are never intentionally rude.

THE TRADITION OF COMRADESHIP

The comradeship of military associates is the strongest and most enduring of Army customs. It is enjoyed by comrades in arms who have served together in some vast experience, such as a great campaign, where individual as well as group pride has developed. Age and grade are submerged here. It is an abiding trust and confidence in one's fellows that may develop swiftly in the crucibles of military service.

Men and women who are true comrades in arms have faith that when the chips are down each may depend fully upon his or her fellows. Ordinary soldiers will often choose the course of great hazard in the accomplishment of mission in preference to revealing themselves as weak in the eyes of their comrades. It is the ultimate in a feeling of belonging.

It is a powerful tradition. Here is the hidden ingredient that binds those who serve the nation with pride and competence as dependable associates, comrades in arms.

Officers' Call or the Stand-To

A special form of unit officer comradeship that has developed is the *stand-to* or *officers' call*. Expect to hear the directive, "All officers stand-to at 1730." This means to join the unit officers at their local club for drinks and conversation. Usually held on Fridays, the custom calls for lighthearted jesting about the events of the week, airing minor gripes, and blowing off a little steam. The point to understand is the totally informal atmosphere in which the commander and the unit officers—and occasionally their spouses—stand together celebrating the week's passing with that good feeling of mission accomplished.

This tradition persists, even with today's stronger laws governing the effects of drinking on public behavior and the official position deemphasizing the use of liquor. Most units make arrangements for designated drivers or other means of safe transportation. Officers should take advantage of these arrangements, so they can enjoy a fine tradition of camaraderie without endangering themselves, those around them, or their careers. Note, however, that consumption of alcohol is not a prerequisite to attendance and enjoyment of the stand-to. All unit officers should attend such functions.

Battalion Parties and Command Performances

Battalion parties and command performance parties are also a periodic custom, especially in areas where officers and their families live off post. Their purpose is to increase and strengthen acquaintances and to weld the interest of all members in their unit. They are held on the occasion of arrivals, departures, promotions, or just for the fun of it. These occasions serve many purposes of building unit cohesiveness and esprit. The term *command performance* is an informal description and is seldom, if ever, used in a formal sense. Still, if the word is passed informally that a battalion party is a command performance, there is a clear implication that your presence is expected. If they cost more than your current resources permit, or if you have sufficient reason to be elsewhere, tell your commander and request permission to be absent. He or she will accept your statement as reasonable and will not assume you to be antisocial, unfriendly, or unresponsive to the commander's implied desires. But it is better to attend and help make the affair successful.

Dining-In

The *dining-in* is a formal dinner function for members of a military organization or unit. The practice of dining-in is believed to have originated in the monasteries and early universities of England. The British military adopted the custom for use in the officers' mess. From there, it was picked up by the U.S. military forces during World Wars I and II and was an integral part of the old regimental mess. The practice of dining-in declined in popularity during and after World War II, but it is again becoming more prevalent.

The dining-in provides an occasion for the officers of a unit to meet socially. It may be used as an opportunity to welcome new officers, to bid farewell to departing officers, to honor distinguished visitors, or merely as a chance for the officers of a unit to get together socially as a means of building unit esprit. The dining-in should be viewed as an opportunity to enjoy the comradeship of one's fellow officers rather than as a mandatory function.

Careful, detailed planning is required to ensure that the occasion proceeds smoothly and enjoyably. The details of the dining-in vary according to its purpose, but those details must be thought through in advance. Formal invitations generally are in order, extended far enough in advance to elicit formal responses so that firm planning can proceed. The dinner menu may consist of from three to seven courses. Toasts are considered a mandatory part of the dining-in. Activities generally are divided into a predinner social period with cocktails, the formal dinner, and an informal period following the formal activities.

The formal portion of the dining-in includes the posting of the colors, an invocation if desired, appropriate toasts, introductory remarks by the presiding officer and introduction of guests, a toast to the guests, dinner service, conduct of the events of the evening, concluding remarks by the presiding officer, retirement of the colors, and adjournment to the informal period. The informal portion of a dining-in is often used for games or other entertainment. Although officers are expected to join in, they must continue to be guided by good taste and officers' behavior during this relaxed period. As with the officers' call or stand-to, most units make arrangements for transportation support for officers who have overindulged, and officers should take advantage of these arrangements.

A variation of the dining-in is the *dining-out,* which follows the general format of the dining-in but also includes the officers' spouses. The Protocol Office of the U.S. Military Academy at West Point produces an informative pamphlet on the conduct of a dining-in, which should be of considerable assistance to anyone planning such a function.

WELCOMES AND FAREWELLS

Reception of a Newly Joined Officer

It is custom that newly joined officers are cordially received and many acts of courtesy extended to the officer and his or her family to make their arrival more pleasant and convenient. It is taken for granted that a newly joined officer knows his or her professional duties and has every intention of performing them ably.

Except when conditions preclude such niceties, the adjutant sends a letter of welcome to an officer under orders to join, with information on local conditions that may be important or interesting for the officer to know before arrival. If the arrival is by train or plane, transportation may be arranged to meet the new arrival.

Most stations and most units welcome incoming families through the sponsor system, under which a designated military member and his or her family on the scene act as hosts and advisers to the new arrivals. Many officers believe that this one custom has been responsible for making more enduring friendships than any other. Certainly the warm welcome and thoughtful courtesies extended to newly arrived members of a unit go a long way to gain the good start.

The adjutant usually introduces the newly joined officer to the commanding officer and at the first assembly to the other officers of the unit. The adjutant should also inform the newcomer as to local regulations and customs that will be needed at once. A copy of the garrison regulations and a map of the post are especially useful to the stranger.

As newcomers, the officer and adult members of the family are usually welcomed at a battalion party, as described earlier. If you are the newcomers, make the most of the opportunity to meet and start acquaintanceships; if you are the old-timers, do your full share to make the occasion useful and pleasant.

Farewell Tendered a Departing Officer

Prior to the departure of an officer from his or her organization or station on change of assignment, a reception or other suitable function is usually given in honor of the departing officer and family. Often one of the unit social functions, called a "Hail and Farewell," is used for this purpose.

Receiving Officers of Sister Services

The officers of the host service accord a high degree of cordiality and hospitality to visiting officers from other services. This may include provisions for quarters, invitation to use an officers mess, extension of club privileges, social invitations, introduction of the visitor to appropriate officers, and the like. But it includes above all else the hand of fellowship and comradeship to a brother or sister officer to stimulate a feeling of being welcomed among friends.

Military Weddings

Military weddings follow the same procedures as any other, except for additional customs that add to their color and tone. Consult your chaplain for details and arrangements that will be suitable in making wedding plans. At military weddings, all officers should wear an appropriate dress uniform. Medals or ribbons may be worn with propriety. Badges may also be worn. Frequently, the national and unit colors are crossed just above and behind the position of the chaplain. The saber? In all likelihood, enough sabers to form the ceremonial arch of older days cannot be found. Perhaps if one is found it may be used for the first cut of the wedding cake as a polite bow to old tradition.

Reception of a Spouse

Bride and groom are usually introduced to the officers of the organization and their spouses at the next appropriate social function. Customs vary with conditions and with regard to official missions and times.

Birth of a Child

When a child is born to the family of an officer, the unit commander may send a personal letter of congratulations to the parents on behalf of the organization. The spouses of the unit officers may purchase a silver cup from their club funds with appropriate engraving. The unit commander sends a letter of congratulations to the enlisted man and his wife or to the enlisted woman and her husband.

Upon request of the parents, the organization color is usually made available for christenings so that the child may receive the ceremony under the colors of the member's organization. For the ceremony of baptism, both the national and organization colors may be made available.

CUSTOMS IN CONNECTION WITH SICKNESS AND DEATH

Visiting the Sick

An officer who is sick in the hospital is visited by the officers of the unit in such numbers as may be permitted by the physician. An officer or soldier of the officer's unit visits the sick officer daily to ensure that his or her comfort or desires receive attention.

An officer's spouse who is sick in the hospital receives flowers sent in the name of the officers of the unit and their wives or husbands.

Death of an Officer or Family Member

When an officer dies, another officer is immediately designated by the commanding officer to render every possible assistance to the bereaved family. A similar courtesy may be tendered, if desired, in the case of the death of a member of an officer's family.

A letter of condolence is written by the unit commander on behalf of the brigade, regiment, group, or similar unit. Flowers are sent in the name of the officers of the unit and their spouses.

Death of an Enlisted Soldier

When an enlisted soldier dies, a letter of condolence is written to the nearest relative by the immediate commander of the deceased soldier. Flowers are sent in the name of the members of the decedent's unit for the funeral. The funeral is attended by all officers and soldiers of the deceased soldier's unit who so desire and whose duties permit.

SUPPORT OF POST AND ORGANIZATION ACTIVITIES

General

An officer is expected to support the activities of the unit, such as a brigade or battalion, to which he or she is assigned, as well as the activities of the entire garrison. The unit to which you are assigned consists of a closely knit group around which are entwined official duties and athletic, social, and cultural activities for the benefit of all. You are a member of an official family. Your assignment must mean more than the place where your required and official duties are performed, important as they may be. You are expected to support and assist, at least by your presence, many events that form a part of military life. Proper interest and pride in all activities of your unit and garrison are factors in stimulating morale.

Each officer should be a good military citizen, sharing with other good citizens responsibility for the unofficial life and activities of the garrison. The development and maintenance of unit cohesion demands it.

The Officers' Club and Mess

The open mess, or officers' club, traditionally has been the nucleus around which revolves much of the off-duty social and recreational life of officers and their spouses. At a large station, there may be branches to serve the needs of separate organizations or of distant areas. Similar establishments are provided for noncommissioned officers. The open mess operates under the control of the station commander, subject to rules set forth in AR 230-60. Membership in the open mess is voluntary but is often strongly encouraged for officers assigned to the station, in some cases becoming almost a requirement.

In recent years, an American cultural change in attitude regarding alcohol consumption, coupled with the Army's zero-tolerance policy toward alcohol abuse, has resulted in a general decrease in club patronage. Many clubs today are struggling to make a profit, which they must do if they are to continue in operation. Particularly overseas, many officers' clubs and NCO clubs now share facilities. Nearly all clubs in the United States welcome station civilian employees to help defray expenses. The traditional role of the open mess as the center of social and recreational activity for officers and their families thus may be changing. Still, if there is an open mess in operation at your station, you are encouraged to become a member and use its facilities.

Attendance at Unit and Organization Parties Sponsored by Enlisted Members

It is customary for officers and their spouses, when invited, to attend special social events sponsored by enlisted members of a unit or organization. Conditions vary so widely throughout the service that no general customs can be identified. The best source of guidance is the commanding officer.

In general, officers, or officers and their spouses, are invited only on special occasions. When invited, officers attend in their official capacity to assist in enhancing pride of service, morale, and esprit. In conduct, they are mindful of the normal social amenities and are guided by the example set by the senior officer present. If the unit or organization is authorized to serve intoxicants, it is accepted practice for the officer to drink in marked moderation; the non-drinker should ask for a soft drink, without excuse. Excessive drinking, exhibitionist dancing, and other ungentlemanly or unladylike behavior would harm the purpose of attendance and are frowned upon. At an appropriate time and after the customary amenities, officers depart with or immediately after the senior officer attending, leaving the party for the enjoyment of its enlisted members.

Attendance at Athletic Events

As a matter of policy, to demonstrate an interest in organization affairs as well as for personal enjoyment, officers should attend athletic events in which their unit teams participate.

Ceremonies at Holiday Dinners

On Thanksgiving, Christmas, and New Year's Day, many organizations have a tradition that the officers visit the companies during the meal or prior to the serving of the meal. The method varies widely. As an example, only the brigade, battalion, or similar commander, his or her staff, and field officers visit the dining facility just prior to the serving of dinner. Officers of the company, their families, and families of married enlisted men of the company may dine with the companies on these holidays.

THE CORRECT USE OF TITLES

Each member of the Army has a military grade, private to general, and this grade becomes his or her military title by force of regulation and custom. In official documents, a member's grade, or title, always accompanies his or her name; it is also used in conversation. Listed below are several illustrations. Through custom and usage, military titles are used between civilians and the military, just as custom has established the usage of "Doctor," "Professor," or "Governor."

A person who has attained a military title carries it permanently, if so choosing, including into retirement.

When addressing a subordinate, preface the soldier's last name with his or her rank. "Sergeant Jones," "Lieutenant Smith," or "Private Henderson" are appropriate means of addressing fellow soldiers of subordinate rank. Conversationally, placing a slight emphasis on the pronunciation of the rank, rather than the name, is pleasing to most ears and is better at eliciting

attention than placing emphasis on the name, which may be more likely to evoke fear or alarm.

When referring to others not present, always use ranks and names. Use of last names only is disrespectful; use of pay grades (e.g. "I was talking to an O-4" or "It was that E-7") is unmilitary and degrading. All soldiers have earned their ranks, from the newest private first class to the most senior general; use them accordingly.

Titles of Commissioned Officers

Lieutenants are addressed officially as "Lieutenant." The adjectives "First" and "Second" are not used except in written communications. The same principle holds for other ranks. In conversation and in nonofficial correspondence (other than in the address itself), brigadier generals, major generals, and lieutenant generals are usually referred to and addressed as "General." Lieutenant colonels, under the same conditions, are addressed as "Colonel."

Senior officers may sometimes address subordinates as "Smith" or "Jones," but this does not give the subordinate the privilege of addressing the senior in any way other than by the senior's proper title.

"Ma'am" may be used in addressing a female officer under circumstances when the use of "sir" would be appropriate in the case of a male officer. All chaplains are officially addressed as "Chaplain," regardless of their military grade or professional title.

Warrant Officers

The warrant officer formally ranks below second lieutenant and above cadet. He or she is extended the same privileges and respect as a commissioned officer and differs only in that there are certain regulated restrictions on command functions. The warrant officer is the Army's top-grade specialist and is addressed as "Mister" or "Miss (Mrs.)," as appropriate. Under less formal situations, warrant officers are often addressed as "Chief."

Titles of Cadets

Cadets of the U.S. Military Academy and the Reserve Officers Training Corps are addressed as "Cadet" officially and in written communications. Under less formal situations, they are addressed as "Mister" or "Miss."

Noncommissioned Officers

Sergeants major are addressed as "Sergeant Major." A first sergeant is addressed as "First Sergeant." Other sergeants, regardless of grade, are addressed simply as "Sergeant," and a corporal is addressed as "Corporal." Specialists are addressed as "Specialist." Privates First Class are addressed as "PFC," whereas privates (in the pay grades E-1 or E-2) are addressed as "Private." The full titles of enlisted members are used in official communications.

Use of Titles by Retired Personnel

Individuals retired from the armed services not on active duty are authorized to use their titles socially and in connection with commercial enterprises, subject to prescribed limitations. Official signatures will include the designated retired status after the grade, thus, "USA Retired" will be used by members on the U.S. Army Retired List (Regulars); "AUS Retired" will be used by those on the Army of the United States List.

CUSTOMS OF RANK

The Place of Honor

The place of honor is on the right. Accordingly, when a junior walks, rides, or sits with a senior, the junior takes position abreast and to the left of the senior. The deference that a young officer should pay to his or her elders pertains to this relationship. The junior should walk in step with the senior, step back and allow the senior to be the first to enter a door, and render similar acts of consideration and courtesy.

Use of the Words "Sir" and "Ma'am"

The words "Sir" and "Ma'am" are used in military conversation by the junior officer in addressing a superior and by all soldiers in addressing officers. It precedes a report and a query; it follows the answer of a question. For example: "Sir, do you wish to see Sergeant Brown?" "Sir, I report as Officer of the Day." "Private Brown, Ma'am." "Thank you, Sir."

Departing Before the Commanding Officer

Officers should remain at a reception or social gathering until the commanding officer has departed.

New Year's Call on the Commanding Officer

It is Army tradition that officers and their spouses make a formal call on the commanding officer during the afternoon of New Year's Day. The pressures of the current Army mission, the desires of the commanding officer, and local or major unit custom bear upon the holding of this event and the way it is done.

As a general guide, when the commanding officer elects to hold the event, timely information is provided as to the time and place and the uniform to be worn. Branch blazers may be authorized. At large stations, the event usually is held at the officers' open mess as a reception with a receiving line; it may include a dance with light refreshments. If the senior commander does not hold the event, commanders of component units such as the brigade or battalion may choose to do so. Official funds are not provided to defray the costs. Officers whose duties of the day permit are expected to attend. In any case, think of it as a pleasant ceremonial social function, adding color to the military scene, starting the New Year in a spirit of general comradeship.

Appointments with the Commanding Officer

It is the custom to ask the adjutant, the executive officer, or an aide, as appropriate, for an appointment with the commander or other senior officer. There is no special formality about it. Just inquire, "May I see the commanding officer?" Often it is appropriate to state the reason. Take your minor administrative problems to an appropriate staff officer of your own headquarters and avoid consuming the time of your commanding officer. Save your personal requests to him or her for major matters that others cannot resolve or resolve as well.

Permission of the First Sergeant

It is the custom that enlisted personnel secure permission from the first sergeant before speaking to the company commander. It is essential to discipline that each soldier knows that he or she has the right to appeal directly to the commander for redress of wrongs.

The Open-Door Policy

The soldier's right to speak to the company commander is echoed by each commander at a higher level. It is the "open-door" policy that permits each person in the Army, regardless of rank, to appeal to the next higher commander. Indeed, this right is checked and enforced by the Inspector General. It is not uncommon for a private soldier to talk to the battalion commander, since many administrative matters are performed by the battalion staff. The officer needs to expect this and not be arbitrary about barring his or her door to soldiers. Usually, if there is disagreement between a soldier and an officer, or a soldier believes that he or she has a real grievance, the soldier has the right to speak to the next senior commander and to have the matter resolved. However, prior to taking a problem to the next higher commander, a soldier should have attempted to resolve the problem using the soldier's chain of command.

TABOOS

Do Not Defame the Uniform

The officer's uniform and official or social position must not be defamed. Conduct unbecoming an officer is punishable under Article 133, Uniform Code of Military Justice. The confidence of the nation in the integrity and high standards of conduct of the officers of the Army is an asset that no individual may be permitted to lower.

Never Slink Under Cover to Avoid Retreat

As a good military person, always be proud and willing to pay homage and respect to the national flag and the national anthem. Now and then, thoughtless people in uniform are observed ducking inside a building or under other cover just to avoid a retreat ceremony and the moment of respect it includes. Or are they merely displaying their ignorance as to the purpose of the ceremony? Never slink away from an opportunity to pay respect to our flag and our anthem.

Spouses and children of Army families will wish to stand at attention and face the colors, too, if the ceremony is explained to them.

Proffer No Excuses

Never volunteer excuses or explain a shortcoming unless an explanation is required. The Army demands results. More damage than good is done by proffering unsought excuses. For the most part, an officer gains respect by admitting a mistake and bearing the consequences.

Do Not Associate Inappropriately

It is strong Army tradition that an officer does not associate with enlisted soldiers as individuals in ordinary social affairs, nor gamble, nor borrow or lend money, nor drink intoxicants with them.

Note, however, that in the Army of today it is increasingly likely that junior officers are assigned quarters in close proximity to NCO or enlisted quarters, perhaps even occupying adjacent units in multiunit buildings. Under such circumstances, socialization by children and spouses is not only unavoidable but is acceptable and even encouraged. Socialization as families is also fine during group cookouts or similar activities. However, care is needed to avoid situations in which such socialization could be construed by others as evidence of favoritism toward the NCO or enlisted member.

Do Not Use Third Person

It is in poor taste for officers to use the third person in conversation with their seniors. For example, do not say, "Sir, does the colonel desire. . . ?" Instead, say, "Sir, is it your desire. . . ?" Most senior officers frown on the use of the third person under any condition, as it is regarded as a form of address implying servility.

Avoid Praising the Commander to His or Her Face

Paying compliments directly to the commander or chief is in poor taste. However genuine your high regard for your chief may be, to express it suggests apple-polishing or flattery and thus may be misinterpreted. If you particularly admire your boss, you can show it by extending the standard military courtesies—and meticulously carrying out his or her policies and doing all in your power to make the organization more effective.

With respect to subordinates, however, recognition of good work on their part is an inherent part of the exercise of command; do not hesitate to commend a subordinate whose actions are praiseworthy.

Use the Phrase "Old Man" with Care

The commanding officer acquires the accolade "the Old Man" by virtue of his position and without regard to his age. When the term is used, it is more often in affection and admiration than otherwise. However, it is never used in the presence of the commanding officer; doing so would be considered disrespectful.

Avoid "Going over an Officer's Head"

The jumping of an echelon of command is called going over an officer's head (for example, a company commander making a request of the brigade commander concerning a matter that should have been presented to the commander of his or her battalion first). The act is contrary to military procedure and decidedly disrespectful. (See the earlier discussion on the open-door policy.)

Avoid Harsh Remarks

The conveying of gossip, slander, harsh criticism, and faultfinding is an unofficerlike practice. In casual conversation, if you can find nothing good to say about a person, it is wiser to say nothing at all.

Avoid Vulgarity and Profanity

Foul and vulgar language larded with profanity is repulsive to most self-respecting men and women. Its use by officers is reprehensible. An officer is expected to be a lady or a gentleman, and however the traditional terms are defined, certainly they exclude the use of vulgarity and profanity in conversation.

Never Lean on a Superior Officer's Desk

Avoid learning or lolling against a senior officer's desk. It is resented by most officers and is unmilitary. Stand erect unless invited to be seated.

Never Keep Anyone Waiting

Report at once when notified to do so. Never keep anyone waiting unnecessarily. On the drill field, when called by a senior officer, go on the double.

Avoid Having People Guess Your Name

Do not assume that an officer whom you have not seen or heard from for a considerable period will know your name when a contact is renewed. Tell him or her at once who you are, and then renew the acquaintance. If this act of courtesy is unnecessary, it will be received only as an act of thoughtfulness; if it happens to be necessary, it will save embarrassment. At official receptions, always announce your name to the aide.

Do Not Carry an Umbrella in Uniform

There is a long-standing Army taboo against a male officer in uniform carrying an umbrella. However, it is both authorized and proper for women in the Army to do so when not in formation.

Do Not Smoke

The Army officially discourages smoking, both for reasons of personal health and in deference to the rights of nonsmokers. Smoking is not permitted in public buildings. Smoking by spectators during outdoor ceremonies, such as parades, also is considered objectionable. Indoors, in quarters or other areas where smoking may be permitted, a considerate officer who smokes should be sensitive to the rights of others.

NCOs Do Not Work on Fatigue

A custom said to be as old as the Army is that which exempts NCOs from performing manual labor while in charge of a fatigue detail or while on fatigue.

LOCAL CUSTOMS: A WORD OF CAUTION

There is a tendency to confuse customs, traditions, and social obligations. Customs of the service that have been treated in this chapter are those that are universally observed throughout the Army. Traditions are much less formal than the recognized customs of the service. There are many more traditions than could be covered here. Many are confined to a particular unit, organization, station, or branch of service, and one is likely to become acquainted with them quickly upon reporting for a new assignment. Such traditions may catch on and become widespread because of the mobile nature of Army life, especially those that have a positive influence on one's personal living.

There is a danger, however, in expecting that others will accept a particular tradition once you are outside the area where it has been observed. For example, many inquiries have been received as to why previous editions of *Army Officer's Guide* offered no counsel about how an officer recognizes his or her promotion in relation to fellow officers and civilian coworkers, if any. Research into this question reveals that, officially, there is no custom of the service to provide guidance, nor is thee any well-entrenched tradition anywhere. Inasmuch as promotion is a personal thing and has differing degrees of meaning at various times and places, an officer may choose to do something or nothing, the former on any scale that befits his or her mood, position, or pocketbook at the time.

You are cautioned to get acquainted with local traditions and customs and to be sure that you are not a party of unjustified criticism of anyone when there is no tangible understanding in the local military community about what one does on any particular occasion.

THE SEVERAL MILITARY SALUTES

History of the Military Salute

Men of arms have used some form of the military salute as an exchange of greeting since the earliest times. It has been preserved and its use continued in all modern armies that inherit their military traditions from the Age of Chivalry. The method of rendering the salute has varied through the ages, as it still varies in form among the armies of today. Whatever form it has taken, it has always pertained to military personnel, and its use has been definitely restricted to those in good standing.

In the Age of Chivalry, the knights were all mounted and wore steel armor that covered the body completely, including the head and face. When two friendly knights met, it was the custom for each to raise the visor and expose his face to the view of the other. This was always done with the right hand, the left being used to hold the reins. It was a significant gesture of friendship and confidence, since it exposed the features and also removed the right hand—the sword hand—from the vicinity of the weapon. Also, in ancient times, the freemen (soldiers) of Europe were allowed to carry arms; when two freemen met, each would raise his right hand to show that he held no weapons in it and that the meeting was a friendly one. Slaves were not allowed to carry arms, and they passed freemen without the exchange of a greeting. In the Middle Ages, gentlemen often went about clothed in heavy capes under which swords were carried; upon meeting a friend, the cloak was thrown back by raising the right arm, thus disclosing that the right hand was not on the sword hilt.

The military salute is given in recognition to a comrade in the honorable profession of arms. The knightly gesture of raising the hand to the visor came to be recognized as the proper greeting between soldiers and was continued even after modern firearms had made suits of armor a thing of the past. The military salute of today is as it has always been, a unique form of greeting between military personnel.

The Different Forms of the Salute

There are several forms in which the prescribed salutes are rendered. The officer normally uses the hand salute; however, when under arms, he or she uses the salute prescribed for the weapon with which armed. Under certain circumstances, when in civilian clothes and saluting the flag or national anthem, the member salutes by placing the right hand over the heart; if a male officer is wearing a headdress, he salutes by first removing the headdress and holding it in his right hand, such that the hand is over the heart while the headdress is over the left shoulder. In this lesson, unless stated otherwise, the hand salute is intended.

When to Use the Hand Salute and the Salute with Arms (AR 600-25)

Outdoors, all Army personnel in uniform are required to salute at all times when they meet and recognize persons entitled to the salute, except in public conveyances, such as trains and buses, or in public places, such as theaters, or when a salute would be manifestly inappropriate or impractical.

Salutes are exchanged between officers (commissioned and warrant) and between officers and enlisted personnel. Salutes are exchanged with personnel of the U.S. Army, Navy, Air Force, Marine Corps, and Coast Guard entitled to the salute. It is customary to salute officers of friendly foreign nations when recognized as such. Civilians may be saluted by persons in uniform when appropriate, but the uniform hat or cap is not raised as a form of salutation.

Military personnel under arms render the salute prescribed for the weapon with which they are armed, whether or not that weapon ordinarily is prescribed as part of their equipment.

If the exchange of salutes is otherwise appropriate, it is customary, although optional, for military members in civilian clothing to exchange hand salutes upon recognition. Civilian personnel, including civilian guards, do not render the hand salute to military personnel or to other civilian personnel.

Except in formation, when a salute is prescribed, the individual either faces the person or colors saluted or turns the head so as to observe the person or colors saluted.

Covered or uncovered, salutes are exchanged in the same manner.

If running, a person comes to a walk before saluting.

The smartness with which the officer or soldier gives the salute indicates the degree of pride the member has in his or her military responsibilities. A careless or halfhearted salute is discourteous.

Methods of Saluting Used by Officers

The hand salute is the usual method. Although in most instances it is rendered while standing or marching at attention, it may be rendered while seated (e.g., an officer seated at a desk who acknowledges the salute of an officer or soldier who is making a report).

The salute by placing the *right hand over the heart* is used under three conditions. At a military funeral, all military personnel dressed in civilian clothes use this form of salute in rendering courtesies to the deceased. Male members of the services in civilian clothes and *uncovered* (without headdress) and female members in civilian clothes, *uncovered* or *covered* (with headdress), salute this way during the national anthem, "To the Color," or "Hail to the Chief." While in the same dress, this salute is used in paying homage to the national flag or color. Males in civilian clothing who are covered stand at attention, holding the hand over the heart with the headdress held in the right hand over the left shoulder as a courtesy to the national anthem or to the national flag or color.

Execution of the Hand Salute

Before the instant arrives to render the salute, stand or walk erectly with head up, chin in, and stomach muscles pulled in. Look squarely and frankly at the person to be saluted. If you are returning the salute of a soldier, execute the movements of the salute in the cadence of marching, *one, two.* If you are saluting a superior officer, execute the first movement and *hold* the position until the salute is acknowledged, and then complete your salute by dropping the hand smartly to your side. Do these things correctly and you will derive many rewards. Your soldiers will be quick to notice it and will vie with you in efforts to outdo their officer—a particularly healthy reaction. Thus you may set the example, which may then be extended to other matters.

To execute the hand salute correctly, raise the right hand smartly until the tip of the forefinger touches the lower part of the headdress or forehead above and slightly to the right of the right eye, thumb and fingers extended and joined, palm to the left, upper arm horizontal, forearm inclined at 45 degrees, hand and wrist straight; at the same time turn the head toward the person saluted. To complete the

salute, drop the arm to its normal position by the side in one motion, at the same time turning the head and eyes to the front.

The junior member executes the first movement, holds the position until it is returned by the senior, and then executes the second movement.

Accompanying the hand salute with an appropriate greeting, such as "Good morning, Sir," and its reply, "Good morning, Sergeant," is encouraged.

The salute is rendered within saluting distance, which is defined as the distance within which recognition is easy. It usually does not exceed 30 paces. The salute is begun when about 6 paces from the person saluted or, in case the approach is outside that distance, 6 paces from the point of nearest approach.

Some of the more frequently observed errors in saluting are these: failure to hold the position of the salute until it is returned by the officer saluted; failure to look at the person or color saluted; failure to assume the position of attention while saluting; failure to have the thumb and fingers extended and joined, a protruding thumb being especially objectionable; a bent wrist (the hand and wrist should be in the same plane); failure to have the upper arm horizontal. Gross errors include saluting with a cigarette in the right hand or in the mouth or saluting with the left hand in a pocket or returning a salute in a casual or perfunctory manner.

Uncovering

Officers and enlisted personnel under arms as a general rule do not uncover except when:

> Seated as a member of or in attendance on a court or board. (Sentinels over prisoners do not uncover.)
>
> Entering places of divine worship.
>
> Indoors when not on duty and it is desired to remain informal.
>
> In attendance at an official reception.

Interpretations of "Indoors" and "Outdoors"

The term *outdoors* includes such buildings as drill halls, gymnasiums, and other roofed enclosures used for drill or exercise of troops. Theater marquees, covered walks, and other shelters open to the sides where a hat may be worn are also considered outdoors.

When the word *indoors* is used, it is construed to mean offices, hallways, dining halls, kitchens, orderly rooms, amusement rooms, bathrooms, libraries, dwellings, or other places of abode.

Meaning of the Term "Under Arms"

The expression *under arms* is understood to mean with arms in hand or having attached to the person a hand, arm or the equipment pertaining directly to the arm, such as cartridge belt or pistol holster.

Cannon Salute

In addition to the salutes rendered by individuals, the regulations (AR 600-25) prescribe the occasions and the procedures for rendering cannon salutes. A salute with cannon (towed, self-propelled, or tank mounted) is fired with a commissioned officer present and directing the firing. Salutes are not fired between retreat and reveille, on Sundays, or on national holidays (excluding Memorial and Independence Days) unless, in the discretion of the officer directing the honors, international courtesy or the occasion requires the exception. They are rendered at the first available opportunity thereafter, if still appropriate. The interval between rounds is normally three seconds.

The *Salute to the Union* consists of firing one gun for each state. It is fired at 1200 hours, Independence Day, at all Army installations provided with necessary equipment.

The *National Salute* consists of 21 guns. It is fired at 1200 hours on Memorial Day. The national flag, displayed at half-staff from reveille until noon on this day, is then hoisted to the top of the staff and so remains until retreat. In conjunction with the playing of appropriate music, this is a tribute to honored dead.

Mourning Salutes are rendered on the occasion of the death and funeral of the President or the Vice President of the United States, and other high civil and military dignitaries, as prescribed in AR 600-25. The number of guns and the accompanying honors to be rendered to high dignitaries are shown in a chart later in this chapter.

The flag of the United States, national color, or national standard is always displayed at the time of firing a salute, except when firing a salute to the Union on the day of the funeral of a President, ex-President, or President-elect. On these occasions, the salute is fired at five-second intervals immediately following lowering of the flag at retreat. Personnel do not salute.

Application of Saluting Rules

The general rules for exchange of salutes are stated in an earlier paragraph. Covered or uncovered, salutes are exchange in the same manner. The salute is rendered only once if the senior remains in the immediate vicinity and no conversation takes place.

A group of enlisted personnel or officers within the confines of military posts, camps, or stations and not in formation, on the approach of a more senior officer, is called to attention by the first person noticing the senior officer; if in formation, by the one in charge. If outdoors and not in formation, they all salute; in formation, the salute is rendered by the person in charge. If indoors, not under arms, they uncover.

Drivers of vehicles salute only when the vehicle is halted. Gate guards salute recognized officers in all vehicles. Salutes otherwise are not required by or to personnel in vehicles, although gate guards normally salute an officer's vehicle when so recognized. Members in civilian attire need not exchange salutes but are encouraged to do so upon recognition. Also, military headgear need not be worn while in other than official vehicles.

Organization and detachment commanders (commissioned and noncommissioned) salute officers of higher grades by bringing the organization to attention before saluting, except when in the field.

In making reports at formations, the person making the report salutes first, regardless of rank. An example of this is the case of a battalion commander rendering a report to the adjutant at a ceremony.

Members of the Army are urged to be meticulous in rendering salutes to, and in returning salutes from, fellow Army members and personnel of the sister services. Such soldierly attitudes enhance the feeling of respect that all should feel toward comrades in arms. *The salute must never be given in a casual or perfunctory manner.*

When Not to Salute

Salutes are *not* rendered by individuals in the following cases:

- An enlisted member in ranks and not at attention comes to attention when addressed by an officer.
- Details (and individuals) at work. The officer or noncommissioned officer in charge, if not actively engaged at the time, salutes or acknowledges salutes for the entire detail.
- When actively engaged in games such as baseball, tennis, or golf.
- While crossing a thoroughfare, not on a military reservation, when traffic requires undivided attention.

- In churches, theaters, or places of public assemblage, or in a public conveyance.
- When carrying articles with both hands, or when otherwise so occupied as to make saluting impractical. Still, a "Good morning, Sergeant," or "Good afternoon, Sir," is manifestly appropriate.
- When on the march in combat, or under simulated combat conditions.
- While a member of the guard who is engaged in the performance of a specific duty, the proper execution of which would prevent saluting.
- On duty as a sentinel armed with a pistol. He or she stands at *raise pistol* until the challenged party has passed.
- The driver of a vehicle in motion is not required to salute.
- Indoors, except when reporting to a senior.

Reporting to a Superior Officer in His or Her office

When reporting to a superior officer in his or her office, the subordinate (unless under arms) removes any headdress, knocks, and enters when told to do so. Upon entering, the subordinate marches up to within about two paces of the officer's desk, halts, salutes, and reports in this manner, for example: "Sir, Private Jones reports to Captain Smith," or "Sir, Lieutenant Brown reports to the Battalion Commander." After the report, conversation is carried on in the first or second person. When the business is completed, the subordinate salutes, executes about-face, and withdraws. A subordinate uncovers (unless under arms) upon entering a room where a senior officer is present.

Courtesies Exchanged When an Officer Addresses a Soldier

In general, when a conversation takes place between an officer and a soldier, the following procedure is correct: Salutes are exchanged; the conversation is completed; salutes are again exchanged. *Exceptions:* An enlisted soldier in ranks comes to attention and does not salute. Indoors, salutes are not exchanged except when reporting to an officer.

Procedures When an Officer Enters a Dining Facility

When an officer enters a dining facility, enlisted personnel seated at meals remain seated at ease and con-

tinue eating unless the officer directs otherwise. An individual addressed by the officer ceases eating and sits at attention until completion of the conversation. In an officers' mess, although other courtesies are observed through custom, the formalities prescribed for enlisted men and women are not in effect.

Procedure When an Officer Enters a Squad Room or Tent

In a squad room or tent, individuals rise, uncover (if unarmed), and stand at attention when an officer enters. If more than one person is present, the first to perceive the officer calls, "Attention."* In officers' quarters, such courtesies are not observed.

Entering Automobiles and Small Boats

Military personnel enter automobiles and small boats in inverse order of rank; that is, the senior enters an automobile or boat last and leaves first. Juniors, although entering the automobile first, take their appropriate seat in the car. The senior is always on the right.

COURTESIES TO THE NATIONAL FLAG

The Flag of the United States

There are four names in use for the flag of the United States: *flag, color, standard,* and *ensign.*

The *national color,* carried by dismounted units, measures 3 feet hoist by 4 feet fly and is trimmed on three sides with golden yellow fringe 2-1/2 inches in width. The *standard,* identical to the *color,* is the name traditionally used by mounted, motorized, or mechanized units. The *ensign* is the naval term for the national flag (or flag indicating nationality) of any size flown from ships, small boats, and aircraft. When we speak of flags we do not mean colors, standards, or ensigns.

There are four common sizes of our national flag. The *garrison flag* is displayed on holidays and special occasions. It is 20 feet by 38 feet. The *post flag,* 10 feet by 19 feet, is for general use. The *storm flag,* 5 feet by 9 feet 6 inches, is displayed during stormy weather. The *grave decorating flag* is 7 inches hoist by 11 inches fly.

---

*On suitable occasions the officer commands "Rest," "As You Were," or "At Ease" when expecting to remain in the room and not desiring them to remain at attention.

Organization colors

Regiments and separate battalions, whose organization is fixed by tables of organization, are authorized to have organization colors symbolic of their branch and past history. Such units are "color-bearing organizations." The size is the same as the national color. The word *color,* when used alone, means the national color; the term *colors* means the national color and the organization or individual color.

Individual Colors

Individual colors, 4 feet 4 inches hoist by 5 feet 6 inches fly, are authorized the President, Vice President, cabinet members and their assistants, the Chairman of the Joint Chiefs of Staff, the Chief of Staff, and the Vice Chief of Staff, U.S. Army.

Pledge to the Flag

According to congressional resolution, 22 December 1942, the following pledge of allegiance should be rendered while standing, with the right hand over the heart:

> I pledge allegiance to the flag of the United States of America and to the republic for which it stands, one nation under God, indivisible, with liberty and justice for all.

Reveille and Retreat

The daily ceremonies of reveille and retreat constitute a dignified homage to the national flag at the beginning of the day, when it is raised, and at the end of the day, when it is lowered. Installation commanders direct the time of sounding reveille and retreat.

At every installation garrisoned by troops other than caretaking detachments, the flag is hoisted at the sound of the first note of reveille. At the last note of retreat, a gun is fired if the ceremony is on a military reservation, at which time the band or field music plays the national anthem or sound "To the Color" and the flag starts to be lowered. The lowering of the flag is regulated so as to be completed at the last note of the music. The same respect is observed by all military personnel whether the national anthem is played or "To the Color" is sounded.

The Flag at Half-Staff

The national flag is displayed at half-staff on Memorial Day until noon as a salute to the honored dead, and upon the death and funeral of military personnel and high civilian dignitaries (AR 600-25).

When the flag is displayed at half-staff it is first hoisted to the top of the staff and then lowered to the half-staff position. Before lowering the flag it is again raised to the top of the staff. For an unguyed flagstaff of one piece, the middle point of the hoist of the flag should be midway between the top and the bottom of the staff.

Memorial Day

On Memorial Day (the last Monday in May) the national flag is displayed at half-staff from reveille until noon at all Army installations. Immediately before noon the band plays an appropriate air, and at 1200 hours the national salute of 21 guns is fired at all installations provided with the necessary equipment for firing salutes. At the conclusion of the salute, the flag is hoisted to the top of the staff and remains so until retreat. When hoisted to the top of the staff, the flag is saluted by playing appropriate patriotic music by a band or a bugler or from a recording, depending on availability. In this manner, tribute is rendered the honored dead.

Independence Day

On Independence Day (4 July), a 50-gun salute to the Union commemorative of the Declaration of Independence is fired at 1200 hours at all Army installations provided with the necessary equipment for firing salutes. When Independence Day occurs on a Sunday, the salute is fired the following day.

Flag Day

Flag Day is celebrated on 14 June, upon proclamation by the President. It calls upon officials of the government to display the flag on all government buildings and urges the people to observe the adoption on 14 June 1777, by the Continental Congress, of the Stars and Stripes as the official flag of the United States of America.

Salute to the President's Flag

When the President of the United States, aboard any vessel or craft flying the President's flag, passes an Army installation that is equipped to fire salutes, the installation commander causes the national salute to be fired.

Salute to Passing Colors

When passing or being passed by the uncased national color, military personnel render honors by executing a salute appropriate to their dress and formation as indicated previously. If indoors and not in formation, personnel assume the position of attention but do not salute. If the colors are cased, honors are not required.

Reception of an Officer on Board a Naval Vessel

The salutes to be exchanged upon boarding a naval vessel and leaving a naval vessel are prescribed in the following paragraph of United States Navy Regulations, to which all members of the Army visiting a naval vessel will conform (AR 600-25):

2108. Salutes to the National Ensign.
  1. Each person in the naval service, upon coming on board a ship of the Navy, shall salute the national ensign if it is flying. He shall stop on reaching the upper platform of the accommodation ladder, or the shipboard end of the brow, face the national ensign, and render the salute, after which he shall salute the officer of the deck. On leaving the ship, he shall render the salutes in inverse order. The officer of the deck shall return both salutes in each case.
  2. When passed by or passing the national ensign being carried, uncased, in a military formation, all persons in the naval service shall salute. Persons in vehicles or boats shall follow the procedure prescribed for such persons during colors.
  3. The salutes prescribed in this article shall also be rendered to foreign national ensigns and aboard foreign men-of-war.

For further information on Navy courtesies and customs, see Navy Customs Army Officers Should Know, later in this reading.

Dipping the Flag or Colors

The flag of the United States, national color, and national standard are never dipped by way of salute of compliment. The organizational color or standard is dipped in salute in all military ceremonies while the U.S. national anthem, "To the Color," or a foreign national anthem is being played, and when rendering honors to the organizational commander or an individual of higher grade, including foreign dignitaries of higher grade, but in no other case.

The U.S. Army flag is considered to be an organizational color and as such is also dipped while the U.S. national anthem, "To the Color," or a foreign national anthem is being played and when rendering honors to the Chief of Staff of the U.S. Army, his direct representative, or individual of higher grade, including foreign dignitary of equivalent or higher grade, but in no other case.

The authorized unit color salutes in all military ceremonies while the national anthem or "To the Color" is being played and when rendering honors to the organizational commander or an individual of higher rank, but in no other case.

Display and Use of the Flag

International usage forbids the display of the flag of one nation above another nation's in time of peace. When the flags of two of more nations are to be displayed, they should be flown from separate staffs, or from separate halyards, of equal size and on the same level.

The national flag, when not flown from a staff or mast, should always be hung flat, whether indoors or out. It should not be festooned over doorways or arches, tied in a bowknot, or fashioned into a rosette. When used on a rostrum, it should be displayed above and behind the speaker's desk. It should never be used to cover the speaker's desk or to drape over the front of the platform. For this latter purpose, as well as for decoration in general, bunting of the national colors should be used, and the colors should be arranged with the blue above, the white in the middle, and the red below. Under no circumstances should the flag be draped over chairs or benches, nor should any object or emblem of any kind be placed above or upon it, nor should it be hung where it can be easily contaminated or soiled. When carried with other flags, the national flag should always be on the right (as color-bearers are facing) or in front. The flag of the United States of America should be at the center and at the highest point of the group when a number of flags of states or localities or pennants of societies are grouped and displayed from staffs.

When flown at a military post, or when carried by troops, the national flag or color is never dipped by way of salute of compliment. The authorized unit color is dipped as a salute when the reviewing officer has the rank of a general officer. This is done by lowering the pike (as the staff of a color is called) to the front so that it makes an angle of about 45 degrees

How To Display the Flag

1. When displayed over the middle of the street, the flag should hang vertically with the union to the north in an east-and-west street or to the east in a north-and-south street.
2. When displayed with another flag from crossed staffs, the U.S. flag should be on the right (the flag's own right), and its staff should be in front of the staff of the other flag.
3. When flying the flag at half-staff, the flag detail should first hoist the flag to the peak and then lower it to the half-staff position, but before lowering the flag for the day, they should again raise it to the peak.
4. When flags of states or cities or pennants of societies fly on the same halyard with the U.S. flag, the U.S. flag should always be at the peak.
5. When the flag hangs over a sidewalk from a rope extending from house to pole at the edge of the sidewalk, the flag should go out from the building, toward the pole, union first.
6. When the flag is on display from a staff projecting horizontally or at any angle from the windowsill, balcony, or front of a building, the union of the flag should go to the peak of the staff (unless the flag is to be at half-staff).
7. When the flag covers a casket, the union should be at the head and over the left shoulder of the deceased. The flag should not be lowered into the grave or allowed to touch the ground.
8. When the flag is on display other than by flying from a staff, it should be flat whether indoors or out. When displayed either horizontally or vertically against a wall, the union should be uppermost and to the flag's own right—that is, to the observer's left. When displayed in a window, it should appear the same way—that is, with the union or blue field to the left of the observer in the street.
9. When carried in a procession with another flag or flags, the U.S. flag should be either on the marching right or, when there is a line of other flags, in front of the center of that line.
10. When a number of flags of states or cities or pennants of societies are grouped on display from staffs with our national flag, the U.S. flag should be at the center or at the highest point of the group.
11. When the flags of two or more nations are on display, they should fly from separate staffs of the same height, and the flags should be of about equal size. International usage forbids displaying the flag of one nation above that of another nation in time of peace.

with the ground. The national flag is used to cover the casket at the military funeral of present or former members of the military service. It is placed lengthwise on the casket with the union at the head and over the left shoulder of the deceased. The flag is not lowered into the grave and is not allowed to tough the ground.

The display and use of the flag by civilian groups is contained in Public Law 829—77th Congress, as amended by Public Law 344—94th Congress.

Display of United Nations Flag

There are no U.S. laws or policies adopted by the United Nations that cause conflict in the display of the U.S. flag in conjunction with the United Nations flag. When the two flags are displayed together, the U.S. flag is on the right, best identified as "the marching right." This is in accordance with U.S. law. The United Nations flag code states that it can be on either side of a national flag without being subordinate to that flag. Both flags should be of the same size and displayed at the same height.

It should be noted that the United Nations flag may be displayed at military installations of the United States or carried by U.S. troops only on very specific occasions, such as the visit of high dignitaries of the United Nations, when the United Nations or high dignitaries thereof are to be honored, or as authorized by the president (AR 840-10).

COURTESIES TO THE NATIONAL ANTHEM

Whenever and wherever the national anthem, "To the Color," or "Hail to the Chief" is played outdoors, at the first note all dismounted personnel in uniform and not in formation, within saluting distance of the flag, face the flag, or the music if the flag is not in view, salute, and maintain the salute until the last note of the music is sounded. This includes personnel in athletic uniform. Men not in uniform remove the headdress with the right hand and hold it at the left shoulder with the hand over the heart. If no headdress is involved, they stand at attention holding the right hand over the heart. Women not in uniform should salute by placing the right hand over the heart.

Vehicles in motion are brought to a halt. Persons riding in a passenger car or on a motorcycle dismount and salute. Occupants of other types of military vehicles and buses remain seated at attention in the vehicle, the individual in charge of each vehicle dismounting and rendering the hand salute. Tank and armored vehicle commanders salute from the vehicle.

The above marks of respect are shown to the national anthem of any friendly country when it is played at official occasions.

When the national anthem is played indoors, officers and enlisted personnel stand at attention and face the music, or the flag if one is present. They do not salute unless under arms. At reveille, the procedures outline above are followed.

The method and personnel required for raising and lowering the flag on a flagstaff are prescribed in FM 26-5, *Interior Guard Duty.*

MILITARY FUNERALS

The military funeral, with its customs, precision, and courtesies, can be a source of great comfort and pride to the bereaved when executed correctly; if not executed correctly, it can add to their grief.

Officers should be thoroughly familiar with the prescribed courtesies to the military dead. This involves a knowledge of the ceremonies incident to the conduct of a military funeral, including correct procedure on the following occasions:

Officer in charge of a funeral.

Honorary pallbearer.

Command of a funeral escort

Attendance as a mourner.

Essential references are AR 600-25 and FM 22-5.

Courtesies at a Military Funeral

At a military funeral, all persons in the military service in uniform attending in their individual capacity face the casket and execute the hand salute at any time when the casket is being moved, while the casket is being lowered into the grave, during the firing of the volley, and while Taps is being sounded. Honorary pallbearers in uniform conform to these instructions when not in motion. Male personnel in civilian clothes, in the above cases and during the service at the grave, stand at attention, uncovered, and hold the headdress over the left breast; if no headdress is worn, the right hand is held over the heart. Female personnel except the active pallbearers follow the example of the officiating chaplain. If he uncovers, they uncover; if he remains covered, they remain covered. When the officiating chaplain wears a biretta (clerical headpiece) during the graveside service, all personnel uncover. When the officiating chaplain wears a yarmulke (skullcap), all personnel remain covered.

The active pallbearers remain covered and do not salute while carrying the casket and while holding the flag over the casket during the service at the grave.

Female military personnel remain covered during military funerals.

Badge of Military Mourning

The badge of military mourning is a straight band of black crepe or plain black cloth 4 inches wide, worn around the left sleeve of the outer garment above the elbow. No badge of military mourning is worn with the uniform, except when prescribed by the commanding officer for funerals, or when specially ordered by the Department of the Army. As family mourning, officers are authorized to wear the sleeve band described above while at the funeral or en route thereto or therefrom (AR 670-5).

Elements of a Military Funeral Ceremony

The military funeral ceremony that has been developed to demonstrate the nation's recognition of the debt it owes to the services and sacrifices of soldiers is based on a few simple customs and traditions. The casket of the soldier is covered with the American flag. It is usually transported to the cemetery on a caisson.† It is carried from the caisson to the grave by six military body bearers. In addition to the body bearers, honorary pallbearers are usually designated who march to the cemetery alongside the caisson. At the cemetery, the casket is placed over the grave, and the body bearers hold the flag-pall waist high

---

†Since caissons are no longer used in the Army, except by the Old Guard at Arlington National Cemetery, the vehicle carrying the casket is generally a civilian hearse or sometimes a light, open Army truck or an ambulance adapted for the purpose. This should be understood whenever the word *caisson* is employed in this description.

over the casket. After the committal service is read by the chaplain, a firing party fires three volleys. A bugler stationed at the head of the grave sounds Taps over the casket, and the military funeral is completed. The body bearers then fold the flag, and it is presented to the next of kin. These basic elements are the foundation of all military funerals, whether last rites are being conducted over a private's casket or final honors are being paid at the grave of a general.

Honorary Pallbearers

The honorary pallbearers arrive at the chapel before the hearse arrives. They take positions in front of the entrance to the chapel in two facing ranks. Upon arrival of the hearse and when the body bearers remove the casket from the hearse, honorary pallbearers execute the hand salute.

When the casket is carried between the two ranks that they have formed, they come to the order of attention, execute the appropriate facing movement, fall in behind the casket, and enter the chapel, the senior preceding the junior and marching to the right. In the chapel, they take places in the front pews to the left of the chapel.

After the chapel service, the honorary pallbearers precede the casket in columns of twos as the two active pallbearers push the church truck to the chapel entrance. The honorary pallbearers again form an aisle from the chapel entrance to the caisson or hearse and uncover or salute as prescribed. When the casket has been placed on the caisson or in the hearse, they enter their conveyances or march. When marching, the honorary pallbearers form columns of files on each side of the caisson or hearse, the leading member of each column opposite the front wheels of the caisson or hearse.

When the entrance to the burial lot is reached, the honorary pallbearers take positions on either side of the entrance. As the body bearers lift the casket from the caisson, the honorary pallbearers execute the hand salute.

When the casket has been carried past them, they come to the order and fall in behind the casket, marching to the grave site in correct precedence of rank, senior to the right and to the front.

At the grave site, they stand in line behind the chaplain at the head of the grave; the senior stands to the right and the junior to the left. They execute the hand salute during the firing of volleys, the sounding of Taps, and the lowering of the casket into the grave.

After the ceremony is over, they march off in two files behind the colors.

Family

The family arrives at the chapel before the casket is received and is seated in pews in the right front of the chapel.

When the chapel service is over, family members follow the casket down the aisle until they reach the vestibule of the chapel, where they wait until the casket is carried outside and secured to the caisson.

When the procession is ready to form, members of the family take their places in the procession immediately behind the body bearers. When the procession arrives at the grave site, the members of the family wait until the band, escort, and colors have taken their positions at the grave, and the casket is carried between the double rows of honorary pallbearers. The members of the family take their positions at the side of the grave opposite the earth mound side for the funeral service.

When the graveside ceremony is finished, a member of the family receives the interment flag from the chaplain, the cemetery representative, the officer in charge of the funeral, or the individual military escort. Upon this ending of the service, it has become customary for close friends to express regrets to the bereaved at the graveside.

Significance of the Military Funeral

The ceremonial customs that constitute the elements of all military funerals are rooted in ancient military usage. In many cases, these traditions are based on expedients used long ago on the battlefield in time of war. The use of a caisson as a hearse, for example, was an obvious combat improvisation. In a similar manner, the custom of covering the casket with a flag probably originated on the battlefield where caskets were not available and the flag, wrapped around the dead serviceman, served as a makeshift pall in which he could be buried. Later, these customs assumed a deeper significance than that of mere expediency. The fact that an American flag is used to cover the casket, for example, now symbolizes the fact that the soldier served in the armed forces of the United States and that this country assumes the responsibility of burying the soldier as a solemn and sacred obligation.

Finally, the sounding of Taps over the grave has an obvious origination in military custom. Since Taps is the last bugle call the soldier hears at night, it is particularly appropriate that it be played over his grave to mark the beginning of his last, long sleep and to express hope and confidence in an ultimate reveille to come.

NAVY CUSTOMS ARMY OFFICERS SHOULD KNOW

Courtesies

There are Navy customs applicable to shore duty and to the special situations of life on board a naval vessel. The courtesies pertaining to a naval vessel are of interest to officers of the Army when they visit or serve aboard a unit of our fleet.

On appropriate occasions when visiting naval vessels, officers of the armed services, except when in civilian clothes, are attended by sailors known as side boys when they come aboard and when they depart. This courtesy is also extended to commissioned officers of the armed services of foreign nations. Officers of the rank of lieutenant to major inclusive are given two side boys, from lieutenant colonel to colonel four side boys, from brigadier to major general six side boys, and lieutenant general and above eight side boys. Full guard and band are given to general officers, and for a colonel, the guard of the day, but no music.

During the hours of darkness or low visibility, an approaching boat is usually hailed "Boat ahoy?" which corresponds to the sentry's challenge, "Who is there?" Some of the answers are as follows:

Answer	Meaning: Senior in boat is:
"Aye aye"	Commissioned officer
"No no"	Warrant officer
"Hello"	Enlisted
"Enterprise"	CO of Enterprise
"Seventh Fleet"	Admiral commanding Seventh Fleet

Similarly, if the commanding general of the 1st Infantry Division is embarked or the commanding general of Fort Monroe, the answers would be "1st Infantry Division" or "Fort Monroe."

On arrival, at the order "Tend the side," the side boys fall in fore and aft of the approach to the gangway, facing each other. The boatswain's mate-of-the-watch takes station forward of them and faces aft. When the boat comes alongside, the boatswain's mate pipes and again when the visiting officer's head reaches the level of the deck. At this latter instant the side boys salute.

On departure, the ceremony is repeated in reverse; the boatswain's mate begins to pipe and side boys to salute as soon as the departing officer steps toward the gangway between the side boys. As the boat casts off, the boatswain's mate pipes again. (Shore boats and automobiles are not piped.)

You uncover when entering a space where men are at mess and in sick bay (quarters) if sick men are present. You uncover in the wardroom at all times except when under arms and passing through. All hands uncover in the captain's cabin and country, except when under arms.

You should not overtake a senior, except in emergency. In the latter case, slow, salute, and say, "By your leave, Sir." Admirals, commanding officers, and chiefs of staff when in uniform fly colors astern when embarked in boats. When officials visit, they also display their personal flags (pennants for commanding officers) in the bow. Flag officers' barges are distinguished by the appropriate number of stars on each side of the barge's hull. Captains' gigs are distinguished by the name or abbreviation of their ships surcharged by an arrow.

Use of Navy Titles

In the Navy it is customary to address officers in the grade of lieutenant commander and below, *socially,* as "Mister" or "Miss," and officers in the grade of commander and above by their titles. *Officially,* officers in both staff and line are addressed by their ranks.

Title of Commanding Officer of a Ship

Any officer in command of a ship, regardless of size or class, while exercising command is addressed as "Captain."

Visiting

Seniors come on board ship first. When reaching the deck, you face toward the colors (or aft if no colors are hoisted) and salute the colors (quarterdeck). Immediately thereafter you salute the officer of the deck (OOD) and request permission to come aboard. The usual form is, "Request permission to come aboard, Sir." The OOD is required to return both salutes.

On leaving the ship, the reverse order is observed. You salute the OOD and request permission to leave the ship. The OOD indicates when the boat is ready (if a boat is used). Each person, juniors first, salutes the OOD, then faces toward the colors (quarterdeck), salutes, and debarks.

The OOD on board ship represents the captain and as such has unquestioned authority. Only the executive and commanding officer may order him or her relieved. The authority of the OOD extends to the accommodation ladders or gangways. The OOD has the right to order any approaching boat to "lie off" and keep clear until the boat can be safely received alongside.

The OOD normally conveys orders to the embarked troops via the troop commander but in emergencies may issue orders direct to you or any person on board.

The *bridge* is the "command post" of the ship when under way, as the quarterdeck is at anchor. The OOD is in charge of the ship as the representative of the captain. Admittance to the bridge when under way should be at the captain's invitation or with his or her permission. You may usually obtain permission through the executive officer.

The *quarterdeck* is the seat of authority; as such it is respected. The starboard side of the quarterdeck is reserved for the captain (and admiral if a flagship). No person trespasses upon it except when necessary in the course of work or official business. All persons salute the quarterdeck when entering upon it. When pacing the deck with another officer the place of honor is outboard, land when reversing direction each turns toward the other. The port side of the quarterdeck is reserved for commissioned officers, and the crew has all the rest of the weather decks of the ship. However, every part of the deck (and the ship) is assigned to a particular division so that the crew has ample space. Not unnaturally, every division considers it has a prior though unwritten right to its own part of the ship. For gatherings such as movies, all divisions have equal privileges at the scene of assemblage. Space and chairs are reserved for officers and for CPOs, where available, and mess benches are brought up for the enlisted personnel. The seniors have the place of honor. When the captain (and admiral) arrives those present are called to attention. The captain customarily gives "carry on" at once through the executive officer or master-at-arms.

Messes

If you take passage on board a naval vessel, you will be assigned to one of several messes on board ship, the wardroom or junior officers' mess. In off-hours, particularly in the evenings, you can gather there for cards, yarns, or reading. A pot of coffee is usually available.

The executive officer is ex-officio the president of the wardroom mess. The wardroom officers are the division officers and the heads of departments. All officers await the arrival of the executive officer before being seated at lunch and dinner. If it is necessary for you to leave early, ask the head at your table for permission to be excused, as you would at home. The seating arrangement in the messes is by order of seniority.

Calls

Passenger officers should call on the captain of the ship. If there are many of you, you should choose a calling committee and consult the executive officer as to a convenient time to call. The latter will make arrangements with the captain.

Ceremonies

Gun salutes in the Navy are the same as in the Army, except that flag officers below the rank of fleet admiral or general of the Army are, by Navy regulations, given a gun salute upon departure only.

Saluting

By custom, Navy personnel do not salute when uncovered, although it is customary for Navy officers to return the salute of Army and Air Force personnel whether covered or not. Aboard ship, seniors are saluted only during the first greeting in the morning. The commanding officer (or any flag or general officer) is saluted whenever met.

AIR FORCE CUSTOMS ARMY OFFICERS SHOULD KNOW

Courtesies

The rules governing saluting, whether saluting other individuals or paying honor to the color or national anthem, are the same for the Air Force as for the Army.

Visiting

It is assumed that the majority of officers visiting an Air Force base are there in conjunction with air travel to or from the base. In addition to the base operations officer, who is the commander's staff officer with jurisdiction over all air traffic, the transient alert crew is charged with meeting all transient aircraft, determining the transportation requirements of transient personnel, and directing them to the various base facilities. General officers and admirals usually are met by a senior base officer. RON (remain overnight) messages may be transmitted through base operations.

Passengers from other services who desire to remain overnight at an Air Force base should make the necessary arrangements with the transient alert crew and not attach themselves to the pilot, who will be busy with his or her own responsibilities. By the same token, passengers of other services who have had a special flight arranged for them should make every effort to see that the pilot and crew are offered the same accommodations that they themselves are using, unless that base has adequate transient accommodations.

Passenger vehicles are never allowed on the ramp or flight lines unless special arrangements have been made with the base operations officer; this permission is granted only under unusual circumstances.

Travel in Military Aircraft

The assigned first pilot, or the airplane commander, is the final authority on the operation of any military aircraft. Passengers, regardless of rank, seniority, or service, are subject to the orders of the airplane commander, who is solely responsible for their adherence to regulations governing conduct in and around the aircraft. In the event it is impractical for the airplane commander to leave his or her position, orders may be transmitted through the copilot, engineer, or crew chief and have the same authority as if given personally by the pilot.

The order of boarding and alighting from military aircraft—excluding the crew—varies somewhat with the nature of the mission. If a special flight is arranged for the transportation of very important persons (VIPs), official inspecting parties or other high-ranking officers of any service, the senior member exits first, and the other members of the party follow either in order of rank or in order of seating, those nearest the hatch alighting first.

In routine transportation flights, officers are normally loaded in order of rank without regard for precedence, except that VIPs are on- and off-loaded first. In alighting, officers seated near the hatch generally debark first, and so on to those who are farthest away. In the event dependents are being carried, they together with their sponsor generally are loaded and unloaded after any VIPs and before the officers.

Aircraft carrying general or flag officers are usually marked with a detachable metal plate carrying stars appropriate to the highest rank aboard and are greeted on arrival by the Air Force base commander, if the destination is an Air Force base. Other aircraft are usually met by the airdrome officer, who is appointed for one day only and acts as the base commander's representative.

Since aerial flights are somewhat dependent on weather, especially when carrying passengers, the decision of the pilot to fly or not to fly or to alter the flight plan en route cannot be questioned by the passengers of whatever rank or service. Regulations governing smoking, the use of seatbelts, and the wearing of parachutes are binding on all classes of passengers.

SALUTES AND HONORS TO DISTINGUISHED OFFICERS

Certain military and civil officials in high position, including foreign officials, are accorded personal honors consisting of cannon salutes, ruffles and flourishes played by field music, and the national anthem of our country or of the foreign country, the "General's March," or a march played by the band. These honors are extended upon presentation of the escort and as part of the parade or review of troops. The accompanying chart (from AR 600-25) states the specific honors of all persons who may be accorded them. A military escort is supplied during their rendition.

Ruffles and Flourishes

Ruffles are played on drums, flourishes on bugles. They are sounded together, once for each star of the general officer being honored and according to the accompanying table of honors for other dignitaries. Ruffles and flourishes are followed by music as prescribed in the table.

Action of the Person Receiving the Honors

It is the usual custom for the person receiving the honors to inspect the escort. The appropriate time to do this is at the conclusion of the honors rendered by the escort upon his or her reception.

During the playing of the ruffles and flourishes and music, as indicated in the chart, the person honored and those accompanying him or her, if members of the armed forces, salute at the first note of the ruf-

ENTITLEMENT TO HONORS

Grade, Title, or Office	Number of Guns Arrival	Departure	Ruffles and Flourishes	Music
President	21	21	4	National anthem or "Hail to the Chief," as appropriate.
Ex-President or President-elect	21	21	4	National anthem.
Sovereign or Chief of State of a foreign country	21	21	4	National anthem of foreign country, "Hail Columbia"
Vice President	19	—	4	
Speaker of the House of Representatives	19	—	4	March.
American or foreign ambassador, or high commissioner while in country to which accredited	19	—	4	National anthem of United States or official's country.
Premier or Prime Minister	19	—	4	National anthem of United States or official's country.
Secretary of Defense	19	19	4	March.
Cabinet members, President protempore of Senate, governor of a state, or Chief Justice of the United States	19	—	4	March.
Deputy Secretary of Defense	19	19	4	March.
Secretary of the Army	19	19	4	March.
Secretary of the Navy or Air Force	19	19	4	March.
Director of Defense Research and Engineering	19	19	4	March.
Chairman, Joint Chiefs of Staff	19	19	4	General's or admiral's march, as appropriate.
Chief of Staff, United States Army; Chief of Naval Operations; Chief of Staff, United States Air Force; or Commandant of the Marine Corps	19	19	4	General's or admiral's march, as appropriate.
General of the Army, Fleet Admiral, or General of the Air Force	19	19	4	General's or admiral's march, as appropriate.
Assistant Secretaries of Defense and General Counsel of the Department of Defense	17	17	4	March.
General or admiral	17	17	4	General's or admiral's march, as appropriate.
Governor of a territory or foreign possession within the limits of his jurisdiction	17	—	4	March.
Chairman of a Committee of Congress	17	—	4	March.
Under Secretary of the Army	17	17	4	March.
Under Secretary of the Navy or Air Force	17	17	4	March.
Assistant Secretaries of the Army	17	17	4	March.
Assistant Secretaries of the Navy or Air Force	17	17	4	March.
American envoys or ministers and foreign envoys or ministers accredited to the United States	15	—	3	March.
Lieutenant general or vice admiral	15	—	3	General's or admiral's march.
Major general or rear Admiral (upper half)	13	—	2	General's or admiral's march, as appropriate.
American ministers resident and ministers resident accredited to the United States	13	—	2	March.
American charges d'affaires and charges d'affaires accredited to the United States	11	—	1	March.
Brigadier general or rear admiral (lower half)	11	—	1	General's or admiral's march.
Consuls general accredited to the United States	11	—	—	March.

fles and flourishes and remain at the salute until the last note of the music. Persons in civilian clothes salute by uncovering.

Action of Persons Witnessing the Honors

Members of the armed forces who witness the salutes and honors render the hand salute, conforming to the action of the official party. Individuals in civilian clothing uncover.

PRECEDENCE OF MILITARY ORGANIZATIONS IN FORMATION

Whenever two or more organizations of different components of the armed forces appear in the same formation, they take precedence among themselves in order as listed below. This means from right to left in line, the senior organization on the right; and from head to tail of a column, the senior organization at the head (AR 600-25).

> Cadets, United States Military Academy
>
> Midshipmen, United States Naval Academy
>
> Cadets, United States Air Force Academy
>
> Cadets, United States Coast Guard Academy
>
> Midshipmen, United States Merchant Marine Academy

United States Army

United States Marine Corps

United States Navy

United States Air Force

United States Coast Guard

Army National Guard of the United States

Army Reserve

Marine Corps Reserve

Naval Reserve

Air National Guard of the United States

Air Force Reserve

Coast Guard Reserve

Other training organizations of the Army, Marine Corps, Navy, Air Force, and Coast Guard in order, respectively

During any period when the U.S. Coast Guard operates as a part of the U.S. Navy, the cadets, U.S. Coast Guard Academy, the U.S. Coast Guard, and the Coast Guard Reserve take precedence, respectively, next after the midshipmen, U.S. Naval Academy, the U.S. Navy, and the Naval Reserve.

CULTURE OF THE ARMY

FM 22-10

When you're first sergeant, you're a role model whether you know it or not. You're a role model for the guy that will be in your job. Not next month or next year, but ten years from now. Every day soldiers are watching you and deciding if you are the kind of first sergeant they want to be.

An Army First Sergeant 1988

3-58.   Culture is a longer lasting, more complex set of shared expectations than climate. While climate is how people feel about their organization right now, culture consists of the shared attitudes, values, goals, and practices that characterize the larger institution. It's deeply rooted in long-held beliefs, customs, and practices. For instance, the culture of the armed forces is different from that of the business world, and the culture of the Army is different from that of the Navy. Leaders must establish a climate consistent with the culture of the larger institution. They also use the culture to let their people know they're part of something bigger than just themselves, that they have responsibilities not only to the people around them but also to those who have gone before and those who will come after.

3-59.   Soldiers draw strength from knowing they're part of a tradition. Most meaningful traditions have their roots in the institution's culture. Many of the Army's everyday customs and traditions are there to remind you that you're just the latest addition to a long line of American soldiers. Think of how much of your daily life connects you to the past and to American soldiers not yet born: the uniforms you wear, the martial music that punctuates your day, the way you salute, your title, your organization's his-

tory, and Army values such as selfless service. Reminders of your place in history surround you.

3-60.   This sense of belonging is vitally important. Visit the Vietnam Memorial in Washington, DC, some Memorial Day weekend and you'll see dozens of veterans, many of them wearing bush hats or campaign ribbons or fatigue jackets decorated with unit patches. They're paying tribute to their comrades in this division or that company. They're also acknowledging what for many of them was the most intense experience of their lives.

3-61.   Young soldiers want to belong to something bigger than themselves. Look at them off duty, wearing tee shirts with names of sports teams and famous athletes. It's not as if an 18-year-old who puts on a jacket with a professional sports team's logo thinks anyone will mistake him for a professional player; rather, that soldier wants to be associated with a winner. Advertising and mass media make heroes of rock stars, athletes, and actors. Unfortunately, it's easier to let some magazine or TV show tell you whom to admire than it is to dig up an organization's history and learn about heroes.

3-62.   Soldiers want to have heroes. If they don't know about SGT Alvin York in World War I, about COL Joshua Chamberlain's 20th Maine during the Civil War, about MSG Gary Gordon and SFC Randall Shughart in the 1993 Somalia fight, then it's up to you, their leaders, to teach them.

3-63.   When soldiers join the Army, they become part of a history: the Big Red One, the King of Battle, Sua Sponte. Teach them the history behind unit crests, behind greetings, behind decorations and badges. The Army's culture isn't something that exists apart from you; it's part of who you are, something you can use to give your soldiers pride in themselves and in what they're doing with their lives.

THE TIES THAT BIND: The Army Officer's Moral Obligations[1]

BY DON M. SNIDER AND GAYLE L. WATKINS

INTRODUCTION

A recent study by respected historians Donald and Frederick Kagan summarizes the effects of United States defense policy in the 1990s as follows: "Beginning in 1994, reports began to surface that the readiness of the armed forces to fight a war on short notice was eroding—training could not be paid for, equipment was breaking down, overworked people were burning out and leaving the services. The House and Senate armed forces committees began taking testimony and uncovered many problems. By 1998 it was widely recognized that the readiness of the armed forces had eroded seriously."[2]

In geopolitical terms, these historians conclude that "the international situation has already begun to slip from our control. The [1991 Gulf War] coalition has shattered; NATO and the United States risk drifting apart. Challengers to the status quo proliferate, along with weapons of mass destruction and the means to deliver them."[3] Moreover, they believe that such measures as are now being taken to remedy the situation are far from adequate: "The military deficit is probably already too great for any 'reasonable' politician to contemplate, and it will only get worse. Not only have readiness and 'quality of life' issues (which affect recruiting and retention of qualified people) suffered badly, but the experiences of even the past few years show that the armed forces are too small. Worse than that, since at least 1995, the Department of Defense has been forced to reprogram money earmarked for modernization toward readiness and current operations. The systems that America will need to fight the major war of 2010 or 2020 are not now in place and are being developed too slowly or not at all. America is not ready now to face a major challenge, and current plans, even in light of current proposals to increase the defense budget, will not make it ready to face a major challenger in the future."[4]

Indeed, since the beginning of the post-Cold War era, the civilian masters of armies throughout the Western world—not alone the United States—seem to have found themselves largely at a loss as to what to do with their sizeable standing armies. For example, they have wondered what their armies' proper jurisdiction should be, what place their armies should occupy in their societies, and what kind of moral standards should be expected of the members of those armies. Evidence of this general air of uncertainty has typically manifested itself in three ways:

1. Drastic defense budget reductions based on the assumption that armies of Cold War proportions are no longer needed;
2. Assignment to those armies of missions well outside the scope of the labor traditionally reserved for armies alone; and
3. Formulation of foreign policies that seek full economic engagement with the world—an engagement totally dependent on international tranquillity—without accounting adequately for the self-serving agendas of power-hungry despots ready to expand their influence as soon as they realize that they will be unopposed militarily.

The answer to questions about what to do with or expect of armies in the twenty-first century may, in fact, be knowable only as more obvious threats to world peace emerge than now seem to exist. However, recognition of this uncertainty does little to assuage the concerns of reflective U.S. Army officers interested not only in the day-to-day performance of individual military duty, but also interested in the long-term welfare of the nation and its Army. Such reflection is healthy and productive for leaders committed to the proposition that the institution entrusted to their care by the nation must survive the test of time. Moreover, the act of questioning what the Army's role should be and how it should set out to accomplish the tasks that lie ahead is certain to produce, as it already measurably has, a desire on the part of its leadership to transform the Army as necessary to ensure that it is relevant to the times. As the 1999 Fletcher Conference observed, "The Army has proclaimed that 'Everything is on the Table' as it pursues transformation."[5] Indeed, *everything should* be on the table if the Army is to gain an honest assessment of its current status and make the changes necessary to maintain its "non-negotiable contract with the American people to fight and win our Nation's wars"[6] in a rapidly changing world.

However, the fact that the Army has placed everything on the table as it undergoes its transformation does not mean, and cannot mean, that everything necessarily must change. Reflective Army leaders certainly realize this as they confront questions of the kind that the leaders of any enduring profession must answer:

1. What does it mean to belong to a profession? That is to say, what obligations does membership in the profession entail?

2. Are there any "fixed points," i.e., professional commitments that never change, or does everything that it means to be a member of the profession hinge ultimately on factors external to the institution (in the case of armies, for example, the international situation or the perceived threat, or perhaps on less glamorous notions such as supply and demand, budget cycles, and the like)?

3. What enduring moral obligations are entailed by membership in the profession? In the case of the U.S. Army, the question becomes, "What is the nature of the moral bond of obligation—if, indeed, such a bond actually exists or should exist—between the U.S. Army officer corps and the nation it serves and the soldiers it leads?"

This reading will argue that, no matter how extensively the Army must change, adapt, or transform in order to be prepared to meet the uncertain challenges of the future, the answers to the moral-philosophical dimension of these questions *must not* change. Furthermore, the U.S. Army officer corps must feel safe in the assurance that the answers *will not* change.[7] Not only must the answers to these questions remain unchanging in the face of the institution's grand transformation, but the answers given to these questions all must point to the following conclusion: *By the nature of the profession of arms, only officers of firm moral character can discharge adequately their professional obligations to the nation and to their subordinates that they are called to lead.*

While it is gratifying that some (hopefully most) Army officers may find this claim to be self-evident and thus not one requiring a rigorously argued defense, it is at the same time true that potent cultural forces are at work that could have the effect of forcing a radical reinterpretation of the nature of the officer corps' bond of moral obligation. With this in mind, let us examine the philosophical grounds for moral obligation within the officer corps.

THE GROUNDS OF MORAL OBLIGATION

The officer corps' moral bond of obligation to the nation and to the Army's soldiers ultimately derives from two sources: (1) the essential and distinguishing characteristics of the profession of arms, and (2) the obligations freely incurred through the oath of office by which officers bind themselves to the Constitution. These will be considered in turn.

The Place of the Profession of Arms among the Professions

A well-established corpus of literature exists on the subject of what constitutes a profession and which human labors properly can be called professions.[8] In this context, the question periodically arises as to whether, properly speaking, the "profession of arms" may, in fact, be considered a profession. However, in order to answer that question, there first must be some agreement as to the nature of professions in general.

For the purposes of this reading, it is not necessary to establish the status of every human endeavor that aspires to be labelled a profession. It merely is necessary to demonstrate that the profession of arms falls completely within that set of human endeavors that may be labelled "the set of all professions" (see Figure 14-1). Given the premise that any human endeavor that falls completely within **B**, the set of all professions, is itself a profession, then it follows that any human endeavor that falls completely within a subset of **B** is likewise a profession. In this case, the subset of **B** at issue is **C**, the set of those segments of society that are recognized widely (if not universally) as legitimately performing functions directly associated with the preservation or termination of human life or freedom in ways accepted by just societies. The qualifying phrase "in ways accepted by just societies" must be added to exclude organizations like the Mafia that engage in the termination of human life but do so illicitly. (For example, the Mafia might claim that, within the context of Mafia subculture, the terminating of human life is legal and otherwise socially acceptable.

To this we may reply, without any harm to the argument, that the killing of Jews may have been legal and otherwise socially acceptable in the context of Nazi culture, but that any reasonable, morally sensitive person might be expected to conclude that the Mafia, the Nazi Party, and other organizations like

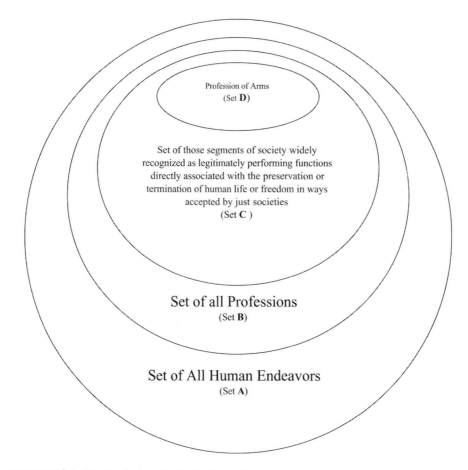

FIGURE 14-1. *Sets Enclosing the Profession of Arms.*

them can be excluded from **C** because of their inherently evil nature.)

This argument embraces the premise that all members of **C** are themselves professions. In this connection, it is worth noting that at least some of the confusion over what counts as a profession exists for semantic reasons rather than logical ones. This is so because of the unfortunate practice in popular culture to elevate the social status of almost any human endeavor by labelling it "professional." Thus, one commonly hears of "professional" hair stylists, "professional" air conditioner installers, and even "professional" golfers and bodybuilders, by which is meant that these pursuits are undertaken on a more or less full-time basis as a source of income.

The confusion could be avoided altogether by applying to these pursuits the traditional vocational titles of "apprentice," "journeyman," and "master" that have been used by tradesmen over the centuries. For example, one can readily imagine an apprentice hair stylist, a journeyman plumber, or even a master golfer or bodybuilder. However, to apply in common, non-technical discourse the term "profession" to a pursuit that has little or nothing to do with the central questions of human existence does a double disservice. First, it artificially elevates the status of some pursuits whose existence is not truly fundamental to a well-ordered society (many societies have functioned without hair stylists, plumbers, and golfers, but few if any have functioned without some form of medical care, legal order, military protection, etc.). Second, it obscures the crucial point that some professions exist in the first place because society has recognized them as essential for the promotion of the public good.

Accordingly, within **C** one finds, among others, the medical profession and the legal profession because both are recognized as having the responsibility to adjudicate issues involving the preservation or termination of life or freedom. However, since **D,** the "profession" of arms, also has as its principal function the preservation or termination of human life or freedom in ways accepted by just societies, one may conclude that **D** is a subset of **C** and therefore also a subset of **B**. Accordingly, given these assumptions, the human endeavor generally denominated the "profession of arms" is, in fact, a profession.

Notice that the logical claim is not that all professions (i.e., the members of **B**) are members of **C**, nor is it necessary for them to be. In fact, it probably is not the case that all things that properly can be called "professions" have as their central function the preservation or termination of human life or freedom. There may be many human endeavors that do not have the central identifying characteristic of **C** but that may be called professions on other grounds. However, it seems reasonable that those segments of society that generally are regarded as having a legitimate claim over matters of life and death, of bondage and freedom, appropriately may be called professions. Accordingly, this argument does not purport to establish the identity of all members of **B,** but merely to establish that among its members, one necessarily finds **D**, the profession of arms.

In a way that is particularly important in light of the aims of the present chapter, it should be noted that regardless of what other sets **D** may intersect or be a subset of, **D** definitely is a member of **C**. This is significant because, as even minimal reflection will reveal, the professions that belong to **C** have *moral* obligations, i.e., obligations derived from the fact that the principal functions of these professions affect the happiness, well-being, flourishing, and, potentially, the life or death of human agents. Indeed, nothing could be more central to the moral enterprise than those matters most directly affecting human existence. Hence, by virtue of its membership in **C**, it must be concluded that **D** is not only a bona fide profession, but also a profession with moral obligations. Thus can be established the claim that Army officers have moral obligations that derive, in part at least, from the fact that they are members of a profession entrusted by society with making decisions that concern the preservation or termination of human life. This is not to say that the profession of arms has *only* moral obligations, nor is it logically necessary to insist that such is the case. It merely is necessary to establish that, among the professional obligations that Army officers have, some of those obligations are properly denominated *moral* ones.

The Place of the Profession of Arms in Society

Since ancient times, the Western intellectual tradition has held that the highest quality of human life could best be realized within the context of the state—the highest form of society. This view was common among the greatest philosophers of ancient Greece and Rome. For example, Cicero regarded the preservation of the state as essential to the moral and physical well-being of the human race. Should this highest form of society cease to exist, man simply would become unable to flourish to the degree otherwise possible, or perhaps at all. Hence, by Cicero's account, the death of any man is less to be lamented than the extinction of the state.[9] In Augustine's paraphrase of Cicero, "Death often rescues individual men from pain, instead of being a disaster to them; but the death of a whole community is always a disaster."[10] Thus, in order to ensure the preservation of this highest form of society, it would seem that, as long as the present bellicose state of human affairs remains, armies will be a sine qua non for any stable state. Similarly, Plato, writing in the *Republic*, pointedly argues that even the ideal state must be prepared to secure itself by having "a special class of guardians"[11] exclusively charged with conducting the "business of fighting"[12] (an enterprise which, one might note with interest, he regards as both an "art and a profession"[13]).

Even Augustine, who takes a radically different view of the state than that found in Plato or Cicero, argues that armies are understandable, if not essential, features of the best of states. The "earthly city," as he refers to human society, never can become an ideal state; that eventuality is reserved for the "city of God" that cannot have its complete realization among fallible human beings. Nevertheless, the earthly city properly has an army to preserve order within, to defend it from without, and even by Augustine's account to serve as an instrument of divine justice. If nothing else, the army properly exists to enable the righteous citizens of the earthly city to cope with their imperfect circumstances until such time as they can partake of perfect justice in the city of God. Whether or not one embraces Augustine's transcendental view (a view which underwrote much of the social and political thought in the West for over one thousand years between Augustine and the Peace of Westphalia), it is nonetheless interesting that even Augustine's worldview includes a privileged place for the profession of arms.

This view of the centrality of the state and the necessity to defend it is by no means restricted to the ancients alone. In fact, no place is this idea plainer than in the writings of the English philosopher Thomas Hobbes (d. 1679). For Hobbes, all human beings live in a constant state of fear of death because of the unremitting forces of the "state of nature," where all humans find themselves as combatants in "the war of all against all": "During the time when men live without a common Power to keep them all in awe they are in that condition called Warre; and such a warre, as is of every man against every other man."[14] According to Hobbes, human beings find refuge from this chaotic world only as they bind together in societies in which they submit their agency to the will of a sovereign (be that one person, such as a monarch, or an assembly of persons, such as in a republic). In exchange for the promise to obey the sovereign, the sovereign "guarantees" (to the extent that it is humanly possible) the security of the members of society by protecting them from the encroaching forces of the state of nature. The sovereign accomplishes this by raising an army. Without such a mechanism to guarantee the security of the state, life is bound to become, in the famous words of Hobbes, "solitary, poore, nasty, brutish, and short."[15]

Armies and Moral Obligation

If the Hobbesean argument is extrapolated one step further, a particularly striking conclusion arises: Since, according to Hobbes, ethical notions such as right and justice cannot exist except within the protected confines of the state,[16] and the state cannot maintain its existence without the guarantee of safety afforded it by an army, the army becomes for Hobbes not only the guarantor of the state's existence but also *the guarantor of morality* (or at least the guarantor of the *potential* for the existence of morality). It may, in fact, be unnecessary to insist upon this latter point. Nevertheless, it is worth noting that in social contractarian moral philosophy of the kind advocated by Hobbes, one can argue that the sovereign is able to "guarantee" the security of the state (i.e., a place where morality can exist—for it cannot exist in the chaotic Hobbesean state of nature) only because he has at his disposal an army. At the very least, and in a similar vein, we can fairly conclude that, to the extent that an army serves as the guarantor of the state's safety, and to the extent that the

preservation of the state represents a moral good, the army has a *moral obligation* to do all within its power to ensure the preservation of the state.

One can arrive at the same conclusion by any number of other avenues. For example, the Kantian moral philosopher might argue that if, as the ancients held, an orderly society is necessary to human flourishing (in which, among other things, the society's members enjoy maximum liberty to discharge their moral obligations), there exists a moral duty to defend such a society's existence. Those officers appointed to lead the state's army, then, might properly be said to have a moral duty to ensure, to the best of their abilities, the preservation of the state from outside danger. On this premise, the state has an army both as a matter of practical necessity and as a matter of moral imperative, and the officers who lead the army are morally obligated to lead it well.

Still another school, the utilitarian moral philosophers, might argue that the interests of the greatest number of society's members are best served when a segment of society devotes itself to the defense of the whole. If this be the case, then the utilitarian could likewise conclude that the army exists as a matter of moral imperative, and that its officers are morally bound by utilitarian principle to lead it well.

In sum, whether one elects to embrace Hobbesean principles, or whether one applies Kantian, utilitarian, or similar tests, all permit the conclusion that armies—and therefore most certainly the officers who lead them—are bound by moral obligation to the societies whose responsibility it is theirs to defend.

The Constitution as a Source of Professional Moral Obligation

The idea of a constitution exists inseparably from the idea of a nation-state. It is one that far transcends the sum total of the meanings of the words contained in a written document, for indeed a constitution need not be written (as in the case of the English constitution). Broadly speaking, each state has a "constitution" in that it exhibits some kind of broadly sanctioned political structure. According to Herbert Spiro, "Aristotle used the Greek word for 'constitution' (*politeia*) in several different senses. The simplest and most neutral of these was 'the arrangement of the offices in a *polis*' (state). In this purely descriptive sense of the word, every state has a constitution, no matter how badly or erratically governed it may be."[17]

In the generally accepted sense of the word today, a "constitutional" state is one in which the institution of government is bound, in some meaningful way, by *contract* with at least some of those it governs.[18] Of all the constitutions in history, none illustrates this idea of "contract" better than the Constitution of the United States. (Inasmuch as the idea of "constitution" transcends the written document itself, one can properly speak of the U.S. Constitution as including not only the governmental structure outlined therein, but also the ideals associated with representative and limited democratic government. It also includes the ideals enshrined in allied documents like the Declaration of Independence and the Bill of Rights, as well as laws made under the authority of the Constitution.)

Given the philosophical, theological, and experimental soil from which sprang the Constitution of the United States, it seems clear that the ultimate aim of the social contract it codifies is not merely law and order, or even merely the preservation of liberty, but rather the promotion of human flourishing—to protect all that is virtuous, lovely, of good report, or praiseworthy[19] while at the same time to serve as a hedge against any malicious influence subversive of that aim. In short, it has the highest of human goods as its aim[20]—an aim that it shares with the moral enterprise.

Against this background, the officer's oath of office assumes a much deeper moral significance than some may suppose. Properly understood, the oath taken by Army officers to "support and defend the Constitution of the United States against all enemies foreign and domestic" comprehends not only the governmental structure itself but also all the *ideals* of government and the way of life (including the protection of all those beliefs and practices that make human flourishing—morality—possible) implicit in them. Furthermore, the oath requires that the gravity of the obligations it entails be acknowledged "without mental reservation or purpose of evasion." It binds the officer not merely to "do his or her job," but to "well and faithfully discharge the duties of the office." It concludes with an invocation of divine assistance in fulfilling the duties of this public trust. If there lingers any doubt as to whether the profession of arms is indeed a profession, let us note that no baker or butcher or hair stylist or golfer in *any* society—as important as these undertakings might be—is ever required to incur such a weighty set of obligations!

It is equally important to note that Army officers do not swear allegiance to any particular person or even to all of the people of the United States in the aggregate. Rather, they swear allegiance to the *ideals* embodied in the Constitution. Hence, the obligation of Army officers to defend the Constitution is a *direct* obligation, whereas the obligation to defend the American people is a *derivative* obligation. It derives from the common allegiance to the Constitution acknowledged both by the American people and by the officers of their Army.

THE ARMY OFFICER AS MORAL EXEMPLAR

Of course, the claim, however well established, that the Army has a moral obligation to defend society does not, in and of itself, imply that the Army's officers themselves have an obligation to be moral persons. However, this logical consideration does not fully account for the complexity of the issue. Logic deals only in what is possible; but when the realities of human nature are superimposed upon the demands of logic, one must be willing to include in his or her calculation the timeless truth that *as a man thinketh in his heart so is he*.[21] This chapter takes as axiomatic that men and women such as Army officers, faced with tasks that require the most exacting capacity for moral reasoning, can best accomplish those tasks if they are themselves morally well-founded persons.

If the Army's officers are themselves bereft of sensitivity for what is moral—a sensitivity which, as Aristotle would tell us, is cultivated by practice and dulled through disuse—then they are no better than the amoral forces of the state of nature. As a practical matter, "if the Army merely replicates the state of nature, as in societies run by warlords, it ceases to be useful to society."[22] Beelzebub cannot cast out Beelzebub, a house divided against itself cannot stand,[23] and the state of nature cannot defend against the state of nature. Hence, the defenders against the state of nature must themselves be of a different—and one might argue better—nature: one that not only recognizes the demands of morality but also one that consistently makes choices that reflect that recognition.

As a result of Army officers' solemn Constitutional obligation to ensure the defense of principle, it is altogether reasonable to expect them to embody the moral virtues enshrined in the Army's own rendition of soldierly values: loyalty to the ideals embodied in the Constitution (as evidenced, among other things, by their strict personal obedience to the laws established under the authority of the Constitution—"the supreme law of the land"[24]), an unwavering commitment to the performance of duty, a spirit of selfless service, and both moral and physical courage.

Even if moral obligations were not inherent in the professional status of Army officers, the oath they take is sufficient to establish de facto that Army officers are themselves bound to live in accordance with a definite and clearly discernible set of moral obligations. More to the point, they are bound to *embody* certain specific moral virtues. This is so because, without these virtues, officers would be unable to fulfil their derivative obligations to the American people. If officers fail to defend the Constitution by being unwilling to perform their duty without regard for the personal risks involved, or to face those risks courageously, selflessly, or even sacrificially, then the American people could not be guaranteed that Army members will do all in their power to defend the people's safety and way of life.

Hence, if soldiers—and thus all the more the officers who lead them—historically occupy a position of unique and recognized status in society (i.e., as instruments appointed by the state to preserve or terminate human life), it seems altogether reasonable to expect that they should be men and women of character who can be counted upon to conduct their task with due sobriety and moral awareness.

The Army Officer as a Moral Exemplar in War

The claim that Army officers have moral obligations in time of war is well established in the history of the profession of arms. For example, according to Augustine, army officers are to be persons of such honor and integrity that they can be counted upon to deal justly even with their enemies. Augustine urged Boniface, a Roman general, that "when faith is pledged, it is to be kept even with the enemy against whom the war is waged."[25]

Likewise, it long has been understood that, inasmuch as Army officers are entrusted by the state with the power to preserve or terminate lives, they must be individuals of character who are committed to the properly constrained use of that power, both in its legal and moral dimensions. Moreover, officers were not to be bound merely by the external constraint of law, but even more so by the internal constraint of

conscience. Augustine urges that officers be guided during war by the desire to achieve a just and lasting peace and not by a lust for blood or a desire to harm: "Even in waging war, cherish the spirit of a peacemaker, that, by conquering those whom you attack, you may lead them back to the advantages of peace."[26] To another officer he writes, "Let necessity, therefore, and not your will, slay the enemy who fights against you."[27] Thus, he urges that the taking of lives in war ought to be minimized to the greatest extent possible. Says Augustine, "For he whose aim is to kill is not careful how he wounds, but he whose aim it is to cure is cautious with his lancet; for the one seeks to destroy what is sound, the other that which is decaying. . . . In all . . . cases, what is important to attend to but this: who were on the side of truth, and who were on the side of iniquity; who acted from a desire to injure, and who from a desire to correct what was amiss?"[28] Augustine unambiguously advocates that a spirit of mercy and forbearance be displayed toward all those who fall into the power of their enemies: "As violence is used towards him who rebels and resists, so mercy is due to the vanquished or the captive, especially in the case in which future troubling of the peace is not to be feared."[29] In the light, then, of such demanding moral imperatives as these, it follows that only men and women of the deepest compassion, clearest sense of justice, and highest integrity would be both able *and willing* in time of war to distinguish between justified and unjustified applications of violence.

The just war tradition has long acknowledged the possibility that the cause for which the state summons its military to war may be less than perfectly just (a morally generous description of at least one side of every war that ever has been fought). On the one hand, therefore, Army officers must be men and women of integrity who, confronted with dark realities, still are willing to do their professional duty, unpleasant though that duty may be, as honorably as they can.

Of equal importance, Army officers are not, and indeed cannot be, automatons. They are moral agents who must recognize their responsibility (1) never to issue an immoral order, and (2) to refuse an order—or even a suggestion—to undertake military operations inconsistent with the ideals they are sworn to defend. Moreover, when an informed judgment leads them to the conviction that an order is morally wrong, they also must possess the maturity to recognize, and the fortitude to accept, the personal consequences of refusal.

The Army Officer as a Moral Exemplar in Peace

That Army officers have fundamental moral obligations in time of peace as well as in war also is well established. For example, according to Plato, those chosen to defend the state "are not to be savage animals, preying on those beneath them, but even if stronger than their fellow-citizens, they will be their friendly allies, and so it is necessary to ensure that they should have the right education and mode of life. . . . [G]old and silver they should neither handle nor touch. And this will be their salvation and the salvation of the State." [30] More recently, the Joint Chiefs of Staff have declared: "Our military service is based on values—those standards that the American military experience has proven to be the bedrock of combat success. These values are common to all the Services and represent the essence of our professionalism." [31]

Unfortunately, there are those in influential positions both in and out of uniform whose conduct suggests a less-than-enthusiastic endorsement of this ideal. For example, given the appalling reality that the citizens of the United States recently were informed from the highest political level that what a public official does in private is not a public concern and, therefore, is no one else's business, [32] there doubtless are those in contemporary society who would shy away from the claim that Army officers have an obligation, by virtue of their privileged position in society, to be moral exemplars not only in war, but also in the conduct of their private, peacetime lives. One version of the argument takes the following form:

> Premise 1. In a democratic republic, those who occupy positions of public trust are expected to act in the public interests.
>
> Premise 2. If such a person functions successfully in that public trust (i.e., "does his or her job"), that person deserves approbation for his or her service, and no other demands can be made on him or her with respect to matters of moral character.
>
> Premise 3. Person X, who holds a public trust, has functioned successfully (as defined above) in his or her office, but has failed miserably in terms of living a virtuous private life.

> Conclusion: Therefore, person X deserves the approbation of the American people for a job well done, regardless of how deep may be the moral flaws evident in person X's private life.

The position of this chapter is that the foregoing argument is unsound by reason of the falsity of Premise 2. This and similar arguments hold a seductive appeal for many members of liberal democratic society. Nevertheless, such arguments are as pernicious as they are seductive. This is particularly so as applied to Army officers. As has already been established, Army officers belong not only to a profession but also to that significant subset of professions whose primary function pertains to the preserving or terminating of human life (recall Figure 14-1, Set **C**). The professional status conferred by society upon members of this subgroup makes of them the moral demand not only that they *know* how to perform their professional tasks but also that they *be* persons of a high moral quality and that they maintain the highest moral standards at all times.

The same is true for other professions in Set **C**. For example, the physician rightly cannot claim moral license to use cocaine in the privacy of his or her off-duty time and then come to the hospital to perform brain surgery. The judge rightly cannot associate with criminals and accept bribes from them during his or her off-duty time and then expect to enjoy the public's confidence that he or she will deal justice to those same criminals facing racketeering charges in court. Likewise, because Army officers are charged to preserve or terminate life in the most untidy of circumstances, they cannot afford to present themselves as persons of whom others might wonder whether their conduct would be cavalier, flippant, or oblivious to the demands of morality in the most demanding of situations. Thus, the Army in transformation must take as its inalterable stance that, even in (what may be an increasingly) liberal democracy, where in many circles recognition of moral verities may be classified politely as postmodern, the Army still will hold itself firmly committed to its traditional ideals of military virtue.

Some may argue that idealized thinking of this kind is fine for ideal societies, but that since American society is itself demonstrably less than ideal, any such talk is out of place in the real world. However, those who argue in this way altogether miss the point because they fail to understand the essential meaning of "America." America is special *not* because it is the realization of any social ideal; it never has been ideal, and perhaps it never will be. America is special because it *aspires* to be ideal; it has always so aspired. America's early pioneers—the Pilgrims, the Founding Fathers, and others—conceived of themselves as men and women with a divine mission. The life they built in the New World was to constitute an ideal—"a city on a hill."[33] As poet Stephen Vincent Benét reflects,

> They were founding Zion, not the United States
> —And the seed is sown, and it grows in the deep earth,
> And from it comes what the sower never dreamed.[34]

Indeed, as long as the current state of human nature prevails, the realization of the perfect society must remain beyond our grasp. Nevertheless, societies, like individuals, that strive for the ideal are bound to come closer to realizing it than those that do not.[35] Likewise, it seems reasonable that any approach to the ideal in the present world would include a professional military led by officers who cling tenaciously to the highest moral standards.

Some may argue that an Army that espouses—or even claims to espouse—moral virtues that are "higher" than those of contemporary society at large cannot but be "out of step." They may claim that such an Army is certain to adopt a sanctimonious, "holier than thou" attitude about the way it regards the society it is sworn to defend. "How could such an Army," they may wonder, "truly possess the motivation necessary to fight the wars of a society it regards as its moral inferior?" However, such questioning also misses the point. The Army never has itself been an ideal organization; it is composed of men and women taken from American society and who possess the same foibles as Americans not in uniform. The taking of the oath of Army officership does not automatically transform, as it were, a "sinner" into a "saint." The point is that by the nature of the demands of professional Army officership, those who would serve the state as Army officers must commit to *strive to transform themselves* into men and women who can live up to and preserve the high ideals of the profession of arms. Officers are not expected to be perfect, but they are expected to live, in the words of the West Point prayer, "above the common level of life."[36]

The suggestion that the nation does not want to be defended by men and women who hold themselves to a higher moral standard than that found in society at large is pure nonsense. No reasonable person who considers the matter would prefer that those charged by the state with the responsibility to make decisions relative to the preserving or terminating of human life be men or women of deficient moral character. On the contrary, such a reasonable person would desire that those who undertake these and similar tasks be among the most virtuous persons that the society can produce. Even the most morally depraved person suffering from a terrible disease would rather be operated upon—all other things being equal—by a medical professional of high moral character who could be counted upon to act in the patient's best interest than by a member of the profession who, although as technically qualified, was a moral derelict. Surely a helpless widow who had lost her life's saving through the actions of an unscrupulous swindler would want the lawyer she engages to be one she could depend on to act vigorously to protect her interests and to right the wrongs done to her—not to compound them for his own selfish purposes. Likewise, any society that entrusts its warring powers to military professionals would want, and indeed *expect*, those professionals to apply judiciously and honorably the powers entrusted to them. (Else, why would a nation full of admittedly less-than-morally-ideal citizens find itself enraged and appalled by the actions of *decidedly* less-than-morally-ideal Army officers at My Lai?) Even in time of peace, those same citizens can be expected to hold those who lead their Army to standards of moral conduct above and beyond what they might find themselves willing to tolerate in society at large. (Else, why the national outrage at neglect of sexual abuse by those in authority at Aberdeen Proving Grounds?)

In short, there is no warrant whatsoever for the claim that the ancient wisdom which for millennia has served as the touchstone for professional military conduct in peace and war suddenly has become irrelevant. Thus, while it may be true that professions in jurisdictional competition that do not adapt are destined to die, it is not clear that the profession of arms can meaningfully exist in a democratic society apart from its foundational moral commitments.

Professions exist because, among other reasons, they lay proper claim to special expertise within the purview of their jurisdiction. Thus, when persons outside the profession of arms foist upon the profession a perspective or a practice that is foreign to and resisted by traditional military culture, there is reason to wonder whether those persons (even if they happen to be political masters) actually possess the professional competence necessary to insist on having their way. It is fully conceded that policy-making authority rests ultimately with civilians outside (and authoritatively above) the profession. Surely, no reflective Army officer questions this arrangement that has served the republic well for over two centuries. By the same token, there is great danger in implementing in the Army politically motivated policies against the considered opinion of the uniformed professionals who have devoted their lives to the *effective* military service of the nation. It is incumbent upon the senior members of the officer corps to articulate this reality to the Army's political masters.

In sum, thus far this chapter has sought to establish the following claims with respect to Army officers and moral obligation:

1. Service as an Army officer is indeed a profession;
2. The profession of arms has moral obligations to society;
3. Constitutional government imposes both explicit and implicit obligations on those who live under the order that government is designed to ensure;
4. Army officers incur a direct moral obligation by binding themselves to defend the Constitution and a derivative moral obligation to defend the people of the United States; and
5. As such, Army officers have a solemn obligation to serve as exemplars of morally well-founded conduct in peace and in war, in public and in private.

With these claims in mind, we now can consider, in moral terms, the kind of professional officer corps that will best enable America's Army to accomplish effectively its aim of winning the nation's wars as that Army marches into the twenty-first century.

TOWARD A MORALLY RENEWED OFFICER CORPS

The value of any philosophical reflection for policymakers is conditioned upon the degree to which philosophical promptings are capable of practical implementation. In the critique that follows, we shall examine two matters of ethical import that, if not dealt with, may effectively erode the bond of moral obligation between the officer corps and the nation, and between the officer corps and the soldiers it leads. The issues discussed are merely representa-

tive, but they merit serious consideration by thoughtful persons who have an interest in the Army's long-term well-being.

The Army as a Business

During the past decade, much has been done to make the Army a more efficient organization (that is, efficient in the commercial sense of generating greater output at less cost). At the same time, some have astutely noted that, in the name of efficiency, the Army has become a less *effective* organization in terms of its raison d'être—its ability to fight and win the nation's wars.

Logic does not dictate any necessary relationship between efficiency and effectiveness. Take, for example, the case of a company that produces replacement parts for tanks and that is under contract with the Army. Since the raison d'être for parts manufacturing companies—like all companies—is to make a profit, the goal the company probably will strive for is to produce the best tank parts (hence, maximum effectiveness) at the least possible costs (hence, maximum efficiency). Both concepts are important, because both help the company to achieve its ultimate aim of making money. Efficiency ensures the minimum expenditure of resources on the front end of the company's investment, while effectiveness ensures that those who buy the company's product will return to buy the product again, thus ensuring continued revenue. Again, however, this end state is merely an ideal, not a logical necessity. For example, if the company undertakes to develop, say, a new kind of replacement part for a tank, one of four possible cases, or outcomes, will obtain:

1. The part will be cheaper to produce (more efficient) and more reliable (more effective); or
2. It will be cheaper to produce (more efficient) but less reliable (less effective); or
3. It will be more expensive to produce (less efficient) but more reliable (more effective); or
4. It will be more expensive to produce (less efficient) and less reliable (less effective).

In Case 1, the project manager overseeing the production of the part gets a promotion. In Cases 2 and 3, the project manager may manage simply to keep his or her job. In Case 4, the project manager gets fired! In any event, an increase or decrease in efficiency does not necessarily imply an increase or decrease in effectiveness—the two variables are log-ically independent.

While this independence is fairly easy to recog-nize in the world of business, it may be somewhat more difficult to see when the notions of efficiency and effectiveness are applied to an organization like the Army that does not have the generation of profits as its purpose. Nevertheless, it is equally true that an Army that costs less to operate (or at least is provided with less resources with which to operate) will not necessarily be more effective at its task of winning the nation's wars.

Since businesses have as their ultimate aim the generation of profits, businesses—even those that supply the Army—may from time to time find it pru-dent to sacrifice effectiveness in order to maximize efficiency. However, no such luxury accrues to the Army; the Army can *never* afford to sacrifice effec-tiveness in the name of efficiency. To do so means that the Army is willing to risk being unable to accomplish its most basic and critical function of defending the nation. Hence those who insist that greater efficiency will necessarily result in a more effective Army ignore the realities of logic. What is worse, they place the Army at a crossroads not unlike the one at which Alice finds herself in Wonderland when she encounters the Cheshire Cat. Alice asks the Cat:

> "Would you tell me, please, which way I ought to go from here?"
> "That depends a good deal on where you want to get to," said the Cat.
> "I don't much care where—" said Alice.
> "Then it doesn't matter which way you go," said the Cat.
> "—so long as I get *somewhere*," Alice added as an explanation.
> "Oh, you're sure to do that," said the Cat, "if you only walk long enough."

So it is when the crucial distinction between effi-ciency and effectiveness is lost. Pursuing the path to efficiency does not necessarily ensure arrival at the aim of effectiveness; it merely ensures arrival *some-where*. If the Army chooses to understand efficiency as the necessary precursor to effectiveness, or worse, if it chooses to become more efficient at the expense of becoming more effective, the whole nature of the institution's moral commitments will require revi-sion. This is so because the business world is, by nature, mercenary in character. People rarely work for businesses because of ideals; they work for busi-nesses out of profit motives. The claim here is not that there is anything wrong with the profit motives of business mercenaries per se, but only that such thinking inappropriate in many military settings. In practical terms, whenever the claim is made that a policy or program will increase efficiency, the Army's leadership must require the claimant to demonstrate how the increase in efficiency will produce a com-mensurate increase in the overall *effectiveness* of the institution or at least avoid producing a decrease in effectiveness. In fact, it may well be that a justifica-tion of this kind should accompany all program pro-posals that require strategic-level approval.

Risk Aversion

Central to the traditional Army ethic is the idea that Army officers are the defenders of the defenseless; officers use the power and the authority of their office *not* to defend themselves, but rather to defend from injustice those that cannot defend themselves. The profession of arms is truly to be a selfless under-taking in which risk to self is understood to be the price of the privilege of being entrusted with the life-taking and life-preserving power of the state.

This point figures into Hobbesean social contract theory. According to Hobbes, the sovereign is able to "guarantee" the security of all members of society *except* those in the sovereign's army, for they must be sacrificed if necessary in order to preserve all else. Hence, if Hobbes conceives morality to mean any-thing at all, he must conceive that the sovereign's army is *morally* bound to protect society, if necessary at the cost of the complete sacrifice of its members' personal interests.

However, one need not adopt Hobbes' concept of morality in order to conclude, with Hobbes, that to suppose that society can be defended without per-sonal risk to those in the army is patently absurd. An army exists to assume risks on behalf of those who rightly lay claim to the army's protection. It exists as a corps of trained professionals who are better equipped to perform the task of defense than any lay-man would be. Risks to the army are not to be miti-gated by never putting it in harm's way, for in harm's way is the place where the army, better than any other organization, is suited to be. Risks to the army are mitigated through the thorough training of offi-cers and soldiers; and, indeed, they require thorough training. As Plato asks: "[A]re we to believe that a man who takes in hand a shield or any other instrument of war springs up on that very day a competent combatant in heavy armor or in any other form of warfare—though no other tool will make a man be an artist or an athlete by his taking it in hand, nor will it be of any service to those who have neither acquired the science of it nor sufficiently practiced themselves in its use?"[37]

Risk assessment as it is currently practiced in contingency operations merits thorough review. The standard applied in training that the death or serious injury of a soldier is unconscionable cannot be conceived as transferring directly to contingency operations. Soldiers must be trained to assume that the environment into which they are being sent is hostile and that they are there to *act* and not to be acted upon. If a task regarded as vital to the national interests requires Americans to go to a place with instructions to "hunker down" and neither get hurt nor allow anyone in their charge to get hurt, the task so described arguably does not belong to the Army. Indeed, the idea that the Army (i.e., the institution, and not its soldiers individually considered) will go anytime, anywhere for *any reason* is a romantic notion that requires thorough reassessment.

While it is understood that the ultimate decision on how to use the Army is one reserved for the highest political level, the Army leadership must articulate this concern vigorously and repeatedly to the Army's controlling but non-professional masters so that the institution's position relative to risk assessment is well understood: If the Army's political masters wish to reduce the risk of death or injury to America's sons and daughters in uniform, the answer is not to avoid sending them to places where they legitimately should be sent or to discipline their officers because someone in the officers' charge gets injured in the line of duty. Rather, the way to reduce risk is to provide the Army with adequate funding and other resources so that its officers can adequately train and equip the soldiers placed in their care and thus prepare them to the greatest possible degree to encounter and overcome risks successfully.

Undoubtedly, there are certain things about the Army that need to transform. As pertaining to those things of moral import that must change, the Army's task is clear:

1. It must examine itself for moral shortcomings, with special attention to those shortcomings that are of its own making (or own allowance). This is an urgent and continuous need because, while the Army cannot cure many of society's ills, it *can* act to remedy its own shortcomings, and then hold itself accountable to fulfil its moral obligations.

2. It must communicate its moral commitments in ways that will appeal to the moral sensitivities of reasonable men and women in a liberal democratic society who may not embrace for themselves the same moral imperatives as does the officer corps. In this regard, even if the American people were either to expect or to require less in terms of moral commitment from its Army officer corps, the officer corps can neither expect nor allow less of itself.

Although the officer corps does, and should, seek to refine its understanding of its own profession and to adapt to the exigencies of the new century, it does not need a new set of moral commitments. It simply must face up squarely to the moral commitments it already has.

The good news is that the task of living in a way that acknowledges the institution's deeply rooted moral commitments is accomplishable by good men and women who are willing to put service before self. Virtue *can* be taught; people *can* be transformed tomorrow into something better than they are today. Moreover, some of the most morally committed men and women to be found anywhere in the world are among the ranks of the U.S. Army—its officers, noncommissioned officers, and soldiers.

However, as the Army transforms, its professional officer corps must take great care to distinguish those things that may or must change from those that must not. Whatever transformation the Army and its officer corps undergo, that transformation must not assume that the work of the officer corps can be divorced from moral considerations—considerations grounded in history and in tradition, as well as in the nature of professions and constitutional government.

NOTES

1. The views and opinions expressed in this chapter are those of the author and are not necessarily those of the Department of the Army or any other U.S. government entity.

2. Donald Kagan and Frederick W. Kagan, *While America Sleeps* (New York: St. Martin's Press, 2000), 432.

3. Ibid., 434.

4. Ibid., 433.

5. 1999 Fletcher Conference—Findings and Recommendations; available from *http://www.army.mil/cmh-pg/documents/fletcher/fletcher-99/F99-F&R.html*; Internet; accessed 20 November 2000.

6. "On the Army Transformation," Congressional Testimony delivered by General Eric K. Shinseki, Chief of Staff, United States Army, before the Airland Subcommittee on Armed Services, United States Senate, Second Session, 106th Congress, 8 March 2000.

7. Naturally, it is hoped that claims of the kind advanced here would find appropriate application to the Army as a whole, the Army's sister services, and, in principle at least, the services of many of America's allies. However, in keeping with the purpose of the present anthology on Army professionalism, the arguments that follow will be tailored to apply directly to the United States Army Officer Corps.

8. Of particular note in the context of the larger study on the Army Profession of which this chapter is a part, an important representative of this corpus of literature on professions is the work of Andrew Abbott entitled *The System of Professions: An Essay on the Division of Expert Labor* (Chicago, IL: University of Chicago Press, 1988).

9. As Cicero argues, "But private citizens often escape those punishments which even the most stupid can feel—poverty, exile, imprisonment and stripes—by taking refuge in a swift death. But in the case of a State, death itself is a punishment, though it seems to offer individuals an escape from punishment; for a State ought to be so firmly founded that it will live forever." Hence, Cicero argues, "There is some similarity, if we may compare small things with great, between the overthrow, destruction, and extinction of a State, and the decay and dissolution of the whole universe" (Marcus Tullius Cicero, *De Re Publica* 3.23, in *De Re Publica* and *De Legibus,* trans. C. W. Keyes [Cambridge, MA: Harvard University Press, 1928], 211-13).

10. Augustine, *City of God*, 22.6, trans. Henry Bettenson (London: Penguin Books, 1984), 1032.

11. Frederick Copleston, *A History of Philosophy* (New York: Bantam Doubleday Dell Publishing Group, Inc., 1985), 1:226.

12. Plato, *The Republic* 2, 374 b, in *The Collected Dialogues*, ed. Edith Hamilton and Huntington Cairns (Princeton, NJ: Princeton University Press, 1961), 620.

13. Ibid.

14. Thomas Hobbes, *Leviathan* (London: Penguin Books, 1985), 185.

15. Ibid., 186.

16. Ibid., 188.

17. *Encyclopaedia Britannica*, 15th ed., s. v. "Constitution and Constitutional Government," by Herbert John Spiro.

18. U.S. Army Col. (Retired) Alexander P. Shine, personal correspondence with the author, 11 March 2001.

19. Philippians 4:8.

20. Shine, 11 March 2001.

21. Proverbs 23:7; see also Isaiah 10:7.

22. Shine, 11 March 2001.

23. Luke 11:17, 18.

24. U.S. Constitution, art. 6.

25. Augustine, *Letters* 189.6, trans. J.G. Cunningham, in *The Nicene and Post-Nicene Fathers*, ed. Philip Schaff, First Series (Grand Rapids, MI: Eerdmans Publishing Company, 1956), 1:554.

26. Ibid.

27. Ibid.

28. Augustine, *Letters* 93.8, 1:385.

29. Augustine, *Letters* 189.6.

30. Copleston 1:228; Plato, *The Republic* 3.417 a 5-6

31. U. S. Department of Defense, Joint Publication 1, *Joint Warfare of the US Armed Forces* (Washington, DC, 11 November 1991), 7.

32. William Jefferson Clinton, nationally televised address, 17 August 1998; available from *http://www.cnn.com/ALLPOLITICS/1998/08/17/speech/transcript.html;* Internet; accessed 13 March 2001.

33. Matthew 5:14.

34. Stephen Vincent Benét, "Pilgrims' Passage."

35. Shine, 11 March 2001.

36. Ibid.

37. Plato, *The Republic* 2.374c, d.

Warrior Ethos

This is the last of a series of seven lessons on the Army Profession and Officership. This lesson builds on earlier lessons focused on the Army Profession and Officership, and the concepts of Honor, Duty, and Country. The theme of this lesson is on the character and characteristics of the warrior, as well as how you can recognize and model the warrior ethos.

The following topics are addressed in this lesson:

- The characteristics of the warrior ethos
- Characteristics of the Army warrior
- Personal goals as they relate to the Army Profession

The following TLO is supported in whole or in part by this lesson:

- Relate the characteristics of a profession to military service as an officer

Following this lesson you will be able to:

- Describe the Army Warrior Ethos
- Distinguish between leaders who possess the Army Warrior Ethos and those who do not

CHARACTER AND THE WARRIOR ETHOS

FM 22-100

2-85. The warrior ethos refers to the professional attitudes and beliefs that characterize the American soldier. At its core, the warrior ethos grounds itself on the refusal to accept failure. The Army has forged the warrior ethos on training grounds from Valley Forge to the CTCs and honed it in battle from Bunker Hill to San Juan Hill, from the Meuse-Argonne to Omaha Beach, from Pork Chop Hill to the Ia Drang Valley, from Salinas Airfield to the Battle of 73 Easting. It derives from the unique realities of battle. It echoes through the precepts in the Code of Conduct. Developed through discipline, commitment to Army values, and knowledge of the Army's proud heritage, the warrior ethos makes clear that military service is much more than just another job: the purpose of winning the nation's wars calls for total commitment.

2-86. America has a proud tradition of winning. The ability to forge victory out of the chaos of battle includes overcoming fear, hunger, deprivation, and fatigue. The Army wins because it fights hard; it fights hard because it trains hard; and it trains hard because that's the way to win. Thus, the warrior ethos is about more than persevering under the worst of conditions; it fuels the fire to fight through those conditions to victory no matter how long it takes, no matter how much effort is required. It's one thing to make a snap decision to risk your life for a brief period of time. It's quite another to sustain the will to win when the situation looks hopeless and doesn't show any indications of getting better, when being away from home and family is a profound hardship. The soldier who jumps on a grenade to save his comrades is courageous, without question. That action requires great physical courage, but pursuing victory over time also requires a deep moral courage that concentrates on the mission.

2-87. The warrior ethos concerns character, shaping who you are and what you do. In that sense, it's clearly linked to Army values such as personal courage, loyalty to comrades, and dedication to duty. Both loyalty and duty involve putting your life on the line, even when there's little chance of survival, for the good of a cause larger than yourself. That's the clearest example of selfless service. American soldiers never give up on their fellow soldiers, and they never compromise on doing their duty. Integrity

underlies the character of the Army as well. The warrior ethos requires unrelenting and consistent determination to do what is right and to do it with pride, both in war and military operations other than war. Understanding what is right requires respect for both your comrades and other people involved in such complex arenas as peace operations and nation assistance. In such ambiguous situations, decisions to use lethal or nonlethal force severely test judgment and discipline. In whatever conditions Army leaders find themselves, they turn the personal warrior ethos into a collective commitment to win with honor.

2-88. The warrior ethos is crucial—and perishable—so the Army must continually affirm, develop, and sustain it. Its martial ethic connects American warriors today with those whose sacrifices have allowed our very existence. The Army's continuing drive to be the best, to triumph over all adversity, and to remain focused on mission accomplishment does more than preserve the Army's institutional culture; it sustains the nation.

2-89. Actions that safeguard the nation occur everywhere you find soldiers. The warrior ethos spurs the lead tank driver across a line of departure into uncertainty. It drives the bone-tired medic continually to put others first. It pushes the sweat-soaked gunner near muscle failure to keep up the fire. It drives the heavily loaded infantry soldier into an icy wind, steadily uphill to the objective. It presses the signaler through fatigue to provide communications. And the warrior ethos urges the truck driver across frozen roads bounded by minefields because fellow soldiers at an isolated outpost need supplies. Such tireless motivation comes in part from the comradeship that springs from the warrior ethos. Soldiers fight for each other; they would rather die than let their buddies down. That loyalty runs front to rear as well as left to right: mutual support marks Army culture regardless of who you are, where you are, or what you are doing.

2-90. That tight fabric of loyalty to one another and to collective victory reflects perhaps the noblest aspect of our American warrior ethos: the military's subordinate relationship to civilian authority. That subordination began in 1775, was reconfirmed at Newburgh, New York, in 1782, and continues to this day. It's established in the Constitution and makes possible the freedom all Americans enjoy. The Army sets out to achieve national objectives, not its own, for selfless service is an institutional as well as an individual value. And in the end, the Army returns its people back to the nation. America's sons and daughters return with their experience as part of a winning team and share that spirit as citizens. The traditions and values of the service derive from a commitment to excellent performance and operational success. They also point to the Army's unwavering commitment to the society we serve. Those characteristics serve America and its citizens—both in and out of uniform—well.

BLACK HAWK DOWN

MARK BOWDEN

In the late afternoon of Sunday, October 3, 1993 an elite group of commandos set out from their base at the Mogadishu, Somalia, airport on what they thought would be a routine mission. Their job was to extract a clan leader and his lieutenants from a safehouse in downtown Mogadishu. The mission was to take place in two stages: a convoy of Delta Force commandos would travel the streets of the city to the target house. Meanwhile, Blackhawk helicopters would insert Army Rangers around the block to secure the area. The entire mission was to take approximately one hour.

What happened has become a study of the problems of modern combat in "peacekeeping situations. Although the vast majority of the force was composed of Army personnel, Navy SEALS and Air Force Parajumpers (CSAR) were also involved and performed heroically, some losing their lives in the fight. The night of October 3rd ninety-nine of America's most elite combat soldiers were trapped in a hostile city. The next morning after the battle, 18 Americans and perhaps several thousand Somalis were dead.

As you read this excerpt from Black Hawk Down, *keep in mind some of the leadership principles you have studied all semester. There is no greater test of leadership than combat and you should try to extract the lessons of this modern battle as they might apply to your leadership, whether in combat or not.*

In the convoy's second-to-last Humvee, where Ruiz was fighting for his life, Sergeant Burns couldn't get through to McKnight on the radio so he took off on foot. He feared if they didn't get Ruiz back to base immediately the young Texas was going to die. Burns noticed that the gunfire that had hurt his ears initially now sounded muffled, distant. His ears had adjusted to it. As he neared the front of the line he saw Joyce stretched out bloody and pale, with a medic working over him furiously on the back of a crowded Humvee. He was about to reach the front when a D-boy grabbed him.

"You've been hit," the Delta operator said.

"No I haven't."

Burns hadn't felt a thing. The D-boy slid his hand inside Burn's vest at his right shoulder and the sergeant felt a vicious stab of pain.

"Having trouble breathing?" the D-boy asked.

"No."

"Any tightness in your chest?"

"I feel all right," Burns said. "I didn't even know I was hit."

"You keep an eye on it," the D-boy said.

Burns made it up to McKnight, who was also bloody, and busy on the radio. So Burns told Sergeant Bob Gallagher about Ruiz. Burns thought they should allow a Humvee or two to speed right back to the base with Ruiz, as they had done earlier with Blackburn. But Gallagher knew the convoy could not afford to lose any more vehicles and firepower now. They still had roughly a hundred men waiting for them around the first crash site, then there was the second crash site.... Gallagher was already kicking himself for sending those three vehicles back with Blackburn. While he knew this might be a death sentence for Ruiz, he told Burns there was no way anybody was leaving.

October 3, 1993

2:49 PM	Two principle targets, Habr Gidr clan leaders, spotted at a residence in central Mogadishu.
3:32 PM	The force launches: nineteen aircraft, twelve vehicles and 160 men.
3:42 PM	The assault begins. The boys hit the target house and four Ranger chalks rope in—one Ranger, Private Todd Blackburn, misses the rope and falls 70 ft. to the street.
3:47 PM	Large crowds of Somalis converging on the target area.
3:58 PM	One of the vehicles, a five-ton truck, is hit and disabled by a rocket propelled grenade, several men are wounded.
4:00 PM	Forces of armed Somalis converging on the target area from all over Mogadishu.

4:02 PM	Assault force reports both clan leaders and about 21 others in custody, as the force prepares to pull out, three vehicles are detached to rush the wounded Private Blackburn back to the base.
4:15 PM	Fighting and confusion delays loading the prisoners and pulling out.
4:20 PM	Black Hawk Super 61 is hit by a rocket propelled grenade and crashes five blocks northeast of the target.
4:22 PM	Crowds of Somalis racing toward the crash site.
4:26 PM	Prisoners loaded, the convoy and ground forces all begin moving toward the downed chopper. Black Hawk Super Six Four, piloted by Michael Durant, takes the downed chopper's place in orbit over the fight.
4:28 PM	Search and rescue team ropes in to assist the downed crew. Both pilot and copilot are dead.
4:35 PM	Convoy makes a wrong turn and begins wandering lost through city streets, sustaining heavy casualties.
4:40 PM	Durant's Black Hawk, Super Six Four, is hit and crashes about a mile southwest of the target. Hostile crowds begin moving toward it.
4:42 PM	Two snipers, Sergeants Randy Shughart and Gary Gordon, are inserted by helicopter to help protect the injured Durant and his crew.
4:54 PM	The Lost Convoy, with more than half of its force wounded or dead, abandons its search for the first downed Black Hawk and begins fighting its way back to the base.
5:03 PM	A smaller, emergency convoy is dispatched in an attempt to rescue the men stranded at Durant's crash site. It encounters immediate obstacles.
5:34 PM	Both convoys, battered and bleeding, link up and abandon the effort to break through to Durant. The remainder of the ground force of Rangers and commandos are converging around the first crash site, sustaining many casualties. Ranger Corporal Jamie Smith is among those shot.
5:40 PM	Somali crowds overrun Durant's crash site, killing Shughart, Gordon, and every member of the crew except Durant, who is carried off by militia through the city.
5:45 PM	Both convoy return to the base. Ninety-nine men remain trapped and surrounded in the city around the first downed Black Hawk, fighting for their lives. Corporal Smith bleeding heavily, medic requests immediate evacuation.
7:08 PM	Black Hawk Super Six makes a daring re-supply run, dropping water, ammo and medical supplies to the trapped force. It is badly damaged, cannot land to evacuate Corporal Smith, limps back to base.
8:27 PM	Corporal Smith dies.
10:00 PM	Giant convoy, two companies of 10th Mt. Division troops along with the remainder of Task Force Ranger, Pakistani tanks and Malaysian armored vehicles, forms at Mogadishu's New Port, and begins planning the rescue.
11:23 PM	The giant rescue convoy moves out, blazing into the city.

October 4, 1993

1:55 AM	Rescue convoy reaches the trapped Ranger force. A second half of the convoy reaches the site of Durant's downed Black Hawk. There is no trace of the crew.
3:00 AM	Forces still struggling to remove the pinned body of Cliff Wolcott, pilot of Super Six One.
5:30 AM	Wolcott's body is finally recovered. Vehicles roll out of the city. Ranger force is left to run out of the city through gunfire—"The Mogadishu Mile."
6:30 AM	The force returns to the Pakistani Stadium. Eighteen dead, 73 injured.

"We have to move to the crash site and consolidate forces," he said.

Disgusted, Burns began to make his way back down the column to his vehicle. He had only gone a few steps when the convoy started rolling again. He jumped on the back of a Humvee. It was already jammed. The rear of the vehicle was slick and sticky with blood. Moaning rose from the pile of Rangers. Beside him, Joyce looked dead, even though a medic was still working on him. Sergeant Galantine was screaming. "My thumb's shot off! My thumb's shot off!" Burns did not want to be on that Humvee.

They were still pointed north. Some of the men were at the breaking point. In the same Humvee with Burns, Private Jason Moore saw some of his Ranger buddies just burying their heads behind the sandbags. Some of the unit's most boisterous chest-beaters were among them. A burly kid from Princeton, New Jersey, Moore had a dip of snuff stuffed under his lower lip and brown spittle on his unshaved chin. He was sweating and terrified. One RPG had passed over the vehicle and exploded with an ear-smarting crack against a wall alongside. Bullet were snapping around him. He fought the urge to lie down. *Either way I'm going to get shot.*

Moore figured if he stayed up and kept on shooting, at least he'd get shot trying to save himself and the guys. It was a defining moment for him, a point of clarity in the midst of chaos. He would go down fighting. He would not consider lying down again.

Not long after he saw Joyce shot, which really shook him up, Private Carlson felt a sudden blow and sharp pain in his right knee. It felt like someone had taken a knife and held it to his knee and then driven it in with a sledgehammer. He glanced down to see blood rapidly staining his pants. He said a prayer and kept shooting. He had been wildly scared for longer than he had ever felt that way in his life, and now he thought he might literally die of fright. His heart banged in his chest and he found it hard to breathe. His head was filled with the sounds of shooting and explosions and visions of his friends, one by one, going down, and blood splashed everywhere oily and sticky with its dank, coppery smell and he figured, *This is it for me.* And then, in that moment of maximum terror, he felt it all abruptly, inexplicably fall away. One second he was paralyzed with fear and pain and the next ... he had stopped caring about himself.

He would think about this a lot later, and the best he could explain it was, his own life no longer mattered. All that did matter were his buddies, his brothers, that *they* not get hurt, and that *they* not get killed. These men around him, some of whom he had only known for months, were more important to him than life itself. It was like when Tescher ran out on the road to pull Joyce back in. Carlson understood that now, and it was heroic, but it also *wasn't* heroic. At a certain level he knew Telscher had made no choice, just as he was not choosing to be unafraid. It had just happened to him, like he had passed through some barrier. He *had* to keep fighting, because the other guys needed him.

In the second of the three Humvees behind the truck, Private Ed Kallman sat behind the wheel amazed and alarmed by what he was seeing. He saw a line of trees on the sidewalk up ahead begin to explode, one after the other, as if someone had placed charges in each and was detonating them at about five-second intervals. Either that or somebody with a big gun was systematically taking out the trees, each about two stories high, thinking that they might be hiding snipers. He found it strange, anyway, the blasts walking their way toward him splintering the trees one by one.

Kallman, who had felt such a rush of excitement an hour earlier as he encountered battle for the first time, now felt nothing but nauseating dread. so far neither he nor anyone in his vehicle had been hit, but it seemed like just a matter of time. He watched with horror as the convoy disintegrated before him. He was a soldier for the most powerful nation on earth. If they were having this much trouble, shouldn't somebody have stepped in? Where was a stronger show of force? Somehow it didn't seem right that they could be reduced to this, battling on these narrow dirt streets, bleeding, dying! This wasn't supposed to happen. He saw men he knew and liked and respected bellowing in pain on the street with gunshot wounds that exposed great crimson flaps of glistening muscle, men wandering in the smoke bleeding, dazed and seemingly unconscious, their clothing torn off. American soldiers. Those who were not injured were covered with the blood of others. Kallman was young and new to the unit. If these more-veteran soldiers were all getting hit, sooner or later he was going to get hit. Oddly, the surprise he felt overshadowed the fear. He kept telling himself, *This is not supposed to happen!*

And Kallman's turn did come. As he slowed down before another intersection he looked out the open window to his left and saw a smoke trail coming straight at him. It all happened in a second. He knew it was an RPG and he knew it was going to hit him. Then it did. He awoke lying on his right side on the front seat with his ears ringing. He opened his eyes and was looking directly at the radio mounted under the dash. He sat up and floored the accelerator. Up ahead he saw the convoy making a left turn and raced to catch them.

Later, when he'd had a chance to inspect his Humvee, he saw that the RPG had hit his door, deeply denting it and poking a hole through the steel. He and the others inside had evidently been spared by the bulletproof glass panel behind the door—Kallman had the window rolled down. The brunt of the grenade's force had been absorbed by the Humvee's outer shell, and the glass barrier had been thick enough to stop it. Kallman's left arm began to swell and discolor, but otherwise he was fine.

■ ■ ■

Dan Schilling felt better whenever they were moving. But the convoy seemed to inch along, stopping, starting, stopping, starting. Whenever they stopped the volume of fire would surge, so many rounds that at times it looked like the stone walls on both sides of the alley were being sandblasted. There were plenty of targets to shoot at. Up in the turret, Pringle unloosed the .50 cal on a group of armed Somalis. Schilling watched as one of them, a tall, skinny man wearing a bright yellow shirt and carrying an AK-47, came apart as the big rounds tore through him. Deep red blotches appeared on the yellow shirt. First an arm came off. Then the man's head and chest exploded. The rest of the Somalis scattered, moving around the next corner, where Schilling knew they'd again be waiting for them to cross.

As the Humvee came abreast of the alley Schilling didn't bother to use his sights, the men were that close. The first man he shot was just ten yards away. He was crouched down and had a painful grimace on his face. Maybe Pringle had hit him earlier. Schilling put two rounds in his chest. He shot the man next to him twice in the chest and as he did he felt a slam and a dull pain in his right foot. When they were through the intersection, Schilling inspected his boot. The door had taken two bullets. One had passed through the outer steel and been

stopped by the bullet-proof glass window inside it. The second had hit lower, and had passed right through the door. The door, which was guaranteed to stop the AK-47's 7.62 mm round, had not stopped either bullet. The glass got the first, and the second had been slowed enough so that it hit with enough force to hurt, but not enough to penetrate the boot.

Pringle had just put doors on the vehicle earlier that day. They'd done the previous six missions without them, and these had just arrived in a shipment from the States. Schilling had mixed feelings about them. He liked the protection, but the doors made it a lot harder to move. When he had checked them out that morning, he couldn't get his window to roll down, so he'd started to remove the door. Pringle stopped him.

"Hey, I just put those on!" he shouted.

Schilling had showed him how the window stuck, and Pringle had fetched a hammer and simply whacked the frame until the window dropped down. Now, Schilling was glad they'd kept the door, but some of the sense of invulnerability he'd felt was gone. Both bullets had gone completely through.

They continued north for about nine blocks, all the way up to Armed Forces Road, one of the main paved roads in Mogadishu. They'd gone past the crash site, only a block west of it, without stopping. The helicopters had directed them to turn right, but the alleyways looked too narrow to Schilling and the others in the lead Humvee. If the trucks got stuck they'd probably all be killed. So they continued on. Some of the men in the convoy saw the downed Black Hawk just a block over as they went past, but no one had told them that it was their objective. Many of the men in the vehicles still thought they were heading back to base. As they approached Armed Forces Street, they stopped again.

Schilling fought back feelings of futility. McKnight seemed dazed and overwhelmed. He was bleeding from the arm and the neck, and not his usual decisive self. Schilling muttered to himself, "We're going to keep driving around until we're all fucking dead."

He then decided to do something himself, since McKnight seemed stymied. Using a frequency he knew helicopter pilots used to talk among themselves, he bypassed the C2 Black Hawk and contacted the observation helicopters flying orbits higher up. Coordinating communications between the air and ground was Schilling's specialty. He asked them to vector him to the crash site. The choppers were eager to oblige. They told him to steer the convoy west on Armed Forces Road, and then hang another left. McKnight gave permission for Schilling to direct them, and the convoy was moving once again.

The made the left turn off Armed Forces and drove through the storm of gunfire for about seven blocks before Schilling saw up ahead the smoldering remains of the five-ton they had torched in front of the target building. They'd come full circle. Schilling hadn't told the observation bird pilots *which* crash site he wanted. The pilots could see how desperate things were around Durant's crash, where Somali mobs had begun to encircle the unprotected downed Black Hawk, and had taken it upon themselves to direct the convoy there. Schilling hadn't realized it until he saw the target house and the Olympic Hotel again.

"We're headed for the second crash site," he told McKnight.

The lieutenant colonel knew only what his orders were. He reiterated that they were to proceed to the *first* crash site.

On the command net, their wanderings had turned to black comedy. Matter were now complicated by the fact that a second vehicle convoy had been dispatched from the base to attempt a rescue at Durant's crash site.

—*Danny, I think you've gone too far west trying to look at the second crash. You seem to have gone about four blocks west and five blocks south, over.*

—*Romeo Six Four* [Harrell], *this is Uniform Six Four* [McKnight]. *Give me a right turn, right turn! Right turn!*

—*Uniform Six Four, this is Romeo Six Four.... You need to go about four blocks south, turn east. There is green smoke marking the site south. Keep coming south.*

A voice came over the busy command frequency pleading for order.

—*Stop giving directions! ... I think you're talking to the wrong convoy!*

—*This is Uniform Six Four, you've got me back in front of the Olympic Hotel.*

—*Uniform Six Four, this is Romeo Six Four. You need to turn east.*

So the convoy now made a U-turn. They had just driven through a vicious ambush in front of the target house and were now turning around to drive right back through it. Men in the vehicles behind could not understand. It was insane! They seemed to be *trying* to get killed.

Things had deteriorated so badly that up in the C2 bird Harrell was considering just releasing the prisoners, their prize, the supposed point of this mission and of all this carnage. He instructed the Delta units on foot now closing in on the first crash site:

—*As soon as we get you linked up with the Uniform element throw all the precious cargo. We're going to try and get force down to the second crash site.*

The voices from various helicopters now trying to steer poor McKnight recorded the frustration of his fruitless twists and turns.

—*Uniform Six Four, this is Romeo Six Four. Next right. Next right! Alleyway! Alleyway!*

—*They just missed their turn.*

—*Take the next available right, Uniform.*

—*Be advised they are coming under heavy fire.*

—*Uniform Six four, this is Romeo Six Four.*

—*God damn it, stop! God damn it, stop!*

—*Right turn! Right turn! You're taking fire! Hurry up!*

In this terrible confusion the men on the convoy saw strange things. They passed an old woman carrying two plastic grocery bags, walking along calmly through the barrage. As the convoy approached, she set both bags down gently, stuck fingers in her ears, and kept on walking. Minutes later, heading in the opposite direction, they saw the same woman. She had the bags again. She set them down, stuck fingers in our ears, and walked away as she had before.

At every intersection now Somalis just lined up, on both sides of the street, and fired at every vehicle that came across. Since they had men on both sides of the street, any rounds that missed the vehicle as it flashed past would certainly have hit the men on the other side of the road. Sergeant Eversmann, who had found some better cover for himself in the back end of his Humvee, watched with amazement. What a strategy! He felt these people must have no regard for even their own lives! The just *did not care!*

The city was shredding them block by block. No place was safe. The air was alive with hurtling chunks of hot metal. They heard the awful slap of bullets into flesh and heard the screams and saw the insides of men's bodies spill out and watched the gray blank pallor rise in the faces of their friends, and the best of the men fought back despair. They were America's elite fighters and they were going to die here, outnumbered by this determined rabble. Their future was setting with this sun on this day and in this place.

Schilling felt disbelief, and now some guilt. He had steered the convoy the wrong way for at least part of the calamity. Stunned by the confusion, he struggled to convince himself this was all really happening. Over and over he muttered, "We're going to keep driving around until we're all fucking dead."

Specialist Spalding was still behind the passenger door in the first truck with his rifle out the window, turned in the seat so he could line up his shots, when he was startled by a flash of light down by his legs. It looked like a laser beam shot through the door and up into his right leg. A bullet had pierced the steel of the door and the window, which was rolled down, and had poked itself and fragments of glass and steel straight up his leg from just above his knee all the way up to his hip. He had been stabbed by the shaft of light that poked through the door. He squealed.

"What's wrong, you hit" shouted Maddox.

"Yes!"

And then another laser poked through, this one into his left leg. Spalding felt a jolt this time but no pain. He reached down to grab his right thigh and blood spurted out between his fingers. He was both distressed and amazed. The way the light had shot through. He still felt no pain. He didn't want to look at it.

Then Maddox shouted, "I can't see! I can't see!"

The driver's helmet was askew and his glasses were knocked around sideways on his head.

"Put your glasses on, you dumb ass," Spalding said.

But Maddox had been hit in the back of the head. The round must have hit his helmet, which saved his life, but hit with such force that it had rendered him temporarily blind. The truck was rolling out of control and Spalding, with both legs shot, couldn't move over to grab the wheel.

The couldn't stop in the field of fire, so there was nothing to do but shout directions to Maddox, who still had his hands on the wheel.

"Turn left! Turn Left! Now! Now!"

"Speed up!"

"Slow down!"

The truck was weaving and banging into the sides of the buildings. It ran over a Somali man on crutches.

"What was that?" asked Maddox.

"Don't worry about it. We just ran over somebody."

And they laughed. They felt no pity and were beyond fear. They were both laughing as Maddox stopped the truck.

One of the D-boys, Sergeant Mike Foreman, jumped from the back of the truck, ran up, and opened the driver's side door to a cabin now splattered with blood.

"Holy shit!" he said.

Maddox slid over next to Spalding, who was no preoccupied with his wounds. There was a perfectly round hole in his left knee, but there was no exit wound. The bullet had evidently fragmented on impact with the door and glass and only the jacket had penetrated his knee. It had flattened on impact with his kneecap and just slid around under the skin to the side of the joint. The remainder of the bullet had peppered his lower leg, which was bleeding. Spalding propped both legs up on the dash and pressed a field dressing on one. He lay his rifle on the rim of the side window, changed the magazine, and, ad Foreman got the truck moving again, resumed firing. He was shooting at everything that moved.

To make room for more wounded on the back of his Humvee, wounded Private Clay Othic, who has been shot in the arm at the beginning of the fight, jumped out the back and ran to the second truck. One of the men riding there proffered a hand to help him climb aboard, but with his broken arm Othic couldn't grab hold of anything. After several failed attempts he ran around to the cab, and Specialist Aaron Hand stepped out to let him squeeze in between himself and the driver, Private Richard Kowalewski, a skinny quiet kid from Texas whom they all called "Alphabet" because they didn't want to pronounce his name.

Kowalewski was new to the unit, and quiet. He had just met a girl he wanted to marry, and had been talking about leaving the regiment when his tour was up in a few months. His sergeant had been trying to convince him to stay. Minutes after Othic slid in next to him, Kowalewski was hit by a bullet in his shoulder, which knocked him back against the seat. He checked out the wound briefly and straightened back up behind the wheel.

"Alphabet, want me to drive?" asked Othic.

"No, I'm okay."

Othic was struggling in the confined space to apply a pressure dressing to the driver's bleeding shoulder when the RPG hit. It rocketed in from the left, severing Kowalewski's left arm and entering his chest. It didn't explode. The two-foot-long missile embedded itself in Kowalewski, the fins sticking out his left side under his missing arm, and point sticking out the right side. He was unconscious, but still alive.

Driverless, the truck crashed into the back end of the one before it, the one with the prisoners in back and with Foreman, Maddox, and Spalding in the cab. The impact threw Spalding against the side door and then his truck careened into a wall.

Othic had been knocked cold. He awakened to Specialist Hand shaking him, yelling that he had to get out.

"It's on fire!" Hand shouted.

The cab was black with smoke and Othic could see the rocket fuse glowing from what looked like inside Alphabet. The grenade lodged in his chest was unexploded, but something had caused a blast. It might have been a flashbang mounted on Kowalewski's vest or rocket propellant from the grenade. Hand jumped out his door. Othic reached over to grab Kowalewski and pull him out, but the driver's bloody clothes just lifted damply off of his pierced torso. Othic stumbled out to the street and noticed his and Hand's helmets had been blown off. Hand's rifle was shattered. They moved numbly and even a little giddily. Death had buzzed past close enough to kill Kowalewski and knock off their helmets but had left them virtually unscathed. Hand couldn't hear out of his left ear, but that was it. Both men found their helmets down the street—they had evidently blown right out the window.

Hand also found the lower portion of Kowalewski's arm. Just the left hand and a bit of wrist. He picked it up, ran back to the Humvee where the D-boys had placed Kowalewski, and put it in the mortally wounded man's pants pockets.

PC A view of the streets of Mgadishu. Official Department of Defense photo.

Still dazed, Othic crawled into a Humvee.

As they set off again he began groping on the floor with his good left hand collecting rounds that guys had ejected from their weapons when they jammed. Othic passed them back to those still shooting.

Many of the vehicles were running out of ammo. They had expended thousands of rounds. Three of the twenty-four Somali prisoners were dead and one was wounded. The back ends of the remaining trucks and Humvees were slick with blood. There were chunks of viscera clinging to floors and inner walls. McKnight's lead Humvee had two flat tires, both on the right side. The vehicles were meant to run on flats, but at nowhere near normal speed. The second Humvee in line was almost totally disabled. It was dragging an axle and was being pushed by the five-ton behind it, the one that had been hit by the grenade that killed Kowalewski. The Humvee driven by the SEALs, the third in line, had three flat tires and was so pockmarked with bullet holes it looked like a sponge. SEAL Howard Wasdin, who had been shot in both legs, had them draped up over the dash and stretched out on the hood. Some of the Humvees were smoking. Carlson's had a gaping grenade hole in the side and four flat tires.

When the RPG hit Kowalewski in the cab of the first truck, it forced everything behind it to a halt. In the noise and confusion, no one in McKnight's lead Humvee noticed, so they proceeded alone up to Armed Forces Road, rolling now at about twenty miles per hour. The observation helicopters called for a right turn (the convoy had driven past the crash site a second time about seven blocks back, this time one block to the east of it, looking in vain for a street wide enough to make a left turn). When they reached Armed Forces Road, Schilling was surprised to find it deserted. They turned right and had gone only about forty yards, planning to turn right again and head back down toward the crash site, when Schilling saw out his right side window a Somali step out into an alley and level an RPG tube at them.

"RPG! RPG!" he shouted.

The Humvee's big turret gun was silent. Schilling turned to see why Pringle wasn't shooting, and saw the gunner down in back grabbing a fresh can of ammo. Pringle raised his hands to cover his head.

"GO!" Schilling screamed at the driver, Private Joe Harosky.

But instead of shooting out of the intersection, Harosky turned into it, and bore straight down on the man with the RPG tube. This happened in seconds. The grenade launched. Schilling saw a puff of smoke and heard the distinctive pop and the big ball of the grenade coming right for them. He froze. He didn't even raise his weapon. The grenade shot straight past the Humvee at door level on his side. He felt it *whoosh* past.

"Back up! Back up!" he shouted.

Schilling got off a few rounds, and Pringle was back up working the .50 cal before they'd cleared the alley. When Schilling turned around, worried they'd ram the Humvee behind them, he discovered they were all alone. Harosky backed out into Armed Forces Road, where they turned around and headed west. They spotted the rest of the column where they'd left it, still facing north just shy of the main road.

McKnight, who had been silent ever since the U-turn back by the Olympic Hotel, seemed to recover himself at this point. He got out of the Humvee and conferred with Sergeant Gallagher outside by the hood of the vehicle. Gallagher was furious about the confusion. But as he confronted McKnight, he was hit with a round that knocked him to the street. He fell right at Schilling's feet. Bright red blood pumped in spurts from his arm. Schilling had never seen such scarlet blood. It was obviously arterial. It shot out in powerful squirts. He pressed his fingers to it and fished for a field dressing in his medical pouch. He patched up Gallagher as best he could, shoving in Curlex (a highly absorbent gauze that is used to help stop bleeding) and bandaging it tightly. It their weeks in Somalia, the PJs had given all the men additional training with field dressings. They'd practiced with live goats, shooting the animals and then having the men work on them, getting their hands in some real gore. The experience helped. Gallagher walked back to his own vehicle, but Schilling kept his weapon. He needed the ammo.

They had been wandering now for about forty-five minutes. McKnight was ready to pack it in. There were now far more dead and wounded in the convoy than there were at the first crash site. He called up to Harrell.

—Romeo Six Four, this Uniform Six Four. We've got a lot of vehicles that will be almost impossible to move. Quite a few casualties. Getting to the crash site will be awful tough. Are pinned down.

Harrell was insistent.

—Uniform Six Four, this is Romeo Six Four. Danny, I really need to get you back to that crash site. I know you turned left on Armed Forces [Road], *what's your status?*

But McKnight and his men had had enough.

—This is Uniform Six Four. I have numerous casualties, vehicles that are halfway running. Gotta get these casualties out of here ASAP.

They weren't home yet.

They began moving, and everyone heartened as word passed back that they were finally pointed back to the base. Maybe some of them would make it out alive after all.

They found Via Lenin, a four-lane road with a median up the center that would lead them back down to the K-4 traffic circle and home. Spalding began to lose feeling in his fingertips. For the first time in the ordeal he felt panic. He thought he must be lapsing into shock. He saw a little Somali boy who looked no more than five years old with an AK-47, shooting wildly from the hip, bright flashes from the muzzle of the gun. Somebody shot the boy and his legs flew up into the air, as though he had slipped on marbles, and he landed flat on his back. It happened like a slow-motion sequence in a movie, or a dream. The D-boy driving, Foreman, was a helluva shot. He had his weapon in one hand and the steering wheel in the other. Spalding saw him gun down three Somalis without even slowing down. He was impressed.

He felt his hands curling up like someone with cerebral palsy.

"Hey, man, let's get the hell back," he said, "I'm not doin' too good."

"You're doin' cool," said Foreman.

SEAL John Gay's Humvee was now in the lead. It was riddled with bullets and smoking and slowing down, running on three rims. There were eight wounded Rangers and Joyce's body in back, with Wasdin's bloody legs splayed out on the hood (he'd been shot once more in the left foot). Wasdin was yelling, "Just get me out of here!" The Sammies had stretched two big underground gasoline tank across the roadway with junk and furniture and other debris and had set it all on fire. Afraid to stop the Humvee for fear it would not start back up, they crashed over and through the flaming debris, nearly flipping, but the wide, sturdy vehicle righted itself and kept on moving. The rest of the column followed.

It was 5:40 P.M. They had been battling through the streets now for more than an hour. Of the approximately seventy-five men in the convoy, soldiers and prisoners, nearly half had been hit by bullets or shrapnel. Eight were dead, or near death. As they approached K-4 circle, they braced themselves for another vicious ambush.

A grenade came from somewhere. It was one of those Russian types that looked like a soup can on the end of a stick. It bounced off the car and then off Specialist Jason Coleman's helmet and radio and then it hit the ground.

Nelson, who was still deaf from Twombly's timely machine-gun blast, pulled his M-60 from the roof of the car and dove, as did the men on both sides of the intersection. They stayed down for almost a full minute, cushioning themselves from the blast. Nothing happened.

"I guess it's a dud," said Lieutenant DiTomasso.

Thirty seconds later another grenade rolled out into the open space between the car and the tree across the street. Nelson again grabbed the gun off the car and rolled with it away from the grenade. Everyone braced themselves once more, and this, too, failed to explode. Nelson thought they had spent all their luck. He and Barton were crawling back toward the car when a third grenade dropped between them. Nelson turned his helmet toward it and pushed his gun in front of him, shielding himself from the blast that this time was sure to come. He opened his mouth, closed his eyes, and breathed out hard in anticipation. The grenade sizzled. He stayed like that for a full twenty seconds before he looked up at Barton.

"Dud," Barton said.

Yurek grabbed it and threw it into the street.

someone had bought themselves a batch of bad grenades. Wilkinson later found three or four more unexploded ones inside the body of the helicopter.

The American forces around Wolcott's downed Black Hawk were now scattered along an L-shaped perimeter stretching south. One group of about thirty men was massed around the wreck in the alleyway, at the northern base of the "L." When they learned that the ground convoy had gotten lost and delayed, they began moving the wounded through the hole made by the falling helicopter into the house of Abdiaziz Ali Aden (he was still hidden in a back room.). Immediately west of the alley (at the bend of the "L") was Marehan Road, where Nelson, Yurek, Barton, and Twombly were dug in across the street at the northwest corner. On the east side of that intersection, nearest the chopper, were DiTomasso, Coleman, Belman, and Delta Captain Bill Coultrop and his radio operator. The rest of the ground force was stretched out south on Marchan Road, along the stem of the "L," which sloped uphill. Steele and a dozen or so Rangers, along with three Delta teams, about thirty men in all, were together in a courtyard on the east side of Marehan Road midway up the next block south, separated from the bulk of the force by half a block, a wide alley, and a long block. Sergeant Howe's Delta team, with a group of Rangers that included Specialist Stebbins, followed by the Delta command group led by Captain Miller, had crossed the wide alley and was moving down the west wall toward Nelson's position. Lieutenant Perino had also crossed the alley and was moving downhill along the east wall with Corporal Smith, Sergeant Chuck Elliot, and several other men.

As Howe approached Nelson's position, it looked to him as though the Rangers were just hiding. Two of his men ran across the alley to tell the Rangers to *start shooting*. Nelson and the others were still recovering from the shock of the unexploded grenades. Rounds were taking chips off the walls all around them, but it was hard to see where the shots were coming from. Howe's team members helped arrange Nelson and the others to set up effective fields of fire and placed Stebbins and machine-gunner Private Brian Heard at the southern corner of the same intersection, orienting them to fire west.

Captain Miller caught up with Howe, trailing his radioman and some other members of his element, along with Staff Sergeant Jeff Bray, an air force combat controller. With all the shooting at that intersection, Howe decided it was time to get off the street. There was a metal gate at the entrance to a courtyard between two buildings on his side of the block. He pushed against the gate, which had two doors that opened inward. Howe considered putting a charge on the door, but given the number of soldiers nearby and the lack of cover, the explosion would probably hurt people. So the burly sergeant and Bray began hurling themselves against the gate. Bray's side gave way.

"Follow me in case I get shot," Howe said.

He plunged into the courtyard and rapidly moved through the house on either side, running from room to room. Howe was looking for people, focusing his eyes at midtorso first, checking hands. The hands told you the whole story. The only hands he found were empty. They belonged to a man and woman and some children, a family of about seven, clearly terrified. He stood in the doorway with his weapon in his right hand pointing at them, trying to coax them out of the room with his left hand. It took a while, but they came out slowly, clinging to each other. The family was flex-cuffed and herded into a small side room.

Howe then more carefully inspected the space. Each of the blocks in this neighborhood of Mogadishu consisted of mostly one-story stone houses grouped irregularly around open spaces, or courtyards. This block consisted of a short courtyard, about two car-lengths wide, where he now stood. There was a two-story house on the south side and a one-story house on the north. Howe figured this space was about the safest spot around. The taller building would shelter them from both bullets and lobbed RPGs. At the west end was some kind of storage shack. Howe began exploring systematically, making a more thorough sweep, moving from room to room, looking for windows that would give them a good vantage for shooting west down the alley. He found several but none that offered a particularly good angle. The alley to the north (the same one that the helicopter had crashed into one block west) was too narrow. He could only see about fifteen yards down in either direction, and all he saw was wall. When he returned to the courtyard, Captain Miller and the others had begun herding casualties into the space. It would serve as their command post and casualty collection point for the rest of the night.

As he reentered the courtyard, one of the master sergeants with Miller told Howe to go back out to the street and help his team. Howe resented the order. He felt he was, at this point, the de facto leader on the ground, the one doing all the real thinking and moving and fighting. They had reached a temporary safe point, a time for commanders to catch their breath and think. They were in a bad spot, but not critical. The next step would be to look for ways to strong-

point their position, expand their perimeter, identify other buildings to take down to give them better lines of fire. The troop sergeant's command was the order of a man who didn't know what to do next.

Howe was built like a pro wrestler, but he was a thinker. This sometimes troubled his relationship with authority—especially the army's maddeningly arbitrary manner of placing unseasoned, less-qualified men in charge. Howe was just a sergeant first class with supposedly narrower concerns, but he saw the big picture very clearly, better than most. After being selected for Delta he had met and married the daughter of Colonel Charlie A. Beckwith, the founder and original commander of Delta. They had met in a lounge by Fort Bragg and when he told her that he was a civilian, Connie Beckwith, a former army officer then herself, nodded knowingly.

"Look," she said. "I know who you work for so let's stop pretending. My dad started that unit."

She had to pull out her driver's license to prove who she was.

Not that Howe had any ambition for formal army leadership. His preferred relationship with officers was for them to heed his advice and leave him alone. He was frequently aghast at the failings of those in charge.

Take this setup in Mogadishu, for instance. It was asinine. At the base, the huge hangar front doors wouldn't close, so the Sammies had a clear view inside at all hours of the day or night. The city sloped gradually up from the waterfront, so any Somali with patience and binoculars could keep an eye on their state of readiness. Every time they scrambled to gear up and go, word was out in the city before they were even on the helicopters. If that weren't bad enough, you had the Italians, some of them openly sympathetic to their former colonial subjects, who appeared to be flashing signals with their headlights out into the city whenever the helicopters took off. Nobody had the balls to do anything about it.

Then there were the mortars. General Garrison seemed to regard mortars as little more than as annoyance. He had walked around casually during the early mortar attacks, his cigar clenched in his teeth, amused by the way everyone dove for cover. "Piddly-assed mortars," he'd said. Which was all well and good, except, as Howe saw it, if the Sammies ever got their act together and managed to drop a few on the hangar, there'd be hell to pay. He wondered if the tin roof was thick enough to detonate the round— which would merely send shrapnel and shards of the metal roof slashing down through the ranks—or whether the round would just poke on through and detonate on the concrete floor in the middle of everybody. It was a question that lingered in his mind most nights as he went to sleep. Then there were the flimsy perimeter defenses. At mealtimes, all the men would be lined up outside the mess hall, which was separated from a busy outside road by nothing more than a thin metal wall. A car bomb along that wall at the right time of day could kill dozens of soldiers.

Howe did not hide his disgust over these things. Now, being ordered to do something pointless in the middle of the biggest fight of his life, he was furious. He began gathering up ammo, grenades, and LAWS off the wounded Rangers in the courtyard. It seemed to Howe that most of the men failed to grasp how desperate their situation had become. It was a form of denial. They could not stop thinking of themselves as the superior force, in command of the situation, yet the tables had clearly turned. They were surrounded and terribly outnumbered. The very idea of adhering to rules of engagement at this point was preposterous.

"You're throwing grenades?" the troop sergeant asked him, surprised when he saw Howe stuffing all of them he could find into his vest pockets.

"We're not getting paid to bring them back," Howe told him.

This was war. The game now was kill or be killed. He stomped angrily out to the street and began looking for Somalis to shoot.

He found one of the Rangers, Nelson, firing a handgun at the window of the building Howe had just painstakingly cleared and occupied. Nelson had seen someone moving in the window, and they had been taking fire from just about ever direction, so he was pumping a few rounds that way.

"What are you doing?" Howe shouted across the alley.

Nelson couldn't hear Howe. He shouted back, "I saw someone in there."

"No shit! There are friendlies in there!"

Nelson didn't find out until later what Howe had been waving this arms about. When he did he was mortified. No one had told him that Delta had moved into that space, but, then again, it was a cardinal sin to shoot before identifying the target.

Already furious, Howe began venting at the Rangers. He felt that were not fighting hard enough. When he saw Nelson, Yurek, and others trying to selectively target armed Somalis in a crowd at the other end of a building on their side of the street, Howe threw a grenade over its roof. It was an amazing toss, but the grenade failed to explode. So Howe threw another, which exploded right where the crowd was gathered. He then watched the Rangers try to hit a gunman who kept darting out from behind a shed about one block north, shooting, and then retreating back behind. it. The Delta sergeant flung one of his golf ball-sized minigrenades over the Rangers' position. It exploded behind the shed, and the gunman did not reappear. Howe then picked up a LAW and hurled it across the road. It landed on the arm of Specialist Lance Twombly, who was lying on his belly four or five feet from the corner wall. The LAW bruised his forearm. Twombly jumped to his knees, angry, and turned to hear Howe bellowing, "Shoot the motherfucker!"

Down on one knee, Howe swore bitterly as he fired. Everything about this situation was pissing him off, the goddamn Somalis, his leaders, the idiot Rangers . . . even his ammunition. He drew a bead on three Somalis who were running across the street two blocks to the north, taking a progressive lead on them the way he had learned through countless hours of training, squaring them in his sights and then aiming several feet in front of them. He would squeeze two or three rounds, rapidly increasing his lead with each shot. He was an expert marksman, and thought he had hit them, but he couldn't tell for sure because they kept running until they crossed the street and were out of view. It bugged him. His weapon was the most sophisticated infantry rifle in the world, a customized CAR-15, and he was shooting the army's new 5.56 mm green-tip round. The green tip had a tungsten carbide penetrator at the tip, and would punch holes in metal, but that very penetrating power meant his rounds were passing right through his targets. When the Sammie were close enough he could see when he hit them. Their shirts would lift up at the point of impact, as if someone had pinched and plucked up the fabric. But with the green-tip round it was like sticking somebody with an ice pick. The bullet made a small, clean hole, and unless it happened to hit the heart or spine, it wasn't enough to stop a man in his tracks. Howe felt like he had to hit a guy five or six times just to get his attention. They used a kid Randy Shughart because he shunned the modern rifle and ammunition and carried a Vietnam era M-14, which shot a 7.62 mm round without the penetrating qualities of the new green tip. It occurred to Howe as he saw those Sammies keep on running that Randy was the smartest soldier in the unit. His rifle may have been heavier and comparatively awkward and delivered a mean recoil, but it damn sure knocked a man down with one bullet, and in combat, one shot was often all you got. You shoot a guy, you want to see him go down; you don't want to be guessing for the next five hours whether you hit him, or whether he's still waiting for you in the weeds.

Howe was in a good spot. There was nothing in front or behind him that would stop a bullet, but there was a tree about twenty feet south against the west wall of the street that blocked any view of him from that direction. The bigger tree across the alley where Nelson, Twombly, and the others were positioned blocked any view of him from the north. So the broad-beamed Delta sergeant could kneel about five feet off the wall and pick off targets to the north with impunity. It was like that in battle. Some spots were safer than others. Up the hill, Hooten had watched Howe and his team move across the intersection while he was lying with his face pressed in the dirt, with rounds popping all around him. *How can they be doing that?* he'd thought. By an accident of visual angles, one person could stand and fight without difficulty, while just a few feet away fire could be so withering that there was nothing to do but dive for cover and stay hidden. Howe recognized he'd found such a safety zone. He shot methodically, saving his ammunition.

When he saw Perino, Smith, and Elliot creeping down to a similar position on the other side of the street, he figured they were trying to do what he was doing. Except, on that side of the street there were no trees to provide concealment.

He shouted across at them impatiently, but in the din he wasn't heard.

Perino and his men had moved down to a small tin shed, a porch really, that protruded from the irregular gray stone wall. They were only about ten yards from the alley where *Super Six One* lay. A West Point graduate, class of 1990, Perino at twenty-four wasn't much older than the Rangers he commanded. His group had gotten out ahead of Captain Steele and most of the Ranger force. They had pushed across the last intersection to the crash site after Goodale had been hit. They had cleared the first courtyard they passed on that block, and Perino had then led several of the men back out in the street to press on down Marehan Road. He knew they were close to linking up with Lieutenant DiTomasso and the CSAR team, which had been their destination when they started this move. The shed was just a few steps downhill from the courtyard doorway.

Sergeant Elliot was already on the other side of the shed. Corporal Smith was crouched behind it and Perino was just a few feet behind Smith. They were taking so much fire it was confusing. Rounds seemed to be coming from everywhere. Stone chips sprayed from the wall over Perino's head and rattled down on his helmet. He saw a Somali with a gun on the opposite side of the street, about twenty yards north of Nelson's position, blocked from those guys' view by the tree they were hiding behind. Perino saw the muzzle flash and cold tell this was where some of the incoming rounds originated. It would be hard to hit the guy with a rifle shot, but Smith had a grenade launcher on his M-16 and might be able to drop a 203 round near enough to hurt the guy. He moved up to tap Smith on the shoulder—there was too much noise to communicate other than face-to-face—when bullets began popping loudly through the shed. The lieutenant was on one knee and a round spat up dirt between his legs.

Across the street, Nelson saw Smith get hit. The burly corporal had moved down the street fast and had taken a knee to begin shooting. Most of the men at that corner heard the round hit him, a hard, ugly slap. Smith seemed jut startled at first. He rolled to his side and, like he was commenting about someone else, remarked with surprise, "I'm hit!"

From where Nelson was, it didn't look like Smith was hurt that badly. Perino helped move him against the wall. Now Smith was screaming, "I'm hit! I'm hit!"

The lieutenant could tell by the sound of Smith's voice that he was in pain. When Goodale had been hit he seemed to feel almost nothing, but the wound to Smith was different. He was writhing. He was in a very bad way. Perino pressed a field dressing into the wound but blood spurted out forcefully around it.

"I've got a bleeder here!" Perino shouted across the street.

Delta medic Sergeant Kurt Schmidt dashed toward them across Marehan Road. Together, they dragged Smith back into the courtyard.

Schmid tore off Smith's pants leg. When he removed the battle dressing, bright red blood projected out of the wound in a long pulsing spurt. This was bad.

The young soldier told Perino, "Man, this *really* hurts."

The lieutenant went back out to the street and crept back up to Elliot.

"Where's Smith?" Elliot asked.

"He's down."

"Shit," said Elliot.

They saw Sergeant Ken Boorn get hit in the foot. The Private Rodriguez rolled away from his machine gun, bleeding, screaming, and holding his crotch. He felt no pain, but when he had placed his hand on the wound his genitals felt like mush and blood spurted thickly between his fingers. He screamed in alarm. Eight of the eleven Rangers in Perino's Chalk One had now been hit.

At the north end of the same block there was a huge explosion and in it Stebbins went down. Nelson saw it from up close. An RPG had streaked into the wall of the house across the alley from him, over near where Stebbins and Heard were positioned. The grenade went off with a brilliant red flash and tore out a chunk of the wall about four feet long. The concussion in the narrow alley was huge. It hurt his ears. There was a big cloud of dust. He saw—and Perino and Elliot saw from across the street—both Stebbins and Heard flat on their backs. *They're fucked up,* Nelson thought. But Stebbins stirred and then slowly stood up, covered from head to foot in white dust, coughing, rubbing his eyes.

"Get down, Stebbins!" shouted Heard. So he was okay, too.

Bullets were hitting around Perino and Elliot with increasing frequency. Rounds would come in long bursts, snapping between them, over their heads, nicking the tin shed with a high-pitched ring and popping right through the metal. Rounds were kicking up dirt all over their side of the street. It was a bad position, just as Howe had foreseen.

"Uh, sir, I think that it would be a pretty good idea if we go into that courtyard," said Elliot.

"Do you really think so?" Perino asked.

Elliot grabbed his arm and they both dove for the courtyard where Schmid was working frantically to save Smith.

Corporal Smith was alert and terrified and in sharp pain. The medic had first tried applying direct pressure on the wound, which had proved excruciatingly painful and obviously ineffective. Bright red blood continued to gush from the hole in Smith's leg. The medic tried jamming Curlex into the hole. Then he checked Smith over.

"Are you hurt anywhere else?" he asked.

"I don't know."

Schmid checked for an exit wound, and found none.

The medic was thirty-one. He'd grown up an army brat, vowing never to join the military, and ended up enlisting a year after graduating from high school. He'd gone into Special Forces and elected to become a medic because he figured it would give him good employment opportunity when he left the army. He was good at it, and his training kept progressing. By now he'd been schooled as thoroughly as any physician's assistant, and better than some. As part of his training he'd worked in the emergency room of a hospital in San Diego, and had even done some minor surgery under a physician's guidance. He certainly had enough training to know that Jamie Smith was in trouble if he couldn't stop the bleeding.

He could deduce that path the bullet had taken. It had entered Smith's thigh and traveled up into his pelvis. A gunshot wound to the pelvis is one of the worst. The aorta splits low in the abdomen, forming the left and right iliac arteries. As the iliac artery emerges from the pelvis it branches into the exterior and deep femoral arteries, the primary avenues for blood to the lower half of the body. The bullet had clearly pierced one of the femoral vessels. Schmid applied direct pressure to Smith's abdomen, right above the pelvis where the artery splits. He explained what he was doing. He'd already run two IVs into Smith's arm, using 14-gauge, large bore needles, and was literally squeezing the plastic bag to push replacement fluid into him. Smith's blood formed an oily pool that shone dully on the dirt floor of the courtyard.

The medic took comfort in the assumption that help would arrive shortly. Another treatment tactic, a very risky one, would be to begin directly transfusing Smith. Blood transfusions were rarely done on the battlefield. It was a tricky business. The medics carried IV fluids with them but not blood. It he wanted to transfuse Smith, he'd have to find someone with the same blood type and attempt a direct transfusion. This was likely to create more problems. He could begin reacting badly to the transfusion. Schmid decided not to attempt it. The rescue convoy was supposed to be arriving shortly. What this Ranger needed was a doctor, pronto.

Perino radioed Captain Steele.

"We can't go any further, sir. We have more wounded than I can carry."

"You've got to push on," Steel told him.

"We CANNOT go further," Perino said, "Request permission to occupy a building."

Steele told Perino to keep trying. Actually, inside the courtyard they were only about fifty feet from Lieutenant DiTomasso and the CSAR force, but Perino had no way of knowing that. He tried to reach DiTomasso on his radio.

"Tom, where are you?"

DiTomasso tried to explain their position, pointing out landmarks.

"I can't see," said Perino. "I'm in a courtyard."

DiTomasso popped a red smoke grenade, and Perino saw the red plume drifting up in the darkening sky. He guessed from the drift of the plume that they were about fifty yards apart, which in this killing zone was a great distance. On the radio, Steel kept pushing him to link up with DiTomasso.

"They need your help," he said.

"Look, sir, I've got three guys left, counting myself. How can I help him?"

Finally, Steele relented.

"Roger, strongpoint the building and defend it."

Schmid was still working frantically on Smith's wound. He'd asked Perino to help him by applying pressure just over the wound so he could use his hands. Perino pushed two fingers directly into the wound up to his knuckles. Smith screamed and blood shot out at the lieutenant, who swallowed hard and applied more pressure. He felt dizzy. The spurts of blood continued.

"Oh, shit! Oh, shit! I'm gonna die! I'm gonna die!" Smith shouted. He knew had had an arterial bleed.

The medic talked to him, tried to calm him down. The only way to stop the bleeding was to find the severed femoral artery and clamp it. Otherwise it was like trying to stanch a fire hose by pushing down on it through a mattress. He told Smith to lean back.

"This is going to be very painful," Schmid told the Ranger apologetically. "I'm going to have to cause you more pain, but I have to do this to help you."

"Give me some morphine for the pain!" Smith demanded. He was still very alert and engaged.

"I can't," Schmid told him. In this state, morphine could kill him. After losing so much blood, he pressure was precariously low. Morphine would further lower his heart rate and slow his respiration, exactly what he did not need.

The young Ranger bellowed as the medic reached with both hands and tore open the entrance wound. Schmid tried to shut out the fact that there were live nerve endings beneath his fingers. It was hard. He had formed an emotional bond with Smith. They were in this together. But to save the young Ranger, he had to treat him like an inanimate object, a machine that was broken and needed fixing. He continued to root for the artery. If he failed to find it, Smith would probably die. He picked through the open upper thigh, reaching up to his pelvis, parting layers of skin, fat, muscle, and vessel, probing through pools of bright red blood. He couldn't find it. Once severed, the upper end of the artery had evidently retracted up into Smith's abdomen. The medic stopped. Smith was lapsing into shock. The only recourse now would be to cut into the abdomen and hunt for the severed artery and clamp it. But that would mean still more pain and blood loss. Every time he reached into the wound Smith lost more blood. Schmid and Perino were covered with it. Blood was everywhere. It was hard to believe Smith had any more to lose.

"It hurts really bad," he kept saying. "It really hurts."

In time his words and movements came slowly, labored. He was in shock.

Schmid was beside himself. He had squeezed six liters of fluid into the young Ranger and was running out of bags. He had tried everything and was feeling desperate and frustrated and angry. He had to leave the room. He got one of the other men to continue applying pressure on the wound and walked out to confer with Perino. Both men were covered with Smith's blood.

"If I don't' get him out of here right now, he's gonna die," Schmid pleaded.

The lieutenant radioed Steel again.

"Sir, we need a medevac. A Little Bird or something. For Corporal Smith. We need to extract him *now.*"

Steele relayed this on the command net. It was tough to get through. It was nearly five o'clock and growing dark. All of the vehicles had turned back to the air base. Steele learned that there would be no relief for some time. Putting another bird down in their neighborhood was out of the question.

The captain radioed Perino back and told him, for the time being, that Smith would just have to hang on.

MEDAL OF HONOR

MEDAL OF HONOR BREAKDOWN
(By War and Service as of 13 May 1997)

Action	Total	Army	Navy	Marine	Air Force	Coast Guard	Posthumous
Civil War	1,520	1,195	308	17	0	0	25
Indian Wars 1861–1898	428	428	0	0	0	0	6
Korea 1871	15	0	9	6	0	0	0
Spanish American War	109	30	64	15	0	0	0
Philippines Samoa	91	70	12	9	0	0	1
Boxer Rebellion	59	4	22	33	0	0	1
Vera Cruz 1914	55	0	46	9	0	0	0
Haiti 1915	6	0	0	6	0	0	0
Dominican Republic	3	0	0	3	0	0	0
Haiti 1919–1920	2	0	0	2	0	0	0
Nicaragua 1927–1933	2	0	0	2	0	0	0
Peacetime 1865–1870	12	0	12	0	0	0	0
Peacetime 1871–1898	103	0	101	2	0	0	0
Peacetime 1899–1911	51	1	48	2	0	0	0
Peacetime 1915–1916	8	0	8	0	0	0	1
Peacetime 1920–1940	18	2	15	1	0	0	4
World War I	124	96	21	7	0	0	32
World War II	440	301	57	81	0	1	250
Korean War	131	78	7	42	4	0	93
Vietnam War	239	155	15	57	12	0	150
Somalia 1993	2	2	0	0	0	0	2
Unknown Soldiers	9	0	0	0	0	0	9
Total	3,427	2,362	745	294	16	1	574

These totals reflect the total number of Medals of Honor awarded. Nineteen (19) men received a second award: fourteen of these men received two separate Medals for two separate actions; five received both the Navy and the Army Medals of Honor for the same action. The total number of Medal of Honor recipients is 3,408.

Total Medals of Honor awarded: 3,427

Total number of Medal of Honor recipients: 3,408

Total number of double recipients: 19

Total number of enlisted personnel: 2,553

As of 13 May 1997, there are 169 living Medal of Honor recipients.

BEAUDOIN, RAYMOND O.

Rank and organization: First Lieutenant, U.S. Army, Company F, 119th Infantry, 30th Infantry Division. Place and date: Hamelin, Germany, 6 April 1945. Entered service at: Holyoke, Mass. Birth: Holyoke, Mass. G.O. No.: 9, 25 January 1946. Citation: He was leading the 2d Platoon of Company F over flat, open terrain to Hamelin, Germany, when the enemy went into action with machineguns and automatic weapons, laying down a devastating curtain of fire that pinned his unit to the ground. By rotating men in firing positions he made it possible for his entire platoon to dig in, defying all the while the murderous enemy fire to encourage his men and to distribute ammunition. He then dug in himself at the most advanced position, where he kept up a steady fire, killing 6 hostile soldiers, and directing his men in inflicting heavy casualties on the numerically superior opposing force. Despite these defensive measures, however, the position of the platoon became more precarious, for the enemy had brought up strong reinforcements and was preparing a counterattack. Three men, sent back at intervals to obtain ammunition and reinforcements, were killed by sniper fire. To relieve his command from the desperate situation, 1st Lt. Beaudoin decided to make a l-man attack on the most damaging enemy sniper nest 90 yards to the right flank, and thereby divert attention from the runner who would attempt to pierce the enemy's barrier of bullets and secure help. Crawling over completely exposed ground, he relentlessly advanced, undeterred by 8 rounds of bazooka fire, which threw mud and stones over him, or by rifle fire, which ripped his uniform. Ten yards from the enemy position he stood up and charged. At point-blank range he shot and killed 2 occupants of the nest; a third, who tried to bayonet him, he overpowered and killed with the butt of his carbine; and the fourth adversary was cut down by the platoon's rifle fire as he attempted to flee. He continued his attack by running toward a dugout, but there he was struck and killed by a burst from a machinegun. By his intrepidity, great fighting skill, and supreme devotion to his responsibility for the well-being of his platoon, 1st Lt. Beaudoin single-handedly accomplished a mission that enabled a messenger to secure help which saved the stricken unit and made possible the decisive defeat of the German forces.

WALKER, DR. MARY E.

Rank and organization: Contract Acting Assistant Surgeon (civilian), U. S. Army. Places and dates: Battle of Bull Run, July 21, 1861; Patent Office Hospital, Washington, D.C., October 1861; Chattanooga, Tenn., following Battle of Chickomauga, September 1863; Prisoner of War, April 10, 1864-August 12, 1864, Richmond, Va.; Battle of Atlanta, September 1864. Entered service at: Louisville, Ky. Born: 26 November 1832, Oswego County, N.Y. Citation: Whereas it appears from official reports that Dr. Mary E. Walker, a graduate of medicine, "has rendered valuable service to the Government, and her efforts have been earnest and untiring in a variety of ways," and that she was assigned to duty and served as an assistant surgeon in charge of female prisoners at Louisville, Ky., upon the recommendation of Major-Generals Sherman and Thomas, and faithfully served as contract surgeon in the service of the United States, and has devoted herself with much patriotic zeal to the sick and wounded soldiers, both in the field and hospitals, to the detriment of her own health, and has also endured hardships as a prisoner of war four months in a Southern prison while acting as contract surgeon; and Whereas by reason of her not being a commissioned officer in the military service, a brevet or honorary rank cannot, under existing laws, be conferred upon her; and Whereas in the opinion of the President an honorable recognition of her services and sufferings should be made: It is ordered, That a testimonial thereof shall be hereby made and given to the said Dr. Mary E. Walker, and that the usual medal of honor for meritorious services be given her.

> Given under my hand in the city of Washington, D.C., this 11th day of November, A.D. 1865.
> Andrew Johnson,
> President
> (Medal rescinded 1917 along with 910 others, restored by President Carter 10 June 1977.)

FOWLER, THOMAS W.

Rank and organization: Second Lieutenant, U.S. Army, 1st Armored Division. Place and date: Near Carano, Italy, 23 May 1944. Entered service at: Wichita Falls,

Tex. Birth: Wichita Falls, Tex. G.O. No.: 84, 28 October, 1944. Citation: For conspicuous gallantry and intrepidity at risk of life above and beyond the call of duty, on 23 May 1944, in the vicinity of Carano, Italy. In the midst of a full-scale armored-infantry attack, 2d Lt. Fowler, while on foot, came upon 2 completely disorganized infantry platoons held up in their advance by an enemy minefield. Although a tank officer, he immediately reorganized the infantry. He then made a personal reconnaissance through the minefield, clearing a path as he went, by lifting the antipersonnel mines out of the ground with his hands. After he had gone through the 75-yard belt of deadly explosives, he returned to the infantry and led them through the minefield, a squad at a time. As they deployed, 2d Lt. Fowler, despite small arms fire and the constant danger of antipersonnel mines, made a reconnaissance into enemy territory in search of a route to continue the advance. He then returned through the minefield and, on foot, he led the tanks through the mines into a position from which they could best support the infantry. Acting as scout 300 yards in front of the infantry, he led the 2 platoons forward until he had gained his objective, where he came upon several dug-in enemy infantrymen. Having taken them by surprise, 2d Lt. Fowler dragged them out of their foxholes and sent them to the rear; twice, when they resisted, he threw hand grenades into their dugouts. Realizing that a dangerous gap existed between his company and the unit to his right, 2d Lt. Fowler decided to continue his advance until the gap was filled. He reconnoitered to his front, brought the infantry into position where they dug in and, under heavy mortar and small arms fire, brought his tanks forward. A few minutes later, the enemy began an armored counterattack. Several Mark VI tanks fired their cannons directly on 2d Lt. Fowler's position. One of his tanks was set afire. With utter disregard for his own life, with shells bursting near him, he ran directly into the enemy tank fire to reach the burning vehicle. For a half-hour, under intense strafing from the advancing tanks, although all other elements had withdrawn, he remained in his forward position, attempting to save the lives of the wounded tank crew. Only when the enemy tanks had almost overrun him, did he withdraw a short distance where he personally rendered first aid to 9 wounded infantrymen in the midst of the relentless incoming fire. 2d Lt. Fowler's courage, his ability to estimate the situation and to recognize his full responsibility as an offi-cer in the Army of the United States, exemplify the high traditions of the military service for which he later gave his life.

ALLWORTH, EDWARD C.

Rank and organization: Captain, U.S. Army, 60th Infantry, 5th Division. Place and date: At Clery-le-Petit, France, 5 November 1918. Entered service at: Corvallis, Oreg. Born: 6 July 1887, Crawford, Wash. G.O. No.: 16, W.D., 1919. Citation: While his company was crossing the Meuse River and canal at a bridge-head opposite Clery-le-Petit, the bridge over the canal was destroyed by shell fire and Capt. Allworth's command became separated, part of it being on the east bank of the canal and the remainder on the west bank. Seeing his advance units making slow headway up the steep slope ahead, this officer mounted the canal bank and called for his men to follow. Plunging in he swam across the canal under fire from the enemy, followed by his men. Inspiring his men by his example of gallantry, he led them up the slope, joining his hard-pressed platoons in front. By his personal leadership he forced the enemy back for more than a kilometer, overcoming machinegun nests and capturing 100 prisoners, whose number exceeded that of the men in his command. The exceptional courage and leadership displayed by Capt. Allworth made possible the re-establishment of a bridgehead over the canal and the successful advance of other troops.

CHILES, MARCELLUS H.

Rank and organization: Captain, U.S. Army, 356th Infantry, 89th Division. Place and date: Near Le Champy Bas, France, 3 November 1918. Entered service at: Denver, Colo. Birth: Eureka Springs, Ark. G.O. No.: 20, W.D., 1919. Citation: When his battalion, of which he had just taken command, was halted by machinegun fire from the front and left flank, he picked up the rifle of a dead soldier and, calling on his men to follow led the advance across a stream, waist deep, in the face of the machinegun fire. Upon reaching the opposite bank this gallant officer was seriously wounded in the abdomen by a sniper, but before permitting himself to be evacuated he made complete arrangements for turning over his command to the next senior officer, and under the inspiration of his fearless leadership his battalion reached its objective. Capt. Chiles died shortly after reaching the hospital.

KEATHLEY, GEORGE D.

Rank and organization: Staff Sergeant, U.S. Army, 85th Infantry Division. Place and date: Mt. Altuzzo, Italy, 14 September 1944. Entered service at: Lamesa, Tex. Birth: Olney, Tex. G.O. No.: 20, 29 March 1945. Citation: For conspicuous gallantry and intrepidity at risk of life above and beyond the call of duty, in action on the western ridge of Mount Altuzzo, Italy. After bitter fighting his company had advanced to within 50 yards of the objective, where it was held up due to intense enemy sniper, automatic, small arms, and mortar fire. The enemy launched 3 desperate counterattacks in an effort to regain their former positions, but all 3 were repulsed with heavy casualties on both sides. All officers and noncommissioned officers of the 2d and 3d platoons of Company B had become casualties, and S/Sgt. Keathley, guide of the 1st platoon, moved up and assumed command of both the 2d and 3d platoons, reduced to 20 men. The remnants of the 2 platoons were dangerously low on ammunition, so S/Sgt. Keathley, under deadly small arms and mortar fire, crawled from 1 casualty to another, collecting their ammunition and administering first aid. He then visited each man of his 2 platoons, issuing the precious ammunition he had collected from the dead and wounded, and giving them words of encouragement. The enemy now delivered their fourth counterattack, which was approximately 2 companies in strength. In a furious charge they attacked from the front and both flanks, throwing hand grenades, firing automatic weapons, and assisted by a terrific mortar barrage. So strong was the enemy counterattack that the company was given up for lost. The remnants of the 2d and 3d platoons of Company B were now looking to S/Sgt. Keathley for leadership. He shouted his orders precisely and with determination and the men responded with all that was in them. Time after time the enemy tried to drive a wedge into S/Sgt. Keathley's position and each time they were driven back, suffering huge casualties. Suddenly an enemy hand grenade hit and exploded near S/Sgt. Keathley, inflicting a mortal wound in his left side. However, hurling defiance at the enemy, he rose to his feet. Taking his left hand away from his wound and using it to steady his rifle, he fired and killed an attacking enemy soldier, and continued shouting orders to his men. His heroic and intrepid action so inspired his men that they fought with incomparable determination and viciousness.

For 15 minutes S/Sgt. Keathley continued leading his men and effectively firing his rifle. He could have sought a sheltered spot and perhaps saved his life, but instead he elected to set an example for his men and make every possible effort to hold his position. Finally, friendly artillery fire helped to force the enemy to withdraw, leaving behind many of their number either dead or seriously wounded. S/Sgt. Keathley died a few moments later. Had it not been for his indomitable courage and incomparable heroism, the overwhelming enemy attacking force might well have annihilated the remnants of 3 rifle platoons of Company B. His actions were in keeping with the highest traditions of the military service.

GORDON, GARY I.

Rank and organization: Master Sergeant, U.S. Army. Place and date: 3 October 1993, Mogadishu, Somalia. Entered service at: — Born: Lincoln, Maine. Citation: Master Sergeant Gordon, United States Army, distinguished himself by actions above and beyond the call of duty on 3 October 1993, while serving as Sniper Team Leader, United States Army Special Operations Command with Task Force Ranger in Mogadishu, Somalia. Master Sergeant Gordon's sniper team provided precision fires from the lead helicopter during an assault and at two helicopter crashes sites, while subjected to intense automatic weapons and rocket propelled grenade fires. When Master Sergeant Gordon learned that ground forces were not immediately available to secure the second crash site, he and another sniper unhesitatingly volunteered to be inserted to protect the four critically wounded personnel, despite being well aware of the growing number of enemy personnel closing in on the site. After his third request to be inserted, Master Sergeant Gordon received permission to perform his volunteer mission. When debris and enemy ground fires at the site caused them to abort the first attempt, Master Sergeant Gordon was inserted one hundred meters south of the crash site. Equipped with only his sniper rifle and a pistol, Master Sergeant Gordon and his fellow sniper, while under intense small arms fire from the enemy, fought their way through a dense maze of shanties and shacks to reach the critically injured crew members. Master Sergeant Gordon immediately pulled the pilot and the other crew members from the aircraft, establishing a perimeter, which placed him and his fellow sniper in the most vulnerable position. Master Sergeant Gordon used his long-range rifle and side arm to kill an undetermined number of attackers until he depleted his ammunition. Master Sergeant Gordon then went back to the wreckage, recovering some of the crew's weapons and ammunition. Despite the fact that he was critically low on ammunition, he provided some of it to the dazed pilot and then radioed for help. Master Sergeant Gordon continued to travel the perimeter, protecting the downed crew. After his team member was fatally wounded and his own rifle ammunition exhausted, Master Sergeant Gordon returned to the wreckage, recovering a rifle with the last five rounds of ammunition and gave it to the pilot with the words, "good luck." Then, armed only with his pistol, Master Sergeant Gordon continued to fight until he was fatally wounded. His actions saved the pilot's life. Master Sergeant Gordon's extraordinary heroism and devotion to duty were in keeping with the highest standards of military service and reflect great credit upon him, his unit and the United States Army.

KAROPCZYC, STEPHEN EDWARD

Rank and organization: First Lieutenant, U.S. Army, Company A, 2d Battalion, 35th Infantry, 25th Infantry Division. Place and date: Kontum Province, Republic of Vietnam, 12 March 1967. Entered service at: Bethpage, N.Y. Born: 5 March 1944, New York, N.Y. Citation: For conspicuous gallantry and intrepidity in action at the risk of his life above and beyond the call of duty. While leading the 3d Platoon, Company A, on a flanking maneuver against a superior enemy force, 1st Lt. Karopczyc observed that his lead element was engaged with a small enemy unit along his route. Aware of the importance of quickly pushing through to the main enemy force in order to provide relief for a hard-pressed friendly platoon, he dashed through the intense enemy fire into the open and hurled colored smoke grenades to designate the foe for attack by helicopter gunships. He moved among his men to embolden their advance, and he guided their attack by marking enemy locations with bursts of fire from his own weapon. His forceful leadership quickened the advance, forced the enemy to retreat, and allowed his unit to close with the main hostile force. Continuing the deployment of his platoon, he constantly exposed himself as he ran from man to man to give encouragement and to direct their efforts. A shot

from an enemy sniper struck him above the heart but he refused aid for this serious injury, plugging the bleeding wound with his finger until it could be properly dressed. As the enemy strength mounted, he ordered his men to organize a defensive position in and around some abandoned bunkers where he conducted a defense against the increasingly strong enemy attacks. After several hours, a North Vietnamese soldier hurled a hand grenade to within a few feet of 1st Lt. Karopczyc and 2 other wounded men. Although his position protected him, he leaped up to cover the deadly grenade with a steel helmet. It exploded to drive fragments into 1st Lt. Karopczyc's legs, but his action prevented further injury to the 2 wounded men. Severely weakened by his multiple wounds, he continued to direct the actions of his men until he succumbed 2 hours later. 1st Lt. Karopczyc's heroic leadership, unyielding perseverance, and selfless devotion to his men were directly responsible for the successful and spirited action of his platoon throughout the battle and are in keeping with the highest traditions of the U.S. Army.

BURKE, LLOYD L.

Rank and organization: First Lieutenant, U.S. Army, Company G, 5th Cavalry Regiment, 1st Cavalry Division. Place and date: Near Chong-dong, Korea, 28 October 1951. Entered service at: Stuttgart, Ark. Born: 29 September 1924, Tichnor, Ark. G.O. No.: 43. Citation: 1st Lt. Burke, distinguished himself by conspicuous gallantry and outstanding courage above and beyond the call of duty in action against the enemy. Intense enemy fire had pinned down leading elements of his company committed to secure commanding ground when 1st Lt. Burke left the command post to rally and urge the men to follow him toward 3 bunkers impeding the advance. Dashing to an exposed vantage point he threw several grenades at the bunkers, then, returning for an Ml rifle and adapter, he made a lone assault, wiping out the position and killing the crew. Closing on the center bunker he lobbed grenades through the opening and, with his pistol, killed 3 of its occupants attempting to surround him. Ordering his men forward he charged the third emplacement, catching several grenades in midair and hurling them back at the enemy. Inspired by his display of valor his men stormed forward, overran the hostile position, but were again pinned down by increased fire. Securing a light machine gun and

3 boxes of ammunition, 1st Lt. Burke dashed through the impact area to an open knoll, set up his gun and poured a crippling fire into the ranks of the enemy, killing approximately 75. Although wounded, he ordered more ammunition, reloading and destroying 2 mortar emplacements and a machine gun position with his accurate fire. Cradling the weapon in his arms he then led his men forward, killing some 25 more of the retreating enemy and securing the objective. 1st Lt. Burke's heroic action and daring exploits inspired his small force of 35 troops. His unflinching courage and outstanding leadership reflect the highest credit upon himself, the infantry, and the U.S. Army.

FIRST LIEUTENANT VERNON J. BAKER

General Order:

Citation: For extraordinary heroism in action on 5 and 6 April 1945, near Viareggio, Italy. Then Second Lieutenant Baker demonstrated outstanding courage and leadership in destroying enemy installations, personnel and equipment during his company's attack against a strongly entrenched enemy in mountainous terrain. When his company was stopped by the concentration of fire from several machine gun emplacements, he crawled to one position and destroyed it, killing three Germans. Continuing forward, he attacked and enemy observation post and killed two occupants. With the aid of one of his men, Lieutenant Baker attacked two more machine gun nests, killing or wounding the four enemy soldiers occupying these positions. He then covered the evacuation of the wounded personnel of his company by occupying an exposed position and drawing the enemy's fire. On the following night Lieutenant Baker voluntarily led a battalion advance through enemy mine fields and heavy fire toward the division objective. Second Lieutenant Baker's fighting spirit and daring leadership were an inspiration to his men and exemplify the highest traditions of the Armed Forces.

MARM, WALTER JOSEPH, JR.

Rank and organization: First Lieutenant (then 2d Lt.), U.S. Army, Company A, 1st Battalion, 7th Cavalry, 1st Cavalry Division (Airmobile). place and date: Vicinity of Ia Drang Valley, Republic of Vietnam, 14 November 1965. Entered service at: Pittsburgh, pa. Born: 20 November 1941, Washington, pa. G.O. No.: 7, 15 February 1967. Citation: For conspicuous gallantry

and intrepidity at the risk of life above and beyond the call of duty. As a platoon leader in the 1st Cavalry Division (Airmobile), 1st Lt. Marm demonstrated indomitable courage during a combat operation. His company was moving through the valley to relieve a friendly unit surrounded by an enemy force of estimated regimental size. 1st Lt. Marm led his platoon through withering fire until they were finally forced to take cover. Realizing that his platoon could not hold very long, and seeing four enemy soldiers moving into his position, he moved quickly under heavy fire and annihilated all 4. Then, seeing that his platoon was receiving intense fire from a concealed machine gun, he deliberately exposed himself to draw its fire. Thus locating its position, he attempted to destroy it with an antitank weapon. Although he inflicted casualties, the weapon did not silence the enemy fire. Quickly, disregarding the intense fire directed on him and his platoon, he charged 30 meters across open ground, and hurled grenades into the enemy position, killing some of the 8 insurgents manning it. Although severely wounded, when his grenades were expended, armed with only a rifle, he continued the momentum of his assault on the position and killed the remainder of the enemy. 1st Lt. Marm's selfless actions reduced the fire on his platoon, broke the enemy assault, and rallied his unit to continue toward the accomplishment of this mission. 1st Lt. Marm's gallantry on the battlefield and his extraordinary intrepidity at the risk of his life are in the highest traditions of the U.S. Army and reflect great credit upon himself and the Armed Forces of his country.

MILLER, GARY L.

Rank and organization: First Lieutenant, U.S. Army, Company A, 1st Battalion, 28th Infantry, 1st Infantry Division. place and date: Binh Duong province, Republic of Vietnam, 16 February 1969. Entered service at: Roanoke, Va. Born: 19 March 1947, Covington, Va. Citation: For conspicuous intrepidity and gallantry in action at the risk of his life above and beyond the call of duty. First Lt. Miller, Infantry, Company A, was serving as a platoon leader at night when his company ambushed a hostile force infiltrating from Cambodian sanctuaries. After contact with the enemy was broken, 1st Lt. Miller led a reconnaissance patrol from their prepared positions through the early evening darkness and dense tropical growth to search the area for enemy casualties. As the group advanced they were suddenly attacked. First Lt. Miller was seriously wounded. However, the group fought back with telling effect on the hostile force. An enemy grenade was thrown into the midst of the friendly patrol group and all took cover except 1st Lt. Miller. who in the dim light located the grenade and threw himself on it, absorbing the force of the explosion with his body. His action saved nearby members of his patrol from almost certain serious injury. The extraordinary courage and selflessness displayed by this officer were an inspiration to his comrades and are in the highest traditions of the U.S. Army.

MEDAL OF HONOR

FM 22-100

Soldiers Are Our Credentials

In September 1944 on the Cotentin Peninsula in France, the commander of a German stronghold under siege by an American force sent word that he wanted to discuss surrender terms. German MG Hermann Ramcke was in his bunker when his staff escorted the assistant division commander of the US 8th Infantry Division down the concrete stairway to the underground headquarters. MG Ramcke addressed BG Charles D. W. Canham through an interpreter: "I am to surrender to you. Let me see your credentials." Pointing to the dirty, tired, disheveled—but victorious—American infantrymen who had accompanied him and were now crowding the dugout entrance, the American officer replied, "These are my credentials."

G A Marshall Continues to Serve

GA George C. Marshall served as Army Chief of Staff from 1939 until 1945. He led the Army through the buildup, deployment, and worldwide operations of World War II. In November 1945 he retired to a well-deserved rest at his home in Leesburg, Virginia. Just six days later President Harry S Truman called on him to serve as Special Ambassador to China. From the White House President Truman telephoned GA Marshall at his home: "General, I want you to go to China for me," the president said. "Yes, Mr. President," GA Marshall replied. He then hung up the telephone, informed his wife of the president's request and his reply, and prepared to return to government service.

President Truman didn't appoint GA Marshall a special ambassador to reward his faithful service; he appointed GA Marshall because there was a tough job in China that needed to be done. The Chinese communists under Mao Tse-tung were battling the Nationalists under Chiang Kai-shek, who had been America's ally against the Japanese; GA Marshall's job was to mediate peace between them. In the end he was unsuccessful in spite of a year of frustrating work; the scale of the problem was more than any one person could handle. However, in January 1947 President Truman appointed GA Marshall Secretary of State. The Cold War had begun and the president needed a leader Americans trusted. GA Marshall's reputation made him the one; his selflessness led him to continue to serve.

MSG Gordon and SFC Shughart in Somalia

During a raid in Mogadishu in October 1993, MSG Gary Gordon and SFC Randall Shughart, leader and member of a sniper team with Task Force Ranger in Somalia, were providing precision and suppressive fires from helicopters above two helicopter crash sites. Learning that no ground forces were available to rescue one of the downed aircrews and aware that a growing number of enemy were closing in on the site, MSG Gordon and SFC Shughart volunteered to be inserted to protect their critically wounded comrades. Their initial request was turned down because of the danger of the situation. They asked a second time; permission was denied. Only after their third request were they inserted.

MSG Gordon and SFC Shughart were inserted one hundred meters south of the downed chopper. Armed only with their personal weapons, the two NCOs fought their way to the downed fliers through intense small arms fire, a maze of shanties and shacks, and the enemy converging on the site. After MSG Gordon and SFC Shughart pulled the wounded from the wreckage, they established a perimeter, put themselves in the most dangerous position, and fought off a series of attacks. The two NCOs continued to protect their comrades until they had depleted their ammunition and were themselves fatally wounded. Their actions saved the life of an Army pilot.

WO1 Thompson at My Lai

Personal courage—whether physical, moral, or a combination of the two—may be manifested in a variety of ways, both on and off the battlefield. On March 16, 1968 Warrant Officer (WO1) Hugh C. Thompson, Jr. and his two-man crew were on a reconnaissance mission over the village of My Lai, Republic of Vietnam.

WO1 Thompson watched in horror as he saw an American soldier shoot an injured Vietnamese child. Minutes later, when he observed American soldiers advancing on a number of civilians in a ditch, WO1 Thompson landed his helicopter and questioned a young officer about what was happening on the ground. Told that the ground action was none of his business, WO1 Thompson took off and continued to circle the area.

When it became apparent that the American soldiers were now firing on civilians, WO1 Thompson landed his helicopter between the soldiers and a group of 10 villagers who were headed for a home-made bomb shelter. He ordered his gunner to train his weapon on the approaching American soldiers and to fire if necessary. Then he personally coaxed the civilians out of the shelter and airlifted them to safety. WO1 Thompson's radio reports of what was happening were instrumental in bringing about the cease-fire order that saved the lives of more civilians. His willingness to place himself in physical danger in order to do the morally right thing is a sterling example of personal courage.

The Will to Persevere

On 8 December 1941, hours after the attack on Pearl Harbor, Japanese forces attacked the American and Filipino forces defending the Philippines. With insufficient combat power to launch a counterattack, GEN Douglas MacArthur, the American commander, ordered his force to consolidate on the Bataan Peninsula and hold as long as possible. Among his units was the 12th Quartermaster (QM) Regiment, which had the mission of supporting the force.

Completely cut off from outside support, the Allies held against an overwhelming Japanese army for the next three and a half months. Soldiers of the 12th QM Regiment worked in the debris of warehouses and repair shops under merciless shelling and bombing, fighting to make the meager supplies last. They slaughtered water buffaloes for meat, caught fish with traps they built themselves, and distilled salt from seawater. In coffeepots made from oil drums they boiled and re-boiled the tiny coffee supply until the grounds were white. As long as an ounce of food existed, it was used. In the last desperate days, they resorted to killing horses and pack mules. More important, these supporters delivered rations to the foxholes on the front lines—fighting their way in when necessary. After Bataan and Corregidor fell,

members of the 12th QM Regiment were prominent among the 7,000 Americans and Filipinos who died on the infamous Bataan Death March.

Though captured, the soldiers of the 12th QM Regiment maintained their will to resist. 1LT Beulah Greenwalt, a nurse assigned to the 12th QM Regiment, personified this will. Realizing the regimental colors represent the soul of a regiment and that they could serve as a symbol for resistance, 1LT Greenwalt assumed the mission of protecting the colors from the Japanese. She carried the colors to the prisoner of war (PW) camp in Manila by wrapping them around her shoulders and convincing her Japanese captors that they were "only a shawl." For the next 33 months 1LT Greenwalt and the remains of the regiment remained PWs, living on starvation diets and denied all comforts. But through it all, 1LT Greenwalt held onto the flag. The regimental colors were safeguarded: the soul of the regiment remained with the regiment, and its soldiers continued to resist. When the war ended in 1945 and the surviving PWs were released, 1LT Greenwalt presented the colors to the regimental commander. She and her fellow PWs had persevered. They had resisted on Bataan until they had no more means to resist. They continued to resist through three long years of captivity. They decided on Bataan to carry on, and they renewed that decision daily until they were liberated. The 12th QM Regiment—and the other units that had fought and resisted with them—remained true to themselves, the Army, and their country. Their will allowed them to see events through to the end.

The Quick Reaction Platoon

On 26 December 1994 a group of armed and disgruntled members of the Haitian Army entered the Haitian Army Headquarters in Port-au-Prince demanding back pay. A gunfight ensued less than 150 meters from the grounds of the Haitian Palace, seat of the new government. American soldiers from C Company, 1-22 Infantry, who had deployed to Haiti as part of Operation Uphold Democracy, were guarding the palace grounds. The quick reaction platoon leader deployed and immediately maneuvered his platoon towards the gunfire. The platoon attacked, inflicting at least four casualties and causing the rest of the hostile soldiers to flee. The platoon quelled a potentially explosive situation by responding correctly and aggressively to the orders of their leader, who knew his mission and the commander's intent.

Self-Control in Combat

An American infantry company in Vietnam had been taking a lot of casualties from booby traps. The soldiers were frustrated because they could not fight back. One night, snipers ambushed the company near a village, killing two soldiers. The rest of the company—scared, anguished, and frustrated—wanted to enter the village, but the commander—who was just as angry—knew that the snipers were long gone. Further, he knew that there was a danger his soldiers would let their emotions get the upper hand, that they might injure or kill some villagers out of a desire to strike back at something. Besides being criminal, such killings would drive more villagers to the Viet Cong. The commander maintained control of his emotions, and the company avoided the village.

BG Jackson at First Bull Run

At a crucial juncture in the First Battle of Bull Run, the Confederate line was being beaten back from Matthews Hill by Union forces. Confederate BG Thomas J. Jackson and his 2,000-man brigade of Virginians, hearing the sounds of battle to the left of their position, pressed on to the action. Despite a painful shrapnel wound, BG Jackson calmly placed his men in a defensive position on Henry Hill and assured them that all was well.

As men of the broken regiments flowed past, one of their officers, BG Barnard E. Bee, exclaimed to BG Jackson, "General, they are driving us!" Looking toward the direction of the enemy, BG Jackson replied, "Sir, we will give them the bayonet." Impressed by BG Jackson's confidence and self-control, BG Bee rode off towards what was left of the officers and men of his brigade. As he rode into the throng he gestured with his sword toward Henry Hill and shouted, "Look, men! There is Jackson standing like a stone wall! Let us determine to die here, and we will conquer! Follow me!"

Character and Prisoners

The morning of [28 February 1991], about a half-hour prior to the cease-fire, we had a T-55 tank in front of us and we were getting ready [to engage it with a TOW]. We had the TOW up and we were tracking him and my wingman saw him just stop and a head pop up out of it. And Neil started calling me saying, "Don't shoot, don't shoot, I think they're getting off the tank." And they did. Three of them jumped off the tank and ran around a sand dune. I told my wingman,

"I'll cover the tank, you go on down and check around the back side and see what's down there." He went down there and found about 150 PWs....

[T]he only way we could handle that many was just to line them up and run them through...a little gauntlet...[W]e had to check them for weapons and stuff and we lined them up and called for the PW handlers to pick them up. It was just amazing.

We had to blow the tank up. My instructions were to destroy the tank, so I told them to go ahead and move it around the back side of the berm a little bit to safeguard us, so we wouldn't catch any shrapnel or ammunition coming off. When the tank blew up, these guys started yelling and screaming at my soldiers, "Don't shoot us, don't shoot us," and one of my soldiers said, "Hey, we're from America; we don't shoot our prisoners." That sort of stuck with me.

Task Force Kingston

1LT Joseph Kingston, a boyish-looking platoon leader in K Company, 3d Battalion, 32d Infantry, was the lead element for his battalion's move northward. The terrain was mountainous, the weather bitterly cold—the temperature often below zero—and the cornered enemy still dangerous. 1LT Kingston inched his way forward, with the battalion adding elements to his force. He had antiaircraft jeeps mounted with quad .50 caliber machine guns, a tank, a squad (later a platoon) of engineers, and an artillery forward observer. Some of these attachments were commanded by lieutenants who outranked him, as did a captain who was the tactical air controller. But 1LT Kingston remained in command, and battalion headquarters began referring to Task Force Kingston.

Bogged down in Yongsong-ni with casualties mounting, Task Force Kingston received reinforcements that brought the number of men to nearly 300. Despite tough fighting, the force continued to move northward. 1LT Kingston's battalion commander wanted him to remain in command, even though they sent several more officers who outranked 1LT Kingston. One of the attached units was a rifle company, commanded by a captain. But the arrangement worked, mostly because 1LT Kingston himself was an able leader. Hit while leading an assault on one enemy stronghold, he managed to toss a grenade just as a North Korean soldier shot him in the head. His helmet, badly grazed, saved his life. His personal courage inspired his men and the soldiers from the widely varied units who were under his control. Task

Force Kingston was commanded by the soldier who showed, by courage and personal example, that he could handle the job.

Trust Earned

In a 1976 interview, Congressman Hamilton Fish of New York told of his experiences as a white officer with the 369th Infantry Regiment, an all-black unit in the segregated Army of 1917. Fish knew that his unit would function only if his soldiers trusted him; his soldiers, all of whom had volunteered for combat duty, deserved nothing less than a trustworthy leader. When a white regiment threatened to attack the black soldiers in training camp, Fish, his pistol drawn, alerted the leaders of that regiment and headed off a disaster.

"There was one thing they wanted above all from a white officer," [Fish recalled in an interview nearly 60 years later] "and that was fair treatment. You see, even in New York City [home of most of his soldiers] they really did not get a square deal most of the time. But if they felt you were on the level with them, they would go all out for you. And they seemed to have a sixth sense in realizing just how you felt. I sincerely wanted to lead them as real soldiers, and they knew it."

Reception on Christmas Eve

An assistant division commander of the 25th Infantry Division told this story as part of his farewell speech:

"I ran across some new soldiers and asked them about their arrival on the island [of Oahu]. They said they got in on Christmas Eve, and I thought to myself, 'Can't we do a better job when we ship these kids out, so they're not sitting in some airport on their first big holiday away from home?' I mean, I really felt sorry for them. So I said, 'Must have been pretty lonesome sitting in a new barracks where you didn't know anyone.' And one of them said, 'No, sir. We weren't there a half-hour before the CQ [charge of quarters] came up and told us to get into class B's and be standing out front of the company in 15 minutes. Then this civilian drives up, a teenager, and the CQ orders us into the car. Turns out the kid was the first sergeant's son; his father had sent him over to police up anybody who was hanging around the barracks. We went over to the first sergeant's house to a big luau [party] with his family and a bunch of their neighbors and friends.'

"My guess is that those soldiers will not only do anything and everything that first sergeant wants, but they are going to tell anyone who will listen that they belong to the best outfit in the Army."

A MESSAGE TO GARCIA: Leading Soldiers in Moral Mayhem[1]

BY DON M. SNIDER AND GAYLE L. WATKINS

When Lt. Col. Pedro Garcia, United States Army, arrived as a student at the Air War College in 1999, he and I soon discovered that we had a great deal in common. Our friendship began by accident. Colonel Garcia was speaking in the corridor to another War College student, Lt. Col. Claude Morgan, when Colonel Morgan saw me nearby, mistaking me as an old friend of his. As we sorted that out, I learned that the two colonels were discussing one of my favorite topics, baseball, and that Colonel Garcia was seeking advice about batting on behalf of his two sons, Dom, 15, and Josh, 13. Dom couldn't catch up to a fastball and Josh had just met a new enemy, the curveball. Before long, Colonel. Garcia—now "Pete" to me—and I were sitting at a table discussing hitting strategies and drills his sons could use. It was the start of a lot of batting practice I was to give the Garcia boys during their time in Montgomery, Alabama, the location of the Air War College.

It was the beginning, too, of a year of lengthy serious conversations between Pete and me on a wide variety of subjects: the state of our country and of the world, the United States Army and his flourishing military career, his reservations about what he perceived as increased tension—Pete called it a "chasm"—between the profession of arms and the American society he loves, the challenges to his faith presented by contemporary military operations, and the ethical cases—Oh! those cases—which we thought through and discussed and debated all year long. My wife Rebecca and Pete's wife Maria became good friends, and Dom and Josh became, if not my "nephews," at least my batting disciples! Pete is a graduate of Notre Dame, where he earned his Army commission through the Reserve Officers' Training Corps. I earned my doctorate at Notre Dame, and my oldest son Chris earned his degree and Army commission at Notre Dame. We often attended mass together, and Pete is an excellent example of commitment to Christian faith. That commitment—although one I shared—led to a number of arguments, one of them very heated, in fact threatening the foundations of our friendship. But I get ahead of myself. I, too, had been an Army infantry officer for one tour of active duty, 1968-1972, though I did not serve in Vietnam. But teaching at a military college (Norwich) and more than ten years of teaching at a War College had kept me at least somewhat current with military matters.

Pete's ten-month course of study at Maxwell Air Force Base zipped by, the highlight of the year proving to be Pete's promotion to colonel, along with the knowledge that he was off to brigade command soon after War College graduation. Much of what we discussed was never settled, so a couple of weeks before Pete left Maxwell, he extorted a promise from me. I remember the conversation:

"Jim, you guaranteed me several months ago that I would ultimately see things your way about ethics and the profession of arms. As it is, the only thing I agree with you about is improving Dom's hand speed to catch up with fastballs."

"That's not fair, Pete. You also agreed with me about teaching Josh to keep his front shoulder in so he could hit the curveball! But as for the rest—well, I wish we could continue our conversations. You've given me a lot to think about, Pete. And I'm sorry—no kidding—that I haven't resolved all your problems. But I should leave something for you to do, after all. Isn't that what we teachers are supposed to do?"

"Of course. But I was thinking . . ."

". . . not again!"

"No, seriously: I was thinking that since Maria and the boys are going to remain here during my tour, I'll have at least some time to continue our conversations. Would you do me a favor? Take a while and write me a letter about some of the problems we've discussed. But no reading assignments and absolutely no quizzes!"

"All right, Pete. I'll do what I can. And maybe I can go you one better. I know your thinking on so many of these subjects that I can anticipate some of your reactions—and objections. I'll try to take these into account as I write."

"That will be great, Jim. Would you object if I shared your correspondence with others?"

"Not at all. But keep in mind that I'll be writing to you from a religious perspective we largely share. I'll be assuming an agreement between us which in most cases clearly exists."

"But, Jim, is it really possible any more, given what we agree is the decline in morality both nationally and internationally, to have a truly ethical American armed force? I could be on the verge

of making military decisions that could result in the deaths of scores of people. I want some answers before I make those decisions!"
Department of Leadership and Ethics
Air War College
Maxwell AFB, AL 36112-6427

Hi Pete:

This is the letter I promised you I'd write. I'm properly going to leave the family talk to Maria and the boys, but I thought I'd assure you that Maria is doing great taking classes at the college, and the boys are really in their element at Catholic High School. I miss batting practice with them, but I've promised to get back out on the diamond with them once basketball season is over. So Dom accuses me of pestering them to read, eh? Guilty! Every time they come over for hamburgers, I hit them with history, politics, and geography. And they get their share of Bible questions—especially from Rebecca! But they're doing great, Pete. Super young men!

POSTMODERN MORAL "STANDARDS"

It's kids like Dom and Josh we need, Pete. I am, as you know, profoundly upset by events in our country over these last thirty years or so. Although Neil Howe and William Strauss assure us that the "Millennial Generation" is bound to be great,[2] I frankly don't think it's getting better. Too often, the examples all around us are of moral squalor. I think we can see that in the person of the ubiquitous cartoon character who, as a decal on the back windows of cars and trucks, urinates on people and things. There have been some great movies recently—I think of *Saving Private Ryan*, *Schindler's List*, and *Glory*—but so much of what appears is trash, or worse. The entertainment industry seems to thrive on sex, violence, brutality of all kinds, and outright hostility towards the virtues and values you and Maria want your kids to grow up with.

You know, I constantly hear that when I was growing up in the late 1950s or when my Mom and Dad were growing up in the 1930s, there were plenty of problems then, too. And that's right. All I have to do is ask African-Americans here in Alabama about that. When I speak favorably of military virtues, I am often greeted with cloaked derision from people who mistakenly think I'm suggesting that the Army dictate values to American civilians. But that's hardly

my position. I do think that the armed forces must practice the virtues—and to the extent that they exemplify the foundational virtues of wisdom; justice or truthfulness; moral and physical courage; and temperance, modesty, or self-control—they can serve as a source of inspiration for all of us.

The armed forces led the way in making integration work. Sometimes I think you guys in uniform don't get enough credit for that. We all know racism hasn't been completely cured in the military, but you've done a great job of making "equal opportunity" a reality and not just a slogan.

So black Alabamians can point with some pride to the fact that, largely because of their courage (and that of one of their own, Dr. Martin Luther King, Jr.), progress in race relations has been made. Things are better now than they were in the segregated 1950s. Certainly, improvements have been made—and in a number of fields. For example, Dom and Josh aren't doing "duck and cover" drills today, getting under their desks at Catholic High, to "protect themselves" in case of nuclear attack. We have made, or so it seems, some progress on the Chemical-Biological-Radiological front. But progress even there can be as illusory, as the 11 September 2001 terrorists attacks on the World Trade Center and Pentagon show.

I grew up loving the Boston Red Sox. Today we have world federation wrestling and "extreme fighting." TV and the movies were bad enough in the 1950s, but *The Lone Ranger* and *Howdy Doody* can't be confused with *Jerry Springer*. The language that kids use routinely today in public I did not hear even in locker rooms years ago. How, for instance, do you compare Eisenhower and Clinton, morally speaking? What passes for comedy today would probably have horrified even teenagers years ago. And even in the 1960s, there was not acceptance of abortion, euthanasia, and infanticide (partial-birth abortion). On the last night of one of the political conventions recently, a local Eagle Scout group was invited to lead the Pledge of Allegiance. Did you read this, Pete? They were met by boos and catcalls from adults in the audience because of the Scouts' position on homosexuals.[3]

I've read numerous books which contain statistics about crime. It's up; it's down; it's more white collar; it's more blue collar; it's more—or less—urban. But use instead as your standard of measurement your old high school. Have you visited your alma mater recently, Pete? It must have been pretty good since your education there got you into Notre Dame. How is it doing today? How are the teachers? Will they patrol the boys' and girls' rooms? How is the level of respect for teaching, for learning, for the school itself? What do the kids talk about? Whom do they admire and seek to emulate? Did you know, Pete, that when I was growing up I didn't even know players on the Red Sox *got paid*! It seems as though money, income, and finances dominate us today as never before. If the love of money really is the root of all evil (1 Tim 6.10), we have much to worry about.

Every kid I knew in the 1950s—including me (if you can believe it!)—was interested in sex. But the picture has changed. When I was in high school, we wouldn't have *publicly* dated girls in which we might have been interested for only one reason. Remember the word *risqué*? It makes no sense any more. Neither does the word *promiscuous*. But when kids are saturated with sex everywhere they watch and read and listen and see, what are they to think of as "right"?

Oops . . . slipped again, didn't I? Talking about "right" as if there were such a thing. Almost all the kids I personally know are cultural or ethical relativists today. What is "right" or "wrong" depends solely upon customs or circumstances, upon friends or gangs, or upon momentary urges or appetites. Glands and gonads dictate, too often I think, what is "right" and what is "true."

I know . . . I can be accused of implicitly talking about a golden age. You and I know such a golden age never existed. We frequently knew as kids, however, that when we misbehaved (another word that is gone by the boards today), we were acting (as teenagers so often do) contrary to a standard. What standard? The church standard. The customary standard. The standard of ladies and gentlemen. So often today, actions are justified—if that's the term to use—by the argument that *there is no standard*. Who are *you* to impose *your* values on *me*?

Well, let me retreat. Maybe there is a standard, after all: the "me" standard. Around us swirl the eddies of moral nihilism. When we have no idea about what truth is, why and how should we concern ourselves about what taste ought to be? So how can we criticize kids—or older people—for bullying, brutal, or bestial behavior (booing kids trying to say the Pledge of Allegiance, for example!) when "everything goes" as long as the cops don't spot it? Parents too frequently on their way to the well-stocked liquor cabinet tell their kids not to use pot. Priests and ministers fall

into pederasty or profit-making. Teachers don't read widely or don't care much, going on strike when they so decide, often despite laws forbidding it. The idea of "student-athlete" is burlesque. Entertainment caters to the basest instincts. Corruption festers in the professions. And our young people see . . . what? At all times and in all professions there have been departures from the standard of right and wrong. But today, we deny the standard itself. There is nothing discourteous, for there is no courtesy. There is nothing indecent, for there is no decency. There is nothing profane, for there is no holiness. What is good or true or beautiful depends only upon "me": my emotions, my desires, my pleasures.

But there's another perspective, too. You know how much I believe in the military ethos—and how firmly I defend it. But I bristle when I hear soldiers cavalierly (and arrogantly) talk about how much better they are than the civilian world. My Lai, Okinawa, Aberdeen, Tailhook. What about the soldiers who have brought shame and infamy to the profession of arms? *The military ethos is morally defensible because—and to the extent that—it is rooted in transcendent truth.* The same is true with the political order in which we find ourselves. Our obedience to our military services and to our political society thus depends upon their fidelity, in turn, to the permanent ideals from which spring our faith. That one adjective, *permanent*, speaks volumes, for it tells us that there are enduring and exceptionless norms (e.g., Ps 119.89-90; Heb 13.8), and that there is a truth to which we owe first and full allegiance (Jn 14.6). That is *really* a counter-cultural view! The idea that some obligations transcend our political-military duties is not a notion that subverts our professionalism, but rather one that endows it with direction and dimension. You are a professional, Pete, because you understand yourself within the settings of both the sacred and the profane; that is the tradition of the virtues, one expression of which is the profession of arms at its best. There are, I fear, too few people today whose education is rooted in the classical virtues.

At Notre Dame we can find students who are committed Catholics, young men and women deeply devoted to the Christian faith. You can find the same kinds of young Protestants at Baylor, say, or at Wheaton—deeply committed to Biblical values. Similarly, you can find many fine young people, committed to Judaism at, for example, Brandeis. Now how many of these intelligent and ethically concerned students are ethical absolutists? How many will say that there are clear and wholly compelling ethical standards which may not be transgressed? I don't have an answer. I have an intuition based upon a number of anecdotal sources telling me that many of these students deny the possibility of an objective moral standard. If they deny that, they do not understand what being Catholic or Protestant or Jewish means. How can one say he believes in God and then deny an absolute standard of morality? I understand cultural and ethical relativism, but I do not for a moment grasp how ostensibly traditional Christians and Jews can accept God on the one hand and implicitly deny the scriptures—Christian and Hebrew—on the other.

The highest good on many campuses is toleration. Remember G. K. Chesterton's thought about that? He believed that toleration is the virtue of people who don't believe in anything. Of course, we should and must practice toleration when it comes to respecting people of different races and religions. But there must be a time, too, to be intolerant. As William Bennett has put it, "A defining mark of a good republic is precisely the willingness of its citizens to make judgments about things that matter." Without being "judgmental," he points out, "Americans would never have put an end to slavery, outlawed child labor, emancipated women, or ushered in the civil rights movement. Nor would we have prevailed against Nazism and Soviet communism, or known how to explain our opposition."[4]

I can tell you only what I've heard from a number of people speaking under the promise of non-attribution: Many, perhaps most, of the young people entering officer accession programs today are, at heart, ethical egoists whose main value is reflected in their mirror. If that's true, then many of the company-grade officers in your command right now are primarily interested in themselves. When you talk about "Army values" of loyalty, duty, respect, *selfless service*, honor, integrity, and personal courage; or when the Air Force talks about integrity, excellence, and *service before self*; or when the Navy and Marine Corps talk about honor, courage, and *commitment*— you're all speaking a foreign language. I don't mean to suggest that these officers are "bad" or that they'll necessarily fail you or their troops in a crisis. On the contrary, they are bright and well schooled in numerous practical skills. But often their ethical frame of reference is decidedly different from that which is at the heart of the traditional military ethic.

Consider this. The heart of all ethics consists in the ability morally to transcend the group. If the group—whatever it is—dictates right and wrong, then there is no Ultimate Standard to which to appeal. It is precisely ultimate standards which are ignored or denied by today's secular culture. We must not think that the privates or second lieutenants in today's Army are importing this ultimate standard with them when they walk into the orderly room to report for duty. The chances are, they do not have this standard to appeal to. For you and me, the Ultimate Standard is God, the Church, the Bible. We have a way of judging the country itself—as well as, of course, the Army and any of its procedures and practices. But you and I also know very good people *without* religious conviction whose actions are wholly consistent with orthodox religious teaching. I would hold, however, that, as Robert Bork has written, they "are living on the moral capital of prior religious generations,"[5] or, as Frank Sheed put it, "we still tend to live by what remains of the Christian ethic, though there is no longer any clear grasp of its foundation; and concessions to human weakness have left it pretty tattered."[6]

But suppose we deny the sacred standard. Then we are left, not with truth, but with, at best, only loyalty. Have I told you what I've heard about the late U.S. Air Force Col. John Boyd? When introducing himself to his commanders, he supposedly said: "Ask for my loyalty and I'll give you my honesty. Ask for my honesty and you'll have my loyalty."[7] But what is honesty or truth if . . . if there is no honesty or truth but only my conception of it? Then I'd better be loyal. But to what? How tough it is for all of us to understand that our first commitment must be to truth, not to society or to country, not to service, not to branch, not to self.

So, when you testify before Congress someday after your command time is done and some two-star tells you to "Get on the team, Colonel Garcia" and reminds you about who writes your OERs and the color of your uniform, then ask yourself what comes first, loyalty or truth? *I know your answer, Pete, but I also know your frame of reference.* Remember the time we boiled it down to this: Soldiers must be prepared to give life or limb for their country—*but not their soul*—for no country can properly ask that of its soldiers. But, you and I, as Catholics, agree about the existence of the soul, with all that implies. What if one denies that existence, *with all that implies*? I can hear you now! "So, Jim, what does that denial mean to me as a commander? What do I do about it *right now?*"

One thing you can't do is to set up command-sponsored religion classes, although the old notion of "Character Guidance" (which we used to have in the Army more than thirty years ago) is a serious and solid idea, as long as it is nondenominational instruction (and best taught by line officers). A couple of years ago, I assisted an Air Force line officer and student from Air Command and Staff College, a Protestant fundamentalist whom I respected for his commitment to his religious values, with some difficulties he was having on a course paper. He told me that in his next assignment, he wanted to use Commander's Time to "win converts for Christ." I told him that he was free at appropriate (read: off-duty) time to proselytize, but that he was legally (and quite correctly) forbidden to use "Air Force time" for such overt religious activity. I insisted that he get prior counseling from the Judge Advocate General, which he did. But what you can do is talk about the Army values: what they mean; what kinds of character they foster; and how incompatible they are with egoism or with ethical relativism. Then you "walk the talk"; you practice what you preach.

Although you and I would contend that the values we cherish derive from religious precept and a treasury of spiritual values, the guidance you provide soldiers must not be rooted in a given religion, for soldiers are free to be either religious or nonreligious. But they are not free to refuse to abide by the warrior ethos. As one of the Army's publications tells us, "The warrior ethos concerns character, shaping who you are and what you do. In that sense, it's clearly linked to Army values such as *personal courage, loyalty to comrades, and dedication to duty*. Both loyalty and duty involve putting your life on the line, even when there's little chance of survival, for the good of a cause larger than yourself. That's the clearest example of *selfless service*."[8] We know that ethical egoism doesn't always clash with military service, but it's very likely to, especially when the chips are down. So I think you can start soldiers on the road to character—on the road to professionalism—by teaching them that loyalty builds organizations and can save lives.

But remember that however necessary loyalty is, it isn't sufficient for the good person or the good soldier. Neither is utilitarianism—or its alter ego, proportionalism. But we'll get to that later.

POSTMODERN MILITARY CHALLENGES

At the same time that recruits to the profession of arms enter, much too frequently, from a background of religious indifferentism, moral confusion, and values anarchy, they are confronted after training with a frenetic deployment schedule and with military-moral situations that would try the wisdom of Solomon and the patience of Job. Have you read Martin Van Creveld's *Transformation of War*? There he talks about how war is becoming the struggles of primitive tribes.[9] Navy Capt. Larry Seaquist uses the term "community wars" to describe the rogue politicos who use fear and brutality to create "soldiers" with no inkling of the law or morality of the West: "The new faces of war are a ragtag collection of ne'er-do-wells, teenagers, and ordinary citizens temporarily dragooned into service by the local thug-in-chief." But, he says, "the rabble regularly outgun us," and they can be viciously efficient, such as when rampaging Hutus slaughtered—with handguns and machetes—some 800,000 of their neighbors in about a hundred days. This is a more lethal record, Seaquist tells us, than that of Hitler's murderers.[10] You read much of Robert Kaplan's stuff when you were at the War College. Sure, he can be incredibly self-promotional, but his admonitions about anarchy on the horizon seem altogether too prescient to ignore. The list is interminable: Rwanda, Haiti, Kosovo, Sierra Leone, Chechnya, Colombia, Bosnia, Liberia, Afghanistan, and on and on. As Army Col. A.M. Coroalles has said about training junior officers in field operations: "You've got to educate folks in [solving] problems they've never seen before."[11]

I am reminded of a passage in a book published in 1989 by Paul Seabury and Angelo Codevilla. The book appeared as the Cold War was ending and the Berlin Wall was coming down. It was a time of great euphoria, remember? Soon we were discussing "peace dividends," and we began to dismantle—to "down-size" and to "right-size"—our armed forces. "Today's world," they wrote, "is filled with more people animated by greater hatred and possessed of more means to make war than ever before."[12] Then came the Gulf War—and a reminder that there really are bad guys out there. In Army circles, T.R. Fehrenbach's book about Korea used to be very popular; it's time to re-read it, for it tells us about the need to fight, and perhaps die, in the mud.[13] And that is not a message that plays well in a postmodern society such as ours, though there seem to be intimations of resolve thus far in American public attitudes toward our military operations in Afghanistan. Although we want to believe well and to act wisely, we know that we live in times of great political and ethical challenge. We know that evil exists and, in a word, we know that life is *tragic*.

When Samuel Huntington's book about the clash of civilizations was published, a number of people criticized it—and occasionally on solid ground. I remember, however, how much you said you got out of it after a careful reading. Remember this point? "The West won the world not by the superiority of its ideas or value or religion . . . but rather by its superiority in applying organized violence. Westerners often forget this fact; non-Westerners never do."[14] Air Force Col. Charles Dunlap's 1996 article "How We Lost the High-Tech War of 2007" put it starkly: the bad guys' strategy was and is "to make warfare so psychologically costly that the Americans would lose their 'will to win.'" Dunlap even theorizes that an enemy state might drop a nuclear weapon— perhaps purloined—on one of its own cities, blaming us. Dunlap quotes Ralph Peters who told us that we will face warriors who have acquired a "taste for killing," who are irrational by our standards, who commit atrocities "that challenge the descriptive powers of language," and who "will sacrifice their own kind in order to survive."[15]

Remember the story I told you about my lecture at the Marshall Center in Germany where I spoke about ethics to a number of officers from eastern European and Soviet successor states? One of the officers, utterly perplexed by my talk, told me essentially that I was "clueless," for it was obvious that I failed to understand that success in warfare meant (1) winning and (2) returning home, regardless of what you had to do or whom you had to kill to accomplish those objectives. When I pressed my points about how it is wrong to violate moral or ethical standards or the Bible or the Koran or . . . whatever, he gave me the same kind of look you might give an otherwise intelligent, cosmopolitan man who expressed serious belief in Santa Claus. The more I talked to him about ethics, the more I felt like Pollyanna or Micawber or some other ultra-idealist from the world of fiction. The only rule that made any sense at all to him was that there are no rules in warfare. I was there that day to teach him; I fear he taught me—and I didn't like the lesson.

Remember a few years ago when North Korea threatened to attack South Korea if international

sanctions were imposed upon them because of their continued noncompliance with the nuclear nonproliferation treaty? The Clinton administration responded by saying that North Korea would receive international assistance in developing peaceful nuclear power, plus hundreds of thousands of barrels of oil. The inspections did not take place. As Donald and Frederick Kagan have pointed out, the Clinton administration "declared victory, but even at the time it was laughably clear that all we had accomplished was to bribe the North Koreans to back away from their threat." Their conclusion is that we have learned to buy off the bad guys. But how long will it last? "Will we," they ask, "like England [in the 1930s], one day find ourselves facing both an urgent need to rearm and insuperable political and economic pressure not to?"[16]

Throughout our history until the Korean War, our national enemies were, at least in terms of military science, often similar to us—the British, the Mexicans, the Spanish, and the Germans of World War I. There is even some such similarity with regard to the Germans and Japanese of World War II in terms of "centers of gravity" and the like. But it's altogether likely that the road-warrior societies of the future—filled as they are with boy-soldiers or with criminals or with approaches to waging war that we would properly regard as ethically insane— will challenge us militarily and morally as never before. The Korean War, of course, is still not legally resolved—and we are still debating today what happened at No Gun Ri more than fifty years ago. The Vietnam War serves in many ways as an example of the kind of "community war" you'll have to wage in the future.[17] And even as a full colonel with more than two decades of Army experience and education, in a sense what you know of Vietnam is what you know of, say, World War I—it is all book learning to you.

Remember that even the Gulf War, which seems to fit into the mold of World War II as a "good war," was unpopular on many campuses and that Congress came very close to denying President George Bush the latitude he needed to prepare for likely combat there. We remember the dissent against the Vietnam War, but we have largely forgotten how unpopular the war in Korea had become by the fall of 1952, when Eisenhower and Stevenson ran for the presidency. To most Americans, the best part of the Gulf War was that it was very short, although we know certainly now that it was too short—and that

Saddam's military might was not destroyed to the extent that it should have been. There most certainly is an American character, and, with all its good and bad, it's manifested in all of us who are or who have been in uniform.

In no way do I mean to challenge or to question your own commitment and courage as a soldier during the Gulf War—or to impugn the professionalism or the patriotism of the thousands of other GIs who faced Iraqi soldiers—but what do you suppose might have happened had Saddam mustered the military might to hold out for many months or even many years (as some, recall, were predicting on the eve of hostilities)? I thought that the *moral* reasons for that war were compelling. Many disagreed, of course, contending that we were trading blood for oil. One of the authors of *Just War and the Gulf War*, George Weigel, has pointed out that much of mainline Protestantism and many in the Catholic Church have abandoned the Christian realism of Reinhold Niebuhr, Paul Ramsey, and John Courtney Murray, substituting in its place "psychologized and quasi-utopian understandings of international public life, which suggest the possibility of a world without conflict."[18] Remember the priest at Notre Dame who told you that you could not be at the same time a soldier and a Catholic? I have run into that (mistaken) sentiment many times in my career, although I think it is profoundly unbiblical—and even heretical, a re-appearance of Pelagianism.

But I guess that gets us where, really, you wanted me to go. Given the realities of a postmodern United States and the increasing geopolitical ugliness of the world which you have to deal with, what is military ethics today all about? How do you maintain true professionalism in the face of the kinds of missions—like your present one—you find yourself committed to? As you once beseeched me, "Tell me how I can deal with ugliness and how I can keep my soldiers from becoming what they're resisting." The new Army Leadership manual touts values, attributes, and character which are utterly at odds with the kind of savagery (think of Bosnia and Kosovo) our soldiers often have to deal with *as peacekeepers*. All soldiers see their own clash of civilizations when they deal with the kinds of military and moral problems beyond their ken. A high-ranking soldier-peacekeeper, speaking at the Air War College under the promise of non-attribution a couple of years before you were here, told us that as "negotiations" began between two warring gangs in his area of

operations, one gang sent its agenda to its rival gang in a large plastic hatbox. Why not in an envelope? Because an ordinary envelope could not have contained the message plus the bloody head of a child from the other gang. Of course that other gang then replied with its own message, together with the head of a child from the first gang.

Someone has said that certain matters in ethics should cause decent people to shudder. Imagine using the head of a murdered child as a macabre visual aid to make a point about your agenda for upcoming negotiations. What kind of savage could do such a thing? And how does it brutalize the mind and soul of the disinterested onlooker? If you can find the time, read Anthony Loyd's book, *My War Gone By, I Miss It So*. It is filled with butchery and barbarism as reported by a journalist who has written from Chechnya, Afghanistan, Sierra Leone, and Kosovo. I could quote at length from some of the stomach-turning scenes painted so powerfully by Loyd, and others like Mark Bowden in *Black Hawk Down*.[19] But you know the stories, Pete. How is it possible for anyone to commit the kinds of atrocities described there? But, similarly, how is it possible for anyone to stick scissors into the head of a baby emerging from the womb into daylight and, through the hole thus created, suck out the baby's brains?

Remember Senator Harry Truman's comment during World War II that we should just sit back and let the German Nazis and the Russian Communists destroy each other? You can read that opinion today about many of the world's conflicts. Just sit back and let the brutal bastards kill one another. But isn't that an indication of how far down the slippery slope of life we've already come? Don't we have a moral—and, arguably, military—duty to intervene to prevent slaughter when and where we can? There is a powerful news film now available that shows how a contingent of international peacekeepers were ordered out of a place in Rwanda in which hundreds of refugees had gathered, pleading with and begging the peacekeepers not to depart, for the refugees knew that when the soldiers left, they would be hacked to death. They even asked the soldiers to shoot them, preferring to die by bullets rather than by machetes. So, what do you do when your commander tells you to leave the helpless, knowing that they are about to be slashed and hacked and murdered, every one? And how long do you stay there? And how many do you evacuate and to where?

MORAL DECISION-MAKING

In the often brutal arena of world politics, how do you find the right course and keep to it? I remember some of our long conversations about this subject, and I can summarize what we agreed upon—en route to what we disputed. In my War College classes and lectures, I try to give students "tools" to use in ethical decision-making. I argue that there are three pieces to the ethical puzzle:[20] customs, rules, and outcomes. *Customs*—the mores, the usual expectations of one's culture—can, to a certain degree, guide us. In Shirley Jackson's short story, "The Lottery," a village held a lottery each year to choose a family; the "winning" family participated in a follow-up lottery to choose one of its members— who was then stoned to death to ensure good crops. Lousy meteorology! But if that is what the society's customs dictate, who are we to challenge them? After all, that would put us in the ranks of those who challenge cultural relativism. But of course we must challenge cultural and ethical relativism (cf. 2 Cor 10.12), provided we see events through the prism of a higher understanding. In this case, of course, empirical science testifies to the sheer stupidity of murdering someone to "ensure" good crops. Nonetheless, customs *are* important, and one should not lightly dismiss tradition. It's part of the picture, but often not the entire thing.

It is certainly critical to soldiers that they not "go native." If in the course of accomplishing their mission, they adopt the customs of savage people—some of whom decapitate little children in order to make "negotiating points"—they will have thereby betrayed not just Army values and American norms, but standards (the permanent things) available to anyone of "ordinary sense and understanding." These standards (so often ignored today as we earlier discussed) are best seen in the Sermon on the Mount, which is, as Father Servais Pinckaers, O.P., has told us in his books, "a model of the ancient moral catechesis" and a "charter of the Christian life."[21] Some things, truly, are written on our hearts (Bar 3.7, Ez 37.26, Jer 31.33, Heb 10.16, Rom 2.15); there are some things we cannot not know, although, as J. Budziszewski has written, we can easily deceive ourselves about what we know.[22] Army values are meritorious, secular reflections of transcendent, sacred virtues; such military core values, understood and properly applied, can help us remain constant to truths "written on our hearts."

In addition to customs, there are *rules* which we should and usually can follow in deciding upon a proper ethical course of action. The rules found in Exodus 20—the Ten Commandments—are not a bad place to start, and one does not have to be Jewish or Christian to accept the spirit of those commandments. We also have the positive or man-made law known as the Uniform Code of Military Justice, whose rules are pretty clear. Beyond that we have Rules of Engagement that can guide soldiers in specific tactical circumstances. When I was in Officer Candidate School at Fort Benning (a long time ago, I admit), we learned the five-paragraph field order which, at that time, did not provide for "Commander's Intent." That is an important concept, proving that there is unlikely to be a single rule which clearly governs soldierly conduct in every circumstance. It's important for subordinates to understand, not just their superiors' literal orders, but also the pattern and purpose of their thinking. I don't mean to sound patronizing about this, and I'm sure you would take great pains in explaining this to your own soldiers, but there are surely times when rules and orders must be broken. One hopes, however, that soldiers who ignore or contravene orders will, when time and circumstances permit, make a clean breast of affairs with their superiors, providing the rationale for their judgment—and not seek to cover up their decisions. Remember Ambrose Bierce's civil war short story, "One Kind of Officer"?[23]

In addition to customs and rules, we must involve ourselves with *outcomes* or *results*. A part of any good ethical judgment is concern with circumstances, including consequences. If we act, for example, out of a fear of death, this can diminish our responsibility for the possible evil of our act. But the teaching we accept is that circumstances "can make neither good nor right an action that is in itself evil" (*Catechism of the Catholic Church*, #1754). The critical point is that good actions are not determined *only* by situation or by circumstance. We begin to approach our major area of disagreement, don't we?

As you used to tell me when you were here at the War College, a soldier may not have time to sit in a library carrel and casually ponder the "tools" of ethical judgment. When the chips are down, you said, soldiers sometimes have to act *now*, and when that is true the sole reliable guide to action is proportionalism. I know you like the idea of "proportionalism"[24] because, as a Christian, you think it's more morally acceptable than utilitarianism or consequentialism, which judges actions only on the basis of outcome or probable outcome. Proportionalism, by contrast, suggests a more measured, more theologically "decent," weighing of alternatives—not excluding the best projected final outcome—a kind of teleological ethics at least partially in keeping with the Church's ancient teaching. My rejoinder that proportionalism is mere crass utilitarianism wearing a miter did not impress you.

Remember the case we used to fight about—Bernard Williams's story?[25] You're on vacation in X-land and, while on a hike, are seized by revolutionaries who also have taken twelve X-lander police captive. They plan to let you go regardless, but tell you that they will shoot all the X-lander police unless you shoot one of the police, which will then prompt them to release unharmed the other eleven. The police tell you that they have reason to believe that the revolutionaries will keep their word and the deal seems rational to them: eleven will live if one dies; all twelve will die if one doesn't. To help you, they're willing to hold a lottery to choose the unlucky sacrificial victim. You will be given a small pistol with one round only. Do you shoot one of the hostages?

Your argument was "yes," citing proportionalism. "The good of the many outweighs the good of the one," you said, prompted by some movie you'd seen. Never take your ethics from movies, Pete, unless maybe you've watched *The Ten Commandments*. Not to act in this circumstance would be sheer cowardice, you told me; not to act would preserve your "purity" but only at the price of twelve deaths. Surely, the greater good would be to shoot one of the hostages.

You know my argument: To shoot one of the hostages is not only doing the terrorists' work for them but it is purely and simply an act of murder. You are implicitly telling me that the life of the hostage you shoot has value only insofar as it is related to others' lives; it has in and of itself no value and is therefore dispensable. But life is sacred—I know you believe that as a Christian.

I well recall your rather heated comeback: that because you believed life is sacred then as a Christian you *must* act—not to take a life but to save eleven lives! I countered with the evidence from a TV show (your movie vs. my TV show—quite an intellectual slugfest!). On a M*A*S*H episode Hawkeye Pierce, some soldiers, and a number of South Koreans are on a stalled bus behind enemy lines in Korea. The North Koreans are sending patrols out into the area, but the bus is camouflaged, waiting for the patrols to depart, allowing the Americans to jumpstart the bus and head back to friendlies. But a baby is crying and may give away the position. Is it all right to smother the child to protect the others from being noticed by the North Koreans? You hesitated. Then I unloaded. It's your wife Maria and Josh as a baby, crying. *Now* is it OK, Pete? *Now does the good of the many outweigh the good of the one?* I know that made you angry—the only time we actually *quarreled* during an "argument."

A few days later, I recall, you told me that I had won only by a debater's tactic—and that it was unfair to personalize the argument. Then you hit me with another example to try to defend proportionalism. A U.S. Army infantry platoon is in prepared positions when armed enemy soldiers approach on line, each soldier carrying a child. You remember I called this example impossibly conjectural (or dumb), and I thought it was—until I read a similar story in Mark Bowden's *Black Hawk Down*.[26] We are back to ugliness, aren't we? So, is it all right to shoot the children in order to retain the positions and, most likely, to keep your soldiers from being shot if they try to retreat to supplementary positions? And how far can those soldiers retreat? Twenty yards? Twenty miles? You were consistent. You told me that, although you'd do everything in your power not to hurt the children, you would not surrender your position or withhold protective covering fire in the event of a pull-back. Your argument is that the likely greater good, in both the short term and long term, is the defense of the positions. Your "clinching" argument is that the injuries to or the deaths of the children, however regrettable, might best be understood as "collateral damage."

Given the ubiquitous evil I talked about early in this letter, I think that, tragically, this kind of situation may well become more common than we care to think about. I never expressed an opinion as to the morally dictated course in this last situation because, as you know, I rather cavalierly dismissed it—until encountering *Black Hawk Down*. Pete, I think . . . well, I think you're right; but I also think you draw the wrong conclusion. There is a parallel, but a slim one, between shooting the hostage policeman and the hostage children. You will have to murder that policeman in cold blood. You intend his death. But when firing at the advancing enemy soldiers, you most certainly do not intend harm to the children they have as hostage. In fact, you'll search for a way out—flanking fire? fire at the exposed parts of the enemy soldiers? getting to them for hand-to-hand combat? Of course, your soldiers will do everything possible, if they fire at the advancing soldiers, not to hit the children. But if I were the lieutenant there, I too would defend my position—even if it meant endangering the children. My small arms fire would, I am afraid, have two results: defense of my position, which is good; and the deaths of one or more of the children, which is bad. We do not seek the bad, either itself or in the course of seeking another end. The good effect is not achieved directly through, or as a consequence of, the bad effect which happens together with the good and which is not wanted or willed by any of us defending our position and ourselves. And the good effect, arguably, outweighs the bad.

Physicians and medical ethicists often use this concept (known as the "Principle of Double Effect") to think through the problem of giving heavy doses of painkiller, which might be life threatening, to terminal patients. If we believe that life is sacred, then we do not wish to hasten death, but we do wish to mitigate pain. A doctor can ethically give the painkiller because, although it's dangerous in this scenario, the bad effect (danger to life) is not intended, is outweighed by the good effect (relief from pain), and does not cause the good effect but is simultaneous with it.

As Catholics, you and I are both absolutists and believe in an objective order of morality. We know that the first and fundamental task—the first absolute of any legitimate warrior ethic and of all genuine soldiers—*is to protect innocent life*. As Gen. Douglas MacArthur said in 1946 when he reviewed the case of Japanese General Yamashita, who had been convicted of war crimes: "The soldier, be he friend or foe, is charged with the protection of the weak and innocent. It is the very essence and reason for his being." But we also know that, in this vale of tears in which we live, such is not always possible or practicable. We know that the innocent can suffer—and have suffered, sometimes terribly. But it may be the Protestant ethicist, Norman Geisler, who helps us the most with the question of whether absolutes can be "compromised." After all, if something is eternally true and perpetually binding, there are no righteous exceptions to it. You and I have just said that we'd shoot toward—although hoping to God we wouldn't hit—babies. And we are prepared to kill our soldier enemies. How do we square

that with the Commandment? Geisler refers to "graded absolutism" (also called "qualified absolutism" or "contextual absolutism").[27] I've used the term Universal Ethical Obligation (UEO). A UEO is a working absolute, but it admits of competing claims to conscience; more precisely, it can give way to another UEO that supersedes it in certain circumstances. For example, I have the obligation to protect my men and my position; I also have the obligation to protect the lives of the children (and, insofar as possible, even the lives of the advancing enemy soldiers). I now have to make a reasoned, prudential, virtuous choice between competing UEOs—what might be thought of as "dueling duties."

We thus come full circle, back to the means by which we make ethical choices in the midst of trial and turbulence, of tragedy and trauma. We explore local and military *customs*; we educate ourselves about that treasury of moral doctrine and dogma which we humans have learned over the centuries—*rules*. We think hard about *outcomes*, both certain and almost certain, realizing that the outcomes must be broadly construed to embrace prudential consideration of attendant circumstances. Then we make a decision, re-adjust as necessary, and report our reactions and results to appropriate authorities as time and events allow. But there is nothing mechanical or formulaic about this decision-making, for the key ingredient is *you* and the *virtues* which are your character (cf. 2 Pt 1.5-9, Gal 5.16-26).

I come back to the proposition that proportionalism is wrong because, no matter how you dress it up, it is sheer utilitarianism. Again, as Catholics, we would agree with Pope Paul VI, quoted by John Paul II in *The Splendor of Truth* (or *Veritatis Splendor*): "Though it is true that sometimes it is lawful to tolerate a lesser moral evil in order to avoid a greater evil or in order to promote a greater good, it is never lawful, even for the gravest reasons, to do evil that good may come of it (cf. Rom 3:8)—in other words, to intend directly something which of its very nature contradicts the moral order. . . ." John Paul adds that "circumstances or intentions can never transform an act intrinsically evil by virtue of its object into an act 'subjectively' good or defensible as a choice."[28]

"DIRTY HANDS"

Thus, there are some wrongs we must never do. Does that imply that there are wrongs you *can* do? Perhaps. So now I will tell you what I did not when you were at the War College: there may be *some* wrongs, in *some* cases, which we must not shrink from doing. And I greatly fear that the moral evil of the world—and your position in it—may put you in circumstances requiring *dirty hands.*

We have fallen a long way here, from absolutes through UEOs and the Principle of Double Effect to Dirty Hands, by which I mean the deliberate commission of a wrong. There is no way to justify this, no way satisfactorily to explain it; doing Dirty Hands business means that you have fashioned your own morality in place of God's, however much you may not want to. The only standard you may be able to apply here is your judgment at the time of crisis; it is the ultimate kind of "situational ethics." Michael Walzer might *disagree* with me when I say that Dirty Hands means his concept of "supreme emergency" at a personal level; but it is as good an explanation as I can make. Trying to use Double Effect in these circumstances is specious, I believe. As the late Elizabeth Anscombe once cogently put it: "It is nonsense to pretend that you do not intend to do what is the means you take to your chosen end. Otherwise there is absolutely no substance to the Pauline teaching [Rom 3.8] that we may not do evil that good may come."[29] There are some things I must never do because they are "always gravely illicit" (*CCC* #1756); in other words, there are things I *absolutely* must not do—e.g., murder—because it is everywhere and always wrong. As one man, I know that I cannot do evil that good might result, regardless of possible or probable consequence.

As a steward of the public good or as a military officer, however, are there times and places for me to do what is evil so that justice might reign? I know you'll agree with me that we have a solemn responsibility to preserve our integrity, our personal moral purity. But as a public steward—as a military officer—you are not free so easily to indulge your conscience, I'll admit. If the Secretary of the Treasury today decides to give all of his personal wealth to a worthy charity, we might well cheer his great generosity. But he is not free to give away *public moneys*, of which he is the custodian or steward. Suppose President Franklin Roosevelt in 1941 had been a pacifist; he might have chosen not to prosecute the war. He could not have ethically surrendered America to Japan, however, so even as a pacifist he might have had to compromise his conscience by leading our country into the just war of 1941.

Are there times when, in your capacity as an infantry officer, you may or must use Dirty Hands— that is, willingly do an evil act? Isn't this only ultimate utilitarianism, which I have just repudiated? Consider: You are, say, a battalion intelligence officer and you have virtually certain information that two enemy soldiers in your custody know the location of units about to ambush your battalion. You're in a helicopter with the prisoners. Can you push one into a net beneath the helicopter, deceiving the other about the "death" of his buddy, probably inducing him to talk when he thinks he's next to go? We know that this is wrong; that it is torture; that it is a war crime. But we know, too, that the pressures of command are compelling; the idea that if you torture—"just a little"—you can gain precious information and perhaps save your men's lives is almost irresistible. So it proved to be recently for an Army officer in Kosovo who held an unloaded weapon to the head of a Kosovo Albanian during interrogation, leading, in time, to his being charged with conduct unbecoming an officer and communicating a threat. The officer later admitted, "I was totally wrong." But isn't that what soldiers do, "communicate threats"? Sure: but not by becoming vigilantes or thugs. One soldier had it right in saying that the unit involved in the "interrogation incident" was "a street gang in Kosovo—an embarrassment to the United States Army."[30] When you torture you destroy, first, your integrity; and, second, your career, for it will follow in flames, as probably it should, for no institution can knowingly tolerate or accept such practice by its members.

When do we cross the line separating tough, hard-nosed, aggressive military operations from intimidation tactics inconsistent with Army values? To lament the difficulties of peacekeeping duties is justifiable, but such duties do not excuse improper behavior. Remember when Maria, Rebecca, you, and I watched the movie *Dirty Harry*? As I recall the plot, policeman Dirty Harry captures a bad guy who, trying to extort money, has buried alive a child whose oxygen supply will shortly run out. Can and should Dirty Harry torture the bad guy to find out where the child is? This is not something he wishes to do *for himself*; but it's not something, either, that can be accepted as police practice. It is the wrong thing to do; but is there, in this single and unrepeatable case, a "*wronger*" thing to do—that is, not to torture the criminal? If this were Dom or Josh, wouldn't you torture that kidnapper-killer in a second? But isn't that why doctors don't operate on their own family members? And isn't that a key reason that we have commissioned officers, whose terrible task it can be to insist upon the dry logic of law and high purpose even in the heat of passion and the desire for information at any cost, for vengeance at any price?

Pete, what I am saying here can be reduced to a simple, yet very harsh, sentence: As a soldier you are prepared to risk your life for your country; but, as a soldier, you may also be risking your *soul* for your country—but *risk* does not mean *relinquish*. You know that Catholic theology tells us to avoid the occasion of sin.[31] One could argue that Christians ought not to involve themselves in either political or military affairs, for, if my reasoning is right, you may be involved in situations, especially in the moral squalor of contemporary world affairs, that could lead to your making decisions that might be deeply troubling from an ethical standpoint. You may be risking your soul for your country. And that is a risk that no country has a right to ask of its citizens or of its soldiers, for we know we must always obey God before men (Acts 5.29). Still, what are we to do? Can we withdraw into a politically quiet shell or enclave, awaiting the Second Coming and disdaining affairs of state? Have we no obligation to love God and neighbor in the realm of politics? We do, of course; and we are obliged to act the very best we can, torn as we will sometimes be between competing obligations. In our country, with its eternal optimism, we forget that life is, at its heart, tragic. I suspect that the years ahead will re-teach us the lessons of life and politics which informed classical political realism. All around us are military situations in which, as Seabury and Codevilla put it, "The only rule is that there is no rule."[32] How do you conduct yourself as a man of character and principle, as a gentleman, and, most critically, as a Christian, in circumstances of moral nihilism? We know that the heart of *jus in bello* is discrimination and proportionality. But maybe Charles Dunlap is right in saying that "when societies propagate evil, democracies must be prepared to visit upon them force so staggering it will produce fundamental change."[33]

CLEAN HEARTS—AND CONSCIENTIOUS LEADERS

Of President Harry Truman, for example, what are we to think? Did he perform his trust wisely and well in the terrible circumstances of August 1945 when he twice ordered atomic bombs to be used? As Christians, we ask mercy on his soul; as Americans we

ask whether he acted and reasoned rightly. I believe he did. Far from contending that the ends always justify the means, I argue only that there can be cases of such extraordinary moral and political import—almost bizarre, very rare, probably unique—that even as there is no precedent *for* them, neither should there be precedent *from* them. *This is why leadership is so critical*, for I am "betting" in these cases, not upon customs or rules or even outcomes (for no one is clairvoyant), but upon men and women of great—one wishes to write "noble"—character.

In situations of momentous military, moral, or political pressure, it is imperative that we have good men—people—as leaders. I do not say here "good leaders" but good men as good leaders. "Army leadership begins with what the leader must BE, the values and attributes that shape a leader's character. It may be helpful to think of these as internal qualities: you possess them all the time, alone and with others. They define who you are; they give you a solid footing. . . ."[34] Retired Air Force Brig. Gen. Malham Wakin once gave us the same advice: "Fully accepting the Aristotelian wisdom that moral character develops out of repeating good actions, that it cannot be ordered but can be exemplified and imitated, our advice to those who aspire to become worthy military leaders can be none other than that of the ancient Chinese sage: 'The way to do is to be.'"[35]

What I am saying is that the good man as a leader knows when to follow orders and when not to. Moreover, he also knows *when to make exceptions*. When a good man is confronted with a horrifying situation such as the one in which enemy soldiers with children as shields are advancing on his troops' perimeter, or when a good man must decide whether to get into the *Enola Gay* and drop an atomic bomb on an enemy, what specific chapter and verse, what precedent, what rule can adequately inform him? In such appalling circumstances, whom does he consult? Here, he needs not information but formation. He must have developed, through continual practice (including reading, study, and prayer or meditation), the strength of character to make, if entirely necessary, Dirty Hands decisions (cf. 2 Chr 30.18-19; Ps 51.12). We are, as Aristotle tried once to tell us, what we continually do. We might add the corollary that we continually do what we fundamentally are.

Now consider our current plight. As Barbara Tuchman has put it, government remains "the paramount field of unwisdom because it is there that men seek power over others—only to lose it over them-selves." And: "Although professionalism can help, I tend to think that fitness of character is what gov-ernment chiefly requires."[36] Well, do the past few years make you optimistic about our likelihood of developing "fitness of character" in our leaders? If our postmodern society is corrosive in its effect on char-acter-building in homes and schools and churches—as I think it is—then where will our genuine leaders come from? How can we trust them?

The military tries to answer these questions as far as officers are concerned. Read your commission again. It is a statement of trust and confidence in your patriotism, valor, fidelity, and abilities. That is the teaching, also, of the Church: "Those too who devote themselves to the military service of their country should regard themselves as the agents of security and freedom of peoples. *As long as they ful-fill this role properly*, they are making a genuine con-tribution to the establishment of peace"[37] Most particularly and most urgently, I as a citizen trust and confidently expect that you as a soldier will make *proper* decisions as a public steward of character and competence. And I believe that you will carry out your duties with honor, not only in routine matters, but in the gravest circumstances, where, ultimately, the decisions you make flow from all you are and all you believe—even to the point of Dirty Hands.

If you must make that kind of decision, I have to trust in *you*. This is not an attempt to deify you or to exalt subjectivism or ethical egotism. All I am say-ing here is that there may be times when your life and even your soul may be on the line. I believe in "virtue ethics" (or aretaic ethics)[38] to the point that I concur with Anton Myrer, author of *Once an Eagle*, which all Army officers ought to read: In it, the pro-tagonist, Col. Sam Damon, tells his son (and us): "If it comes to a choice between being a good soldier and a good human being—try to be a good human being."[39] No one has ever put it more concisely, more cogently.

I want you as a commander to have a well-formed conscience. I hope you will follow the dic-tates of that conscience, *despite* the rules we know and accept, if exigent circumstances so demand. And I hope you then face squarely and manfully the con-sequences of your decision and your action. But what your fellow citizens expect of you as a soldier—and the report of your stewardship that you must ren-der—is, in fact, not much different from our higher obligation (as in Rom 2.6-11 or 1 Pt 4.10).

Remember the early 1960s film *Fail-Safe*? The United States has accidentally dropped a nuclear weapon on Moscow due, principally, to technologi-cal failure. The Soviets are about to retaliate when the U.S. president, trying to avert World War III, orders a U.S. Air Force officer to drop a nuclear weapon on New York City—to placate the Soviets. Talk about Dirty Hands! Can the President order that? Can he, given the scenario, *not* order that? Can the officer fly the plane and drop the bomb? (By the way, in the film, the officer's wife and children are in New York City that day, as is the President's wife.) The officer flies the plane, drops the bomb, and then kills himself.

How do you read me, Pete? I should decide that dropping the bomb is a terrible necessity. Right? My Dirty Hands moral theory must come into play here, mustn't it? No. I cannot drop that bomb, nor can I applaud the President for ordering it or the officer for doing it. I understand the President's decision, but I cannot condone it. These are wholly innocent American citizens; international nuclear war is not a certainty (although as painted for us in the film and book such war is admittedly very likely); and the President and the Air Force officer, finally, cannot kill their own countrymen in the name of national secu-rity. I'm saying that the ends here do not justify the means.

I know: I just finished saying that it's possible, *but extremely rare*, that good ends can justify bad means. Here, in the *Fail-Safe* scenario, I cannot accept that rationale. Upon reflection, neither would you. For we can never justifiably call "collateral damage" what is, in fact, "the indiscriminate destruction of whole cities or vast areas with their inhabitants" (*CCC #* 2314). To do such a thing would not merely dirty our hands; it would poison our hearts and pollute our souls.

THE THINGS WE CANNOT NOT KNOW

In 1972, Barbara Tuchman, whom I mentioned in a different context above, spoke at the Army War College on the subject of "Generalship." She told the audience that the West Point motto of "Duty, Honor, Country" may no longer suffice. "Country," she said, "is clear enough, but what is Duty in a wrong war? What is Honor when fighting is reduced to 'wasting' the living space—not to mention the lives—of a peo-ple that never did us any harm? The simple West Point answer," she continued, "is that Duty and Honor consist in carrying out the orders of the government. That is what the Nazis said in their defense, and we tried them for war crimes nevertheless." Tuchman appealed to the soldiers assembled there at Carlisle Barracks *to think*.[40]

But Tuchman actually did not have to urge the soldiers to think. Thinking *should* be regarded as essential to professionalism. The *Manual for Courts-Martial*, for example, tells military personnel that "it is a defense to any offense that the accused was acting pursuant to orders unless the accused knew the orders to be unlawful or *a person of ordinary sense and understanding* would have known the orders to be unlawful."[41] We may understand the phrase *ordinary sense and understanding* to refer to conscience. The central idea, after all, is that if you receive an order from your two-star, you are to obey it unless you know the order is unlawful or unless *you should know* (because it's "written on your heart") it to be unlawful. In other words, the *Manual for Courts-Martial* insists that there is a standard of general knowledge and of ordinary morality according to which our actions may be judged. The ordinary private in Lt. William Calley's platoon at My Lai, if he actually did not know that the order given there to murder Vietnamese was wrong, should have known. All decent people know that! It is no defense to say, "I didn't know such-and-such was wrong," for the rejoinder is that you most certainly should have known. We are back to an earlier point: *There are some things that we can't not know.* That is very, very important. It takes us, if we let it, into theological waters, such as those found in 2 Cor 3.3, in Heb 8.10, and in *CCC* # 1958.

Some would argue that, in a multicultural society, we can do little in the way of discussing ends or purposes or substance. That is why the military oath of office is sworn in support of the Constitution. At the same time, however, Pete, you and I realize as Christians that our first and foremost obligation is to God. Remember Sacred Heart Basilica at Notre Dame, where under the archway of one of the doors are chiseled the words *God, Country, Notre Dame*? To us, God must always come before country. We have what we might call a *perfect duty* of obedience to God through our formed conscience and a compelling but still *imperfect duty* to the state and its representatives and officers (as in Mt 22.21, Rom 13.1-7, 1 Pt 2.13-17, Ti 3.1, *CCC* #1880).

You've heard my argument on this before. We live in a society in which we often hear about *rights* (and perhaps not enough about duties). But we very rarely hear about *Right*. The various core values of the armed services are pathways to *Right*, by which I mean virtuous ends. If all of what our services do to maintain our national security is done without concern for—or in violation of—standards of good and evil, of honor and shame, that are obvious to anyone of "ordinary sense and understanding," then we have paid too high a price, and we have destroyed what we ostensibly sought to preserve. If we are going to become like the barbarians who routinely murder and commit other savage practices (such as allowing rape by soldiers as a means of terrorizing the populace, thus facilitating military control over the defeated country), then why not simply join the barbarians?

The object of military ethics, after all, is to help soldiers understand that there are things they cannot do, lines they cannot cross, means they cannot employ—even if they thereby sacrifice certain military advantages—because, by so doing, they destroy, not just *rights* but *Right* itself. *Right* refers to those things we cannot not know; it is prima facie virtue, a perception of what is true and transcendent, despite what divergent (and occasionally defective) cultures might say; it is an understanding of the mind and heart about what makes life itself holy. As John Paul II has written, people exist in particular cultures but are *not* "exhaustively defined by that same culture." And: "If there is no transcendent truth, in obedience to which man achieves his full identity, then there is no such principle for guaranteeing just relations between people. Their self-interest as a class, group, or nation would inevitably set them in opposition to one another. If one does not acknowledge transcendent truth, then the force of power takes over, and each person tends to make full use of the means at his disposal in order to impose his own interests or his own opinion."[42]

Isn't that, essentially, what it's all about? Isn't that, finally, why the military ethic is *good*? To the extent to which the warrior ethos, the military ethic, or the profession of arms participates in what is good and true (cf. Phil 4.8), you as a soldier *owe*—a very important verb—allegiance to that ethic, and those you command in the name of that ethic similarly owe obedience. But when countries or commanders or specific orders depart from or, worse, violate a transcendent standard, then citizens and soldiers alike—people of ordinary sense and understanding—must very carefully consider whether the country has forfeited its claim upon them (as in the case of Germany in World War II) or whether the commander's orders have become immoral and therefore illegal.

But there must be a standard—and that, I fear, is what the new barbarism denies and what our post-modern society increasingly scorns. Remember how impressed you were with José Ortega y Gasset's argument that "barbarism is the absence of standards to which appeal can be made"?[43] His book first appeared about seventy years ago; what do you think he'd say of *today's* moral nihilism? Probably much the same thing that Alasdair MacIntyre might say: that "modern politics itself expresses in its institutional forms a systematic rejection of [the tradition of the virtues]," for contemporary government "does not express or represent the moral community of the citizens, but is instead a set of institutional arrangements for imposing a bureaucratized unity on a society which lacks genuine moral consensus." The problem is that "the nature of political obligation becomes systematically unclear."[44]

TEACHING WHAT WE ARE

So, finally, after all this, you'd want me to say how all this can be taught! The services have different words for their core values, even though the meanings are similar. They are necessary, I think, but not sufficient. Philosophy and theology do offer us four virtues (not just "values") which now, in turn, I offer to you. The first is *wisdom,* for without it we can hardly expect to differentiate good from evil. I define it as the ability reasonably to evaluate (and to bring order to) the temporary in light of the eternal and the changeable in light of the changeless. Human nature doesn't change. If it does, how can we expect to read Sophocles or Euripedes or Herodotus or Homer and truly appreciate the emotions expressed there? Some of the lessons, for example, of the Peloponnesian War are timeless. We spend much time seeking information superiority when, so often, the problem we have is wisdom deficiency. And, no, I am not trying to make either you or your men philosophers! But you have a *legal obligation* to judge immoral orders. How can you hope to do that unless there is some serious and substantial education given to soldiers along with solid, hard-nosed training? The cardinal virtues are sometimes referred to as *hinge virtues* because all the others depend upon these four, which in effect are one virtue.

Justice (or truthfulness) is the second cardinal virtue. It refers to habitual right thinking and speaking and worthiness of conduct. *Fortitude* or courage is the third cardinal virtue, meaning firmness in difficulty and constancy of purpose toward the good. *Temperance* or moderation or self-control is the fourth, and it refers to direction and discretion with respect to appetites, instincts, and urges. I regard these four virtues as a composite; you can't have one without the others. What we have built here is a four-component image of the good man or woman. These are not debatable "values"; they are essential virtues, and virtue is conformity to standards of Right (cf. Wis 8.7, Rom 12.2; Col 1.9-12; *CCC* #1804-1809).[45]

So where does the "standard of Right" come from in the U.S. Army, which is a secular armed service of a secular state? It comes from you and from the culture and confraternity of your fellow leaders at all levels, insofar as it conforms to what is the eternal standard (cf. Jn 5.30, 1 Cor 2.14-16, 1 Thess 4.1; *CCC* # 215). And you already know the standard because it is found and exemplified daily by those you respect and admire (although certainly not in all of us and never perfectly in any of us). Every commander—every good teacher—knows that, in the end, he or she will be followed, not because of rank or special privilege or particular position, but because he and she are people worthy of trust and confidence. Those words appearing on your commission mean so much because they, not power or rank, are ultimately what your soldiers will follow when the chips are down. They will follow you, not just because you are *Colonel Garcia* (although that of course is an important part of it), but because you are *Pedro Garcia*, who has the competence of the good soldier and the character of the good man.

You will teach the standard of Right to your soldiers, not just because you *do* it but because you *are* it. When FM 22-100 says "Be, Know, and Do," it has leadership exactly right. Every time you make a serious moral judgment, you become that judgment; every time you issue a command, you not only tell your subordinates what to do but what to be. That is why, in the horrible circumstances in which you or your soldiers might find yourselves in the months ahead in a world seemingly gone morally mad, I trust in you because of the moral compass which is yours from your education, your experience, your expertise. You *do* on the basis of your information; you *are* on the basis of your formation. Ethics, in the final analysis, is caught, not just taught. Your command will do right because of the example you'll set, helping its members to be right.

Well, Pete, it's time to quit. I've tried to write from the heart as well as from the head. You know I like Anton Myrer's novel, which I've already quoted to you once here. I can't resist closing with another excerpt. Colonel Damon tells his son: "That's the whole challenge of life—to act with honor and hope and generosity, no matter what you've drawn. You can't help when or what you were born, you may not be able to help how you die; but you can—and you should—try to pass the days between as a good man."[46] I believe, Pete, that if we try sincerely to know and to do what is good, we can become, if not good, then at least better men. In that effort—toward which the cardinal virtues compel us—lies, not just character, but the fulfillment of doing a noble job nobly.

All the best, Pete!
—Jim

NOTES

1. Although I am solely responsible for any errors of fact, interpretation, or expression in this chapter, I wish to thank Col. Alexander Shine (USA, Ret.) for his keen interest and significant contributions to this effort. The opinions expressed in this chapter, of course, do not imply the endorsement of the Department of Defense, the Department of the Army, the Department of the Air Force, Air University, or the Air War College.

2. Neil Howe and William Strauss, *Millennials Rising: The Next Great Generation* (New York: Vintage, 2000).

3. *Montgomery Advertiser*, 9 September 2000.

4. William Bennett, *The Death of Outrage* (New York: The Free Press, 1998), 121.

5. Robert Bork, *Slouching Toward Gomorrah* (New York: Regan, 1996), 275.

6. Frank Sheed, *Theology and Sanity* (San Francisco, CA: Ignatius, 1978), 394.

7. Quoted by Grant T. Hammond, *The Mind of War* (Washington, DC: Smithsonian Institution, 2001), 211.

8. Headquarters, Department of the Army, FM 22-100, *Army Leadership: Be, Know, Do* (Washington, DC: U.S. Government Printing Office, 1999), 2-21.

9. Martin Van Creveld, *The Transformation of War* (New York: Free Press, 1991).

10. Larry Seaquist, "Community War," *U.S. Naval Institute Proceedings* 126 (August 2000): 56-59.

11. *Baltimore Sun*, 4 September 2000.

12. Paul Seabury and Angelo Codevilla, *War: Ends and Means* (New York: Basic Books, 1989), 14.

13. T.R. Fehrenbach, *This Kind of War* (New York: Macmillan, 1963).

14. Samuel Huntington, *The Clash of Civilizations and the Remaking of World Order* (New York: Simon and Schuster, 1996), 51.

15. Charles J. Dunlap, Jr., "How We Lost the High-Tech War of 2007," *Weekly Standard*, 29 January 1996, 22-28.

16. Donald Kagan and Frederick Kagan, "Peace for Our Time?" *Commentary* 110 (September 2000): 45-46; see also their book *While America Sleeps* (New York: St. Martin's Press, 2000), 400-35.

17. On this theme, see David Donovan [Terry Turner], *Once a Warrior King* (New York: McGraw-Hill, 1985). This is an excellent study of use to company- and field-grade officers.

18. James Turner Johnson and George Weigel, *Just War and the Gulf War* (Washington, DC: Ethics and Public Policy Center, 1991), 85.

19. Anthony Loyd, *My War Gone By, I Miss It So* (New York: Atlantic Monthly Press, 1999); and Mark Bowden, *Black Hawk Down* (New York: Atlantic Monthly Press, 1999).

20. Theologians often contend that there are three sources of a morally good act: the object chosen, the end or the intention, and the circumstances. See *Catechism of the Catholic Church* [hereafter *CCC*] (New York: Doubleday, 1994), #1750.

21. Servais Pinckaers, O.P., *Morality: The Catholic View*, trans. Michael Sherwin, O.P. (South Bend, IN: St. Augustine's Press, 2001), 8.

22. J. Budziszewski, *The Revenge of Conscience* (Dallas, TX: Spence, 1999), ch. 2.

23. This story, from Bierce's collection *Can Such Things Be?* (1893), tells of Captain Ransome's fire on his own troops because of the faulty orders of his general. The general is killed in battle, leaving Ransome to be punished for his general's error.

24. For a study of proportionalism, see Sean Fagan, S.M., *Does Morality Change?* (Dublin: Gill and Macmillan, 1997). There is much in this book that is mistaken, however. Cf. the encyclical let-

ter of Pope John Paul II, *The Splendor of Truth* (Boston, MA: St. Paul [1993]), #32.

25. See E. L. Miller, *Questions That Matter* (Boston, MA: McGraw-Hill, 1998), 395.

26. Bowden, *Black Hawk Down*, 106.

27. Norman Geisler, *Christian Ethics* (Grand Rapids, MI: Baker House, 1989), 97-132.

28. *The Splendor of Truth*, sections 80 and 81.

29. Michael Walzer, *Just and Unjust Wars*, 2d ed. (New York: Basic, 1977), ch. 16; Elizabeth Anscombe, "War and Murder," in *War, Morality, and the Military Profession*, 2d ed., ed. Malham M. Wakin (Boulder, CO: Westview Press, 1986), 294.

30. *Washington Post*, 19 October 2000.

31. *CCC, #408, 1768, 1865-1869.*

32. Seabury and Codevilla, *War: Ends and Means*, 10.

33. Charles Dunlap, Jr., "Rethinking Noncombatancy in the Post-Kosovo Era: The End of Innocence," *Strategic Review* 28 (Summer 2000): 17.

34. FM 22-100, *Army Leadership*, 1-4.

35. *War, Morality, and the Military Profession*, 197.

36. Barbara W. Tuchman, "An Inquiry into the Persistence of Unwisdom in Government." *Parameters* 10 (March 1980): 8-9.

37. Vatican Council II, *Gaudium et Spes* (7 Dec 1965), no. 79; my emphasis.

38. Aretaics is the "science of virtue—contrasted with *eudaemonics*"(*Webster's Third New International Dictionary of the English Language Unabridged*, 1968).

39. Anton Myer, *Once an Eagle* (New York: Berkley, 1968), 913; in the HarperCollins edition of 1997, see 936.

40. Barbara W. Tuchman, "Generalship," *Parameters* 2 (1972): 11.

41. Joint Service Committee on Military Justice, *Manual for Courts-Martial, United States*, 1995 Edition (Washington, DC: U.S. Government Printing Office, 1995), rule 916 (II-109), my emphasis.

42. *The Splendor of Truth*, sections 53 and 99.

43. José Ortega y Gasset, *The Revolt of the Masses* (New York: W.W. Norton, 1957), 72.

44. Alasdair MacIntyre, *After Virtue*, 2d ed. (Notre Dame, IN: University of Notre Dame Press, 1984), 254-55. For MacIntyre's comments about the extent to which modern barbarianism has infected us, see 263.

45. In *Morality*, Father Pinckaers writes that "the cardinal virtues are simply four forms of charity" (21; cf. 87).

46. Myer, *Once an Eagle*, 660; in the HarperCollins edition of 1997, see 677-678.

Officership Case Study I

This is the first case study in a set of five case studies on the evolution of the Army. The intent of this lesson is to have you gain familiarity with the historic context in which the U.S. became involved in the Vietnam Conflict, to identify the policies and practices of the Vietnam Conflict, and the lessons that need to be learned from that era. In addition, you will learn about the Threads of Continuity, the Six Imperatives, and how they can be applied so as to recognize and guide an organization in change.

The following topics are addressed in this lesson:

- The history of American involvement
- The policies and practices of the Vietnam Conflict
- The conduct of the Officer corps
- The Threads of Continuity
- The Six Imperatives

The following TLO is supported in whole or in part by this lesson:

- Institute change in an organization

Following this lesson you will be able to:

- Identify the key elements needed to institute a change within an organization
- Analyze the evolution of the Army using the Threads of Continuity

VIETNAM'S FORGOTTEN LESSONS

Twenty-five years after the end of the war, does the Pentagon remember the causes of America's defeat?

By Richard J. Newman

Lyndon Johnson once boasted that during the Vietnam War, "I had more control over the generals than any other civilian President in history." But President Clinton had one advantage Johnson didn't: "POTUS slides." During the war against Yugoslavia last year, intelligence analysts produced viewgraphs exclusively for the President of the United States—POTUS, in administration speak. Each contained detailed information on targets NATO commanders wanted to bomb. There was a picture of the target and data on what kind of bomb would be used. Better, yet, the slides estimated how much damage would be done to nearby buildings, and how many civilians and enemy troops would be killed. If the numbers looked good, Clinton gave a thumbsup, and bombs would fly. Key European capitals had to agree, of course, but in the end many targets were deemed too risky and relegated to the "no-strike" list.

A week into the war, Gen. Wesley Clark, NATO's top commander, was bristling. Politicians in Washington and Europe were refusing to attack targets in Belgrade, the Yugoslav capital. Command bunkers and other critical targets were ruled off-limits. Serb forces, meanwhile, were marauding through Kosovo, "Clark said, 'This is impossible,'" according to a NATO official involved in the process. "We need blanket [target] approval." The NATO chief implored his political bosses to approve more targets. He even launched warplanes toward unapproved targets, hoping to get an OK once he explained that the jets were already airborne. The ploy didn't work—not once. Only after about a month of bombing did the restrictions ease significantly, as the Serbs proved far tougher than expected.

Futility. That's no way to fight a war—at least according to the lessons the American military learned in Southeast Asia a quarter century ago. The fall of Saigon and the communist victory in Vietnam brought to a close one of the most painful—but instructive—epochs in the nation's history. The image of defeat is indelible: a Marine Corps chopper plucking desperate Americans from a Saigon rooftop while North Vietnamese troops swarm through the city. It epitomized the futility of Vietnam, a conflict fought valiantly on the ground but lost by the bull-headed decisions of those in high office. Twenty-five years later, the denunciations of the war are muted—but still accurate: 58,219 Americans died in Vietnam because shortsighted political leaders misused the nation's military.

From all the waste, however, something valuable did emerge: a military that learned how *not* to fight an enemy. "It was a very frustrating war for a lot of us," recalls Gen. Mike Ryan, the Air Force chief of staff, who flew 100 missions over North Vietnam in an F-4 fighter-bomber. On many of those flights, North Vietnamese MiG fighters would engage U.S. jets, flying from air bases American pilots were forbidden to bomb. It was that kind of insanity that taught Ryan and others of his generation how to fight to win: Establish clear objectives. Give military leaders broad authority. Don't micro-manage the war from Washington. And "if you're going to use American might," says Ryan, "use it in a way so we don't prolong that war." The showcase for those lessons was the 1991 Persian Gulf war, a furious, 43-day onslaught in which the U.S.-led coalition pulverized Saddam Hussein's Air Force, crippled his infrastructure, and routed 300,000 of his troops. "By God," declared President George Bush at the end of the war, "we've kicked the Vietnam syndrome once and for all."

Nearly a decade later, however, the U.S. military is beset by an identity crisis. Many of the lessons of Vietnam have been lost, forgotten, or cast aside, deemed inconvenient or irrelevant. Few members of the Vietnam generation remain in uniform. Only 1,379 of the Army's 475,000 soldiers, for instance, served in Vietnam. Many generals still remember Vietnam vividly, but the war has virtually vanished from the cultural memory of the rank and file. "Vietnam is history, and it's been forgotten, especially for the younger soldiers," says Command Sgt. Maj. Robert Seiler of the Division of Engineers, 4th Infantry Division at Fort Hood, Texas, who spent 27 months on the ground in Vietnam. Clothing stores at Fort Hood don't even carry Vietnam-era ribbons for soldier's dress uniforms; they have to be specially ordered.

At a higher level, Pentagon brass have increasingly blessed practices denounced after Vietnam: gradual increases in military pressure, bombing to signal American resolve, indefinite involvement in overseas disputes. "In Kosovo," says a retired general who flew combat missions over North Vietnam, "we had the exact same things happening as in the Vietnam

War—picking targets at the White House, micro-managing the conflict in ways reminiscent of [Defense Secretary Robert] McNamara and LBJ."

Other parallels haunt. In the Persian Gulf, U.S. warplanes drop bombs on Iraq weekly, in attacks reminiscent of the limited responses to enemy aggression ordered by Lyndon Johnson. In Bosnia, Kosovo, and Columbia, the indefinite deployment of American ground troops represents the kind of "stumbling forward" strategy that prevailed in Vietnam, according to another retired four-star general.

Surprises. The difference today, of course, is that few Americans are dying in overseas missions. And a debacle on the scale of the Vietnam War seems inconceivable. But military experts worry that trends similar to those during the Vietnam years could produce ugly surprises for the Pentagon. "There's the illusion that we can rely on technology before we have to go bloody somebody," says Marine Corps Gen. John Sheehan, who led an infantry company through the Vietnamese jungle. "But at some point, you're going to run across the Chechens. I can see 30, 40, or 50 killed because they're not going to be ready, or there won't be enough of the right guys." Retired Army Col. Rich Dunn, who led a company of engineers in Vietnam, argues that "because of the passing of the Vietnam generation, we're forgetting the lessons of Vietnam. We're starting to see things reappear that broke the Army in the 1970s."

The U.S. military—and the Army in particular—was reeling by the nd of the Vietnam War. "The American Army emerged from Vietnam cloaked in anguish," wrote Maj. Gen. Robert Scales, who is now commandant of the Army War College, in *Certain Victory,* a 1993 account of how the Army evolved into the force that prevailed in Operation Desert Storm. The military draft, with its tolerance for felons and its escape hatches for privileged youth, produced a dysfunctional force. In the Army, 41 percent of soldiers scored in the lowest of four categories on mental aptitude tests. Drug use and discipline problems became rampant. Many career noncommissioned officers—the experienced sergeants who make units hum—quit when faced with a second or third tour in Vietnam. Dunn's battalion in Vietnam in 1971 suffered just one combat death—but 18 deaths from drug overdoses. As a young Marine commander dealing with discipline problems, says Gen. James Jones, now the commandant of the Marine Corps, "I had many Marines standing before me saying, "Well, I'm

here because the judge said either I go to the Marines or I go to jail for grand theft auto.' It was exhausting."

After the war, military leaders began recasting the services to avoid the kinds of problems they saw in Vietnam. The Army and Marine Corps gave commanders broader authority to give troublemakers the boot. Command assignments were lengthened so battalion commanders would get to know their units, instead of blithely rotating through every six months to punch another ticket as they moved up the career ladder—the common practice during the war.

At the same time, the military was adapting to the need of the draft in 1973 and the start of the all-volunteer force. That move—bitterly opposed by the brass beforehand and almost universally applauded today—eventually helped the Pentagon recruit more qualified troops. By 1990, more than 95 percent of new Army recruits were high school graduates, compared with about 60 percent 20 years earlier. To test the new force, the services established some of the toughest training programs and facilities in the world, including the Air Force's Red Flag exercises and the Army's National Training Center in the California desert. In exercises, units faced an "opposition force" meant to stimulate the best the Soviet Union might throw at them; often, they got clobbered—but they learned how to fight and fight smart.

Powell's way. But the biggest advances were in strategy, most notably, the so-called Powell Doctrine, named after Gen. Colin Powell, the chairman of the Joint Chiefs of Staff from 1989 to 1993. The Powell Doctrine, which actually derived from a speech Defense Secretary Caspar Weinberger gave in 1984, held that U.S. forces should be sent to war only when a "vital national interest" is at stake, when there is a clear intention of winning, and when the American public and Congress support a specific operation. Once determined to go to war, the United States should use overwhelming force to defeat the enemy as quickly as possible. In short, Powell's principles addressed virtually all the mistakes he had observed during two tours on the ground in Vietnam.

The Powell Doctrine was the ethos that inspired the Pentagon plan to repel the Iraqi troops that invaded Kuwait. Around the clock, from Day 1, hundreds of U.S. and coalition warplanes hammered targets throughout Iraq, including sensitive sites like command bunkers and power grids. "We made an absolute commitment," says retired Air Force Col. John Warden, a key architect of the plan, "that when we decide to risk the lives of our own people, we ought to be certain we are doing so as decisively as we can."

That conviction no longer prevails. The Kosovo war, for instance, was designed from the start to be a "phased" operation, which NATO gradually increasing the pressure until Serbian leader Slobodan Milosevic caved. Air Force commanders and the Joint Chiefs of Staff lobbied vigorously for a more aggressive campaign. But the U.S. and European civilians they were appealing to recalled not the lessons of Vietnam but the lessons of Bosnia. When NATO finally intervened in that war in 1995, it took less than two weeks of bombing to halt the Bosnian Serb military campaign and ultimately compel them to sign a peace agreement. But the NATO bombing coincided with a ground campaign by the Serbs' opponents that left the Serbs vulnerable to air attacks, an advantage NATO air forces didn't have in Kosovo. "We walked into incrementalism [in Kosovo] because of NATO's experience in the past, and there was no way to move them off that as a starting point," says a senior Pentagon official. "Did we want to get into this in an incremental way? Absolutely not. But it was incrementalism or don't go."

Whose rules? This is a modus operandi military officials may have to get used to, even though it challenges one of the principal lessons military officers took away from Vietnam: that once a president has decided to go to war, he should turn the conduct of the campaign over to military professionals. "It's the wrong lesson," says Tom McNaugher of Rand, a government-supported think tank. "I don't know any way around incrementalism. Massing forces is nice, if you can get it. But if you can't get that kind of freedom of action, are you going to stand by and do nothing? That's like saying we'll only fight the wars where we get to play by our rules."

Eventually, during the Kosovo war, NATO and U.S. authorities granted permission to strike the targets military leaders wanted to hit at the outset: Power plants, TV and radio transmitters, political headquarters in Belgrade. Since NATO ultimately won—with zero combat deaths—Defense Secretary William Cohen and others have argued that incremental bombing worked. But there was a cost: The war probably went on much longer than it had to. "There were probably 30 or 40 good targets in Belgrade," says Warden, the Desert Storm strategist. "The whole war could reasonably have been done in less than 10

days—with fewer sorties, fewer attacks, fewer targets. The refugee flow never would have happened. There is a feeling that the humane way to conduct military operations is gradually, but you end up with the opposite effects. You end up killing more people."

An eerier echo of Vietnam may be the "containment" of Iraq. The plan, implemented in 1992, relies on U.S. and British jets flying patrols over northern and southern Iraq. In December 1998, Washington and London approved an intensive four-day bombing campaign against Iraq. Since then, American and British pilots have been fired at regularly by Iraqi air-defense guns and missiles. When such attacks occur, U.S. commanders choose from a number of "response options" deemed appropriate to the level of provocation. The result has been hundreds of U.S. attacks on Iraqi air defense sites, including seven so far this month.

That kind of tit-for-tat reminds many Vietnam experts of the "retaliatory" strikes against North Vietnam during the 1960s. The missions were meant not to win the war; but to signal Americas resolve against North Vietnamese aggression. After North Vietnamese attacks on a U.S. installation in Pleiku in February of 1965 that killed eight and wounded more than 100, for instance, an outraged Lyndon Johnson ordered the bombing of several North Vietnamese barracks and staging areas. But he stressed that the response was "carefully limited to military areas" and was "appropriate and fitting.... We seek no wider war," Johnson assured the North Vietnamese.

Is the United States committing the same mistake again in Iraq? "There's no way you can plausibly argue that the bombing of Iraq will lead to the overthrow of Saddam or any kind of political outcome," says Andrew Bacevich, a retired Army colonel, Vietnam veteran, and professor of international relations at Boston University. "It's using force for signal sending and demonstrating our determination. That was completely—completely—discredited after Vietnam." Military commanders accede to the policy, Bacevich says, because "they need to demonstrate their relevance," in order to justify continued funding from Congress.

Are there no better solutions for the military challenges the United States faces today? "We have a lot of angst about [Iraq]," admits one senior Pentagon official." But if containment in the long run works, it will be declared a victory." Even Warden, a strong advocate of overwhelming force, agrees that "in the

The Healing Process Is Far From Done

Perry Buck, 72, a veteran of World War II and Korea, thought he knew everything about the horrors of war. But the Vietnam War, says Buck, one of the nation's first Navy Seals, proved him wrong.

In the steamy mangrove forests of Southeast Asia, Buck came in contact with Agent Orange, the dioxin-laced herbicide used by the U.S. military to defoliate the jungle and give U.S. soldiers a defense against the guerrilla warfare of the enemy Viet Cong. In the peak years for Agent Orange use, 1965 to 1967, Buck was on missions where, he says, "we were caught in the bushes when they sprayed the foliage with it."

Once home, Buck's right lung collapsed. His chest and back were covered with rashes. Then in 1992, he was diagnosed with prostate cancer. The Department of Veterans Affairs did not see these conditions as "service connected" to Agent Orange exposure.

It was not until 1994, nearly 20 years after the last Americans left Vietnam, that a congressional ordered review of Agent Orange by the national Institute of Medicine linked the defoliant to skin rashes, called chloracne, and soft-tissue and lymphatic cancers. "That was the breakthrough," says Mark Brown of the VA, which began compensating for these conditions in 1996. That same year, the government added prostate cancer, multiple myeloma, respiratory cancers, and spina bifida, a crippling birth defect in the children of exposed veterans, to its growing list of Agent Orange-related illnesses. The Institute of Medicine is now reviewing the herbicide's possible links to diabetes.

Unsung survivors. Advances in surgery, drugs, and wound treatment meant that, unlike in previous wars, "in Vietnam, you had a high proportion of very seriously injured people who lived, lots of bilateral, lower leg amputees," says Thomas Holohan, VA chief of patient care services. But the public's antiwar sentiment made adjusting to these disabilities both physically and psychologically challenging. "When they came home, they were called "baby killers,'" adds Holohan. "It was difficult to reconcile the sacrifice they made with the view that it was totally meaningless."

Because there was no effective hepatitis C test until 1992, many of the transfusions used to keep soldiers alive in Vietnam were likely to be contaminated with the virus. Hepatitis is endemic in Southeast Asia, so association with local people, blood on the battlefield from infected soldiers, and intravenous drug use all made the risk of infection high. Hepatitis C has a 10-to-30-year latency; many veterans don't yet know they are infected with a virus that can cause liver failure and death. Gary Rozelle, director for infectious diseases for the VA, evaluated the 54,682 new cases of hepatitis C diagnosed by the VA during 1989-99. His study found that 62.7 percent were in Vietnam-era vets.

The Vietnam Veterans of America has petitioned the VA for a "presumptive service connection for hep C," making compensation automatic. A bill pending in Congress, H.R. 1020, would do the same.

But little has been done to address the psychological fallout to the three million Americans who served in Southeast Asia. "Doctors didn't recognize post-traumatic stress disorder," says Terry Baker of the Vietnam Veterans of America. PTSD was not accepted by the American Psychiatric Association until 1980. "When the WWII guys came back," Baker adds, "they were able to talk about the war. With Vietnam, vets had to change their clothes in the bus station because people would spit on them. The biggest health problem Vietnam vets still face is our lack of self-esteem." —*Amanda Spake*

---

scheme of things, {containment of Iraq] has been pretty cheap. We have exercised control at a pretty low price."

The need for soldiers to do things other than fight and win wars is forcing the Pentagon's top officers to question whether the lessons they learned in Vietnam still apply. "The debate should be more sophisticated than to say we have a military just to use in case of fire," says Jones, the Marine Corps commandant. "For the United States to remain in a position of leadership, we're going to have to engage [in foreign countries]. In my opinion, we do windows."

Mogadishu moment. The willingness to mop up messes that don't directly affect the United States might have surfaced earlier if not for the deaths of 18 soldiers in Somalia in October 1993. A force of more than 25,000 U.S. troops that entered the African nation to help end a famine caused by tribal warfare had dwindled to just 4,000. But then the mission changed. The new objective? Hunting down warlords. When the Battle of Mogadishu erupted on Oct. 3, 1993, the U.S. force lacked the armor to extract soldiers trapped in alleys by armed and angry Somali clansmen. Only after the battle did the U.S. ramp up the force again. "It was the Powell Doctrine again after 3 October," says retired Maj. Gen. Carl Ernst, who commanded the U.S. relief force. "Then it got real quiet."

Those lessons of Mogadishu have colored every American ground mission since. U.S. troops entered

Bosnia in 1996—after four years of debate over whether they should ever get involved there—with enough tanks and artillery to defeat the entire army of most nations. Unlike their European counterparts, U.S. troops in Bosnia and Kosovo must wear flak jackets and Kevlar helmets virtually everywhere they go. While it's hard to argue against the value of protecting soldiers, some analysts believe the Powell Doctrine has become so rigid that it makes the military ineffective. "The Army is hung up on the Powell doctrine, and it's going to make them irrelevant," says one veteran of Vietnam who works as a consultant for the Army. "You ask for 24 helicopters and they give you 5,200 guys," he moans, referring to the two months it took the Army to deploy 24 Apache attack helicopters to Albania last year and prepare them for the Kosovo War. The Apaches and their crews were deemed fully ready to fight just days before the war ended. They were never used.

Others see pernicious effects in the Pentagon's seeming obsession with avoiding casualties, a corollary of the Powell Doctrine. In a paper published in December, three West Point instructors argued that such airtight "force protection" is eroding the military principle of self-sacrifice. The result, they claim is "a major breakdown in ... the professional military ethnic within the United States Army."

Slowly, the Pentagon is shifting away from the Powell Doctrine, even as it continues to oppose broader rules for its troops, like taking on routine police functions in Kosovo and Bosnia. Army Chief of Staff Gen. Eric Shinseki has vowed to transform heavy Army units that take weeks to get to overseas conflicts into fast-deploying shock troops that can be fighting within days. Last week, an independent panel reviewing national security policy, led by former Sens. Gary Hart and Warren Rudman, issued a report urging the Pentagon to prepare more of its force for "constabulary" missions around the world—the very sort of operation General Powell opposed as chairman of the Joint Chiefs.

Echoes. Other changes are transforming the military Powell left behind. The Army is losing captains—field-grade officers with four to 10 years of experience—at a record rate. Few experienced NCOs stay in the Army past the 20-year point at which they are eligible for retirement benefits. A recent survey of hundreds of Army majors at the Command and General Staff College at For Leavenworth, Kan., revealed that young officers question the value of many Army missions and are losing respect for their leaders. "Senior leaders are devoted to micromanagement and their own career advancement—they spend most of their time avoiding mistakes instead of explaining to soldiers why they are on a deployment and what impact they are making," reads one summary of the survey.

Those complaints sound hauntingly familiar to some old-timers. A ground-breaking Army study from 1970, which sought to explain the disarray wrought by Vietnam, found that "the existing climate includes ... selfish behavior that places personal success ahead of the good of the Service; looking upward to please superiors instead of looking downward to fulfill the legitimate needs of subordinates; [and] preoccupation with the attainment of trivial short-term objectives."

There's no doubt that today's Army is far better trained and staffed than it was 30 years ago, but there *are* some signs of trouble. "There're lots of data showing that morale throughout the armed forces is the lowest it's been in a long time," says retired Lt. Gen. Walt Ulmer, who conducted the 1970 Army study and helped lead a recent survey of 12,000 service members. The Army has formed two "blue ribbon" panels to study the problem. But if it doesn't manage to stop the current "hemorrhaging of talent," says Ulmer, "we won't have any good people left in three or four years—and we might not know until we lose the next war."

IMPRESSIONS OF AN INFANTRYMAN IN VIETNAM, 1967-1969

BY LTC (RET) BARRY GASDEK

The "grunts" as they were affectionately called, not only reflected their closeness to *mother earth* as "ground pounders" (infantry) but also the noises they made as they donned their 70-80 pound packs and *walked for endless miles* through the plains, jungles and highlands of Vietnam.

As I reflect back upon my experience in Vietnam I think of the *strong bond* and *camaraderie* that existed in my infantry outfit during that war. In a combat situation your survival depended on you or your fellow soldiers reactions to situations as they present themselves, *doing what they were trained to do.* In many instances, actions went beyond what was expected, because in a firefight you either did what you were trained to do, or you probably didn't survive. Unfortunately, *you were not* usually given a second chance during an ambush or meeting engagement to *ponder your options! Luck* also had to be on your side.

Vietnam was unique from other wars in that there were actually no real defined friendly lines. The firebase you were in or your unit perimeter defense was usually the only secure or safe area you had. The rest of the real estate belonged to "Charlie" (Viet Cong). This was especially true in I Corps between Chu Lai and Da Nang, north to the DMZ and east/west from the South China Sea to the Laotian border. I was an Infantry Company Commander, Delta Company, and operated as an independent unit throughout this area of operation (AO). We were part of the 4th Battalion, 21st Infantry, 11th Brigade, American Division in northern South Vietnam. It was imperative that infantry company personnel knew how to *call in artillery fire, close air support, medical evacuations* and of course, be able to *read a map* with precision. Knowing where you were, was obviously necessary to accomplish the above. Any of those skills, at one time or another, *could* and *probably did* save your life or that of your men.

A typical day in combat consisted of some of the following prior to a tactical operation. First, you were briefed by the battalion operations officer (S-3) and the intelligence officer (S-2). The missions varied form searching an area or village to trying to make contact with either the local Viet Cong (VC) or the

North Vietnamese Army (NVA). We normally would break our company down into platoon size elements and saturate an area looking for the enemy. We could easily consolidate if contact was made and their force was much larger than ours.

These "search and destroy" operations many times were *dry wells* with little or no contact. War in Vietnam usually consisted of long periods of boredom occasionally overlaid by short or brief periods of extreme violence! You had to guard against complacency, because when you *made contact* with the enemy, you'd better be prepared! If not, your company/men would pay the price, *usually in lives lost!*

As one might imagine, with the thick vegetation and many times, operating in triple canopy jungle, you had to almost move in single file, with limited flank security. That's why, at least in the highlands, it made battalion size operations impractical, if not impossible, unless operating out of a firebase or fixed location, in company size units.

Vietnam was a *Company Commander's war* because this size unit was large enough to sustain itself, yet small enough to operate in this type of environment. We would operate from a firebase and extend outward, sometimes on 35-45 day operations or missions. We would get re-supplied by air, normally helicopters, every two or three days and get periodic intelligence updates either at our field location or get evacuated back to headquarters, get briefed and then back to the field positions. This way the company could continue the operations from day to day, remaining in the bush for longer periods of time.

The *"point"* or *lead man* was rotated every so often as this was one of the most dangerous/tedious positions in the company. He was basically the "eyes and ears" of the lead element of the company. The point man's *survival,* and that of the unit, many times depended upon his skills, *reaction, instinct and training.* "Kill or be killed" was understood, and *one's finger was never very far from the trigger.* The same principle applied to *"tunnel rats",* soldiers who had to go into tunnels to search for the enemy. The .45 caliber pistol was the weapon of choice for this dangerous task. Usually you had a skilled fearless soldier who enjoyed the kind of "rush" volunteer for that dangerous and potentially life shortening duty.

Personal hygiene was important, not only for sanitary reasons, but to *instill discipline* in your unit. When you were engaged in a firefight, the more *disciplined and trained* you were, the less casualties you took. *"Sweat in training saved lives on the battle-field!"* How true that was!

General George Patton had it right when he said, "The idea of warfare was to have that poor SOB die for his country rather than you for yours." Unfortunately, it did not always work or turn out that way. Many times *aggressiveness* paid dividends by surprising the enemy as to your intentions. The less the enemy knew about your tactics, the more successful you were in accomplishing your mission.

We would "dig in" every evening, call in artillery defensive fires, close to our positions, in case we needed to adjust it, or got attacked. Shrapnel coming near your perimeter was not only an incentive for your unit to dig in, but also a deterrent to enemy attack at night. Ambush patrols were sent out nightly to guard routes into your location—an early warning system you could not afford to be without. This *was not* normally a popular duty, but necessary for security of the company perimeter. Claymore or "mechanical ambushes" using claymore mines, which shot out hundreds of ball bearings, proved to be very effective. One night when the company perimeter was about to be attacked, an NVA soldier was just about to pick up one of the claymores when it was detonated. All that was left of this individual was two hands in front of where the mine was located. All of my men carried at least one claymore mine.

Our infantry company seldom got attacked, unless a chance meeting, as we were mobile and seldom in the same spot for more than a day. Fixed installations/fire bases took the brunt of both *Tet/counter Tet* operations by both the VC/NVA. We watched many a firebase get attacked from miles away at our field location. Units would ask where the rocket/mortar fire was coming from, and usually it was "Sappers" (Specially trained infiltration outfits of the VC/NVA) getting inside their firebase perimeters and raising havoc. The fact that they had infiltrated the firebase was usually confirmed the next day when they found enemy bodies inside the area. One morning we found 19 enemy bodies still in the wire whom were killed. Ten motor pool vehicles had *chicom grenades* in them, but none went off. It must have been a bad lot of enemy grenades.

It became hard to establish strong friendships after having a few close friends killed. It was easier emotionally and psychologically to do your job to the best of your ability, be friendly, but not get too personally involved, other than taking care of the needs of your men. This may have been a mild form of Post-Traumatic Stress Disorder (PTSD) that enabled one to tolerate some of the rigors of combat. Leadership decisions you made many times were potential life and death decisions for you and your men. As a leader, you had to live with that decision and its outcome. Again, quality training enabled one to make the best decision possible!

River and stream crossings were great in that one could do their laundry, bathe, shave, and be ready to go for a few more days on the other side of the river. This was, of course, after you set up proper security. Uniform changes were made every 30-45 days whether *you needed it or not!* Underwear was seldom worn, and the thought of a "flush toilet" again was only *dreamed about!* Basic survival needs ruled most of the time, as an infantryman needed just food, water, and *ammunition* to survive. Maslow's hierarchy of needs was experienced in its most rudimentary form. *Priority* in your pack and what you carried was *ammunition,* water, and food last. Malaria pills (both large and small ones) were taken daily, plus water purification pills (iodine tablets) were always used. Kool Aid sent in "care packages" from the U.S.A. helped flavor the water from the "nasty" iodine taste. Mosquito and leach repellent also helped make life in the jungle more bearable. Cigarette butts were also effective in removing leaches.

"Flak jackets" were also available, but seldom used except for fire base duties. The extra weight carried in the jungle heat was *not worth* the effort unless it was *ammunition.* Nobody complained about carrying *ammunition!* New recruits were normally given a *week or two* to adapt to the extreme heat and humidity, before being "farmed out" to infantry units in the field. Some times this *was not enough!* One day, we had five new recruits sent to our company field location, and all five were med-evac'd out that evening for heat exhaustion. We were operating in 14 foot high elephant grass and 119 degrees Fahrenheit temperatures. A tough environment to adapt to! I normally carried 28 each, 20 round magazines of M-16 ammunition, 4 each clips of .45 caliber ammunition, a M-16 rifle, a .45 caliber pistol, 8 each Fragmentary Grenades, 5 each Smoke Grenades, compass, maps, and my Poncho and Poncho liner. *Creature comfort* items such as sleeping bags, air mattresses, and ground pads were not used because of the weight and environment. After "humping" (walking) all day and each evening *digging in,* it was not too hard to fall asleep.

You never fell in a "deep sleep" awakening at the least strange battlefield noise. I've slept, or cat "napped" on a pile of rocks to foxholes filled with water during the monsoons. During one three week period of continuous rain, the war almost came to a halt, as neither could operate. Islands of land jutted out into a sea of water. It was an undeclared temporary truce! Resupply and medevacs were also hampered by the monsoons. If the ceiling was too low, aircraft could not fly, nor could you get close tactical air support.

Well, what lessons were learned from this Vietnam infantryman's combat experience? First, *effective training* can save you or your men's lives— *pure and simple!* Respect, confidence, support and dependability on your fellow man could help save your life! *Luck* could even save your life! However, being at the wrong spot at the wrong time could prove to be very detrimental to your health and well being. Lucky charms were not uncommon, and were often worn or carried. The belief that you would not be a casualty sometimes helped. Once your men had confidence in you as a leader, they would follow you anywhere. You became an *"extended family".*

After spending 14 years overseas, I've learned a *love and respect* of country that no book or school could ever teach! It's called *the school of "hard knocks".* Never expect your men to do something you would not do yourself. Be an *assertive and proactive leader!* Lead by example. This is the style of leadership I used and it served me well. Others used different styles that served them well.

Help honor the veterans of this great nation for their sacrifice, unselfish service, and that of families/friends who helped share that sacrifice. Attend all veteran events and memorials. *The price of freedom is not free!* The numerous cemeteries throughout our nation and overseas will attest to that fact. *Respect* your *fellow man, community, country* and *flag* as the symbol of our freedom and way of life.

Finally, it is O.K., and never too late to *tell a veteran—Thanks!* You'll be amazed how proud they are of their service. One only has to travel to troubled or war torn countries to know the difference between freedom and tyranny. *Help keep the United States of America great!* Be proud of and respect *yourself, family, friends, and community—because it all starts there!*

Officership Case Study II: The Hollow Army of the 1970's

This is the second case study in a set of five case studies on the evolution of the Army. This lesson focuses on the post Vietnam challenges and the leaders who tackled the problems, and rebuilt the Army. This lesson covers the state of the Army in the early 1970's after Vietnam. The lesson covers the character and vision of outstanding officers, including Creighton Abrams, who led the Army out of what has been described as the Army's darkest period since the days of General Washington at Valley Forge.

The following topics are addressed in this lesson:

- Challenges of leadership in the post-Vietnam environment
- The framework for the changes that would take place under the new Chief-of-Staff
- Key people involved in rebuilding the Army

The following TLO is supported in whole or in part by this lesson:

- Integrate military history into education of officers

Following this lesson you will be able to:

- Describe the conduct of officers in the post Vietnam era
- Identify the challenges facing the post Vietnam Army
- Summarize the major changes initiated by General Abrams in the post Vietnam Army

TO CHANGE AN ARMY

BY GENERAL DON STARRY

Change is a constant for today's armed forces. With frequently shifting requirements as well as advancing technology, it is imperative that any reforms contribute to a force's ability to operate on the battlefield. The author reviews some changes that have occurred in the past, points out certain requirements associated with change and calls for creative solutions to future needs.

"This framework (below) is necessary to bring to bear clearly focused intellectual activity in the matter of any change, whether in concepts for fighting, equipment, training, or manning the force."

1. There must be an *institution* or *mechanism* to identify the need for change, to draw up parameters for change and to describe *clearly* what is to be done and how that differs from what has been done before.
2. The educational background of the principal staff and command personalities responsible for change must be sufficiently rigorous, demanding and relevant to bring common cultural bias to the solution of the problems.
3. There must be a *spokesman* for the change. The spokesman can be a person, one of the mavericks; an institution such as a staff college; or staff agency.
4. Whoever or whatever it may be, the spokesman *must build a consensus* that will give the new ideas, and the need to adopt them, a wider audience of converts and believers.
5. There must be *continuity among the architects of change* so that consistency of effort is brought to bear on the process.
6. *Someone at or near the top* of the institution must be willing to hear out arguments for change, agree to the need, embrace the new operational concepts and become at the least a supporter, if not the champion, of the cause for change.
7. The changes proposed must be *subjected to trials.* Their relevance must be convincingly demonstrated to a wide audience by experiment and experience, and necessary modifications must be made as a result of such trial outcomes.

*This article is adapted from an address made by General Don Starry, 10 June 1982, to the U.S. Army War College Committee on a Theory of Combat, Carlisle Barracks, Pennsylvania. The entire article is available from Military Review, U.S. Army Command and General Staff College, Fort Leavenworth, Kansas

THE HOLLOW ARMY

BY EDWARD C. MEYER and R. MANNING ANCELL w/ JANE MAHAFFEY

After a brief period of public support prompted by the end of the draft, the American public and Congress's interest in the volunteer Army quickly dissipated. To induce recruitment, the Nixon administration raised soldier salaries 61 percent in 1973. But in spite of large-scale inflation, salaries remained essentially frozen for seven years thereafter. Earlier pay raises were targeted toward first-term enlistees, while noncommissioned officers, considered already hooked by the system, received proportionately less. The consequent pay compression meant that an experienced sergeant earned only 30 percent more than the newest private. In real terms, purchasing power for sergeants dropped from $20,000 per year in 1973 to $14,000 by 1979. Entitlements, which military families considered essential for economic survival, lost value in proportion to pay. Moving allowances for a family of four remained at 10 cents per mile—unchanged since the Eisenhower administration. Young sergeants, in the best of circumstances barely able to make ends meet, found themselves thrown hopelessly into debt with unexpected movement orders. By 1979, the salary of junior enlisted soldiers had dropped so low that a corporal with a small family was officially below the prescribed government poverty level. In that same year Army commissaries accepted almost $10 million in food stamps.[10] The soldiers' plight grew considerably worse in Europe. As large numbers of wives streamed overseas to join their soldier husbands, the problem of poor or nonexistent housing was compounded by poverty wages. With no money to spend, soldiers and families had little to do but try to survive.

In the lean years following Vietnam, the Army created the conceptual outline for a future force fundamentally different from any American Army of the past. Accepting the mantle of steward from Weyand in 1976, General Bernard Rogers embraced Abrams' goal of creating a force consisting of 16 Active and 8 Reserve component combat divisions. At the same time, he continued to work on ways to improve soldiers' quality of life. However, while Rogers paved the way to improved readiness and worked on long-term sustainability in an effort to pull the Army out of the intellectually and physically stagnant period of the volunteer Army, his task was severely hampered by budget woes.

In the late seventies, the Army witnessed drastic cuts in funding for maintenance and training. By 1979, 6 of 10 Stateside Army divisions were, by the Army's own liberal standards of measurement, not combat-ready. Even though Europe was the Army's front line, one of the four divisions stationed there was not combat-ready. Serious shortages of qualified soldiers, spare parts, and replacement equipment grew alarmingly. The Commander in Chief, US Army Europe, General Frederick Kroesen, long noted for his frankness, confessed publicly that the European Army had become obsolescent. Kroesen and other senior officers began to speak openly of a "hollow army." Although the Army could boast 16 divisional flags, the content and quality of those divisions was diminishing rapidly.

Soldier quality, never particularly high during the early years of the volunteer Army, started another precipitous drop after 1976. The numbers recruited in mental Categories I, II, and IIIa, which measure the upper half of mental aptitude among American youth, shrank from 49 percent in 1973 to 26 percent in 1980. Only 50 percent of those recruited in 1980 had graduated from high school.[11] Statistics for drug addiction, unauthorized absences, and crimes, while still below the immediate post-Vietnam War figures, were still alarmingly high. The Army recruited so many poor-quality soldiers during the late seventies that it dismissed 40 percent for indiscipline or unsuitability before they completed their first enlistment.

Meanwhile, in late 1979, the Islamic fundamentalists' removal of the Shah of Iran and the Soviet invasion of Afghanistan began to shake the American public from its lethargy.

CRISES OPEN THE COFFERS

The failed attempt to rescue American hostages held in Iran in 1980 marked one of the lowest points in American military performance since the end of the Vietnam War. The spectacle of broken Marine helicopters and crashed Air Force C-130 aircraft and the tales that emerged from Desert One of confusion, overcentralization, poor communication, and botched planning brought to light publicly what the pros had foretold for some time. As so often happens in American military history, a military debacle was necessary to wrench the Services back from the brink of ruin.

The furor following Desert One alerted the American public to chronic institutional problems that had remained shrouded since Vietnam. The Army realized that reduced budgets had left equipment inoperative, shortened training exercises, and delayed the arrival of new weapons. The Army leadership also recognized that the Army could not achieve real combat readiness unless it could, as a first priority, populate itself with good soldiers. In the wake of Desert One, the cry grew more shrill for a return to the draft. A volunteer army, so the argument went, would only draw from the poorest and most poorly educated segment of the population. In time the Army would consist only of the socially disenfranchised. While ostensibly volunteer, the Army was still "drafting," but using economics rather than the Selective Service System to force enlistments.[12] Some pro-draft sentiment could still be found within the Army, but by and large, most Army leaders favored the all-volunteer concept. The flaw, they believed, was in how the volunteer system was implemented. The draft was over. Simply opening doors was not enough to induce quality men and women to enlist. America's youth had to be convinced that service in the Army was right for them. Needing a marketeer to sell itself, the Army found its salesman in the person of Major General Maxwell "Max" Thurman.

Thurman began his tenure as head of the Army Recruiting Command by selecting only the best soldiers to be recruiters. Instead of long-term recruiting professionals, he brought in officers and noncommissioned officers from the field for short-term assignments. Their job was to recruit the same soldiers that they would later have to train. The recruiting market moved from the streets to high schools. High school students were harder to recruit, but research proved that a diploma was the most reliable indicator of future success as a soldier.[13] Each of Thurman's subordinate commanders negotiated a contract with him to produce a certain quality of soldier in a certain number, balancing the demands of the Army against the particular demographic and economic circumstances of the region. Thurman recognized the power of advertising. With the enthusiastic support of Vice Chief of Staff General John Vessey, he convinced Congress to appropriate approximately a half-billion dollars to finance Army recruiting and bonuses. The "Be All You Can Be" campaign achieved instant recognition among American youth. Thanks to positive image-making and the improving quality of life within the Army, the "Willie and Joe" image inherited from the drafted Army gave way for the Army's new image as a caring, challenging, high-tech outfit.[14]

A Congress increasingly alarmed by the Army's declining readiness and sympathetic to the plight of soldiers and their families responded by increasing soldiers' salaries 25 percent between 1981 and 1982. Army research found that the most important reason for the smartest soldiers to enlist was money for college. After Congress reinstated the GI Bill and initiated the Army College Fund, the quality gap began to close.[15]

While Army recruiting continued to experience occasional growing pains, the quality of young men and women recruits steadily climbed, keeping pace with the public's increasingly favorable image of the Army. By 1991, more than 98 percent of the applicants were high school graduates. Seventy-five percent scored in the upper mental categories, less than one percent in the lowest. Fully 41 percent chose to enroll in the Army College Fund. As quality increased, traditional indicators of indiscipline dropped off the charts. Desertions and unauthorized absences dropped 80 percent and courts-martial 64 percent. Positive indications of drug abuse dropped from 25 percent in 1979 to less than 1 percent a decade later.[16]

As defense budgets increased, the temptation grew to expand the size of the Army to meet the growing Soviet threat. However, with end-strength capped at 780,000 soldiers, meeting the goal of 16 Active divisions was difficult enough, let alone trying to expand the force. General Edward "Shy" Meyer, Chief of Staff from 1979 to 1983, chose to hold the line on total numbers. He reasoned that any large increase, given the limited number of available high-quality prospective recruits, would substantially lower overall quality. The most glaring shortage would be made up by the Reserves.

The political argument for greater integration of the Reserves had its roots in Vietnam. President Johnson chose to rely on the draft alone to prosecute the war in order to cause as little disruption on the home front as possible and thereby dampen popular opposition. While successful during the early years, Johnson's policy created an army in the field made up largely of the very young, the poor, and the disaffected. As the war dragged on and casualties mounted, a rift was inevitable between the people and this unfamiliar, unrepresentative body of men fighting an unpopular war. For that reason, General Abrams, during his short tenure as Chief of Staff, had insisted that the Army could not go to war again without the involvement and tacit approval of the American people. A call-up of the Reserves would bring home to Americans from the beginning that they had a personal stake in the conflict. Therefore, Abrams had sought to weave Reserve forces so inextricably into established deployment schemes that no force would be able to fight a major war in the future without them.

The creation of what was to become the Total Force Policy began gradually during the mid-seventies as the Army shifted combat support and combat service support necessary to sustain the Active Army in a large-scale European conflict into the National Guard and Army Reserve. The plan was to increase the total number of Active divisions to 16 while staying within mandated end-strength ceilings by "rounding out" selected Army divisions so that they consisted of two regular and one Reserve component brigade. A number of separate Reserve component battalions were also included in the roundout program. Roundout brigades were expected to join their parent division after a period of muster and postmobilization training, which was originally postulated to require at least 30 days. By the late eighties, the Total Force Policy had been so firmly embedded in the Army's structure that 52 percent of combat forces and 67 percent of other forces were Guard or Reserve. Seven Reserve component brigades—six from the National Guard and one from the Army Reserve—rounded out Active Army divisions, while 10 separate battalions, all in the Guard, served additionally as roundout augmentation to the Active Army.[17]

THE RENAISSANCE

BY EDWARD C. MEYER and R. MANNING ANCELL w/ JANE MAHAFFEY

One of the most visible legacies a chief of staff leaves when he retires is the senior leadership of the Army, the choosing of whom he can take most—if not all—the credit. After all, the selection and development of his generals is one of the chiefs prime responsibilities. The Army's Pentagon team that Shy Meyer left in place was, at his retirement in September 1983, one of the finest in recent history. General Andy Goodpaster, a distinguished former SACEUR and recently retired superintendent of the Military Academy, described the senior staff of the Army under his successor, John Wickham, "as capable as I've ever seen." Four of the five deputy chiefs—Max Thurman, Fred Mahaffey, Art Brown and Richard Thompson—went on to four-stars. Like the chiefs before him, Shy spent a great deal of time making certain good people were identified and developed. "He has no more important duty than that, because he should be preparing for the future and should have these people lined up coming along," Goodpaster agreed. "It is very important to make sure you give them the experience that gives breadth and view, how to work with allies, how to work with the other services effectively, how to command forces of several services. You look to see that they have had that kind of experience along the way. That needs a lot of conscious thought, especially as people move up to two-star and three-star grade."[1]

It's interesting to note that Wickham's West Point classmate General Charlie Gabriel had been chief of staff of the Air Force for a year when he became Army chief. Wickham was one of ten young captains who worked for General Bill Knowlton when he was associate professor of social sciences at the United States Military Academy. Knowlton watched Wickham's ascendancy to the top of the mountain with great interest and later made an important point about the value, all too often overlooked, of people in high positions who work together behind the scenes. "They were good friends and they knew and trusted one another," Knowlton said of Wickham and Gabriel.

> They got together and said you know, there are a lot of areas of duplication between the Army and Air Force but we ought to be able to sort out and settle a whole list of things. This will go to the Army, this will go

to the Air Force, but it will do for both. Almost all of these things were done at a tremendous saving in material, people and particularly money, yet no one in Congress seemed a damn bit interested. The $600 toilet seat is the kind of thing they beat people to death on instead of saying hundreds of millions of dollars had been saved by the Army and the Air Force getting together and doing these things.[2]

By the early 1980s the role and influence of the four-star had changed considerably from the World War II–Korean War era. In many ways it evolved from the sheer weight of numbers. During the Second World War only seventeen Army officers rose to four-star general. During the Vietnam War at least a dozen full generals were on active duty at anyone time, many with much less a public awareness as a Westmoreland or Abrams. "Obviously, this was a position of tremendous prestige in the nineteenth century when there were so few of them, and four-stars were often celebrities in war time," observed Gene Zuckert. "Conversely, since World War II—in my experience—the majority of many four-star generals' public recognition quotient would be zero. You can find a parallel to this is business: Sloan and Knudsen, for example, were giants. I'll buy anybody a drink who can name two out of the last three presidents of General Motors. And look at service secretaries: contrast Henry Stimson as secretary of War with the unknown who has the comparable job today."[3]

Zuckert's point was well taken. It can't be overlooked that the "lessened influence of the senior military on policy decisions," as Douglas Kinnard has noted, coincided with "the rise of other influential groups. . . . The increased influence of Congress on defense policy is one such reality. This has been occasioned by political events, such as the public reaction to the Vietnam War, and also by their increased staff support in the defense area. Another reality is the permanent and powerful staff supporting the National Security Council and the importance of the presidential assistant for national security affairs, who heads the staff."[4]

About one hundred miles from the coast of South America sits Grenada, a dot on the map as the southernmost of the Windward Islands, 133 square miles in size with a population of no more than ninety thousand. After two centuries of British rule, Grenada became independent in early 1974, but by 1983 the government was in the hands of Prime Minister

Maurice Bishop, a Marxist and protégé of Cuba's Fidel Castro. On October 19 of that year leftists even more radical than Bishop overthrew the government in a bloody coup, and Bishop along with four of his cabinet officers were executed. Fearing a spread of terror to neighboring islands, five members of the Organization of Eastern Caribbean States sent a message to the White House: help us stage an invasion of Grenada to restore democracy. President Reagan, on a weekend golf outing in Georgia, received a telephone call from Bud McFarlane, in his fourth day as the new national security adviser, at four in the morning. In a matter of minutes the scenario had been laid out. "I asked McFarlane how long the Pentagon thought it would need to prepare a rescue mission on Grenada," Reagan wrote. "He said the Joint Chiefs of Staff believed it could be done in forty-eight hours. I said, 'Do it.'"[5]

Planning had already been underway in the Pentagon since October 20, the day after Bishop's murder. The Joint Staff gave chairman Jack Vessey a list of options which he translated for Secretary of Defense Caspar Weinberger, who wrote that the "broad objectives of the plan called for us to move as quickly as possible to Point Salines to seal off the new airfield, which was not yet fully operational, as well as the older and operational airport at Pearls, on the eastern side of the island; to secure the two campuses of the medical school in the southwestern portion of the island, so that our students could be freed and brought home; and to rescue the Governor General and other political prisoners from imprisonment."[6]

President and Mrs. Reagan, still at the Augusta National Golf Course, went to bed early on October 23 but were awakened at 2:30 A.M. by another phone call from Bud McFarlane. It was grim news. "He said a suicide bomber had just driven a truckload of dynamite past our sentries and smashed into the Marine barracks at the Beirut Airport," Reagan said. "According to the first reports, at least one hundred Marines had been killed. There was to be no more sleep for us that night. I got on the phone with the Pentagon to make sure that everything possible was being done to protect the remaining Marines in Beirut, then met with George Shultz and Bud for several hours in the same living room where we'd spent much of the night before. As dawn approached, the news from Beirut became grimmer and grimmer."[7]

Secretary of Defense Weinberger, back in Washington, took the news of the Beirut incident

with a feeling that he hadn't been "persuasive enough" in numerous previous meetings to insist upon the withdrawal of United States Marines from the international force. He had "argued and reargued" that the "international force as constituted was totally incapable of carrying out the mission of interposing itself as peace keepers between withdrawing Israeli and Syrian troops."[8] The reason was simple. Syrian and Israeli troops were not withdrawing.

By the afternoon of October 24 the death toll of United States Marines and Navy personnel in the Beirut bombing stood at 241. A similar explosion at a French paratroop barracks nearby, which occurred almost simultaneously, claimed forty lives. The tragedy in Lebanon was an excellent example of missed cues and limited understanding in the relationships among America's senior military and the administration. The military rationale behind having a Marine unit in Beirut was always questionable. The JCS had not supported its presence, but it was directed to return by the President. On the other hand, once it was clear that American forces would be there for some time, the military did little to address what sort of forces would be best suited and where they could best be located for specific military reasons. The long, convoluted chain of command through the European Command in Stuttgart, down to the JCS in Washington, contributed to some of the confusion. This incident reinforced the arguments those in favor of the Goldwater-Nichols Bill to reform the JCS.

As in the aborted rescue of Iranian hostages three years earlier, secrecy surrounded the invasion of Grenada. In order to reduce the possibility of a leak, Reagan elected not to inform any allies of the impending mission, including Britain's Prime Minister Thatcher, a staunch American supporter. "Frankly, there was another reason I wanted secrecy," Reagan admitted. "It was what I call the 'post-Vietnam syndrome,' the resistance of many in Congress to the use of military force abroad for any reasons, because of our nation's experience in Vietnam."[9] There was also a dearth of information—of intelligence—on the island of Grenada, the layout of key buildings and installations, the placement of troops and, as Mark Adkin wrote, "in knowing nothing about the 400 or so students outside True Blue (the medical school grounds), in having no proper maps, and all this despite Grenada's having been the center of Communist activity in the region for over four years."[10] Secretary

Weinberger's response to sketchy intelligence was to order that "whatever forces the field commander said he would need" should be doubled. The day of the invasion he told General Vessey, "Be sure we have enough strength."[11] This was in contrast to the measured responses in Vietnam, which led to the conclusion by many that it's best to have more than is needed but don't take on a mission with "just enough" because despite how cost effective that might sound, how much is enough in warfare is not quantifiable despite what systems analysts might argue.

For some inexplicable reason the contingency plan for Grenada, established earlier, was replaced by one fashioned by the Atlantic Command, headed by Admiral Wesley R. McDonald. It was hastily put together by inexperienced naval officers whose primary goal seemed to be the integration of forces from every possible source in order to give "jointness" to the operation. The chain of command flowed from General Vessey to Admiral McDonald—the CINC—to Vice Admiral Joseph Metcalf, head of Joint Task Force 120, whose deputy was Major General Norm Schwarzkopf. Beneath them on the organization chart were forces from the Military Airlift Command (Air Force), Readiness Command (Joint), Seals (Navy), Delta Force (Army), 82nd Airborne Division (Army), Amphibious Squadron Four (Navy) and four Marine Corps elements. There was a sense of doubt among those involved in this incursion into Grenada as to whether it would actually occur. If so, it would be only the second use of military might by the United States—after the aborted hostage rescue attempt in Iran—since the end of the Vietnam War. "I will never forget flying out of Norfolk and down to Grenada," said Schwarzkopf. "The prevailing thinking was, 'We're going, but it's not going to happen.' I can remember sitting in the dining area on the *Guam* and all of a sudden the watch officer or someone came in and said, 'It's a go.' And we all said, 'A go?' 'Yeah, tomorrow morning.' All of a sudden everybody stopped eating and left the table to do what they had to do. I remember standing outside the command bridge in the dark of night saying, 'Gee, we're going into Grenada. This is a military operation involving lethal force. Are we getting into another Vietnam?'"[12]

Despite the lack of intelligence, bad timing, poorly selected targets, little coordination among units of different services, the inability to communicate from unit to unit, no interservice close air support to speak of and widespread confusion, the invasion succeeded.

How? It was largely due to the individual initiative and heroism of small units. As Norm Schwarzkopf put it, "Even though higher headquarters screws it up every way you can possibly screw it up, it is the initiative and valor on the part of small unit leadership that will win for you every time."[13]

One aspect of the Grenada invasion deserved special mention for the precedent it set—the decision to keep the media out of range of the action during the initial stage. As soon as President Reagan had publicly announced that the United States and six Caribbean neighbors had mounted an invasion of Grenada, a wave of reporters—more than three hundred at first count—swept into the area. They were able to get no closer than the island of Barbados, some 160 miles from Grenada. The task force commander, Vice Admiral Joseph Metcalf, insisted that no one from the media be allowed to go into Grenada with the landings "until a secure beachhead had been obtained," explained Secretary Weinberger. He reinforced the need for secrecy and pointed to the "limited transport available" as well as "critical and few communications facilities" in Barbados. "In matters of this kind, and although aware of the unhappiness the decision would cause, I felt the commander should be supported; so I accepted and agreed to the task force commander's request, with the understanding we would make every effort to get the press in at the end of the first day."[14] As it turned out, two more days passed until the first handful of media were allowed into Grenada. Inevitably the media took pot shots at the administration and particularly at Weinberger. The editorial page of *The New York Times* mentioned the famous photograph of Marines raising the flag on Iwo Jima in World War II with the comment, "How much safety does he think was guaranteed to Joe Rosenthal of the Associated Press, who took the famous picture?" In a televised address thirteen days after giving the approval for armed intervention in that tiny Caribbean nation, President Reagan told the American people: "Grenada was a Soviet-Cuban colony being readied as a major military bastion to export terror and undermine democracy. We got there just in time."[15]

While successful, the invasion of Grenada in late October of 1983 was not as well executed an exercise as could have been expected. For the senior leaders involved in that operation, from the chairman of the Joint Chiefs on down, Shy Meyer would give a "C." It rates only a "C" because for such a small-sized operation there were so many operational problems. Part of this can be attributed to the naval command structure carrying out essentially an air-land operation. The recommendations of the Special Operations Forces commander were preempted, and the operation probably would have been more successful if the original plan hadn't been changed by higher headquarters. Many lessons about joint operations were learned from this experience. In the long run it was a relatively cheap way to learn lessons that would serve us well in the future. And we won!

In May 1984, following nine months as number two at FORSCOM under General Dick Cavazos, Bill Livsey picked up a fourth star and headed for Korea as the new CINC, relieving General Bob Sennewald, the new commander at FORSCOM. Cavazos was retiring after more than thirty-three years in uniform, nearly all of them in front of troops, and his reputation was Army-wide. "Every one of us, at some time or another, runs into an ego problem," said Livsey. "I'm not sure Cavazos ever had too much of an ego problem—he's a genuine hero. He doesn't have any phony medals on his chest. The soldiers loved him from the first. He and I were in the same division in Korea; we didn't know each other closely at that time, but he's a genuine hero. He was inspirational. He didn't always agree with the Pentagon—I didn't either."[16]

That June Lieutenant General Fred Mahaffey, an up-and-comer in the Army since his graduation from the ROTC program at the University of Denver in 1955, took over command of REDCOM from General Wally Nutting, who was retiring. Mahaffey had spent nearly two and a half years as the DCSOPS, having been brought to Washington specifically for that job by Meyer in early 1983. Lieutenant General Richard Trefry, the Army's inspector general the final six years of his career, recalled that his last year overlapped with Mahaffey's first as the DCSOPS, and Fred left a most favorable impression. "I'll tell you something about Fred. One of the things that made Fred a hell of a lot different than other people is I'd say, 'Fred, I've got to see you,' and of all the guys that were in DCSOPS—even including Jack Vessey—Fred was the only guy who came down to my office. And if I had said I need to see him, within hours I would get a call that Fred was on the way down to see me."[17]

As inevitably happens, officers reach that point in time when they must hang up their uniforms and turn over their commands to younger men. For generals in particular there's a deeply rooted desire to

leave behind something for which they will be remembered. When Jack Vessey retired at the end of September 1985, he left behind a legacy of dealing squarely with officers at all levels of the Army. The highly decorated chairman of the JCS, who had earned a commission on the battlefield in World War II, was known in Washington as a man of action. "He ran the joint system pretty much like he's run other organizations that he's been in, by dealing directly with his subordinates one-on-one," said Paul Gorman.

> In those dealings he always conveyed profound understanding and respect for that subordinate, he always handled them with humor and grace. I can't think of a single instance in which Jack Vessey made an enemy unnecessarily nor through an awkward choice of words caused an offense to be given. To the contrary, he was always warm, effective and decisive. One of the best things about dealing with Vessey was that you could call him virtually anytime, day or night, and he would give you an answer. If he couldn't give it himself he'd get it in a matter of minutes.[18]

Vessey was succeeded, the day after his retirement, by a naval officer with a different background than most of his predecessors, Admiral Bill Crowe. The new chairman was an imposing figure in the corridors of the Pentagon. Tall and solid—he could have donned a different kind of uniform and occupied the starting line of The Buffalo Bills with no questions asked—Crowe towered over his civilian boss, Secretary of Defense Cap Weinberger. While their relationship was cordial and professional, Crowe admitted that the chairman and the Defense secretary are traditionally "at odds all the time" and he was exasperated by the animosity between Weinberger and Secretary of State George Shultz. By statute, the chairman of the Joint Chiefs of Staff is the highest ranking uniformed officer charged with advising the President, the Defense secretary and the National Security Council. Schultz wanted Crowe to provide advice directly to him; Weinberger didn't want him conferring with Schultz unless he was present. It put Admiral Crowe in a continuously awkward position. "The chairman has a problem if he's going to take issue with the secretary of Defense," Crowe explained. "The Congress has never really faced up to this. It's one of the reasons to put the chairman in the chain of command so the chairman has his own constituencies. Not that he would disobey the secretary of Defense—it would mean he would be in on everything whether the secretary of Defense likes it or not. As it is now, the secretary of Defense doesn't even have to ask for the chairman's advice." It's long been a bone of contention in the JCS that while they're responsible for providing military advice, there's no requirement that it be accepted. The secretary of Defense can, if he wishes, completely ignore the chairman and the other members of the Joint Chiefs. "This poses a big problem for the chairman," Crowe continued. "No matter what he does, if he wants to be effective and play in the ball game, he in some fashion has to obtain the trust and confidence of the secretary or he won't be in the game. If he disagrees with the secretary on everything he may as well resign, because he isn't going to be very effective. Pretty soon the secretary is going to say, 'I'm going to quit dealing with that son-of-a-bitch.'"[19]

The summer of 1986 there was a change in the top job at the Army's two major commands. On the heels of two years commanding the I Corps at Seattle, Lieutenant General Joseph T. Palastra relieved General Bob Sennewald as FORSCOM commander. A little later, after one year as the DCSOPS, Carl Vuono picked up a fourth star and moved to Fort Monroe as commanding general of TRADOC. He was, by that time, intimately knowledgeable of the inner workings at the command, having spent two years there in 1979–1981 as deputy chief for combat developments. His predecessor, Bill Richardson, had retained throughout his career the boyish good looks Meyer first encountered when they were cadets. Within recent years the Army's four-stars have concentrated increasingly on the art and science of war, knowing that the complexities of war are enhanced by constantly changing technology. As head of TRADOC, Bill witnessed evolutionary changes in our senior generals. "The four-stars are steeping themselves in it naturally and, as a result, they are not only more knowledgeable about the art and science of war but they want to involve themselves in it," Richardson said. "At TRADOC, as well as elsewhere, we were far more concerned with the important aspects—the essentials—of war fighting as opposed to management practices which may have been the case of four-stars in years past. As we got into the post-Vietnam era four-stars knew their business, in my estimation, by and large to a far greater extent than their prede-

cessors. They were out practicing it, training it, teaching others about it."[20]

Since 1947, when the War and Navy Departments were replaced by the Department of Defense and a new civilian bureaucracy began to grow, generals and admirals often were at odds with their civilian bosses over excesses of one sort or another and misinterpreted policies. Many of the inherent problems between the civilian side of the Defense Department and the uniformed chiefs were put to rest in the fall of 1986 with the passage of the landmark Goldwater-Nichols Bill. This legislation, which passed over the objections of the JCS and Secretary of Defense Weinberger—they felt that the current system at that time was adequate—brought about a major change in the way in which senior military commanders operated together. Former JCS chairman David C. Jones had long felt that structural and procedural changes in the Joint Chiefs of Staff were in order. In 1981 he formed a study group of retired four-stars and several others, to examine closely the intricacies of the joint system. "When I first became convinced that some very major surgery was required, I sat down and tried to figure out the strategy," General Jones recalled. "I concluded that if it were an initiative from the Pentagon to Congress it would not succeed. There had been efforts before to get the Director of the Joint Staff a fourth star, and a lot of other things, but we couldn't get it through the Congress. I became convinced that the initiative had to come from the Hill."[21] Meyer, who shared Jones's view, wrote an article for the *Armed Forces Journal* which proposed even greater changes than those suggested by General Jones. They both rallied support from key members and staff of the House and Senate.

Goldwater-Nichols made several significant changes to the command structure within the Department of Defense. First, it placed the chairman of the Joint Chiefs of Staff in the position as principal adviser to the secretary of Defense and the President on military matters. Previously the JCS as a body had held that role. This created what has commonly been called the "lowest common denominator of advice." While that term is overly critical of the way the system worked, nonetheless it's indicative of the fact that the system required an agreed upon position for a paper that went to the President or Defense secretary. If agreement could not be reached, a paper went forward with differing solutions supported by certain members of the JCS. From 1966 to 1983 only two papers went forward with split positions. This is understandable, since the chiefs and the chairman gave up some of their strength if they forwarded a split paper and left the decision to the secretary of Defense. Equally important, the Goldwater-Nichols legislation created historical change in relationships between the commanders of the combined and unified commands—more commonly known as CINCs, or commanders in chief—the chairman, the secretary of Defense and the chiefs of each service. The CINCs were given direct access to the secretary through the chairman and not necessarily through the JCS. It put the CINCs in a more dominant role, placing the people who were going to prepare and execute the plans in a position where they could influence the resources that were going to be spent. Further, they were going to be able to have their voices heard directly without first having them translated by the service chiefs.

A third aspect of Goldwater-Nichols that will have impact on all officers of the Armed Forces for years to come was the creation of a requirement that all officers serve in a joint staff position before they can be selected for promotion to general or flag officer. The Army and Air Force had long sent outstanding officers to the joint staff and considered that to be part of their development, but placed no requirement on such assignments for promotion, while the Navy had never considered the joint staff to be an essential assignment for its officers. "It's obviously a trade-off on how much time an officer spends in joint duty and time in his own service," noted Admiral Bill Crowe. "It's my own view that if we can work out the mechanical problems, joint duty will have a positive effect. It has to be tempered with good judgment and not overdone."[22]

Mentorship, too, will take a different form in the future as a result of Goldwater-Nichols. "Purple-suited" CINCs of unified commands will be more involved in mentoring individuals who are not of their own service. They will be able to influence their promotions more than they have been able to in the past because they'll have more say about their ultimate assignments either in the joint arena or back in the service. The CINCs will also have more to say about assignments when officers are with the joint command. The Army colonels, as well as others, will be exposed to officers of the other services. If the brigadier general or rear admiral for whom they're working becomes the chief of staff or CNO they may be in a position to benefit even though they are from a different service. An example of that was Jack Vessey, who promoted an Air Force general who had been his director of the Joint Staff, as, chief of staff of SHAPE. Bernie Rogers picked Bill Crowe over someone else to be CINCSOUTH because of his knowledge of him as DCNO plans, policy and operations and therefore got him started. He saw him perform in a joint kind of environment. More of that is going to happen in the future where we see combined or unified commanders mentoring people from other services in a way that hadn't existed in the past. Being closely observed by the other services will carry greater risk, but that's a healthy aspect of the change. If they're going to fail, it's better that they fail during the mentoring process than at the point in time at which they get to be in a position of vital national security. A good example was Tom Kelley. He would never have gotten promoted to three-star general if it hadn't been for Bill Crowe. When Crowe needed a good Army guy over in CINCSOUTH, Meyer sent Tom Kelly to him as a brigadier general. Crowe brought Kelly back to the Joint Staff; promoted him to major general there and then promoted him to three stars over the objections of the Army. There will be many more instances of that where joint mentorship takes place. If Schwarzkopf had stayed around, he would have been able to help people of other services who had worked for him in various wartime positions.

Those far-reaching shifts implemented in Goldwater-Nichols to aid the flow of information to and from virtually anywhere in the world were supported by a continuing growth in the technology of information processing and retrieval. Admiral Ron Hays, in his multi-hatted job as commander in chief Pacific, saw firsthand the effect of new technologies on all the services, "It's had a profound impact," Hays said. "Today a vast amount of information is available that was denied the commander in days past. Command and control arrangements allow us to do a far better job of remaining aware of the status of the battlefield. With this knowledge appropriate actions can be taken. Warfare has become far more complex and far more deadly; you've got to be a whole lot smarter about it, otherwise you'll be killed. The technological influence makes us smarter."[23]

The Army, like the other services, will find an increasing need for specialists—technicians—to assemble and analyze the massive amounts of data being produced by new technology. "In a division there must be twenty-two, conservatively, sensors that pick up information from the enemy of one kind or another," explained General Glenn Otis.

> You intercept that, put it together with the data bases and draw conclusions. All of that has had to be analyzed. There isn't any commander that I know of that could take an aerial photograph with a stereoscopic image and go in there and pick out which things were which. It took technicians. But it's not going to substitute in the next ten or fifteen years for the human, so you're going to need staffs. More and more the staff guys are going to be the technicians. They're going to have to know how to assess that this particular correlation program in the computer is weak in this area and strong in that. Those are the kind of staff guys you're going to need.[24]

It also became apparent during this period of growth in new technology that space was going to be an important venue in future operations. Satellites in space assisted command and control of troops in the air, on the ground and at sea. As a result, Space Command was created so that the resources of all the services could be focused, and that space assets could be orchestrated. This new command increased the number of people assigned in headquarters and added key personnel dedicated to a facet of warfare over and above the traditional functions all the services perform.

After almost three years as military assistant to Secretary of Defense Weinberger, Colin Powell picked up a third star in the summer of 1986 as well as the command opportunity he had been seeking for so long—the V Corps in Europe. He'd had no say about his assignments for some time.

> In my recent history over the last eight years my life has been shaped to a large extent by what civilians have done. I had a very checkered path over the last five years, especially, as a result of the influence of civilian officials who mentored me. The record will reflect I never asked for any of those assignments. I just went wherever I was told to go. I went to V Corps and son of a gun, six months later I start getting these phone calls from Mr. Carlucci—who has been made national security adviser— asking me to come back and be the deputy. I said no. Then Mr. Carlucci really pressed and said this is really something I need you to do and the President wants you to do it.

> I said I'm a corps commander, I can't just walk out on the corps because we've got a bureaucratic problem unless the President calls. The President did call. There's no other answer when the President calls—I said yes, sir.[25]

Late in 1986 the Army lost one of its finest young generals. Fred Mahaffey, a native of New Mexico and the only Army four-star ever from that state, fell victim to a brain tumor in October at the age of fifty-two. There was little doubt that Fred would have been a leading contender for chief of staff that year, and probably more. He had already attracted the attention of the Army's senior leaders, including General Andy Goodpaster, for a number of years. "He was a man I had my eye on, thinking he might be a future SACEUR," Goodpaster said. "He was commanding Readiness Command, a four-star command. I had known him as the deputy chief of staff for operations for the Army—he was then three stars—and I've seen him when he was of a lesser grade. I just sensed he was a man with that kind of ability."[26] To fill the spot opened up by Mahaffey's untimely death, Chief of Staff John Wickham tapped Lieutenant General James J. Lindsay, commanding general of the XVIII Airborne Corps at Fort Bragg since the spring of 1984. An exceptionally capable field commander who spent much of his career with the 82nd Airborne, Lindsay—only the fourth OCS graduate to become a full general—earned a fourth star on October 10, his fifty-fourth birthday.

Another benchmark was reached in the spring of 1987 with the selection of Carl Vuono to be chief of staff. Heralded Army-wide, his appointment sent a signal that yes, there was room at the top for a soldier who makes his way to the seat of government, who wins acceptance from his civilian bosses and still relates to the grassroots needs of the Army. That June, when General John Wickham retired, Vuono took over as chief of staff. The selection of Carl as the new chief paved the way for the appointment of General Max Thurman as TRADOC commander. Max, who had just spent four years as the vice chief, had served at TRADOC in the mid-seventies as a fresh-cut brigadier general. He was known as an innovative, inquisitive, take-charge general who constantly poked around looking for ways to improve the quality of training.

> When I got to TRADOC, one of the first things I said was, 'Look fellows, you've got

to take apart all the rotations at the National Training Center and tell me what went on there.' I wasn't interested in the performance of any particular unit, I was interested in the trend-line data. One of the things that fell out of that was that defeating the Red Force out there requires a fellow to be able to manipulate his own forces on the field of battle based upon the fragments of information that come in through his intelligence assets and subordinate commands. So what's new? Well, the answer is that nothing is new. But the real issue is, if you are a chess player and you are going up against the Russians in an international chess competition, how many chess games should you play to prepare yourself? The answer might be several hundred a year. Now, how many battalion attacks does a young battalion commander get a chance to command and control with all of his principal forces? The answer is maybe eight or ten over a two-year period, because there is not enough money to go out and run a battalion attack every day with the troops. There just is not enough Op Tempo [operational tempo] money."

Thurman analyzed the data available to him and then created a computerized war game at Fort Leavenworth which an officer preparing for battalion command can utilize. It's an interactive system developed by the Livermore National Laboratory. "I have talked to some battalion commanders who have been through that who say it is the biggest single advance in the preparation of young officers who will command battalions we have ever had," Thurman continued. "We call that the tactical commanders training program. Now every combat officer who is going to command works the computer for a couple of weeks. So he may, in a couple of weeks, fight ten battalion attacks before he arrives at his battalion. He gets the tactics right in his head, the weapons, ranges, equipment, relative speeds of maneuver and all of that."[27]

Other important moves occurred that month high in the Army hierarchy. After a record eight years as Supreme Allied Commander in Europe, General Bernie Rogers traded Mons, Belgium, for retirement in suburban Virginia. Because the SACEUR must be voted on and approved by our NATO allies, the nomination of General Jack Galvin had already been made several months before and quickly approved. A 1954 graduate of West Point,

Galvin was one of those late bloomers who flourished with each new assignment and promotion. By the time he had earned four-stars in 1985, as head of the Southern Command, his reputation was known throughout the Army—and the Air Force. "Jack Galvin was a fellow you could see grow every day of the week," said General Mike Dugan. "Even though he's a very senior citizen, he's one of the few Army officers I know who has studied what air does or ought to do very thoroughly. If you wanted to have a conversation with Jack Galvin about air power you had better be prepared. He was well prepared, a very valuable and gracious fellow to work for."[28]

After a little more than three years as commander in chief United Nations Command in Korea, General Bill Livsey retired and came home to live near Atlanta. The new CINC, Louis C. Menetrey, knew the territory well, having served as commanding general of the Combined Field Army—U.S. and Korean troops—from 1983 to 1985. In another part of the world Lieutenant General Fred Woerner was given a fourth star and moved from command of the 6th Army at the Presidio to Quarry Heights, Panama, as commander in chief of Southern Command. Woerner was a foreign area specialist on Latin and Central America. Many of the finest officers earn such specialties, but managing Woerner's career to ensure he had a chance to bring his knowledge to bear on this region was a major undertaking.

Training has always been extremely important to the Army, and Carl Vuono instituted through TRADOC a leadership development program built on what he termed "three pillars." The concept had begun well before he became chief but took on special emphasis under his tutelage. "One is what I call institutional training," he explained. "That starts before a kid gets commissioned. That's precommissioning training, that's ROTC, West Point and OCS. Then it goes to formalized schooling: basic course, advanced, then the regular Leavenworth course and the War College." Through each "block" of leadership training there was particular emphasis on history, case studies and lessons from the past. Then came the second pillar, operational assignments. "I look on it as leader development actions," Vuono continued. "There has to be a conscious effort on the part of the leader to say to the subordinate going into his job here is what I expect you to accomplish while you are in that job, here is what is not negotiable with me. In other words, value and honesty."[29] The third pillar, and probably the most difficult for the

Army to track, is self-development. Each officer must take stock of his strengths and weaknesses and buttress his individual skills.

At the highest operational level of the Army—the corps and division—the Battle Command Training Program was designed to keep senior commanders performing at the peak of proficiency. During his time as chief of staff, Carl Vuono saw to it that this unique training was a fundamental part of the Army's mission. "We put all these division commanders, brigade commanders and staff into a room with some observer controllers and they talk about their business," Vuono said. "They spend a lot of time on their war plan. At a later date, some three to four months after that, we give them a command post exercise for seven to ten days. We have a complete team that goes and administers that." The team was headed by three retired Army generals with impeccable credentials—two four-stars and a three-star. Their assessment of a corps or division's war fighting capability was honest, candid and meaningful. Only the commanding general received a copy of the after-action report so that he alone could follow up and initiate changes or corrections without worrying about punitive reactions from anywhere else in the Army structure. "This is as close as any of these guys are going to see of combat," Vuono concluded.[30]

Throughout 1987 and into 1988 the United States government struggled with its policy toward Panama. We wanted Noriega out of the picture. The United States "no longer cared to be seen with him in public, and had, besides, serious qualms as to his trustworthiness," wrote R. M. Koster and Guillermo Sanchez, journalists with a keen knowledge of the heart and soul of Panama. "Thirty years of policy, from building the Guardia into an army to supporting its rule to enacting the Canal treaties, had one underlying purpose: keeping the Isthmus of Panama in friendly hands. Did Noriega's regime fit that description? The visible government didn't think so. Its invisible counterpart may well have agreed, but its members had made Noriega their accomplice, had trusted him too deeply to risk making him angry."[31]

Second only to Robert McNamara in tenure as secretary of Defense—and by only three months—Caspar Weinberger resigned on November 23, 1987. He was succeeded by his deputy and longtime public servant Frank Carlucci, who served until the end of the Reagan administration. Carlucci's move from national security adviser to secretary of Defense opened the door for Colin Powell to become national security adviser in the White House—another civilian job initiated by his mentors Weinberger and Carlucci. This key position allowed Powell to utilize his growing capabilities in the political and military arena.

When the smoke cleared on election day, November 8, 1988, the country had a new President, George Herbert Walker Bush, and the Republicans secured another four years in the White House. Few modern Presidents possessed the breadth of experience enjoyed by Bush: two-term congressman from Texas, ambassador to the United Nations, director of Central Intelligence Agency and, most recently, eight years of working at Reagan's elbow as vice president.

The day before Thanksgiving, Norm Schwarzkopf pinned on a fourth star as commander in chief Central Command. While his career in the Army had been a mixed bag for the first twenty-five years after graduation from West Point in 1956—some troop command, stints as a student or instructor and plenty of staff assignments—the last seven years had provided him a solid base of current experience on both sides of the fence: first a couple of years as assistant commander of the 8th Infantry Division in Germany, followed by nearly a year learning the personnel business in the Pentagon, then two years as commanding general of the 24th Infantry Division. Following a little less than a year as assistant DCSOPS under Fred Mahaffey, he was sent to command the I Corps at Fort Lewis as a lieutenant general. The summer of 1987 he came back to the Pentagon as the DCSOPS and, like so many of those who have held that key position, went on to four-stars.

At the height of the summer of 1989, Secretary of Defense Dick Cheney announced the retirement of General Fred Woerner as head of the Southern Command. In actuality Woerner was being fired for publicly criticizing the Bush administration in recent weeks for lacking a cohesive policy for its actions—largely reactive—in Central America. A short while later Cheney released word of the nomination of Colin Powell as the next chairman of the Joint Chiefs of Staff. That summer also marked the two-year point for General Carl Vuono's term as Army chief of staff as well as his West Point class's thirtieth reunion. Without question he had done well for himself over the previous thirty years but close friends said he retained an unusual level of humility. "That he was the Army's first soldier was only apparent because we classmates knew that to be true," said West Point classmate Raymond Bell. "He walked with everyone else, sat with his class friends, participated like anyone else. Most interesting was that the highest ranking flag flown was the three-star flag for the superintendent—not General Vuono's four-star flag. That was a real mark of the man General Vuono."[32]

When Max Thurman was handpicked to take over the Southern Command in Panama, following Woerner's quick departure, Carl Vuono brought in Lieutenant General John W. Foss, the DCSOPS, to be the new head trainer at TRADOC. Amazingly, his assignment on the General Staff was his *first* tour of duty in the Pentagon after thirty-one years in uniform. "I think I was probably a token for awhile," Foss admitted.

> I mean I was used as a token, as an example of one who was able to stay out in the field and not necessarily go to Washington. But you would be surprised how many young brigadiers—I just sat on the brigadier board—how many of those have not served in Washington at high levels. You know, you really have two levels of Army leadership. You have those that command units and then you have an Army leadership that's part of Washington that has to deal with other factors—the secretary of Defense, the JCS, the Congress—and tell the Army's story and understand how to deal with those things very well. One is not necessarily greater than the other; we've seen very effective people in that area.[33]

A short while before Max Thurman left Fort Monroe for his new assignment at Quarry Heights, he phoned Lieutenant General Carl Stiner, who had the XVIII Airborne Corps at Fort Bragg. "You're going to be my joint task force commander if anything happens down there and I want you to understand that," Thurman said. "I know how you think and you know how I think. Carlos, you're going to be my man if anything happens and we need to talk." Stiner laughed.

> It was funny. On the phone he always called me Carlos. Then I ran into General Vuono about a week later and he said, 'Have you talked to Max Thurman?' I said, 'I've talked with him on the phone and he's coming to Bragg shortly and I'm going to brief him on some ideas I've got.' And he said, 'You need to talk to him.' So Max came to Bragg. I had been looking at the plan

that existed for Panama and I didn't like it because I thought I could do it better. It utilized more troops than I thought was necessary and it took a long time to get them there, so there was not the possibility of achieving surprise. The way I looked at it, it would cause more casualties and it could be done in a more surgical way than that.[34]

Knowing he had responsibility for anything the Army might do in Panama—and the situation there was heating up by the week—Stiner put his planners on the task of reworking the operational plan that the previous commanders of Southern Command had approved. Later, at the TRADOC change of command, Stiner talked to Thurman about the plan. "I want you to come down, we need a session or two," Thurman told me. By that time I had this plan pretty well wrapped up. I went down there and briefed him on it and he pretty much bought it right down the line. So we went back and I started rehearsing this plan. Planned in detail and we started rehearsing it."

Six weeks after John Foss took over TRADOC, following General Colin Powell's promotion to chairman of the Joint Chiefs, Ed Burba became commander in chief of Forces Command. Thin as a whip with very closely cropped hair, the fifty-three-year-old general had risen rapidly in rank and responsibility. Only six years earlier he had been a full colonel. There was no question that the Army was his life; he once said "light reading" was taking home a couple of Army field manuals to read over a weekend.

The retirement of Admiral Bill Crowe in October 1989 and the appointment of Colin Powell as the new chairman ended one important era and began another. Crowe was the first chairman to serve under the aegis of the landmark Goldwater-Nichols Act that put considerably more clout in the hands of the chairman and strengthened his relationship with the CINCs spread throughout the world. Powell, on the other hand, was not only the first black to serve as chairman but the only chairman to have spent 69 percent of his career as a general officer—85 out of the previous 124 months—working for his civilian bosses in the White House or Pentagon. To Powell's thinking, politics and generalship work hand in hand in the nation's capitol. "Show me a general in Washington who is successful, who isn't a political general, and I'll show you someone who is telling a fib," he asserted. "We work for civilians and they are politicians—anybody who is going to be successful working for civilians has to understand the political problems that civilians want you to help them solve. All problems are political, not military."[35] Colin Powell had cut his teeth working for the secretary of Defense and that gave him a significant edge as the JCS chairman. Each of the services tries to get its man in the secretary's office as aide. It's very competitive. You get the very top people assigned up there—that's where Powell and all that crew came from, out of that environment. Powell knew all those people in Defense as a result of having been assigned to jobs there earlier. What happens to the aides, though, is the job politicizes them to a higher degree than it should because it doesn't give them the opportunity to get as much experience in the art of war as it should. In the case of Colin Powell, he was denied the opportunity to do things that would have prepared him better for the military side of soldiering. On the other hand it prepared him well for the role as an integrator of strategic issues and political issues as a result of having seen it all at the very highest level. There is one possible downside, and that's the possibility of introducing political issues into the equation too early in the development of a military option. There is merit in developing military options based on military rationale and then adjusting them later to accommodate political needs rather than the other way around. Such procedures ensure that both the military and the political leaders understand the real trade-offs.

In Panama, meanwhile, forces loyal to Manuel Noriega turned back an attempted coup and the dictator responded by tightening the screws on his country. Reports from Panama indicated Noriega's brutal paramilitary forces—dignity battalions he called them, which was the furthest thing from the truth—rounded up, tortured and killed as many as seventy-five men who participated in the aborted coup. America's official reaction to the turmoil in Panama came on October 6 from President Bush, who acknowledged that there were those in the government who urged him to take action against Noriega. "But that's not prudent," the President remarked, "and that's not the way I plan to conduct the military or foreign affairs of this country."[36] Late in the week of December 11 the situation in Panama neared the boiling point. Noriega declared himself "maximum leader" of his country and boasted that a "state of war" existed with the United States. "We the Panamanian people will sit along the banks of the canal to watch the dead bodies of our enemies pass by," he said. Then that weekend, on Saturday the sixteenth, four off-duty American officers got lost while looking for a restaurant and ran into a Panama Defense Force (PDF) roadblock. A PDF soldier opened a door of the car and attempted to pull one of the officers onto the street. The driver reacted by speeding away and PDF troops opened fire, mortally wounding First Lieutenant Robert Paz. A Navy lieutenant and his wife, in another car, witnessed the shooting. They were abruptly taken into custody and driven to PDF headquarters, where the lieutenant was kicked and beaten and his wife threatened with rape before they were finally released. The next day Lieutenant General Tom Kelley, director of operations for the Joint Staff, phoned Stiner at his Fort Bragg quarters and brought him up to date on events of the last twenty-four hours. Then he asked Stiner if there was anything he wanted to say. Stiner replied yes. "Tell the chairman I would like for him to emphasize—he probably knows this already—but my point is that we can't do anything to bring Lieutenant Paz back—he's gone. We can't correct that situation. If we're going to do it, it needs to be done right."[37] He asked for forty-eight hours to get his airplanes together and "approval of the total package."

Just eight days before Christmas, after President Bush had decided the United States had seen and heard enough from Manuel Noriega, he gave the green light to Secretary of Defense Dick Cheney and Chairman Powell. Cheney chose the name, Operation Just Cause. No more than two or three hours later, Kelley called back. "It's a go," he said. "You got your forty-eight hours. Notify Wayne Downing [commanding general of Southern Command's Joint Special Operations Command at Fort Bragg]." Stiner replied, "Roger that."

He decided to remain at Bragg for another twenty-four hours to make sure all the pieces of the complex puzzle were coming together. Monday evening, December 18, Stiner took twelve members of the JTF and boarded a plane for Panama. Major General Downing and his assault command post (CP) took a second plane. "As soon as I got there, I gathered up my commanders from Panama that were already in place," Stiner continued. They included Air Force and Navy contingents permanently assigned there, plus the Army's 193rd Brigade, a battalion from the 7th Infantry Division, another battalion out of the 5th Mechanized Division at Fort Polk, and a reinforced Marine battalion with light armored vehicles, or LVYs. "I had a good bit of combat power there. To preserve operational security, nobody other than just the commanders had been brought in on this plan. So I had to get down there and get them all briefed at the right time because if it were to be compromised I was afraid it would be on that end. With all the dependents, everybody going home and telling their wives and so on, even though we had ten thousand dependents in all that we had to protect, we couldn't tell them or it would have been compromised for sure."[38]

Not long after Stiner arrived in Panama, he got a call from Colin Powell. "The President's been briefed in great detail on the plan and he's got great confidence in your ability to do this," Powell said. "I guess the best thing that I can do is to try to keep the Pentagon off your back for the first twenty-four to thirty-six hours." Stiner replied, "I sure would appreciate that." The following afternoon the Military Airlift Command began moving some seven thousand troops from six bases—Forts Lewis, Ord, Polk, Bragg, Benning and Stewart—toward a rendezvous point in the Pacific Ocean off the coast of Panama. The attack was set for one A.M. the next morning, Wednesday, December 20.

At 12:45 A.M. Stiner decided to launch the attack early for fear the movement of troops might have alerted Noriega that something was in the offing. Moving swiftly, American units struck simultaneously at the PDF headquarters in Panama City, sealed off the only route into the city from the west—the Bridge of the Americas, moved onto Paitilla Airfield on the edge of the city and blocked Fort Amador, where potential PDF replacements were stationed. Fifteen minutes later two Ranger battalions parachuted onto Torrijos Airport, supported by Apache gunships. "We had to do this quickly and surgically and we had to limit ourselves in the kind of weapons that we used in order to do this," Stiner explained. "The rules of engagement that I imposed upon them were they could use nothing but direct fire weapons—machine guns, AT-4 anti-tank weapons and LAVs and tanks. We dropped in Sheridan tanks and we could use Apache helicopters firing Hellfire missiles with laser designation control because they are very accurate. They could use artillery but in a direct fire role only. They could not use mortars in any built-up area and they could not use air strikes."[39]

As CNN and the television networks later confirmed, Operation Just Cause was well planned, well executed and quickly consummated. It was, as TRADOC's John Foss commented, "an eight-hour battle followed by about four days of lighter conflict. The decision had been reached by nine o'clock in the morning. There was no question that there was no longer a Panamanian government, Noriega was no longer in charge of that, and the Panamanian army units had been defeated."[40] Although Noriega evaded capture and took refuge in the Vatican Embassy, his fate was sealed.

What did we learn from Operation Just Cause? "As you move away from global confrontations to regional confrontations certainly the first and last battles are very often the same," observed General Foss. That held true in Panama. Carl Stiner, however, later said "we didn't really learn anything new" but we certainly validated a great deal. Most importantly, we validated that training—the right training—pays off. "I went to Panama right after the troops went in," said Carl Vuono. "I was talking to one battalion commander down there who had a rotation [assignment] at the Joint Readiness Center at Chafee about a month and one-half before he went to Panama. I said, 'How was it?' He said, 'The training center was much tougher than this.' That's what you want him to say."[41] General Mike Davison, the former commander of United States Army forces in Europe, wholeheartedly agreed. "The peacetime training today is probably the best it has ever been but budgetary support is waning," he said. "Congress always cuts the operations money first. Thus, we may be forced into mediocrity. However, for the time being the Army is capable of performing well as a result of its training—witness Operation Just Cause."[42]

Within the XVIII Corps, Carl Stiner had preached intensive small-unit training at the rifle-squad or tank-crew level. It was practiced time and again until it became rote. Then the command issued all the troops small booklets containing seven or eight battle drills that were common to the missions of their units. "For a rifle squad, for example, these additional drills were how to clear a trench line, how to attack a bunker, how to move through a built-up area, how to attack and clear a building, how to breach and obstacle, and those sorts of things," Stiner explained. "When the units hit those kinds of things they didn't have to stop and come up with a plan to do it. They knew it automatically. They just went right into it and there was no loss of momentum."[43]

Perhaps it had to do with the makeup of the Bush administration, but Operation Just Cause proved that the system worked. It's based on the way things are supposed to be done: the civilians make the decisions and the military carries them out. "I think the actions of our civilian leadership had a tremendous impact, very beneficial impact, on the outcome of Panama because we were allowed to develop a plan—the military—we had a good, sound plan which was briefed all the way up the tape, all the way up to the President, and that plan was approved," Stiner said. "And then our civilian leaders had enough confidence in the ability of their military leaders to allow them to execute that plan without meddling, or without micro-managing. So far as I am concerned, it is exactly the way it ought to be, a situation of mutual trust and confidence. Charge the military with that responsibility and them let go at it."[44]

The invasion of Panama also helped strengthen the relationship between the Army's senior generals and the media, if only on a small scale. Reporter Tom Donnelly of the *Army Times* caught up one afternoon with Carl Vuono and Lieutenant General Gordon Sullivan, the DCSOPS, as they were inspecting the battlefield in the aftermath. Donnelly particularly remembered Sullivan.

> He seemed a quiet, reserved man, but one who would step out of Vuono's official party from time to time, pulling aside the nearest soldier to ask him what he did and what his impressions were of the fighting in Panama. At one point, we stopped outside the shattered barracks of the Panama Defense Forces at Fort Amador. The buildings were pocked with holes from everything from rifle rounds to 105mm howitzer shells. As we listened to Colonel Mike Snell, commander of the 193rd Infantry Brigade, tell the story of the assault on Fort Amador, Vuono's and Sullivan's attention perked when they heard Snell explain how he had told his men to avoid destroying the mausoleum of General Omar Torrijos, the father of Panamanian nationalism. We stopped closer to the shrine, just yards from the gutted barracks. It had but one nick in it. Vuono put his arm around me, and together the two generals made sure I got the point. I could feel their warm pride in the professionalism of their soldiers, a palpable presence on the cool, dewy morning.[45]

In retrospect the invasion of Panama displayed an extraordinary juxtaposition of leadership. Colin Powell, while not as well versed in the art of war as many others, was exceptionally proficient in integrating the military capabilities with the political. He understood his shortcomings and relied upon the CINCs in the field. By that time Goldwater-Nichols was in place, allowing the CINCs in the field to deal directly with the chairman, the secretary of Defense and the President. General Max Thurman, the overall commander in Panama, was someone who had not had a lot of experience on the operational side but knew how to deal with Washington very well. He had a lot of experience in Washington, knew the Washington scene and could deal well with the media and Congress. General Glenn Otis saw the Panama invasion as "a shining example of the right way to do something" and gave thumbs-up to the marching orders for Thurman, adding that "if you're going to do something in an area that's assigned to a joint CINC that's the guy who gets the message to do it. Panama is a shining example of that."[46] We had in Lieutenant General (later General) Carl Stiner, the principal planner and executor of the operation, someone who had spent all of his career as an operator. We were fortunate to have in place an officer who possessed the right sort of background and experience. Therefore, for the invasion of Panama Meyer gives the U.S. military an "A minus." We still hadn't evolved some of the kinds of equipment that we should have to be able to deal with this sort of warfare, nor were we as well prepared for it as we should have been. It also taught us that we need some forms of nonlethal weaponry for the future.

Our country's response to other activities during the eighties—the Soviet invasion of Afghanistan, the events that took place in Nicaragua, El Salvador and ultimately in Panama—demonstrated that the Armed Forces were operating in an area in which they were very unfamiliar: the very low end of the spectrum of warfare. Our military operated as an adjunct to some of the activities that were handled by the Central Intelligence Agency and the White House, and the interface was not always as good as it should have been. In the military's ability to be able to operate in that changing environment and its lack of knowledge and understanding of how to meet the requirements of low-intensity warfare they get a "D." The senior officers were more skilled at the art of conventional and nuclear war versus the U.S.S.R. than they were at being able to handle wars at the edge. Something positive came out of it, however: the development of Special Operations Command, the increased capability of Southern Command, the willingness of the military forces to look at the development of forces to take care of the other kind of wars. The senior generals and admirals began to learn from it and undertook changes in the way in which the services and joint commands function so that they would be more responsive in the future.

At the beginning of the summer of 1990, Lieutenant General Robert W. RisCassi, one of many senior Army generals to have experience as the DCSOPS, took over as commander in chief United Nations Command Korea from retiring General Lou Menetrey. At the same time, due in large part to his exemplary performance late the previous year as commanding general of the XVIII Corps, Lieutenant General Carl Stiner was given a fourth star as head of the Army's new Special Operations Command at MacDill Air Force Base.

For the previous few months Iraq's President Saddam Hussein had openly expressed contempt toward his neighbor Kuwait. Suddenly, with no warning, on August 2 Iraqi troops stormed the border of Kuwait and poured into the tiny nation. The United Nations Security Council reacted by condemning the invasion, while President Bush banned all trade with Iraq. Four days later the U.N. authorized economic sanctions against Iraq. With tens of thousands of Iraqi troops now on Kuwaiti soil, equipped with hundreds of Soviet-built tanks, the leaders of Saudi Arabia became openly concerned that their oil-rich country was vulnerable to attack. King Fahd put out a plea for assistance from the West. On August 7, responding quickly to the Saudi request, Operation Desert Shield was launched, and the following day the first U.S. Army units—paratroopers from Fort Bragg—arrived in the Gulf, By August 22 more than 400,000 American troops had been ordered to the Gulf and President Bush announced additional deployments. A week later, in only the second time in history, the United Nations Security Council authorized, in Resolution Number 678, use of "all necessary means" to thwart the Iraqi occupation of Kuwait.

One day after excerpts from a wide-ranging interview with General Mike Dugan, the recently appointed Air Force chief of staff, appeared on the front pages of *The Washington Post* and the *Los Angeles Times,* he was abruptly fired by Secretary of Defense Dick Cheney. Stating that Dugan "did not, in my mind, reveal an adequate understanding of the situation and what is expected of him as chief of staff of the Air Force," Cheney accused Dugan of revealing classified information. "I was concerned about the lack of judgment involved in wide-ranging speculation about decisions which may or may not be made in the future by the President," Cheney added. Reporters from the two newspapers and a third from *Aviation Week & Space Technology* had interviewed Dugan and five other Air Force generals on a trip to Saudi Arabia the week before. "I told a story about Air Force doctrine and it got printed on the front page of the paper," Dugan said. "Nobody ever prints Army or Air Force doctrine on the front page of the paper. Now they printed, exaggerated, embellished it a little bit, but it was a story about Air Force doctrine. If I had to do it over again, I'd probably do it again and in that regard maybe Mr. Cheney made a good choice. I am at peace with myself. I read the transcript of my story and I'm not embarrassed about any of it."[47]

In effect Mike Dugan was dismissed for being too open and candid with the media. There was little if anything in the newspaper articles that wasn't generally known; he simply put his own spin on it. For example, he said that "air power is the only answer that's available to our country" to avoid a bloody land war. That reflects a certain Air Force bias but as it was to turn out, air power did make the decisive difference in Desert Storm. Further, Dugan was quoted as being disdainful of the Iraqi Armed Forces. "Their air force has very limited military capability," Dugan said. "They did not distinguish themselves in the war against Iran, often missing targets by miles." Iraq possesses "an incompetent army," he added. "With 5,000 tanks one should have been able to do something against Iran." Again, Dugan was very prescient. The Iraqi Air Force, for the most part, flew out of the country once the war began. And the Iraqi Army, with a few exceptions, was inept. Meyer believed Mike Dugan was an outstanding Air Force general. On July 5, shortly after Dugan had assumed his duties as chief of staff, they met in his office in the Pentagon. Meyer discussed issues concerning the Air Force and the future. As he was ready to leave Shy mentioned how important he thought it was for the head of a service to develop good relationships with a few key members of the media. The day Mike's dismissal was announced Meyer felt somehow complicit.

Meanwhile the congressional debate over President Bush's desire to counter Iraqi aggression with United States troops was continuously televised. The sessions were lengthy, repetitive, all too often partisan and at times acrimonious. The War

Powers Act required the President to either seek the concurrence of Congress before committing America's Armed Forces in a war, or if he exercised his powers and committed them as a national emergency, they must be withdrawn within a prescribed length of time. President Bush didn't want his hands tied, so he sought a vote of confidence from Congress. After much hand-wringing and heated discussion Congress, on January 12, 1991, gave President Bush its reluctant blessing. The final vote was very close, signifying a sharply divided Congress, but he now possessed unquestioned authority to use force in the Gulf.

On January 15 the United Nations deadline for Iraq to withdraw from Kuwait came and passed. There had been no sign of any movement by Iraqi forces; on the contrary, they were dug in and presumably girded for battle. General Schwarzkopf had, by that time, already given a pep talk to U.S. troops that set the stage for the inevitable clash with the Iraqis on the ground. "There was never any doubt in my mind that we were going to get air superiority very quickly and were going to control the air, but what I need is the tank killers in here," Schwarzkopf said. "Now I've got the tank killers in here and I've got the people that are going to maintain them and the people flying and we're all feeling a lot better about the situation. Let's face it. If he dares to come across that border I'm completely confident we're gonna kick his butt when he gets here and that's because of you folks right here." The following day, Desert Storm was launched by the coalition forces. Forty-eight hours after the attack began, air raid sirens wailed as Iraq fired its first SCUD missiles at Saudi Arabia and Israel. That attack provided a milestone for the Patriot missile, which scored its first kill.

While President Bush enjoyed the overwhelming support of the American people, there were the inevitable protesters against America's role in the Gulf. On college campuses across the country there were scattered incidents of protest marches and flag burnings by students too young to remember Vietnam. It forced us to remember that the words "consensus" and "majority" sometimes have little meaning in a country in which democracy permits the most divergent and often outrageous outpourings of public sentiment.

After more than five weeks of around-the-clock pummeling by coalition aircraft, Iraqi forces were hit by a massive ground attack. Elements of the XVIII Airborne Corps under the command of Lieutenant General Gary Luck pounded into Iraq from the southwest and then drove eastward toward Kuwait, while Lieutenant General Frederick M. Franks's VII Corps, situated north of King Khalid Military City, struck central Iraq and spearheaded its attack toward the Iraq-Kuwait border. At the same time the Joint Forces Command North, Marine Central Command and Joint Forces Command East converged on Kuwait City. From his headquarters in Riyadh, Saudi Arabia, Schwarzkopf called the shots on the massive force moving swiftly across the immense Iraqi battlefield.

On the morning of the second day of the campaign, February 25, Schwarzkopf awoke to find that the VII Corps was sitting in essentially the same position it had occupied the night before. The 24th Infantry Division (Mechanized) had moved twice as far as planned and outdistanced VII Corps' 1st and 3rd Armored Divisions, which were positioned to move against the Republican Guard. Franks's plan called for sequencing the divisions for a coordinated drive against the guard but Schwarzkopf, fearing the elite Iraqi unit would slip out of the vise, wanted Franks to step up the attack. He complained to Lieutenant General John Yeosock, commanding the 3rd Army, that if Franks "couldn't handle the job, I'll get someone who can. I've got Waller chomping at the bit."[48] A phone call to Schwarzkopf, in which Franks explained his strategy, cleared the air for the moment. He agreed to turn up the heat against the Iraqi opposition. Franks told his commanders, "We are going to drive the corps hard for the next twenty-four to thirty-six hours, day and night, to overcome all resistance and to prevent the enemy from withdrawing."

In subsequent fighting two Iraqi divisions were decimated and two others badly mauled, with minimum casualties on friendly forces and equipment. Enemy resistance was piecemeal, and by February 27 the Iraqi Army was out of business. The "mother of all battles," as Saddam Hussein had boasted of the clash in Kuwait, turned out to be what Secretary of Defense Dick Cheney called "the mother of all retreats." Although Schwarzkopf's Central Command forces had not yet reached the goals he envisioned, Washington pulled the plug at midnight—one hundred hours into the ground war. Measured against United States losses, the Iraqi army was humiliated; thousands of soldiers had died, hundreds of tanks lay destroyed in the desert. Yet most of the Iraqi air force sat unharmed on airfields in Iran while Saddam languished in his virtually indestructible bunker below the streets of Baghdad.

Did the one hundred-hour war quell any doubts about America's ability to muster its forces and respond to an emergency halfway around the world? TRADOC's John Foss, who had responsibility for training Army troops during the year preceding the Persian Gulf incursion, said the Army was well set for battle. "I think we have trained our officer corps so that it is trained to fight well every battle, and that's what units do. Now the Army itself has to figure out whether it is willing to possibly lose the first battle or to win the last battle. I don't see that as a choice—if you lose the first battle you might never get to the last battle."[49]

Foss brought up an important point. Future conflicts are likely to be lightning quick with little or no time to debate doctrine or tactics and even less to determine the mettle of the troops and their leaders. General Bill Rosson, one of a handful of senior officers who spent much of the Vietnam War in-country, warned that the jury was not yet out on the Army's performance in Desert Storm.

> I followed the whole thing as closely as I could without having access to things in Washington, knowing what was going on in the Pentagon I pondered the significance. In my view the key to the success that was achieved out there lay in the air campaign which was apparently very effective and eliminated the Iraqi Air Force as a factor and rendered the Iraq Army rather helpless in many respects. It must have been very punishing from the viewpoint of morale as well as support. Defenses were simply not cohesive, the will to stand and fight was not widespread and the resistance simply crumbled and broke up. This does not take anything away from what I consider to be rather brilliant planning and execution that we witnessed. The end run concept, the 'Hail Mary concept,' certainly stands forth as a lesson in applying a maneuver to best advantage. Everything considered, we would be wrong to view the outcome of the gulf campaign as indicative of what we're going to encounter in the future and as a paradigm as to how we should organize and conduct the action.[50]

The biggest show of force since Vietnam, Desert Storm was the war Norm Schwarzkopf argued left no doubts about United States military leadership now or in the future. The Persian Gulf War was an extraordinary event. The air part of the war was handled in a superb manner. The use of firepower instead of manpower was exactly what each of the commanders learned from their experiences in Vietnam. As General Carl Vuono said recently, "The group of leaders who are in the key positions, we were all about the same rank during the Vietnam days, majors and lieutenant colonels, and I think all of us were shaped by that, all of us were shaped by the low point in the military in the early '70s."[51] They knew that the Armed Forces had to maintain the support of the American people and the President had to have achievable goals laid out for the campaign. Things that went wrong in Vietnam didn't go wrong in Desert Storm because the senior leadership had learned from their studies and experience the importance of agreement with the President, the importance of firepower over manpower and the necessity to have a plan of operation that everyone understood. This demonstrated the viability of the Goldwater-Nichols Act in that we had a joint force there that could work well together. For the first time in the history of warfare we saw elements of the United States Navy under the operational control of a commander not in a Navy uniform. The integration of those forces made Desert Storm clearly rate an "A."

However, having said that, it is well to note that we were fortunate to have had particular officers in particular places. We had in Colin Powell, as chairman, someone who possessed a great understanding of the interface between military and political power and was able to work very well with the White House and the secretary of Defense in its integration. As for his colleagues on the Joint Chiefs of Staff; he accepted their views but in the end the advice given to Secretary Cheney and the President had a decidedly Powell flavor. "I don't have to get a committee decision," he said bluntly.

> After we're through debating something I say okay guys, here's what I think I heard you say, here's what I think, here's what I'm going to tell the secretary. Here's where I come out on this, here is what I'm going to tell him. Anybody disagree? If they disagree I take their disagreement, tell the secretary what I think and say by the way, Al Gray or Carl Vuono or Gordie Sullivan doesn't agree with me but this is what I think, this is my advice. So I don't have to get a paper chopped by anyone. Often I write it myself and don't even show it to my own staff. It's none of their business either. The whole process of bureaucracy has been simplified, the grooves turn a lot faster and we give

crisper advice to the secretary and the President—advice that has a political content to it and is conscious of public relations implications but is fundamentally sound militarily.[52]

Powell's human and political tendencies were apparent. For example, he might not have said that one hundred hours was a nice way to end the war. He might have said there was a military objective rather than a number of hours. The simple fact is the lines between war fighting capabilities and the political and economic dimensions of national security have become increasingly blurred in the modern world. "This is more attributable to advanced technology, especially in information sciences, than to misjudgment," argued former Secretary of State Al Haig.

It has meant that combat leadership has had to share the stage with management skills and technology competence. All have contributed to a new range of leadership progression criteria favoring the advancement of leaders who would not risk making waves in this complex military environment. In such an environment, effective leaders must seek subordinates who are willing to deliver advice that their superiors *should* hear rather than advice that they believed their superiors *wanted* to hear. Notwithstanding, my experience confirmed that the percentage of our leaders who followed that course is still respectable although declining. Unfortunately, the new system with the infusion of modern technology is less tolerant of those who, when rendering such advice, are guilty of misjudgment. Frequently the Army personnel system is the main culprit. This system must always be willing to forgive isolated misjudgments in the interest of nurturing bold and innovative battlefield skills.[53]

The Army had in Norm Schwarzkopf an individual with a lot of experience with troops. Many of our division commanders in Desert Storm had served tours as brigade or battalion commanders during a time when the length of those tours was up to three years in length. They had, therefore, more time in command than some of their predecessors and probably some of their successors. We also enjoyed the benefits of cohort units who were enlisted, trained and fought together and unit cohesion brought about

by units that were together six months prior to the time the war started. And we cannot overlook the benefits of intensive, realistic training. Carl Vuono and Larry Welch—a former chief of staff of the Air Force—conducted a battle review with members of the 2nd Armored Cavalry Regiment after the Gulf war. This came up in the question and answer session:

"None of you have ever been in combat before," Vuono said. "In previous wars, never have we been able to be so successful in first engagements. How do you explain your great success in your first battle?" Carl was referring to the Battle of 73-Easting on February 26, 1991, as he queried a group of captains.

"Sir, this was not our first battle," answered one of the officers. "This was our tenth battle! We fought three wars at the National Training Center, Fort Irwin, California; we fought four wars at the Combat Maneuver Training Center, Hoenfels, Germany; and a lot of other simulations like SIMNET, COFT and BCTP. Yes, sir, we had been 'shot at' before. Many times. This war was just like our training."

All of these contributed significantly to our success. However, this should not lead us to conclude that we have solved all our leadership problems, that our leadership development program is such that we can pluck any general or admiral from any tree and put him in command of a force anywhere in the world and be confident of victory.

Leadership of the Army changed hands at the very top in June of 1991 when President Bush chose as the new chief of staff Gordon R. Sullivan, fifty-three, who had been vice chief for the last year. Like many of his predecessors—Douglas MacArthur in the thirties and Matthew B. Ridgway in the early fifties, for example—Sullivan was handed the scepter to preside over a dwindling kingdom, an Army destined only to get smaller. And as the Army downsizes, the onus is on the officer corps, which is squeezed anyway in good times or bad. As John Foss pointed out, the chief in the nineties and beyond must play an ever-increasing role in selecting, training and motivating young leaders who will be the generals one day. "You start to pick your better leaders obviously for battalion command," Foss said. "That's a critical command. Then we continue the process, and it's almost a winnowing out, because only one out of three battalion commanders is going to be a brigade commander. Partly what was painful was sitting on the board this year is that while we picked a lot of good war fighters—we knew they could do that role—there were an awful lot of other very capable people that were just about the same quality which you couldn't pick."[54]

That means a lot of talented people are going to be gone at the twenty-year mark. What does the Army do with these officers? "What we have to do is keep the very best and give them the opportunity," said Carl Vuono. "If he says I really want to compete for battalion and brigade command and he realizes that everybody who competes for those commands doesn't make it—very small percentages make it—then we have to say to that officer there is a good career for you for the next ten years or whatever it is."[55] The Army's former IG, retired Lieutenant General Dick Trefry, had an additional thought.

> We have to go back and think in terms of a thirty-year career, that there are honorable things in the Army besides being a battalion commander and being in a TOE unit, or being a brigade commander. What is it that officers really do? The first thing you do is you know how to fight. That's a given, and hopefully we all know how to do that. That's what the school system is all about. The second thing is, and most people don't think about it, is we're teachers—because fighting is an unnatural act. Everybody wants to be a nice guy, nobody wants to be a son of a bitch. So you have to teach people how to fight and teach people how to protect themselves from the time you get off the bus and meet the guy with the Smoky Bear hat. What they're trying to teach you is instant reaction and instant discipline. That's what makes us different from civilians.[56]

Early in June 1991 John Foss, the Army's visionary guru, retired as TRADOC's head. A distinguished West Pointer who commanded at every level from platoon to corps, he left a legacy that emphasized the importance of training. "TRADOC has two jobs and they are different time spans," Foss said. "One is training the Army and the other is building the Army of the future. The training of the Army of today is the easier job. The Army of the future is a more difficult job because you have to bridge where you are now and where you want to take the Army, and you have to understand that a large part of the Army is not interested in changing."[57]

By the spring of 1992 the world map had been redrawn. The death of communism in Eastern Europe and the dissolution of the Soviet Union left the United States with no major protagonists in the Western Hemisphere for the first time in nearly half a century. "I applaud the changes we are witnessing," said General John T. Chain. "I hope they continue. I hope the wheels of change that have been set in motion are irreversible. The good news is that the strategy of containment, which had been in effect since the end of World War II has been successful. Much of the credit for what's happening in Eastern Europe today must be given to that containment strategy, a healthy NATO, strong United States military forces and the failure of the communist system."[58]

Concurrent with the reshaping of Europe and the emergence of Russia as the dominant power in the former Soviet Union, Warsaw Pact and NATO forces agreed that there would be a reduction of their conventional forces. This not only has changed the size and structure of our Armed Forces, particularly the United States Army, but it highlights an important fact for the future. The makeup of our military forces will be highly influenced by arms-control agreements, confidence-building measures and other such factors. "Undeniably those who became generals during the eighties still faced a massive Soviet threat," said General John Shalikashvili, "but were receiving the weapons, superb soldiers and national focus of being prepared to defend our interests against Communism. Today's new generals have the challenge of facing an unknown threat which is perhaps at a lesser level, but with fewer forces, a downward trend in modernization and spending, and a national focus on purely internal matters like the economy. In each way, the challenge is significant, but clearly any officer would prefer the former over the latter."[59] In many instances the nature of our forces in the future will be governed by factors other than our own desires and our approach toward what those requirements are. The Conventional Forces in Europe Reduction Act that followed the mutual balance in force reduction process, which began in August 1973, is now—more than twenty years later—in the process of bringing about real force reductions.

Inevitably, the U.S. Army's presence overseas will change markedly. On April 15, 1992, VII Corps was inactivated in Germany, as was the 8th Infantry Division, and the 3rd Armored Division returned to the United States, leaving only two divisions in Europe—the 3rd Infantry at Wurzburg and the 1st Armored at Bad Kreuznach, which comprise the V Corps. Once again there are rumblings about reducing the number of troops assigned to South Korea, despite the lack of any move on the part of North Korea to lessen tensions across the border.

In October 1993 Colin Powell retired from the Army and President Clinton named General John M. Shalikashvili, fifty-seven, the new chairman of the Joint Chiefs of Staff. A native of Poland who served as an enlisted man before earning a commission through OCS, Shali had been in Europe as SACEUR only a few months when the surprise announcement came. Not only did he bring an unusually broad knowledge of Eastern and Western Europe, but as Powell's successor he has a firsthand knowledge of what's expected of the chairman. Prior to becoming SACEUR, Shali served as Powell's three-star deputy and some of Powell's way of doing things was likely to have rubbed off.

General support for the military peaked in the Reagan and Bush administrations but now, well after the wake of Desert Storm and in a Democratic administration intent on change and cost cutting, major reductions are in store. It is projected that over the next five years the United States Armed Forces will reduce by 25 percent in actual resources spent. The biggest force, and the hardest hit, will be the Army, where manpower will plunge to 550,000 *at the very least* in this five-year period. Congressman Les Aspin brought with him, when he joined the Clinton administration as secretary of Defense, a plan that the new President had openly endorsed during the 1992 presidential campaign. Aspin's "Option C: would reduce the Army 10 percent below the base force to 483,000 active duty personnel, a force level the Army said cannot do the job. "The new administration under Mr. Aspin began by articulating a strategy known colloquially as 'win-hold-win,'" observed General William G. Tuttle, "in which case he was proposing that we fight a war in the Mid East essentially as was articulated in the Bush administration's National Military Strategy. Then, if there was simultaneously an attack in Korea, we 'hold' these using air and naval forces and the troops on the ground as best we could until such time as we were done with the Mid East conflict and then put the effort into winning in Korea. Of course that strategy has now been modified based on the reactions of the Koreans—and I presume the Japanese—to the instability which that kind of articulated strategy might induce in East Asia."[60]

"Getting to a downsized Army is the hard part," confirmed Lieutenant General Tom Jaco, commander of the 4th Infantry Division in Desert Storm. "If we make the transition without losing public support, without losing credibility, without reducing the standard—then we will have achieved success." The problem, Jaco added, is whether the Army can perform at force levels below those necessary to get the job done. He believes it can't be done, and the result would be "low strength, mediocre units that do little to standard, units that cannot accomplish their mission. A hollow force."[61]

The demands placed upon the Army's senior leaders in these leaner times will only get tougher. As Admiral Lee Baggett recently observed, it takes "inspired leadership to wage peace. In a period of violent peace we must keep our Armed Forces ready to respond to a wide range of options. There are no enemies upon which the wrath of our National consciousness can be vented, no focal point for our fighting men to direct their fury. All we have is the potential enemy against which we prepare to fight."[62]

NOTES

1. General Andrew J. Goodpaster, interview with R. Manning Ancell, 23 October 1986.
2. General William A, Knowlton, interview with R. Manning Ancell, 29 October 1986.
3. Eugene M. Zuckert, letter to R. Manning Ancell, 1 August 1977.
4. Douglas Kinnard, *The Secretary of Defense* (Lexington: University Press of Kentucky, 1980), 205.
5. Ronald Reagan, *An American Life: The Autobiography* (New York: Simon and Schuster, 1990), 450.
6. Caspar W. Weinberger, *Fighting For Peace: Seven Critical Years in the Pentagon* (New York: Warner Books, 1990), 110.
7. Reagan, *American Life*, 452–53.
8. Weinberger, *Fighting for Peace*, 116.
9. Reagan, *American Life*, 451.
10. Major Mark Adkin, *Urgent Fury—The Battle for Grenada* (Lexington, Massachusetts: D. C. Heath and Company, 1989), 336.
11. Weinberger, *Fighting for Peace*, 113.
12. *US. News and World Report*, October 1990, 34.
13. Quoted by Adkin in *Urgent Fury*, 336.
14. Weinberger, *Fighting for Peace*, 115.
15. Reagan, *American Life*, 454.
16. Livsey, interview.

17. Lieutenant General Richard G. Trefry, interview with Jane Mahaffey, 1990.

18. Gorman, interview.

19. Admiral William J. Crowe, interview with R. Manning Ancell, 30 August 1990.

20. General William R. Richardson, interview with R. Manning Ancell, 2 November 1986.

21. General David C. Jones, interview with R. Manning Ancell, 12 October 1991.

22. Crowe, interview.

23. Admiral Ronald J. Hays, interview with R. Manning Ancell, 22 August 1986.

24. General Glenn K. Otis, interview with Jane Mahaffey, October 1990.

25. Powell, interview.

26. General Andrew J. Goodpaster, interview with R. Manning Ancell, 28 October 1986.

27. *Army Times,* 16 October 1989, 15.

28. General Michael Dugan, interview with Jane Mahaffey, October 1990.

29. General Carl B. Vuono, interview with Jane Mahaffey, October 1990.

30. Vuono, interview.

31. R. M. Koster and Guillermo Sanchez, *In the Time of the Tyrants—Panama: 1968-1990* (New York: W. W. Norton and Company, 1990), 354.

32. Bell, letter.

33. General John W. Foss, interview with Jane Mahaffey, October 1990.

34. Stiner, interview.

35. Powell, interview.

36. Quoted in *Newsweek,* January 1990, 18.

37. Stiner, interview.

38. Stiner, interview.

39. Stiner, interview.

40. Foss, interview.

41. Vuono, interview.

42. General Michael S. Davison, letter to R. Manning Ancell, 3 May 1990.

43. Stiner, interview.

44. Stiner, interview.

45. Tom Donnelly, *Army Times,* 29 April 1991, 1.

46. Otis, interview.

47. Dugan, interview.

48. Quoted by Tom Donnelly in *Army Times,* 2 March 1992, 16.

49. Foss, interview.

50. General William B. Rosson, interview with R. Manning Ancell, 1 October 1991.

51. General Carl B. Vuono, *U.S. News and World Report,* October 1990, 30.

52. Powell, interview.

53. Alexander M. Haig, letter to R. Manning Ancell, 1 June 1990.

54. Foss, interview.

55. Vuono, interview.

56. Trefry, interview.

57. Foss, interview.

58. General John T. Chain, speech delivered at Tuskegee University, 16 February 1990.

59. General John M. Shalikashvili, letter to R. Manning Ancell, no date.

60. General William G. Tuttle Jr., letter to R. Manning Ancell, 22 July 1993.

61. Lieutenant General Neal T. Jaco, letter to R. Manning Ancell, 6 August 1993.

62. Admiral Lee Baggett Jr., letter to R. Manning Ancell, 1 December 1986.

Officership Case Study III: Transformation

This is the third case study in a set of five case studies on the evolution of the Army. This lesson draws a direct connection between the success of the Army and the doctrine and training philosophy. The lesson covers the critical role of the NCOs and describes the "Big Five" weapons program and how this has contributed to success in battle. Special emphasis is placed on the basic principles of General Starry's AirLand Battle doctrine.

The following topics are addressed in this lesson:

- The "Big Five" weapons program
- The critical role NCOs play in our Army
- The transformation of the Army

The following TLO is supported in whole or in part by this lesson:

- Integrate military history into education of officers

Following this lesson you will be able to:

- Describe the change in training doctrine that occurred with creation of the Combat Training Centers (CTCs)
- Explain the importance of the resurgence of the NCO corps during the period

THE BIG FIVE

BY Brigadier General ROBERT H. SCALES, JR.

While General Abrams committed the Army to producing world-class soldiers, he also sought to develop first-class material. Following Vietnam, the obstacles to achieving that commitment were seemingly insurmountable. The Soviets had exploited the Army's Vietnam diversion to close the gap in weapons technology. Popular opinion at the time did not appear to favor significant funding increases for new weaponry. Since the Army traditionally spent proportionately more than the other Services on people programs, not enough developmental money was available to buy every weapon the Army needed. The Army was fortunate to have Abrams at the helm. He was an officer who continued to maintain the trust and respect of Congress and the public through the Army's troubled times. He had a congenital distrust of Pentagon bureaucracy. Perhaps his obvious discomfort with Washington was one reason Congress listened to him so attentively. Abrams drew copiously from this wellspring of political credibility to rebuild the Army, but first he had to deal with the bureaucracy.

The Army material development community consisted of dozens of constituents, all of whom believed that their particular weapon or program deserved funding priority. Legions of young officer-analysts labored intently to produce tightly argued, amply documented justifications to prove the worth of their particular systems. However, even within each community, opinions varied. To Abrams, the Army seemed reluctant to make up its mind or to keep to an established course once it made material decisions and only he could discipline the process. He began by selecting five weapons the Army had to have: a new tank, an infantry fighting vehicle, two helicopters—an attack helicopter and a utility transport to replace the ubiquitous Huey of Vietnam fame—and an air defense missile. Other programs would be proposed and some would ultimately survive Congressional scrutiny, but having put his reputation on these Big Five, Abrams would tolerate no further dissention within the Army.

As the development of the Big Five weapons systems began during the period of constrained military budgets, Abrams' successors continued to fight to keep the programs alive. With the efforts in recruiting, training and doctrinal reforms, and new weapons systems all running concurrently, Army leaders continued to seek better ways to bring all of these improvements together.

BIRTH OF THE COMBAT TRAINING CENTERS

Studies of combat experience in World War II, Korea, and Vietnam revealed a disturbing propensity for units to suffer very high casualties in their first exposure to direct combat. The problem was particularly perplexing because the human cost in first battles did not seem to be lessened by the time spent in training prior to deployment. Some divisions like the 90th prepared for war in Europe for more than two years, yet suffered more than 100 percent casualties in the hedgerows of Normandy. A method was needed in peacetime, as DePuy had noted, to steepen the seasoning Curve without paying in blood. Curiously, the Navy showed the Army how to practice fighting for real. In early air-to-air combat over Vietnam, Navy pilots achieved a kill ratio against North Vietnamese MiGs of only two to one. A careful study showed a seasoning curve increase for pilots after combat as dramatic as Army studies had found for ground soldiers. Forty percent of all pilot losses occurred in their first three engagements. However, 90 percent of those who survived three engagements went on to complete a combat tour. In 1969 the Navy began a program that sought to provide a pilot his first three missions risk-free. *Top Gun* pitted novice airmen against a mock aggressor skilled in North Vietnamese aerial tactics. Combat was bloodless yet relatively unfettered. Uncompromising instructors recorded and played back every maneuver and action. The results were dramatic. From 1969 until the end of the air war, the Navy's kill ratio increased sixfold.

A similar method of battle seasoning was needed for Army training, and General DePuy handed the task to his TRADOC deputy chief of staff for training, Major General Paul Gorman. However, technological problems in creating a ground-based *Top Gun* were daunting. Aircraft came equipped with their own on-board radars and computers. Aircraft instruments could easily be linked to ground-based sensors to track and record every aerial track and maneuver for later playback and critique. But how do you keep track of thousands of soldiers shooting at each other among the folds and foliage of normal terrain? Gorman again got the answer from the Navy. In 1973, he discovered a young technician who was experimenting with a method for sailors to practice marksmanship indoors. The technician simply attached a laser to a pistol and fabricated a laser-sensitive target to record hits. Gorman expanded the "laser pistol" idea into what eventually became the Multiple Integrated Laser Engagement System (MILES) with devices that could be attached to all weapons from rifles to tank guns. MILES was a sophisticated version of the "laser pistol" concept that used coded signals to record kills and to discriminate among the types of weapons firing so that rifles "killed" only soldiers and not tanks. To replicate the Navy's successful program, planners had to devise an instrumentation system capable of tracking units, vehicles, and individuals and linking them all together through a master computer. The Core Instrumentation System (CIS) that evolved for the National Training Center utilized state-of-the-art technology with video cameras and multiple radio monitoring stations.

To exploit the promise of MILES and CIS, Gorman pursued an Army version of *Top Gun*, which was ultimately created at Fort Irwin, California. The exercise area was vast, and MILES permitted combat units to be pitted against each other in relatively free-play, force-on-force engagements. An observation center equipped with CIS near Fort Irwin kept track electronically of MILES kills, individual vehicle movement, and radio transmissions from the evaluated units. The center resembled a dimly lighted video arcade with monitors and television screens depicting real vehicles engaged in mock combat. Elaborate data-processing equipment provided instantaneous information on unit locations, troop concentrations, heavy weapons positions, the number of shots fired by caliber, and hits and misses. Remote-control cameras located on mountaintops provided total video coverage of the battle area. Observer-controllers accompanied every unit throughout the rotation, unobtrusively recording actions that were then combined with electronic data for the after-action reviews (AARs).

The resounding success of the National Training Center was the result not so much of its technology, but of the effect of its real-world, real-time, no-nonsense combat simulation on how the Army prepared for war. Each successive iteration or rotation of a unit through the NTC experience increased that unit's ability to survive and win in combat. The experience was grueling indeed and often, at first, very humbling. The opposing force, or OPFOR, regiment

that daily hammered the novice commander was finely practiced in Soviet tactics and offered no quarter. Four hours after each instrumented engagement, leaders of the evaluated unit faced the harsh realities of watching their performance played back during an AAR. The conduct of an AAR embodied, perhaps more than any other single event, the commitment of the Army to no-nonsense training. In silence, each commander watched on video as the observer-controller dispassionately explained, vehicle by dead vehicle, how the OPFOR took the unit apart. The observer-controllers did not intend the AAR to be cruel. Units that did not do well were not necessarily bad units; the more numerous and highly skilled OPFOR was tough to beat. The AAR simply brought home to every leader the realities of combat. Lieutenant General Frederick Brown, former deputy chief of staff for training at TRADOC, saw the AAR process as the "truly revolutionary characteristic of the NTC." There was no precedent for exposing a unit's chain of command to a no-holds-barred battle against an OPFOR where a leader's failure was evident in exquisite detail to his subordinates. "No army—including the Israeli army—has dared to do this," Brown said.[1] After leaving the briefing van, the commander knew whether his skill at drawing arrows on the map was equaled by his ability to infuse his soldiers with the confidence, leadership, and combat skills necessary to make his battle plan work in the harsh, unforgiving world of real combat. Almost a decade of continuous exposure to NTC and other derivative exercises at the Joint Readiness Training Center at Fort Chaffee in Arkansas and the Combat Maneuver Training Center at Hohenfels in Germany infused in field commanders an institutional obsession to train realistically for combat. With each successive rotation, the Army moved inexorably and bloodlessly a notch higher along the combat learning curve.

In 1984, *America's First Battles,* a volume produced under the auspices of the Army Command and General Staff College (CGSC), Fort Leavenworth, Kansas, appeared and caused an instant stir among senior leaders throughout the Army. The final chapter concluded what American soldiers had known intuitively for some time. The American Army performed poorly in the opening battles of all its wars not so much because of poorly prepared soldiers but because senior leaders—division and corps commanders—were not up to the task of commanding and controlling large units in the field. Lieutenant General Jerry Bartlett, then commander at the Combined Arms Center and CGSC, believed that this problem could be substantially solved by applying the learning curve to generals as well as privates. What the Army needed was an NTC-like experience for generals and their staffs. Divisions and corps were too large to be routinely placed in the field to conduct realistic force-on-force combat. Therefore, the Army created a computer-driven OPFOR to be manned by experienced controllers capable of electronic force-on-force interaction. To put as much of the fog of battle as possible into the Battle Command Training Program, or BCTP, the simulation was taken to units in the field so that the war game could be played using the tested division's headquarters staff and communications equipment. Whenever possible, Bartlett's controllers would exercise the division's existing war plans.

BCTP would provide the same realism, stress, and harsh, objective reality for generals and their staffs as NTC provided for colonels. The problem was the dreaded AAR. Holding colonels accountable for their errors in front of troops was difficult enough, but what about generals? The Army solved the dilemma by bringing in three retired four-star generals, each known and respected throughout the Army as experienced war fighters, to supervise the exercise. Initially, the Army in the field balked at such frank exposure. However, General Carl Vuono, then Chief of Staff, insisted that the BCTP continue.[2]

Unit-level training is the focus of the NTC, the ARTEP, and the BCTP. Units and their leaders perform mission-essential tasks that can be observed and evaluated against measurable standards under specific conditions. Within units, the leadership skills required by increasingly sophisticated weapons systems and training tools called for a simultaneous revamping of the Noncommissioned Officer Education system (NCOEs).

THE NONCOMMISSIONED OFFICER EDUCATION SYSTEM

In late November 1990, Command Sergeant Major of the Army Julius Gates accompanied General Vuono to the Soviet Union at the invitation of General Valetin Varennikov, the Soviet Ground Forces Commander-in-Chief and a hero of the battle of Vilnius in World War II. Near Kiev, Vuono, Gates, and another Soviet General, Boris Gromov, stood together as they watched two young Soviet officers lead a platoon of trainees through a demonstration of close-order drill. Soviet officers did not quite know what to make of Gates. A master paratrooper and a Ranger, Gates' many years with light infantry units had kept him trim and fit. Yet the sight of a sergeant purported to be a personal advisor and confidant to the highest-ranking officer in the Army seemed incongruous to them, to say the least. Gates was not terribly impressed with what he saw. As the soldiers wheeled about in intricate evolutions, Gates turned to Gromov, pointed to the officer drillmasters, and remarked dryly, "You know, in our army sergeants would be doing that—junior sergeants."

"Yes, I know," the Soviet replied through an interpreter. "That's what makes your army so good. We use officers because we don't have sergeants like you."

Soldiers have long recognized that sergeants are the backbone of an army, particularly the American Army, which has traditionally given noncommissioned officers a great deal of authority and responsibility. But 10 years of war in Vietnam damaged the NCO Corps physically, morally, and psychologically—more than any other segment of the institution. The strain imposed by back-to-back combat tours in Vietnam exacted a terrible toll on young NCOs. Tens of thousands died or were wounded, and many more left the Army frustrated and fatigued as soon as their hitch was up. Morale continued to plummet after the war. NCOs found themselves in an unfamiliar army where the message to new volunteer soldiers was not one of discipline and combat readiness but rather "the Army wants to join you." Pay compression made NCOs almost as poor as their privates. Those who remained stood by and watched anxiously as their authority steadily eroded in a progressively more permissive and ill-disciplined environment.

The near ruin of the NCO Corps during Vietnam caused the Army leadership to take a careful look at how the Army developed noncommissioned officers. Without a comprehensive schooling system, NCOs were expected, for the most part, to learn on the job. In 1969 General William Westmoreland, at the urging of his Vice Chief, General Ralph Haines, had instituted a system of NCO training and selection that in many respects paralleled the officer system. The concept called for four levels of training. The primary level was similar to the old NCO academies. Basic and advanced levels required board selection for attendance and included advanced skill development balanced with a strong dose of leadership and training evaluation. The fourth and highest level was the Sergeants Major Academy founded at Fort Bliss, Texas, in 1972. The Academy curriculum paralleled that of the Army War College, and selection became as highly prized among senior NCOs as the War College has traditionally been among officers. The NCOES added rigor to NCO career development. A Sergeant had to prove himself to his leaders in order to advance to each level, and at each level he learned the skills necessary to succeed at the next higher grade.

As the NCOES produced better sergeants, the trust of officers in their NCOs returned in full measure and then began to grow. With trust came increased responsibility and in turn confidence began to reappear among the "new breed" of well-trained and well-educated NCOs. As pay and quality of life for NCOs improved, so too did the quality of the NCOs themselves. Of the SMA's first graduating class in 1973, fewer than 8 percent had attended college. Of the soldiers who joined the Army that year and who rose through the ranks to attend the academy 18 years later, 88 percent had attended college; nearly half had earned degrees.[3] In addition to education, the NCO Corps maintained with equal strictness standards for job performance, personal conduct, physical fitness, and, most importantly, demonstrated leadership ability. By the time units deployed for Desert Shield, the transformation of the NCO Corps was virtually complete. Sergeants performed in the desert with unequaled initiative, professionalism, skill, and concern for soldier welfare. Brighter, better educated NCOs also required the best possible officer leaders.

AIRLAND BATTLE DOCTRINE

Most of the Army's senior leadership, with General Starry in the lead, had grown increasingly uncomfortable with the 1976 version of FM 100-5. In 1977, a year after taking command of V Corps, Starry stood on the Golan Heights looking east toward Damascus as Israeli General Rafael Eitan explained how, in the desperate hours of October 6, 1973, he watched as waves of Syrian tanks formed successive echelons as far as the eye could see.[4] Although force ratios clearly called for the Syrians to win, they lost because of

intangibles. To Starry, the battle of Kuneitra proved conclusively that the side that seized the initiative and demonstrated superior fighting skill and determination would prevail.

The Soviet invasion of Afghanistan in 1979 underscored to General Meyer that Europe might not be the only probable future battlefield. Meyer was particularly concerned that fixation on the active defense, whether intended or not, might affect the morale and fighting spirit of young officers. General Richard Cavazos had a heightened respect for unquantifiable aspects of warfare that FM 100-5 tended to ignore. Commander of Forces Command (FORSCOM) at the time, Cavazos spoke about the value of leadership, courage, endurance, and will as principal determinants of combat effectiveness: "What's important is how soldiers, not systems, fight."

The 1982 version of FM 100-5, for the first time, moved decisively away from force ratios to intangibles as predominant factors on the battlefield. It listed leadership as an element of combat equal to firepower and maneuver and went on to underscore the validity of training, motivation, and boldness—the ability to perceive opportunity, to think rapidly, to communicate clearly, and to act decisively. The success of AirLand Battle depended on four basic tenets: *initiative, depth, agility,* and *synchronization,* each demanding as much from the intellect of the commander as from the physical power of his force.

The 1982 manual also introduced AirLand Battle doctrine. General Glenn Otis, Starry's successor as TRADOC commander, recognized that the size and complexity of the air and land battlefield had outgrown the narrow tactical focus that DePuy had imposed on Army operations in FM 100-5. Otis chose, therefore, to introduce the operational level of war in the 1982 version as an intermediate level between tactics and strategy. By the time the Army developed the 1986 edition, AirLand Battle had become synonymous with the operational level of war.[5]

AirLand Battle doctrine sought to find a method for defeating second- and third-echelon forces. A defending force waiting passively for the enemy to appear would be swept aside by successive Soviet echelons. In order to have any chance of winning against such unfavorable odds, the defender would have to seize the initiative by attacking follow-on echelons before they appeared. The manual proposed two methods of attack. The first was to use distant fires and electronic warfare to slow, confuse, and damage as many early arriving forces as possible, executing distant strikes in a carefully conceived pattern. The object was to create gaps in the enemy's battle array that could then be exploited with the second means of attack: lightning-fast offensive maneuver using mechanized forces supported by tactical air power and attack helicopters. Fires became, therefore, not merely a means to attrit the enemy, but also a mechanism for setting the terms of battle. Fires would freeze the enemy and stun him long enough for maneuver forces to strike deep to destroy following echelons.

The imperative to strike deep forced the writers of FM 100-5 to observe the battlefield from a higher perspective. In the 1976 version, the view from the division commander's perch, essentially a tactical view, was high enough to observe the direct fire-fight at the point of collision between two opposing forces. But to see and strike echelons not yet committed demanded a higher-level perspective. In terms of time and space, three echelons attacking in column formation occupied ground to a depth of 150 kilometers and required about three days to close on the point of contact. In 1982 the maneuver commander had few weapons or means of observation capable of reaching that far. The Air Force, however, did have a deep capability, so the need to extend the battlefield and strike deep gave the corps commander an even greater interest in how air power was employed. Since World War II, the Air Force had considered aerial deep attack, or interdiction, to be an essential mission, but they had not, in the past, so closely linked the interdiction effort to the corps commander's maneuver scheme. However, the Air Force did accept the Army's contention that success on the ground depended on deep strikes to shape the battlefield. Beginning in 1979, the Tactical Air Command at Langley Air Force Base, Virginia, and TRADOC headquarters, just 20 minutes away, began to develop a joint doctrinal vision that included a system for Army fires to suppress enemy air defenses and air interdiction (AI) to attack the second echelon.

In 1984 General John Wickham and General Charles Gabriel, the Army and Air Force Chiefs of Staff, announced the acceptance of 31 initiatives specifically designed to enhance joint employment of AirLand Battle doctrine. The initiatives resulted from a year of discussions, war-gaming, and intellectual free-for-alls by members of a joint force development group. The group's charter, simply stated,

was "to create a means to design and field the best affordable AirLand combat force."[6] A focal point of their effort was to reach an agreed method for using air interdiction as an integral part of combat power. As a result, the group redefined air interdiction as an attack on targets beyond the corps commander's area of interest and established a new category, battlefield air interdiction (BAI). Initiative 21 stated in part that BAI was:

> *Air action against hostile surface targets nominated by the ground commander and in direct support of ground operations. It is the primary means of fighting the deep battle at extended ranges. BAI isolates enemy forces by preventing their reinforcement and supply and restricting their freedom of maneuver. It also destroys, delays, or disrupts follow-on enemy units before they can enter the close battle. . . .*[7]

Operational art and the increasing importance of joint operations demanded more from commanders and their staffs than ever before. As these demands increased, so would the need for educating officers more capable of understanding and applying the new concepts.

SCHOOL OF ADVANCED MILITARY STUDIES (SAMS)

General William Richardson was commandant at the Command and General Staff College during the period when the 1982 version of FM 100-5 was being written. He lamented the Army's system of officer education, which had not adequately provided the intellectual rigor necessary to grapple with the complexities of the operational level of war. The intellectual ferment surrounding the birth of the new doctrine rekindled interest throughout the Army in military history as the most practical laboratory for learning the art of War and applying intangibles to its execution. The result was a concept, first offered in 1981, to create an advanced second-year course for a small, select group of perhaps 50 first-year graduates of CGSC. They would study the art of war in an intensive program of reading military history, practicing computer war games, and writing extensively. Recitations in class would be scrupulously critiqued by their peers and a faculty selected for their own intellectual acumen and knowledge of military history.

Instituted in 1983, SAMS was so rigorous that it initially overwhelmed its students. Long hours of concentrated study and intense pressure to perform led some students to wonder if this "academic Ranger school" was really worth the effort. To avoid any appearance of elitism, graduates received no special favors other than a guaranteed position in division— or corps-level staffs. As its motto SAMS adopted the unofficial maxim of the German general staff, "Be more than you appear to be," and the director admonished graduates that they must be an elite with a humility that bears no trace of elitism.[8] The intention of the program to infuse a common body of thought—a common *cultural bias*—throughout the Army by means of its graduates worked beyond anyone's expectation.

By the time the Gulf War began, SAMS graduates had established a reputation as some of the best staff officers in the Army. They were present on all planning staffs and were heavily involved in the conception, development, and execution of the strategic and operational plans that would win the war so convincingly.

LIGHT FORCES RENAISSANCE

Despite the focus on armor and mechanized forces fighting on the Central European plain, which had been sharpened by the October 1973 Arab-Israeli War, the Army could not ignore light and Special Operations forces. General Abrams recognized the value of highly trained and disciplined light infantry when he instituted the formation of two Ranger battalions in 1974. He intended to create a core of light fighters that would set the standards for the rest of the Army. The 1-75th Infantry (Ranger) was formed at Fort Stewart, Georgia, and the 2-75th at Fort Lewis, Washington. Many Ranger-qualified soldiers actively sought assignment to these tough units that they knew to be bastions of discipline and pride.

As the seventies progressed and terrorism increased, the Rangers and other Special Operations forces received more attention. The Army described a spectrum of conflict that compared the likelihood of engagement in combat to the risk or magnitude of danger. The high risk of total war up to and including nuclear holocaust seemed less likely than terror-

ism and brush wars at the low-risk end. This model argued for balance at both ends.

The Ranger battalions did indeed set the standards throughout the Army for training, physical fitness, and discipline. Parallel to the resurrection of the Rangers, the Army's Special Forces also underwent a renaissance to throw off the lethargy of Vietnam. Expanded several times over during that conflict, the Special Forces had lost the professional edge that had made them such an elite force. Like other elements of the Army, the Green Berets returned to basics—in their case, teaching indigenous forces to fight unconventional wars. After Desert One, the role of Special Forces expanded considerably to include counterterrorism and difficult direct-action missions that required specialized equipment and training.

In 1980 General Meyer established the High-Technology Test Bed in the 9th Infantry Division at fort Lewis. Meyer's idea was to increase the mobility and firepower of the division while simultaneously making it smaller and lighter. Technology would cover the combat power gap created by smaller size and greater deployability. During its early years, the 9th Infantry Division under Major General Robert Elton, and later under Major General Robert RisCassi, tested emerging equipment in the midst of its development cycles, bought off-the-shelf items, and restructured itself to test Meyer's concept. Shortly after becoming Chief of Staff in 1983, General John Wickham carried Meyer's initiatives one step farther with the creation of light infantry divisions. Driven by the shortage of airlift, the high likelihood of conflict at the lower end of the risk spectrum, and the constrained end-strength of the Army, Wickham foresaw an ascending role for light divisions. These divisions would not replace the heavy force, but would increase responsiveness and provide a complementary force optimized to fight where heavy armor and mechanized units could not go.

NOTES

1. Paul F. Gorman, *The Secret of Future Victories* (Alexandria, VA: Institute for Defense Analyses, October 1991), p. 86.
2. *Ibid.*
3. On Kelly, 'The Crippling Squeeze on Pay in the Services," *U.S. News & World Report,* March 31, 1980, p. 49.

4. William Bowman, Roger Little, and G. Thomas Sicilia, *All-Volunteer Force After a Decade: Retrospect and Prospect* (Washington, DC: Pergamon-Brassey's, 1986), p. 270.

5. Senator J. James Exon as quoted in "Navy Chief Breaks with Carter, Urges Return to Military Draft," *Washington Post,* June 20, 1981, p. Al (UPI, September 4, 1981).

6. Interview with General (Retired) Maxwell Thurman, February 25, 1992.

7. Bowman and Little, pp. 266–286, and interview with General Thurman, March 7, 1992.

8. *Ibid.*

CERTAIN VICTORY: THE U.S. ARMY IN THE GULF WAR

BY ROBERT H. SCALES

ONE HUNDRED HOURS

On 24 February, when ground operations started in earnest, coalition forces were poised along a line that stretched from the Persian Gulf westward 300 miles into the desert. The XVIII Airborne Corps, under Lt. Gen. Gary E. Luck, held the left, or western, flank and consisted of the 82d Airborne Division, the 101st Airborne Division (Air Assault), the 24th Infantry Division (Mechanized), the French 6th Light Armored Division, the 3d Armored Cavalry, and the 12th and 18th Aviation Brigades. The VII Corps, under Lt. Gen. Frederick M. Franks, Jr., was deployed to the right of the XVIII Airborne Corps and consisted of the 1st Infantry Division (Mechanized), the 1st Cavalry Division (Armored), the 1st and 3d Armored Divisions, the British 1st Armored Division, the 2d Armored Cavalry, and the 11th Aviation Brigade. Between them these two corps covered about two-thirds of the line occupied by the huge multinational force.

Three commands held the eastern one-third of the front. Joint Forces Command North, made up of formations from Egypt, Syria, and Saudi Arabia and led by His Royal Highness Lt. Gen. Prince Khalid ibn Sultan, held the portion of the line east of VII Corps. To the right of these allied forces stood Lt. Gen. Walter E. Boomer's I Marine Expeditionary Force, which had the 1st (or Tiger) Brigade of the Army's 2d Armored Division as well as the 1st and 2d Marine Divisions. Joint Forces Command East on the extreme right, or eastern, flank anchored the line at the Persian Gulf. This organization consisted of units from all six member states of the Gulf Cooperation Council. Like Joint Forces Command North, it was under General Khalid's command.[1]

After thirty-eight days of continuous air attacks on targets in Iraq and Kuwait, President George H. Bush directed Central Command to proceed with the ground offensive. General Schwarzkopf unleashed all-out attacks against Iraqi forces very early on 24 February at three points along the allied line. In the far west the French 6th Light Armored and the 101st Airborne Divisions started the massive western envelopment with a ground assault to secure the allied left flank and an air assault to establish forward support bases deep in Iraqi territory. In the approximate cen-

ter of the allied line, along the Wādī al Bāṭin, Maj. Gen. John H. Tilelli, Jr.'s 1st Cavalry Division attacked north into a concentration of Iraqi divisions, whose commanders remained convinced that the coalition would use that and several other wadies as avenues of attack. In the east two Marine divisions, with the Army's Tiger Brigade, and coalition forces under Saudi command attacked north into Kuwait. Faced with major attacks from three widely separated points, the Iraqi command had to begin its ground defense of Kuwait and the homeland by dispersing its combat power and logistical capability.[2]

DAY ONE: 24 FEBRUARY 1991

The attack began from the XVIII Airborne Corps sector along the left flank. At 0100 Brig. Gen. Bernard Janvier sent scouts from his French 6th Light Armored Division into Iraq on the extreme western end of General Luck's line. Three hours later the French main body attacked in a light rain. Their objective was As Salmān, little more than a crossroads with an airfield about 90 miles inside Iraq. Reinforced by the 2d Brigade, 82d Airborne Division, the French crossed the border unopposed and raced north into the darkness.

But before they reached As Salmān, the French found some very surprised outposts of the Iraqi *45th Infantry Division.* General Janvier immediately sent his missile-armed Gazelle attack helicopters against the dug-in enemy tanks and bunkers. Late intelligence reports had assessed the 45th as only about 50-percent effective after weeks of intensive coalition air attacks and psychological operations, an assessment soon confirmed by feeble resistance. After a brief battle that cost them two dead and twenty-five wounded, the French held 2,500 prisoners and controlled the enemy division area, now renamed ROCHAMBEAU Janvier pushed his troops on to As Salman, which they took without opposition and designated Objective WHITE. The French consolidated WHITE and waited for an Iraqi counterattack that never came. The allied left flank was secure.[3]

Maj. Gen. James H. Johnson, Jr.'s 82d Airborne Division carried out a mission that belied its "airborne" designation. While the division's 2d Brigade moved with the French, its two remaining brigades, the 1st and 3d, trailed the advance and cleared a two-lane highway into southern Iraq—main supply route TEXAS—for the troops, equipment, and supplies supporting the advance north.

The XVIII Airborne Corps' main attack, led by Maj. Gen. J. H. Binford Peay III's 101st Airborne Division, was scheduled for 0500, but fog over the objective forced a delay. While the weather posed problems for aviation and ground units, it did not abate direct support fire missions. Corps artillery and rocket launchers poured fire on objectives and approach routes. At 0705 Peay received the word to attack. Screened by Apache and Cobra attack helicopters, 60 Black Hawk and 40 Chinook choppers of XVIII Airborne Corps' 18th Aviation Brigade began lifting the 1st Brigade into Iraq. The initial objective was the forward operating base COBRA, a point some 110 miles into Iraq. A total of 300 helicopters ferried the 101st's troops and equipment into the objective area in one of the largest helicopter-borne operations in military history.[4]

Wherever they went in those initial attacks, Peay's troops achieved tactical surprise over the scattered and disorganized foe. By midafternoon they had a fast-growing group of stunned prisoners in custody and were expanding COBRA into a major refueling point 20 miles across to support subsequent operations. Heavy Chinook helicopters lifted artillery pieces and other weapons into COBRA, as well as fueling equipment and building materials to create a major base. From the Saudi border, XVIII Corps support command units drove 700 high-speed support vehicles north with the fuel, ammunition, and supplies to support a drive to the Euphrates River.[5]

As soon as the 101st secured COBRA and refueled the choppers, it continued its jump north. By the evening of the twenty-fourth its units had cut Highway 8, about 170 miles into Iraq. Peay's troops had now closed the first of several roads connecting Iraqi forces in Kuwait with Baghdad.[6]

Spearhead units were advancing much faster than expected. To keep the momentum of the corps intact, General Luck gave subordinate commanders wider freedom of movement. He became their logistics manager, adding assets at key times and places to maintain the advance. But speed caused problems for combat support elements. Tanks that could move up to 50 miles per hour were moving outside the support fans of artillery batteries that could displace at only 25 to 30 miles per hour. Luck responded by leapfrogging his artillery battalions and supply elements, a solution which cut down on fire support, since only half the pieces could fire while the other

half raced forward. As long as Iraqi opposition remained weak, the risk was acceptable.[7]

In XVIII Corps' mission of envelopment, the 24th Infantry Division had the central role of blocking the Euphrates River valley to prevent the escape north of Iraqi forces in Kuwait and then attacking east in coordination with VII Corps to defeat the armor-heavy divisions of the *Republican Guard Forces Command*. Maj. Gen. Barry R. McCaffrey's division had come to the theater better prepared for combat in the desert than any other in Army Central Command. Designated a Rapid Deployment Force division a decade earlier, the 24th combined the usual mechanized infantry division components—an aviation brigade and three ground maneuver brigades, plus combat support units—with extensive desert training and desert-oriented medical and water purification equipment.

When the attack began, the 24th was as large as a World War I division, with 25,000 soldiers in thirty-four battalions. Its 241 Abrams tanks and 221 Bradley fighting vehicles provided the necessary armor punch to penetrate *Republican Guard* divisions. But with 94 helicopters, and over 6,500 wheeled and 1,300 other tracked vehicles—including 72 self-propelled artillery pieces and 9 multiple rocket launchers—the division had given away nothing in mobility and firepower.[8]

General McCaffrey began his division attack at 1500 with three subordinate units on line, the 197th Infantry Brigade on the left, the 1st Brigade in the center, and the 2d Brigade on the right. Six hours before the main attack the 2d Squadron, 4th Cavalry, had pushed across the border and scouted north along the two combat trails that the division would use, X-RAY on the left and YANKEE on the right. The reconnaissance turned up little evidence of the enemy, and the rapid progress of the division verified the scouts' reports. McCaffrey's brigades pushed about 50 miles into Iraq, virtually at will, and reached a position roughly adjacent to Objective WHITE in the French sector and a little short of forward operating base COBRA in the 101st's sector.

In their movement across the line of departure, and whenever not engaging enemy forces, battalions of the 24th Division generally moved in "battle box" formation. With a cavalry troop screening 5 to 10 miles to the front, four companies, or multi-platoon task forces, dispersed to form corner positions. Heavier units of the battalion—whether tanks or

Bradleys—occupied one or both of the front corners. One company, or smaller units, advanced outside the box to provide flank security. The battalion commander placed inside the box the vehicles carrying ammunition, fuel, and water needed to continue the advance in jumps of about 40 miles. The box covered a front of about 4 to 5 miles and extended about 15 to 20 miles front to rear.[9]

Following a screen of cavalry and a spearhead of the 1st and 4th Battalions, 64th Armor, McCaffrey's division continued north, maintaining a speed of 25 to 30 miles per hour. In the flat terrain the 24th kept on course with the aid of long-range electronic navigation, a satellite-reading triangulation system in use for years before DESERT STORM. Night did not stop the division, thanks to more recently developed navigation technology. Unit commanders and vehicle drivers used image-enhancement scopes and goggles, and searched for targets with infrared- and thermal-imaging systems sensitive to personnel and vehicle heat signatures. Small units used hand-held Trimpack and Magellan global positioning systems. Around midnight McCaffrey stopped his brigades on a line about 75 miles inside Iraq. Like the rest of XVIII Airborne Corps, the 24th Division had established positions deep inside Iraq against surprisingly light opposition.

Command and control, as well as protection against fratricide, were accomplished with the transmitting device Budd Light, named for its inventor, Henry C. "Budd" Croley of the Army Materiel Command. Consisting of infrared light-emitting diodes snapped onto the tops of commercial batteries, Budd Lights were placed on vehicle antennas in varying numbers to distinguish command or guide vehicles from others. Easily visible up to 1.2 miles through night vision goggles, the purplish glow of 10,000 Budd Lights enabled the 24th Division and other units to move safely at night. Other safety measures included marking all coalition vehicles with inverted V's, rather than the insignia of each participating country, in a reflective infrared paint.[10]

The VII Corps had the mission of finding, attacking, and destroying the heart of President Saddam Hussein's ground forces, the armor-heavy *Republican Guard* divisions. In preparation for that, Central Command had built up General Franks' organization until it resembled a mini-army more than a traditional corps. The "Jayhawk" corps of World War II fame had a 3d Infantry Division (Mechanized) brigade attached to the 1st Armored Division and four field artillery

brigades, the 42d, 75th, 142d, and 210th. To make deep attacks, to ferry infantry units into trouble spots, and to help armor crews kill tanks, the corps also had the 11th Aviation Brigade. Franks' command numbered more than 142,000 soldiers, compared with Luck's 116,000. To keep his troops moving and fighting, Franks used more than 48,500 vehicles and aircraft, including 1,587 tanks, 1,502 Bradleys and armored personnel carriers, 669 artillery pieces, and 223 attack helicopters. For every day of offensive operations, the corps needed 5.6 million gallons of fuel, 3.3 million gallons of water, and 6,075 tons of ammunition.[11]

The plan of advance for VII Corps paralleled that of Luck's corps to the west: a thrust north into Iraq, a massive turn to the right, and then an assault to the east into Kuwait. Because Franks' sector lay east of Luck's—in effect, closer to the hub of the envelopment wheel—VII Corps had to cover less distance than XVIII Airborne Corps. But intelligence reports and probing attacks into Iraqi territory in mid-February had shown that VII Corps faced a denser concentration of enemy units than did XVIII Corps farther west. Once the turn to the right was complete, both corps would coordinate their attacks east so as to trap *Republican Guard* divisions between them and then press the offensive along their wide path of advance until Iraq's elite units either surrendered or were destroyed.

General Schwarzkopf originally had planned the VII Corps attack for 25 February. But XVIII Corps advanced so fast against such weak opposition that he moved up his armor attack by fourteen hours. Within his own sector Franks planned a feint and envelopment much like the larger overall strategy. On VII Corps' right, along the Wādī al Bāṭin, the 1st Cavalry Division would make a strong, but limited, attack directly to its front. While Iraqi units reinforced against the 1st, Franks would send two divisions through berms and mines on the corps' right and two more divisions on an "end around" into Iraq on the corps' left.

On 24 February the 1st Cavalry Division crossed the line of departure and hit the Iraqi *27th Infantry Division*. That was not their first meeting. General Tilelli's division had actually been probing the Iraqi defenses for some time. As these limited thrusts continued in the area that became known as the Ruqī Pocket, Tilelli's men found and destroyed elements of five Iraqi divisions, evidence that the 1st succeeded in its theater reserve mission of drawing and holding enemy units.

The main VII Corps attack, coming from farther west, caught the defenders by surprise. At 0538 Franks sent Maj. Gen. Thomas G. Rhame's 1st Infantry Division forward. The division plowed through the berms and hit trenches full of enemy soldiers. Once astride the trench lines, it turned the plow blades of its tanks and combat earthmovers along the Iraqi defenses and, covered by fire from Bradley crews, began to fill them in. The 1st neutralized 10 miles of Iraqi lines this way, killing or capturing all of the defenders without losing one soldier, and proceeded to cut twenty-four safe lanes through the minefields in preparation for passage of the British 1st Armored Division. On the far left of the corps sector, and at the same time, the 2d Armored Cavalry swept around the Iraqi obstacles and led 1st and 3d Armored Divisions into enemy territory.[12]

The two armored units moved rapidly toward their objective, the town of Al Buṣayyah, site of a major logistical base about 80 miles into Iraq. The 1st Armored Division on the left along XVIII Corps' boundary and the 3d Armored Division on the right moved in compressed wedges 15 miles wide and 30 miles deep. Screened by cavalry squadrons, the divisions deployed tank brigades in huge triangles, with artillery battalions between flank brigades and support elements in nearly 1,000 vehicles trailing the artillery.

Badly mauled by air attacks before the ground operation and surprised by Franks' envelopment, Iraqi forces offered little resistance. The 1st Infantry Division destroyed two T-55 tanks and five armored personnel carriers in the first hour and began taking prisoners immediately. Farther west, the 1st and 3d Armored Divisions quickly overran several small infantry and armored outposts. Concerned that his two armored units were too dispersed from the 1st Infantry Division for mutual reinforcement, Franks halted the advance with both armored elements on the left only 20 miles into Iraq. For the day, VII Corps rounded up about 1,300 of the enemy.[13]

In the east Marine Central Command (MARCENT) began its attack at 0400. General Boomer's I Marine Expeditionary Force aimed directly at its ultimate objective, Kuwait City. The Army's Tiger Brigade, 2d Armored Division, and the 1st and 2d Marine Divisions did not have as far to go to reach their objective as did Army units to the west—Kuwait City lay between 35 and 50 miles to the northeast, depending on the border crossing point—but they faced more elaborate defense lines and a tighter concentration of the enemy. The 1st Marine Division led from a position in the vicinity of the elbow of the southern Kuwait border, and immediately began breaching berms and rows of antitank and antipersonnel mines and several lines of concertina wire. The unit did not have Abrams tanks, but its M60A3 tanks and TOW-equipped high mobility multipurpose wheeled vehicles, supported by heavy artillery, proved sufficient against Iraqi T-55 and T-62 tanks. After the marines destroyed two tanks in only a few minutes, 3,000 Iraqis surrendered.[14]

At 0530 the 2d Marine Division, with Col. John B. Sylvester's Tiger Brigade on its west flank, attacked in the western part of the Marine Central Command sector. The Army armored brigade, equipped with M1A1 Abrams tanks, gave the marines enough firepower to defeat any armored units the Iraqis put between Boomer's force and Kuwait City. The first opposition came from a berm line and two mine belts. Marine M60A1 tanks with bulldozer blades quickly breached the berm, but the mine belts required more time and sophisticated equipment. Marine engineers used mine clearing line charges and M60A1 tanks with forked mine plows to clear six lanes in the division center, between the Umm Qudayr and Al Wafrah oil fields. By 1615 the Tiger Brigade had passed the mine belts. As soon as other units passed through the safe lanes, the 2d Marine Division repositioned to continue the advance north, with regiments on the right and in the center and the Tiger Brigade on the left tying in with the allied forces.[15]

To maintain command and control and to measure progress beyond the mines, Boomer's staff had drawn a series of parallel east-west phase lines, most of which followed power lines or desert trails. Reaching daily objectives on the approach to Kuwait City, the 2d Marine Division would cross phase lines RED, HORSE, WOLF, BEAR, and OX. The last two phase lines were modern multilane highways leading to Kuwait City. Navigation between phase lines became easier after the Iraqis ignited oil fields, for these became reliable landmarks.[16]

Moving ahead a short distance to phase line RED near the end of the day, the 2d Marine Division captured intact the Iraqi *9th Tank Battalion* with thirty-five T-55 tanks and more than 5,000 men. Already on the first day of ground operations the number of captives had become a problem in the Marine sector. After a fight for Al Jaber airfield, during which the 1st Marine Division destroyed twenty-one tanks, another 3,000 prisoners were seized. By the end of the day the I Marine Expeditionary Force had worked its way about 20 miles into Kuwait and taken nearly 10,000 Iraqi prisoners.[17]

DAY TWO: 25 FEBRUARY 1991

On 25 February XVIII Airborne Corps units continued their drive into Iraq. The 82d Airborne Division began its first sustained movement of the war, although, to the disappointment of General Johnson and his troops, the division had to stay on the ground. The 82d followed the French 6th Light Armored Division along phase line SMASH. While the 82d entered As Salmān-Objective WHITE—the 101st Airborne Division sent its 3d Brigade out of COBRA on a jump north to occupy an observation and blocking position on the south bank of the Euphrates River, just west of the town of An Nāşīnyah.[18]

In the early morning darkness of the same day, General McCaffrey put his 24th Division in motion toward its first major objective. Following close air support and artillery fires, the division's 197th Brigade attacked at 0300 toward Objective BROWN in the western part of the division sector. Instead of determined opposition, the brigade found hungry prisoners, dazed by the heavy artillery preparation. By 0700 the 197th had cleared the area around BROWN and established blocking positions to the east and west along a trail, which was then being improved to serve as XVIII Corps main supply route VIRGINIA. Six hours later the division's 2d Brigade followed its own artillery fires and attacked Objective GREY on the right, encountering no enemy fire and taking 300 prisoners. After clearing the area, the brigade set blocking positions to the east.[19]

At 1450, with the 2d Brigade on GREY, the 1st Brigade moved northwest into the center of the division sector and then angled to the division right, attacking Objective RED directly north of GREY. Seven hours later the brigade had cleared the RED area, set blocking positions to the east and north, and processed 200 captives. To the surprise of all, the 24th Division had taken three major objectives and hundreds of men in only nineteen hours while meeting weak resistance from isolated pockets of Iraqi soldiers from the *26th* and *35th Infantry Divisions*. By

the end of the day XVIII Airborne Corps had advanced in all division sectors to take important objectives, establish a functioning forward operating base, place brigade size blocking forces in the Euphrates River valley, and capture thousands of prisoners of war—at a cost of two killed in action and two missing.[20]

In VII Corps General Franks faced two problems. The British 1st Armored Division, one of the units he had to have when he met the *Republican Guard* armored force, had begun passage of the mine breach cut by the 1st Infantry Division at 1200 on the twenty-fifth, and would not be completely through for several hours, possibly not until the next day. With the 1st and 3d Armored Divisions along the western edge of the corps sector, and the British not yet inside Iraq, the 1st Infantry and 1st Cavalry Divisions lay vulnerable to an armored counterattack.

A more troubling situation had developed along VII Corps' right flank. The commitment of some coalition contingents had concerned General Schwarzkopf months before the start of the ground war. Worried about postwar relations with Arab neighbors, some Arab members of the coalition had expressed reluctance to attack Iraq or even enter Kuwait. If enough of their forces sat out the ground phase of the war, the entire mission of liberating Kuwait might fail. To prevent such a disaster, Schwarzkopf had put the 1st Cavalry Division next to coalition units and gave the division the limited mission of conducting holding attacks and standing by to reinforce allies on the other side of the Wādī al Bāţin. If Joint Forces Command North performed well, the division would be moved from the corps boundary and given an attack mission. Action on the first day of the ground war bore out the wisdom of holding the unit ready to reinforce allies to the east. Syrian and Egyptian forces had not moved forward, and a huge gap had opened in the allied line. Central Command notified the 2d Armored Cavalry to prepare to assist the 1st Cavalry Division in taking over the advance east of the Wādī al Bāţin.[21]

But Franks could not freeze his advance indefinitely. The VII Corps had to press the attack where possible, and that meant on the left flank. Maj. Gen. Ronald H. Griffith's 1st Armored Division and Maj. Gen. Paul E. Funk's 3d Armored Division resumed their advance north shortly after daybreak. Griffith's troops made contact first, with outpost units of the Iraqi *26th Infantry Division,* and turned on the enemy the tactical sequence that brought success throughout the campaign. With the 1st Armored Division still about 35 to 40 miles away from its objective, close air support strikes began, followed by attack helicopter strikes. As the division closed to about 10 to 15 miles, artillery, rocket launchers, and tactical missile batteries delivered preparatory fires. As division lead elements came into visual range, psychological operations teams broadcast surrender appeals. If the Iraqis fired on the approaching Americans, the attackers repeated artillery, rocket, and missile strikes. In the experience of the 1st Armored Division, that sequence was enough to gain the surrender of most Iraqi Army units in a given objective. Only once did the Iraqis mount an attack after a broadcast, and in that instance a 1st Armored Division brigade destroyed forty to fifty tanks and armored personnel carriers in ten minutes at a range of 1.2 miles.[22]

By late morning of 25 February Joint Forces Command North had made enough progress to allow VII Corps and Marine Central Command on the flanks to resume their advance. That afternoon and night in the 1st Infantry Division sector, the Americans expanded their mine breach and captured two enemy brigade command posts and the *26th Infantry Division* command post, with a brigadier general and complete staff. Behind them, the British 1st Armored Division made good progress through the mine breach and prepared to turn right and attack the Iraqi *52d Armored Division.* [23]

Approaching Al Buṣayyah in early afternoon, the 1st Armored Division directed close air support and attack helicopter sorties on an Iraqi brigade position, destroying artillery pieces, several vehicles, and taking nearly 300 prisoners. That night the 2d Armored Cavalry and 3d Armored Division oriented east and encountered isolated enemy units under conditions of high winds and heavy rains.[24]

With the allied advance well under way all along the line, a U.S. Navy amphibious force made its final effort to convince the Iraqi command authority that Central Command would launch a major over-the-beach assault into Kuwait. Beginning late on 24 February and continuing over the following two days, the Navy landed the 7,500-man 5th Marine Expeditionary Brigade at Al Mish'āb, Saudi Arabia, about 28 miles south of the border with Kuwait. Once ashore, the 5th became the reserve for Joint Forces Command East. Later investigation showed that the presence of the amphibious force in Persian Gulf waters before the ground war had forced the Iraqi command to hold in Kuwait as many as four divisions to meet an amphibious assault that never materialized.[25]

At daybreak on 25 February Iraqi units made their first counterattack in the Marine sector, hitting the 2d Marine Division right and center. While Marine regiments fought off an effort that they named the "Reveille Counterattack," troops of the Tiger Brigade raced north on the left. In the morning the brigade cleared one bunker complex and destroyed seven artillery pieces and several armored personnel carriers. After a midday halt, the brigade cleared another bunker complex and captured the Iraqi *116th* brigade commander among a total of 1,100 prisoners of war for the day. In the center of the corps sector the marines overran an agricultural production facility, called the "Ice Cube Tray" because of its appearance to aerial observers.[26]

By the end of operations on 25 February General Schwarzkopf for the second straight day had reports of significant gains in all sectors. But enemy forces could still inflict damage, and in surprising ways and places. The Iraqis continued their puzzling policy of setting oil fires—well over 200 now blazed out of control—as well as their strategy of punishing Saudi Arabia and provoking Israel. They launched four Scuds, one of which slammed into a building housing American troops in Dhahran. That single missile killed 28 and wounded more than 100, causing the highest one-day casualty total for American forces in a war of surprisingly low losses to date.[27]

DAY THREE: 26 FEBRUARY 1991

On 26 February the XVIII Airborne Corps units turned their attack northeast and entered the Euphrates River valley. With the French and the 101st and 82d Airborne Divisions protecting the west and north flanks, the 24th Division spearheaded Luck's attack into the valley. The first obstacle was the weather. An out-of-season *shamal* in the objective area kicked up thick clouds of swirling dust that promised to give thermal-imaging equipment a rigorous field test through the day.

After refueling in the morning, all three brigades of the 24th moved out at 1400 toward the Iraqi airfields at Jalībah and Tallil. The 1st Brigade went north, then east about 40 miles to take a battle position in the northeast corner of the corps sector; the 2d Brigade moved 35 miles north to a position along the eastern corps boundary and then continued its advance another 25 miles until it was only 15 miles south of Jalībah; and the 197th Brigade went northeast about 60 miles to a position just south of Tallil. Meanwhile, the 3d Armored Cavalry screened to the east on the division's south flank.

In these attacks the 24th encountered the heaviest resistance of the war. The Iraqi *47th* and *49th Infantry Divisions,* the *Nebuchadnezzar Division* of the *Republican Guard,* and the *26th Commando Brigade* took heavy fire but stood and fought. The 1st Brigade took direct tank and artillery fire for four hours. For the first time in the advance the terrain gave the enemy a clear advantage. McCaffrey's troops found Iraqi artillery and automatic weapons dug into rocky escarpments reminiscent of the Japanese positions in coral outcroppings on Pacific islands that an earlier generation of 24th Infantry Division soldiers had faced. But Iraqi troops were not as tenacious in defense as the Japanese had been, and the 24th had much better weapons than its predecessors. American artillery crews located enemy batteries with their Firefinder radars and returned between three and six rounds for every round of incoming. With that advantage, American gunners destroyed six full Iraqi artillery battalions.[28]

In the dust storm and darkness American technological advantages became clearer still. Thermal-imaging systems in tanks, Bradleys, and attack helicopters worked so well that crews could spot and hit Iraqi tanks at up to 4,000 meters (2.5 miles) before the Iraqis even saw them. American tank crews were at first surprised at their one-sided success, then exulted in the curious result of their accurate fire: the "pop-top" phenomenon. Because Soviet-made tank turrets were held in place by gravity, a killing hit blew the turret completely off. As the battle wore on, the desert floor became littered with pop-tops. A combination of superior weaponry and technique—precise Abrams tank and Apache helicopter gunnery, 25-mm. automatic cannon fire from the Bradleys, overwhelming artillery and rocket direct support and counterbattery fire, and air superiority—took the 24th Division through enemy armor and artillery units in those "valley battles" and brought Iraqi troops out of their bunkers and vehicles in droves with hands raised in surrender. After a hard but victorious day and night of fighting, the 2d Brigade took its position by 2000 on the twenty-sixth. The other two brigades accomplished their missions by dawn.[29]

In VII Corps' sector on 26 February the 1st Armored Division fired heavy artillery and rocket preparatory fires into Al Buṣayyah shortly after dawn, and by noon had advanced through a sandstorm to overrun the small town. In the process, General Griffith's troops completed the destruction of the Iraqi *26th Infantry Division* and, once in the objective area, discovered they had taken the enemy *VII Corps* headquarters and a corps logistical base as well. More than 100 tons of munitions were captured and large numbers of tanks and other vehicles destroyed. The 1st Armored Division pressed on, turning northeast and hitting the *Tawakalna Division* of the *Republican Guard.* Late that night Griffith mounted a night assault on the elite enemy unit and, in fighting that continued the next day, killed 30 to 35 tanks and 10 to 15 other vehicles.[30]

In the 3d Armored Division sector Funk's men crossed the intercorps phase line SMASH just after daylight and attacked Objective COLLINS, east of Al Busayyah. Through the evening the division fought its toughest battles in defeating elements of the *Tawakalna Division.* With the capture of COLLINS and nearby enemy positions, VII Corps reached the wheeling point in its advance. From here, General Franks' divisions turned east and assaulted *Republican Guard* strongholds. Meanwhile, the 1st Infantry Division was ordered north from its position inside the mine belt breach. As the attack east began, VII Corps presented in the northern part of its sector a front of three divisions and one regiment: the 1st Armored Division on the left (north); the 3d Armored Division, the 2d Armored Cavalry, and the 1st Infantry Division on the right (south). Farther south, the British 1st Armored Division, with over 7,000 vehicles, cleared the mine breach at 0200 and deployed to advance on a separate axis into Objective WATERLOO, and on to the juncture of phase line SMASH and the corps boundary. From ARCENT headquarters came word that General Luck's corps would soon be even stronger. At 0930 the ARCENT commander, Lt. Gen. John J. Yeosock, released 1st Cavalry Division from its theater reserve role to VII Corps.[31]

In the early afternoon Col. Leonard D. Holder, Jr.'s 2d Armored Cavalry advanced east of COLLINS in a *shamal.* The regiment, screening in front of 1st Infantry Division, had just arrived from the mine belt along the Saudi border that it had breached the first day of the ground war. The cavalrymen had only a general idea of the enemy's position. The Iraqis had long expected the American attack to come from the south and east and were now frantically turning hundreds of tanks, towed artillery pieces, and other vehicles to meet the onslaught from the west. On the Iraqi side, unit locations were changing almost by the minute. As Holder's men neared phase line TANGERINE, 20 miles east of COLLINS, one of the cavalry troops received fire from a building on the 69 Easting, a north-south line on military maps. The cavalrymen returned fire and continued east. More enemy fire came in during the next two hours and was immediately returned. Just after 1600 the cavalrymen found T-72 tanks in prepared positions at 73 Easting. The regiment used its thermal imaging equipment to deadly advantage, killing every tank that appeared in its sights. But this was a different kind of battle than Americans had fought so far. The destruction of the first tanks did not signal the surrender of hundreds of Iraqi soldiers. The tanks kept coming and fighting.[32]

The reason for the unusually determined enemy fire and large number of tanks soon became clear. The cavalrymen had found two Iraqi divisions willing to put up a hard fight, the *12th Armored Division* and the *Tawakalna Division*. Holder's regiment found a seam between the two divisions, and for a time became the only American unit obviously outnumbered and outgunned during the ground campaign. But, as the 24th Division had found in its valley battles, thermal-imaging equipment cut through the dust storm to give gunners a long-range view of enemy vehicles and grant the fatal first-shot advantage. For four hours Holder's men killed tanks and armored personnel carriers while attack helicopters knocked out artillery batteries. When the battle of 73 Easting ended at 1715, the 2d Armored Cavalry had destroyed at least 29 tanks and 24 armored personnel carriers, as well as numerous other vehicles and bunkers, and taken 1,300 prisoners. That night, the 1st Infantry Division passed through Holder's cavalrymen and continued the attack east.[33]

Farther to the south, the British 1st Armored Division attacked eastward through the *48th Infantry* and *52d Armored Divisions* and remnants of other Iraqi units trying to withdraw north. This attack marked the start of nearly two days of continuous combat for the British, some of the toughest fighting of the war. In the largest of this series of running battles, the British destroyed 40 tanks and captured an Iraqi division commander.[34]

To the east, the Marine advance resumed on the twenty-sixth with the two Marine divisions diverging from their parallel course of the first two days. The 2d Marine Division and the Army's Tiger Brigade, 2d Armored Division, continued driving directly north, while the 1st Marine Division turned northeast toward Kuwait International Airport. The Army tankers headed toward Mutlā Ridge, an extended upfold only about 25 feet high. The location next to the juncture of two multilane highways in the town of Al Jahrah, a suburb of Kuwait City, rather than the elevation, had caught General Boomer's attention weeks earlier. By occupying the ridge the brigade could seal a major crossroads and slam the door on Iraqi columns escaping north to Baghdad.[35]

The brigade advanced at 1200 with the 3d Battalion, 67th Armor, in the lead. Approaching Mutlā Ridge, the Americans found a minefield and waited for the plows to cut a safety lane. On the move again, the brigade began to find enemy bunker complexes and dug-in armored units. Enemy tanks, almost all of the T-55 type, were destroyed wherever encountered, and most bunkers yielded still more prisoners. During a three-hour running battle in the early evening, Tiger tankers cleared the Mutlā police post and surrounding area. Moving up and over Mutlā Ridge, the 67th's tanks found and destroyed numerous antiaircraft artillery positions. Perimeter consolidation at the end of the day's advance was complicated and delayed by the need to process an even larger number of prisoners of war than the day before: 1,600.[36]

The Tiger Brigade now controlled the highest point for hundreds of miles in any direction. When the troops looked down on the highways from Mutlā Ridge, they saw the largest target an armored brigade had probably ever seen. The previous night Air Force and Navy aircraft had begun destroying all vehicles spotted fleeing from Kuwait. Now the brigade added its firepower to the continuous air strikes. On the "Highway of Death" hundreds of burning and exploding vehicles of all types, including civilian automobiles, were visible. Hundreds more raced west out of Kuwait City unknowingly to join the deadly traffic jam. Here and there knots of drivers, Iraqi soldiers, and refugees fled into the desert because of the inferno of bombs, rockets, and tank fire. These lucky ones managed to escape and join the ranks of the growing army of prisoners.[37]

At the close of allied operations on 26 February a total of twenty-four Iraqi divisions had been defeated. In all sectors the volume of prisoners continued to grow and clog roads and logistical areas. Iraqi soldiers surrendered faster than Central Command could count them, but military police units estimated that the total now exceeded 30,000.[38]

The day ended with at least one other major logistical problem. The 24th Division had moved so fast in two days that fuel trucks had difficulty keeping up. After taking positions on the night of the twenty-sixth, the lead tanks had less than 100 gallons of fuel on board. Brigade commanders had the fuel, but lead elements were not sure where to rendezvous in the desert. The problem was solved by the kind of unplanned actions on which victories often turn. A small number of junior officers took the initiative to lead tank truck convoys across the desert at night with only a vague idea of where either brigade fuel supplies or needy assault units were located. By approaching whatever vehicles came into view and asking for unit identity, those leaders managed to refuel division vehicles by midnight.[39]

DAY FOUR: 27 FEBRUARY 1991

On the morning of 27 February XVIII Airborne Corps prepared to continue its advance east toward Al Baṣrah. But before the assault could be resumed, the 24th Division had to secure its positions in the Euphrates River valley by taking the two airfields toward which it had been moving. Tallil airfield lay about 20 miles south of the town of An Nāṣirīyah; Jalībah airfield lay 40 miles east southeast, near the lake at Hawr al Malih. The task of taking the airfields went to the units that had ended the previous day in positions closest to them. While the 1st Brigade would conduct a fixing attack toward the Jalībah airfield, the 2d Brigade planned to move east about 25 miles and turn north against the same objective. Moving north, the 197th Brigade would take Tallil.

Following a four-hour rest, the 2d Brigade attacked at midnight, seized a position just south of Jalībah by 0200 on the twenty-seventh, and stayed there while preparatory fires continued to fall on the airfield. At 0600 the 1st Brigade moved east toward the airfield, stopped short, and continued firing on Iraqi positions. At the same time, the 2d Brigade resumed the attack with three infantry-armor task forces and crashed through a fence around the runways. Although the airfield had been hit by air strikes for six weeks and a heavy artillery preparation

by five battalions of XVIII Corps' 212th Field Artillery Brigade, Iraqi defenders were still willing to fight. Most Iraqi fire was ineffectual small arms, but armor piercing rounds hit two Bradleys, killing two men of the 1st Battalion, 64th Armor, and wounding several others in the 3d Battalion, 15th Infantry. As nearly 200 American armored vehicles moved across the airfield knocking out tanks, artillery pieces, and even aircraft, Iraqis began to surrender in large numbers. By 1000 the Jalībah airfield was secure.[40]

At midday heavy artillery and rocket launcher preparations, followed by twenty-eight close air sorties, were directed on the Tallil airfield. As the fires lifted, the 197th Brigade advanced across the cratered runways and through weaker resistance than that at Jalībah. But like the 2d Brigade at Jalībah, the 197th killed both armored vehicles and aircraft on the ground and found large numbers of willing prisoners.[41]

As the 197th Brigade assaulted Tallil, General McCaffrey realigned his other units to continue the attack east centering on Highway 8. The 1st Brigade took the division left (north) sector, tying in with the 101st Airborne Division. The 2d Squadron, 4th Cavalry, the 24th's reconnaissance unit, moved east from the Hawr al Mālih lake area to set up a tactical assembly area behind the 1st Brigade. The 2d Brigade left its newly won airfield position and assumed the center sector of the division front. The 3d Armored Cavalry took the right sector, tying in with VII Corps to the south. With the 24th Division now oriented east after its northern advance of the first two days, a new series of phase lines was drawn between the Tallil airfield and the Ar Rumaylah oil fields, just southwest of Al Basrah. From the line of departure east of the Jahbah airfield, McCaffrey's units would advance across phase lines AXE, KNIFE, VICTORY, and CRUSH.[42]

The run down the highway showed more clearly than any other episode the weaknesses of Iraqi field forces and the one-sidedness of the conflict. Through the afternoon and night of 27 February the tankers, Bradley gunners, and helicopter crews and artillery—men of the 1st and 4th Battalions, 64th Armor, fired at hundreds of vehicles trying to redeploy to meet the new American attack from the west, or simply to escape north across the Euphrates River valley and west on Highway 8. With no intelligence capability left to judge the size or location of the oncoming American armored wedges and attack helicopter swarms, as well as insufficient communications to coordinate a new defense, Iraqi units stumbled into disaster. Unsuspecting drivers of every type of vehicle, from tanks to artillery prime movers and even commandeered civilian autos, raced randomly across the desert or west on Highway 8 only to run into General McCaffrey's firestorm. Some drivers, seeing vehicles explode and burn, veered off the road in vain attempts to escape. Others stopped, dismounted, and walked toward the Americans with raised hands. When the division staff detected elements of the *Hammurabi Division* of the *Republican Guard* moving across the 24th's front, McCaffrey concentrated the fire of nine artillery battalions and an Apache battalion on the once elite enemy force. At dawn the next day, the twenty-eighth, hundreds of vehicles lay crumpled and smoking on Highway 8 and at scattered points across the desert. The 24th's lead elements, only 30 miles west of Al Baṣrah, set up a hasty defense along phase line VICTORY.[43]

The 24th Division's valley battles of 25-27 February rendered ineffective all Iraqi units encountered in the division sector and trapped most of the *Republican Guard* divisions to the south while VII Corps bore into them from the west, either blasting units in place or taking their surrender. In its own battles the 24th achieved some of the most impressive results of the ground war. McCaffrey's troops had advanced 190 miles into Iraq to the Euphrates River, then turned east and advanced another 70 miles, all in four days. Along the way they knocked out over 360 tanks and armored personnel carriers, over 300 artillery pieces, over 1,200 trucks, 500 pieces of engineer equipment, 19 missiles, and 25 aircraft, and rounded up over 5,000 enemy soldiers. Just as surprising as these large enemy losses were the small numbers of American casualties: 8 killed in action, 36 wounded in action, and 5 nonbattle injuries. And in the entire XVIII Airborne Corps, combat equipment losses were negligible: only 4 M1A1 tanks, 3 of which were repairable.[44]

In VII Corps' sector the advance rolled east. The battles begun the previous afternoon continued through the morning of 27 February as General Franks' divisions bore into *Republican Guard* units trying to reposition or escape. As the assault gained momentum, Franks for the first time deployed his full combat power. The 1st Cavalry Division made good progress through the 1st Infantry Division breach and up the left side of VII Corps' sector. By midafternoon,

after a high-speed 190-mile move north, General Tilelli's brigades were behind 1st Armored Division, tying in with the 24th Division across the corps boundary. Now Franks could send against the *Republican Guard* five full divisions and a separate regiment. From left (north) to right, VII Corps deployed the 1st Armored Division, 1st Cavalry Division, the 3d Armored Division, the 1st Infantry Division, the 2d Armored Cavalry, and the British 1st Armored Division.[45]

The dust storms had cleared early in the day, revealing in VII Corps' sector the most awesome array of armored and mechanized power fielded since World War II. In a panorama extending beyond visual limits 1,500 tanks, another 1,500 Bradleys and armored personnel carriers, 650 artillery pieces, and supply columns of hundreds of vehicles stretching into the dusty brown distance rolled east through Iraqi positions, as inexorable as a lava flow. To Iraqi units, depleted and demoralized by forty-one days of continuous air assault, VII Corps' advance appeared irresistible.

Turning on the enemy the full range of its weapons, VII Corps systematically destroyed Iraqi military power in its sector. About 50 miles east of Al Buṣayyah, the 1st and 3d Armored Divisions tore into remnants of the *Tawalzalaa, Madina,* and *Adnan Divisions* of the *Republican Guard.* In one of several large engagements along the advance the 2d Brigade, 1st Armored Division, received artillery fire and then proceeded to destroy not only those artillery batteries but also 61 tanks and 34 armored personnel carriers of the *Madina Division* in less than one hour. The 1st Infantry Division overran the *12th Armored Division* and scattered the *10th Armored Division* into retreat. On the south flank the British 1st Armored Division destroyed the *52d Armored Division,* then overran three infantry divisions. To finish destruction of the *Republican Guard Forces Command,* General Franks conducted a giant envelopment involving the 1st Cavalry Division on the left and the 1st Infantry Division on the right. The trap closed on disorganized bands of Iraqis streaming north in full retreat. The only setback for VII Corps during this climactic assault occurred in the British sector. American Air Force A-10 Thunderbolt aircraft supporting the British advance mistakenly fired on 2 infantry fighting vehicles, killing 9 British soldiers.[46]

At 1700 Franks informed his divisions of an imminent theater-wide cease-fire but pressed VII Corps' attack farther east. An hour later the 1st Squadron, 4th Cavalry, 1st Infantry Division, set a blocking position on the north-south highway connecting Al Baṣrah to Kuwait City. The next morning corps artillery units fired an enormous preparation involving all long-range weapons: 155-mm. and 8-inch (203-mm.) self-propelled pieces, rocket launchers, and tactical missiles. Attack helicopters followed to strike suspected enemy positions. The advance east continued a short time until the cease-fire went into effect at 0800, 28 February, with American armored divisions just inside Kuwait.[47]

In ninety hours of continuous movement and combat, VII Corps had achieved impressive results against the best units of the Iraqi military. Franks' troops destroyed more than a dozen Iraqi divisions, an estimated 1,300 tanks, 1,200 infantry fighting vehicles and armored personnel carriers, 285 artillery pieces, and 100 air defense systems, and captured nearly 22,000 men. At the same time, the best Iraqi divisions destroyed only 7 M1A1 Abrams tanks, 15 Bradleys, 2 armored personnel carriers, and 1 Apache helicopter. And while killing unknown thousands of enemy troops, VII Corps lost 22 soldiers killed in action.[48]

In the Marine Central Command's sector on 27 February the Tiger Brigade, 2d Armored Division, and the 2d Marine Division began the fourth day of the ground war by holding positions and maintaining close liaison with Joint Forces Command North units on the left flank. The next phase of operations in Kuwait would see Saudi-commanded units pass through General Boomer's sector from west to east and go on to liberate Kuwait City. At 0550 Tiger troops made contact with Egyptian units, and four hours later Joint Forces Command North columns passed through 2d Marine Division. During the rest of the day Tiger troops cleared bunker complexes, the Ali Al Salem Airfield, and the Kuwaiti Royal Summer Palace, while processing a continuous stream of prisoners of war. The Army brigade and the 2d Marine Division remained on Mutlā Ridge and phase line BEAR until the ceasefire went into effect at 0800 on 28 February. Prisoner interrogation during and after combat operations revealed that the Tiger Brigade advance had split the seam between the Iraqi *III* and *IV Corps,* overrunning elements of the *14th, 7th,* and *36th Infantry Divisions,* as well as brigades of the *3d Armored, 1st Mechanized,* and *2d Infantry Divisions.* During four days of combat Tiger Brigade task forces destroyed or captured 181 tanks, 148 armored personnel carriers, 40 artillery pieces, and 27 antiaircraft systems while killing an estimated 263 enemy and capturing 4,051 prisoners of war, all at a cost of 2 killed and 5 wounded. [49]

CEASE-FIRE

When the cease-fire ordered by President Bush went into effect, ARCENT divisions faced the beaten remnants of a once-formidable force. The U.S. Army had contributed the bulk of the ground combat power that defeated and very nearly destroyed the Iraqi ground forces. The Iraqis lost 3,847 of their 4,280 tanks, over half of their 2,880 armored personnel carriers, and nearly all of their 3,100 artillery pieces. Only five to seven of their forty-three combat divisions remained capable of offensive operations. In the days after the cease-fire the busiest soldiers were those engaged in the monumental task of counting and caring for an estimated 60,000 prisoners. And these surprising results came at the cost of 148 Americans killed in action. In the theater of operations Army Central Command had won the fastest and most complete victory in American military history.[50]

Of the many successful aspects of Army operations in Operation DESERT STORM, three stand out. First, Army units moved so fast that they found their enemy consistently out of position and oriented in the wrong direction. In 100 hours of combat XVIII Airborne Corps moved its lead elements 190 miles north into Iraq and then 70 miles east. Even the armor-heavy VII Corps drove 100 miles into Iraq and then 55 miles east. Iraqi units showed themselves unable to reposition even short distances before Army units were upon them.

Second, American forces enjoyed substantial technological advantages, most notably in night vision and electro-optics. Two types of vision-enhancing technology had been incorporated into Army operations preceding the deployment to the Persian Gulf. One of these aids to vision represented advanced development of a device first field tested during the Vietnam War, the image intensification system known as Starlight. Gathering and concentrating the faint light of the moon and stars, Starlight offered a view of terrain out to about 100 yards in shades similar to a photographic negative. It did not depend on a transmitted beam that an adversary could detect. Still, it had drawbacks, among them the system's need for a clear night as well as expense, weight, and size. So the early Starlight scopes had been distributed only to specialized units, such as long-range patrol and sniper teams.

By 1991 image intensification systems had been refined to the point that small lightweight units could be used by individual soldiers, in the forms of night vision goggles and weapon sights. Among an entire family of night vision and electro-optical devices, three particular types showed the wide battlefield applicability of the technology. The AN/PVS-4 individual-served weapon sight could be used with the M16 rifle, the M60 machine gun, the M72 rocket launcher, and the M203 grenade launcher. Detached from these weapons, the sight offered commanders the ability to carry out night surveillance. The AN/PVS-7 night vision goggle was a head-mounted monocular unit for ground vehicle operation, map reading, navigation, maintenance, and first aid. The AN/AVS-6 aviation night vision imaging system was a binocular system that allowed helicopter pilots to conduct nocturnal missions as close to the ground as possible.[51]

Another category of vision enhancement technology—thermal imaging—avoided the need of image intensification systems for clear night skies and retained the advantage of passivity. By reading the heat signatures of vehicle engines and human bodies at distances beyond 2 miles, thermal-imaging systems penetrated visual barriers created by nighttime, dust storms, and rain or snow. These systems proved particularly useful on M1A1 tanks, Bradleys, TOW missile launchers, and Apache helicopters. When combined with laser range-finding systems on armored vehicles, thermal imaging gave crews the ability to fire on targets—the troops called them "hot spots"—before the enemy even knew they were there.[52]

Soldiers at all levels enthusiastically praised all of the imagery devices. American troops were able to carry out night or day combat operations with virtually the same efficiency. This equipment vastly surpassed the obsolescent Soviet equipment used by the Iraqis and overturned the age-old assumption that the force fighting on its own territory had an inherent advantage. By seeing the heat signatures of Iraqi tanks and other vehicles on their thermal-imaging scopes before their own appeared on Iraqi scopes, Americans could engage targets in heavy rain, dust storms, and darkness. So, throughout the ground war

the Iraqis, on their own familiar territory, were continually subjected to accurate fire in conditions, at distances, and from directions they did not expect.[53]

Other products of advanced technology contributed significantly to success. Two location and navigation devices, named Trimpack and Magellan by their manufacturers, minimized disorientation on the ground, a perennially serious problem that was magnified by the featureless desert environs of Southwest Asia. Trimpack (officially called the small lightweight global positioning system receiver) was dubbed "Slugger" by the troops. Both devices weighed about six pounds and were small enough to fit in a pack. They had solid-state electronics that read transmissions from orbiting satellites and gave their users precise coordinate locations. Both also determined firing data for artillery units, corrected azimuth bearings to objectives, and measured angles of descent for aircraft heading for landing zones or targets. Magellan and Trimpack rendered the age-old problems of map or terrain-reading errors obsolete.

Among weapons, the AH-64A Apache attack helicopter, armed with HELLFIRE missiles, belied its reputation as an overly complex, breakdown-prone system. The Apache proved a highly effective tank killer. The multiple launch rocket system and Army tactical missile system demonstrated great effect against entrenched enemy and in counterbattery missions in their own right. When combined with the Firefinder device to locate the source of enemy fire, the rocket and missile systems suppressed Iraqi artillery fire quickly and permanently. Because of the Firefinder advantage, enemy batteries were rarely heard from in XVIII Airborne Corps' sector after the first two days of the conflict, a great relief to Army commanders concerned about one of the few advantages of the Iraqis—the greater range of their newer artillery. The older mainstays of Army artillery, 155-mm. and 8-inch (203-mm.) pieces, underlined their well-founded reputations as accurate and dependable direct support systems.[54]

Just as impressive as the high-technology Army inventory at the beginning of the crisis in late 1990 was the ability of American defense agencies to answer demands from Central Command for new products. A dramatic example of this response capability came in the days before the ground war. The successful allied counterattack on the city of R'as al Khafji in the first week of February was marred when American support fire killed several CENTCOM troops. General Schwarzkopf ordered accelerated research on antifratricide methods. A joint research team, coordinated by the Defense Advanced Research Projects Agency, immediately went to work on the problem of making American vehicles and positions visible only to American armored vehicles and aircraft. Just nineteen days later Central Command distributed the results of the agency's work: On the Army side of the research effort the Center for Night Vision and Electro-Optics at Fort Belvoir, Virginia, came up with the Budd Light and over twenty other solutions to the problem, some of which were fielded before the end of the war.[55]

Third, American soldiers outperformed their Iraqi enemies. Particularly gratifying to higher-echelon commanders was the conduct of personnel in the all-important middle-level action positions: junior officers and noncommissioned officers. Those were the lieutenants and sergeants who took the initiative to lead convoys across dangerous desert expanses at night to resupply the advance; found and engaged thousands of enemy tanks and positions in the confusion of heavy rains and blinding dust storms; and, when called for, treated a defeated enemy with dignity and care. As General McCaffrey observed of his junior officers and noncommissioned officers during the 24th Division's dash to the Euphrates River valley, "They could have done it without us."[56]

The impressive overall performance notwithstanding, problems requiring postwar attention did occur. Several types of equipment drew criticism from commanders. American field radios proved unreliable, and commanders who had the opportunity to try British-made Iraqi radios pronounced them superior. Fortunately, the initiative of key commissioned and enlisted personnel at the battalion and company levels bridged communications gaps at crucial times. In a curious split decision on a weapon, the M109 155-mm. field artillery piece won praise for fire effect on targets, but its self-propelling component proved underpowered to keep pace with mechanized and armored assaults. One piece of combat engineer equipment earned similar criticism. The M9 armored combat earthmover cut through berms easily but could not keep up with assaults over open terrain.

Despite its brevity, the 100-hour Persian Gulf war lasted long enough to provoke an update of the age-old postwar lament, criticism of the supply effort.

This time, the speed of the advance exposed a shortcoming: helicopters, tanks, and Bradleys outdistanced supply trucks. Lifting fuel tanks and ammunition pallets by helicopter provided a quick fix, but choppers carrying fuel gulped it almost as fast as they delivered it. If the ground war had lasted longer, General Schwarzkopf would have had to halt the advance to fill forward operating bases. On the morning of 27 February, as VII Corps prepared to complete the destruction of the *Republican Guard Forces Command,* 1st and 3d Armored Division tanks were almost out of fuel.[57]

After isolating and evaluating various aspects of Army operations and systems, questions remained about the overall course of the war and its outcome. Was the Army really as good as the overwhelming victory and one-sided statistics of the war suggested? Was Iraq's military really that weak? Complete answers awaited more careful analysis of the combatants, but in the immediate aftermath of the ground campaign two conclusions seemed justified.

First, Iraq's military was not prepared for a war of rapid movement over great distances. The Iraqis, in their most recent combat experience against Iran, had developed skills at slow-paced, defense-oriented warfare. Those skills proved inadequate to stop an army with high-speed armor capabilities.

Second, Central Command used its air arm to devastating advantage. With air supremacy established more than a month before the ground war began, the success of General Schwarzkopf's well-conceived and dreadfully misnamed "Hail Mary" play—the huge corps-size envelopment to the west—was assured. The relentless day and night pounding of aerial bombardment made easier the task of coalition units not in the envelopment, for when they attacked straight ahead into Iraqi positions, they found enemy units less than 50-percent effective. The combination of a powerful air offensive, followed by a fast moving armor-reinforced ground campaign, proved extremely effective in the desert environs of Southwest Asia.

NOTES

[1] Unless otherwise noted, material in this chapter is based on U.S. Department of Defense, *Conduct of the Persian Gulf War, An Interim Report to Congress* (Washington, D.C.: Government Printing Office,

1991), p. 4-6, Third U.S. Army, After Action Review, 12 Mar 91, Draft MS, Swain, Operational Narrative, and Robert H. Scales, Jr., *Certain Victory: The United States Army in the Gulf War* (Washington, D.C.: Office of the Chief of Staff, United States Army, 1993).

[2] *Army Focus,* Jun 91, p. 22.

[3] XVIII Airborne Corps Sitrep, 24 Feb 91\; Peter David, *Triumph in the Desert* (New York: Random House, 1991), p. 78; Interv (telephone), Charles R. Anderson with Maj. Robert K. Wright, command historian, XVIII Airborne Corps, May 91.

[4] *Army Times*, 11 Mar 91, p. 15; Wright interview.

[5] Ibid.

[6] Wright interview.

[7] Ibid.

[8] Desert Shield and Desert Storm Operations Overview, 9 May 1991, prepared for United States Senate Armed Services Committee, Document no. 77 in HQ, 24th Infantry Division (Mech.), *Historical Reference Book* (Fort Stewart, Ga., 1992), copy in CMH.

[9] Interv, Maj. William H. Thomas III with Lt. Col. Edwin W. Chamberlain III, commander, 1/18th Infantry, 197th Infantry Brigade, 24th Infantry Division (Mech.), 16 May 91.

[10] Interv, Charles R. Anderson with Walter B. Morrow, Center for Night Vision and Electro-Optics, U.S. Army Communications-Electronics Command, Fort Belvoir, Va., 2 Jul 92.

[11] MS, Doughty, War in the Persian Gulf, p. 15; Draft MS, Carver, Narrative of VII Corps in Operation DESERT STORM, pp. 3-4.

[12] *Army Focus,* Jun 91, p. 22; *Washington Post*, 12 and 13 Sep 91; 1st Infantry Division (Mech.), Operations DESERT SHIELD and DESERT STORM Command Rpt, 19 Apr 91, p. 4; VII Corps Commander's Sitrep (Combat) 38, 24 Feb 91.

[13] VII Corps Sitrep, 24 Feb 91; MS, Maj. Guy C. Swan, 1st Armored Division in Combat, 21-28 February 1991, p. 1; Draft MS, Carver, Narrative of VII Corps in Operation DESERT STORM, p. 4.

[14] *Army Times*, 11 Mar 91, pp. 14-15, Lt. Gen. Walter E. Boomer, Command Brief: Persian Gulf Campaign; U.S. Marine Corps Operations, n.d.; Intervs, Charles R. Anderson with Lt. Col. Ronald J. Brown, U.S. Marine Corps Reserve (USMCR) and Maj. Charles D. Melson (USMC, U.S. Marine Corps History and Museums Division, 2 Jul 91, Washington, D.C.

[15] 1st Brigade, 2d Armored Division, Commander's Summary, n.d.

[16] Brown interview.

[17] Boomer, Command Brief: Persian Gulf Campaign; U.S. Marine Corps Operations, n.d., Army Times, 11 Mar 91, p. 15.

[18] Third U.S. Army, After Action Review, 12 Mar 91.

[19] Maj. Gen. Barry R. McCaffrey, 24th Infantry Division (Mech.): Operation DESERT STORM Post-Attack Summary, 18 Mar 91.

[20] Ibid.; Interv, Maj. William H. Thomas III with Col. John Lemoyne, commander, 1st Brigade, 24th Infantry Division (Mech.), 7 Mar 91; XVIII Airborne Corps Sitrep, 25 Feb 91.

[21] VII Corps, Desert Sabre Operations Summary.

[22] Ltr, Mal Paul J. Jacobsmeyer to Col. K. Hamburger, Department of History, USMA, 7 Mar 91.

[23] VII Corps, Desert Sabre Operations Summary; VII Corps Commander's Sitrep (Combat) 39, 25 Feb 91.

[24] MS, Swan, 1st Armored Division in Combat, 21-28 February 1991, p. 1; Ltr, Capt. Kevin McKedy to "Dear Mil [*sic*] Artists," 9 Mar 91.

[25] *Army Times*, 11 Mar 91, p. 14.

[26] Brown interview; 1st Brigade, 2d Armored Division, Commander's Summary, n.d.

[27] ODCSINT Intelligence Summaries 404, 25 Feb 91, and 406, 26 Feb 91.

[28] McCaffrey, 24th Infantry Division (Mech.): Operation DESERT STORM Post-Attack Summary, 18 Mar 91, Lemoyne interview.

[29] Ibid.; Wright interview.

[30] VII Corps Sitrep, 27 Feb 91; VII Corps Commander's Sitrep (Combat) 40, 26 Feb 91; 1st Armored Division Executive Summary—Operation DESERT STORM, 19 Apr 91.

[31] VII Corps Sitrep, 27 Feb 91; VII Corps Commander's Sitrep (Combat) 40, 26 Feb 91; Third U.S. Army, After Action Review, 12 Mar 91; 1st Infantry Division (Mech.), Operations DESERT SHIELD and DESERT STORM Command Rpt, 19 Apr 91, p. 5; 3d Armored Division, Historical Overview of the 3AD in the Persian Gulf War, p. 10.

[32] Memo, Col. Michael D. Krause for Gen. Gordon R. Sullivan, 19 Apr 91, sub: Battle of 73 Easting.

[33] Ibid.; VII Corps Sitrep, 27 Feb 91.

[34] VII Corps Sitrep, 27 Feb 91; VII Corps Commander's Sitrep (Combat) 40, 26 Feb 91; VII

Corps, Desert Sabre Operations Summary; VII Corps DESERT SHIELD/DESERT STORM After Action Rpt, 29 May 91.

[35] Brown interview.

[36] Boomer, Command Brief: Persian Gulf Campaign; U.S. Marine Corps Operations, n.d., 1st Brigade, 2d Armored Division, Commander's Summary, n.d.

[37] Brown interview.

[38] ODCSINT Intelligence Summaries 406, 26 Feb 91, and 408, 27 Feb 91.

[39] Interv, S Sgt. Warren B. Causey, 317th Military History Detachment, with Lt. Col. Raymond Barrett, commander, 3/15th Infantry, 2d Brigade, 24th Infantry Division, 1 Mar 91.

[40] Ibid.

[41] McCaffrey, 24th Infantry Division (Mech.): Operation DESERT STORM Post-Attack Summary, 18 Mar 91.

[42] Ibid.

[43] Ibid.; Interv, Maj. William H. Thomas with Maj. Gen. Barry R. McCaffrey, 28 Feb 91, Interv, Thomas with Lt. Col. David Jensen, commander, 3/7th Infantry, 1st Brigade, 24th Infantry Division, 9 Mar 91.

[44] Ibid.; Wright interview.

[45] Third U.S. Army, After Action Review, 12 Mar 91.

[46] Ibid., MS, Swan, 1st Armored Division in Combat, 21-28 February 1991, pp. 2-3; MS, VII Corps Public Affairs Office, VII Corps DESERT STORM History, p. 5; VII Corps, Desert Sabre Operations Summary; VII Corps Commander's Sitrep (Combat) 41, 27 Feb 91; 1st Armored Division Executive Summary— Operation DESERT STORM, 19 Apr 91.

[47] MS, Doughty, War in the Persian Gulf, p. 16; MS, Swan, 1st Armored Division in Combat, 21-28 February 1991, p. 3.

[48] MS, Doughty, War in the Persian Gulf, p. 17; MS, Carver, Narrative of VII Corps in Operation DESERT STORM, p. 7.

[49] Boomer, Command Brief: Persian Gulf Campaign; U.S. Marine Corps Operations, n.d., 1st Brigade, 2d Armored Division, Commander's Summary, n.d.

[50] Third U.S. Army, After Action Review, 12 Mar 91; ODCSINT Intelligence Summary 412, 1 Mar 91; *Washington Post*, 13 Jun 91.

[51] Ibid.; Wright interview.

[52] VII Corps Sitrep, 27 Feb 91.

[53] MS, Lt. Col. Gregory Fontenot, commander, 2/34th Armor, Attack on Objective NORFOLK, 26 Mar 91, p.1.

[54] Wright interview.

[55] John F. Morton, "DARPA, Industry Fielded Antifratricide Device in 19 Days," *Armed Forces Journal International* (May 1991): 58, 60; Interv, Charles R. Anderson with Walter B. Morrow, Center for Night Vision and Electro-Optics, 27 Jun 91, Fort Belvoir, Va.

[56] McCaffrey interview.

[57] Ibid.; Chamberlain interview; Memo, Lt. Col. Fontenot, 8 Mar 91, sub: Operation DESERT STORM After Action Report; MS, Swan, 1st Armored Division in Combat, 21-28 February 1991, p. 2.

Officership Case Study IV

This is the fourth case study in a set of five case studies on the evolution of the Army. Whereas the earlier lessons in this set focused on the negative impact of policies and practices during the Vietnam era, the struggles of Army leaders to overcome a variety of challenges, and the changes that visionary leaders gradually implemented, this lesson shows the results. The work that was done paid off—the Army has transformed itself. The initiatives begun by General Abrams in the early 1970s are being witnessed in the success in the Gulf War.

The following topics are addressed in this lesson:

- The fruition of initiatives started in the early 1970s
- The Threads of Continuity
- Clausewitz's Trinity: The relationship among the people, nation, and the Army
- The conduct of the officer corps

The following TLO is supported in whole or in part by this lesson:

- Integrate military history into education of officers

Following this lesson you will be able to:

- Compare and contrast how the Gulf War was conducted versus the Vietnam War
- Use the Threads of Continuity to describe some of the initiatives initiated in the 1970s that contributed to the success of the Gulf War
- Describe how the Combat Training Centers (CTC) contributed to the victory in the Gulf War

OPERATION DESERT SHIELD/DESERT STORM

CHRONOLOGY OF EVENTS

2 Aug 90-11 Apr 91

2 Aug 90 Iraq invades Kuwait. Kuwaiti air defense units equipped with U.S. HAWK antiaircraft missiles down about 22 Iraqi aircraft & one combat helicopter during the invasion. Iraqi forces capture U.S.-made HAWK & TOW missiles in Kuwait. U.N. Security Council Resolution 660 condemns the Iraqi invasion of Kuwait. The Chief of the MICOM Plans & Operation Office extends operation of the MICOM EOC to 14 hours while planning a full 24-hour manning level. William Hollingsworth, a MICOM civilian technical specialist assigned to Kuwait, and his wife Nancy are detained by the Iraqi Army.

3 Aug 90 The PATRIOT PM directs the prime contractor & other program subcontractors to surge production to support anticipated needs in SWA.

6 Aug 90 U.N. Security Council Resolution 661 imposes economic sanctions against Iraq. Saudi Arabia requests U.S. assistance in its defense. The MICOM EOC goes to full 24-hour operation. The acceleration of PATRIOT PAC 2 missile production receives formal approval.

7 Aug 90 Operation Desert Shield begins (C-Day). BG Larry R. Capps, MICOM DCG, formally orders the activation of the MICOM EOC, with operations to continue on a 24-hour basis until further notice. Contractors begin the accelerated delivery schedule for PATRIOT PAC 2 missiles.

8 Aug 90 The first U.S. forces arrive in Saudi Arabia. AMC tasks its subordinate commands for critical items lists for surge possibilities.

9 Aug 90 U.N. Security Council Resolution 662 declares the Iraqi annexation of Kuwait null & void. Lead Army elements from the 82d Airborne Division arrive in theater. The TOW Project Office receives word that the 82d, 101st, & 24th Divisions will deploy immediately to SWA. The 1st Cavalry Division, elements of the 2d Armored Division, & the 3d Armored Cavalry Regiment would follow shortly. Analysis shows that only the 82d has the latest version of the TOW 2 missile guidance set with new software for improved tracking in a desert environment.

10 Aug 90 Coalition military activities in SWA are designated Operation Desert Shield. HQDA directs the TOW Project Office to immediately apply the latest software modification to the TOW 2 launchers & the ITV launch rail modification on TOW 2 systems before units deploy to SWA. Within 72 hours of their arrival in Saudi Arabia, all U.S. Air Force combat aircraft have their missile jammers upgraded to counter U.S.-made HAWK missiles captured in Kuwait by invading Iraqi forces.

11 Aug 90 The first MICOM LAR deployed for Operation Desert Shield arrives in SWA.

12 Aug 90 LTC James D. Fagan is appointed MICOM SCR for SWA.

13 Aug 90 The first ship departs Savannah with the equipment of the 24th Infantry Division (Mechanized). The arrival of Battery B, 2d Battalion, 7th ADA, 11th ADA Brigade in Saudi Arabia marks the first PATRIOT battery in-country. PERSCOM begins requesting Redstone soldiers in certain specialties to fill vacancies at deploying units. Of the first 67 processed out, 33 belong to OMMCS; 9 are MICOM; 12 are TMDE.

14 Aug 90 The 82d Airborne Division Ready Brigade-1 arrives in theater and moves to secure ports.

17 Aug 90 The first U.S. Army prepositioned ship arrives in Saudi Arabia. After the TOW modification team completes its mission at Fort Hood, deploying units have the most up-to-date TOW 2 equipment available.

18 Aug 90 U.N. Security Council Resolution 664 calls for the immediate release of foreigners from Iraq & Kuwait. The MICOM SCR for SWA arrives in Saudi Arabia.

22 Aug 90 By this date, CHAPARRAL/FAAR Project Office engineers have developed a new FAAR carrier conversion kit initially using a 2 1/2-ton M35A2 truck as the carrier for the radar.

25 Aug 90 U.N. Security Council Resolution 665 authorizes the use of force to halt maritime shipping to & from Iraq.

26 Aug 90 The Iraqi army releases Nancy Hollingsworth, who returns to the United States.

27 Aug 90 U.S. Central Command now considers PATRIOT to be "in-country & functional" although hardware began arriving almost 2 weeks earlier.

29 Aug 90 The 82d Airborne Division arrives in theater. HQDA orders Army TACMS low rate initial production to be accelerated.

31 Aug 90 The first PATRIOT PAC 2 missiles roll off the production line, 5 months ahead of schedule.

10 Sep 90 The first group deployment from Redstone Arsenal in support of ODS involves a squad-size group of soldiers from the 95th Maintenance Company.

12 Sep 90 Major combat elements of 24th Infantry Division (Mechanized) arrive in theater.

13 Sep 90 U.N. Security Council Resolution 666 establishes guidelines for humanitarian aid to Iraq & Kuwait.

15 Sep 90 The Army TACMS low rate initial production contract is modified to accelerate delivery in support of Operation Desert Shield.

16 Sep 90 U.N. Security Council Resolution 667 condemns Iraq & demands protection of diplomatic personnel.

19 Sep 90 ISC-MICOM printing plant employees complete the last batch of the first printing of 250,000 copies of the pocket guide, "The Iraqi Threat and How They Fight."

24 Sep 90 U.N. Security Council Resolution 669 authorizes the examination of requirements for economic assistance under U.N. Article 50.

25 Sep 90 U.N. Security Council Resolution 670 condemns Iraq & confirms the economic embargo.

Sep 90 The first PATRIOT PAC 2 missiles produced under the accelerated production contract are air transported directly to troops in SWA.

2 Oct 90 ODCSOPS suspends FAAR system deactivation & tasks MICOM to bring the system to full readiness.

5 Oct 90 MAJ Walter E. Lorchiem is appointed MICOM SRO.

6 Oct 90 The 101st Airborne Division (Air Assault) arrives in the theater of operation.

16 Oct 90 Less than a month after printing an initial 250,000 copies of a guide about Iraqi troops & weapons, the ISC-MICOM printing plant prepares a second run for shipment to the Middle East.

18 Oct 90 MAJ Walter E. Lorcheim, a reserve officer appointed as MICOM SRO, arrives in SWA.

22 Oct 90 The 1st Cavalry Division, deployed with its AVENGER systems, arrives in theater.

29 Oct 90 U.N. Security Council Resolution 674 condemns Iraq & calls for the release of third-country nationals & the provision of food. The Iraqi army releases William Hollingsworth, who returns to Redstone Arsenal.

Oct 90 Lockheed Sanders, prime contractor for the FAAR, begins converting the system to the 5-ton truck configuration in support of Operation Desert Shield. The accelerated hand off of AVENGER fire units begins in support of Operation Desert Shield.

9 Nov 90 The HELLFIRE Project Office offers equipment check-out assistance to HELLFIRE/APACHE units alerted for deployment to SWA. Findings from the assistance visits indicate serious readiness problems with the subsystem. MLC sends a team to SWA in support of PATRIOT. This support team will remain in theater until 18 Apr 91.

11 Nov 90 The G/VLLD Exchange Program for SWA begins in Germany to provide a calibrated eyesafe LD/R. An advance team from MICOM tests, repairs, & modifies 107 G/VLLD assets belonging to units scheduled to deploy to SWA.

18 Nov 90 The PEO Fire Support sends a team to SWA in support of TOW. This support team will remain in theater until 13 Mar 91.

21 Nov 90 VII Corps units begin deployment to SWA.

23 Nov 90 MICOM receives the order to deploy two PATRIOT fire units to Israel within 120 days.

28 Nov 90 U.N. Security Council Resolution 677 condemns Iraqi attempts to alter Kuwaiti demographics. The United States & Saudi Arabia sign an FMS case for the sale of PATRIOT fire units. Valued at more than $1 billion, it is implemented on 30 Nov 90. The PEO Air Defense sends a team to SWA in support of PATRIOT subsystems. This support team will remain in theater until 24 Mar 91.

29 Nov 90 U.N. Security Council Resolution 678 authorizes the use of force to uphold resolutions unless Iraq withdraws by the 15 Jan 91 deadline.

30 Nov 90 MICOM informs HQDA that the contractor will accelerate delivery of CHAPARRAL missiles. By this date, the TOW 2 optical protection sight exchange program is completed in SWA. MLC sends another team to SWA in support of PATRIOT. This support team will remain in theater until 21 Apr 91.

Nov 90 The deployment of STINGER-RMP missiles to SWA begins. The Saudi Arabia National Guard is provided TOW night sights, giving them night fighting capability used effectively during Desert Storm.

1 Dec 90 The XVIII Airborne Corps arrives in the theater of operation. Initially deployed with the XVIII is the 6/27th Field Artillery Battalion, which arrives in SWA with two Army TACMS batteries.

3 Dec 90 SAMD sends two teams to SWA in support of MLRS & HAWK. The MLRS team returns on 6 Dec 90, while the HAWK team returns on 15 Jan 91.

14 Dec 90 RD&E Center sends a team to SWA in support of MLRS. This support team will remain in theater until 8 May 91.

31 Dec 90 A letter contract is issued for FMS customer Saudi Arabia for PATRIOT fire units & missiles.

Dec 90 The accelerated delivery of items under the Army TACMS low rate initial production contract modification of 15 Sep 90 is completed. A "Quick Fix" team deploys to SWA to modify MLRS launchers. The team installs metal panels on 70 launchers before 15 Jan 91. The HELLFIRE Project Office dispatches a contractor technical representative contact team to SWA to locate & make the necessary adjustments & repairs to restore the HELLFIRE/APACHE units to a high readiness posture. This effort is completed the following month.

1 Jan 91 The PEO Fire Support sends a team to SWA in support of HELLFIRE. This support team remains in theater until 13 Jan 91.

3 Jan 91 The AMC DCG for Material Readiness directs the MICOM Commanding General to coordinate with DESCOM to determine echelon above division back-up maintenance capability/capacity that could be used to reduce maintenance backlogs of the M-901 ITV.

8 Jan 91 The 3343d U.S. Army Hospital of Mobile, Alabama, is mobilized to augment Fox Army Community Hospital, Redstone Arsenal. The advance party arrives on 11 Jan; the first increment of the main body reaches Redstone on 15 Jan; & the final increment reports on 4 Feb.

10 Jan 91 An eight-member MICOM G/VLLD team departs Redstone Army Airfield for Dhahran.

14 Jan 91 The MICOM G/VLLD team begins exchanging LD/Rs on the front lines in the theater of operation.

15 Jan 91 The U.N. sets this date as the deadline for Iraq to withdraw from Kuwait.

16 Jan 91 By this date, the number of soldiers at Redstone Arsenal processed for possible duty in Saudi Arabia totals 225: 167 departed, 14 pending departure, the rest on standby. LTC Daniel M. Prescott, MICOM SCR, & MAJ James Fowler, MICOM SRO, arrive in SWA.

17 Jan 91 The Operation Desert Storm air war begins (D-Day). Laser-guided HELLFIRE missiles, fired by U.S. Army 101st Aviation Brigade APACHE helicopters strike the first coalition blow against two Iraqi early-warning radar sites, destroying both within 4 minutes thereby opening a corridor for the first air strikes against targets inside Iraq. U.S. Marine Corps AH-1T COBRA helicopter gunships destroy an Iraqi command post with TOW missiles following Iraq's sporadic shelling of the Khafji area near the Saudi- Kuwaiti border.

A total of 36 MICOM LARs and 2 supervisors are on site in Saudi Arabia by this date.

18 Jan 91 Iraq fires the first Scud missiles at Israel & Saudi Arabia. Battery A, 2d Battalion, 7th ADA, 11th ADA Brigade scores the first combat kill for the PATRIOT system after successfully intercepting the first Scud over Dhahran, Saudi Arabia. A Battery, 6th Battalion, 27th Field Artillery, attached to VII Corps, fired the first two Army TACMS missiles of Operation Desert Storm in counterattacks against Iraqi artillery at the Kuwaiti border firing on Saudi Arabia. These are the first rounds fired in anger by VII Corps since World War II as well as the first rounds fired by U.S. Army field artillery in the Persian Gulf War.

19 Jan 91 DOD announces the deployment of USAEUR PATRIOT missiles & crews to Israel.

20 Jan 91 XVIII Airborne & VII Corps (minus elements of the 3d Armored Division) begin movement to forward assembly areas for the ground phase of the campaign. MLC sends two teams to Israel in support of PATRIOT. The first team returns on 31 Mar 91 and the second team returns on 4 Apr 91.

22 Jan 91 WSMD sends a team to SWA in support of G/VLLD. This support team remains in theater until 2 Feb 91.

25 Jan 91 The PEO Air Defense sends a team to SWA in support of PATRIOT. This support team remains in theater until 8 Feb 91.

26 Jan 91 The VCSA directs another acceleration of PATRIOT PAC 2 missile production & delivery which is to be sustained through Aug 91.

28 Jan 91 A second acceleration of Army TACMS low rate initial production is issued.

29 Jan 91 Iraqi troops attack Khafji, Saudi Arabia. After AMC tasks MICOM to manage the M901 ITV, a WSMD team begins to identify problems & their solutions that result in raising system readiness rates from 80 percent to 95 percent.

30 Jan 91 Saudi-led coalition forces, which included U.S. Marine Corps units, storm the Iraqi-held Saudi town of Khafji, but are forced to retreat not only by Iraqi resistance but by "friendly fire" from the Qatari armored unit assigned to protect the Saudis from the rear.

31 Jan 91 MLC sends a team to Turkey in support of PATRIOT. This support team remains in country until 31 Mar 91. The second Saudi-led attack successfully retakes Khafji. During the series of fire fights constituting the first major ground battle of Operation Desert Storm, many Iraqi tanks and armored cars are reportedly immobilized by TOW antitank missiles.

Jan 91 MICOM LARs upgrade software packaged on STINGER-RMP gripstocks deployed to SWA.

2 Feb 91 LTC James D. Fagan, the first MICOM SCR in SWA, returns to Redstone Arsenal & assumes duties as senior operations officer in the MICOM EOC.

3 Feb 91 XVIII Airborne & VII Corps complete movement to the forward assembly areas.

6 Feb 91 VII Corps closes in theater with the arrival of the last elements of the 3d Armored Division.

13 Feb 91 Alpha Battery, 21st Field Artillery launches the first MLRS munitions to be fired in combat.

16 Feb 91 Coalition forces begin day & night artillery raids along front lines.

23 Feb 91 The deadline for Iraq to withdraw from Kuwait before the beginning of the ground war is set for 12 Noon (8 p.m. in Baghdad). The MICOM Commanding General dispatches a message on the effects of crude oil smoke on EO sensors & laser designators specifying the potential impact on operations. The PEO Air Defense sends a team to Israel in support of PATRIOT. This support team remains in country until 6 Mar 91.

24 Feb 91 Coalition forces begin the ground phase of the campaign (G-Day).

25 Feb 91 An Iraqi Scud missile destroys a U.S. barracks in Dhahran, killing 28 American soldiers.

27 Feb 91 A MICOM Quality Assurance Technician completes the task of handing off TOW 2 equipment to the Royal Saudi Land Forces.

28 Feb 91 President Bush orders the cessation of offensive operations.

Feb 91 Lockheed Sanders ships 22 FAARs in the new 5-ton truck configuration to SWA.

1 Mar 91 Cease fire terms are negotiated in Safwan, Iraq. TASK FORCE FREEDOM begins emergency recovery operations in Kuwait. The PATRIOT PM sends a retrograde support team to SWA. This team remains in country until 13 Mar 91.

2 Mar 91 U.N. Security Council Resolution 686 demands that Iraq cease all hostile actions & abide by the previous U.N. resolutions.

7 Mar 91 DOD announces the first troop deployment home.

8 Mar 91 Redeployment of the 24th Infantry Division (Mechanized) begins. Class IX shipments to SWA are suspended.

Mar 91 The PATRIOT PAC 2 missile production acceleration effort of 26 Jan 91 is terminated.

Mar 91 By this time, MICOM Transportation had coordinated the movement of 58,700 short tons of Class V material in support of Operation Desert Shield/Storm.

3 Apr 91 U.N. Security Council Resolution 687 sets forth a permanent cease fire.

6 Apr 91 Iraq officially accepts U.N. cease fire terms & Security Council resolutions.

11 Apr 91 The cease fire takes effect.

Officership Case Study V: Into the 21st Century

This is the last case study in a set of five case studies on the evolution of the Army. This lesson identifies a number of the post-Cold War challenges and the activities of the current Army as it undergoes transformation. The purpose of this lesson is to describe the challenges and risks of the 21st century, and to generate ideas as to how risks can be minimized and opportunities seized.

The following topics are addressed in this lesson:

- The conduct and effect of the post-Cold War downsizing
- The evolving missions of the Army
- Ongoing Army transition and modernization initiatives

The following TLO is supported in whole or in part by this lesson:

- Integrate military history into education of officers

Following this lesson you will be able to:

- Identify the types of current missions facing the Army today
- Describe the challenges facing the post-Cold War Army
- Summarize an officer's unique responsibilities to the future of the Army

THE DOWNSIZED WARRIOR

BY DAVID McCORMICK

AN AGENDA FOR REFORM

An Officer Corps for the Twenty-First Century

> *An end of war can be a time of rebirth for the Army or a time of psychological let down. We need to seize the moment for reforming and modernizing our officer corps. . . . That is the best way to build for the future. But time is short. When the transition to peace is ended, it will become increasingly difficult to promote fundamental change.*
>
> —William L. Hauser and Zeb Bradford,
> *Army,* December 1971

In 1993, Yale professor Paul Bracken created something of a buzz in defense policy circles by criticizing the propensity of policymakers to conceptualize military posture in terms of the "next military"—the one existing trends will produce in ten years given the character of current military problems and the fine-tuning of existing operational strategies. Too little emphasis, he argued, was being given to "the military after next"— the dramatically changed military organization that would emerge in twenty years in light of the transformations likely to occur in technology, the nature of warfare, and the international environment (1993, 175). With this insightful admonition in mind, let us ponder for a moment the qualities the army should seek to develop in its officers to ensure they are prepared for the unknown challenges of the future.[1]

Within a decade, the present generation of lieutenant colonels and colonels will be the army's senior leaders. Likewise, today's captains and majors will be the lieutenant colonels and colonels of the next army, and the colonels and generals of the army of 2015— the army after next. Two notable trends promise new challenges for these future army leaders. First, and most obvious, the world has changed. Despite the dangers of the bipolar standoff during the Cold War, there was an element of stability and consistency in international affairs that was oddly comforting. The abrupt end of the Cold War, however, has created a wholly different world—complex, dangerous and unpredictable—in which we are faced with a plethora of small-scale wars, waged as often by "terrorists, guerrillas, bandits and robbers" as by traditional armies (van Creveld 1993, 197).

Despite these uncertainties, the outlines of future military operations within the new world order are beginning to emerge. It is already clear that the military's role in the conduct of U.S. foreign affairs has changed markedly. As a precondition for domestic acceptability of military interventions abroad, the U.S. Army is likely to deploy forces in small numbers, often as part of multilateral coalitions, for specific and achievable purposes, with commanders held accountable for needless collateral damage (Bacevich 1990, 22). Military force is but one instrument among the many that the United States is likely to employ. And the army is certain to be used for a host of missions that fall outside the purview of traditional combat roles. The changing nature of the military mission, coupled with the dramatic decline of defense resources, have in a few short years caused not only the U.S. Army but armies around the world to change shape, shrink in size, and in some cases wither away.

Second, the rate of technological change in the decades ahead, particularly with respect to microchip technology, will be an order of magnitude greater than that of the past decade and will continue to accelerate. Advances in technology are changing not only the way nations trade and communicate but also the way they fight their wars. The post-Cold War era has been accompanied by what some commentators have labeled a revolution in military affairs. Since World War II, technological change has steadily fragmented the military organization into a growing number of specialties and has required increasing reliance on officers with "nonmilitary" expertise (Wood 1988, 30). Recently, this trend has quickened due to advances in computer and communications technology (Krepinevich 1994b; Bracken 1993, 162). These dramatic changes, first fully evident during the Gulf War, promise profound changes in the shape and size of military organizations as well as in their doctrine. Decentralized command and control, precision-guided weaponry, and a blurring of distinctions between the front lines and rear areas are likely to be characteristics of future battlefields and military organizations.

Together, these trends will alter traditional conceptions of professional military expertise, making it more difficult to distinguish between warriors and nonwarriors, commanders and noncommanders, and technicians and nontechnicians. Future military operations will require not only competencies outside the realm of traditional "military expertise" but also a level of political and technical sophistication unknown and unneeded by military leaders in the past. "The army may require a very different kind of officer in the future . . . as we move into these fuzzy situations that put a premium on [officers] with cultural sensitivity and an ability to adapt rapidly" (Andrew Krepinevich as cited in Ricks 1995, 1). Moreover, the increasing sophistication of high-tech warfare will enlarge the body of knowledge pertinent to military operations and require a corps of officers who are comfortable with technology, ambiguity, and decentralized command and control (Toffler and Toffler 1993, 74).

Given this growing complexity, the post-Cold War army will require leaders at all levels with specialized knowledge. There will be a demand for officer with political expertise—men and women with in-depth knowledge of certain regions, language skills, the capacity to work on joint (interservice) staffs, an understanding of international and domestic political affairs, and the ability to provide civilian leaders in the administration and Congress with sage military advice. There will be a growing demand for officers with technical expertise—leaders with skills and experience in personnel, administration, logistics, and technology who can be counted upon to master the growing complexities of the modern computer-based military organization. And, of course, there will be a continuing need for officers with expertise in command—leaders who spend the majority of their careers "with troops" preparing for or serving in command. Tomorrow's commanders, however, must be capable not only of leading soldiers in operations from peacekeeping to high-intensity combat but also of developing tactics and doctrine appropriate for the twenty-first century.[2]

In the past, officers have served in all three of these roles, often rotating among them sequentially as they progressed through the ranks. In the future, however, given the growing complexities of each, few officers will be capable of such a feat. Occasionally, an exceptionally gifted leader will have the ability to contribute in more than one area, but for the most part these roles will be mutually exclusive. As former army Chief of Staff Edward C. Meyer concludes: "Some will argue that a good generalist can keep all three balls in the air at the same time. When our world was bipolar that may have been true, but tomorrow's world is changing so rapidly that we are unlikely to have time to permit generalists to become specialists" (1995, 227). Moreover, the costs associated with training and educating officers in a range of

needed specialties is increasing rapidly. Thus, there will be growing pressure to gain maximum return from these specialists through repetitive assignments in their areas of expertise (Thie and Brown 1994, 23). In short, the post-Cold War era will strain traditional occupational categories that have defined the officer corps in the past. The future army will be led by a corps of highly trained specialists with diverse technical and nontechnical expertise.

Across all specialties, however, the army's leadership must comprise officers who not only know one field deeply but who possess the broad range of leadership skills, confidence, experience, and intellectual flexibility required to adapt to present and future uncertainties. As Chairman of the Joint Chiefs of Staff General John Shalikashvilli observes: "The unexpected has become so routine; we need people who are comfortable in an uncertain world" (as quoted in Rokke 1995, 21). Moreover, in the long run, the army's effectiveness will depend on its ability to innovate—more specifically on the existence of bright, ambitious officers with the willingness to ask and pursue difficult questions, the curiosity to seek knowledge outside the nuts and bolts of their own area of expertise or of the military profession more generally, and the self-confidence to test and relentlessly pursue promising new ideas. In sum, the army's future success will depend on the capacity of top leaders to create an organizational culture of generating intellectual capital, expertise, adaptability, and innovation.

TROUBLING TRENDS

This idealized image of the post-Cold War officer corps is distinctly at odds with the officer corps of today or of the immediate future. Today's officer corps is demoralized and less committed, more careerist and increasingly tentative. In addition, as a result of shortened assignments and more turbulent career patterns, officers are less tactically and technically proficient than they were before downsizing began. Moreover, the retrenchment of junior officers to muddy boots career patterns is particularly alarming in light of the challenges posed by this new era. While these problems are largely a function of downsizing, the army's rigid and outdated officer management system has exacerbated these deleterious trends.

Declining Professionalism

The professional fiber of the army officer corps has been strained by the uncertainty and turmoil of downsizing.[3] Although experts have long argued over the definition of military professionalism, Samuel Huntington's concept, first presented in his 1957 classic, *The Soldier and the State,* is still widely accepted by professional soldiers. "In this formulation, the distinguishing characteristics of any profession are expertise, social responsibility, and "corporateness."[5] The competence of the military professional lies in the "management of violence," a distinct sphere of proficiency common to all, or almost all, officers.[6] The professional soldier is not motivated by economic incentives but rather feels a special responsibility, a commitment, to the society he serves and to his craft. The corporate character of the military profession is manifest in a certain organic unity (esprit de corps) and consciousness within the profession of the military as a group apart from laymen (1957, 8-11).

The army officer corps is less professional today than it was when the Cold War "officially" ended with the fall of the Berlin Wall in 1989 and planning for downsizing began in earnest. The corporateness and esprit de corps of the officer corps has been undermined by downsizing. Likewise, the corps' commitment to both the army in particular and the military profession in general has been weakened. These effects might have been anticipated, for in some respects the notion of unexpectedly separating competent and committed officers is antithetical to professionalism. A sense of security is one of several attributes that "anchors" an individual to a certain profession and to a certain organization (Strand 1993, 140).

Additionally, the military is unique among professions in that the "expertise" of the professional soldier has only limited applicability outside the military organization. While other professionals—doctors, lawyers, and accountants, for example—may depart the organization for which they work and remain members of their profession as independents or in a range of other public and private enterprises, the military profession can be practiced only within the military institution. It is for this reason, perhaps, that military professionals place added faith in an informal contract—an implicit agreement between them and the military organization of what each can expect from the other (Elton and Malone 1972). In return for enduring the hardships of military life and fulfilling the obligations of a professional soldier, the state provides special privileges, career opportunity, and a reasonable modicum of security. Downsizing is viewed by officers as a violation of contract.

What is more difficult to anticipate is the magnitude of these changes in attitude and behavior and whether they will be temporary or enduring. This task is further complicated by the fact that they are neither recent phenomena nor solely the consequence of downsizing; they have simply become more conspicuous because of it. During and after the Vietnam War, military professionalism within the army officer corps declined significantly, which, many argued, contributed to America's defeat.[7] In the late 1970's sociologist Charles Moskos recast this discussion by arguing that the "econometric mindset" in military manpower policy underlying the introduction of the all-volunteer force had accelerated a "creeping occupationalism" in the armed forces. Moskos argued that the military career had traditionally been legitimated in terms of values and norms and a purpose transcending self-interest in favor of a presumed higher good, a notion consistent with conventional conceptions of professionalism. Conversely, occupations are legitimated in terms of the marketplace, that is, a level of monetary compensation established by market dynamics is awarded for equivalent competencies (1977, 43). With this shift, Moskos maintained that military service was increasingly becoming more like a job than a calling, and that this had serious implications for military effectiveness (Moskos and Wood 1988b).

At the core of this debate is the contention that in the philosophy governing manpower policy has fundamentally changed the ethos of U.S. military organizations. On one level, this shift in rationale—which some label (after Max Weber) bureaucratic rationalism—is manifest in the language, analyses, and decisionmaking processes of military policymakers (Faris 1988).[8] On another level, this trend is evident in the corrosion of traditional values and norms among military personnel (Segal 1989, 57). Downsizing is viewed by some as a manifestation of a fundamental shift toward organizational rationalization and depersonalization that runs throughout American society (A. Bennett 1990). If one extends this reasoning to the army, it would not be surprising if downsizing has contributed to occupationalism within the officer corps.[9]

The potential consequences of these trends for military effectiveness are significant. Occupationalism undermines moral, cohesion, expertise, initiative, and the moral climate within the office corps. Numerous examples of less-than-successful military operations during and after the Vietnam War show the devastating effects of these trends.[10] Quite simply, "a functioning military requires bonds of trust, sacrifice and respect within its rank, and similar bonds of support and respect between an army and the nation it represents" (Fallows 1981, 171). Professionalism within today's officer corps is in decline because the bonds on which it depends have been severely strained by downsizing.

Declining Military Competence

Downsizing has also undermined military competence or expertise, another crucial component of military professionalism. Turbulence within the officer corps has increased dramatically as a consequence of the growing requirements for officers coupled with the limited professional development opportunities available to them. Ironically, in an attempt to "develop" as many officers as possible to serve as future battalion commanders, the army has diluted the quality of preparation available to those select few who will actually be given this opportunity.

The length of officer assignments has always been somewhat controversial within the army. During and after the Vietnam War, for example, critics chastised the army for its shortened assignment policy (most company, battalion, and brigade commanders and staff officers served between six and twelve months in Vietnam) as both a cause and a consequence of pervasive careerism. Moreover, the less time officers spend in key command and staff positions, the less likely they are to develop a close knowledge of their responsibilities, their men, and their unit's abilities (Gabriel 1985, 9). In the mid-1970s, tour lengths for both battalion and brigade commanders were first lengthened to eighteen months and then to thirty months and finally reduced to twenty-four months where they have remained for the last fifteen years (Hauser 1985, 5).

Despite these changes, the rapid rotation of captains though company command positions and majors through battalion staff jobs has persisted, and has been substantially worsened by the stresses and strains of downsizing. The persistence of this phenomenon is due to fundamental shortcomings in officer management practices, the content of which are considered shortly. For now it is enough to note that the time officers spend in key professional development jobs has declined precipitously. This change has alarming implications for the "seasoning" of the army's future combat commanders.

Based on current assignment policy, the battalion commanders of the year 2005 are likely to have had substantially less of the crucial preparatory time in troop units than was enjoyed by their predecessors. The majority of captains will serve fifteen to eighteen months as company commanders, a 23-32 percent decline in the amount of time officers have traditionally served in this position. Likewise, most majors will serve a mere twelve months as a battalion operations officer (S-3) or a battalion executive officer (XO), a 43-45 percent decline from the past. In short, the battalion commanders of the future are likely to have had as little as twenty-four months of crucial professional development experience in combat battalions. The impact of these changes on the quality, competence, and confidence of future battalion commanders remains to be seen. It is clear, however, that in an attempt to qualify and develop as many future battalion commanders as possible, the army is on average giving significantly less preparation to those few who will actually have that opportunity.

Muddy Boots Career Patterns

Despite the explicit rules governing officer career management, individual officers (and the senior officers who "sponsor" them) exercise considerable initiative in selecting their assignments. The army's downsizing experience has influenced these choices. There is a growing emphasis being placed in strictly muddy boots career patterns, at the expense of full-time civilian graduate schooling and nontraditional assignments. Intellectual activities within the army appear to be getting short shrift, not necessarily because officers do not want to participate, but because they don't believe they can do so and remain competitive for promotion. It is particularly noteworthy that the number of officers willing to pursue graduate study in the hard sciences (math, science, or engineering) and the utilization tours that follow has declined markedly (*The Science and Engineering Requirements* 1996, 12). These trends are significant because the career decisions and the development experiences of today's junior and mid-career officers will have profound consequences for the next army and the army after next.

For a number of reasons, this scenario might have been predicted. In times of uncertainty, it is common for individuals to make conservative career choices, and professional soldiers are no exception: "The military professional, confronted with an unpredictable and uncontrollable external environment, has traditionally responded with a drive for internal order and internal consistency" (Lang 1964, 78). Additionally, there is a tendency on the part of organizational leaders to reward individuals with the types of backgrounds with which they are most familiar and comfortable, particularly during periods of uncertainty. For this reason, it is crucial during such periods that army leaders make a conscious effort to avoid becoming fatally inbred, for as the force shrinks, promotion boards predictably tend to reward "standard issue" career patterns (Peters 1993).

Both these undesirable tendencies have been evident during downsizing. As opportunity has declined and competition increased, a growing number of junior and mid-career officers who aspire to military careers are retrenching to traditional career patterns, fearing to stray far, if at all, from the muddy boots army. Concurrently, assignment officers are encouraging officers on the "fast track" who want to stay there to adhere to traditional career patterns in the expectation that nontraditional assignments will be viewed unfavorably by future promotion boards. These trends are directly at odds, however, with developing the kinds of specialized, intellectually adaptable officers who will be required in the post-Cold War era. In short, the army has failed to create the professional climate and the formal and informal institutional structures needed to develop an officer corps for the twenty-first century.

OUTDATED ASSUMPTIONS AND MISPLACED PRIORITIES

In a large extent, the decline in professionalism and the described alterations in career choices are inevitable consequences of the uncertainty created by prolonged and incremental downsizing, a process largely outside the army's control. At the same time, the traditional norms within the officer corps and the rigidity of the Officer Personnel Management System (OPMS) have exacerbated these problems. And army leaders have been unacceptably slow in adjusting officer management practices to meet the challenges of this new age.

Recent history offers some insight into the present situation. Career management systems are important not only because they affect the technical competence of the officer corps but also because they shape the character, content, and values of the institution. With this in mind, perhaps army Chief of Staff William Westmoreland directed the Deputy Chief of Staff for Personnel in August 1970 to develop a new officer management system that would increase professional competence by instituting more concentrated assignment patterns in various specialties and by ensuring equitable promotion opportunity across these specialties, that is, to create a number of viable paths to the top.[11] The eventual outcome of this directive was the Officer Personnel Management System, which was implemented after several sets of revisions in 1974. For the past twenty-three years, OPMS has, with only marginal changes, remained intact. It established dual career patterns in which officers select a functional area, or secondary specialty between their fifth and eighth years of service. From that point forward, most officers rotate between assignments in their functional areas and their basic branches through the remainder of their careers.

Military organizations are unique in that they grow their own executive talent. For the army, OPMS provides both the framework and the formula for acquiring, developing, and ultimately separating or retiring each generation of army leaders (Strand 1993, 4). Three main policy areas—strength management (identifying officer requirements and overseeing officer procurement, separation, and distribution), performance evaluation, and professional development (education, training, and assignments)—fall under the purview of OPMS. The system was designed to be evolutionary, adjusting as necessary to meet unforeseen officer development needs (*Commissioned Officer Development and Career Management* 1995, 1). Officer professional development is the key pillar within this triad, reflecting the emphasis army doctrine places on the ability of decentralized leaders at every level to made decisions (Military Leadership 1990).

To its credit, the army places a higher premium on the professional development of its officer corps, particularly future commanders, than the other services. Institutional training, rotation through key operational assignments, and self-development make up the army's approach to leadership development.[12] Despite its benefits, however, the emphasis placed on the professional development of the officer corps and, more specifically, on preparing future commanders, has bred inefficiencies. As noted, the professional development process is designed around the goal of preparing officers to command battalions or higher units through a set sequence of schooling and operational assignments. This persists despite the fact only a small fraction of the officer corps will be afforded the opportunity for such commands. In part, this is a reflection of the army's desire to indoctrinate all junior and mid-career officers with the "heroic leader" mindset through successive field assignments early in their careers.[13] More than anything else, however, the army's officer development process is the product of the army's history, tradition, and organizational culture.

Officer personnel policy is profoundly influenced by the deeply ingrained institutional value that the army places on command: "Deep in the soul of most professional military men is the desire to lead. The military institution . . . remains primarily committed to the belief that a command career is the best road to success and personal fulfillment" (Sarkesian 1975, 80). Moreover, the system assumes a close correlation between command experience and the army's management needs; a proven commander is capable, this philosophy holds, of performing successfully in most other assignments in the army. As a consequence, battalion command assignments are virtually mandatory for the officer who hopes to advance to the rank of colonel, despite the original intent of OPMS (Strand 1993, 121).[14]

Not surprisingly, the officer corps adheres to this relatively narrow conception of military professionalism and officers generally equate command with success. And, senior army leaders perpetuate these notions. For example, in an article on professionalization and the army, Chief of Staff Carl Yuono describes a military professional as "an expert in the profession of arms . . . responsible for soldiers and units" (1990, 3). Given such statements, it is no wonder that the majority of officers participate in relentless rivalry for command or preparatory assignments leading up to command. Predictably, the system is generally unforgiving for those who deviate from this practice.

Additionally, three interrelated organizational priorities, conceived by military and civilian leaders in the aftermath of World War II, continue to influence profoundly officer personnel practices, despite the fact that they are arguably outdated in the post-Cold War era. First, the army places significant institutional emphasis on maintaining its mobilization capability.[15] The army began World War II with an officer corps that was not only too small but too old.[16] To avoid repeating this mistake, it sought to develop a core of well-trained officers at all levels able to serve as operational commanders in case it needed to expand rapidly in the future (Rostker et al. 1993, 3-8).[17] This logic still persists in the army today, despite the growing reliance placed on reserve forces) with their own complement of officers) and the fact that future wars are increasingly likely to be "come as you are," over and done with before there is an opportunity to mobilize conscripts or reserves.[18]

The "generalist" ideal also remains a powerful tradition and significantly influences the design of the officer management system. This also springs from the army's World War II experience when it was observed that "broad-gauged" officers, rather than specialists, coped better when thrust into unforeseen roles (Hauser 1984, 452). The generalist ideal is therefore grounded in the aforementioned notion that gifted operational commanders could fulfill most officer roles throughout the army and that they should be exposed to a variety of command and staff assignments as they advanced through the ranks. While OPMS attempted to alter this tradition by placing greater emphasis on specialization by creating "many roads to the top," generalist career patterns remain distinct criteria for promotion (Strand 1993, 121). The army's reluctance to acknowledge or accept the challenge of a wider, more demanding body of relevant professional knowledge is in distinct contrast to the specialization that has evolved in other professions.

Finally, officer management and development are greatly affected by the army's up-or-out system and the institutional emphasis placed on a young and vigorous officer corps. This priority affected not only the way the army downsized but also the way it develops its officer corps. Legislated guidance on promotion timing (and the mandatory curtailment of officers' careers) cramps the officer development sequence, forcing officers to race through their development requirements at each rank in order to be fully qualified for promotion to the next rank.[19] While DOPMA legislation is outside the army control, "youth and vigor" is also a priority the army's leadership has supported, and sometimes enthusiastically embraced, over the past decade. As with the other post-World War II insights, however, youth and vigor is arguably no longer an appropriate criterion for manning the modern military. Yet, if one compares the officer career management system put in place in 1948 with that which exists today there are striking similarities.[20] While there is still some justification for considering mobilization capability, generalist career patterns, and youth and vigor, an officer management system founded primarily on these principles is inappropriate in the post-Col War era.

Furthermore, the army has contributed to the dysfunctional aspects of this management system by taking the notion that "leaders are made and not born" to unhealthy extremes. Over the past several decades, the army has created an officer professional development model guided by the notion that predetermined set of experiences is optimal for "building" future leaders.[21] This logic has resulted in an increasingly rigid and unforgiving management system in which officers must adhere with great precision to career "templates' and timelines during each phase of their careers to remain competitive for promotion. The army even publishes schematic diagrams showing ideal career patterns, which suggests that to deviate from these traditional patterns is to decrease the quality of an officer's professional experience and therefore to limit his or her career potential. The current system allows little latitude for the officer of exceptional talent to rise to the top without having done all the things that the "prototypical" career pattern requires. And promotion boards reinforce the importance of strict adherence to this progression. It is alarming to think that an Eisenhower or a Marshall, who both had somewhat nontraditional career patterns, would be unlikely to be successful in today's army (Strand 1993, 132).

It is understandable that as the number of opportunities for key development positions has decreased during downsizing, so too has the willingness of career-minded junior and mid-career officers to test uncharted waters in making their career choices. Increased competition for key "branch-qualifying" jobs has contributed to careerism, attenuated cohesion, and stifled initiative. The effects of downsizing are troubling because they have significant implications for the army's current effectiveness. Even more disturbing, however, is the effect that downsizing will have on successive generations of future army leaders. If these patterns persist, the next several generations of leaders are likely to be less diverse collectively, as well as within their individual career patterns, than the leaders of today. Future battalion commanders will have spent significantly less time in key development assignments than their predecessors, as a relatively larger number of officers are rotated through a decreasing number of operational development opportunities. Moreover, it is increasingly less likely that future army leaders will have attended full-time civilian graduate schools (particularly in the hard sciences) or have served in fellowships or trained with industry. They will be less likely to have worked closely with, or studied among, their civilian contemporaries. As Sarkesian writes: "Nothing could be more dangerous to military professionalism than to develop a world view that is unidimensional, omni-competent, and limited in its intellectual scope" (1981, 189). It is not unreasonable to conclude that this observation will likely apply to the next generation of army leaders, or even more likely to the leaders of the army after next.

REFORM FOR THE TWENTY-FIRST CENTURY

The problems that exist in today's army are due at least partially to forces outside its control. Regardless of their causes, however, these problems will not be solved by others. Moreover, they will require the army to respond in a manner that is most difficult for a large organization—through self-generated change. How should officer management practices be reformed not only to address the immediate aftereffects of downsizing but also to prepare better army leaders for the post-Cold War era? What should army leaders do to strengthen professionalism within the officer corps in the short run and modify the officer management system in the long run? And what is the desired role of civilian policymakers—in Congress and the Department of Defense—in addressing these very serious questions?

Reprofessionalization

Recently army leaders have begun to recognize the devastating effects of downsizing on military professionalism and to address these problems with surprising and admirable candor. In a February 1996 article in the journal *Military Review*, Chief of Staff Dennis Reimer conceded publicly that micromanagement, careerism, and a zero-defects mindset are among the unfortunate side effects of the turmoil created by the downsizing of the army (1996, 9). Obviously, recognizing that such problems exist is the first important step toward correcting them.

(Indeed, the army's leadership should make an even greater effort in the future to convey its sensitivity to the special problems and uncertainties brought about by downsizing.) Despite the recognition, however, the army has taken little action thus far to arrest the decline in professionalism or to modify existing officer management practices. Further, the changes that are likely to result from current reform efforts are too cautious, too static, and too shortsighted to overcome the army's current problems or to meet the challenges of the post-Cold War era.

One of the paradoxes of change is that trust among juniors and seniors alike is hardest to establish when you need it the most (Duck 1993, 115). This observation accurately describes the army's downsizing dilemma. Since 1989, the "ground rules" concerning opportunity, stability, and security have changed continually, and this has eroded trust within the officer corps. Officers are less trusting of one another, of civilian leaders in Congress and the administration, and of the army's leadership—what it tells them and how it evaluates, assigns, and promotes them. Declining professionalism is the outcome of this loss of trust. Yet, trust is what is needed most during this time of extraordinary organizational change.

As a first step toward addressing this problem, the army's leadership should assess the indirect effects of downsizing on the officer management system, focusing on those aspects of the professional climate cited above.[22] Armed with this assessment, it should take steps to "reinstitutionalize" the officer corps by stressing traditional military values. It should also seek to broaden the definition of professionalism and success by introducing some modest changes into current officer management practices.[23] As in the early 1980s, when the army and the other services undertook like-minded institution-building efforts to counter a perceived increase in occupational tendencies over the previous decade (Moskos 1988, 23), the army should now renew its efforts in this area to counter the ill effects of downsizing. From their "bully pulpits," army leaders (civilian and military) should articulate the distinctive characteristics of the military organization and profession. In this time of uncertainty, they must clarify the meaning and importance of military professionalism and reinforce selfless service and absolute integrity. They should emphasize an officer corps ethos that is nation-centered, not organization-centered; mission-centered, not career-centered; group-centered, not individual-centered; and service-centered, not work-centered (Cotton 1988, 53). Recent articles in military journals by senior army generals addressing these issues are indications that the leadership is moving in this direction (Reimer 1996; Stroup 1996).

But army leaders must not deceive themselves that such efforts are sufficient, for they have been only marginally successful in the past and are likely to be similarly so today. The army leadership must also broaden the notion of professionalism and modify entrenched assumptions about the definition of a successful military career. Because the "management of violence" is perceived throughout the army to be the military professional's distinctive competence, officers are more unwilling than ever to deviate from muddy boots career patterns and the quest for command. Moreover, as the army has attempted to "qualify" as many officers as possible for command, it has inadvertently heightened turbulence by rotating officers at an accelerating pace. This has undermined the professional development of future commanders by significantly reducing the amount of time they spend in key preparatory assignments.

These outcomes are telling indications that the narrow conception of professionalism on which the army has relied in the past is insufficient to describe what is actually required of a modern fighting force in the post–Cold War era. Certainly combat expertise is the single most vital skill for the officer corps, but this should not exclude all the other skills essential to the present and future army. Obviously, members of the officer corps who are not commanders but instead serve as staff officers or who step out of the muddy boots track altogether to become foreign area officers, permanent faculty members at West Point or at the other service schools, acquisition officers, and the like make a crucial contribution to the army's short-term and long-term effectiveness, and ultimately to its fighting power. While its leaders acknowledge this is the case, the army's institutional priorities—as demonstrated by who gets promoted, where the most high-touted officers are assigned, and the perceptions held by the majority of officers—belie this assertion.

Along these same lines, the army should make a concerted effort to so define success for career military officers as something other than simply selection for battalion command. There continues to be a commonly held belief within the officer corps that "to lead is to command." But this long-standing premise is increasingly imprecise in its conception, obscure in its perspective, and inadequate in its application, particularly in the post–Cold War era (Sarkesian 1981, 219). Not only is there a diminishing need for operational commanders, but there is also a growing demand for officers of exceptional quality to serve in assignments distinctly different from "transitional" command. This outmoded conception of what constitutes a "successful" military career accounts for many of the problems the army faces.

The army is likely to see some progress in these two areas by simply ensuring that a greater proportion of qualified officers who do not adhere to strictly traditional career patterns, and who have not served as battalion commanders, are promoted to colonel or higher. The promotion system is a clear-cut demonstration of institutional priorities, and these priorities should be made more transparent. By manipulating the promotion system in this way, the army's leadership will send a message that will not be lost on the officer corps. Over time, officers will modify their behavior and perceptions accordingly. A 1994 RAND study describes this phenomenon well:

> The outcomes of the promotion process . . . are carefully studied in an effort to identify trends and prepare for the future. . . . Career patterns of promoted officers are studied to identify the type of assignments that are prevalent. If certain types of assignments (duty with the reserves, recruiting assignments, ROTC duty, teaching at service schools) are common among selected officers, this type of assignment is considered "career enhancing." The converse is also true.

(Thie and Brown 1994, 278)

Finally, the army's leadership should take steps to reduce the rigidity—to loosen the bolts—in the current officer development process. The effects of downsizing have been exacerbated by the fact that officers must satisfy an inflexible set of requirements at each level of professional development in order to be considered "branch-qualified," and, for all practical purposes, to get promoted. Each development requirement is well-conceived and serves an important and useful purpose. Collectively, however, this deluge of requirements is dysfunctional. "Timing,"

rather than technical skills and expertise, professional maturity, or general knowledge (or cost-effectiveness, for that matter) has become the crucial criterion in officer management. Officers race from one assignment to the next frantically trying to "pass through all the gates" before being considered for the next promotion.

There are three possible approaches to solving these problems. Each poses varying degrees of difficulty and probability of success, and each addresses different aspects of the same problems. First, policymakers in Congress and the administration should modify the existing up-or-out officer management system mandated by the Defense Officer Personnel Management Act to allow for longer and more secure careers. Second, the army should independently make dramatic changes in the Officer Personnel Management System, modifying those aspects of its predicated on outdated assumptions. Third, the army should make minor adjustments in the existing system in order to create added flexibility. The first two will undoubtedly require more time for consideration and implementation than the third. Thus, army leaders should begin with the third course of action immediately and begin on the other two over the next year.

What are these minor adjustments? First, across all branches, the army should expand the types of assignments at each rank that it classifies as mandatory for advancement, or branch-qualifying, particularly at the rank of major.[24] This would reduce competition for these assignments and would lengthen the amount of time that majors who do adhere to "command" career patterns spend in key development jobs. Second, the army should consider adjusting its requirements concerning "utilization" tours following full-time civilian graduate school. As the policy now stands, officers go immediately from graduate school to a tour in which they purportedly utilize their newly acquired skills. This large block of time away from troop assignments not only deters officers from pursuing this option but also creates management dilemmas, as the officers who do attend civilian graduate school attempt to squeeze their other "requirements" into an abbreviated period before being considered for promotion to lieutenant colonel. By allowing officers to defer, or perhaps occasionally waive, the utilization requirement, the army would inject some much-needed flexibility in the current system.

Third, the army should consider waiving occasionally the requirement that officers complete mandatory military schooling before serving in key development assignments.[25] Brigade commanders on every army installation (at the post commander's discretion) should be permitted to select a small number of outstanding junior captains or senior captains and majors (say, 10–20 percent) to serve as company commanders, battalion operations officers, and executive officers.[26] Finally, the army should make promotion boards for lieutenant colonels six to twelve months later, thereby adding some flexibility to the officer development process. Between 1990 and 1995, the army shifted lieutenant colonel promotion boards forward by seven months. This reduced the amount of time officers of this rank had to wait for promotion, but it unnecessarily "cramped" majors in their professional development and contributed to the army's present management dilemmas.

Collectively, these minor adjustments would introduce some diversity and flexibility into career patterns, de-emphasizing the need to follow one, and only one, career path for promotion. These steps would also decentralize marginally the selection process for key development jobs by allowing brigade commanders to identify and reward the army's finest performers and future commanders. These changes would introduce additional efficiency and flexibility into officer management. At best, however, these suggestions are only short-term measures for addressing a number of very serious and deep-seated organizational problems. They do not address the myriad shortcomings in the current Officer Personnel Management System—shortcomings that have become increasingly evident and detrimental during downsizing.

Officer Management Reform

The army's leadership appears to have recognized that current officer management practices are outmoded. In 1996, it initiated an in-depth study of the current officer management system. It is uncertain what the Officer Personnel Management System (OPMS) XXI Task Force charged with this review will recommend. If past history is any guide, however, we might expect to see a relatively conservative set of recommendations that do little to challenge the status quo. Even under the most optimistic of scenarios—one in which a bona fide program for reform is recommended—it is likely to be years before any

significant alterations in officer management practices are made. What follows, therefore, is a broad set of recommendations for creating a viable and visionary officer management system for the post–Cold War era.

Officer management consists of strength management, officer evaluation, and professional development. In each of these areas, there is a compelling need for reform. In the case of strength management, the manner in which officer requirements are identified by the army, particularly TDA billets, must be improved. This argument, which was made in chapter 3, is not repeated in detail here. Simply stated, requirements for officers in the army's infrastructure, or TDA, are distorted by the fact that the senior officers who oversee TDA organizations play a significant role not only in identifying their officer requirements but also in authorizing them. Not surprisingly, the system is undisciplined and has placed a heavy burden on the officer management system, particularly during downsizing. Past efforts at reform in this area have failed. But in this period of declining resources, and with the demand for officers in other areas growing rapidly as a result of congressional mandates, the army must rationalize this process and streamline the officer-rich TDA army.

The army wisely refrained from instituting a new officer evaluation report in the midst of downsizing. This decision appears to have been based largely on its post-Vietnam experience, in which the introduction of a new report in the midst of dramatic personnel cuts had a disastrous effect. As downsizing has continued, however, the existing report has become increasingly inflated, contributing to a zero-defects mindset and a less innovative organizational culture. The army has had a new report ready to implement since the late 1980s. The new evaluation system should be implemented in conjunction with the re-professionalization efforts described above.[27]

The army's professional development system is the third component of OPMS. Dramatic changes in the professional development system—the way officers are educated, trained, and assigned—must be made in light of the demands likely to be imposed on the army in the future. The army is likely to require officers who not only are highly trained specialists but are capable of adapting to the uncertainties that inevitably accompany new technologies and unprecedented military missions. The shortcomings in the current system, particularly the institutional emphasis on preparing officers for command, runs counter to this requirement. Moreover, the original intent of OPMS—to establish varied and widely recognized "paths to the top"—has been subverted. This phenomenon was troubling enough during the Cold War, but it will spell disaster for the army in the post–Cold War era. An updated paradigm for officer professional development is needed for the next generation of army leaders, and for the generation after next.

An officer corps of specialists, with expertise across a range of technical and nontechnical areas, is needed for the future. In a recent book, former Chief of Staff Edward C. Meyer and several colleagues make a similar observation, suggesting that the army of the future will require an officer corps of specialists in three areas of expertise—politico-military, manager/technician, and operational command (1995, 225). The role of the professional development system would be to assist officers in gaining specific expertise, while also equipping them with the depth of experience and breadth of perspective necessary for the future. Meyer's proposal is a useful point of embarkation for sketching the skeleton of a future officer corps professional development system. The following pages are not a blueprint for transforming the army but rather a construct for exploring how a significantly modified professional development system might evolve. Clearly the current system is outmoded, and a new system that develops an officer corps of diverse specialties with multiple paths to the top is absolutely necessary.

The argument for a specialist officer corps, comprising officers not only on a command track but in a host of other specialties as well, has been considered by the army in the past. Indeed, this was one of the primary, though unrealized, objectives of OPMS. Additionally, during the reform movement of the 1970s, a number of authors made recommendations for a "pluralist" officer corps comprised of small core of institutionally oriented command specialists serving mostly in the fighting army and a larger group of occupationally oriented specialists serving mostly in the support army (Hauser 1973, 208; Bradford and Brown 1973, 193).[28] Fortunately, effective professional development for the twenty-first century requires nothing quite as bold as dividing the military profession into two parts. Indeed, in retrospect, these past proposals appear somewhat simplistic.[29] What is needed, however, is an institutional and professional framework that allows officers to concentrate during their careers in one of the three broad areas of expertise outlined above. Moreover, rather than explicitly dividing officers into separate categories of traditional military professionals and those with civilian-oriented specialties, an attempt should be made to broaden institutional conceptions of professionalism in recognition of the critical contributions made by each facet of the officer corps.

Ideally, a professional development system consistent with these principles would seek to identify officers for each area of expertise between their fifth and seventh years of service. This is a controversial point for many traditionalists who argue that making this decision so early in an officer's career does not permit the "late bloomer" to demonstrate a strong propensity for command. The obvious response to this argument, of course, is that a downsized Army does not have the luxury of retaining hundreds of unneeded junior and mid-career officers in command career patterns in the hope of discovering the occasional late bloomer.

As currently, officers would be commissioned into basic branches and spend their first two active duty tours as company grade officers in the field army. As is also presently the case, each officer would be required to command a company during this period in order to be branch-qualified.[30] At this point, however, the traditional officer development models would change dramatically. During this initial five years, the army should ruthlessly cull each cohort, as officers will have had ample opportunity to demonstrate specific aptitudes and potential for continued service. Between their fifth and seventh years of service, on the basis of their preferences, academic background, and performance, officers would choose one of the three career tracks—politico-military, manager/technical, and operational command. The majority of officers would be dedicated to the first two career patterns, while a minority (approximately twice the number of officers who ultimately would be selected for battalion command) would be permitted to pursue the command track. The outcome of this concept would be an army in which every field grade officer might legitimately be called a specialist.

The numbers of officers dedicated to each career track should be determined, of course, on the basis of the army's projected needs. Thus, after rationalizing the officer requirements process, the army should strive to code all, or most, field grade officer billets into one of these three specialties, from the general ranks on down. Obviously, such changes would have significant implications for the branch structure and the current specialty modes of the officer corps. The current branches should be reevaluated and expanded, shrunk, or eliminated, depending on the army's present and projected needs. A certain percentage of officers from each branch, depending on the new officer requirements, could logically serve in the three major specialties. There would, for example, be positions for officers from the transportation branch or the engineer branch in the command track, the managerial/technical track, and perhaps even in the politico-military track. The same would hold true for most other branches. Functional areas would fall within one of these three broad specialties, thus the choice of a functional area would be consistent with the choice of a career track.[31]

It would be imperative, of course, to create viable career patterns and a reasonable development sequence within each specialty. As is now the case, there should be ample opportunity for officers in each of the three specialties to serve with increasing responsibility in various positions between their tenth and twentieth years of service. Within the army, politico-military specialists would generally serve on high-level staffs, division level and above. They would also fill the majority of assignments external to the army—as members of joint staffs, interagency groups, congressional liaison teams, State Department staffs, or as military attachés. Managerial/technical specialists would also have ample field assignments down to the brigade level in the areas of logistics, maintenance, and personnel. Moreover, they would fill the large majority of assignments in these areas as well as in budgeting, procurement, and research and development, and other technical areas in the Pentagon and in other major army headquarters.

Finally, officers in the operational command track would serve on operations staffs at the battalion, brigade, and division levels, thereby avoiding staff assignments only peripherally related to command.[32] Moreover, officers in the operational command track would be primarily responsible for staffing the army's training centers and for serving as evaluators and advisors for the Army National Guard and the Army Reserve. It would also be necessary and important to identify additional points during an officer's career (following battalion command, and prior to attending the War College, for example) in which he or she

might change specialties. One option would be to allow successful battalion commanders who have demonstrated a certain expertise to change into the politico-military or managerial/technical track. However, this possibility should only be open to a small percentage of talented officers who have demonstrated the ability to make significant contributions across specialties.

It is foolish to think, of course, that a one-star or two-star general who served admirably as a brigade commander or division commander is, on the basis of that performance alone, prepared or qualified to serve in a senior position in logistics, procurement, or politico-military affairs, yet the army currently makes such assignments routinely.[33] Under this proposal, general officer positions would for the most part be designated for officers within each of the three career tracks. Division and corps commanders and regional commanders in chief (CINCs) would clearly be designated as part of operational command track, while other senior positions on the Joint Staff or Army Staff would fall in the politico-military area. Some general officer billets such as the Chief of Engineers, the Deputy Chief of Staff for Logistics, and the Commanding General of the Army Material Command would be designated as part of the managerial/technical track. Some general officer positions such as Superintendent of West Point, the Commanding General of the Army War College, and the Chief of Staff of the Army should be open to officers from all three.

Of course, in instituting such changes myriad factors must be considered. How should officers be trained and educated? What are the common principles that should guide professional development across all three categories? And, in what areas should professional development models vary significantly? Three issues in particular—flexibility within career patterns, civilian graduate education, and professional military schooling—will be crucial in the future.

Flexible Career Patterns

Flexible career patterns will be crucially important for the next officer corps, and for the officer corps after next. The army must avoid cookie-cutter career patterns at all costs. As Tracy Goss et al. write: "There is an obscure law of cybernetics—the law of requisite variety—that postulates that any system must encourage and incorporate variety internally if it is to cope with variety externally" (1993, 106). The logic of this

law applies not only to the career patterns of individual army officers but to the officer corps at large,
and it should be a guiding principle for the army as it
develops new career patterns for the post–Cold War
era. In practice, it implies that an effort should be
made to introduce flexibility by allowing officers
periodically to serve in assignments and participate
in educational opportunities outside traditional
career patterns. At first blush, this might seem to
contradict the notion that officers of the future
should be specialists. On the contrary, however, variety need not imply "generalist" career patterns in
which officers rotate through myriad developmental
assignments, becoming jacks of all trades and masters
of none. Rather, it simply means that no "ideal" career
pattern exists.

The idea of permitting (even encouraging), officers to partake in educational opportunities and to
serve in assignments outside their specialties (after
they have developed their expertise through consecutive assignments and schooling) has certain advantages. It would contribute to cross-fertilization,
benefiting the army by introducing expertise and
new perspective into different components of the
organization while adding valuable breadth to an officer's outlook. Although such developmental practices might be viewed as frivolous in corporate
America, they would be vital to professional development in an organization that places such a high
premium on adaptive leadership.

Variance and flexibility in career patterns within
each specialty and across specialties will also
improve the quality of organizational decisionmaking. Senior leaders would be more likely to bring
with them to high-level positions a diversity of views
and experiences, thereby enhancing the quality of
the decisionmaking process. Organizations in which
there is homogeneity in terms of members' social
background, ideology, and professional development
are more susceptible to "groupthink"—a myopic
mode of thought that exists when people, deeply
involved in a cohesive "in group," allow their desire
for unanimity to override any motivation to appraise
realistic alternatives (Janis 1982). Varied career patterns will help the army avoid the dangers of groupthink throughout its hierarchy.

Historical experience also suggests that officers
with somewhat various career patterns are more successful and more effective army leaders. In a 1950
sample of the army's elite, for example, Janowitz

found that 72.5 percent had "adaptive" career patterns, concluding that "most officers who have
entered the top one-half of one percent of the hierarchy had complied with conventional career forms,
but (have) . . . frequently had specialized and inno-
vating experiences which have increased their usefulness to the military profession."[34] Moreover, army
leaders who had been most decisive were characterized by pronounced unconventionality in their career
patterns (1960, 151, 169). Others have even gone so
far as to conclude that the effectiveness of military
leaders varies inversely with their exposure to a conventional routinized military career (Davis, as cited in
Janowitz 1960, 151). Similarly, military historian
Russell Weigley concludes that the adaptability and
thoughtfulness among senior military leaders resulting from such unconventionality "constitutes a prime
assurance of [the army's] ability to serve the country
adequately in an uncertain future" (1984, 554).

By introducing flexibility into officer career patterns, and specifically into officer assignment and
promotion policies, the army may also improve the
likelihood of successful peacetime innovation. In his
book, *Winning the Next War,* Stephen Rosen finds
that "peacetime innovation has been possible when
senior military officers with traditional credentials
. . . have acted to create a new promotion pathway
for junior officers practicing a new way of war"
(1991, 251). In other words, peacetime innovation
was successful when senior officers were able to convince bright, young, talented officers that they would
be protected—that is, continue to advance to the
highest levels of the army—if they veered from traditional career patterns.[35] Flexible career patterns
would thus enhance the likelihood of innovation.

Given these findings, the army's leadership
should introduce both variety and flexibility into
future career patterns. They should not be so rigid
or so unforgiving as to discourage completely nontraditional career choices on the part of ambitious
and talented officers as they do now. With formalized specialist career patterns, the officer corps will
have significantly more time to develop true expertise in their fields. The army should encourage officers to participate periodically in schooling or
nontraditional assignments outside designated career
paths by ensuring that certain managerial/technical
or politico-military assignments are periodically filled
with officers from the operational command track,
and vice versa. An officer corps made up of individ-

uals with myriad development experiences, disparate intellectual skills and training, and diversified specialties will be best prepared to adapt successfully to the uncertainties of the post–Cold War era.

Full-Time Civilian Graduate School

The army should also incorporate full-time advanced civilian graduate education into the careers of most officers, including those on the operational command track. As retired colonel A. J. Bacevich writes, "American army officers pride themselves on being doers rather than thinkers" (1990, 13). But thinking, which is not mutually exclusive with doing, is arguably more important in a peacetime army. In the past, the army has generally offered full-time civilian graduate training to officers who agreed to serve in specific follow-on positions for which specialized training was purportedly needed (Sarkesian 1981, 179). In the future, full-time civilian graduate schooling for the majority of officers across all three main specialties—including command specialists—and in a range of disciplines, will help create and sustain a vibrant intellectual climate. The merits and drawbacks of full-time civilian graduate schooling have been debated within the army for decades and the particulars of that debate will not be repeated here. There are three reasons why full-time civilian graduate schooling for most officers is a good idea in the post–Cold War era.[36]

First and most obviously, this will be necessary in an officer corps of specialists—officers with politico-military, managerial/technical, and operational command expertise. In the first two categories, there is a clear need for specialized education in political science, foreign area specialties, international affairs, law, management, science, mathematics, and engineering. Not surprisingly, the army is incapable of providing top-quality education as inexpensively and efficiently as civilian institutions. Civilian graduate schooling is equally valuable for the breadth it provides, particularly for officers who remain on the operational command track. There will be the tendency among many senior officers to exclude combat leaders from civilian schooling, on the argument that they will have neither the time or the need for such a luxury. This would be a terrible mistake. As retired general Andrew Goodpaster writes:

> The effective command of complex military units and organizations remains as much an

art as a science. Development of the capacity for exercising command effectively is advanced by studies ranging from history and the understanding of the human condition to ethics and psychology of leadership before the processes of decision, the capabilities of weapons, the elements of alliance relationships, the thought patterns, culture and doctrine of possible opponents, and the whole gamut of professional military knowledge are even broached.

(As quoted in Sarkesian 1981, 184)

Civilian graduate schooling also helps the army to avoid intellectual isolation.[37] The injection of new ideas, combined with heightened competence and broadened perspective, instills a dynamism within the officer corps that the military cannot hope to achieve through purely professional military education (Sarkesian 1981, 132). Moreover, it provides the opportunity for active duty officers to establish relationships and interact (in a non-political) environment with present and future civilian leaders—members of Congress, the media, appointed officials—foreign nationals, and other national and international personages—with whom they are likely to have greater interaction in the post–Cold War era. And as the number of civilians with military experience steadily declines, it is important that future policymakers gain some knowledge of and experience with members of the armed forces.[38] Finally, there is evidence that the promise of army-sponsored civilian graduate schooling is a powerful retention tool, particularly among company grade officers.[39]

In brief, the army should place an even greater emphasis on civilian graduate education in the post–Cold War era than it has in the past. Specialist career patterns will provide officers with the flexibility to attend civilian schools and gaining expertise in their fields will often require them to do so. Civilian education should not be viewed as a luxury, or limited to a certain number of slots annually. Nor should it be rigidly programmed into an officer's career pattern. Officers in all career specialties should be encouraged to attend civilian graduate schools. In many cases officers should be required to do so and in most cases they should be rewarded for doing so.[40]

Professional Military Schooling

Robust intellectual centers, dedicated not only to the professional development of the officer corps but also to the cultivation of ideas about tactics, doctrine, and strategy, will be instrumental in creasing a vibrant and visionary peacetime army. The army's intellectual community—service schools, operational training centers, and laboratories—should receive high priority, not only in terms of financial resources (within budget limitations) but also in terms of the quality of the officers assigned to it. The army's experience in the period leading up to World War II reinforces the importance of military intellectual centers during peacetime. Despite dissatisfaction over slow promotions, perennial unhappiness over poor pay, and chronic low morale, the army retained and maintained a vibrant, versatile, and extraordinarily talented officer corps. Many attribute this success to the institutional emphasis placed on professional education and the core of outstanding officers who served on the faculties of the army's professional schools during the interwar period (1918–1941). Some of the army's most illustrious historical figures—Marshall, Eisenhower, and Patton, for example—were assigned to the Infantry School, the Command and General Staff College, the War College, and Army Industrial College and "formed a self-conscious elite" that proved instrumental to the army's success in World War II (Miller 1973, 47). Similarly, some have attributed the army's smashing success in the Gulf War to the professional schooling received by a generation of senior officers in the 1970s and 1980s (Kitfield 1991).

With these experiences in mind, several reforms in the army's professional schooling programs should be considered. First, the army should take steps to overcome the perception (reinforced by the SERB experience) that the faculties at the Command and General Staff College at Fort Leavenworth and the Army War College are "graveyards" in which disenchanted majors, lieutenant colonels, and colonels serve out the final years of their stalled careers. Duty on these faculties should be seen as career-enhancing—not only as an opportunity to mentor and teach the army's future leadership but as a chance for independent research, doctrinal development, and personal reflection.[41] Senior army leaders and personnel assignment officers must both play a role in changing these perceptions by continually emphasizing the importance of such assignments in word and in deed. The most talented officers at every rank should be routinely assigned instructor duty at West Point, the War College, and Leavenworth and regularly promoted from these assignments to positions of higher responsibility.

The professional schooling system will also require rethinking to ensure its integration with a new officer management system. Given an officer corps of specialists, army leaders should consider whether attendance at the Command and General Staff College and the War College is appropriate for every part of the officer corps. If so, how should the curricula be adjusted to meet the joint development needs of these three groups of specialists? If the army were to place added emphasis on civilian graduate schooling, its professional schools would be able to shift their focus toward the military topics relevant to the post–Cold War era and away from such "civilian" subjects as management and political science, which are better taught and learned elsewhere.[42] As Meyer et al. write:

> The military education program has evolved into a very responsive system for preparing officers for combat. It is less effective in preparing them for other challenges they are likely to face. . . . The sophistication required in many of the "peace" related roles that our troops will be called upon to perform indicates that [officer] education needs to be more complete if our armed forces are to be successful in these roles." (1999, 225)

With this in mind, there will undoubtedly be a need to modify the curricula of the Command and Staff College and the War College. While an initial phase of instruction focusing on subjects common to all three career tracks—ethics, leadership, and military history, for example—would still be plausible, there would also be a need for separate sequences of course work projects, and independent study, with supporting faculty in each. In the event that the army decides that attendance at CGSC or the War College is no longer appropriate for certain groups of officers, it must take steps to ensure that cohesiveness within the officer corps, which is reinforced through the professional schooling system, is maintained.

SUMMARY

These changes would create an officer corps with true and enduring expertise. Field grade officers would be required to serve in consecutive assignments in their designated fields. A substantial reduction in the number of officers on the "command track" would mitigate the unhealthy competitiveness and careerist tendencies that now exist. This approach would permit the army to extend the period that officers spend in key command, staff, and technical assignments, and to reduce turbulence, as officers would no longer be required to change locations or assignments so frequently.

With this approach, the operational commanders in the military after next would be more seasoned, having had the opportunity to develop "war-fighting skills" throughout a career of tough, sequential, operational assignments. The same would be true for officers serving in politico-military and managerial/technical career patterns. The army would add significant flexibility to officer management by separating officers into distinct specialist patterns earlier in their careers. As a consequence, an officer's career progression would be pliant enough, for example, to permit twelve to twenty-four months of full-time civilian graduate schooling, as well as occasional assignments outside traditional career patterns without fear of permanent damage to long-term career prospects. In short, this approach will develop army leaders appropriate for the twenty-first century—a corps of officers with expertise in a range of technical and nontechnical skills, but adaptable and sophisticated enough to function effectively amidst the complexities and uncertainties of future military operations.

John Kotter and James Heskett observe that in any organization "who gets promoted says more about real values than any mission statement or credo" (1992, 144). This is true of the army. Formal and widely publicized modifications to army promotion policy will be necessary if such revolutionary changes are to be accepted and lasting. The army must deliver on promises of equal opportunities for advancement to the highest levels if it is to attract the best young officers into all three specialties.[43] Undoubtedly, the logic of this approach will be lost on many senior military leaders who are products of the current system and cling tenaciously to outdated conceptions of military professionalism and officer development. Likewise, despite the army's assurances, junior officers will be reluctant at first to strike out on managerial/technical or politico-military career patterns for fear that promised advancement opportunities will not materialize. Initially, it is likely that the army will be required to assign a certain percentage of each officer cohort (depending on officer requirements) to each of these three career tracks.[44]

With time, however, as these career patterns are established and refined, and as officers in each specialty climb steadily to the highest echelons of the army, anxiety will subside, each career track will be viewed as credible, and a more healthy and vital professional climate will prevail:

> With equal opportunities for advancement in a command, staff or other specialized career, there would be no stigma attached to whatever path an officer took—in concert with the needs of the army, of course, and the army could build pools from which qualified, motivated officers could be pulled for specific requirements requiring specific backgrounds. In that way, the army will have modern versions of the Pattons and Eisenhowers we require.
>
> (Meyer et al. 1995, 225)

Regardless of promotion opportunities, officers in the command track will remain the army's elite. This is inevitable and appropriate. However, the army will only achieve the much-needed balance of "talent" across the officer corps by equitably distributing promotion opportunities among the three career tracks.

CONGRESS AND THE DEPARTMENT OF DEFENSE: LEGISLATIVE REFORM

Civilian leaders too must take steps to build an officer corps for the twenty-first century. Most important, they must become more sensitive to the strains imposed on the army officer corps by incremental and prolonged downsizing. The army's projected size has steadily been chipped away as the political and budgetary landscapes have grown increasingly treacherous. After having already been cut by 30 percent, the army's "final" target from strength has declined further since 1993, from 535,000 to 520,000 to 495,000, with further cuts on the horizon. This is not to suggest that significant cuts in endstrength were not necessary, or that additional cuts may not be warranted in the future. It is clear, however, that as policymakers in Congress and the Department of Defense have haggled over endstrength numbers of divisions, modernization dollars, and readiness, they have overlooked the bonds of trust, sacrifice, and respect that atrophy as those in uniform look around and wonder who will be next. These bonds are important in any organization, but they are essential for an effective fighting force. By prolonging the uncertainty of downsizing, policymakers have undermined the faith of the professional officer corps in its leaders, weakened their confidence that successful, productive careers are possible, and engendered attitudes and behaviors antithetical to a professional volunteer army. Civilian leaders must factor the devastating effects of personnel cuts on these "intangibles" into future downsizing decisions.

Additionally, administration policymakers and congressional leaders must replace the existing officer management legislation (DOPMA) with rules and regulations more appropriate to the downsized military services. The possibility of such reform has already been raised. Two recent RAND studies—a 1993 retrospective assessment of DOPMA and a 1994 analysis of future officer career management systems—found substantial shortcomings in the current system and presented various alternatives (Rostker et al. 1993; Thie and Brown 1994).[45] Among other things, the RAND work confirmed that DOPMA was far better suited for periods of growth and stability than for the period of dramatic personnel reductions carried out between 1990 and 1996, though it also noted that even in periods of stability the legislation had shortcomings (Rostker et al. 1993, 69). The numerous waivers and special provisions that Congress authorized to manage officer cuts during this period are testimony to DOPMA's inflexibility. Moreover, DOPMA is based on the assumption that there is a need for uniformity in promotion opportunity timing and grade structure across the services. While uniformity is an understandable objective, it fails to account for differences in service cultures, missions, and officer requirements. Third, DOPMA was designed with the intent of controlling officer growth and "grade creep." Thus, a sliding-scale grade table included in the legislation is used to control officer inventory directly, as the officer requirements generated by the services are generally, and understandably, not believed (This may be one of the few cases in which deeper congressional involvement and oversight is justified.) Still, the DOPMA approach fails to account for the dynamic nature of officer requirements, which may grow or diminish over time, particularly during periods of dramatic organizational change.

In addition, the 1981 DOPMA legislation codified in a single act a combination of beliefs and assumptions based on the military's experiences in World War II. The up-or-out principle and mandatory early retirement, in particular, reflect the desire to ensure a young and vigorous fighting force. This assumption, in particular, has been outdated for decades:

> Military manpower policies have been based on the claim that "youth and vigor" are by far the most important qualifications for military service. But how valid is this claim? The military has opted for a youthful force, judging it is better able to endure the hardships of military duty and hence more effective in maintaining defense readiness. . . . The relationship in which age is a proxy for physical fitness is neither as clear, nor as simple as that implied by past and current military manpower policies. . . . The requirement for youthfulness and vigor is neither overwhelming nor applicable to all of the jobs in the military services

(Binkin 1986, 24, 28).

The benefits of the up-or-out approach and mandatory early retirement are few. These policies ensure a constant flow of "new blood" through the officer corps, arguably providing officers with incentives to perform at high levels throughout their careers. This approach also ensures generous advancement opportunity at every level, through a process of forced attrition. The disadvantages of these policies, however, are equally apparent. The current system is inordinately expensive, as highly trained and effective officers are continually discharged from active duty, despite the fact that they have the ability to provide valuable service for years, sometimes decades, after retirement.[46] Moreover, shortened military careers crowd the officer professional development process and increase turbulence in the officer corps. As one reformer writes: "The chief obstacle to . . . meaningful improvement in [the] development of officers is the short and hurried nature of the military career."[47] Finally, as the 1994 RAND study concludes: "The forced-attrition mechanism diminishes long-term commitment" among officers (Thie and Brown 1994, 78). These phenomena were magnified across the entire officer corps by downsizing.

The creation and implementation of a new officer career management system will obviously require much time and research as well as numerous congressional hearings and negotiations before it becomes a reality. However, the army's current management dilemmas and the insightful and comprehensive work done by RAND suggest several fundamental features that should be part of any new system. First, there should be some variation of "up and stay." While it may be desirable to have a high turnover of officers during the first ten years of service to whittle the corps down to an appropriately sized career force, the large majority of those who remain after that point should be retained for an entire career. Second, army careers should be extended for officers with the capacity for continued service to thirty-five to forty years, though under such a system it would be crucial to develop mechanisms for selectively weeding out poor performers. Third, defense planners should consider a more portable retirement system, under which officers and enlisted members could take with them their accrued benefits regardless of the stage of their careers when they depart the army.

These changes would yield many improvements over the current system. First, the proposed system would be more efficient. The services would no longer be forced to separate competent, highly trained officers simply because they had not been promoted. Retention could be solely performance-based. And, indeed, it would be crucially important to develop an effective mechanism for separating retirement-eligible officers who are no longer productive while retaining those who continue to make an important contribution. In addition, these changes would lengthen the period that officers would have to develop and utilize the specialized skills gained throughout successive assignments in their specialties, with a far greater overall return on investment for the army. By extending officers' careers and permitting retention without the necessity for continued promotion, the incentives for careerism and ticket punching will be reduced dramatically. Additionally, the anxiety many officers feel late in their careers as they approach mandatory retirement and the uncertain prospects of civilian employment at middle age will decline.[48]

Third, there is no reason why the grade structure for the services in the future necessarily needs to be a pyramid. For example, the grade structure could be designed like an aircraft carrier—the junior grades are below the decks, the career force begins with the bulge of majors on the carrier deck, and the higher grades of lieutenant colonel, colonel, and general are represented by the narrower superstructure in the center of the ship (Thie and Brown 1994, 194). Admittedly, promotion timing and opportunity would be less certain with alternative grade structures, but

this might cause the importance of these variables to diminish. This is a trade-off that should be considered. Finally, legislative reform must take place sooner rather than later. There is no time to waste—officer management reform should be a top priority of both Congress and the current administration.

LEADERSHIP FOR THE MILITARY AFTER NEXT

Some will call these recommendations a "radical" reform agenda. However, the army's current officer management system, and the legislation that governs it, are too antiquated to create the kind of specialized and adaptable officer corps needed for the future. Moreover, the rigidity of the current system has exacerbated the undesirable effects of downsizing. A new system is clearly needed to confront these shortcomings. If "radical" means ridding the army's personnel management system of outmoded assumptions and worn out ideas, then this agenda is radical indeed.

The recommendations I make are relatively straightforward. The army should modify its officer management system, particularly its current professional development model. During their first five to seven years of service, officers should be assigned to one of three career tracks—politico-military, managerial/technical, or operational command. Through sequential assignments, military schooling, and civilian graduate education, officers will develop true expertise in these specialties. In the post–Cold War era, the army should also place added emphasis on maintaining flexible career patterns, avoiding at all costs cookie-cutter approaches to professional development. Likewise, full-time civilian graduate schooling should be a top priority for all officers, even those in the operational command track. Additionally, the army should take steps to build an intellectually vital social architecture within its professional schooling system. Finally, Congress should write, debate, refine, and pass new officer management legislation permitting longer careers based on the principle of "up and stay."

None of these propositions is completely new. Variations of each have been debated inside and outside the army for decades. During the reform movement in the early 1970s, a number of friendly and some not-so-friendly critics offered numerous recommendations for the improvement of officer management and professional development to correct the professional malaise the officer corps suffered during and after the Vietnam War. In the post–Cold War era, the army faces a somewhat different problem. While it is true that professionalism within the officer corps has been strained by downsizing, an equally pressing challenge is to modify the army's officer management system to ensure it develops the kinds of specialized, adaptable leaders who will be needed in the future.

The ideas proposed here are ambitious. Even if civilian and military leaders supported them, time would be needed for their implementation. The army, like any large bureaucratic organization, will be slow to transform itself, particularly in areas as sensitive as officer management. It is more likely that there will be significant resistance among many senior military leaders to some, perhaps all, of these proposals. An increased emphasis on specialization, longer careers, an up-and-stay career system, and a broader conception of military professionalism all run counter to deeply entrenched institutional norms. In addition, these recommendations have some very legitimate dangers associated with them.

First, some might argue that it is impossible to draw such definitive conclusions or make such radical recommendations on the basis of one research effort. However, the attitudinal and behavioral problems I observe are consistent with the findings of studies conducted by the Army Strategic Fellows Program and the Department of the Army Inspector General in 1994. Likewise, the 1995 *Army Assessment,* an army-wide survey focusing specifically on this issue, reportedly portrays a professional climate even more alarming than that which is described in this book (Reimer 1996). The army's leadership has already begun to acknowledge these problems. It is time now to do something about them.

Along the same lines, some senior officers and civilians contend that the undesired effects of downsizing will subside once stability has returned to the personnel system, making a reform agenda unnecessary. While this contention is not totally incorrect, it grossly underestimates the damage already done. Most of the problems described here will linger even if personnel reductions were to end once and for all (an unlikely prospect until at least 2000 and beyond). Following the Vietnam War, it took the better part of a decade to correct similar problems in the officer corps (Dunnigan and Macedonia 1993). In any case, the army does not have the luxury of waiting for stability to implement organizational change, for the current officer management system is simply inappropriate for developing officers to meet the challenges of the twenty-first century. This assertion holds regardless of the state of professionalism within the officer corps.

It might also be argued that specialized career patterns will pose significant challenges for the army's leadership, perhaps creating problems that outweigh their benefits. There is a legitimate concern, for example, that subdivisions of this sort would destroy the homogeneity and peer group associations among officer cohorts, creating an "us-them" mentality within the officer corps.[49] In addition, critics would be correct in observing that developing and educating an officer corps of specialists would be costly, an expense some will surely say the army cannot afford.[50] Despite these disadvantages, they are far outweighed by the benefits of a specialized officer corps.

Experts in politico-military affairs, management and technology, and operational command are needed if the army is to be successful when faced by the myriad roles it will be expected to play in the future. Intellectual capital of this sort will be as important as the next generation of high-tech weaponry to the army's effectiveness, perhaps more so. In addition, the costs of these recommendations for the army's personnel budget would be less than one might at first believe, for there are efficiencies to be gained as well. With specialist career patterns, it will no longer be necessary to rotate officers as regularly through branch-qualifying assignments (thereby reducing the frequency of moving expenses). Moreover, with a corps of officers dedicated to particular specialties, the overall number of officers required, and their respective costs, are likely to decrease, particularly if the army streamlines its officer requirements process and Congress approves longer careers and a substantially less expensive up-and-stay management system.[51]

Fourth, some will argue that three specialist career tracks and an added emphasis on civilian schooling will undermine the army's warrior ethos, diverting the officer corps' focus from its single most important mission—fighting and winning the nation's wars. This is a legitimate concern—one that requires the utmost consideration—but this problem, too, is avoidable. It is true that with many paths to the top, significantly more officers in what might be considered nonwarrior career patterns will become senior army leaders. This is both sensible and necessary. Just as it would be unreasonable for the executive ranks of Ford Motor Company to be filled exclusively by managers from the manufacturing division, so too is it nonsensical to suggest that it is appropriate to lead a modern army solely with operational commanders. At the same time, there are very real dangers in creating an army managed by senior officers too far removed from the point of the spear to have an intuitive feel for the needs and appropriate priorities of a military organization.

For this reason, operational commanders should, and undoubtedly will, continue to dominate at the highest levels of the organization and many (though not all) of the army's most promising young leaders should be assigned to the operational command career track. But the army must strike a more appropriate balance between the various types of military leaders that dominate at each level of its hierarchy. The army has always had senior officers who could be roughly categorized as politico-military generals, military managers, and operational commanders. This proposal simply formalizes the developmental process for each. The first two are likely to gain some influence at the expense of the third, but they will not and should not displace operational commanders as the "elite" in the organization. Additionally, within the command track, the army's warriors should have the opportunity through longer, sequential, and demanding troop assignments to become truly proficient operational commanders. In short, the army's warriors should be afforded the opportunity to focus predominantly on fighting and winning future wars. These points notwithstanding, the army's senior leaders should make maintaining the warrior ethos, throughout the officer corps, in reality as well as symbolically a top priority during the transition to a new system. Strong leadership in this area will be crucial to the army's future success.

There may also be criticisms that the proposed officer development process devotes too much energy and too many resources to developing in junior and mid-career officers the talents or skills only needed by the very few who will be promoted to the highest levels of the army. According to a retired general of an earlier era, "Problems arise when too much attention is given the qualifications a man must have in order that he may be considered for selection to general officer rank, rather than to the experience needed in the less exalted ranks of service" (Smith 1971, 28). In the post–Cold War era, however, specialized expertise, political sophistication, and adaptability are needed at all levels of the army hierarchy. The infantry captains charged with

monitoring compliance with the Dayton Peace Accords in Bosnia, the staff officers who recently planned humanitarian relief operations in northwestern Iraq, and the lieutenant colonels overseeing the development of the next generation of army weapons systems, for example, all must make rapid and independent decisions in an environment far more complicated and politically volatile than their predecessors. Such challenges will be even more numerous and complex in the future.

Finally, some might argue that this reform agenda—particularly the politico-military career track and the emphasis on civilian graduate education—will ultimately "politicize" the officer corps. In this case, politicization refers to partisan politics—activities that subordinate the interests of the country to the parochial interests of the army or particular individuals, thereby undermining military professionalism. This view is consistent with traditional conceptions of professionalism, which hold that civilian control is best maintained by keeping the military separate from society (Huntington 1957). In contrast to the traditional view, however, this proposal presumes a more mature conception of professionalism, recognizing that it has a political dimension. Military professionals should not become politicians, but in the post–Cold War era they must be more astute, more knowledgeable about and sensitive to the political imperatives of domestic and international societies than ever before. As Bacevich writes: "Those who protest the danger of soldiers becoming involved in politics miss the point. The exclusion of soldiers from politics does not guarantee peace. It only guarantees that those who command armies in wartime will be politically obtuse" (1990, 19).

In conclusion, this chapter is a call for action. Developing exceptional leaders for the next military, and for the military after next, will require sustained and visionary action. By creating three career tracks—politico-military, managerial/technical and operational command—the army will be better able to prepare officers for the uncertainties of this new era. Officers will have the opportunity to develop the expertise needed to maneuver within increasingly tenuous political situations, manage increasingly complex military organizations, and lead soldiers successfully in increasingly complicated and diverse military operations. Moreover, this approach will be far more efficient because officers will no longer be herded through a rigid and outdated professional development process. Finally, by modifying officer management legislation, congressional leaders may once and for all free the military services of outmoded post–World War II planning assumptions.

Instituting these changes will be difficult. It will require dramatic changes in the way military and civilian leaders think about officer management. Many of these changes will be particularly difficult for the army to make because they conflict with deeply entrenched elements of its institutional culture. Moreover, they will require the transfer of resources for specialized training, civilian graduate schooling, and nontraditional military assignments, the benefits of which are unlikely to be understood by green-shade budgeteers. Although change will be difficult and perhaps unpopular, it is nonetheless necessary. The complexity and difficulty of the tasks ahead are no excuse for inaction.

RESOURCES

URLs ACCESSED DURING THIS COURSE

Blackboard: *http://rotc.blackboard.com/*

HOOAH 4 Health: *http://hooah4health.com*

HOOAH 4 YOU: *http://hooah4health.com/4You/default.htm*

Health Goals Checklist:
http://www.hooah4health.com/4You/hgoalsadultsurvey.asp

Food Pyramid Game:
http://www.hooah4health.com/body/pyramidinteractive.htm

Learning Style Inventory:
http://www.metamath.com//lsweb/dvclearn.htm

Learning Style Inventory Survey:
http://www.metamath.com//multiple/multiple_choice_questions.cgi

COPYRIGHT ACKNOWLEDGMENTS

MODULE I

Lesson Two

Donatelle, Rebecca J., *Access to Health* (7th ed.). San Francisco: Benjamin Cummings. 2002. (ISBN: 0-205-33664-7). "Putting Health in Perspective", pages 3 through 5, "Improving Your Health", pages 15 through 17, and "Psychosocial Health", pages 32 through 57

Lesson Three

Insel, Paul and Roth, Walton. "Eating Healthy" in *Core Concepts in Health* (9th ed.). New York: McGraw Hill, 2002. (ISBN: 0-7674-2370-4) Pages 314–327 and 352

MODULE II (Part I)

Lesson Four

Hughes, R. L., Ginnett, R. C., & Curphy, G. J. *"Setting Goals" in Leadership, Enhancing the Lessons of Experience (4th ed.).* New York: Irwin McGraw-Hill, 2002. (ISBN: 0-07-244529-7). Pp. 467–475

MODULE III (Part I)

Lesson Six

Feldman, Robert S. *Power Learning: Strategies for Success in College and Life.* Robert S. Feldman. McGraw-Hill Higher Education. 2000. (ISBN: 0-0-73-65505-8). pp. 55–63, Discovering Your Learning Styles

Lesson Seven

STP 21-1-SMCT *Soldier's Manual of Common Tasks (Skill Level 1)*(1994/10/01). Table of Contents.

Lesson Eight

COL Gregory Fontenot *Military Review.* January 1993. *Fright Night: Task Force 2-34 Armor.*

Lesson Nine

Colonel Harry Summers Jr., US Army, Retired. *Full Cirlce: World War II to the Persian Gulf.* © 1992.

Lesson Eleven

Center for Military History Publication 19-6, *The Korean War–The Outbreak.* Pages 16 through 26.

Lesson Twelve

Cross, David F. *Mantled in Fire and Smoke.* America's Civil War magazine; AMERICA'S CIVIL WAR: VOLUME 12 * NUMBER 3 * JULY 1999.

Norton, Oliver Willcox. *The Attack and Defense of Little Round Top, Gettysburg, July 2, 1863.* Dayton, Ohio: Morningside Bookshop, 1978. (ISBN: 0-890-29041-5). Report of Col. Joshua L. Chamberlain, 20th Maine Infantry, pages 210 through 218 and map "Chamberlain at Gettysburg July 2, 1863."

MODULE II (Part II)

MODULE III (Part III)

Lesson Fourteen

Nairne, James S. "Solving Problems" in *Psychology: The Adaptive Mind* (2nd ed.). Wadsworth Publishing Co, 2000. (ISBN: 0-534-72432-9). Pages 362 through 375.

MODULE IV

Lesson Twenty-five

Bonn, Keith E. (LTC Ret.). *Army Officer's Guide* (48th Ed.). Mechanicsburg, PA: Stackpole Books, 1999. (ISBN 0-8117-2659-2). Preface.

The Oath of Office for Commissioned Officers (DA Form 71).

The Officers Commission (DD Form 1A).

Don M Snider and Gayle L. Watkins. *The Future of the Army Profession.* McGraw-Hill Primis Custom Publishing. 2002. (ISBN 0-07-255268-9). Pages 3–18, "Introduction."

Lesson Twenty-six

Nye, Roger. "The Commander's Concept of Duty," *The Challenge of Command.* New Jersey: Avery Publishing Group, Inc, 1986. Pp 115–130. (Reprinted by permission in West Point's Perspectives on Officership: Published for the Class of 2004. Alliance Press. (ISBN: 0-7593-0646-X). Copyright 2001 by United States Military Academy at West Point. pp. 71-82)

Lesson Twenty-seven

Bonn, Keith E. (LTC Ret.). *Army Officer's Guide* (48th Ed.). Mechanicsburg, PA: Stackpole Books, 1999. (ISBN 0-8117-2659-2). Pages 46 through 63.

Don M Snider and Gayle L. Watkins. *The Future of the Army Profession.* McGraw-Hill Primis Custom Publishing. 2002. (ISBN 0-07-255268-9). Pages 379–395, "Backbone vs. Box: The Choice between Principled and Prescrptive Leadership."

Lesson Twenty-nine

Thie, Harry, et al. *Future Career Management Systems for U.S. Military Officers.* New York: Rand Corporation, 1994. (ISBN: 0-833-01572-9). Appendix B, Officership

Huntington, Samuel P. "Officership as a Profession" in *The Soldier and the State.* New York: Vintage Books, 1957. pp. 7–18. (Reprinted by permission in West Point's Perspectives on Officership: Published for the Class of 2004. Alliance Press. (ISBN: 0-7593-0646-X). Copyright 2001 by United States Military Academy at West Point. pp. 95-102)

Blumenson, Martin. "On Entering The Military Profession" in *Army Magazine* (September 1996). pp. 13–15. (Reprinted by permission in *West Point's Perspectives on Officership: Published for the Class of 2004.* Alliance Press. (ISBN: 0-7593-0646-X). Copyright 2001 by United States Military Academy at West Point. pp. 117-120.)

Don M Snider and Gayle L. Watkins. *The Future of the Army Profession.* McGraw-Hill Primis Custom Publishing. 2002. (ISBN 0-07-255268-9). Pages 19–38, "Expertise Jurisdiction and Legitimacy of the Military."

Lesson Thirty

Bonn, Keith E. (LTC Ret.). *Army Officer's Guide* (48th Ed.). Mechanicsburg, PA: Stackpole Books, 1999. (ISBN 0-8117-2659-2). Pages 2 through 45.

Don M Snider and Gayle L. Watkins. *The Future of the Army Profession.* McGraw-Hill Primis Custom Publishing. 2002. (ISBN 0-07-255268-9). Pages 293–311, "The Ties That Bind: The Army Officer's Moral Obligations."

Lesson Thirty-one

Bowden, Mark. *Black Hawk Down,* New York: Atlantic Monthly Press, 1999. (ISBN: 0-871-13738-0) (Excerpt reprinted by permission of Atlantic Monthly Press in *Leadership and Management.* Boston: Pearson Custom Publishing, 2000. (ISBN 0-536-62210-8) Pages 590 through 610.)

Don M. Snider and Gayle L. Watkins. *The Future of the Army Profession.* McGraw-Hill Primis Custom Publishing. 2002. (ISBN 0-07-255268-9). Pages 313–336, "A Message to Garcia: Leading Soldiers in Moral Mayhem."

Lesson Thirty-two

Newman, Richard J. Vietnam's forgotten lessons, Copyright 2000 *U.S. News & World Report,* L.P. Reprinted with permission. Pgs 30–40.

Lesson Thirty-three

WHO WILL LEAD? SENIOR LEADERSHIP IN THE U.S. ARMY, Edward Meyer, Manning Ancell & Jane Mahaffey. Copyright (c) 1995 by Greenwood Publishing Group. Reproduced with permission of Greenwood Publishing Group, Inc., Westport, CT. Pgs 189–220.

Meyer, Edward, Ancell, Manning R. & Mahaffey, Jane (1995) The Renaissance. In Edward Meyer, R. Ancell Manning & Jane Mahaffey, Who Will Lead? (pp. 189–219). Westpoint Connecticut: Preager.

Lesson Thirty-four

Scales, Robert H. *Certain Victory: The U.S. Army in the Gulf War.* Washington: U.S. Government Printing Office, 1993. (ISBN: 0-160-61107-5). Pages 15 through 29.

Center for Military History Publication 70-30, *THE WHIRLWIND WAR: THE UNITED STATES ARMY IN OPERATIONS DESERT SHIELD AND DESERT STORM,* gen. eds. Frank N. Schubert and Theresa L. Kraus. U.S. Government Printing Office, 1994. (ISBN: 9-995-77747-9). Chapter 8, pages 174 through 205.

Lesson Thirty-five

Gulf War chronology from the web site (http://www.redstone.army.mil/history/netstorm/appen.html)

Lesson Thirty-six

McCormick, David. (1998). The Downsized Warrior. New York: New York University Press, 1998. (ISBN: 0-914-75584-4). Pages 157–194.